C0-AWT-050

The Scarecrow Author Bibliographies

1. John Steinbeck (Tetsumaro Hayashi). 1973.
2. Joseph Conrad (Theodore G. Ehrsam). 1969.
3. Arthur Miller (Tetsumaro Hayashi). 2d ed. 1976.
4. Katherine Anne Porter (Waldrip & Bauer). 1969.
5. Philip Freneau (Philip M. Marsh). 1970.
6. Robert Greene (Tetsumaro Hayashi). 1971.
7. Benjamin Disraeli (R. W. Stewart). 1972.
8. John Berryman (Richard W. Kelly). 1972.
9. William Dean Howells (Vito J. Brenni). 1973.
10. Jean Anouilh (Kathleen W. Kelly). 1973.
11. E. M. Forster (Alfred Borrello). 1973.
12. The Marquis de Sade (E. Pierre Chanover). 1973.
13. Alain Robbe-Grillet (Dale W. Frazier). 1973.
14. Northrop Frye (Robert D. Denham). 1974.
15. Federico Garcia Lorca (Laurenti & Siracusa). 1974.
16. Ben Jonson (Brock & Welsh). 1974.
17. Four French Dramatists: Eugène Brieux, François de Curel, Emile Fabre, Paul Hervieu (Edmund F. Santa Vicca). 1974.
18. Ralph Waldo Ellison (Jacqueline Covo). 1974.
19. Philip Roth (Bernard F. Rodgers, Jr.). 1974.
20. Norman Mailer (Laura Adams). 1974.
21. Sir John Betjeman (Margaret Stapleton). 1974.
22. Elie Wiesel (Molly Abramowitz). 1974.
23. Paul Laurence Dunbar (Eugene W. Metcalf, Jr.). 1975.
24. Henry James (Beatrice Ricks). 1975.
25. Robert Frost (Lentricchia & Lentricchia). 1976.
26. Sherwood Anderson (Douglas G. Rogers). 1976.
27. Iris Murdoch and Muriel Spark (Tominaga & Schneidermeyer). 1976.
28. John Ruskin (Kirk H. Beetz). 1976.
29. Georges Simenon (Trudee Young). 1976.
30. George Gordon, Lord Byron (Oscar José Santucho). 1976.
31. John Barth (Richard Vine). 1977.
32. John Hawkes (Carol A. Hryciw). 1977.
33. William Everson (Bartlett & Campo). 1977.
34. May Sarton (Lenora Blouin). 1978.
35. Wilkie Collins (Kirk H. Beetz). 1978.
36. Sylvia Plath (Lane & Stevens). 1978.
37. E. B. White (A. J. Anderson). 1978.
38. Henry Miller (Lawrence J. Shifreen). 1979.
39. Ralph Waldo Emerson (Jeanetta Boswell). 1979.
40. James Dickey (Jim Elledge). 1979.
41. Henry Fielding (H. George Hahn). 1979.
42. Paul Goodman (Tom Nicely). 1979.
43. Christopher Marlowe (Kenneth Friedenreich). 1979.
44. Leo Tolstoy (Egan & Egan). 1979.
45. T. S. Eliot (Beatrice Ricks). 1980.
46. Allen Ginsberg (Michelle P. Kraus). 1980.
47. Anthony Burgess (Jeutonne P. Brewer). 1980.
48. Tennessee Williams (Drewey Wayne Gunn). 1980.
49. William Faulkner (Beatrice Ricks). 1980.
50. Lillian Hellman (Mary Marguerite Riordan). 1980.
51. Walt Whitman (Jeanetta Boswell). 1980.
52. Jack Kerouac (Robert J. Milewski). 1981.
53. Herman Melville (Jeanetta Boswell). 1981.
54. Horatio Alger (Scharnhorst & Bales). 1981.
55. Graham Greene (A. F. Cassis). 1981.
56. Henry David Thoreau (Jeanetta Boswell). 1981.

WILLIAM FAULKNER:

A Bibliography of Secondary Works

compiled by
BEATRICE RICKS

The Scarecrow Author Bibliographies,
No. 49

The Scarecrow Press, Inc.
Metuchen, N.J., & London
1981

Library of Congress Cataloging in Publication Data

Ricks, Beatrice.
William Faulkner, a bibliography of secondary works.

(The Scarecrow author bibliographies ; no. 49)
Includes indexes.
1. Faulkner, William, 1897-1962--Bibliography.
I. Title.
Z8288.R53 [PS3511.A86] 016.813'52 80-15251
ISBN 0-8108-1323-8

Manufactured in the United States of America

Dedicated to the Staff of the
Ward Edwards Library
of
Central Missouri State University

PREFACE

This bibliography of secondary references, consisting of over 8,000 items, is comprised of the following sections: Biography; Works (Novels and Stories, Articles-Essays-Sketches, Interviews, Letters, Poetry, Speeches); General Criticism; Bibliography; Topical Index; and Index of Critics.

The Topical Index in which cross-references are given by item numbers has been designed to suggest facets of study, persons important in the life and work of William Faulkner, authors whose influence on Faulkner has been noted, or authors influenced by Faulkner. References under this Index are not and cannot be exhaustive for the reason that so very many areas of study of Faulkner have been pursued. It is hoped, however, that sufficient areas are noted to indicate possibilities for further study.

Each section of this bibliography has been developed independently to eliminate constant cross-reference as to authors, editors, or publication data.

Although, as stated, articles and books pertaining to a specific work are listed under the particular novel or story, reference should also be made to General Criticism, for very often many novels and stories will be examined in one comprehensive study.

The material has not been separated into independent sections as to articles and books for the reason that articles are frequently expanded and/or revised for publication in books, and it should be helpful to have this information in proximity.

The compiler expresses deepest gratitude to Dr. Ronald McReynolds of the English Department of Central Missouri State University for suggesting this study of William Faulkner, and for his frequent counsel and encouragement.

B. R.

TABLE OF CONTENTS

ABBREVIATIONS AND PUBLICATIONS

A	Action
Ab	Arbalète
ABC	American Book Collector
Accent	Accent
Aegis	Aegis: A Periodical in Literature and Language
AF	Aspects de la France
AgeN	Age nouveau
AGR	American Germanic Review
AH	American Heritage
AI	American Imago
Aikamme	Aikamme
AION-SG	Annali Istituto Universitario Orientale, Napoli, Sezione Germanica
AIQ	American Indian Quarterly
AJMD	American Journal of Mental Deficiency
AL	American Literature
ALitASH	Acta Litteraria Academiae Scientiarum Hungaricae (Budapest)
ALR	American Literary Realism
AmBC	American Book Collector
America	America: A Journal of Today
Americas	Americas
Amerika	Amerika
AmLR	American Literary Review (Tokyo)
AmMerc	American Mercury
AmR	American Review
AmRep	American Reporter (New Delhi)
AmSch	American Scholar
AmSpec	American Spectator
AN&Q	American Notes and Queries (New Haven, Conn.)
Anglia	Anglia
Anglica	Anglica (Kansai U. , Osaka)
Anglo-Am	Anglo-Americana (Vienna-Stuttgart)
AntiochR	Antioch Review

Approach	Approach
Approdo	L'Approdo Letterario (Roma)
AQ	American Quarterly
Arbor	Arbor
Archiv	Archiv für das Studium der neueren Sprachen und Literaturen
Aretusa	Aretusa
ArielE	Ariel: A Review of International English Literature
ArL	Arts et Lettres
ArlQ	Arlington Quarterly
ArQ	Arizona Quarterly
ArRep	Arizona Republic
Arts	Arts
ARund	Die Amerikanische Rundschau
AS	American Speech
A&S	Arts and Sciences (New York University)
ASRC	American Studies Research Centre Newsletter (Hyderabad)
AŞUI	Analele Ştiinţifice ale Universităţii Iaşi
Atl	Atlantic Monthly
AtlJ	Atlanta Journal
B	Bataille
BA	Books Abroad
BAASB	British Association for American Studies Bulletin
B&B	Books and Bookmen
BAcaR	Black Academy Review
BB	Bulletin of Bibliography
BBr	Books at Brown
BCGE	Bulletin Collection of General Education (Tohoku University, Sendai, Japan)
BCLF	Bulletin Critique du livre français
BColl	Book Collector
BFLS	Bulletin de la Faculté des Lettres de Strasbourg
BKom	Bücher-Kommentare
BLM	Bonniers Litterära Magasin (Stockholm)
Bookman	Bookman
BookW	Book Week
BRMMLA	Bulletin of the Rocky Mountain Modern Language Association

Brotéria	Brotéria
BSTCF	Ball State Teachers College Forum
BSUF	Ball State University Forum
BUJ	Boston University Journal
BuR	Bucknell Review
BUSE	Boston University Studies in English
BYUS	Brigham Young University Studies
BzJA	Beihefte zum Jahrbuch für Amerikastudien (Heidelberg, Carl Winter)
C	Carrefour
CamR	Cambridge Review
Candide	Candide
CanForum	Canadian Forum
CanL	Canadian Literature
CarQ	Carolina Quarterly
Carrell	The Carrell: Journal of the Friends of the University of Miami (Florida) Library
CaSE	Carnegie Series in English
CathW	Catholic World
CC	La Civita Cattolica
CCTE	Proceedings of Conference of College Teachers of English of Texas
CdSud	Cahiers du Sud
CE	College English
CEA	CEA Critic
CEJ	California English Journal
CentR	Centennial Review (Michigan State Univ.)
Cf	Confluences
CHA	Cuadernos Hispanoamericanos (Madrid)
Chimera	Chimera
ChiR	Chicago Review
ChrC	Christian Century
ChronOkla	Chronicles of Oklahoma
ChS	Christian Scholar
CimR	Cimarron Review (Oklahoma State University)
Cithara	Cithara
CL	Comparative Literature
Cl	Climats
CLAJ	College Language Association Journal (Morgan State College, Baltimore)
ClassB	Classical Bulletin

CLM	Cahiers des Langues Modernes
CLS	Comparative Literature Studies (University of Illinois)
CollL	College Literature
ColQ	Colorado Quarterly
ColuF	Columbia Forum
Combat	Combat (Paris)
Comment	Comment (University of Alabama)
Commentary	Commentary
Commercial Appeal	(Memphis)
CompD	Comparative Drama
Confluences	Confluences
ConL	Contemporary Literature (University of Wisconsin)
ConnR	Connecticut Review (Bertram D. Sarason)
Contemp	Contemporaneo
Contemporanul	Contemporanul
Conv	Convivium (Barcelona)
Costerus	Costerus: Essays in Language and Literature Concerning Poetry (West Washington State College)
CQ	The Cambridge Quarterly
CRAS	The Centennial Review of Arts and Sciences (Michigan State)
CRB	Cahiers de la Compagnie Madeleine Renaud-Jean, Louis Barrault
CrB	Critisch Bulletin (Arnheim)
CRevAs	Canadian Review of American Studies
Criterio	Criterio
Critic	Critic
Criticism	Criticism (Wayne State)
Critique	Critique: Studies in Modern Fiction
Critique(P)	Critique (Paris)
CritQ	Critical Quarterly
CSE	Carnegie Series in English
CSMM	Christian Science Monitor Magazine
CurL	Current Literature
Cw	Commonweal
CWCP	Contemporary Writers in Christian Perspective
DA	Dissertation Abstracts
Daedalus	Daedalus
Dagens Nyheter	Dagens Nyheter (Copenhagen)
DAI	Dissertation Abstracts International
DanskUd	Dansk Udsyn (Askov)

Debonair	Debonair
Delta	Delta (Cambridge, England)
DeltaR	The Delta Review: The Magazine of Memphis and the Mid-South
DenverQ	Denver Quarterly
Descant	Descant
Dialoghi	Dialoghi
Diogenes	Diogenes
Discourse	Discourse (Concordia College)
Diss	Dissertation
DLD	Das literarische Deutschland
DNR	Die Neue Rundschau
DPL	De Proprietatibus Litterarum
DQR	Dutch Quarterly Review of Anglo-American Letters
DR	Dalhousie Review
DRu	Deutsche Rundschau
DUJ	Durham University Journal
EA	Etudes Anglaises
EAm	Estudios Americanos (Seville)
E&S(T)	Essays and Studies in British and American Literature (Tokyo Joshi Daigaku)
Ed&Pub	Editor and Publisher (New York)
Edda	Edda
EdL	Education Leader
EibKen	Eibungaku Kenkyu (Meiji University, Tokyo)
EIE	English Institute Essays
EigoS	Eigo Seinen (The Rising Generation) (Tokyo)
EJ	English Journal
EL	Ephemerides liturgicae (Roma)
ELH	ELH: Journal of English Literary History
ELN	English Language Notes (University of Colorado)
ELT	Essays in Literature and Thought (Fukuoka Women's University)
Encounter	Encounter (London)
Eng&AL	English and American Literature (Kwansei Gakuin University)
English	English (London)
EngLit	English Literature (Waseda)
EngQ	English Quarterly
EngRec	English Record (New York State English Council)

ER	Europdische Revue
ES	English Studies
Es	Esprit
ESA	English Studies in Africa
EsAm	Estudios Americanos
ESELL	Essays and Studies in English Language and Literature (Sendai, Japan)
Espace	Espace (Paris)
ESPSL	Estado de São Paulo, Suplemento Literário
ESQ	Emerson Society Quarterly
Esquire	Esquire
ESRS	Emporia State Research Studies
ETJ	Educational Theatre Journal
Etudes	Etudes
EUQ	Emory University Quarterly
Europaische	Europäische
Europe	Europe
ExEx	Exercise Exchange
Expl	Explicator
Express	Express
F&C	Forum and Century
FCN	Faulkner Concordance Newsletter
FHA	Fitzgerald/Hemingway Annual
FilmQ	Film Quarterly
FL	Figaro Littéraire
FlaQ	Florida Quarterly
FLe	La Fiera Letteraria (Italy)
FMLS	Forum for Modern Language Studies (University of St. Andrews, Scotland)
FMod	Filología Moderna (Madrid)
FN	Filologičeskie Nauki
FnR	Fortnightly Review
Fontaine	Fontaine
ForLit	Foreign Literature
Forum	The Forum
ForumH	Forum (Houston)
FourQ	Four Quarters (La Salle)
FR	French Review
FS	Faulkner Studies
FSUS	Florida State University Studies
FT	Finsk-Tidskrift
Furioso	Furioso
FurmanMag	Furman Magazine

FurmS	Furman Studies (Furman University, Greenville, S. C.)
G	Gavroche
Gambit	Gambit
GaR	Georgia Review
Genre	Genre (University of Illinois at Chicago Circle)
GHQ	Georgia Historical Quarterly
GLet	Gazette des Lettres
GLit	Gazeta Literară
GR	Germanic Review
Gr	Gringoire
Griffin	The Griffin
GW	Guardian Weekly (Manchester)
GypsyS	Gypsy Scholar
HA	Harvard Advocate
HAB	Humanities Association Bulletin (Canada)
H&H	Hound and Horn
HarpB	Harper's Bazaar
HarpM	Harper's Magazine
HarpMM	Harper's Monthly Magazine
Hasifrut	Hasifrut: Quarterly for the Study of Literature
HemN	Hemingway Notes
HINL	History of Ideas Newsletter
Hispam	Hispamerica: Revista de Literatura
HitJA&S	Hitotsubashi Journal of Arts & Sciences (Tokyo)
HLQ	Huntington Library Quarterly
HM	Hommes et Mondes
Hochland	Hochland
Holiday	Holiday
HollinsC	Hollins Critic
HopR	Hopkins Review
Horizon	Horizon
HPCS	High Point Colorado Studies
HSELL	Hiroshima Studies in English Language and Literature (Hiroshima, Japan)
HSL	Hartford Studies in Literature
HudR	Hudson Review
Humanist	Humanist
Humanitas	Humanitas, Revista di Cultura (Brescia, Italy)

ICS	Italia che scrive
Idea	Idea
IeD	Informations et documents
IEY	Iowa English Yearbook
IJAS	Indian Journal of American Studies
IL	Inostrannaya Literatura (Foreign Lit.)
IllQ	Illinois Quarterly
IlP	Il Ponte; revista mensile di politica e letteratura
IM	Il Mondo
InL	Inostrannaya literatura (Moscow)
Interpretations	Interpretations
IQ	Italian Quarterly
JA	Jahrbuch für Amerikastudien
JAF	Journal of American Folklore
JAmS	Journal of American Studies
JCWH	Journal of Civil War History
JdP	Journal de Psychologie Normale et Pathologique (Paris)
JEGP	The Journal of English and Germanic Philology
JHopM	Johns Hopkins Magazine
JHR	Journal of Human Relations
JHS	Journal of Historical Studies
JIAS	Journal of International American Studies
JMissH	Journal of Mississippi History
JML	Journal of Modern Literature (Temple University)
JNT	Journal of Narrative Technique
JOFS	Journal of Ohio Folklore Society
JO'L	John O'London's
JPC	Journal of Popular Culture
JSH	Journal of Southern History
JSL	Journal of the School of Languages
JSSTC	Journal of Spanish Studies: Twentieth Century
KAL	Kyusha American Literature (Fukuoka, Japan)
Kam	Kamereon (Kamereon Society)
KBAA	Kieler Beiträge zur Anglistik und Amerikanistik

KCS	Kobe College Studies (Kobe, Japan)
Kerygma	Kerygma
KFR	Kentucky Folklore Record
KM	Kansas Magazine
KN	Kwartalnik Neofilologiczny (Warsaw)
Knji	Knjíževnost (Belgrade)
KR	Kenyon Review
Kritika	Kritika (Budapest)
KRQ	Kentucky Romance Quarterly
KSE	Kent Studies in English
KuL	Kunst und Literatur
Kult	Kultuurleven
L	Littéraire
LaH	Louisiana History
Landfall	Landfall
Lang&S	Language and Style
LanM	Les Langues Modernes
LaS	Louisiana Studies (Northwestern State College)
L&I	Literature and Ideology (Montreal)
L&L	Life and Letters
L&P	Literature and Psychology (University of Hartford, New York)
LaurelR	Laurel Review (West Virginia Wesleyan College)
LCrit	Literary Criterion (University of Mysore, India)
LCUT	Library Chronicle of University of Texas
LE	Liberte de l'Esprit
Let	Letteratura
LetM	Letterature Moderne (Milan)
LetN	Lettres Nouvelles
LF	Lettres Françaises
LFQ	Literature/Film Quarterly
LibChron	Library Chronicle (University of Pennsylvania)
LibJ	The Library Journal
Life	Life
Lit	Literature
Litera	Litera
Literatur	Die Literatur
LitM	Litterature Moderne
LitU	Literaturna Ukrajina
LivA	Living Age
LM	Le Monde

LonM	London Magazine
LonMerc	London Mercury
LRd'I	La Rassegna d'Italia
LRN	La Revue Nouvelle
LS	London Spectator
LSUSHS	Louisiana State University Studies, Humanities Series
LTLS	London Times Literary Supplement
Luc	Luceafărul (Bucharest)
LWU	Literatur in Wissenschaft und Unterricht (Kiel)
MA	Magazine of Art
Madamoiselle	Madamoiselle
MagY	Magazine of the Year
MAQR	Michigan Alumnus Quarterly Review
MarkR	Markham Review
MASJ	Midcontinent American Studies Journal (University of Kansas, Lawrence)
Mass&Main	Masses and Mainstream
MassR	Massachusetts Review
Match	Match (Paris)
MCR	Melbourne Critical Review (University of Melbourne)
MdF	Mercure de France
Meanjin	Meanjin
Merkur	Merkur (Deutsche Zeitschrift für europäisches Denken)
MFS	Modern Fiction Studies
MichA	Michigan Academician
MichQR	Michigan Quarterly Review
Midamerica	Midamerica: The Yearbook of the Society for the Study of Midwestern Literature
MidwJ	Midwest Journal
MidwQ	Midwest Quarterly (Pittsburg, Kansas)
MidwR	Midwest Review (Nebraska State Teachers College at Wayne)
MinnR	Minnesota Review
MissFR	Mississippi Folklore Register
MissLN	Mississippi Library News
MissQ	Mississippi Quarterly
MLN	Modern Language Notes

MLQ	Modern Language Quarterly
MN	Monde nouveau
MN-P	Monde nouveau-Paru
ModA	Modern Age (Chicago)
ModD	Modern Drama
ModQ	Modern Quarterly
ModSpr	Moderna Språk
Mon/AmLS	Monographs/American Literary Scholarship (Duke University)
Mon/Aug	Augustana College Press Monograph Series (Rock Island, Ill.)
MonF	Monde français
Mon/Or	Proceedings of the 1970 Steinbeck Conference, Oregon State and Ball State Universities
MonOc	Modern Occasions
Mosaic	Mosaic: A Journal for the Comparative Study of Literature and Ideas
MSCS	Mankato State College Studies [Mankato Studies in English No. 1]
MSE	Massachusetts Studies in English
MSLC	Modernist Studies: Literature and Culture, 1920-1940
MTJ	Mark Twain Journal
MTQ	Mark Twain Quarterly
MundusA	Mundus Artium: A Journal of International Literature and Arts
MVC	Mississippi Valley Collection of the Brister Library (Memphis State University
Names	Names (Potsdam, New York)
N&Q	Notes and Queries
NAR	North American Review
NasR	Nassau Review (Nassau Community College)
Nation	Nation
NatlGeo	National Geographic
NatlObs	National Observer
NatlR	National Review
NcaFJ	North Carolina Folklore Journal
NConL	Notes on Contemporary Literature
NCr	La Nouvelle Critique
NDEJ	Notre Dame English Journal
NDQ	North Dakota Quarterly
Nef	La Nef (Paris)
NEG	New England Galaxy

NEMLA	Northeast Modern Language Association
Neophil	Neophilologus (Groningen)
NewL	New Leader
New Lit Hist	New Literary History
NGR	North Georgia Review
Nimrod	Nimrod
NineC	Nineteenth Century
NL	Nouvelles littéraires
NM	Neuphilologische Mitteilungen (Helsinki)
NMAL	Notes on Modern American Literature
NMQR	New Mexico Quarterly Review
NMW	Notes on Mississippi Writers
NNRF	Nouvelle Nouvelle Revue Française
NOrlR	New Orleans Review
NorthR	Northern Review
NotaBene	Nota Bene (Lake Erie College, Painesville, Ohio)
Novel	Novel: A Forum on Fiction (Brown University)
NPZ	Neuphilologische Zeitung
NR	New Republic
NRF	La Nouvelle Revue Française
NRs	Neue Rundschau
NS	Die Neueren Sprachen
NSt	New Statesman
NS&N	New Statesman and Nation
Numero	Número
NWR	Northwest Review
NY	New Yorker
NyA	Nya Argus
NYHTB	New York Herald Tribune Books
NYPost	New York Post
NYSN	New York Sunday News
NYTBR	New York Times Book Review
NZ	Neuphilologische Zeitschrift
NZZ	Neue Zürcher Zeitung
Obs	Observer
OffC	Off Campus
OJES	Osmania Journal of English Studies (Osmania University, Hyderabad)
Okt	Oktjabr': Literaturno-Khudozestvennyi i Obscestven no-Politicheski Zurnal (Moscow)
Opportunity	Opportunity: Journal of Negro Life

OUR	Ohio University Review (Athens)
P	Paru
PacS	Pacific Spectator
PADS	Publications of the American Dialect Society
Pan	Pan (Milan)
Panorama	Panorama (Lisboa and also Washington)
PAPA	Publications of the Arkansas Philological Association
Paragone	Paragone
ParisR	Paris Review
PBSA	Papers of the Bibliographical Society of America
PC	Pensiero Critico
PELL	Papers on English Language and Literature
Pergale	Pergale (Vilnius)
Person	The Personalist
Persona	Persona
Perspective	Perspective (Washington University)
Phylon	Phylon
PLL	Papers on Language and Literature
PMASAL	Papers of the Michigan Academy of Science, Arts and Letters
PMLA	Publications of the Modern Language Association of America
PoeN	Poe Newsletter (Washington State University)
PoeS	Poe Studies
Poésie	Poêsie
Poetry	Poetry
PostDisp	Post Dispatch (St. Louis)
PQ	Philological Quarterly (Iowa City)
PR	Partisan Review
Preuves	Preuves
Pro	Profils
Proof	Proof: Yearbook of American Bibliographical and Textual Studies
Prospetti	Prospetti
Prov	Provincial
PrS	Prairie Schooner
PS	Pacific Spectator
PSA	Papeles de Son Armadans (Mallorca, Madrid)
PTL	A Journal for Descriptive Poetics and Theory

PubW	Publishers Weekly
PULC	Princeton University Library Chronicle
PULQ	Princeton University Library Quarterly
Punch	Punch
PURBA	Panjab University Research Bulletin (Arts)
Pursuit	Pursuit Society
Putevi	Putevi
QQ	Queen's Quarterly
R	Réforme
RAA	Revue Anglo-Américaine
RA&A	Recherches Anglaises et Américaines
RALS	Resources for American Literary Studies
Ramparts	Ramparts
RANAM	Recherches Anglaises et Américaines
RBPH	Revue Belge de Philologie et d'histoire (Brussels)
RCCI	Recherches et débats du Centre Catholique des Intellectuels Français
RDM	La Revue des deux mondes
RdO	Revista de occidente
RdP	Revue de Paris
Re: A&L	Re: Arts and Letters
ReadDig	Reader's Digest
Réalités	Réalités
Réforms	Réforme
REL	Review of English Literature (Leeds)
RelL	Religion in Life
Renascence	Renascence
Reporter	The Reporter
Republic	Republic
Republika	Republika (Zagreb)
RevBib	Revista Bibliotecilor (Library Review)
RevG	Revue générale
RevI	Revista de las Indias (Bogotá)
RevP	Revue de Paris
RF	Revue Française
RG	Revue générale
RH	Revue hebdomadaire

Abbreviation	Publication
RIP	Rice Institute Pamphlet
RJefNl	Robinson Jeffers Newsletter
RLC	Revue de Littérature Comparée
RLM	Revue des Lettres Modernes
RLMC	Riv. di Letterature Moderne e Comparate (Firenze)
RLV	Revue des Langues Vivantes (Bruxelles)
RM	Revue mondiale
RN	Revue nouvelle
RockyMR	Rocky Mountain Review
RoLit	Romănia Literară
RoR	Romanian Review
RPol	Review of Politics (Notre Dame)
RS	Research Studies (Washington State University)
RSH	Revue des Sciences Humaines
RT	Revue theatrale
RUCR	Revista de la Universidad de Costa Rica
RUS	Rice University Studies
RyF	Razón y fe (Madrid)
SA	Studi Americani (Roma)
SAB	South Atlantic Bulletin
SAF	Studies in American Fiction
SAH	Studies in American Humor
SALit	Studies in American Literature
SamF	Samtid och Framtid
SamS	Samedi Soir
SAQ	South Atlantic Quarterly
SatR	Saturday Review
SatEP	Saturday Evening Post
SatRL	Saturday Review of Literature
SB	Studies in Bibliography: Papers of the Bibliographical Society of the University of Virginia
SB&AL	Studies in British and American Literature (University of Osaka Prefecture)
SBL	Studies in Black Literature
SCB	South Central Bulletin (Tulsa, Oklahoma, Studies by Members of South Central Modern Language Association)
SCE	Study of Current English (Tokyo)
SCR	South Carolina Review

Scrutiny	Scrutiny
SDD-UW	Summaries of Doctoral Dissertations --University of Wisconsin
SDR	South Dakota Review
SEL	Studies in English Literature
SELit	Studies in English Literature (English Literary Society of Japan)
SELL	Studies in English Literature and Language (Kyushu University, Fukuoka, Japan)
Semiotica	Semiotica: Revue Publiée par l'Association Internationale de Sémiotique
Serif	Serif (Kent, Ohio)
SFQ	Southern Folklore Quarterly
Shenandoah	Shenandoah
SHR	Southern Humanities Review
SHum	Studies in the Humanities
Sigma	Sigma: Rivista Trimestrale di Letteratura (Turin)
SIR	Studies in Romanticism
Situation(Paris)	Situation (Paris)
SLJ	Southern Literary Journal
SM	Semaine dans le monde
SNNTS	Studies in the Novel (North Texas State University)
SoF	Samtid och Framtid (Stockholm)
SoLiv	Southern Living
SoLJ	Southern Literary Journal
SoLM	Southern Literary Messenger
SoQ	Southern Quarterly (Hattiesburg, Miss.)
SoR	Southern Review (Louisiana State University)
SoRA	Southern Review: An Australian Journal of Literary Studies (University of Adelaide)
SovL	Soviet Literature
SovR	Soviet Review
SPe	Lo Spettatore Italiano
Spectator	Spectator
Sphinx	The Sphinx: A Magazine of Literature and Society
SR	Sewanee Review
SS	Scandinavian Studies
SSF	Studies in Short Fiction
SSH	Stetson Studies in the Humanities

SSJ	Southern Speech Journal
SSL	Studies in Scottish Literature (Texas Tech. College, Lubbock, Texas)
Stampa	La Stampa
STC	Studies in Twentieth Century (Russell Sage Coll.)
SteinbeckQ	Steinbeck Quarterly
StHum	Studies in the Humanities
Studiekamraten	Studiekamraten (Lund)
Style	Style (Arkansas University)
SuF	Sinn und Form
Sur	Sur (Buenos Aires)
SUS	Susquehanna University Studies (Selinsgrove, Pa.)
SWR	Southwest Review
SXX	Secolul XX (Bucharest)
Sylvan	Sylvan Society
Symposium	Symposium
Synthèses	Synthèses
TC	Twentieth Century
TCDA&A	Travaux du Centre d'Etudes Anglaises et Americaines
TCL	Twentieth Century Literature
TFSB	Tennessee Folklore Society Bulletin
TH	Terre humaine
ThA	Theatre Arts
Theoria	Theoria: A Journal of Studies in the Arts, Humanities and Social Sciences
Thoth	Thoth (English Department, Syracuse University)
Thought	Thought
THQ	Tennessee Historical Quarterly
TimesDis	Times-Dispatch (Richmond, Va.)
TkJ	Tamkang Journal (Taipei City, Taiwan)
TLS	Times Literary Supplement (London)
TM	Les Temps Modernes
Tomorrow	Tomorrow
Topic	Topic: A Journal of the Liberal Arts
Torre	La Torre
TP	Temps Présent
TQ	Texas Quarterly (Texas University)
TR	Table Ronde (France)
TSE	Tulane Studies in English

TSL	Tennessee Studies in Literature
TSLL	Texas Studies in Language and Literature
TsudaR	Tsuda Review (Tokyo)
T&T	Time and Tide
TUSAS	Twayne's United States Authors Series
TVG	TV Guide
UA	United Asia
UCM	University of Chicago Magazine
UCSLL	University of Colorado Studies in Language and Literature
UES	Unisa English Studies
UKCR	University of Kansas City Review
UMissAR	University of Mississippi Alumni Review
UMPEAL	University of Miami Publications in English and American Literature
UMSE	University of Mississippi Studies in English
Unisa ES	Unisa English Studies
Univ	Universitas (Stuttgart)
University	University: A Princeton Magazine
UPortR	University of Portland Review
UR	University Review (Kansas City, Missouri)
USCAD	University of Southern California Abstracts of Dissertations
Ushione	Ushione
UTQ	University of Toronto Quarterly
UTSH	University of Tennessee Studies in the Humanities (Nashville)
UVM	University of Virginia Magazine
UWR	University of Windsor Review (Windsor, Ontario)
VBQ	Visva-Bharati Quarterly (Santiniketan, India)
Venture	Venture
Verri	Verri
VF	Világirodalmi Figyelö
Vindrosen	Vindrosen
Vinduet	Vinduet (Oslo)
VlG	De Vlaamse Gids
VLit	Voprosy Literatury
VMU	Vestnik Moskovskogo Universiteta. Filologiya.

VQR	Virginia Quarterly Review
Wake	Wake
WAL	Western American Literature
WallStJ	Wall Street Journal
WeltS	Welt-Stimmen (Stuttgart)
WestR	Western Review
WGCR	West Georgia College Review
WHR	Western Humanities Review
WilsonBul	Wilson Library Bulletin
WisSL	Wisconsin Studies in Literature
WLit	World Literature
WmM	Westminster Magazine
WmR	Westminster Review
Works	Works
WR	Western Review
WritersD	Writer's Digest
WSCL	Wisconsin Studies in Contemporary Literature
WVUPP	West Virginia University Philological Papers
XUS	Xavier University Studies
YES	Yearbook of English Studies (MHRA)
YFS	Yale French Studies
YLM	Yale Literary Magazine
YR	Yale Review
YULG	Yale University Library Gazette
ZAA	Zeitschrift für Anglistik und Amerikanistik (East Berlin)
ZL	Zycie Literackie
Znak	Znak (Kraków)
Znamja	Znamja

I. BIOGRAPHY

1 Anderson, Sherwood. "A Meeting South," Dial, 78 (April, 1925), 269-279.
Biographical implications in the character David. Cf., Wm. Van O'Connor. The Tangled Fire. Minneapolis: 1954, p. 24.

2 Anon. Faulkner (William): Biography and Criticism, 1951-1954. Eugene, Oregon: 1955.

3 Anon. "Faulkner Country," Life, 55, #5 (August 2, 1963), 46B-53.

4 Anon. "The Postmaster," NY, 46 (November 21, 1970), 50.

5 Anon. "William Faulkner," Wilson Bulletin, 4 (February, 1932), 252. Repr., in Living Authors: A Book of Biography. Dilly Tante, ed. New York: H. W. Wilson, 1931, pp. 121-122.

6 Basso, Hamilton. "William Faulkner, Man and Writer," SatR, 45 (July 28, 1962), 11-14.

7 Beaver, Harold. "The Count of Mississippi," TLS, No. 3821 (May 30, 1975), 600-601.
Essay review, Blotner's Faulkner Biography, #11 below.

8 Bishop, William Avery. "Tales of the British Air Service," NatlGeo, 33 (January, 1918), 27-35.
Background of Faulkner's R. A. F. service.

9 Blotner, Joseph. Faulkner: A Biography. 2 vols. New York: Random House, 1974.
Reviews: Adams, Richard P. AL, 46 (1974), 392-393; Brown, Calvin S. CL, 28 (1976), 362-4; Clemons, W. Newsweek, 83 (March 25, 1974), 91-92; Gray, P. Time, 86 (March 25, 1974), 86f; Heller, T. ArizQt, 30 (Wntr, 1974), 355-357; Littlejohn, D. NewRep, 170 (March 23, 1974), 25-7; McHaney, T. Cw, 100 (July 26, 1974), 412-13; Newman, C. Harper, 248 (April, 1974), 98-100; Polk, Noel. Costerus, 4 (1975), 173-79; Yoder, E. M., Jr. NatlR, 26 (July 5, 1974), 767.

10 ________. "Faulkner in Hollywood," in Man and the Movies.

W. R. Robinson and George Garrett, eds. Baton Rouge: Louisiana State U. P., 1967, pp. 261-303.

11 _______. "The Falkners and the Fictional Families," GaR, 30 (Fall, 1976), 572-592.
Faulkner's depiction of his own family in his novels.

12 _______, ed. Selected Letters of William Faulkner. New York: Random House, 1977.

13 _______. "William Faulkner: Committee Chairman," Themes and Directions in American Literature. R. B. Browne and D. Pizer, eds. Lafayette, Indiana: Purdue Univ. Studies, 1969, pp. 200-219.
Faulkner's activities in Eisenhower's "People-to-People Program."

14 _______. "William Faulkner, Roving Ambassador," International Educational and Cultural Exchange (U. S. Advisory Commission on International Educational Affairs), (Summer, 1966), 1-22.
Faulkner's government-sponsored trips, 1954-1960.

15 Bradford, M. E. "Blotner's Faulkner," Triumph, 9, #v (1974), 32-34.

16 Brown, Andrew. "The First Mississippi Partisan Rangers, C. S. A.," JCWH, 1 (December, 1955), 371-399.

17 Brown, Calvin S., Jr. "Billy Faulkner, My Boyhood Friend," in William Faulkner of Oxford. James W. Webb and A. Wigfall Green, eds. Baton Rouge, Louisiana: Louisiana State U. P., 1965, pp. 40-48.

18 Brown, Maggie. "Hunt Breakfast, Faulkner Style," in William Faulkner of Oxford. James W. Webb and A. Wigfall Green, eds., pp. 119-123.

19 Brown, Maud Morrow. "An Old Friend Remembers Fondly," in William Faulkner of Oxford. James W. Webb and A. Wigfall Green, eds., pp. 37-39.

20 Brown, Ruth. "The Falkners of Mississippi," SatR, 45 (July 28, 1962), 17.

21 Browne, Olivia. "The Flying Faulkners," Memphis Commercial Appeal, Section 4 (November 8, 1959).

22 Burson, Harold. "Mr. Faulkner Sees a Cub," in William Faulkner of Oxford. James W. Webb and A. Wigfall Green, eds., pp. 116-119.

23 Buttitta, Anthony. "William Faulkner: That Writin' Man of Oxford," SatRL, 18 (May 21, 1938), 6-8.

24 Cabaniss, Allen. "To Scotch a Monumental Mystery," NMW, 3 (1970), 79-80.
Notes an error in M. C. Falkner's The Falkners of Mississippi concerning date of erection of Oxford Square's Confederate monument.

25 Cantwell, Robert. "The Faulkners: Recollections of a Gifted Family," in New World Writing. Second Mentor Selection. New York: 1952, pp. 300-315. Repr., in Three Decades of Criticism. Frederick Hoffman and Olga Vickery, eds. East Lansing: Michigan State College Press, 1960, pp. 51-66.

26 Capps, Jack L. "Introduction: William Faulkner and West Point," U. S. Military Academy Library Occasional Papers, No. 2 (1974), 1-5.

27 _______. "West Point's William Faulkner Room," GaR, 20 (Spring, 1966), 3-8.

28 _______. "William Faulkner and West Point," Die deutsche Literatur in der Weimarer Republik. Wolfgang Rothe, ed. Stuttgart: Reclam, 1974, pp. 1-5.

29 Carter, Hodding. "Faulkner and His Folk," PULC, 18 (Spring, 1957), 95-107.

30 _______. "The Forgiven Faulkner," JIAS, 7 (1965), 137-147.
Local resentment in Oxford toward Faulkner's racial views gradually dispelled.

31 Cerf, Bennett. "From William Faulkner's Publisher," SatRL, 45(July 28, 1962), 12.

32 Clark, Thomas D. "The Greenskeeper," in William Faulkner of Oxford. James W. Webb and A. Wigfall Green, eds., pp. 68-76.

33 Cochran, Louis. "A Front Steps Interview," in William Faulkner of Oxford. James W. Webb and A. Wigfall Green, eds., pp. 101-107.

34 _______. "William Faulkner: A Personal Sketch," in William Faulkner of Oxford. James W. Webb and A. Wigfall Green, eds., pp. 215-224.

35 _______. "William Faulkner, Literary Tyro of Mississippi," Commercial Appeal (Memphis), (November 6, 1932), Mag. Sec., 4.

36 Cofield, J. R. "Many Faces, Many Moods," in William Faulkner of Oxford. James W. Webb and A. Wigfall Green, eds., pp. 107-113.

37 Coindreau, Maurice Edgar. "Faulkner tel que je l'ai connu,"

Preuves, No. 144 (February, 1963), 9-14; translated "The Faulkner I Knew," Shenandoah, 16 (Winter, 1965), 27-35.

38 Collins, Carvel, ed. "Faulkner at the University of Mississippi," William Faulkner: Early Prose and Poetry. Boston: Little, Brown & Co., 1962, pp. 3-33.

39 Commins, Dorothy B. "William Faulkner in Princeton," JHS, 2 (1969), 179-185.

40 Coughlan, Robert. "The Private World of William Faulkner," Life, 35 (September 28, 1953), 118-136; (October 5, 1953), 55-68. Repr., in Prize Articles, 1954. New York: Ballantine Books, 1954, pp. 121-156; also in Life (Periodical), Great Reading from Life, New York: Harper & Bros., 1960, pp. 204-216.

41 ________. The Private World of William Faulkner. New York: Harper & Brothers, 1954; Cooper Square Pubs., 1972.

42 Cowley, Malcolm. Exiles Return. New York: Viking, 1951, p. 291; 2nd printing, 1959; 3rd, 1961.

43 ________. "Faulkner: The Yoknapatawpha Story," in A Second Flowering: Works and Days of the Lost Generation. New York: Viking Press, 1956, 1973, pp. 130-155.

44 ________. The Faulkner-Cowley File: Letters and Memories, 1944-1962. New York: Viking, 1966; London: Chatto & Windus, 1966.

45 Cullen, John B. "As I Knew William Faulkner," The Oxford Eagle, July 12, 1962, Sec. 2, p. 1.

46 ________, and Floyd C. Watkins. Old Times in the Faulkner Country. Chapel Hill: North Carolina U.P., 1961.
Cullen's letters and reminiscences of his acquaintance with Faulkner.

47 Dahl, James. "Faulkner Reminiscence: Conversations with Mrs. Maud Falkner," JModLit, 3 (April, 1974), 1026-30.

48 Douds, Edith Brown. "Recollections of William Faulkner and the Bunch," in William Faulkner of Oxford. James W. Webb and A. Wigfall Green, eds., pp. 48-53.

49 Duclos, Donald Philip. "Son of Sorrow: The Life, Works, and Influence of Colonel William C. Falkner, 1825-1889," DA, 23 (Michigan: 1962), 233.

50 Duvall, Howard, Jr. "Captain Ahab and the Sloop," in William Faulkner of Oxford. James W. Webb and A. Wigfall Green, eds., pp. 174-180.

51 Eades, Robbie. "A Love of Drawing," in William Faulkner of Oxford. James W. Webb and A. Wigfall Green, eds., pp. 22-24.

52 Emerson, O. B. "Bill's Friend Phil," JMiH, 32 (May, 1970), 135-145.
Phil Stone's relationship with Faulkner.

53 Evans, Medford. "Oxford, Mississippi," SWR, 15 (Winter, 1929), 46-63.
A report on the town's view of the young novelist.

54 Falkner, Murry C. "The Coming of the Motor Car," SoR, 10 (January, 1974), 170-180.

55 _______. "The Day the Balloon Came to Town," AmHer, 17, #1 (December, 1965), 46-49.

56 _______. The Falkners of Mississippi: A Memoir. Baton Rouge: Louisiana State U. P., 1967.
General family background.

57 _______. "The Falkners of Oxford: The Enchanted Years," SoR, 3 (April, 1967), 357-386; included in The Falkners of Mississippi.

58 _______. "The Wonderful Mornings of Our Youth," in William Faulkner of Oxford. James W. Webb and A. Wigfall Green, eds., pp. 9-22.

59 Fant, Joseph L., and Robert Ashley, eds. Faulkner at West Point. New York: Random House, 1964; trans., O. Falk. Utrecht: A. W. Bruna & Zoon, n.d.
Reviews: Irvin Malin, BA, 39 (1965), 342; TLS (July 16, 1964), 629.

60 Faulkner, Jim. "Auntee Owned Two," SoR, 8 (October, 1972), 836-844.
Family memoirs.

61 _______. "The Picture of John and Brother Will," DeltaR, 7 (Fall, 1970), 12-14.

62 Faulkner, John. "His People on the Square," William Faulkner of Oxford. James W. Webb and A. Wigfall Green, eds., pp. 212-213.

63 _______. My Brother Bill: An Affectionate Reminiscence. New York: Trident Press, 1963.
Reviews: Daniel Aaron, NSt, 68 (1964), 25; Hubert Creekmore NYTB (September 15, 1963), 6; Granville Hicks, SatR (Sept. 21, 1963), 31-2; Tony Tanner, Spec (June 19, 1964), 826; Lawrance Thompson, NYHTB (Sept. 15, 1963), 4, 16.

64 _______. "My Brother Bill: An Affectionate Reminiscence," VQR, 40 (Winter, 1964), xxvi.

65 _______. "A Tender-hearted Someone: My Brother Bill," Time (September 13, 1963), 110.

66 Ferris, William R., and Emily Stone. "William Faulkner and Phil Stone: Interview," SAQ, 68 (Autumn, 1969), 536-542.

67 Fontaine, John E. "Never the Ordinary Genius," in William Faulkner of Oxford. James W. Webb and A. Wigfall Green, eds., pp. 30-37.

68 Ford, Margaret Patricia, and Suzanne Kincaid. "Biographical Sketch," Who's Who in Faulkner. Baton Rouge: Louisiana State U.P., 1963, pp. 3-12.

69 Foster, R. E. "A Review of William Faulkner: The Journey to Self-Discovery, by H. Edward Richardson," SAQ, 69 (Summer, 1970), 427-429.

70 Franklin, Malcolm A. Bitterweeds: Life with Faulkner at Rowan Oak. Irving, Texas: The Society for the Study of Traditional Culture, 1977.
Rev. by Thomas L. McHaney, MissQ, 31 (Summer, 1978), 447-479.

71 _______. "A Christmas in Columbus," MissQ, 27 (Summer, 1974), 319-322.
Reminiscences.

72 Fuller, Edmund. "Faulkner on Campus: Two Self-Portraits," WallStJ, 163 (May 8, 1964), 14.
Review-article of Joseph Fant and Robert Ashley, eds. Faulkner at West Point and Frederick Gwynn and Joseph Blotner, eds., Faulkner in the University.

73 Geher, István. "Ole Grandfather: The Presence of a Missing Link in Faulkner's Life and Work," Studies in English and American, Vol. II. Erzsêbet Perênyi and Frank Tibor, eds. Budapest: Dept. of Eng., L. Eotvos Univ., 1975, pp. 215-275.

74 Goldsborough, Murray Lloyd. "Sitting for a Portrait," William Faulkner of Oxford. James W. Webb and A. Wigfall Green, eds., pp. 196-197.

75 Gotten, Henry B. "Oxford," DeltaR, 5 (December, 1968), 14-16, 80-81.
Cf., Allen Cabaniss, "To Scotch a Monumental Mystery," NMQ, 3 (1970), 79-80.

76 Green, A. Wigfall. "First Lectures at a University," in William Faulkner of Oxford. James W. Webb and A. Wigfall Green, eds., pp. 127-139.

77 _______. "William Faulkner at Home," SR, 40 (July-September, 1932), 294-306. Repr., in William Faulkner: Two Decades of Criticism, Hoffman, F. J., and O. W. Vickery, eds., pp. 33-47.

78 _______. "William Faulkner's Flight Training in Canada," UMSE, 6 (1965), 49-57.

79 Gwynn, Frederick L., and Joseph L. Blotner. Faulkner in the University. Charlottesville, Virginia: Virginia U.P., 1959.

80 Hale, Nancy. "Col. Sartoris and Mr. Snopes," Vogue (August 1, 1963), 112-113, 135-136, 138-139.

81 Harmon, J. W. "Hometown Actor," William Faulkner of Oxford. James W. Webb and A. Wigfall Green, eds., pp. 89-94.

82 Healy, George W., Jr. "No Beck and Call for Bill," William Faulkner of Oxford. James W. Webb and A. Wigfall Green, eds., pp. 57-60.

83 Helztynski, Stanislaw. "Okreg Yoknapatawpha w Tworczosci William Faulkner," Kwartalnik Neofilogoczcy (1959), 305-320.

84 Hines, Tom S., Jr. "The Crusader," William Faulkner of Oxford. James W. Webb and A. Wigfall Green, eds., pp. 113-115.

85 Hoar, Jere R. "William Faulkner of Oxford, Mississippi," WritersD (July, 1961), 15-16, 77-78.

86 Hoar, Victor. "Colonel William C. Falkner in the Civil War," JMissH, 27 (February, 1965), 42-62.
William Faulkner's great-grandfather.

87 Holley, John Reed. "Halloweens at Rowan Oak," William Faulkner of Oxford. James W. Webb and A. Wigfall Green, eds., pp. 85-89.

88 Howell, Elmo. "William Faulkner's Graveyard," NMW, 4, #3 (Winter, 1972), 115-118.

89 Howorth, Lucy S. "Bill Faulkner at Ole Miss," DeltaR, 2, #3 (July-August, 1965), 38-39, 73.

90 Hudson, Bill. "Faulkner Before Sanctuary" CarolinaMag, 69 (April, 1935), 11-14.

91 Hull, Cecil. "He Nodded or Spoke," William Faulkner of Oxford. James W. Webb and A. Wigfall Green, eds., pp. 123-124.

92 Inge, M. Thomas. "Faulkner, the Man and His Masks: A Biographical Note," SoQ, 11 (March, 1964), 55-59.

93 ________. "Intruding on Faulkner," Chron. of Higher Ed, 13 (February 7, 1977), 14.
Art.-rev. of Meta Carpenter Wilde's A Loving Gentleman. New York: 1976.

94 ________. "The Virginia Face of Faulkner," Va. Cavalcade, 24 (Summer, 1974), 32-39.

95 Israel, Calvin. "The Last Gentleman," PR, 35 (Spring, 1968), 315-319.

96 Kalb, B. "Biographical Sketch," SatR, 37 (July 31, 1954), 11.

97 Keith, Don L. "Faulkner in New Orleans," DeltaR, 6 (May, 1969), 46-49.
Faulkner's relations with William Spratling, Sherwood Anderson, and Harold Levy in New Orleans.

98 Kielty, Bernardine. "William Faulkner" (biographical note), A Treasury of Short Stories. New York: Simon & Schuster, 1948.

99 King, Larry L. "Requiem for Faulkner's Home Town," Holiday, 45, #3 (March, 1969), 60, 74-76.

100 Leary, Lewis. William Faulkner of Yoknapatawpha County. New York: Crowell, 1973.
A general biographical and critical survey of the life and career of Faulkner, with chapters on particular novels.

101 Linder, Felix. "A Gentleman of the First Order," William Faulkner of Oxford. James W. Webb and A. Wigfall Green, eds., pp. 171-173.

102 Linscott, Elizabeth. "Faulkner in Massachusetts," NEG, 10, #3 (Winter, 1969), 37-42.
Reminiscences.

103 Linscott, Robert N. "Faulkner Without Fanfare," Esquire, 60, #1 (July, 1963), 36-38.

104 Littlejohn, D. "How Not to Write a Biography," NR, 170 (March 23, 1974), 25-27.
Essay-review of Joseph Blotner's Faulkner: A Biography.

105 Lloyd, James B. "The Oxford Eagle, 1902-1962: A Census of Locations," MissQ, 29, #3 (Summer, 1976), 423-431.

106 Lumpkin, Ben Gray. "The Awesome Postmaster," William Faulkner of Oxford. James W. Webb and A. Wigfall Green, eds., pp. 54-56.

107 McAlexander, Hubert, Jr. "William Faulkner--The Young

Poet in Stark Young's The Torches Flare," AL, 43, #4 (1972), 647-649.
Resemblances between the young Faulkner and Eugene Oliver, a minor character in Young's novel of 1928.

108 McHaney, Thomas L. "The Falkners and the Origin of Yoknapatawpha County: Some Corrections," MissQ, 25, #3 (Summer, 1972), 249-264.
Cf., Calvin S. Brown. Appendix, A Glossary of Faulkner's South, pp. 223ff.

109 Malley, Terence. "Thoughts, Hopes, Endeavors, Failures," MarkhamR, 4 (1974), 78-80.
Rev. article on J. Blotner's Faulkner: A Biography.

110 Markette, John Ralph. "Railroad Days," William Faulkner in Oxford. James W. Webb and A. Wigfall Green, eds., pp. 28-30.

111 Meriwether, James B., ed. "And Now What's to Do," MissQ, 26 (Summer, 1973), 399-402.
Notes the "very clear autobiographical element" in the manuscript.

112 _______. "Blotner's Faulkner," MissQ, 28 (Summer, 1975), 353-369.

113 _______. "Faulkner's Correspondence with The Saturday Evening Post," MissQt, 30, #3 (Summer, 1977), 461-475.

114 "Milestones," Time (April 30, 1956), 80.
Birth of first child to Jill Faulkner Summers.

115 Millgate, Michael. "The Career," The Achievement of William Faulkner. New York: Random House, 1966, pp. 1-57.

116 _______. "Faulkner in Toronto: A Further Note," UTQ, 37, #2 (January, 1968), 197-202.
Supplementary facts about Faulkner's RAF service.

117 _______. "William Faulkner, Cadet," UTQ, 35, #2 (January, 1966), 117-132.

118 _______. "William Faulkner: A Biographical Sketch," excerpt from "William Faulkner" in Bear, Man, and God. F. L. Utley, et al., eds. New York: Random House, 1963, pp. 121-127.

119 Minchero, Vilasaro Angel. "William Faulkner, descendiente de gobernadores ...," Diccionario universal de escritores (San Sebastian), 1 ([1957]), 117-118.

120 Minter, David. "Faulkner and the Uses of Biography," GaR,

28 (Fall, 1974), 455-465.
Essay-review of Joseph Blotner's Faulkner: A Biography.

121 Mitchell, Julian. "God's Own Country," NSt, (October 25, 1974), 582-583.
Rev.-art., Joseph Blotner. Faulkner: A Biography. Chatto, 1974.

122 Moeller, Charles. "Faulkner tel qu'en lui-même.... L'amour ne meurt pas, c'est vous qui mourez," Informations catholiques internationales, No. 173-174 (August, 1962), 31-32.

123 Mullen, Phillip E. "The Fame and the Publicity," William Faulkner of Oxford. James W. Webb and A. Wigfall Green, eds., pp. 162-165.

124 Nichols, Lewis. "In and Out of Books," NYTBR (April 19, 1964), 8.
Note on Faulkner at West Point. Joseph L. Fant and Robert Ashley, eds.

125 O'Connor, William Van. "William Faulkner's Apprenticeship," SWR, 38 (Winter, 1953), 1-14; repr., in The Tangled Fire of William Faulkner. pp. 16-36. (Pages 3-15, 146-157, also biographical.)

126 Ohashi, Kenzaburo. "Faulkner: A Biography wo Yonde," EigoS, 120 (1974), 234-235.

127 Olson, Ted. "Faulkner and the Colossus of Maroussi," SAQ, 71 (Spring, 1972), 205-212.
Faulkner's trip to Athens, Greece.

128 Pate, Willard. "Pilgrimage to Yoknapatawpha," FurmanM (Winter, 1969), 6-13.

129 Pfeiffer, Andrew H. "Eye of the Storm: The Observers' Image of the Man Who Was Faulkner," SoR, 8, n.s. (October, 1972), 763-773.
Impressions of Faulkner the man.

130 Pivano, Fernanda. "Vita di Faulkner," LRd'I, 4 (June, 1949), 638-645.

131 Plummer, William. "Three Versions of Faulkner," HudR, 31, #3 (Autumn, 1978), 466-482.

132 Price-Stephens, Gordon. "Faulkner and the Royal Air Force," MissQ, 17, #3 (Summer, 1964), 123-128.

133 Pruett, D. F. "Papers of John Faulkner," MVC Bul, 3 (Fall, 1970), 81-84.
Papers in the Mississippi Valley Collection of Brister Library at Memphis State University.

134 Raimbault, R. N. Faulkner. Paris: Editions Universitaires, 1963.
Review: Michel A. Gresset, "Faulkneriana," MdF, 350 (April, 1964), 658-661.

135 Reed, Mack. "Mr. Mack Remembers Bill," William Faulkner Souvenir Edition, Oxford Eagle (April 22, 1965), Part 3, p. 2.

136 Reed, W. McNeill. "Four Decades of Friendship," William Faulkner of Oxford. James W. Webb and A. Wigfall Green, eds., pp. 180-188.

137 Richards, Robert Fulton, ed. "Faulkner, William," Concise Dictionary of American Literature. New York: Philosophical Library, 1955, pp. 78-80.

138 Richardson, H. Edward. "The Ways That Faulkner Walked: A Pilgrimage," ArQ, 21 (Summer, 1965), 133-145.

139 ______. William Faulkner: The Journey to Self-Discovery. Columbia: Missouri U. P., 1969.
Reviews: Richard P. Adams, AL, 42 (1970), 117-118; R. E. Foster, SAQ, 69 (1970), 427-429; James B. Meriwether, MFS, 17 (1971-72), 649-650.

140 Roberts, Bramlett. "A Soft Touch, a Great Heart," William Faulkner of Oxford. James W. Webb and A. Wigfall Green, eds., pp. 150-153.

141 Rowland, Rose. "William and His Grandmother," William Faulkner of Oxford. James W. Webb and A. Wigfall Green, eds., pp. 24-27.

142 Rutledge, Wilmuth S. "How Colonel Faulkner Built His Railroad," MissQ, 20 (Summer, 1967), 166-170.

143 Seay, J. Aubrey. "A Day at the Lake," William Faulkner of Oxford. James W. Webb and A. Wigfall Green, eds., pp. 188-196.

144 Shaw, Marybec Miller. "From Playmate to Maid," William Faulkner of Oxford. James W. Webb and A. Wigfall Green, eds., pp. 145-147.

145 Simpson, Lewis P. "Foreword--Yoknapatawpha and the World of Murry Falkner," The Falkners of Mississippi: A Memoir by Murry C. Falkner. Baton Rouge: Louisiana State U. P., 1967.

146 ______. "The Loneliness of William Faulkner," SLJ, 8 (Fall, 1975), 126-143. Essay-review of Blotner's Faulkner: A Biography.

147* Smith, Claude Maxwell. "He Just Wanted to Be Old Bill," in William Faulkner of Oxford. James W. Webb and A. Wigfall Green, eds., pp. 62-68.

148 Smith, Marshall J. "Faulkner of Mississippi," Bookman, 74 (December, 1931), 411-417.

149 Spratling, William. "Chronicle of a Friendship: William Faulkner of New Orleans," TQ, 9, #1 (Spring, 1966), 34-40.

150 ________. File on Spratling: An Autobiography. Boston: Little, Brown & Co., 1932, 1967, pp. 21ff.

151 Stern, Richard G. "Faulkner at Home," BA, 39 (Autumn, 1965), 408-411.

152 Stock, Jerold Howard. "Suggestions of Death-Anxiety in the Life of William Faulkner," DAI, 38 (West Virginia: 1977), 2130A-31A.

153 Stone, Emily Whitehurst. "Faulkner Gets Started," TQ, 8 (Winter, 1965), 142-148.
Phil Stone and Faulkner.

154 ________. "Some Arts of Self-Defense," William Faulkner of Oxford. James W. Webb and A. Wigfall Green, eds., pp. 95-100.

155 Stone, Phil. "Count No Count," Saturday Review Treasury. New York: Simon & Schuster, 1957, pp. 230-232. Repr., from SatR, 25, #38 (September 19, 1942).

156 ________. "I Know William Faulkner," Oxford Eagle (November 11, 1950), 1.

157 ________. Letter by Phil Stone, December 28, 1931, to Louis Cochran, William Faulkner of Oxford. James W. Webb and A. Wigfall Green, eds., pp. 225-229.

158 ________. "The Man and the Land," William Faulkner of Oxford. James W. Webb and A. Wigfall Green, eds., pp. 3-9.

159 ________. "William Faulkner and His Neighbors," SatR, 25, #38 (September 19, 1942), 12.

160 ________. "William Faulkner, the Man and His Work," Oxford Magazine (Oxford, Mississippi), Copy 1 (April 1, 1934), 13-14; Copy 2 (June 4, 1934), 11-15; Copy 3 (November 1, 1934), 3-10.

161 Stone, William Evans. "Our Cotehouse," William Faulkner of Oxford. James W. Webb and A. Wigfall Green, eds., pp. 76-85.

162 Sullivan, Walter. "Allen Tate, Flem Snopes, and the Last Years of William Faulkner," in _Death by Melancholy: Essays on Modern Southern Fiction_. Baton Rouge: Louisiana State U. P., 1972, pp. 3-21, passim.

163 Talmey, Allene. "Faulkner at West Point," Vogue, 140 (July, 1962), 70-73, 114, 116.

164 Taylor, Mrs. Guy B., Sr. "William Stocks His Farm," _William Faulkner of Oxford_. James W. Webb and A. Wigfall Green, eds., pp. 143-144.

165 Turner, Arlin. "William Faulkner: The Growth and Survival of a Legend," SHR, 9 (Winter, 1975), 91-97.
Essay-review of Blotner's _Faulkner: A Biography_.

166 Vance, William. "Faulkner: Life and Art," BUJ, 23, i (1975), 65-72.
Rev.-art. on Joseph Blotner. _Faulkner: A Biography_.

167 Waddle, Mary Betsy. "A Late Dinner with the Faulkners," _William Faulkner of Oxford_. James W. Webb and A. Wigfall Green, eds., pp. 139-142.

168 Wagner, Linda W. "Joseph Blotner, _Faulkner: A Biography_," SCR, 7, i (1974), 102-106.

169 Watkins, Floyd C. "Faulkner, Faulkner, Faulkner," SR, 82 (Summer, 1974), 518-527.
Review of Joseph Blotner's _Faulkner: A Biography_, 1974.

170 ________, in collaboration with John B. Cullen. _Old Times in the Faulkner Country_. Chapel Hill: North Carolina U. P., 1961.

171 Webb, Clifton Bondurant. "Swing Low for Sweet Callie," _William Faulkner of Oxford_. James W. Webb and A. Wigfall Green, eds., pp. 124-127.

172 Webb, James W. "Rowan Oak, Faulkner's Golden Bough," UMSE, 6 (1965), 39-47.

173 ________. "William Faulkner Comes Home," _William Faulkner of Oxford_. James W. Webb and A. Wigfall Green, eds., pp. 198-211.

174 ________, and A. Wigfall Green, eds. _William Faulkner of Oxford_. Baton Rouge: Louisiana State U. P., 1965.
Reviews: Melvin Backman, WHR, 21 (1967), 79-80; Lynn Z. Bloom, ABC, (March, 1966), 3-4; Joseph Blotner, NYTB (Nov. 28, 1965), 72; John Wm. Corrington, GaR, 19 (1965), 485-486; Ernest G. Griffin, HAB, 17 (1966), 92-5; Granville Hicks, SatR, (Oct. 2, 1965), 37-8; Lester G.

McAllister, Encounter, 27 (1966), 367-8; James B. Meriwether, MissQ, 20 (1967), 181-183; Michael Millgate, MLR, 62 (1967), 517-18; Lawrence R. Thompson, BW, (Jan. 2, 1966), 5, 17; Thomas D. Young, JMissH, 28 (1966), 88-90; Otis B. Wheeler, SAQ, 65 (1966), 419; AL, 37 (1966), 521; TLS (November 25, 1965), 1052.

175 West, Anthony. "The Real and the Trivial," B&B, 21 (1976), 50-52.
Rev.-art. Joseph Blotner. Faulkner: A Biography.

176 Who's Who in America, 1954-1955. Vol. 28. Chicago: Marquis, 1954, p. 833.
Material for entry supplied by William Faulkner.

177 Wilde, Meta Carpenter and Orin Borsten. A Loving Gentleman: The Love Story of William Faulkner and Meta Carpenter. New York: Simon & Schuster, 1976.
Cf., art.-rev., by Malcolm Cowley. NYTBR (December 19, 1976), Section 7, 2, and M. T. Inge, Chron. Higher Ed, 13 (1977), 14.

178 Wilde, Meta Doherty. "An Unpublished Chapter from A Loving Gentleman," MissQt, 30, # 3 (Summer, 1977), 449-460.

179 Williams, Dorothy Roane. "Food for Friends," William Faulkner of Oxford. James W. Webb and A. Wigfall Green, eds., pp. 148-149.

180 Wolfe, Peter. "Faulkner: A Biography by Joseph Blotner," CLAJ, 18 (June, 1975), 591-593.

181 Wortham, Earl. "So I Could Ride Along with Him," William Faulkner of Oxford. James W. Webb and A. Wigfall Green, eds., pp. 165-170.

182 "Yoknapatawpha Possum," Newsweek (April 30, 1962), 58.
On Faulkner at West Point.

183 Young, Stark. "New Year's Craw," NR, 93 (January 12, 1938), 283-284.

184 _______. The Pavillion. New York: Scribner's, 1951, pp. 59-60.
Reminiscences of Young's acquaintance with William Faulkner.

OBITUARY NOTICES

185 Allsop, Kenneth. Daily Mail (July 7, 1962).

186 Antonini, Giacomo. "E'morto Faulkner," Nazione (Florence) (July 9, 1962), 3.

187 Atkinson, Justin Brooks. "Death of Faulkner," Tuesdays and Fridays. New York: Random House, 1963, pp. 260-262.

188 Brand, David. Humanist, 78, #2 (February, 1963), 46-47.

189 Britannica Book of the Year 1963. Chicago: Encyclopaedia Britannica, 1963, pp. 868-869.

190 "The Death of William Faulkner," SatEP (July 13, 20, 1962).

191 "Faulkner l'universal," Figaro litteraire (July 14, 1962), 8.

192 Gourlay, Logan. Daily Express (July 7, 1962).

193 Grant, Douglas. Yorkshire Post (July 7, 1962).

194 Hempstead, Frank. (July 7, 1962).

195 Hicks, Granville. "Requiem for the Famous Son," SatRL, 46, #38 (September 21, 1963), 31-32.

196 King, L. L. "Requiem for Faulkner's Home Town," Holiday, 45 (March, 1969), 60-61.

197 "The Last of William Faulkner," TLS, #3160 (September 21, 1962), 726.

198 Marshall, Lenore. "The Power of Words," SatRL, 45, #29 (July 28, 1962), 16-17.

199 "Memory of William Faulkner," SatEP, 238 (October 9, 1965), 88.

200 Nouvelles litteraires (July 12, 1962), 1.

201 "Obituary," LondonN, 241 (July 14, 1962), 69.

202 PubW, 182 (July 16, 1962), 33-35.

203 Quinton, Anthony. Sunday Telegraph (July 8, 1962).

204 Robbins, Alfred. "Yoknapatawpha Notes Faulkner's Death," Journal-American (New York) (July 6, 1962), 30.

205 Rudd, Hughes. "The Death of William Faulkner," SatEP, #26 (July 13/July 20, 1963), 32-34, 37.

206 Smith, Norman. "Enduring Literary Legacy Left by William Faulkner," Arts & Men (July, 1962), 5.

207 Snow, Sir Charles (Interviewed), NYT (July 7, 1962), 7.

208 Styron, William. "William Faulkner, 1897-1962: A Great-

hearted Writer Belongs to the Ages," Life (July 20, 1962), 4, 36-36B, 39-42.

209 Taillefer, Anne. "As Faulkner Lies Dead," Catholic Worker, 29 (September, 1962), 2, 8.

210 Tate, Allen. "William Faulkner, 1897-1962," SR, 71, #1 (Winter, 1963), 160-164. Repr., from New Statesman (London), 64 (September 28, 1962), 108.

211 Thompson, Lawrance R. "A Dim Light in September," Post Book Review (Washington) (September 15, 1963), 4, 16.

212 Thompson, Ray M. "Mississippi's William Faulkner," Down South, 12 (September-October, 1962), 7, 16, 26.

213 "A Titan Passes--William Faulkner," Times (Los Angeles) (July 8, 1962), Section A, p. 2.

214 Toynbee, Philip. The Observer (July 8, 1962).

215 Weatherby, W. J. The Guardian (July 7, 1962).

216 [William Faulkner], CSMM (July 10, 1962), 14.

217 [William Faulkner], Daily Oklahoman (Okla. City), (July 11, 1962), 14.

218 [William Faulkner], Dallas Morning News (July 7, 1962), IV, 2.

219 [William Faulkner], Kansas City Times (July 7, 1962), 38.

220 "William Faulkner," Livres choisis, n. s., No. 19 (November, 1962), 1-2.

221 [William Faulkner], National Observer (July 9, 1962), 17.

222 "William Faulkner, 1897-1962," Ramparts, 1 (November, 1962), 8-9.

223 "William Faulkner: Faith That Man Will Prevail," Newsweek, 60 (July 16, 1962), 52-53.

224 "William Faulkner, RIP," NatlRev (July 31, 1962), 54.

II. WORKS

NOVELS AND STORIES

ABSALOM, ABSALOM!
(New York: Random House, 1936)

225 Adamowski, Thomas H. "Children of the Idea: Heroes and Family Romances in Absalom, Absalom!" Mosaic, 10 (Fall, 1976), 115-131.

226 _______. "Dombey and Son and Sutpen and Son," SNNTS, 4, #3 (Fall, 1972), 378-389.
Similarities between those "who desire autonomy."

227 Adams, Richard P. "Work: Absalom, Absalom!" Faulkner: Myth and Motion. Princeton, New Jersey: Princeton U. P., 1968, pp. 172-214.

228 Aguilar, Esperanza. Yoknapatawpha, Propiedad de William Faulkner. Santiago de Chile: Editorial Universitaria, 1964, pp. 66-73.

229 Allen, Walter. The Modern Novel in Britain and the United States. New York: E. P. Dutton, 1964, pp. 121-124.

230 _______. The Urgent West: The American Dream and the Modern Man. New York: E. P. Dutton, 1969, pp. 88-90.

231 Anderson, Charles R. "Faulkner's Moral Center," EA, 7 (January, 1954), 48-58.

232 Angell, Leslie E. "The Umbilical Cord Symbol As Unifying Theme and Pattern in Absalom, Absalom!" MSE, 1 (Fall, 1968), 106-110.

233 Anon. "Doom in Mississippi," TLS, #1829 (February 20, 1937), 128.

234 Anon. "Faulkner Has Nightmare About the South in Civil War Days," Newsweek, 8 (October 31, 1936), 26.

235 Anon. "Reviewing Reviews," SatRL, 15 (December 5, 1936), 58.

236 Anon. "Southern Cypher," Time, 28 (November 2, 1936), 67.

237 Antrim, Harry T. "Faulkner's Suspended Style," UKCR, 32 (Winter, 1965), 122-128.

238 Arnavon, Cyrille. "Absalon, Absalon!," RLM, Nos. 40-42 (Hiver, 1958-59), 250-270.

239 Arthos, John. "Ritual and Humor in the Writing of William Faulkner," Accent, 9 (Autumn, 1948), 17-30.

240 Aswell, Duncan. "The Puzzling Design of Absalom, Absalom!," KR, 30, #1 (Winter, 1968), 67-84.

241 Atkins, Anselm. "The Matched Halves of Absalom, Absalom!" MFS, 15, #2 (Summer, 1969), 264-265.

242 Aury, Dominique. "Le Pêché des origines," NRF, 1 (November, 1953), 886-893.

243 Backman, Melvin. "Absalom, Absalom!" in Twentieth Century Interpretations of Absalom, Absalom! Arnold Goldman, ed. Englewood Cliffs, New Jersey: Prentice-Hall, 1971, pp. 59-75.

244 _______. "Faulkner's Sick Heroes: Bayard Sartoris and Quentin Compson," MFS, 2 (Autumn, 1956), 95-108.

245 _______. "Sickness and Primitivism: A Dominant Pattern in Faulkner's Work," Accent, 14 (Winter, 1954), 61-73.

246 _______. "Sutpen and the South: A Study of Absalom, Absalom!" PMLA, 80, #5 (December, 1965), 596-604.

247 Baldanza, Frank. "Faulkner and Stein: A Study in Stylistic Intransigence," GaR, 13, #3 (Fall, 1959), 274-286.
Similarities between Faulkner's novel and Gertrude Stein's The Making of Americans.

248 Barjon, Louis. "Retour aux enfers de Faulkner: Absalon, Absalon!" Etudes (Paris), 279 (November, 1953), 225-236.

249 Barklund, Gunnar, tr. Absalom, Absalom! Stockholm: Albert Bonniers Forlag, 1969. Swedish translation.

250 Barth, J. Robert. "Faulkner and the Calvinist Tradition," Thought, 39 (March, 1964), 110-111.

251 Bashiruddin, Zeba. "The Lost Individual in Absalom, Absalom!" ASRC Newsletter (Hyderabad), No. 11 (December, 1967), 49-52.

252 Bates, H. E. "A Black Pudding of Dynamite and Thunder," Morning Post, (February 19, 1937), 14.

253 Beach, Joseph Warren. "William Faulkner: The Haunted South," in American Fiction, 1920-1940. New York: Macmillan, 1960, pp. 138-143, 164-169.

254 Beck, Warren. "Faulkner and the South," AntiochR, 1 (Spring, 1941), 82-94.

255 _______. "William Faulkner's Style," American Prefaces, 6 (1941), 195-211. Repr., in Two Decades of Criticism. Hoffman and Vickery, eds., pp. 147-164.

256 Behrens, Ralph. "Collapse of Dynasty: The Thematic Center of Absalom, Absalom!" PMLA, 89 (January, 1974), 24-33.

257 Beja, Morris. "A Flash, a Glare: Faulkner and Time," Renascence, 16 (Spring, 1964), 137-141.

258 _______. "William Faulkner: A Flash, a Glare," in Epiphany in the Modern Novel. Seattle: Washington U.P., 1971, pp. 182-210.

259 Beresford, J. D. "Four Novels," Manchester Guardian (February 19, 1937), 7. Review.

260 Berrone, Louis C., Jr. "Faulkner's Absalom, Absalom! and Dickens: A Study of Time and Change Correspondence," DAI, 34 (Fordham: 1973), 5158A.

261 Billingslea, Oliver L. "The Monument and the Plain: The Art of Mythic Consciousness in William Faulkner's Absalom, Absalom!" DA, 32 (Wisconsin: 1971), 3293A.

262 Björk, Lennart. "Ancient Myths and the Moral Framework of Faulkner's Absalom, Absalom!" AL, 35 (May, 1963), 196-204.

263 Blakeston, Oswell. "Novels," Life and Letters Today, 16 (Summer, 1937), 155-156. Review.

264 Bowling, Lawrence E. "William Faulkner: The Importance of Love," DR, 43 (Winter, 1963), 476-477.

265 Boyd, Gary Michael. "The Reflexive Novel: Fiction as Critique," DAI, 37 (Madison, Wis.: 1975), 293A-94A.

266 Bradford, Melvin E. "Brother, Son, and Heir: The Structural Focus of Faulkner's Absalom, Absalom!" SR, 78, #1 (January-March, 1970), 76-98.

267 _______. "'New Men' in Mississippi: Absalom, Absalom! and Dollar Cotton," NMW, 2, #2 (Fall, 1969), 55-66.
Parallels between Faulkner's novel and that of his brother John.

268 Breaden, Dale G. "William Faulkner and the Land," AQ, 10 (Fall, 1958), 344-357.

269 Breit, Harvey. Introduction, Absalom, Absalom! New York: Modern Library, 1951, pp. v-xii.

270 Brick, Allen. "Absalom Reconsidered," UTQ, 1 (October, 1960), 45-57.
Sees Faulkner as more concerned with defining the South than in portraying "the modern tragic hero."

271 Brickell, Herschel. "William Faulkner's New Novel Once More Sets Forth Theory That the South Is Doom-Ridden," New York Post (October 26, 1936), 13.
See also Rev. of Reviews, 94 (December, 1936), 15.

272 Brooks, Cleanth. "Absalom, Absalom!: The Definition of Innocence," SR, 59 (October, 1951), 543-558.

273 _______. "The American 'Innocence': In James, Fitzgerald, and Faulkner," Shenandoah, 16, #1 (Autumn, 1964), 21-37.
Christopher Newman, Jay Gatsby, and Thomas Sutpen are examples of American innocents.

274 _______. "Faulkner's Vision of Good and Evil," MassR, 3 (Summer, 1962), 692-712; repr., in The Hidden God. New Haven: Yale U.P., 1963, pp. 22-43.

275 _______. "History, Tragedy, and the Imagination in Absalom, Absalom!" YR, 52 (March, 1963), 340-351; revised and expanded in William Faulkner: The Yoknapatawpha Country, New Haven: 1963, pp. 295-324, 424-443.

276 _______. "The Narrative Structure of Absalom, Absalom!" GaR, 29 (Summer, 1975), 366-394.

277 _______. "On Absalom, Absalom!" Mosaic, 7, #1 (Fall, 1973), 159-183.

278 _______. "The Poetry of Miss Rosa Canfield," [sic], Shenandoah, 20 (Spring, 1970), 199-206.
"Canfield" for "Coldfield"--a printing error.

279 _______. William Faulkner: The Yoknapatawpha Country. New Haven and London: Yale U.P., 1963, pp. 295-324.

280 Brophy, John. "New Novels," Time and Tide, 18 (February 20, 1937), 245-248.

281 Brown, William R. "Mr. Stark on Mr. Strawson on Referring," Lang&S, 7 (Summer, 1974), 219-224.

282 Brumm, Ursula. "Geschichte als Geschehen und Erfahrung:

Eine Analyse von William Faulkners Absalom, Absalom!" Archiv, 204, #1 (May, 1967), 26-50.

283 _______. "Geschichte als Geschehen und Erfahrung: Eine Analyse von William Faulkners Absalom, Absalom!" Miscellanea Anglo-Americana: Festschrift für Helmut Viebrock. Kuno Schuhmann, et al., eds. München: Pressler, 1974, pp. 258-274.

284 _______. "Thoughts on History and the Novel," CLS, 6, #3 (September, 1969), 317-330.
Sees the two plots of Absalom, Absalom! as a historical novel and a novel on history.

285 Brylowski, Walter. Faulkner's Olympian Laugh. Detroit: 1968, pp. 17-42, 120-121.

286 Burgum, Edwin Berry. "William Faulkner's Patterns of American Decadence," Novel and the World's Dilemma. New York: Oxford U. P., 1947, pp. 221-222.

287 Burns, Stuart L. "Sutpen's 'Incidental' Wives and the Question of Respectability," MissQt, 30 (Summer, 1977), 445-447.

288 Callen, Shirley. "Planter and Poor White in Absalom, Absalom!--'Wash,' and The Mind of the South," SCB, 23, #4 (Winter, 1963), 24-36.

289 Cambon, Glauco. "Absalom, Absalom! di William Faulkner. Un'epica comme all'autore e al personaggio," FLe, No. 44 (November 2, 1952), 1-2.

290 _______. "'Assalonne, Assalonne!': Il Demone della memoria," La lotta con proteo. Milan: Bompiani, 1963, pp. 215-222.

291 _______. "My Faulkner: The Untranslatable Demon," in Proceedings of the Comparative Literature Symposium. Vol. IV. William Faulkner: Prevailing Verities and World Literature. Wolodymyr T. Zyla and Wendell M. Aycock, eds. Lubbock: Interdept. Comm. on Comp. Lit. Texas Tech U., 1973, pp. 77-93.

292 _______. "Prefazione," Assalonne, Assalonne! by William Faulkner. Milano: Mondadori, 1954, pp. 7-17.

293 Campbell, Harry Modean. "Faulkner's Absalom, Absalom!" Expl. 7 (December, 1948), Item 24.

294 _______, and Ruel E. Foster. William Faulkner: A Critical Appraisal. Norman, Oklahoma: Oklahoma U. P., 1951, pp. 31-35, 74-76.

295 Cargill, Oscar. "The Primitivists," Intellectual America. New York: Macmillan, 1941, pp. 370-386.

296 Carrouges, Michel. "Faulkner le voyant," Monde Nouveau Paru, No. 75 (January, 1954), 74-79. Review.

297 Chikamori, Kazue. "Unity of Theme and Technique in Absalom, Absalom!" E&S(T), 11 (Summer, 1963), 65-88.

298 Church, Margaret. "William Faulkner: Myth and Duration," in Time and Reality: Studies in Contemporary Fiction. Chapel Hill: North Carolina U.P., 1963, pp. 227-250.

299 Church, Richard. "New Books," John O'London's Weekly, 36, #933 (February 26, 1937), 897. Review.

300 Clark, C. C. "'Mistral': A Study in Human Tempering," MissQ, 21 (Summer, 1968), 195-204.
Anticipates the narrative form of Absalom, Absalom!

301 Clark, Edward Depriest. "Six Grotesques in Three Faulkner Novels," DAI, 33 (Syracuse: 1972), 302A.

302 Clark, William Bedford. "The Serpent of Lust in the Southern Garden," SoR, 10, #4 (October, 1974), 805-822.

303 Clark, William G. "Is King David a Racist?" UR, 34 (December, 1967), 121-126.

304 Cleopatra, Sr. "Absalom, Absalom! The Failure of the Sutpen Design," LHY, 16 (January, 1975), 74-93.

305 Coanda, Richard. "Absalom, Absalom!: The Edge of Infinity," Renascence, 11 (Autumn, 1958), 3-9.

306 Coindreau, Maurice E. "Absalon, Absalon! par William Faulkner," NRF, 280 (janvier 1, 1937), 123-126. Review.

307 _______. "William Faulkner y su último gran libro," La Nación (diciembre 13, 1936). Review.
"Más que una novela, Absalon, Absalon! es un vasto poema bárbaro."

308 Colum, Mary. "Faulkner's Struggle with Technique," Forum, 97, #1 (January, 1937), 35-36.
Comparison of Absalom, Absalom! with Wuthering Heights.

309 Connolly, Thomas E. "Fate and 'The Agony of Will': Determinism in Some Works of William Faulkner," in Essays on Determinism in American Literature. S. J. Krause, ed. Kent Studies in English No. 1. Kent State U.P., 1964, pp. 45-47.

310 _______. "A Skeletal Outline of Absalom, Absalom!" CE, 25 (November, 1963), 110-114.

311 Cook, Albert. The Meaning of Fiction. Detroit: Wayne State U. P., 1960, pp. 236-239.

312 Cook, Richard M. "Popeye, Flem, and Sutpen: The Faulknerian Villain As Grotesque," SAF, 3 (Spring, 1975), 3-14.

313 Cowley, Malcolm. "An Introduction to William Faulkner," in Critiques and Essays on Modern Fiction. John W. Aldridge, ed. New York: Ronald Press, 1952, pp. 432-437.

314 _______. "Poe in Mississippi," NR, 89 (November 4, 1936), 22.

315 _______. "William Faulkner's Legend of the South," SR, 53 (Summer, 1945), 343-361.

316 Crane, John Kenny. "The Jefferson Courthouse: An Axis Exsecrabilis Mundi," TCL, 15 (April, 1969), 19-23.
Discussion of Jefferson in terms of Mircea Eliade's theory of civilization.

317 Darragh, Vicki. "Wordy Warfare," Daily Worker (March 10, 1937), 7.

318 Davenport, F. Garvin, Jr. "William Faulkner," The Myth of Southern History: Historical Consciousness in Twentieth-Century Southern Literature. Nashville: Vanderbilt U. P., 1970, pp. 82-130.

319 Delgado Nieto, Carlos. "Absalón, Absalón!" Revista de las Indias, No. 114 (August, 1950), 411-412.

320 DeVoto, Bernard. "Witchcraft in Mississippi," SatRL, 15, #1 (October 31, 1936), 3-4, 14. Repr., Minority Report. Boston: Little, Brown, 1940, pp. 209-218.

321 Dickerson, Lynn. "A Possible Source for the Title Absalom, Absalom!" MissQ, 31, #3 (Summer, 1978), 423-424.
Grace Lumpkin's To Make My Bread a possible source.

322 Dillingham, William B. "William Faulkner and the 'Tragic Condition,'" Edda, 66 (Heft 5, 1966), 322-335.

323 Donley, Carol Cram. "Modern Literature and Physics: A Study of Interrelationships," DAI, 36 (Kent State: 1975), 3684A.

324 Donohoe, Eileen Marie. "Psychic Transformation Through Memory: Work and Negation in William Faulkner's Absalom, Absalom," DAI, 39 (Notre Dame: 1978), 1546A-47A.

325 Doody, Terrence. "Shreve McCannon and the Confessions of Absalom, Absalom!" SNNTS, 6, #4 (Winter, 1974), 454-469.

326 Edmonds, Irene C. "Faulkner and the Black Shadow," Southern Renascence: The Literature of the Modern South. Louis D. Rubin, Jr., and Robt. D. Jacobs, eds. Baltimore: 1953, pp. 192-206.

327 Edwards, Duane. "Flem Snopes and Thomas Sutpen: Two Versions of Respectability," DR, 51 (Winter, 1971-72), 559-570.
Parallels between the two characters.

328 Eigner, Edwin M. "Faulkner's Isaac and the American Ishmael," JA, 14 (1969), 107-115.

329 Everett, Walter K. Faulkner's Art and Characters. Woodbury, New York: Barron's Educ. Series, 1969, pp. 1-6.

330 Ewell, Barbara N. "To Move in Time: A Study of the Structure of Faulkner's As I Lay Dying, Light in August, and Absalom, Absalom!" DA, 30 (Florida State: 1969), 3940A.

331 Fadiman, Clifton. "Faulkner, Extra-special, Double-distilled," NY, 12 (1936), 78-80.

332 Fane, Vernon. "The World of Books," Sphere, 148, #1939 (March 20, 1937), 462. Review.

333 "Faulkner Has Nightmare About South in Civil War Days," Newsweek (October 31, 1936), 26.

334 Fazio, Rocco R. "The Fury and the Design-Realms of Being and Knowing in Four Novels of William Faulkner," DA, 25 (Rochester: 1964), 1910.

335 Fiedler, Leslie A. Love and Death in the American Novel. New York: Criterion Books, 1960, pp. 394-398.

336 Flint, R. W. "Faulkner as Elegist," HudR, 7 (Summer, 1954), 246-257.

337 Foran, Donald J., S.J. "William Faulkner's Absalom, Absalom! An Exercise in Affirmation," DAI, 34 (So. California: 1973), 4259A.

338 Ford, Daniel Gordon. "Comments on William Faulkner's Temporal Vision in Sanctuary, The Sound and the Fury, Light in August, Absalom, Absalom!" SoQ, 15 (April, 1977), 283-290.
Use of the calendar, characters, and the clock in the four novels.

339 ________. "Uses of Time in Four Novels by William Faulkner," DAI, 35 (Auburn: 1974), 1654A.

340 Forrer, Richard. "Absalom, Absalom!: Story-telling As a Mode of Transcendence," SLJ, 9 (Fall, 1976), 22-46.

341 Foster, Ruel E. "Social Order and Disorder in Faulkner's Fiction," Approach, 55 (Spring, 1965), 20-28.

342 Franklin, Rosemary F. "Clairvoyance, Vision, and Imagination in the Fiction of William Faulkner," DA, 29 (Emory: 1969), 3135A.

343 Friedling, Sheila. "Problems of Perception in the Modern Novel: The Representation of Consciousness in Works of Henry James, Gertrude Stein, and William Faulkner," DAI, 34 (Wisconsin: 1973), 3391A.

344 Frondizi, Josefina B. de. "Absalon, Absalon!," Asomante, 7, #1 (January-March, 1951), 93-95.

345 Fuller, Timothy. "The Story of Jack and Jill," SatRL, 15 (December 19, 1936), 10.

346 Gannett, Lewis. "Books and Things," NYHT (October 31, 1936), 17.

"He can write with a beauty and a power granted no other American of his generation."

347 Garzilli, Enrico. "Myth, Story, and Self: Absalom, Absalom!" Circles Without Center: Paths to Discovery and Creation of Self in Modern Literature. Cambridge: Harvard U.P., 1972, pp. 52-60.

348 Gegerias, Mary. "Michel Butor and William Faulkner: Some Structures and Techniques," DA, 30 (Columbia: 1969), 712A.

349 Geismar, Maxwell. Writers in Crisis. Boston: Houghton Mifflin, 1942, pp. 170-176.

350 Giannitrapani, Angela. "Wistaria: Le immagini in Faulkner," SA, 5 (1959), 243-280.

Wisteria imagery in Absalom, Absalom! and in earlier works.

351 Giordano, Frank R., Jr. "Absalom, Absalom! as a Portrait of the Artist," in From Irving to Steinbeck: Studies of American Literature in Honor of Harry R. Warfel. Motley Deakin and Peter Lisca, eds. Gainesville, Florida: Florida U.P., 1972, pp. 97-107.

352 Glicksburg, Charles Irving. "William Faulkner and the Negro Problem," Phylon, 10 (June, 1949), 153-156.

353 ________. "The World of William Faulkner," ArQ, 5 (Spring, 1949), 46-58.

354 Gold, Joseph. William Faulkner: A Study in Humanism from Metaphor to Discourse. Norman: Oklahoma U.P., 1966, pp. 30-38.

355 Goldman, Arnold, ed. Introduction. Twentieth Century Interpretations of Absalom, Absalom! Englewood Cliffs, New Jersey: Prentice-Hall, 1971, pp. 1-11.

356 Gossett, Louise Y. "The Climate of Violence," Violence in Recent Southern Fiction. Durham: Duke U.P., 1965, pp. 35-38.

357 Gray, Richard. "The Meanings of History: William Faulkner's Absalom, Absalom!" DQR, 3 (1973), 97-110.

358 Greene, Graham. "The Furies in Mississippi," LonMerc, 35 (March, 1937), 517-518. Repr., in Faulkner: A Collection of Critical Essays. Robert Penn Warren, ed., pp. 276-277.

359 Guerard, Albert. Conrad the Novelist. Cambridge, Mass.: 1958, pp. 129-134.

Cf., W. J. Harvey. Character and the Novel. Ithaca, New York: 1965, pp. 197-198. Takes issue with Guerard's discussion of Absalom, Absalom!

360 ________. "Absalom, Absalom!: The Novel as Impressionistic Art," The Triumph of the Novel: Dickens, Dostoevsky, Faulkner. New York: Oxford U.Pr., 1976, pp. 302-339.

361 Guetti, James. "Absalom, Absalom!" The Limits of Metaphor: A Study of Melville, Conrad, and Faulkner. Ithaca, New York: Cornell U.P., 1967, pp. 69-108.

Rev., C. Hugh Holman, AL, 40 (1968), 243-244.

362 ________. "The Failure of the Imagination: A Study of Melville, Conrad, and Faulkner," DA, 25 (Cornell: 1965), 4145-6.

363 Gustavson, Leif V. "Om William Faulkner och hans Romanexperiment 'Absalom, Absalom!'" Studiekamraten, 48 (1966), 70-73.

364 Gwynn, Frederick L., and Joseph L. Blotner, eds. Faulkner in the University: Class Conferences at the University of Virginia, 1957-1958. Charlottesville: Virginia U.P., 1959, passim.

365 H., C. H. "Novels from America," Oxford Times (February 26, 1937), 22. Review.

366 Hagan, John. "Déjà vu and the Effect of Timelessness in Faulkner's Absalom, Absalom!" BuR, 11 (March, 1963), 31-52; repr., in Makers of the Twentieth-century Novel. H. R.

Garvin, ed. Lewisburg, Pa.: Bucknell U.P., 1977, pp. 192-207.

367 _______. "Fact and Fancy in Absalom, Absalom!" CE, 24 (December, 1962), 215-218.

368 Hagopian, John V. "Absalom, Absalom! and the Negro Question," MFS, 19 (Summer, 1973), 207-211.

369 _______. "The Biblical Background of Faulkner's Absalom, Absalom!" CEA Critic, 36, #2 (January 1974), 22-24.

370 Hammond, Donald. "Faulkner's Level of Awareness," FlaQ, I, #2 (1967), 75-78.

371 Hansen, Harry. "William Faulkner's New Book a Dark and Terrible Story. Its Prose a Triumph," New York World-Telegram (October 26, 1936), 19.

372 Hardy, John E. "William Faulkner: The Legend Behind the Legend," Man in the Modern Novel. Seattle: Washington U.P., 1964, pp. 143-146.

373 Hartman, Geoffrey. "The Aesthetics of Complicity," GaR, 28 (Fall, 1974), 384-403.

374 Hartt, Julian N. The Lost Image of Man. Baton Rouge: Louisiana State U.P., 1963, pp. 39-41.

375 Harvey, W. J. "The Retreat from Character," Character and the Novel. Ithaca, New York: Cornell U.P., 1965, pp. 197-198.

Cf., Albert Guerard. Conrad the Novelist, pp. 129-134.

376 Haury, Beth. "The Influence of Robinson Jeffers' 'Tamar' on Absalom, Absalom!" MissQ, 25, #3 (Summer, 1972), 356-358.

Finds the novel's characterization closer to the Jeffers poem than to 2 Samuel.

377 Hawkins, E. O. "Faulkner's 'Duke John of Lorraine,'" AN&Q, 4 (October, 1965), 22.

Suggests John V of Armagnac was Faulkner's Duke John of Lorraine.

378 Hedin, Anne Miller. "The Self as History: Studies in Adams, Faulkner, Ellison, Belyj, Pasternak," DAI, 36 (Virginia: 1975), 6074A.

379 Henderson, Harry B., III. "Faulkner," Versions of the Past: The Historical Imagination in American Fiction. New York: Oxford U.P., 1974, pp. 253-269.

380 Hicks, Granville. "The Meaning of Tragedy," SatR, 42 (March 28, 1959), 19.

381 Hlavsa, V. V. "The Vision of the Advocate in Absalom, Absalom!" Novel, 8 (Fall, 1974), 51-70.

382 Hodgson, John A. "'Logical Sequence and Continuity': Some Observations on the Typographical and Structural Consistency of Absalom, Absalom!" AL, 43, #1 (March, 1971), 97-107.

383 Hoffman, A. C. "Faulkner's Absalom, Absalom!" Expl, 10 (November, 1951), Item 12.

384 _______. "Point of View in Absalom, Absalom!" UKCR, 19 (Summer, 1953), 233-239.

385 Hoffman, Frederick J. "The Tangled Web--Absalom, Absalom!" in William Faulkner. New York: Twayne Pubs., 1966, rev., pp. 74-79.

386 _______. "William Faulkner," American Winners of the Nobel Literary Prize. W. G. French, and W. E. Kidd, eds. Norman, Oklahoma: Oklahoma U.P., 1968, pp. 150-152.

387 Holden, Sarah Holland. "Changes in the Novel: A Structuralist Comparison of Middlemarch, The Confidence Man, and Absalom, Absalom!" DAI, 38 (Rice: 1977), 1409A.

388 Holman, C. Hugh. "Absalom, Absalom! The Historian as Detective," SR, 79, #4 (Autumn, 1971), 542-553.

389 _______. "Absalom, Absalom! The Historian as Detective," in The Roots of Southern Writing. Athens, Georgia: Georgia U.P., 1972, pp. 168-176.

390 _______. "William Faulkner: The Anguished Dream of Time," Three Modes of Southern Fiction: Ellen Glasgow, William Faulkner, Thomas Wolfe. Athens: Georgia U.P., 1966, pp. 27-47.

391 Holmes, Edward M. Faulkner's Twice Told Tales: His Re-Use of His Material. The Hague: Mouton, 1966, pp. 83-87.

392 Hopper, Vincent F. "Faulkner's Paradise Lost," VQR, 23 (Summer, 1947), 405-420.

393 Howe, Irving. William Faulkner: A Critical Study. Revised, ed. New York: Vintage Books, 1962, pp. 71-78.
Statement of the gothic qualities of Absalom, Absalom!

394 Howell, Elmo. "Faulkner's Wash Jones and the Southern Poor White," BSUF, 8, #1 (Winter, 1967), 8-12.

395 _______. "William Faulkner: The Substance of Faith," BYUS, 9 (Summer, 1969), 453-462.

396 Hunt, John W. "The Theological Center of Absalom, Absalom!" William Faulkner: Art in Theological Tension. Syracuse U. P., 1965, pp. 101-136; excerpt in Religious Perspectives in Faulkner's Fiction. J. R. Barth, ed. Notre Dame, Indiana: Notre Dame U. P., 1972, pp. 141-169.

397 Irwin, John T. Doubling and Incest, Repetition and Revenge: A Speculative Reading of Faulkner. Baltimore and London: Johns Hopkins U. P., 1975.

398 Isaacs, Neil D. "Gotterdammerung in Yoknapatawpha," TSL, 8 (1963) 47-55.

399 J. H. P. Cambridge Review, 59, #1436 (October 22, 1937), 34. Review.

400 Jack, Peter Monro. "Nightmares of Evil," NYSun (October 30, 1936), 30. Review.

401 Jackson, Naomi. "Faulkner's Woman: 'Demon-Nun and Angel-Witch,'" BSUF, 8 (Winter, 1967), 12-20.

402 Jacobs, Robert D. "Faulkner and the Tragedy of Isolation," in Southern Renascence. Louis D. Rubin and Robt. D. Jacobs, eds. Baltimore: Johns Hopkins, 1966, pp. 170-191.

403 _______. "How Do You Read Faulkner?" Prov, 1, #4 (April, 1957), 3-5.
Analysis of style and structure in Absalom, Absalom!

404 _______. "William Faulkner: The Passion and the Penance," in South: Modern Southern Literature in Its Cultural Setting. Louis D. Rubin, Jr., and Robt D. Jacobs, eds. Garden City, New York: Doubleday, 1961, pp. 163-169.

405 Justus, James H. "The Epic Design of Absalom, Absalom!" TSLL, 4, #2 (Summer, 1962), 157-176.

406 Kartiganer, Donald M. "Faulkner's Absalom, Absalom!: The Discovery of Values," AL, 37, #3 (November, 1965), 291-306.

407 _______. "Process and Product: A Study of Modern Literary Form," MassR, 12 (Autumn, 1971), 297-328, 789-816.

408 _______. "The Role of Myth in Absalom, Absalom!" MFS, 9, #4 (Winter, 1963-64), 357-369.

409 Kellner, R. S. "A Reconsideration of Character: Relationships in Absalom, Absalom!" NMW, 7 (Fall, 1974), 39-43.

410 Kierszys, Zofia, tr. Absalomie, Absalomie. Warsaw: Państwowy Instytut Wydawniczy, 1959.

411 Kinney, Arthur F. "Form and Function in Absalom, Absalom!" SoR, 14 (October, 1978), 677-691.

412 Kinoian, Vartkis. Review Notes and Study Guide to Faulkner's Absalom, Absalom! [and other novels]. New York: Monarch Press, 1964.

413 Kirk, Robert W., and Marvin Klotz. Faulkner's People. Berkeley: California U.P., 1963, pp. 84-93.

414 Klotz, Marvin. "The Triumph Over Time: Narrative Form in William Faulkner and William Styron," MissQ, 17 (Winter, 1964), 9-20.

415 Knox, Robert H. William Faulkner's Absalom, Absalom! Diss. Harvard: 1959.

416 Kohler, Dayton. "William Faulkner and the Social Conscience," CE, 11 (December, 1949), 119-127.

417 Korenman, Joan S. "Faulkner and 'That Undying Mark,'" SAF, 4 (Spring, 1976), 81-91.
Faulkner's "obsession" with time in Absalom, Absalom! Cf., Ruth M. Vande Kieft, SoR, 6 (1970), 1100-1109.

418 Korn, Karl. "Moira und Schuld," NRs, No. 49 (December, 1938), 603-616.

419 L., M. "Cult of Infantilism," AmSpec (February-March, 1937), 13-14.

420 Labatt, Blair P., Jr. "Faulkner the Storyteller," DAI, 34 (Virginia: 1974), 7761A.

421 Langford, Gerald. Faulkner's Revision of Absalom, Absalom!: A Collation of the Manuscript and the Published Book. Austin: Texas U.P., 1971.
Cf., Noel Polk. "The Manuscript of Absalom, Absalom!" MissQ, 25 (Summer, 1972), 359-367; Jack Capps, SLJ, 6 (Fall, 1973), 117-121.

422 Larsen, Eric. "The Barrier of Language: The Irony of Language in Faulkner," MFS, 13 (1967), 19-31.

423 Laws, Frederick. "New Novels," NS&N, 13, #315 (March 6, 1937), 380. Review.

424 Lawton, Mary. "Different," Constitution (Atlanta) (November 23, 1936), M9. Review.

425 Leary, Lewis. "Absalom, Absalom!" William Faulkner of Yoknapatawpha County. New York: Crowell, 1973, pp. 96-113.

426 Leaska, Mitchell A. "The Rhetoric of Multiple Points of View in Selected Contemporary Novels," DA, 29 (N.Y.U.: 1969), 3145A-46A.
Absalom, Absalom! one of the novels analyzed.

427 LeBreton, Maurice. "Technique et psychologie chez William Faulkner," EA, 1 (septembre, 1937), 418-438.

428 Lensing, George S. "The Metaphor of Family in Absalom, Absalom!" SoR, 11, #1 (January, 1975), 99-117.

429 Lenson, David R. "Classical Analogy: Giraudoux versus Faulkner," Achilles' Choice: Examples of Modern Tragedy. Princeton, New Jersey: Princeton U.P., 1975, pp. 98-116.

430 _______. "Examples of Modern Tragedy," DAI, 32 (Princeton: 1972), 6433A-34A.

431 Levin, David. "Absalom, Absalom!: The Problem of Recreating History," In Defense of Historical Literature. New York: Hill & Wang, 1967, pp. 118-139.

432 Levins, Lynn Gartrell. Faulkner's Heroic Design: The Yoknapatawpha Novels. Athens: Georgia U.P., 1976.

433 _______. "The Four Narrative Perspectives in Absalom, Absalom!" PMLA, 85 (January, 1970), 35-47.

434 _______. "William Faulkner: The Heroic Design of Yoknapatawpha," DAI, 34, #5 (North Carolina at Chapel Hill: 1973), 2635A.

435 Lillqvist, Holger. "Det förflutnas närvaro och fantasins styrka," NyA, 63 (1970), 55-57.

436 Lind, Ilse Dusoir. "The Design and Meaning of Absalom, Absalom!" PMLA, 70 (December, 1955), 887-912. Repr., in Three Decades, Hoffman and Vickery, eds., pp. 278-304.

437 Lisk, Thomas David. "Love, Law and the Nature of Character," DAI, 36 (Rice: 1975), 2198A.

438 Litz, Walton. "William Faulkner's Moral Vision," SWR, 37 (Summer, 1952), 200-209.

439 Longley, John L., Jr. The Tragic Mask: A Study of Faulkner's Heroes. Chapel Hill: North Carolina U.P., 1963, pp. 200-218.

440 Lorch, Thomas M. "Thomas Sutpen and the Female Principle," MissQ, 20 (Winter, 1966-67), 38-42.

441 Loughrey, Thomas F. "Aborted Sacrament in *Absalom, Absalom!*" FourQ, 14, #1 (November, 1964), 13-21.

442 Lynd, Robert. News Chronicle (February 24, 1937). Review.

443 McClennen, Joshua. "*Absalom, Absalom!* and the Meaning of History," PMASAL, 42 (1956), 357-369.

444 McCole, Camille. "The Nightmare Literature of William Faulkner," CathW, 141 (August, 1935), 576-583. Repr., in *Lucifer at Large*. New York: Longmans Green, 1937, pp. 203-228.

445 McDonald, Walter R. "Coincidence in the Novel: A Necessary Technique," CE, 29 (February, 1968), 373-388.

446 MacLure, Millar. "Allegories of Innocence," DR, 40 (Summer, 1960), 145-156.

447 Magill, Frank N., ed. *Masterplots: First Series*: New York: Salem Press, 1957, pp. 5-7.

448 Major, Sylvia B. B. "*Absalom, Absalom!*: A Study of Structure," DAI, 34 (No. Texas State: 1973), 5188A.

449 Makuck, Peter Landers. "Faulkner Studies in France: 1953-1969," DA, 32 (Kent State: 1971), 3314A.

450 Mălăncioiu, Ileana. "*Absalom, Absalom!* sau tragicul absolut," RoLit, 11 (August, 1977), 20-21.

451 Malin, Irving. *William Faulkner: An Interpretation*. Stanford U. P., 1957, *passim*.

452 Mann, Dorothea Lawrence. "William Faulkner As Self-Conscious Stylist," Boston Evening Transcript (October 31, 1936), 6. Review.

453 Marlow, Young. "Novelists Face Up to Big Themes," Reynolds News (February 21, 1937), 13. Review.

454 Marshall, Sarah L. "Fathers and Sons in *Absalom, Absalom!*" UMSE, 8 (1967), 19-29.

455 Mascitelli, David W. "Faulkner's Characters of Sensibility," DA, 29 (Duke: 1968), 608A-9A.

456 Mathews, James W. "The Civil War of 1936: *Gone with the Wind* and *Absalom, Absalom!*" GaR, 21 (Winter, 1967), 462-469.

457 Matlack, James H. "The Voices of Time: Narrative Structure in *Absalom, Absalom!*" SoR, 15, #2 (April, 1979), 333-354.

458 Mayoux, Jean-Jacques. "La Creation du Reel chez William Faulkner," EA, 5, #1 (février, 1952), 25-29; tr. by F. J. Hoffman, and repr., in Three Decades, Hoffman and Vickery, eds., pp. 156-173.

459 Meriwether, James B. "Absalom, Absalom!" The Literary Career of William Faulkner. Columbia: South Carolina U.P., 1971, pp. 26-27.

460 Middleton, John. "Shreve McCannon and Sutpen's Legacy," SoR, 10 (Winter, 1974), 115-124

461 Miller, David M. "Faulkner's Women," MFS, 13 (Spring, 1967), 3-17.

462 Miller, Douglas T. "Faulkner and the Civil War: Myth and Reality," AQ, 15 (Summer, 1963), pp. 205-206.

463 Miller, James E. "William Faulkner: Descent into the Vortex," Quests Surd and Absurd: Essays in American Literature. Chicago: Chicago U.P., 1967, pp. 52-53, 55, 58-59.

464 Millgate, Michael. "Absalom, Absalom!" The Achievement of William Faulkner. New York: Random House, 1966, pp. 150-164.

465 ________. "The Firmament of Man's History: Faulkner's Treatment of the Past," MissQ, 25 (Spring, 1972), 25-35.

466 ________. William Faulkner. New York: Grove Press, 1961. Revised, 1966; repr., Capricorn Books, 1971.

467 Miner, Ward L. The World of William Faulkner. Durham, North Carolina: Duke U.P., 1952, pp. 141-143.

468 Minter, David L. The Interpreted Design as Structural Principle in American Prose. New Haven: Yale U.P., 1969, pp. 191-219.

469 Moloney, Michael Francis. "The Enigma of Time: Proust, Virginia Woolf, and Faulkner," Thought, 32 (Spring, 1957), 69-85.

470 Monaghan, David M. "Faulkner's Absalom, Absalom!" Expl, 31 (December, 1972), Item 28.
Parallels between Absalom and Oedipus Rex.

471 Morris, Wright. "The Violent Land: Some Observations on the Faulkner Country," Magazine of Art, 45 (March, 1952), 99-103.

472 Moses, Henry C. "History as Voice and Metaphor: A Study of Tate, Warren, and Faulkner," DA, 29 (Cornell: 1969), 4014A.

473 Moussy, Marcel. "Absalon! Absalon!" LetN, 1 (October, 1953), 1030-1035.

474 Muehl, Lois. "Faulkner's Humor in Three Novels and One 'Play,'" LibrChron, 24 (Spring, 1968), 78-93.

475 Muhlenfeld, Elisabeth S. "Shadows with Substance and Ghosts Exhumed: The Women in Absalom, Absalom!" MissQ, 25 (Summer, 1972), 289-304.

476 ______. "'We have waited long enough': Judith Sutpen and Charles Bon," SoR, 14 (January, 1978), 66-80.

477 Narain, S. K. "Absalom, Absalom! by William Faulkner: An Interpretation," LitCrit, 6 (Summer, 1964), 116-122.

478 Nelson, Beatriz Florencia, tr. Absalón, Absalón!" Buenos Aires: Emece, 1950.

479 Nilon, Charles H. Faulkner and the Negro. New York: Citadel Press, 1965, pp. 93-96, 105-106.

480 Nishiyama, Tamotsu. "The Structure of Absalom, Absalom!" KAL, No. 1 (June, 1958), 9-13.

481 O'Brien, Matthew C. "A Note on Faulkner's Civil War Women," NMW, 1 (Fall, 1968), 56-63.

482 O'Connor, William Van. "Faulkner's Legend of the Old South," WHR, 7 (Autumn, 1953), 294-299. Repr., with revisions in The Tangled Fire of William Faulkner. 1954, pp. 94-100.

483 ______. "Protestantism in Yoknapatawpha County," in HopR, 5 (Spring, 1952), 26-42; repr., in Southern Renascence, Louis D. Rubin, Jr., and Robt D. Jacobs, eds. 1953, pp. 153-169.

484 ______. The Tangled Fire of William Faulkner. Minneapolis: Minnesota U. P., 1954, pp. 94-100.

485 ______. William Faulkner. Minneapolis: Minnesota U. P., 1964, pp. 25-28.

486 O'Donnell, George Marion. "Faulkner's Mythology," KR, 1 (Summer, 1939), 285-299. Repr., in Three Decades. Hoffman and Vickery, eds., pp. 82-93; also in Two Decades, pp. 49-62.

487 Ohki, Masako. "The Technique of Handling Time in Absalom, Absalom!" Kyushu Am Lit (Fukuoka, Japan), 15 (1974), 89-94.

488 Ostendorf, Berndt. "Faulkner: Absalom, Absalom!" Der

amerikanische Roman: Von den Anfangen bis zur Gegenwart. Hans-Joachim Lang, ed. Dusseldorf: August Bagel, 1972, pp. 249-275.

489 Oswell, D. "The Puzzling Design of Absalom, Absalom!" KR, 30 (Winter, 1968), 65-84.

490 Otomo, Yoshiro. "Young Thomas Sutpen in Absalom, Absalom!" BCGE, 12, #2 (1971), 90-104.

491 Otten, Terry. "Faulkner's Use of the Past: A Comment," Renascence, 20 (Summer, 1968), 198-207, 214.

492 P., J. H. "Mississippi Miasma," CamR, (October 22, 1937), 34. Review.

493 Parker, Hershel. "What Quentin Saw 'Out There,'" MissQ, 27 (Summer, 1974), 323-326.

494 Parks, D. W. "Can't Tell Story and Be Through," PostDisp (November 1, 1936), 4-J. Review.

495 Parks, Edd Winfield. "Six Southern Novels," VQR, 13 (Winter, 1937), 154-156. Repr., in Segments of Southern Thought. Baltimore: Waverly Press, 1938, pp. 129-130.

496 Parr, Susan Dale R. "'And by Bergson, Obviously'--Faulkner's The Sound and the Fury, As I Lay Dying and Absalom, Absalom! from a Bergsonian Perspective," DAI, 32 (Wisconsin: 1972), 6996A.

497 ________. "The Fourteenth Image of the Blackbird: Another Look at Truth in Absalom, Absalom!" ArizQt, 35 (Summer, 1979), 153-164.

498 Paterson, Isabel. "An Unquiet Ghost Out of the Old South," NYHTB (October 25, 1936), 3.

499 Paterson, John. "Hardy, Faulkner, and the Prosaics of Tragedy," CentR, 5 (Spring, 1961), 156-175.

500 Patten, Mercury. "Books in General," NSt (February 14, 1933), 163. Review.

501 Patterson, Alicia. "Notes on Some of the Season's Better Books," NYSN (November 22, 1936), 90. Review.

502 Perry, Bradley T. "Absalom, Absalom!--Faulkner Critics: A Bibliography Breakdown," FS, 2 (Spring, 1953), 11-14.

503 Pfister, Kurt. Deutsche Zukunst, 6 (October 2, 1938), 10. Review.

504 Phillips, Elizabeth G. "Absalom, Absalom!"--A Critical Commentary. New York: Monarch Press, 1965. Study Guide, pp. 664-663.

505 Piacentino, Edward J. "Another Possible Source for Absalom Absalom!" NMW, 10 (Winter, 1977), 87-93.
T. S. Stribling's trilogy, The Forge, The Store, and Unfinished Cathedral suggested as a source.

506 Pinsker, Sanford. "Thomas Sutpen and Milly Jones: A Note on Paternal Design in Absalom, Absalom!" NMAL, 1 (1976). Item 6.

507 Pires, Sister Mary Dolorine. "Plot Manipulation and Kaleidoscoping of Time As Sources of Tragic Perception in William Faulkner's Absalom, Absalom!" DAI, 31 (St. Louis: 1970), 4176A.

508 Plomer, William. "Fiction," Spectator (February 26, 1937), 376. Review.

509 Poirier, William R. "'Strange Gods' in Jefferson, Mississippi: Analysis of Absalom, Absalom!" SR, 53 (Summer, 1945), 44-56. Repr., in William Faulkner: Two Decades of Criticism. Hoffman and Vickery, eds. 1951, pp. 217-243.

510 Polek, Fran James. "The Fourteenth Blackbird: Refractive Deflection in Absalom, Absalom!" UPortR, 28, #1 (Spring, 1976), 23-34.

511 ________. "From Renegade to Solid Citizen: The Extraordinary Individual and the Community," SDR, 15 (Spring, 1977), 61-72.
Discusses Thomas Sutpen in Absalom, Absalom!

512 Polk, Noel. "The Manuscript of Absalom, Absalom!" MissQ, 25, #3 (Summer, 1972), 359-367.
Essay-review of Gerald Langford's Faulkner's Revision of Absalom, Absalom! (1971).

513 Pouillon, Jean. "A propos d'Absalon, Absalon!" TM, 9 (October, 1953), 742-752.

514 Praz, Mario. "L'ultimo Faulkner," Omnibus, (April 3, 1937); included in Cronache letterarie anglosassoni. Roma: Edizioni di Storia e Letteratura (1951), II, 246-256.

515 Putzel, Max. "What Is Gothic About Absalom, Absalom!" SLJ, 4, #1 (Fall, 1971), 3-19.

516 Rahv, Philip. "Faulkner and Destruction," New Masses (November 24, 1936), 20-21. Review.

517 Raimbault, R. N., tr., avec le collaboration de Ch. P. Vorce. Absalon! Absalon! Paris: Gallimard, 1953.

518 Randel, Fred V. "Parentheses in Faulkner's Absalom, Absalom!" Style, 5 (1971), 70-87.

519 Raper, J. R. "Meaning Called to Life: Alogical Structure in Absalom, Absalom!" SHR, 5, #1 (Winter, 1971), 9-23.

520 Reed, Joseph W., Jr. "Absalom, Absalom!" Faulkner's Narrative. New Haven: 1973, pp. 145-175.

521 _______. "Appendix C--Absalom, Absalom!" Faulkner's Narrative. New Haven, pp. 286-288.

522 Reznicek, Felicitas von. Deutsche Rundschau, 258 (1939), 149. Review.

523 Richardson, Kenneth E. Force and Faith in the Novels of William Faulkner. The Hague: Mouton, 1967 (Studies in American Literature, 7), pp. 29-35.

524 Rinaldi, Nicholas M. "Game Imagery in Faulkner's Absalom, Absalom!" ConnR, 4, #1 (October, 1970), 73-79.

525 Ringold, Francine. "The Metaphysics of Yoknapatawpha County: 'Airy Space and Scope for Your Delirium,'" HSL, 8 (1976), 223-240.

526 Roberts, James L. Absalom, Absalom!--Notes. Lincoln, Nebraska: Cliff's Notes, 1964. Rev. ed., 1970.

527 Robin, Régine. "Absalom, Absalom!" Views and Reviews of Modern German Literature. Festschrift für Adolf D. Klarmann. Karl S. Weimar, ed. München: 1974, pp. 67-129.

528 Robinson, Cecil. "The Fall of 'The Big House' in the Literature of the Americas," ArQ, 24 (Spring, 1968), 23-41.

529 Rodewald, F. A. "Faulkner's Possible Use of The Great Gatsby," FHA (1975), 97-101.

530 Rodnon, Stewart. "The House of the Seven Gables and Absalom, Absalom!" StHum, 1, #2 (Winter, 1969), 42-46.

531 Rollyson, Carl E., Jr. "Faulkner and Historical Fiction: Redgauntlet and Absalom, Absalom!" DR, 56 (Winter, 1976-77), 671-681.

532 _______. "The Re-creation of the Past in Absalom, Absalom!" MissQ, 29, #3 (Summer, 1976), 361-374.

533 Rome, Joy. "Love and Wealth in Absalom, Absalom!" UES, 9 (March, 1971), 3-10.

534 Rose, Maxine A. "From Genesis to Revelation: The Grand Design of Faulkner's Absalom, Absalom!" DAI, 34 (Alabama: 1974), 6656A.

535 Rosenman, John B. "[Sherwood] Anderson's Poor White and Faulkner's Absalom, Absalom!" MissQ, 29, #3 (Summer, 1976), 437-438.

536 _______. "A Matter of Choice: The Locked Door Theme in Faulkner," SAB, 41, #2 (May, 1976), 8-12.

537 Rosenzweig, Paul. "The Narrative Frames in Absalom, Absalom!: Faulkner's Involuted Commentary on Art," ArizQt, 35 (Summer, 1979), 135-152.

538 Ross, Stephen M. "Conrad's Influence on Faulkner's Absalom, Absalom!" SAF, 2 (Autumn, 1974), 199-209.

539 Rota, Bertram. "Contemporary Collectors, VII: The George Lazarus Library," BColl (London), 4 (Winter, 1955), 279-284.
On the holograph manuscript of Absalom, Absalom!

540 Roueché, Berton. "Absalom, Absalom!" UR, 3 (Winter, 1936), 137-138.

541 Rouse, H. Blair. "Time and Place in Southern Fiction," Southern Renascence. L. D. Rubin and Robert Jacobs, eds. Baltimore: Johns Hopkins Pr., 1966, pp. 141-143.

542 Rousseaux, André. "Absalon, Absalon!" FL, 8, #383-384 (August 22-29, 1953), 2.

543 _______. "L'enfer de Faulkner," Littérature de vingtième siècle. (5th ser.) Paris: Editions Albin Michel, 1955, pp. 115-133.

544 Rubin, L. D., Jr. "Chronicles of Yoknapatawpha: The Dynasties of William Faulkner," Faraway Country: Writers of the Modern South. Seattle: Washington U. Pr., 1963, pp. 43-71.

545 _______. "Looking Backward," NR, 171 (October 19, 1974), 20-22.
Essay-review of Versions of the Past: The Historical Imagination in American Fiction by Harry B. Henderson, III, with comments on Absalom, Absalom!

546 _______. "Scarlett O'Hara and the Two Quentin Compsons," The South and Faulkner's Yoknapatawpha. Evans, Harrington and Ann J. Abadie, eds. Jackson, Miss.: Miss. U. P., 1977, pp. 168-194.

547 Sabiston, Elizabeth. "Women, Blacks, and Thomas Sutpen's Mythopoeic Drive in Absalom, Absalom!" MSLC, 1, iii (1974), 15-26.

548 Sachs, Viola. "Absalom, Absalom!" The Myths of America. The Hague: Mouton, 1973.

549 Scheid, Mark Stacy. "Structuralism and the Modern Novel," DAI, 33, # 5 (Rice: 1972), 2393A.

550 Scherer, Olga. "Faulkner et le fratricide: pour une théorie dans la littérature," EA, 30 (July-Sept., 1977), 329-336.

551 Schneider-Schelde, Rudolf. "Absalom, Absalom! Roman von William Faulkner, Literatur (Berlin-Stuttgart), 40 (July, 1938), 693-694.

552 Schoenberg, Estella. Old Tales and Talking: Quentin Compson in William Faulkner's Absalom, Absalom! and Related Works. Jackson: Mississippi U. P., 1977.
Rev. by Elisabeth Muhlenfeld, MissQ, 30 (1977), 489-492.

553 ________. "Quentin Compson and the Fictive Process: A Four-Dimensional Study of Absalom, Absalom!" DAI, 35 (Tulsa, Okla.: 1974), 6732A-33A.

554 Scholes, Robert E. "The Modern American Novel and the Mason-Dixon Line," GaR, 14 (Summer, 1960), 193-204.

555 ________, and Robert Kellogg. The Nature of Narrative. New York: Oxford U. P., 1966, passim.

556 Schönemann, Freiderich. [Absalom, Absalom!] Zeitschrift (1939), 120.

557 Schrank, B. "Patterns of Reversal in Absalom, Absalom!" DR, 54 (Winter, 1974), 648-666.

558 Schrero, Elliott M. "Another Country and the Sense of Self," (BAcaR, 2, # 1&2 (Spring-Summer, 1971), 91-100.
Baldwin's novel Another Country compared with Absalom, Absalom!

559 Scott, Arthur L. "The Faulknerian Sentence," PrS, 27 (Spring, 1953), 91-98.

560 ________. "The Myriad Perspectives of Absalom, Absalom!" AQ, 6 (Fall, 1954), 210-220.

561 Seiden, Melvin. "Faulkner's Ambiguous Negro," MassR, 4 (Summer, 1963), 675-690.

562 Sewall, Richard B. "Absalom, Absalom!" The Vision of

Tragedy. New Haven and London: Yale U. P., 1959, pp. 133-147.

563 Singleton, Marvin K. "Personae at Law and Equity: The Unity of Faulkner's Absalom, Absalom!" PLL, 3 (Fall, 1967), 354-370.

564 Skaggs, Merrill Maguire. "The Tradition in the Twentieth Century," The Folk in Southern Fiction. Athens: Georgia U. P., 1972, pp. 221, 231-234.

565 Slabey, Robert M. "Faulkner's 'Waste Land' Vision in Absalom, Absalom!" MissQ, 14 (Summer, 1961), 153-161.

566 _______. "Quentin Compson's 'Lost Childhood,'" SSF, 1 (Spring, 1964), 173-183.

567 Slatoff, Walter J. "The Major Fiction--Absalom, Absalom!" Quest for Failure. Ithaca: Cornell U. P., 1960; 2nd pr., 1961, pp. 198-203.

568 Smith, Henry Nash. "Notes on Recent Novels," SoR, 3 (Winter, 1937), 577-593.
Comparison of Absalom, Absalom! with Kay Boyle's Death of a Man.

569 _______. "William Faulkner Continues to Depict Decadence of South," Dallas Morning News (November 29, 1936), Sec. II, 9; also reviewed in SoR, 2 (1937), 583-585.

570 Sowder, William J. "Colonel Thomas Sutpen as Existentialist Hero," AL, 33 (January, 1962), 485-499.

571 Spring, Howard. Evening Standard (February 18, 1937). Review.

572 Stafford, William T. "A Whale, an Heiress, and a Southern Demigod: Three Symbolic Americas," CollL, 1 (1974), 100-112.
"The rise and fall of Thomas Sutpen and his family recapitulates--perhaps prescribes--the American experience...."

573 Stark, John. "The Implications for Stylistics of Strawson's 'On Referring,' with Absalom, Absalom! as an Example," Lang&S, 6 (1973), 273-280.

574 Steinberg, Aaron. "Absalom, Absalom!: The Irretrievable Bon," CLAJ, 9 (September, 1965), 61-67.

575 _______. "Faulkner and the Negro," DA, 27 (N. Y. U.: 1966), 1385A.

576 Stewart, David H. "Absalom Reconsidered," UTQ, 30 (October, 1960), 31-44.

577 Straumann, Heinrich. "Faulkner und der amerikanische Süden: Zur Interpretation von Absalom, Absalom!" NZZ (September 22, 1962), 22-23.

578 Strauss, Harold. "Mr. Faulkner Is Ambushed in Words," NYTBR (November 1, 1936), 7. Review.

579 Stresau, Hermann, tr. Absalom, Absalom! Berlin: E. Rowohlt Verlag, 1938.
The translation was called "meisterlich" by Kurt Pfister, Deutsche Zukunst, 6 (October, 1938), 10.

580 Sullivan, Walter. "Southern Novelists and the Civil War," Southern Renascence: The Literature of the Modern South. Louis D. Rubin, Jr., and Robert Jacobs, eds. Baltimore: Johns Hopkins Press, 1953, pp. 122-123.

581 ________. "The Tragic Design of Absalom, Absalom!" SAQ, 50 (October, 1951), 552-566.

582 Sullivan, William P. "William Faulkner and the Community," DA, 22 (Columbia: 1962), 4355.

583 Swiggart, Peter. "A Puritan Tragedy: Absalom, Absalom!" The Art of Faulkner's Novels. Austin: Texas U.P., 1962, pp. 149-70.

584 Tanaka, Hisao. "Quentin Doomed As a Southerner: A Study of Absalom, Absalom!" SALit (Hiroshima U.), 7 (1971), 1-14.

585 Taylor, Walter. "Faulkner's Curse," ArQ, 28 (Winter, 1972), 333-338.
Concludes that "the curse is slavery."

586 TeSelle, Sallie McFague. Literature and the Christian Life. New Haven and London: Yale U.P., 1966, pp. 181-185.

587 Thomas, Douglas M. "Memory-Narrative in Absalom, Absalom!" FS, 2, #2 (Summer, 1953), 19-22.

588 Thompson, Lawrance. "A Defense of Difficulties in William Faulkner's Art," Carrell, 4 (December, 1963), 7-16

589 ________. William Faulkner. New York: Barnes and Noble, 1963, pp. 53-65.
Examination of Absalom, Absalom! in relation to Greek myth and Bible story.

590 Tindall, William York. Literary Symbol. Bloomington: Indiana U.P., 1955, pp. 264-267.

591 Tobin, Patricia. "The Time of Myth and History in Absalom, Absalom!" AL, 45, #2 (May, 1973), 252-270.

592 Towne, Charles H. "Pity Poor Reviewer on a Day Like This," American (New York) (October 27, 1936), 36. Review.

593 Troy, William. "The Poetry of Doom," Nation, 143, #18 (October 31, 1936), 524-525. Review.

594 Tuck, Dorothy. Crowell's Handbook of Faulkner (1964), pp. 56-66.

595 Tuso, Joseph F. "Faulkner's 'Wash,'" Expl, 27 (November, 1968), Item 17.
The meaning of the name "Wash" in the story and in Absalom.

596 Vande-Kieft, R. M. "Faulkner's Defeat of Time in Absalom, Absalom!" SoR, 6 (Autumn, 1970), 1100-1109.
A study of the theme of time and point of view in the novel.

597 Vandenbergh, John, tr. Absalom, Absalom! Hasselt: Heideland, 1966.

598 Van Gelder, Robert. "Books of the Times," NYT (October 25, 1936), 15. Review.

599 Van Nostrand, A. D. Everyman His Own Poet. New York: McGraw-Hill, 1968, pp. 184-189.

600 Vauthier, Simone. "Absalom, Absalom! un deliemme américain," BFLS, 38 (May-June, 1960), 381-397.
The Negro problem as interpreted in the novel.

601 Vickery, Olga W. "The Idols of the South: Absalom, Absalom!" The Novels of William Faulkner: A Critical Interpretation. Rev. ed., Baton Rouge: Louisiana State U. P., 1964, pp. 84-100.

602 Visentin, Giovanni. "Absalon, Absalon!" Idea, 6 (April 25, 1954), 2.

603 Volpe, Edmond L. A Reader's Guide to William Faulkner N. Y.: Noonday, (1964). pp. 184-212, 387-392.

604 Wad, Soren. "I: William Faulkner; II: Absalom, Absalom!" in Six American Novels: From New Deal to New Frontier: A Workbook. Jens Bøgh and Steffen Skovmand, eds. Aarhus: Akademisk Boghandel, pp. 85-118.

605 Waggoner, Hyatt H. "The Historical Novel and the Southern Past: The Case of Absalom, Absalom!" SLJ, 2, #2 (Spring, 1970), 69-85.

606 ________. Introduction. The House of the Seven Gables by Nathaniel Hawthorne. Boston: Houghton Mifflin, 1964.
Comparison of Hawthorne's novel with Absalom.

607 ________. William Faulkner: From Jefferson to the World. Lexington: Kentucky U. P., 1959, pp. 148-169. Repr., in Faulkner: A Collection of Critical Essays. Robt. Penn Warren, ed. pp. 175-185.

608 Wagner, Charles A. "Books," Mirror (New York) (October 31, 1936), 12. Review.

609 Walters, P. S. "Hallowed Ground: Group Areas in the Structure and Theme of Absalom, Absalom!" Theoria, 47 (1976), 35-55.

610 Warren, Robert Penn. "Faulkner: The South and the Negro," SoR, 1 (July, 1965), 515, 518-519.

611 Watkins, Evan. "The Fiction of Interpretation: Faulkner's Absalom, Absalom!" The Critical Act: Criticism and Community. New Haven, Conn.: Yale U. P., 1978, pp. 188-212.

612 Watkins, Floyd C. "Thirteen Ways of Talking About a Blackbird," The Flesh and the Word. Nashville: Vanderbilt U. P., 1971, pp. 216-233.
"The distinction between doing and merely talking, ... is central in Absalom, Absalom!"

613 ________. "What Happens in Absalom, Absalom!?" MFS, 13 (Spring, 1967), 79-87.

614 Watson, Francis. "Absalom, Absalom!" Fortnightly, 141 (April, 1937), 510-511. Review.

615 Watson, James G. "'If Was Existed': Prophets and the Patterns of History," MFS, 21, #4 (Winter, 1975-76), 499-507.
Faulkner's concept of time in the interpretation of Absalom, Absalom!

616 Weatherby, H. L. "Sutpen's Garden," GaR, 21 (Fall, 1967), 354-369.

617 Wee, Morris Owen. "Confronting the Ghost: Quentin Compson's Struggle with His Heritage in Faulkner's Absalom, Absalom!" DAI, 35 (Boston College: 1974), 6166A.

618 Weinstein, Arnold L. "Vision as Feeling: Bernanos and Faulkner," Vision and Response in Modern Fiction. Ithaca, New York: Cornell U. P., 1974, pp. 91-153.

619 Weisgerber, Jean. "Faulkner's Monomaniacs: Their Indebtedness to Raskolnikov," CLS, 5 (June, 1968), 181-193.

620 Whan, Edgar W. "Absalom, Absalom! As Gothic Myth," Perspective 3 (Autumn, 1950), 192-201.

621 White, William Allen. "Books of the Fall," SatRL 14 (October 10, 1936), 16, 26. Review.

622 Wigley, Joseph Alexander. "An Analysis of the Imagery of William Faulkner's Absalom, Absalom!" DA, 16 (Northwestern: 1956), 2464-65.

623 ______. "Imagery and the Interpreter," Studies in Interpretation. Esther M. Doyle and Virginia H. Floyd, eds. Amsterdam: Rodopi N. V., 1972, pp. 171-190.

624 Williams, Philip E. "The Biblical View of History: Hawthorne, Mark Twain, Faulkner, and Eliot," DA, 25 (Pennsylvania: 1968), 608A-9A.

625 ______. "Faulkner's Satan Sutpen and the Tragedy of Absalom, Absalom!" ESELL, Nos. 45-46 (Winter, 1964), 179-199.

626 Wilson, Mary Ann T. "Search for an Eternal Present: Absalom, Absalom! and All the King's Men," ConnR, 8, #1 (October, 1974), 95-100.

627 Wolfe, Humbert. "Strange Tales from America," Observer (February 21, 1937), 7. Review.

628 Woodward, Robert H. "Poe's Raven, Faulkner's Sparrow, and Another Window," PoeN, 2, #1-2 (1969), 37-38.

629 Yu, Beong-Cheon. "Quentin's Troubled Vision," ELL, 18 (Summer, 1966), 112-119.

630 Zink, Karl E. "William Faulkner: Form As Experience," SaQ, 53 (July, 1954), 384-403.

631 Zoellner, Robert H. "Faulkner's Prose Style in Absalom, Absalom!" AL, 30 (January, 1959), 488-502.

"AD ASTRA"
(American Caravan IV [March 27, 1931], 164-181)

632 Campbell, Harry Modean, and Ruel E. Foster. William Faulkner: A Critical Appraisal. Norman: Oklahoma U. P., 1951, pp. 23-24.

633 Day, Douglas. "The War Stories of William Faulkner," GaR, 15 (Winter, 1961), 385-394.

634 Dillon, Richard T. "Some Sources of Faulkner's Version of the First Air War," AL, 44, #4 (January, 1973), 629-637.

635 Moses, W. R. "Victory in Defeat: 'Ad Astra' and A Farewell to Arms," MissQ, 19 (Spring, 1966), 85-89.

636 TLS, No. 1652 (September 28, 1933), 648. Review.

"AFTERNOON OF A COW"
("L'Apres-midi d'une Vache," Fontaine, 27-28 (1943); Furioso, 2 (1947), 5-17.

637 Coindreau, Maurice E., trad., and Prêface. "L'Après-midi d'une vache," Poêsie, 43 (juillet-août, 1943), 19-29; and Fontaine (juin-juillet, 1943), 66-81.

638 Faulkner, John. "Earnest Truehart," My Brother Bill. New York: Trident Press, 1963, p. 172.

639 Holmes, Edward M. Faulkner's Twice Told Tales: His Re-Use of His Material. The Hague: Mouton, 1966, pp. 19-45, 87-88.

640 McIlwaine, Shields. "Faulkner Begins a Trilogy About the Snopes Family," Commercial Appeal (Memphis) (April 14, 1940), IV, 10.
The reviewer thought the episode of Ike's affair with the cow the most brilliant prose he had ever read.

641 O'Connor, William Van. ["Afternoon of a Cow"] The Tangled Fire of William Faulkner. Minneapolis: Minnesota U.P., 1954, pp. 120-121.

"ALL THE DEAD PILOTS"
(These 13, 1931, pp. 81-109; repr., Collected Stories, 1950)

642 Day, Douglas. "The War Stories of William Faulkner," GaR, 15 (Winter, 1961), 385-394.

643 Hall, James B., and Joseph Langland, eds. The Short Story. New York: Macmillan, 1956, pp. 64-66.

644 O'Connor, William Van. ["All the Dead Pilots"], The Tangled Fire of William Faulkner. Minneapolis: 1954, p. 67.

"ARTIST AT HOME"
(Story, 3 (August, 1933), 27-41; repr., in Collected Stories, 1950).

645 Bradford, M. E. "An Aesthetic Parable: Faulkner's 'Artist at Home,'" GaR, 27 (Summer, 1973), 175-181.

"AS I LAY DYING"
(New York; Jonathan Cape: Harrison Smith, 1930).

646 Adams, Richard P. Faulkner: Myth and Motion. Princeton: Princeton U.P., 1968, pp. 71-84.

647 Aguero, Luis. Prólogo. Mientras agonizo. La Habana, Editora del Consejo Nacional de Cultura. Editorial Nacional de Cuba, 1965.

648 Aguilar, Esperanza. Yoknapatawpha, Propiedad de William Faulkner. Santiago de Chile: Editorial Universitaria, 1964, pp. 47-53.

649 Alldredge, Betty Jean Edwards. "Levels of Consciousness: Women in the Stream of Consciousness Novels of Joyce, Woolf, and Faulkner," DAI, 37 (Oregon: 1976), 3610A.

650 _______. "Spatial Form in Faulkner's As I Lay Dying," SLJ, 11, #1 (Fall, 1978), 3-19.

651 Allen, Charles A. "William Faulkner: Comedy and the Purpose of Humor," ArQ, 16 (Spring, 1960), 59-69.

652 Anderson, Charles. "Faulkner's Moral Center," EA, 7 (January, 1954), 48-58.

653 Angelis, Giulio de., tr. Mentre morivo; romanzo. Milano: Mondadori, 1958.

654 Annas, Pamela J. "The Carpenter of As I Lay Dying," NMW, 8 (Winter, 1976), 84-99.

655 Anon. London Mercury, 33 (November, 1935), 89. Review.

656 Anon. "New Novels: Savage Continents," Glasgow Herald (September 26, 1935), 4. Review.

657 Anon. "As I Lay Dying," Times (September 27, 1935), 6. Review.

658 Anon. TLS, No. 1756 (September 26, 1935), 594. Review.

659 Anon. "A Witch's Brew: As I Lay Dying," NYTBR (October 19, 1930), 6. Review.

660 Anon. "Twenty-four Novels of the Season," LitD (January 24, 1931), 18. Review.

661 Anon. NR, 65 (November 19, 1930), 27. Review.

662 Arthos, John. "Ritual and Humor in the Writings of William Faulkner," Accent, 9 (Autumn, 1948), 17-30. Repr., in Two Decades of Criticism. Frederick Hoffman and Olga Vickery, eds., 1951, pp. 101-118.

663 B., H. Manchester Guardian (October 4, 1935). Review.

664 B., J. K. W. "Literature and Less," Times-Picayune (October 26, 1930), 33. Review.

665 Backman, Melvin. Faulkner: The Major Years. Bloomington: Indiana U. P., 1966), pp. 50-66.

666 ______. "Sickness and Primitivism: A Dominant Pattern in William Faulkner's Work," Accent, 14 (Winter, 1954), 61-73.

667 ______. "Tandis que j'agonise," RLM, Nos. 40-42 (Hiver, 1958-59), 309-330.

668 Baker, Carlos. "William Faulkner: The Doomed and the Damned," The Young Rebel in American Literature. Carl Bode, ed. New York: Praeger, 1960, pp. 145-169.

669 Baker, James R. "The Symbolic Extension of Yoknapatawpha County," ArQ, 8 (Autumn, 1952), 223-228.

670 Barrault, Jean-Louis, et M. E. Coindreau. "Ce qu'ils pensent de Faulkner," Carrefour (Novembre 14, 1950), 9.

671 Barth, J. Robert. "Faulkner and the Calvinist Tradition," Thought, 39 (March, 1964), 100-120.

672 Beach, Joseph Warren. "William Faulkner: The Haunted South--Novels of Social Reference, Cast and Color," American Fiction, 1920-1940. New York: Macmillan, 1941, pp. 132-135.

673 Beauvoir, Simone de. "Faulkner's Novels As I Lay Dying and Sanctuary," The Prime of Life. Peter Green, tr. Cleveland: World, 1962, pp. 149-150.

674 Beck, Warren. "Tandis que j'agonise," RLM, 5 (1957-58), 309-326.

675 Bedient, Calvin. "Pride and Nakedness: As I Lay Dying," MLQ, 29 (March, 1968), 61-76.

676 Beidler, Peter G. "Faulkner's Techniques of Characterization: Jewel in As I Lay Dying," EA, 21 (July-September, 1968), 236-242.

677 Blakestone, Oswell. "As I Lay Dying," Life and Letters Today, 13, #2 (December, 1935), 198. Review.

678 Bleikasten, André. Faulkner's As I Lay Dying. Paris: 1970. Trans., with author's collaboration, by Roger Little. Revised and enlarged ed., Bloomington: Indiana U. P., 1973.

679 Blotner, Joseph L. "As I Lay Dying: Christian Lore and Irony," TCL, 3 (April, 1957), 14-19.

680 Booth, Wayne C. The Rhetoric of Fiction. Chicago: Chicago U. P., 1961, passim.

681 Bowling, Laurence Edward. "William Faulkner: The Importance of Love," DR, 43 (Winter, 1963-64), 474-482.

682 Bradford, M. E. "Addie Bundren and the Design of *As I Lay Dying*," SoR, 6 (Autumn, 1970), 1093-1099.

683 Brady, Ruth H. "Faulkner's *As I Lay Dying*," Expl, 33 (March, 1975), Item 60.

684 Branch, Watson G. "Darl Bundren's 'Cubistic' Vision," TSLL, 19 (Spring, 1977), 42-59.

685 Breaden, Dale G. "William Faulkner and the Land," AQ, 1 (Fall, 1958), 344-357.

686 Bridgman, Richard. "As Hester Prynne Lay Dying," ELN, 2 (June, 1965), 294-296.
The Scarlet Letter as source for *As I Lay Dying*.

687 Brooks, Cleanth. "Faulkner's Vision of Good and Evil," MassR, 3 (Summer, 1962), 692-712.

688 _______. "Odyssey of the Bundrens," *William Faulkner: The Yoknapatawpha Country*. New Haven: Yale U.P., 1963, pp. 141-166.

689 Brophy, John. "New Fiction," Time and Tide, 16, #42 (October 19, 1935), 1489-1491. Review.

690 Brylowski, Walter. "The Comic Vision," *Faulkner's Olympian Laugh: Myth in the Novels*. Detroit: Wayne State U.P., 1968, pp. 86-96.

691 Burgum, Edwin Berry. "William Faulkner's Patterns of American Decadence," *The Novel and the World's Dilemma*. New York: Oxford U.P., 1947, pp. 215-217.

692 Burnham, James. "Trying to Say," Symposium, 2 (January, 1931), 356.

693 Campbell, Harry M. "Experiment and Achievement: *As I Lay Dying* and *The Sound and the Fury*," SR, 51 (April, 1943), 305-320.
Cf., Reply by G. M. O'Donnell, SR, 51 (July, 1943), 446-447.

694 _______, and Ruel E. Foster. *William Faulkner: A Critical Appraisal*. Norman: Oklahoma U.P., 1951, pp. 27-29, 107-108.

695 Capote, Truman. "Faulkner Dances," ThA, 33 (April, 1949), 49.
Review of Valerie Bettis ballet adaptation of *As I Lay Dying*.

696 Capps, Jack L., ed. As I Lay Dying: A Concordance to the Novel. Ann Arbor, Michigan: Univ. Microfilms International, 1977.

697 Cargill, Oscar. "The Primitivists," Intellectual America. New York: Macmillan, 1941, pp. 370-386.

698 Chase, Richard. "Faulkner--The Great Years: As I Lay Dying," The American Novel and Its Tradition. New York: Doubleday Anchor Books, 1957, pp. 207-210.

699 Church, Margaret. "William Faulkner: Myth and Duration," Time and Reality. Chapel Hill: North Carolina U.P., 1963, pp. 235-237.

700 Clark, Eulalyn. "Ironic Effects of Multiple Perspective in As I Lay Dying," NMW, 5, #1 (Spring, 1972), 15-28.

701 Coffee, Jessie A. "Empty Steeples: Theme, Symbol, and Irony in Faulkner's Novels," ArQ, 23 (Autumn, 1967), 197-206.

702 Coindreau, Maurice E. Aperçus de Litterature Americaine. Paris: 1946, pp. 121-122.
Noted similarities between As I Lay Dying and anecdote in The World's Illusion by Jacob Wasserman, New York: 1930, pp. 165-167.

703 _______. "Dewey Dell," (extrait de Tandis que j'agonise.) Jeune littérature prolétarienne aux États-Unis. Paris, 1948, p. 22.

704 _______, tr. Tandis que j'agonise. Paris: Gallimard, 1934.

705 _______. "William Faulkner en France," YFS, 10 (Autumn, 1952), 85-91.

706 Collins, Carvel. "The Pairing of The Sound and the Fury and As I Lay Dying," PULC, 18 (Spring, 1957), 114-123.

707 Connelly, Thomas E. "Fate and 'The Agony of Will,' Determinism in Some Works of William Faulkner," Essays on Determinism in American Literature. Kent, Ohio: Kent State U.P., 1964, pp. 36-52.

708 Cross, Barbara M. "Apocalypse and Comedy in As I Lay Dying," TSLL, 3 (Summer, 1961), 251-258.

709 Cullen, John B. "The Yocona River and As I Lay Dying," Old Times in the Faulkner Country. Chapel Hill: North Carolina U.P., 1961, pp. 84-88.

710 Dabit, Eugene. As I Lay Dying. Europe (September 18, 1934); (October 15, 1934), 294-296. Reviews.

711 Davenport, Basil. "In the Mire," SatRL, 7 (November 22, 1930), 362. Review.

712 Davidson, Donald. "The 43 Best Southern Novels for Readers and Collectors," PubW, 127 (April 27, 1935), 1675-1676.

713 Dawson, Margaret Cheney. "Beside Addie's Coffin," NYHTB (October 5, 1930), 6. Review.

714 Degenfelder, E. Pauline. "Yoknapatawphan Baroque: A Stylistic Analysis of As I Lay Dying," Style 7 (1973), 121-156.

715 Delay, Florence, and Jacqueline de Labriolle. "Márquez est-il le Faulkner colombien?" RLC, 47 (1973), 88-123. Comparison of Hojarasca (1955) by Gabriel García Márquez with As I Lay Dying.

716 Despain, Norma LaRene. "Stream of Consciousness Narration in Faulkner: A Redefinition," DAI, 37 (Conn.: 1975), 306A-07A.

717 Dickerson, Mary Jane. "As I Lay Dying and The Waste Land: Some Relationships," MissQ, 17 (Summer, 1964), 129-135.

718 ________. "Some Sources of Faulkner's Myth in As I Lay Dying," MissQ, 19 (Summer, 1966), 132-142.

719 Dickmann, Max, tr., and Preface. Mientras yo agonizo. Buenos Aires: Santiago Rueda, 1942; 2nd ed., 1952; 3rd ed., 1953.

720 ________. "William Faulkner, escritor diabólico," Revista de las Indias, 13, #39 (March, 1942), 107-116.

721 Dillingham, William B. "William Faulkner and the 'Tragic Condition,'" Edda, 53 (1966), 322-335.

722 Ditsky, John M. "'Dark, Darker Than Fire': Thematic Parallels in Lawrence and Faulkner," SHR, 8 (Fall, 1974), 497-505.

723 ________. "Faulkner's Carousel: Point of View in As I Lay Dying," LaurelR, 10, #1 (Spring, 1970), 74-85.

724 Douglas, Harold J., and Robert Daniel. "Faulkner and the Puritanism of the South," TSL, 2 (1957), 1-13.

725 Everett, W. K. Faulkner's Art and Characters. Woodbury, New York: Barron's Educational Series, 1969, pp. 7-15.

726 Ewell, Barbara N. "To Move in Time: A Study of the Structure of Faulkner's As I Lay Dying, Light in August, and Absalom, Absalom!" DAI, 30 (Florida State: 1970), 3940A.

727 Fadiman, Clifton. "Morbidity in Fiction," Nation, 131 (November 5, 1930), 500-501. Repr., "William Faulkner," Party of One. Cleveland: World Pub. Co., 1955, pp. 98-99, 102-104.

728 Fant, Joseph L., and Robert Ashley, eds. Faulkner at West Point. New York: Random House, 1964, pp. 96-97.

729 Fazio, Rocco R. "The Fury and the Design: Realms of Being and Knowing in Four Novels of William Faulkner," DA, 25 (Rochester: 1964), 1910.

730 Flint, R. W. "What Price Glory," HudR, (Winter, 1955), 604.

731 Foster, Ruel E. "Social Order and Disorder in Faulkner's Fiction," Approach, 55 (Spring, 1965), 20-28.

732 Franklin, Ralph W. Narrative Management in As I Lay Dying," MFS, 13 (Spring, 1967), 57-65.

733 Franklin, Rosemary. "Animal Magnetism in As I Lay Dying," AQ, 18 (Spring, 1966), 24-34.

734 Franklin, Rosemary F. "Clairvoyance, Vision, and Imagination in the Fiction of William Faulkner," DA, 29 (Emory: 1969), 3135A.

735 Friedman, Melvin J. "Le Monologue Intérieur dans As I Lay Dying," RLM, Nos. 40-42 (Hiver, 1958-59), 331-344.

736 Garrett, George P. "Some Revisions in As I Lay Dying," MLN, 73 (June, 1958), 414-417.

737 Garrison, Joseph M., Jr. "Perception, Language, and Reality in As I Lay Dying," ArQ, 32 (Spring, 1976), 16-30.

738 Garzilli, Enrico. "Myth, Story, and Self: As I Lay Dying," Circles Without Center: Paths to Discovery and Creation of Self in Modern Literature. Cambridge: Harvard U.P., 1972, pp. 60-65.

739 Geismar, Maxwell. "The Negro and the Female," Writers in Crisis. Boston: Houghton Mifflin, 1942, pp. 161-162.

740 Glasgow Herald (September 26, 1935). Review.

741 Glicksburg, Charles I. "William Faulkner and the Negro Problem," Phylon, 10 (June, 1949), 153-160.

742 ________. "The World of William Faulkner," ArQ, 5 (Spring, 1949), 46-58.

743 Goellner, Jack Gordon. "A Closer Look at *As I Lay Dying*," Perspective, 7 (Spring, 1954), 42-54.

744 Goethals, Thomas. *As I Lay Dying: A Critical Commentary.* New York: American R. D. M. Corp., 1965.

745 Gold, Joseph. "'Sin, Salvation and Bananas': *As I Lay Dying*," Mosaic, 7, #1 (Fall, 1973), 55-73.
In conclusion, quotes Faulkner, "... I was writing about people. I took these people ... this family and subjected them to the two greatest catastrophes which man can suffer --flood and fire, that's all...."

746 _______. *William Faulkner: A Study in Humanism.* Baton Rouge: Louisiana State U.P., 1963.

747 Gossett, Louise Y. "The Climate of Violence," *Violence in Recent Southern Fiction.* Durham, North Carolina: Duke U.P., 1965, pp. 32-34.

748 Gould, Gerald. "Six Books in Search of a Theory," Observer (September 29, 1935), 6.

749 Green, Martin. "Faulkner" The Triumph of Rhetoric," *Re-Appraisals: Some Commonsense Readings in American Literature.* New York: Norton, 1965, passim.

750 Greenberg, Alvin. "Shaggy Dog in Mississippi," SFQ, 29 (December, 1965), 284-287.
Folklore material.

751 Gresset, Michel, ed. Introduction. *William Faulkner: As I Lay Dying.* Paris: Armand Colin, 1970.

752 _______. *Dictionnaire des Oeuvres Contemporaines.* Paris: Laffont-Bompiani, 1968, pp. 693-694.

753 _______. "Le 'parce que' chez Faulkner et le 'donc' chez Beckett," LetN, 9 (November, 1961), 124-138.

754 Gwynn, Frederick L., and Joseph L. Blotner, eds. *Faulkner in the University, 1957-1958.* Charlottesville: Virginia U.P., 1959, pp. 109-115, *passim.*

755 Hammond, Donald. "Faulkner's Levels of Awareness," FlaQ, 1, #2 (1967), 78-81.

756 Handy, William J. "*As I Lay Dying*: Faulkner's Inner Reporter," KR, 21, #3 (Summer, 1959), 437-451.

757 _______. "Faulkner's *As I Lay Dying*," *Modern Fiction: A Formalist Approach.* London: Feffer & Simons, Inc.; Carbondale and Edwardsville: Southern Illinois U.P., 1971, pp. 75-93.

758 Harwick, Robert D. "Humor in the Novels of William Faulkner," DA, 26 (Nebraska: 1965), 1646.

759 Hauck, Richard B. "The Comic Christ and the Modern Reader," CE, 31 (February, 1970), 498-506.

760 Hemenway, Robert. "Enigmas of Being in As I Lay Dying," MFS, 16 (Summer, 1970), 133-146.

761 Henderson, Philip. The Novel Today: Studies in Contemporary Attitudes. London: John Lane, 1936, pp. 147-150.

762 Hess, Albert, and Peter Schunemann, trs. Als ich im Sterben lag. Zürich: Fretz & Wasmuth Verlag; Stuttgart: Henry Goverts Verlag, 1961.

763 Hewes, Henry. "Broadway Postscript," SatR, 43 (June 4, 1960), 30.
Dramatic adaptation of As I Lay Dying by Robert Flynn.

764 Hicks, Granville. "The Past and Future of William Faulkner," Bookman, 74 (September, 1931), 17-24.

765 Hiers, John Turner. "Traditional Death Customs in Modern Southern Fiction," DAI, 35, #2 (Emory: 1974), 1103A.

766 Hoffman, Frederick J. Freudianism and the Literary Mind. Baton Rouge: Louisiana State U. P., 2nd ed., 1957, pp. 129-130.

767 _______. Introduction. William Faulkner: Three Decades of Criticism. Frederick J. Hoffman and Olga W. Vickery, eds. East Lansing: Michigan State U. P., 1960, pp. 1-50.

768 _______. "The Original Talent: As I Lay Dying," William Faulkner. New York: Twayne Author Series. 2nd ed., Revised, 1966, pp. 60-65.

769 Howe, Irving. William Faulkner: A Critical Study. 2nd ed. New York: Vintage Books, 1962, pp. 52-56, 175-191.

770 Howell, Elmo. "Faulkner's Jumblies: The Nonsense World of As I Lay Dying," ArQ, 16 (Spring, 1960), 70-78.

771 Hughes, Allen. "Dance: Literary Evening," NYT (March 5, 1965), 36).
Critique of ballet version of As I Lay Dying.

772 Humphrey, Robert. Stream of Consciousness in the Modern Novel. Berkeley and Los Angeles: California U. P., 1954, pp. 20-21, 36-37, 64-65, 72-73, 104-106.

773 Inge, M. Thomas. "Donald Davidson Selects the Best Southern

Novels," MissQ, 24 (Spring, 1971), 155-158.
Repr., of 1935 article by Davidson which included As I Lay Dying and The Sound and the Fury.

774 ________. "William Faulkner and George Washington Harris: In the Tradition of Southwestern Humor," TSL, 7 (1962), 47-59.

775 Jacobs, Robert D. "William Faulkner: The Passion and the Penance," South: Modern Southern Literature in Its Cultural Setting. Louis D. Rubin, Jr., and Robert D. Jacobs, eds. Garden City, New York: Doubleday, 1961, pp. 153-155.

776 Jones, E. B. C. "As I Lay Dying," The Adelphi, 11 (February, 1936), 318. Review.

777 Josephson, Matthew. "The Younger Generation: Its Young Novelists," VQR, 9 (April, 1933), 250-253. Review.

778 Juhasz, Leslie. As I Lay Dying: A Critical Commentary. New York: Monarch Press, 1965.

779 Kelly, H. A., S.J. "Consciousness in the Monologues of Ulysses," MLQ, 24, #1 (March, 1963), 3-12.
Excludes Faulkner from the stream of consciousness category.

780 Kerr, Elizabeth M. "As I Lay Dying as Ironic Quest," WSCL, 3, #1 (Winter, 1962), 5-19.

781 King, Roma, Jr. "The Janus Symbol in As I Lay Dying," UKCR, 21 (June, 1955), 287-290.

782 Kinoian, Vartkis. "As I Lay Dying" in Review Notes and Study Guide to Faulkner's "As I Lay Dying." New York: Monarch Press, 1964, pp. 110-113.

783 Kirk, Robert W. "Faulkner's Anse Bundren," GaR, 19 (Winter, 1965), 446-452.

784 ________, and Marvin Klotz. Faulkner's People. Berkeley: California U.P., 1963, pp. 50-57.

785 Komar, Kathleen Lenore. "The Multilinear Novel: A Structural Analysis of Novels by Dos Passos, Döblin, Faulkner, and Koeppen," DAI, 38 (Princeton: 1977) 2101A.
Faulkner's As I Lay Dying.

786 Kowalczyk, Richard L. "From Addie Bundren to Gavin Stevens: The Direction from Reality," CEJ, 2, #1 (Winter, 1966), 45-52.

787 L., R. N. "Faulkner--Pity and Terror," ScribnerMag (December, 1930), 58, 60.

788 Lanati, Barbara. "Il primo Faulkner: As I Lay Dying," Sigma, 19 (1968), 83-119.

789 Larbaud, Valéry. "As I Lay Dying," in Oeuvres Completes. III. Paris: Gallimard, 1951.

790 _______. Preface. Tandis que j'agonise. M. E. Coindreau, tr. Paris: Gallimard, 1934.

791 _______. "Un Roman de William Faulkner: 'Tandis que j'agonise,'" Ce Vice impuni, la lecture. Domaine anglais. Paris: Gallimard, 1936, pp. 218-222.

792 Lassaigne, J. RM (juillet, 1934), 32. Review.

793 Leary, Lewis. "As I Lay Dying," in William Faulkner of Yoknapatawpha County. New York: Thos. Crowell, 1973, pp. 63-77.

794 Leath, Helen Lang. "'Will the Circle Be Unbroken?' An Analysis of Structure in As I Lay Dying," SwAL, 3 (1973), 61-68.

795 Leaver, Florence. "Faulkner: The Word As Principle and Power," SAQ, 57 (1958), 464-476; repr., in Three Decades. Frederick J. Hoffman and Olga W. Vickery, eds., 1960, pp. 199-209.

796 Le Breton, Maurice. "Le Thème de la Vie et de la Mort dans As I Lay Dying," Configuration Critique de William Faulkner, No. 3. Paris: 1958-1959, pp. 292-309.

797 Leek, John. "As I Lay Dying," Daily Oklahoman (Oklahoma City), (February 22, 1931), 11. Review.

798 Lewis, R. W. B. "William Faulkner: The Hero in the New World," The Picaresque Saint. Philadelphia: Lippincott, 1959, pp. 218-219.

799 Lilly, Paul, Jr. "Caddy and Addie: Speakers of Faulkner's Impeccable Language," JNT, 3 (September, 1973), 170-182.

800 Little, Matthew. "As I Lay Dying and 'Dementia Praecox' Humor," SAH, 2 (April, 1975), 61-70.

801 Litz, Walton. "William Faulkner's Moral Vision," SWR, 37 (Summer, 1952), 200-209.

802 McCole, Camille John. "The Nightmare Literature of William Faulkner," CathW, 141 (August, 1935), 576-583; repr., in Lucifer at Large. New York: Longmans, 1937, pp. 203-28.

803 McIlwaine, Shields. "Naturalistic Modes: The Gothic, the Ribald, and the Tragic--William Faulkner and Erskine Cald-

well, " in The Southern Poor-White. Norman: Oklahoma U. P., 1939, pp. 217-240.

804 Macmillan, A. "Books To-day," Scottish Standard, 1, #10 (November, 1935), 28. Review.

805 Magill, Frank N., ed. Masterplots: Combined Edition. New York: Salem Press, 1960, pp. 171-173.

806 Makuck, Peter L. "As I Lay Dying," "Faulkner Studies in France, 1953-1969," DAI, 32 (Kent State: 1971), 3314A.

807 Malin, Irving. William Faulkner: An Interpretation. Stanford: Stanford U. P., 1957, pp. 47-53.

808 Marks, Margaret Louise. "Flannery O'Connor's American Models: Her Work in Relation to That of Hawthorne, Faulkner, and West," DAI, 38 (Duke: 1977), 4830A.

809 May, John R. "Words and Deeds: Apocalyptic Judgment in Faulkner, West, and O'Connor," in Toward a New Earth: Apocalypse in the American Novel. Notre Dame: Notre Dame U. P., 1972, pp. 92-144.

810 Mellard, James M. "Faulkner's Philosophical Novel: Ontological Themes in As I Lay Dying," Person, 48 (Autumn, 1967), 509-523.

811 Meriwether, James B. "As I Lay Dying," in The Literary Career of William Faulkner. Princeton University Library, 1961, pp. 17-18.

812 _______. "A Prefatory Note by Faulkner for the Compson Appendix," AL, 43, #2 (May, 1971), 281-284.

813 Middleton, David. "Faulkner's Folklore in As I Lay Dying: An Old Motif in a New Manner," SNNTS, 9 (Spring, 1977), 46-53.

814 Miller, David M. "Faulkner's Women," MFS, 13 (Spring, 1967), 3-17.

815 Miller, James E. "William Faulkner: Descent into the Vortex," Quests Surd and Absurd: Essays in American Literature. Chicago: Chicago U. P., 1967, pp. 49, 54, 57-60.

816 Millgate, Michael. The Achievement of William Faulkner. New York: Random House, 1966, pp. 104-112.

817 _______. William Faulkner. New York: Grove Press, 1961; revised, 1966, pp. 34-39. Repr., New York: Capricorn Bks., 1971.

818 Miner, Ward L. "Faulkner and Christ's Crucifixion," NM, 57 (1956), 260-269.

819 Moloney, Michael. "Faulkner, the Enigma of Time," Thought, 35 (1957), 69-85.

820 Monaghan, David M. "The Single Narrator of As I Lay Dying," MFS, 18, #2 (Summer, 1972), 213-220.

821 Moore, Robert, ed. The Faulkner Concordance Newsletter, No. 3 (May, 1974).

822 Muir, Edwin. "New Novels," Listener, 14 (October 16, 1935), 681. Review.

823 Murray, Trudy Kehret. "Tricked by Words: Syntax and Style in Faulkner's As I Lay Dying," DAI, 36 (Washington: 1974), 3660A.

824 Nadeau, Robert L. "The Morality of Act: A Study of Faulkner's As I Lay Dying," Mosaic, 6, #3 (Spring, 1973), 23-35.

825 Nakamura, Junichi. "A Study in the English of William Faulkner's As I Lay Dying," Kobe College Studies (Kobe, Japan), 2 (June, 1954), 7-20.

826 Nilon, Charles H. Faulkner and the Negro. New York: Citadel Press, 1965.

827 Noble, David W. "After the Lost Generation," The Eternal Adam and the New World Garden. New York: Braziller, 1968, pp. 161-176.

828 O'Connor, William Van. "Protestantism in Yoknapatawpha County," HopkinsR, 5 (Spring, 1952), 26-42; repr., in The Tangled Fire of William Faulkner. Minneapolis: Minnesota U.P., 1954, pp. 45-53.

829 ________. William Faulkner. Minneapolis: Minnesota Press, 1959, pp. 14-17; repr., in Seven Modern American Novelists. William Van O'Connor, ed. Minneapolis: 1964, pp. 128-131.

830 O'Donnell, George Marion. "Faulkner's Mythology," KR, 1 (Summer, 1939), 285-299.

831 ________. "Reply," SR, 51 (July, 1943), 446-447.
Cf., Harry M. Campbell, SR, 51 (April, 1943), 305-320.

832 O'Faolain, Sean. "As I Lay Dying," Fortnightly, 138 (December, 1935), 637-638. Review.

833 ________. "William Faulkner or More Genius than Talent," The Vanishing Hero: Studies in Novelists of the Twenties. London: Eyre & Spottiswoode, 1956, pp. 99-134.

834 Orfali, Ingrid. "Silences de Tandis que j'Agonise," Delta, 3 (November, 1976), 19-21.

835 Page, Sally R. "The Female Idealist: As I Lay Dying and The Wild Palms," in Faulkner's Women. DeLand, Florida: 1972, pp. 111-135.

836 Palliser, Charles. "Fate and Madness: The Determinist Vision of Darl Bundren," AL, 49 (January, 1978), 619-633.

837 Parr, Susan D. R. "'And by Bergson, Obviously,' Faulkner's The Sound and the Fury, As I Lay Dying, and Absalom, Absalom! from a Bergsonian Perspective," DAI, 32 (Wisconsin: 1972), 6996A.

838 Parsons, Thornton H. "Doing the Best They Can," GaR, 23 (Fall, 1969), 292-306.

839 Patten, Catherine Mary. "A Study of William Faulkner's As I Lay Dying Based on the Manuscript and Text," DAI, 34 (New York University: 1972), 331A.

840 Pedrolo, Manuel de. Pròleg. Mentre agonitzo. Camarasa, R. Folch, tr. Barcelona: Edicions Proa, 1968.

841 Peek, Charles A. "The Signboard for New Hope: Faulkner's As I Lay Dying," DAI, 32 (Nebraska: 1971), 4015A.

842 Perlis, Alan D. "As I Lay Dying As a Study of Time," SDR, 10, #1 (1972), 103-110.

843 Pitavy, François. "William Faulkner: As I Lay Dying and Light in August. Paris: Librarie Armand Colin, 1970; rev. and enlarged. Gillian E. Cook, ed. and tr. Bloomington: Indiana U.P., 1973.

844 Presley, Delma E. "Is Reverend Whitfield a Hypocrite?" RS, 36, #1 (March, 1968), 57-61.

845 Price-Stephens, Gordon. "The British Reception of William Faulkner--1929-1962," MissQ, 18 (Summer, 1965), 119-200.

846 Quennell, Peter. "As I Lay Dying," NS&N, 10, #241 (October 5, 1935), 453-454. Review.

847 Rabi. "Faulkner et la génération de l'exil," Esprit, 19 (January, 1951), 56; repr., Faulkner: Two Decades of Criticism. Frederick J. Hoffman and Olga W. Vickery, eds. East Lansing: 1951, p. 129.

848 Raines, Charles A. Faulkner's As I Lay Dying: A Critical Commentary. New York: Barrister, 1966.

849 Randall, Julia. "Some Notes on As I Lay Dying," HopR, 4 (Summer, 1951), 47-51.

850 Ransom, John Crowe. "Modern with the Southern Accent," VQR, 11 (April, 1935), 184-200.

851 Reaver, J. Russell. "This Vessel of Clay: A Thematic Comparison of Faulkner's As I Lay Dying and Latorre's The Old Woman of Peralillo," FSUS, 14 (1954), 131-140.

852 Reed, Joseph W., Jr. "Appendix A--Narrative Structure of As I Lay Dying," in Faulkner's Narrative. New Haven: 1973, p. 283.

853 _______. "As I Lay Dying," in Faulkner's Narrative. New Haven: 1973, pp. 84-111.

854 Rhynsburger, Mark. "Student Views of William Faulkner," MoOc, 1, #2 (Winter, 1971), 264-269.

855 Richardson, Kenneth E. Force and Faith in the Novels of William Faulkner. The Hague: Mouton, 1967, pp. 73-76.

856 Richmond, Lee J. "The Education of Fardaman Bundren in Faulkner's As I Lay Dying," Renaissance and Modern: Essays in Honor of Edwin M. Moseley. Murray J. Levith, ed. Saratoga Springs: Skidmore Coll. 1976, pp. 133-142.

857 Rinaldi, N. M. "Game Imagery and Game-Consciousness in Faulkner's Fiction," TCL, 10 (October, 1964), 108-118.

858 Roberts, James L. As I Lay Dying: Notes. Lincoln, Nebraska: Cliff's Notes, 1964.

859 _______. "The Individual and the Family: Faulkner's As I Lay Dying," ArQ, 16 (Spring, 1960), 26-38.

860 Rooks, George. "Vardaman's Journey in As I Lay Dying," ArizQt, 35 (Summer, 1979), 114-128.

861 Rosenman, John B. "Another Othello Echo in As I Lay Dying," NMW, 8, #1 (Spring, 1975), 19-21.

862 _______. "As I Lay Dying: A Study of the Poor White in Faulkner," DAI, 31 (Kent State: 1970), 6069A-70A.

863 _______. "A Note on William Faulkner's As I Lay Dying," SAF, 1 (1973), 104-105.

864 _______. "Physical-Spatial Symbolism in As I Lay Dying," CollL, 4 (Spring, 1977), 176-177.

865 Rosenthal, M. L. "On Teaching Difficult Literary Texts," CE, 20 (January, 1959), 157-158. Notes on As I Lay Dying.

866 Ross, Stephen M. "Shapes of Time and Consciousness in As I Lay Dying," TSLL, 16 (Winter, 1975), 723-737.

867 Rossky, William. "*As I Lay Dying*: The Insane World," TSLL, 4 (Spring, 1962), 87-95.

868 Rubin, Louis D., Jr. "Chronicles of Yoknapatawpha: The Dynasties of William Faulkner," *The Faraway Country: Writers of the Modern South.* Seattle: Washington U.P., 1963, pp. 62-63.

869 ______. "The Difficulties of Being a Southern Writer Today: Or Getting out from under William Faulkner," JSH, 29, #4 (November, 1963), 486-494. Repr., *The Curious Death of the Novel.* Baton Rouge: Louisiana State U.P., 1967, pp. 282-293.

870 ______. "The Great American Joke," SAQ, 72, #1 (Winter, 1973), 82-94.

871 ______, ed. Introduction. *The Comic Imagination in American Literature.* New Brunswick: Rutgers U.P., 1973.

872 ______. "Notes on a Rear-Guard Action," *The Idea of the South: Pursuit of a Central Theme.* Frank E. Vandiver, ed. Chicago: Chicago U.P., 1964, pp. 27-41.

873 ______. "The South and the Faraway Country," VQR, 38 (Spring, 1962), 444-459.

874 ______. "Southern Literature: A Piedmont Art," MissQ, 23, #1 (Winter, 1969-70), 1-16.

875 ______, and Robert D. Jacobs, eds. Introduction. *South: Modern Southern Literature in Its Cultural Setting.* Garden City: Doubleday, 1961, pp. 142-176.

876 ______, and ______, eds. "William Faulkner: The Novelists of the South," *Southern Renascence.* Baltimore: Johns Hopkins Press, 1953; 2nd pr., 1954, *passim.*

877 ______, and John Rees Moore, eds. *The Idea of an American Novel.* New York: Thomas Y. Crowell, 1961, *passim.*

878 ______, et al. "Modern Novelists and Contemporary American Society: A Symposium," Shen, 10 (Winter, 1959), 3-31.

879 Rule, Philip C. "The Old Testament Vision As in *As I Lay Dying*," in *Religious Perspectives in Faulkner's Fiction.* J. R. Barth, ed. Notre Dame U.P., 1972, pp. 107-116.

880 Ryakhesoo, Ya. "Afterword to Estonian Translation of "*As I Lay Dying.*" Tallin: Periodika, 1971.

881 Sadler, David F. "The Second Mrs. Bundren: Another Look at the Ending of *As I Lay Dying*," AL, 37 (March, 1965), 65-69.

882 Sandeen, Ernest. "William Faulkner: Tragedian of Yoknapatawpha," in *Fifty Years of the American Novel*. H. C. Gardiner, ed. New York: Scribner's, 1951, pp. 165-182.

883 Sanderlin, Robert R. "*As I Lay Dying*: Christian Symbols and Thematic Implications," SoQ, 7 (January, 1969), 155-166.

884 Sawyer, K. B. "Hero in *As I Lay Dying*," FS, 3 (Summer-Autumn, 1954), 30-33.

885 Scholes, Robert E., and Robert Kellogg. *The Nature of Narrative*. New York: Oxford U. P., 1966, pp. 262-263, *passim*.

886 Seib, Kenneth. "Midrashic Legend in Faulkner's *As I Lay Dying*," NMAL, #2 (1977), Item 5.

887 Seltzer, Leon F. "Narrative Function vs. Psychopathology: The Problem of Darl in *As I Lay Dying*," L&P, 25, No. 2 (1975), 49-64.

888 ________, and Jan Viscomi. "Natural Rhythms and Rebellion: Anse's Role in *As I Lay Dying*," MFS, 24, #4 (Winter, 1978-79), 556-564.

889 Sherwood, J. C. "The Traditional Element in Faulkner," FS, 3 (Summer-Autumn, 1954), 17-23.

890 Shoemaker, Alice. "A Wheel Within a Wheel: Fusion of Form and Content in Faulkner's *As I Lay Dying*," ArizQt, 35 (Summer, 1979), 101-113.

891 Simon, John K. "Faulkner and Sartre: Metamorphosis and the Obscene," CL, 15 (Summer, 1963), 216-225.
Comparison of *La Nausie* with *As I Lay Dying* and *Sanctuary*.

892 ________. "The Glance of the Idiot: A Thematic Study of Faulkner and Modern French Fiction," DA, 25 (Yale: 1964), 1220.

893 ________. "The Scene and the Imagery of Metamorphosis in *As I Lay Dying*," Criticism, 7 (Winter, 1965), 1-22.

894 ________. "What Are You Laughing At, Darl?" CE, 25 (November, 1963), 104-110.

895 Simon, M. Jean. Roman amêricain au XXe siècle. Paris: Boivin & Cie, 1950.

896 Skaggs, Merrill M. "The Tradition in the Twentieth Century," *The Folk of Southern Fiction*. Athens: Georgia U. P., 1972, pp. 224-225.

897 Slabey, Robert M. "As I Lay Dying As an Existential Novel," BuR, 11, #4 (December, 1963), 12-23.

898 Slatoff, Walter J. "As I Lay Dying," Quest for Failure. Ithaca: Cornell U.P., 1960; 2nd pr., 1961, pp. 158-173.

899 Smith, Harrison. "A Troubled Vision: As I Lay Dying," SWR, 16 (January, 1931), 16-17.

900 Solery, Marc. "Addie Bundren: du corps au groupe," Sud, 14 (1975), 117-127.

901 Southern, Terry. "Dark Laughter in the Towers," Nation (April 23, 1960), 348-350.

902 Spring, Howard. Evening Standard (September 26, 1935).

903 Stallman, Robert W. "A Cryptogram: As I Lay Dying," in The Houses That James Built. East Lansing: Michigan State U.P., 1961, pp. 200-211.

904 Stein, Jean. "William Faulkner," Paris Review, 4 (Spring, 1956), 32-33.

905 Stitch, K. P. "A Note on Ironic Word Formation in As I Lay Dying," NMW, 8 (Winter, 1976), 100-103.

906 Stonesifer, Richard J. "In Defense of Dewey Dell," Educational Leader, 22 (1958), 27-33.

907 Stonum, Gary Lee. "Dilemma in As I Lay Dying," Renascence, 28 (Winter, 1976), 71-81.

908 Sutherland, Ronald. "As I Lay Dying: A Faulkner Microcosm," QQ, 73, #4 (Winter, 1966), 541-549.

909 Swiggart, Peter. "A Modern Mock-Epic," in The Art of Faulkner's Novels. Austin: Texas U.P., 1962, pp. 108-130.

910 Thiébaut, Marcel. "Que j'Agonise," Revue de Paris, 41 (July 15, 1934), 474-476.

911 Thompson, Alan Reynolds. "The Cult of Cruelty," Bookman, 74 (January-February, 1932), 477-487.

912 Thompson, Frederick. "Second Best of a First-Rater," Cw, 13, #12 (January 21, 1931), 335. Review.

913 TLS, #1756 (September 26, 1935), 594. Review.

914 Times (September 27, 1935). Review.

915 Toesca, Maurice. ["Tandis que j'agonise"] Gazette des Lettres (janvier, 1947), 9.

916 Tuck, Dorothy. Crowell's Handbook of Faulkner. New York: Crowell, 1964, pp. 34-39.

917 Van Nostrand, A. D. "The Poetic Dialogues of William Faulkner," Everyman His Own Poet. New York: McGraw Hill, 1968, pp. 175-196.

918 Vergara-Misito, Noemi. "William Faulkner: Mientras yo agonizo," Nosotros, 18, 2d series, No. 77 (August, 1942), 215-217.

919 Vickery, Olga. "As I Lay Dying," Perspective, 3 (Autumn, 1950), 179-191. Also in Vickery, O. W. Novels of William Faulkner, pp. 50-65; and in Hoffman, F. J., and O. W. Vickery, eds. Two Decades of Criticism, pp. 189-205.

920 _______. "The Dimensions of Consciousness: As I Lay Dying," in The Novels of William Faulkner. 1959, pp. 50-65.

921 Volpe, Edmond L. A Reader's Guide to William Faulkner. New York: Noonday Press, 1964, pp. 126-140, 377-382.

922 Wade, John D. "The South in Its Fiction," VQR, 7 (January, 1931), 124-126.

923 Waggoner, Hyatt H. "Vision," William Faulkner: From Jefferson to the World. Lexington: Kentucky U. P., 1959, pp. 62-87.

924 Wagner, Linda W. "As I Lay Dying: Faulkner's All in the Family," CollQ, 1 (1974), 73-82.

925 _______. "Faulkner's Fiction: Studies in Organic Form," JNT, 1 (January, 1971), 1-14.

926 Walton, Edith H. "An Eccentric Novel," NY Sun (November 7, 1930), 31. Review.

927 Warren, Robert Penn. "Cowley's Faulkner," NR, 115 (August 12, 1946), 176-180; (August 26, 1946), 234-237.

928 _______. "Faulkner: The South and the Negro," SoR, 1, n.s. (Summer, 1965), 501-529.

929 Wasiolek, Edward. "As I Lay Dying: Distortion in the Slow Eddy of Current Opinion," Critique, 3 (Spring-Fall, 1959), 15-23.

930 Watkins, Floyd C. "As I Lay Dying: The Dignity of Earth," In Time and Place: Some Origins of American Fiction. Athens: Georgia U. P., 1977, 175-189.

931 _______. "The Word and the Deed in Faulkner's First Great

Novels," The Flesh and the Word. Nashville: Vanderbilt U. P., 1971, pp. 181-202.

932 ________, and W. B. Dillingham. "The Mind of Vardaman Bundren," PQ, 39 (April, 1960), 247-251.

933 Weatherby, H. L. "Sutpen's Garden," GaR, 21 (Fall, 1967), 354-369.

934 Weber, Robert W. "Raskol'nikov, Addie Bundren, Meursault: Sur la Continuitê d'un Mythe," Archiv, 202 (1966), 81-92.

935 Westland, Olga. "As I Lay Dying," Perspective, 3 (Autumn, 1950), 179-191.

936 White, Kenneth. "As I Lay Dying," NR, 65 (November 19, 1930), 27.

937 White, Michael. "Inverse Mimesis in Faulkner's As I Lay Dying," ArQ, 32 (Spring, 1976).

938 Wilder, Amos N. "Faulkner and the Vestigal Moralities," Theology and Modern Literature. Cambridge: Harvard U. P., 1958, pp. 113-131.

939 Williams, Ora G. "The Theme of Endurance in As I Lay Dying," LaS, 9, #2 (Summer, 1970), 100-104.

940 Winn, James A. "Faulkner's Revisions: A Stylist at Work," AL, 41 (May, 1969), 231-250.

941 Woodbery, Potter. "Faulkner's Numismatics: A Note on As I Lay Dying," RS, 39 (1971), 150-151.

942 Woodworth, Stanley D. William Faulkner en France (1931-1952). Paris: M. J. Minard, 1959, p. 49.

943 Wynne, Carolyn. "Aspects of Space: John Marin and William Faulkner," AQ, 16 (Spring, 1964), 59-71.

Dramatic Productions of As I Lay Dying

944 Artaud, Antonin. "Un Spectacle magique," NRF, 45 (July, 1935), 136-138; repr., in Cahiers de la Compagnie Madeleine Renaud-J.-L. Barrault, II, 7ème cahier. Paris: Julliard, 1954, pp. 39-42.

945 Barrault, Jean-L. Rêflexions sur le thêâtre. Paris: Jacques Vautrain, 1949, pp. 41-53.
In June, 1935, Barrault presented the stage production of As I Lay Dying under the title of Autour d'une mère.

946 Capote, Truman. "Faulkner Dances," ThA, 33 (April, 1949),

49.
On the dance adaptation of As I Lay Dying by Valerie Betti.

947 Flynn, Robert L. "From Yoknapatawpha to UNESCO, the Dream," SatR, 42 (November 14, 1959), 21.

"BARN BURNING"
(Harper's, 179 (June, 1939), 86-96; repr., in Collected Stories, 1950)

948 Baumbach, Jonathan, and Arthur Edelstein. Instructor's Manual to Moderns and Contemporaries. New York: Random House, 1968.

949 Bowen, James K., and James A. Hamby. "Colonel Sartoris Snopes and Gabriel Marcel: Allegiance and Commitment," NMW, 3, #3 (Winter, 1971), 101-107.

950 De Jovine, F. Anthony. The Young Hero in American Fiction: A Motif for Teaching Literature. New York: Appleton-Century-Crofts, 1971, p. 47, passim.

951 Fisher, Marvin. "The World of Faulkner's Children," UKCR, 27 (October, 1960), 13-18.

952 Franklin, Phyllis. "Sarty Snopes and 'Barn Burning,'" MissQ, 21 (Summer, 1968), 189-193.
Cf., Elmo Howell. "Colonel Sartoris Snopes and Faulkner's Aristocrats," CarQ, 11 (1959), 13-19.

953 Havighurst, Walter. Instructor's Manual: Masters of the Modern Short Story. New York: Harcourt, 1955, pp. 7-8.

954 Hays, Peter L. The Limping Hero: Grotesques in Literature. New York: New York U.P., 1971, pp. 163-164.

955 Howe, Irving. "A Note on the Stories: 'Barn Burning,'" William Faulkner: A Critical Study. New York: Vintage, 1952, pp. 265, 266.

956 Howell, Elmo. "Colonel Sartoris Snopes and Faulkner's Aristocrats: A Note on 'Barn Burning,'" CarQ, 11 (Summer, 1959), 13-19.
Cf., Phyllis Franklin. "Sarty Snopes and 'Barn Burning,'" MissQ, 21 (1968), 189-193.

957 Johnston, Kenneth G. "Time of Decline: Pickett's Charge and the Broken Clock in Faulkner's 'Barn Burning,'" SSF, 11, #4 (Fall, 1974), 434-436.

958 Kashkin, I. Ob avtore [Concerning the author]. in Faulkner: W. Podzhigatel ["Barn Burning"]. Moscow, 1959, pp. 3-6.

959 Malin, Irving. William Faulkner: An Interpretation. Stanford U.P., 1957, p. 81.

960 Meriwether, James B. "Barn Burning," The Literary Career of William Faulkner. Columbia: South Carolina U.P., 1971, p. 70, passim.

961 Mitchell, Charles. "The Wounded Will of Faulkner's Barn Burner," MFS, 11 (Summer, 1965), 185-189.

962 Nicolaisen, Pater. "Hemingways 'My Old Man' und Faulkners 'Barn Burning': Ein Vergleich," in Amerikanische Erzählungen von Hawthorne bis Salinger: Interpretationen. Paul G. Buchloh, ed. (KBAA 6.) Neumünster, 1968, pp. 187-223.

963 Nicolet, William P. "Faulkner's 'Barn Burning,'" Expl, 34 (November, 1975), Item 25.

964 Raimbault, R. N., tr. "L'incendiaire," AN, No. 74-76 (June-August, 1952), 12-31.

965 Stein, William Bysshe. "Faulkner's Devil," MLN, 76 (December, 1961), 731-732.

966 Trilling, Lionel. The Experience of Literature: Fiction. New York: Holt, Rinehart & Winston, 1967, pp. 745-748.

967 Wilson, Gayle E. "'Being Pulled Two Ways': The Nature of Sarty's Choice in 'Barn Burning,'" MissQ, 24 (Summer, 1971), 279-288.

968 Youngblood, Sarah. "Teaching a Short Story: Faulkner's 'Barn Burning,'" Kinescript from Commission on English. Princeton, New Jersey: College Entrance Exam. Board, 1965, pp. 1-44.

"THE BEAR"
(Sat. Ev. Post, 214 (May 9, 1942), 30-31, passim)

969 Adamowski, T. H. "Isaac McCaslin and the Wilderness of the Imagination," CentR, 17 (1973), 92-112.

970 Adams, Richard P. "Focus on William Faulkner's 'The Bear': Moses and the Wilderness," American Dreams, American Nightmares. David Madden, ed. Carbondale, Edwardsville: So. Ill. U.P., 1970, pp. 129-135.

971 ________. "Moral," Faulkner: Myth and Motion. Princeton: Princeton U.P., 1968, pp. 145-149, passim.

972 Altenbernd, Lynn. "A Suspended Moment: The Irony of History in William Faulkner's 'The Bear,'" MLN, 75 (November, 1960), 572-582.

973 Anon. "'The Bear' and Huckleberry Finn: Heroic Quests for Moral Liberation," MTJ, 12 (Spring, 1963), 12-13, 21.

974 Arthos, John. "Ritual and Humor in the Writing of William Faulkner," Accent, 9 (Autumn, 1948), 18.

975 Backman, Melvin. "The Wilderness and the Negro in Faulkner's 'The Bear,'" PMLA, 76 (December, 1961), 595-600.

976 Baumgarten, Murray. "The Language of Faulkner's 'The Bear,'" WHR, 15 (Spring, 1961), 180-182.

977 Beauchamp, Gorman. "The Rite of Initiation in Faulkner's 'The Bear,'" ArQ, 28 (Winter, 1972), 319-325.

978 Beck, Warren. "The Bear," Faulkner: Essays by Warren Beck. Madison: Wisconsin U.P., 1976, pp. 382ff.

979 Bell, H. H., Jr. "A Footnote to Faulkner's 'The Bear,'" CE, 24 (December, 1962), 179-183. On Boon.

980 Beresford, J. D. Manchester Guardian (October 9, 1942). Review.

981 Blum, Irving D. "The Parallel Philosophy of Emerson's 'Nature' and Faulkner's 'The Bear,'" ESQ, No. 13 (4th Qt., 1958), 22-25.

982 Bradford, Melvin E. "Brotherhood in 'The Bear': An Exemplum for Critics," ModA, 10 (Summer, 1966), 278-281.

983 ________. "The Gum Tree Scene: Observations on the Structure of 'The Bear,'" SHR, 1 (Summer, 1967), 141-150.

984 Breaden, Dale G. "William Faulkner and the Land," AQ, 10 (Fall, 1958), 344-357.

985 Brocki, Sr. Mary Damascene. "Faulkner and Hemingway: Values in a Modern World," MTJ, 11 (Summer, 1962), 5-9.

986 Brooks, Cleanth. "The Story of the McCaslins: Earlier Versions of 'The Bear,'" in William Faulkner: The Yoknapatawpha Country. New Haven: Yale U.P., 1963, 1964, pp. 414-416.

987 ________. "William Faulkner: Vision of Good and Evil," Religion and Modern Literature. G. B. Tennyson and E. E. Ericson, Jr., eds. Grand Rapids, Mich.: Wm. B. Eerdmans, 1975, pp. 310-315.

988 Brumm, Ursula. "Wilderness and Civilization: A Note on William Faulkner," PartisanR, 22 (Summer, 1955), 349-350.

989 Brunauer, Dalma H. "Worshiping the Bear-God," Ch&L, 23, # 3 (Spring, 1974), 7-35.

990 Buckler, William E., and Arnold B. Sklare. "A Suggested Interpretation," in _Stories from Six Authors._ New York: McGraw-Hill, 1960, pp. 269-270.
On the short version of "The Bear."

991 Butler, John F. "Faulkner: 'The Bear," _Exercises in Literary Understanding._ Chicago: Scott-Foresman, 1956, pp. 45-47.

992 Butor, Michel. "Les relations de parentê dans _l'Ours_ de William Faulkner," LetN, 4 (May, 1956), 734-745. Also in _Rêpertoire: Études et conferences, 1948-1959._ Paris: Editions de Minuit, 1960, pp. 250-261.

993 Campbell, Harry M., and R. E. Foster. "Faulkner's Uses of Imagery and Humor," excerpt from _William Faulkner: A Critical Appraisal_ in _Bear, Man, and God._ Francis L. Utley, et al., eds. New York: 1963, pp. 347-349.

994 _______. "Structural Devices in the Works of William Faulkner," Perspective, 3 (Autumn, 1950), 215-218.

995 Carpenter, Thomas P. "A Gun for Faulkner's Old Ben," AN&Q, 5 (May, 1967), 133-134.

996 Chapman, Arnold. "Pampas and _Big Woods:_ Heroic Initiation in Güiraldes and Faulkner," CL, 11 (Winter, 1959), 61-67.

997 Collins, Carvel. "Are These Mandalas?" L&P, 3 (November, 1953), 3-6.
Cf., "A Note on the Conclusion of 'The Bear,'" FS, 2 (1954), 58-60.

998 _______. "Faulkner and Certain Earlier Southern Fiction," CE, 16 (November, 1954), 96-97.

999 _______. "A Note on the Conclusion of 'The Bear,'" FS, 2, # 4 (Winter, 1954), 58-60.

1000 Connolly, Thomas E. "Fate and 'the Agony of Will': Determinism in Some Works of William Faulkner--'The Bear,'" in _Essays in Determinism in American Literature._ S. J. Krause, ed. Kent, Ohio: Kent State U. P., 1964, pp. 47-49.

1001 Cowley, Malcolm. "William Faulkner's Legend of the South," SR, 53 (Summer, 1945), 349-351, 360-361; repr., in Allen Tate, _A Southern Vanguard_, pp. 18-19, 26-27; _The Wind and the Rain,_ 248-249, 255; Ray B. West, _Essays in Modern Literary Criticism_, 518-519, 525-526; John W. Aldridge,

Critiques and Essays on Modern Fiction, 436-437, 441-442.

1002 _______. "Editor's Note," and "The Bear," in The Portable Faulkner. New York: Viking Press, 1949, pp. 225-226, 227-363.

1003 Cullen, John B. Old Times in the Faulkner Country. Chapel Hill: North Carolina U. P., 1961, pp. 27-44.

1004 Dabney, Lewis M. "The Bear," The Indians of Yoknapatawpha. Baton Rouge: 1974, pp. 135-157, passim.

1005 _______. "Faulkner, the Red, and the Black," ColuF, 1, #2 (Spring, 1972), 52-54.

1006 Darnell, Donald G. "Cooper and Faulkner: Land, Legacy, and the Tragic Vision," SAB, 34 (March, 1969), 3-5.

1007 Davis, Walter A. The Act of Interpretation: A Critique of Literary Reason. Chicago: Chicago U. P., 1978.
"The Bear" used as a test for three critical approaches.

1008 De Jovine, F. Anthony. The Young Hero in American Fiction: A Motif for Teaching Literature. New York: Appleton-Century-Crofts, 1971, p. 41, passim.

1009 Devlin, Albert J. "Faulknerian Chronology: Puzzles and Games," NMW, 5 (Winter, 1973), 98-101.

1010 Dussinger, Gloria R. "Faulkner's Isaac McCaslin as Romantic Hero Manqué," SAQ, 68 (Summer, 1969), 377-385.

1011 Early, James. "The Bear," in The Making of "Go Down, Moses." Dallas: Southern Methodist U. P., 1972, pp. 29-67.

1012 Ellison, Ralph, and Irving Howe. "The Bear," Invitation to Learning Reader, No. 9. New York: Random House, 1953, pp. 40-46.

1013 Fiedler, Leslie A. "From Redemption to Initiation," NewL, 41 (May 26, 1958), 20-23.

1014 Flanagan, John T. "Folklore in Faulkner's Fiction," PLL, 5 (Summer, 1969), 119-144.

1015 Flint, R. W. "Faulkner as Elegist," HudR, 7 (Summer, 1954), 253-254.

1016 Foster, Ruel E. "A Further Note on the Conclusion of 'The Bear,'" FS, 3 (Spring, 1954), 4-5.

1017 ________. "Primitivism," in William Faulkner. Campbell and Foster. Norman: Oklahoma U. P., 1951, pp. 146-158.

1018 Gelfant, Blanche H. "Faulkner and Keats: The Ideality of Art in 'The Bear,'" SLJ, 2 (Fall, 1969), 43-65.

1019 Giles, Barbara. "The South of William Faulkner," Mass& Main, 3 (February, 1950), 33-36.

1020 Gillespie, Gerald. "Novella, Nouvelle, Novella, Short Novel? --A Review of Terms," Neophil, 51 (July, 1967), 225-229.

1021 Gilley, Leonard. "The Wilderness Theme in Faulkner's 'The Bear,'" MQ, 6 (July, 1965), 379-385.

1022 Grenier, Cynthia. "The Art of Fiction: An Interview with William Faulkner, September, 1955," Accent, 16 (Summer, 1956), 167-177.

1023 Harrison, Robert. "Faulkner's 'The Bear': Some Notes on Form," GaR, 20 (Fall, 1966), 318-327.

1024 Hart, John A. "That Not Impossible He: Faulkner's Third-Person Narrator," Studies in Faulkner. Carnegie Series in English, No. 6. Pittsburgh: Carnegie Institute of Technology, 1961, pp. 29-41.

1025 Hassan, Ihab. Radical Innocence: Studies in the Contemporary American Novel. Princeton: Princeton U. P., 1961, pp. 57-58.

1026 Havighurst, Walter. Masters of the Modern Short Story. New York: Harcourt, Brace & Co., 1955, passim.

1027 Hess, Judith W. "Traditional Themes in Faulkner's 'The Bear,'" TFSB, 40 (June, 1974), 57-64.

1028 Hettich, Blaise. "A Bedroom Scene in Faulkner," Renascence, 8 (Spring, 1956), 121-126.

1029 Hiers, John T. "Faulkner's Lord-to-God Bird in 'The Bear,'" AL, 47 (January, 1976), 636-637.

"... Faulkner's Lord-to-God bird, like his old bear, illustrates the almost supernatural grandeur of an old order come to fruition and thus to the threshold of extinction."

1030 Hoffman, Daniel. "William Faulkner: 'The Bear," in Landmarks of American Writing. Hennig Cohen, ed. New York: Basic Books, 1969, pp. 341-352.

1031 Hotchner, A. E. Papa Hemingway: A Personal Memoir. New York: Random House, 1966, pp. 69-70.

Quotes Hemingway as saying "... You ever read his story

'The Bear'? Read that and you'll know how good he once was...."

1032 Howe, Irving. William Faulkner: A Critical Study. New York: Vintage Books, 1962, pp. 60-70, 186-189.

1033 Howell, Elmo. "Faulkner's Elegy: An Approach to 'The Bear,'" ArlQ, 2 (Winter, 1969-70), 122-132.

1034 _______. "William Faulkner and the Chickasaw Funeral," AL, 36 (January, 1965), 523-525.

1035 Hughes, Charles W. "Man Against Nature: Moby Dick and 'The Bear,'" DAI, 32 (Texas Tech: 1971), 5230A.

1036 Hutchinson, E. R. "A Footnote to the Gum Tree Scene," CE, 24 (April, 1963), 564-565. A note on "The Bear."

1037 "Insignificant Fyce Baits a Bear," Life, 39 (November 14, 1955), 194.

1038 Jelliffe, Robert A. Faulkner at Nagano. Tokyo: Kenkyusha, 1956, pp. 50-51, 92-93.

1039 Jensen, Eric G. "The Play Element in Faulkner's 'The Bear,'" TSLL, 6 (Summer, 1964), 170-187.

1040 Jobe, Phyllis. "'The Bear': A Critical Study," Nimrod, 2 (Winter, 1958), 27-30.

1041 Jonason, Olov, tr. Björnen. Stockholm: Aldus Bonniers, 1964.

1042 Josephs, Mary J. "The Hunting Metaphor in Hemingway and Faulkner," DAI, 34 (Michigan State: 1973), 1282A-83A.

1043 Kazin, Alfred. "Faulkner in His Fury," The Inmost Leaf. New York: Harcourt Brace, 1955, pp. 266-267.

1044 Kern, Alexander C. "Myth and Symbol in Criticism of Faulkner's 'The Bear,'" Myth and Symbol: Critical Approaches and Applications. Bernice Slote, ed. Lincoln: Nebraska U.P., 1963, pp. 152-161.

1045 Kinney, Arthur F. "'Delta Autumn': Postlude to 'The Bear,'" in Bear, Man, and God. F. L. Utley, et al., eds. New York: Random House, 1963, pp. 384-395.

1046 _______. "Faulkner and the Possibilities for Heroism," SoR, 6 (October, 1970), 1110-1125.

1047 Knight, Karl F. "'Spintrius' in Faulkner's 'The Bear,'" SSF, 12 (Winter, 1975), 31-32.

1048 Kohler, Dayton. "William Faulkner and the Social Conscience," CE, 11 (December, 1949), 124-125.

1049 Kolodny, Annette. "'Stript, shorne and made deformed': Images on the Southern Landscape," SAQ, 75, #1 (Winter, 1976), 55-73.

1050 LaBudde, Kenneth. "Cultural Primitivism in William Faulkner's 'The Bear,'" AQ, 2 (Winter, 1950), 322-328.

1051 Lehan, Richard. "Faulkner's Poetic Prose: Style and Meaning in 'The Bear,'" CE, 27 (December, 1965), 243-247.

1052 Lewis, R. W. B. "The Hero in the New World: William Faulkner's 'The Bear,'" KR, 13 (Autumn, 1951), 641-660.

1053 ________. "William Faulkner: The Hero in the New World--'The Bear': America Transcended," The Picaresque Saint. New York: Lippincott, 1959, pp. 193-209.

1054 Litz, Walton. "Genealogy as Symbol in Go Down, Moses," FS, 1 (Winter, 1952), 49-53.

1055 ________. "William Faulkner's Moral Vision," SWR, 37 (Summer, 1952), 205-207.

1056 Ludwig, Richard, and Marvin B. Perry, Jr. Nine Short Novels. Boston: Heath, 1952, pp. xxxiii-xxxvii.

1057 Lupan, Radu. Traducere si prefata. Ursal. Nuvelle. Bucuresti: Editura Pentru Literatura, 1966.

1058 Lydenberg, John. "Nature Myth in Faulkner's 'The Bear,'" AL, 24 (March, 1952), 62-72. Repr., Myth and Literature. J. B. Vickery, ed. Lincoln: Nebraska U. P., 1966, pp. 257-264.

1059 ________. "Romanciers Amêricains ... A la Recherche d'un Monde Perdu," TCDA&A, 1 (1962), 29-46.

1060 Lytle, Andrew. "The Son of Man: He Will Prevail," SR, 63 (Winter, 1955), 127-128.

1061 McDonald, Walter R. "Faulkner's 'The Bear': Part IV," CEA, 34 (January, 1972), 31-32.

1062 ________. "Faulkner's 'The Bear': The Sense of Its Structure," EngRec, 18 (December, 1967), 8-14.

1063 Maclean, Hugh. "Conservatism in Modern American Fiction," CE, 15 (March, 1954), 322-325.

1064 Madeya, Ulrike. "Interpretationen zu William Faulkners 'The Bear': Das Bild des Helden und die Konstellation der Charaktere," LWU, 3 (1970), 45-60.

1065 Malin, Irving. William Faulkner: An Interpretation. Stanford: Stanford U.P., 1957, pp. 26-28, 70-73, 85-86.

1066 Maud, Ralph. "Faulkner, Mailer, and Yogi Bear," CRevAS, 2 (Fall, 1971), 69-75.
Comparison of initiation in "The Bear" and Why Are We in Vietnam?

1067 Merton, Thomas. "'Baptism in the Forest': Wisdom and Initiation in William Faulkner," CathW, 207 (June, 1968), 124-130.

1068 Miner, Ward L. The World of William Faulkner. Durham, North Carolina: Duke U.P., 1952, pp. 149-151.

1069 Moses, W. R. "Water, Water Everywhere: Old Man and A Farewell to Arms," MFS, 5 (Summer, 1959), 172-174.

1070 ________. "Where History Crosses Myth: Another Reading of 'The Bear,'" Accent, 13 (Winter, 1953), 21-33.

1071 Motoda, Shuichi. "William Faulkner: 'The Bear,'" Essays in Literature and Thought, 23 (March, 1962), 38-54.

1072 Mulqueen, James E. "Foreshadowing of Melville and Faulkner," AN&Q, 6 (March, 1968), 102.
Comparison of a story of Whig Review (1845) with Faulkner's "The Bear" and Melville's "Metaphysics of Indian Hating."

1073 Nagel, James. "Huck Finn and 'The Bear': The Wilderness and Moral Freedom," ESA, 12 (March, 1969), 59-63.

1074 Nelson, Malcolm A. "'Yr Stars Fell' in 'The Bear,'" AN&Q, 9 (March, 1971), 102-103.

1075 Nelson, Raymond S. "Apotheosis of the Bear," RS, 41 (1973), 201-204.

1076 Nestrick, William V. "The Function of Form in 'The Bear,' Section IV," TCL, 12 (October, 1966), 131-137.

1077 O'Connor, William Van. "The Wilderness Theme in Faulkner's 'The Bear,'" Accent, 13 (Winter, 1953), 12-20. Repr., Three Decades, Hoffman and Vickery, eds., pp. 322-347.

1078 Otten, Terry. "Faulkner's Use of the Past: A Comment," Renascence, 20 (Summer, 1968), 198-207, 214.

1079 Page, Sally R. Faulkner's Women. DeLand, Florida: Everett/Edwards, 1972, pp. 186-187.

1080 Perluck, Herbert A. "'The Bear': An Unromantic Reading," in Religious Perspectives in Faulkner's Fiction. J. R. Barth, ed. Notre Dame: Notre Dame U. P., 1972, pp. 173-198.

1081 ________. "'The Heart's Driving Complexity': An Unromantic Reading of 'The Bear,'" Accent, 20 (Winter, 1960), 23-46.

1082 Pinsker, Sanford. "The Unlearning of Ike McCaslin: An Ironic Reading of William Faulkner's 'The Bear,'" Topic, 12, #23 (Spring, 1972), 35-51.

1083 Poirier, Richard. A World Elsewhere: The Place of Style in American Literature. New York: Oxford U. P., 1966, pp. 78-84.

1084 Pounds, Wayne. "Symbolic Landscapes in 'The Bear': Rural Myth and Technological Fact,'" GypsyS, 4 (Winter, 1977), 40-52.

Leo Marx's landscapes in "The Bear."

1085 Prasad, V. R. N. "The Pilgrim and the Picaro: A Study of Faulkner's 'The Bear' and The Reivers," in Indian Essays in American Literature: Papers in Honour of Robert E. Spiller. Sujit Mukherjee, et al., eds. Bombay: Popular Prakashan, 1969, pp. 209-221.

1086 Pritchard, William. "Related Exercises on Joyce and Faulkner," ExEx, 10 (November, 1962), 4-5.

1087 Radomski, James Louis. "Faulkner's Style: A Syntactic Analysis," DAI, 35 (Kent State: 1974), 6154A.

1088 Roberts, Ann T., with the assistance of Daliah Singer. "The Bear," Views and Reviews of Modern German Literature. Festschrift für Adolf D. Klarmann. Karl S. Weimar, ed. München: Delp, 1974, pp. 182-198.

1089 Robinson, Cecil. "The Fall of 'The Big House' in the Literature of the Americas," ArQ, 24 (Spring, 1968), 23-41.

1090 Rollins, Ronald G. "Ike McCaslin and Chick Mallison: Faulkner's Emerging Southern Hero," WVUPP, 14 (1963), 74-79.

1091 Roth, Russell. "William Faulkner: The Pattern of Pilgrimage," Perspective, 2 (Summer, 1949), 251-254.

1092 Rubin, Louis D., Jr. William Elliott Shoots a Bear: Essays on the Southern Literary Imagination. Baton Rouge: Louisiana State U. P., 1975, pp. 13-16.

1093 Ruotolo, Lucio P. "Isaac McCaslin," Six Existential Heroes: The Politics of Faith. Cambridge: Harvard U.P., 1973, pp. 57-78.

1094 Sachs, Viola, ed. Le Sacré et le profane: "The Bear" de William Faulkner. Paris: Département Anglo-Américain, Université de Paris, 1971.
A collective explication of "The Bear" by twenty-eight French undergraduate students.

1095 ________. The Myths of America. The Hague: Mouton, 1973, p. 147.

1096 Schamberger, J. Edward. "Renaming Percival Brownlee in Faulkner's Bear," CollL, 4 (Winter, 1977), 92-94.
On the significance of Spintrius as a name for Brownlee.

1097 Sequeira, Isaac. "'The Bear': The Initiation of Ike McCaslin," OJES, 9 #1 (1972), 1-10.

1098 Short, Raymond W., and Richard B. Sewall. "The Bear," Manual--Short Stories for Study. New York: Holt, 1956, pp. 37-39.
On the short version of "The Bear."

1099 Simpson, Lewis P. "Isaac McCaslin and Temple Drake: The Fall of New World Man," LSUS, 15 (1965), 88-106; repr., in part in Bear, Man and God. Francis L. Utley, et al., eds. 2nd ed., pp. 202-209.

1100 Snell, George. "The Fury of William Faulkner," WR, 11 (Autumn, 1946), 39-40; repr., George Snell. Shapers of American Fiction. New York: Dutton, 1947, pp. 102-103.

1101 Stanzel, Franz. "Die Zeitgestaltung in William Faulkners 'The Bear,'" NS, 3 (1953), 114-121.

1102 Starke, Catherine J. Black Portraiture. New York: Basic Books, 1971, pp. 192-193.

1103 Stephens, Rosemary. "Ike's Gun and Too Many Novembers," MissQ, 23 (September, 1970), 279-287.

1104 Stewart, David H. "The Purpose of Faulkner's Ike," Criticism, 3 (1961), 333-342, repr., Bear, Man and God. Francis L. Utley, et al., eds., pp. 327-336; 2nd ed., pp. 212-220.

1105 Stewart, Randall. American Literature and Christian Doctrine. Baton Rouge: Louisiana State U.P., 1958, pp. 136-139.

1106 ________. "Hawthorne and Faulkner," CE, 17 (February,

1956), 258-262; repr., in Regionalism and Beyond: Essays by Randall Stewart. George Core, ed. Nashville: Vanderbilt U.P., 1968, pp. 126-135.

1107 ________, and Dorothy Bethurum. Living Masterpieces of American Literature. Vol. 3. Chicago: Scott, Foresman, 1954, pp. 106-110.

1108 Stone, Edward. "More on Moby-Dick and 'The Bear,'" NMAL, 1 (1977), Item 13.

1109 Stone, Emily Whitehurst. "How a Writer Finds His Material," HarpersM, 231 (November, 1965), 157-161. Possible genesis of "The Bear."

1110 Stonesifer, Richard J. "Faulkner's 'The Bear': A Note on Structure," CE, 23 (December, 1961), 219-223.

1111 Sultan, Stanley. "Call Me Ishmael: The Hagiography of Isaac McCaslin," TSLL, 3 (Spring, 1961), 50-66.

1112 Tanner, Tony. City of Words: American Fiction, 1950-1970. New York: Harper & Row, 1971, pp. 367-368, passim.

1113 Tindall, William Y. The Literary Symbol. Bloomington: Indiana U.P., 1955, pp. 164-166.

1114 Trimmer, Joseph F. Black American Literature: Notes on the Problem of Definition. (Ball State Monograph, No. 22), Muncie, Indiana: Ball State U.P., 1971, p. 23.

1115 Umphlett, Wiley Lee. "Ike McCaslin and the 'Best Game of All,'" The Sporting Myth and the American Experience: Studies in Contemporary Fiction. Lewisburg, Pa.: Bucknell U.P., 1975, pp. 58-69.

1116 Utley, Francis L., Lynn Z. Bloom, and Arthur F. Kinney, eds. Bear, Man, and God: Seven Approaches to Faulkner's 'The Bear.'" New York: Random House, 1963; revised as Eight Approaches.... 1971.

1117 Van Nostrand, A. D. "The Bear," Everyman His Own Poet. New York: McGraw-Hill, 1968, pp. 189-196.

1118 Vickery, Olga W. "God's Moral Order and the Problem of Ike's Redemption," The Novels of William Faulkner. Baton Rouge: Louisiana State U.P., 1959, rev., 1964; and in Bear, Man, and God, 2nd ed., pp. 209-212.

1119 Walton, Gerald. "Tennie's Jim and Lucas Beauchamp," AN&Q, 8 (October, 1969), 23-24.

1120 Warren, Joyce W. "The Role of Lion in Faulkner's 'The Bear': Key to a Better Understanding," ArQ, 24 (Autumn, 1968), 252-261.

1121 Warren, Robert P. "William Faulkner," NR, 115 (August 12, 1946), 176-180; (August 26, 1946), 234-237; repr., Wm. Van O'Connor, Forms of Modern Fiction, pp. 125-143; repr., Hoffman and Vickery, eds., Two Decades, pp. 82-101.

1122 Watkins, Floyd C. "Faulkner's Inexhaustible Voice," in The Flesh and the Word. Nashville: Vanderbilt U.P., 1971, pp. 241-243, 250-251.

1123 Welty, Eudora. "The Bear," Short Stories. New York: Harcourt Brace, 1949, pp. 39-47.

1124 _______. "The Reading and Writing of Short Stories," Atl, 183 (March, 1949), 48; repr., Wm. Van O'Connor. Modern Prose: Form and Style. New York: Crowell, 1959, pp. 440-442.

1125 Wertenbaker, T. J. "Faulkner's Point of View and the Chronicle of Ike McCaslin," in Bear, Man and God. Francis L. Utley, et al., eds., pp. 261-272.

1126 _______. "Faulkner's Point of View and the Chronicle of Ike McCaslin," CE, 24 (December, 1962), 169-178.

1127 West, Ray B., Jr. The Short Story in America: 1900-1950. Chicago: Henry Regnery, 1951, pp. 101-105.

1128 Wheeler, Otis B. "Faulkner's Wilderness," AL, 31 (May, 1959), 126-136.

1129 Wilner, Herbert. "Aspects of American Fiction: A Whale, a Bear, and a Marlin," Americana-Austriaca: Festschrift des Amerika--Instituts der Universität Innsbruck anlässlich seines zehnjährigen Bestehens. Klaus Lanzinger, ed. (Beiträge zur Amerikakunde, Band 1.) Wien, Stuttgart: W. Braumuller Univ.-Verl, 1966, pp. 229-246.

1130 Woodruff, Neal, Jr. "'The Bear' and Faulkner's Moral Vision," Studies in Faulkner. Carnegie Series in English No. 6. Pittsburgh: Carnegie Institute of Technology, 1961, pp. 43-67.

1131 Yoshida, Hiroshige. "Comments on 'The Bear' and 'The Old Man and the Sea,'" HSELL, 18 (1971), 69-77.
In Japanese.

"A BEAR HUNT"
(Sat. Ev. Post, (February 10, 1934), 3-9, passim; repr., in Collected Stories, 1950)

1132 Breaden, Dale G. "William Faulkner and the Land," AQ, 10 (Fall, 1958), 354-355.

1133 Rouberol, Jean. "Les Indiens dans l'Oeuvre de Faulkner," EA, 26 (March, 1973), 54-58.

"BEYOND"
(Harper's (September, 1933); repr., in Doctor Martino, 1934; Collected Stories, 1950)

1134 Kazin, Alfred. "William Faulkner: The Short Story--'Beyond,'" Contemporaries. Boston: Little, Brown & Co., 1962, p. 157.

1135 Raimbault, R. N., tr. "Au-dela," Fontaine (mai 1946), 711-728.

1136 Voss, Arthur. The American Short Story. Norman, Oklahoma: Oklahoma U. P., 1973, p. 244.

"THE BIG SHOT"
(Cf. Meriwether, J. B., Proof, 1 (1971), 313)

1137 Lang, Beatrice. "An Unpublished Faulkner Story: 'The Big Shot,'" MissQ, 26 (Summer, 1973), 312-324.

1138 Meriwether, James B. The Literary Career of William Faulkner. Princeton: Princeton U. P., 1961, pp. 35, 87.

1139 ________. "The Short Fiction of William Faulkner: A Bibliography," Proof, 1 (1971), 293-329.

1140 Millgate, Michael. ["The Big Shot"], The Achievement of William Faulkner. New York: Random House, 1965, passim.

BIG WOODS
(New York: Random House, 1955)

1141 Bradley, Van Allen. ChiDN (1955). Review.

1142 Burggraf, David Leroy. "The Genesis and Unity of Faulkner's 'Big Woods,'" DAI, 36 (Ohio: 1975), 6679A-6680A.

1143 Chapman, Arnold. "Pampas and Big Woods: Heroic Initiation in Güiraldes and Faulkner," CL, 11 (Winter, 1959), 61-77.

1144 Cowley, Malcolm. "Life of the Hunter," NYTBR (October 16, 1955), 4, 44. Review.

1145 Kierszys, Zofia and Jan Zakrzewski, trs. Wielki las. Warszawa: Panstwowy Instytut Wydawniczy, 1962.

1146 McHaney, Thomas L. "A Deer Hunt in the Faulkner Country," MissQ, 23 (Summer, 1970), 315-320.

1147 Rosenberger, Coleman. "Four Faulkner Hunting Stories, Rich in Narrative and Symbol," NYHT (October 16, 1955), 1, 16. Review.

1148 Smith, Harrison. "Big Woods," SatRL, 38 (October 29, 1955), 16. Review.

1149 Stresau, Hermann, and Elizabeth Schnack, trs. Der grosse Wald. Stuttgart: Henry Goverts Verlag, 1964.

1150 Wheeler, Otis B. "Faulkner's Wilderness," AL, 31 (May, 1959), 126-136.

"BLACK MUSIC"
(Doctor Martino, 1934; repr., in Collected Stories, 1950)

1151 Garnett, David. "Books in General," NS&N, 8, n.s. (September 29, 1934), 396.

1152 Meriwether, James B. The Literary Career of William Faulkner. Princeton U. Library, 1961, pp. 82, 170.

1153 Solery, Marc. "Black Music ou La Metamorphose du regard," Delta, 3 (November, 1976), 35-43.
The ironic effects of perspective.

"THE BROOCH"
(Scribner's (January, 1936), 7-12; repr., in Collected Stories, 1950)

1154 "Baptism of Faulkner," Newsweek, 41 (April 13, 1953), 56.
Description of the filming of the story for Lux Video Theater.

1155 Garrison, J. M., Jr. "Faulkner's 'The Brooch': A Story for Teachers," CE, 36 (September, 1974), 51-57.

1156 Gould, Jack. "'The Brooch' on TV," NYT (April 12, 1953), II, 11.

1157 Hult, Sharon Smith. "William Faulkner's 'The Brooch': The Journey to the Riolama," MissQ, 27 (Summer, 1974), 291-305.
Faulkner's use in "The Brooch" of William Henry Hudson's Green Mansions.

1158 Meriwether, James B. The Literary Career of William Faulkner. Princeton U. Library, 1961, passim.

1159 "New Blood: Lux Video Theater," Time, 61 (April 13, 1953), 71-72.
CBS production of "The Brooch" by Calvin Kuhl.

1160 Raimbault, R. N., tr. "The Brooch," FL, 17 (July 14, 1962), 8.

"BY THE PEOPLE"
(Mademoiselle (October, 1955); incorporated in The Mansion, 1959)

1161 Meriwether, James B. The Literary Career of William Faulkner. Columbia, S.C.: South Carolina U.P., 1961, 1971, pp. 43-44.

"CARCASSONE"
(These 13, 1931; repr., in Collected Stories, 1950)

1162 Gwynn, Frederick L., and Joseph L. Blotner, eds. "Carcassone," Faulkner in the University. Charlottesville: Virginia U.P., 1959, p. 22.

1163 Hamblin, Robert W. "'Carcassone': Faulkner's Allegory of Art and the Artist," SoR, 15, #2 (April, 1979), 355-365.

1164 Meriwether, James B. "The Short Fiction of William Faulkner," Proof, 1 (1971), 299.

1165 Milum, Richard A. "Faulkner's 'Carcassone': The Dream and the Reality," SSF, 15, #2 (Spring, 1978), 133-138.

"CENTAUR IN BRASS"
(AmMerc, (February, 1932); repr., in Collected Stories, 1950; The Town, 1957)

1166 Campbell, Harry Modean. "Mr. Roth's Centaur and Faulkner's Symbolism," WR, 16 (Summer, 1952), 320-321.

1167 Meriwether, James B. The Literary Career of William Faulkner. Columbia, S.C.: South Carolina U.P., 1971, passim.

1168 Nilon, Charles H. Faulkner and the Negro. New York: Citadel Press, 1962, pp. 48-54.

1169 Raimbault, R. N., tr. Le centaure de bronze. Paris: 1961.

1170 Roth, Russell F. "The Centaur and the Pear Tree," WR, 16 (Spring, 1952), 199-205.
Cf., Harry Modean Campbell. "Mr. Roth's Centaur and Faulkner's Symbolism," WR, 16 (1952), 320-321.

COLLECTED STORIES
(New York: Random House, 1950)

1171 "A. P. D." Yorkshire Even Press (April 3, 1958); (September 18, 1959). Review.

1172 Anon. Jackson Daily News (August 29, 1950), 9. Review.
"... What Faulkner writes about the eroded people and lands of the 1920's is tragically accurate."

1173 Anon. Glasgow Herald (September 21, 1933). Review.

1174 Anon. Time (August 28, 1950), 79. Review

1175 Bowen, Elizabeth. Tatler and Bystander, 228, #2963 (April 23, 1958), 197. Review

1176 C. F. Oxford Mail (October 9, 1933). Review.

1177 Carter, Hodding. "William Faulkner's Collected Stories Reveal Growing Hope for the Eroded South," Sunday Journal-Constitution (Atlanta), (August 27, 1950), F-3. Review.

1178 "Collected Stories of William Faulkner," HudR, 3 (Winter, 1950), 631-633.

1179 Dunsany, Lord. "Great Short Stories," JO'LW (October 26, 1951), 652. Review.

1180 Fiedler, Leslie. "Style and Anti-Style in the Short Story," KR, 13 (Winter, 1951), 164-166.

1181 Garnett, David. NSt, n.s. (September 30, 1933), 387.

1182 Gregory, Horace. "In the Haunted, Heroic Land of Faulkner's Imagination," NYHTBR (August 20, 1950), 1, 12.

1183 "Haunted Landscapes," Time, 56 (August 28, 1950), 79.

1184 Haxton, Josephine A. "The Collected Stories of William Faulkner," Delta Democrat Times (August 20, 1950), 20.

1185 Haynes, Michael Allen. "The Unity of Collected Stories," DAI, 39, #5 (Ball State: 1978), 2938A.

1186 Hicks, Granville. New Leader (November 20, 1950), 20-22.

1187 Hunt, John. "Collected Stories," Wake, 9 (1950), 122-124.

1188 Kazin, Alfred. "Big Chips Off the Old Block," Griffin, (New York) (May, 1961), 2-7.

1189 Kierszys, Zofia, tr. Opowiadania. Warszawa: Panstwowy Instytut Wydawniczy, 1967. [Translation of Collected Stories.]

1190 Krim, Seymour. "Short Stories by Six," HudR, 3 (Winter, 1951), 626-633.

1191 Momberger, Philip. "A Critical Study of Faulkner's Early Sketches and Collected Stories," DAI, 33 (Johns Hopkins: 1970), 2386A.

1192 Muir, Edwin. Listener, 10 (October 4, 1933), 519.
Adverse criticism.

1193 Parsons, Luke. Fortnightly, 170 (December, 1951), 866-867.

1194 Peden, William. "Sartoris, Snopes and Everyman," SatRL, 33 (August 26, 1950), 12.

1195 Price-Stephens, Gordon. MissQ, 17 (Summer, 1964), 123-128.

1196 Rosenfeld, Isaac. "Faulkner and Contemporaries," PR, 18, #1 (January-February, 1951), 106-112.

1197 Skelton, Bill. "Faulkner, Best, Worst, and Inimitable," Jackson Clarion-Ledger (September 10, 1950), Sec. 4, p. 3.

1198 Smith, Henry. "More Gold Medals," SatRL, 34 (March 17, 1951), 22-23.
Noted that Faulkner was awarded the National Book Award for Collected Stories published in 1950.

1199 Sylvester, Harry. NYTBR (August 20, 1950), 1. Review.

1200 Toynbee, Philip. The Observer (February 1, 1959). Review.

1201 Urquhart, Fred. Time and Tide, 39, #16 (April 19, 1958), 498. Review.

"A COURTSHIP"
(SR, 56 (1948), 634-653; repr., in Collected Stories, 1950)

1202 Cantrell, Frank. "Faulkner's 'A Courtship,'" MissQ, 24 (Summer, 1971), 289-295.

1203 _______. "Faulkner's Late Short Fiction," DAI, 31 (South Carolina: 1971), 5391A.

1204 Dabney, Lewis M. "A Courtship," The Indians of Yoknapatawpha. Baton Rouge: Louisiana State U.P., 1974, pp. 57-71, 101.

1205 _______. "Faulkner, the Red, and the Black," ColuF, 1, #2 (Spring, 1972), 52-54.

1206 Howell, Elmo. "Inversion and the 'Female' Principle: William Faulkner's 'A Courtship,'" SSF, 4 (Summer, 1967), 308-314.

1207 _______. "William Faulkner and the Mississippi Indians," GaR, 21 (December, 1967), 386-396.

1208 Langford, Beverly Young. "History and Legend in William Faulkner's 'Red Leaves,'" NMW, 6 (Spring, 1973), 19-24.

1209 Longley, John L., Jr. The Tragic Mask: A Study of Faulkner's Heroes. Chapel Hill: North Carolina U.P., 1963, pp. 122-125.

1210 Meriwether, James B. The Literary Career of William Faulkner. Columbia: South Carolina U.P., 1971, pp. 35, 82, 85.

1211 Milum, Richard A. "Ikkemotube and the Spanish Conspiracy," AL, 46 (November, 1974), 389-391.

1212 Rouberol, Jean. "Les Indiens dans L'oeuvre de Faulkner," EA, 26 (March, 1973), 54-58.

1213 Yglesias, Jose. "Neurotic Visions," Masses and Mainstream, 2 (December, 1949), 74-76.

"CREVASSE"
(See also "Victory"--"Crevasse" was once a part of "Victory.")

1214 Day, Douglas. "The War Stories of William Faulkner," GaR, 15 (Winter, 1961), 385-394.

1215 Meriwether, James B. The Literary Career of William Faulkner. Columbia: South Carolina U.P., 1971, p. 86.

1216 Millgate, Michael. The Achievement of William Faulkner. New York: Random House, 1965, pp. 260, 261, 273.

1217 O'Connor, William Van. The Tangled Fire of William Faulkner. Minneapolis: Minnesota U. P., 1954, p. 67.

1218 Reed, Joseph W. Faulkner's Narrative. New Haven: Yale U. P., 1973, p. 55.

1219 Smith, Raleigh W., Jr. "Faulkner's 'Victory': The Plain People of Clydebank," MissQ, 23 (Summer, 1970), 241-249.
"Crevasse" illuminates "Victory."

"DEATH DRAG"
(Scribner's (January, 1932); repr., in Doctor Martino, 1934; Collected Stories, 1950).

1220 Connolly, Francis. The Types of Literature. New York: Harcourt, Brace, 1955, pp. 705-706.

1221 Gwynn, Frederick L., and Joseph L. Blotner, eds. Faulkner in the University. Charlottesville: Virginia U. P., 1959, pp. 48, 68.

1222 Hagopian, John V., and Martin Dolch. Insight I: Analyses of American Literature. Frankfurt am Main: Hirschgraben-Verlag, 1962, pp. 55-59.

1223 Howe, Irving. "A Note on the Stories--'Death Drag,'" William Faulkner: A Critical Study. New York: Vintage, 1952, p. 264.

1224 Meriwether, James B. The Literary Career of William Faulkner. Columbia: South Carolina U. P., 1971, pp. 25, 82, 171.

1225 Millgate, Michael. The Achievement of William Faulkner. New York: Random House, 1965, pp. 138, 148, 273.

1226 O'Connor, William Van. The Tangled Fire of William Faulkner. Minneapolis: Minnesota U. P., 1954, p. 89.

"DELTA AUTUMN"
(Story, 20 (1942); revised for Go Down, Moses, 1942; part of that version revised for ending of Big Woods, 1955.)

1227 Ackerman, R. D. "The Immolation of Isaac McCaslin," TSLL, 16 (Fall, 1974), 557-565.

1228 Adamowski, T. H. "Isaac McCaslin and the Wilderness of the Imagination," CentR, 17 (1973), 92-112.

1229 Cate, Hollis L. "Faulkner's Delta-shaped Land in 'Delta Autumn,'" RS, 38 (1970), 156.

1230 Douglas, Kenneth. "Masterpieces of the Modern World," World Masterpieces. Maynard Mack, et al., eds. Vol. 2, 3rd ed. New York: Norton, 1962, pp. 1381-1382.

1231 Dussinger, Gloria R. "Faulkner's Isaac McCaslin as Romantic Hero Manqué," SAQ, 68 (1969), 377-385.

1232 Early, James. "Delta Autumn," The Making of "Go Down, Moses." Dallas: Southern Methodist U.P., 1972, pp. 86-93.

1233 Flanagan, John T. "Folklore in Faulkner's Fiction," PLL, 5, Supp. (Summer, 1969), 123.

1234 Gwynn, Frederick L., and Joseph L. Blotner, eds. Faulkner in the University. Charlottesville: Virginia U.P., 1959, pp. 46, 277.

1235 Harter, Carol C. "The Winter of Isaac McCaslin: Revisions and Irony in Faulkner's 'Delta Autumn,'" JML, 1 (1970), 209-225.

1236 Jackson, James Turner. "Delta Cycle," Chimera, 5 (Autumn, 1946), 3-14.

1237 Kinney, Arthur F. "'Delta Autumn': Postlude to 'The Bear,'" in Bear, Man, and God. F. L. Utley, et al., eds. New York: 1964, pp. 384-395.

1238 _______. "'Delta Autumn': William Faulkner's Answer for David H. Stewart," PMASAL, 49 (1963), 541-549; repr., Modern Short Stories: The Uses of the Imagination. Arthur Mizener, ed. New York: Norton, 1971, 3rd ed., pp. 625-628.

1239 _______. "Faulkner and the Possibilities for Heroism," SoR, 6 (1970), 1110-1125.

1240 Kolodny, Annette. "'Stript, shorne and made deformed': Images on the Southern Landscape," SAQ, 75, #1 (Winter, 1976), 55-73.

1241 LaCroix, Annie. "Delta Autumn," Views and Reviews of Modern German Literature: Festschrift für Adolf D. Klarmann. Karl S. Weimar, ed. München: Delp, 1974, pp. 199-210.

1242 Litz, Walton. "Genealogy as Symbol in Go Down, Moses," FS, 1 (Winter, 1952), 50-51.

1243 Meriwether, James B. The Literary Career of William Faulkner. Columbia: South Carolina U. P., 1971, pp. 31, 39, 74, 80.

1244 Millgate, Michael. The Achievement of William Faulkner. New York: Random House, 1965, p. 213.

1245 Miner, Ward L. The World of William Faulkner. Durham, North Carolina: Duke U. P., 1952, pp. 154-156.

1246 Mizener, Arthur, ed. Modern Short Stories: The Uses of the Imagination. Rev. ed. New York: Norton, 1967, pp. 545-550, 738-740.

1247 O'Connor, William Van. The Tangled Fire of William Faulkner. Minneapolis: Minnesota U. P., 1954, pp. 133-134.

1248 ________. "The Wilderness Theme in Faulkner's 'The Bear,'" Accent, 13 (Winter, 1953), 19-20.

1249 Ohashi, Kenzaburo, ed. "Notes," "Delta Autumn" and Three Other Stories. Tokyo: Kenkyusha, 1966.

1250 Ross, Woodburn O., and A. Dayle Wallace. "Delta Autumn," Short Stories in Context. New York: American Bk. Co., 1953, pp. 337-341.

1251 Ruotolo, Lucio P. "Isaac McCaslin--'Delta Autumn,'" Six Existential Heroes: The Politics of Faith. Cambridge: Harvard U. P., 1973, pp. 57-78.

1252 Stewart, David H. "The Purpose of Faulkner's Ike," Criticism, 3 (Fall, 1961), 332-342.
Cf., Arthur F. Kinney. "'Delta Autumn': An Answer for David H. Stewart," PMASAL, 49 (1963), 541-549.

1253 Warren, Robert P. "William Faulkner," NR, 115 (August 12, 1946), 176-180; (August 26, 1946), 234-237.

1254 Winkel, Carol A. G. "Faulkner's Style and Its Relation to Theme: A Stylistic Study of Two Stories from Go Down, Moses," DAI, 35 (Delaware: 1974), 3017A.

"THE DEVIL BEATS HIS WIFE"
(Cf., Meriwether, James B., #1256 below)

1255 Meriwether, James B. The Literary Career of William Faulkner. Columbia: South Carolina U. P., 1971, p. 81.

1256 ________. "The Short Fiction of William Faulkner," Proof, 1 (1971), 313-314.
States that the story "Christmas Tree" is apparently a

version of "The Devil Beats His Wife," a three-page manuscript "which Faulkner kept in his papers."

1257 Millgate, Michael. The Achievement of William Faulkner. New York: Random House, 1965, p. 23.
Faulkner abandoned the story, but his friend, Ben Wasson, used the title for a novel.

1258 Richardson, H. Edward. William Faulkner: The Journey to Self-Discovery. Columbia: Missouri U.P., 1970, p. 165.

"DIVORCE IN NAPLES"
(These 13 (1931); repr., in Collected Stories, 1950)

1259 Meriwether, James B. The Literary Career of William Faulkner. Columbia: South Carolina U.P., 1971, pp. 82, 171.

1260 Millgate, Michael. The Achievement of William Faulkner. New York: Random House, 1965, pp. 260, 262, 274.

1261 O'Connor, William Van. The Tangled Fire of William Faulkner. Minneapolis: Minnesota U.P., 1954, p. 70.

"DOCTOR MARTINO" and DOCTOR MARTINO AND OTHER STORIES
(The story "Doctor Martino," in Harper's, 163 (1931); repr., in Doctor Martino and Other Stories, 1934; and in Collected Stories, 1950)

1262 Abramov, A. Review of Dr. Martino and Other Stories, Inostrannaia kniga, No. 3 (1935), 17-18.

1263 "A. P. D." Yorkshire Evening Press (February 12, 1959). Review.

1264 Benêt, William Rose. "Fourteen Faulkner Stories," SatRL, 10 (April 21, 1934), 645.

1265 Blanzat, Jean. "Le Docteur Martino et autres histoires," FL (décembre 18, 1948), 5.

1266 Brickell, Herschel. "The Literary Landscape," NAR, 237 (June, 1934), 570.

1267 Crickmay, Edward. Sunday Referee (October 7, 1934). Review.

1268 Garnett, David. NS&N, 8 (September 29, 1934), 396. Review.

1269 Gould, Gerald. Observer (September 30, 1934). Review.

1270 Hale, Lionel. News Chronicle (October 10, 1934). Review.

1271 Hansen, Harry. NYTel (April 16, 1934). Review.

1272 Knieger, Bernard. "Faulkner's 'Mountain Victory,' 'Doctor Martino,' and 'There Was a Queen,'" Expl, 30 (February, 1972), Item 45.

1273 Kronenberger, Louis. NYT (April 22, 1934), 9.

1274 Lang, Béatrice. "Dr. Martino: The Conflict of Life and Death," Delta, 3 (November, 1976), 23-33.
The story is called "a good introduction" to the study of "closure and finality."

1275 Leary, Lewis. William Faulkner of Yoknapatawpha County. New York: Crowell, 1973, pp. 32, 135.

1276 Lebesque, M. [Dr. Martino and Other Stories] Climats (décembre 1948), 12.

1277 Le Breton, Maurice. RAA (édition anglaise) (août 1935), 565.

1278 London Mercury, 31, #181 (November, 1934), 87. Review.

1279 Malin, Irving. William Faulkner: An Interpretation. Stanford U.P., 1957, p. 82.

1280 Marsh, F. T. "Books," NYHT (April 15, 1934), 7. Review.

1281 Matthews, T. S. NR, 79 (May 23, 1934), 51. Review.

1282 Meriwether, James B. The Literary Career of William Faulkner. Columbia: South Carolina U.P., 1971, pp. 24-25.

1283 Millgate, Michael. The Achievement of William Faulkner. New York: Random House, 1965, pp. 259, 265, 273, 274.

1284 Monicelli, Giorgio, and Attilio Landi, trs. Il Dottor Martino e altri racconti. Milan: Arnoldo Mondadori Editore, 1968.

1285 O'Connor, William Van. The Tangled Fire of William Faulkner. Minneapolis: Minnesota U.P., 1954, pp. 88-90, 160.

1286 Plomer, William. Spectator, 153 (September 28, 1934), 454. Review.

1287 Raimbault, R. N., and Ch. P. Vorce, trs. Le Docteur Martino et autres histoires. Paris: Gallimard, 1948.

1288 Rice, Philip Blair. "The Art of William Faulkner," Nation, 138 (April 25, 1934), 478.

1289 Spring, Howard. Evening Standard (September 13, 1934). Review.

1290 Toynbee, Philip. The Observer (February 1, 1959). Review.

1291 Vallette, J. MdF (fêvrier, 1949), 354.

"DRY SEPTEMBER"
(Scribner's, 89 (1931); revised and repr., These 13, 1931; Collected Stories, 1950.

1292 Bache, William B. "Moral Awareness in 'Dry September,'" FS, 3 (Winter, 1954), 53-57.

1293 Carey, Glenn O. "Social Criticism in Faulkner's 'Dry September,'" EngRec, 15, #2 (December, 1964), 27-30.

1294 Coindreau, M. E., tr. "Septembre ardent," NRF, 220 (janvier, 1932), 49-65.

1295 Dabney, Lewis M. The Indians of Yoknapatawpha. Baton Rouge: Louisiana State U.P., 1974, pp. 91-92, 98.

1296 Davis, Robert Gorham. Instructor's Manual for Ten Modern Masters. New York: Harcourt, 1953, pp. 44-45.

1297 Faulkner, Howard. "The Stricken World of 'Dry September,'" SSF, 10 (Winter, 1973), 47-50.

1298 Ford, Arthur L. "Dust and Dreams: A Study of Faulkner's 'Dry September,'" CE, 24 (December, 1962), 219-220. Concentration on "repetition of key images."

1299 Franulic, Lenka, tr. "Septiembre ardiente," Antología del cuento norteamericano. Santiago: Ercilla, 1943, pp. 233-246.

1300 Griffin, William J. "How to Read Faulkner: A Powerful Plea for Ignorance," TSL, 1 (1956), 28-30.

1301 Günter, Bernd. "William Faulkner's 'Dry September,'" NS, 72 (n.s., 22) (November, 1973), 607-616.

1302 Hamada, Seijiro. "Dry September No Atmosphere," EigoS, 120 (1974), 122-124.

1303 Hamalian, Leo, and Frederick R. Karl. The Shape of Fiction. New York: McGraw-Hill, 1967, pp. 79-81.

1304 Howard, Daniel F., ed. Instructor's Manual to The Modern Tradition. Boston: Little, Brown & Co., 1968, pp. 17-18.

1305 Johnson, Ira. "Faulkner's 'Dry September' and Caldwell's 'Saturday Afternoon': An Exercise in Practical Criticism," Tradition et innovation, littérature et paralittérature: Actes du Congrès de Nancy (1972). Soc. des Anglicistes de l'Enseignement Supérieur. Paris: Didier, 1975, pp. 269-278.

1306 McDermott, John V. "Faulkner's Cry for a Healing Measure: Dry September," ArQ, 32 (Spring, 1976), 31-34.

1307 Meriwether, James B. The Literary Career of William Faulkner. Columbia: South Carolina U.P., 1971, pp. 83, 172.

1308 "Movies Do a Hard-Driving and Memorable Job on Faulkner's Story," Life, 27 (December 12, 1949), 149-150f.

1309 Nilon, Charles H. Faulkner and the Negro. New York: Citadel Press, 1965, pp. 43-44.

1310 O'Connor, William Van. The Tangled Fire of William Faulkner. Minneapolis: Minnesota U.P., 1954, p. 68.

1311 Oliver, María Rosa. "La novela norteamericana moderna," Sur, 59 (August, 1939), 43-45.

1312 Page, Sally R. Faulkner's Women: Characterization and Meaning. DeLand, Florida: Everett/Edwards, 1972, pp. 99-103.

1313 Reed, Joseph W., Jr. Faulkner's Narrative. New Haven: Yale U.P., 1973, pp. 50-55, passim.

1314 Sato, Susumu. "The Style and Theme of Faulkner's 'Dry September,'" Pursuit, 2 (July, 1963), 35-46.

1315 Schnack, Elizabeth, tr. Dürrer September und acht andere erzählungen. Zurich: Diogenes, 1968.

1316 Simon, Jean. "French Studies in American Literature and Civilization," AL, 6 (May, 1934), 184.

1317 Vickery, John B. "Ritual and Theme in Faulkner's 'Dry September,'" ArQ, 18 (Spring, 1962), 5-14.

1318 Waggoner, Hyatt. William Faulkner: From Jefferson to the World. Lexington: Kentucky U.P., 1959, pp. 196-199.

1319 Weiss, Daniel. "William Faulkner and the Runaway Slave," NwRev, 6 (Summer, 1963), 71-79.

1320 Winslow, Joan D. "Language and Destruction in Faulkner's 'Dry September,'" CLAJ, 20 (March, 1977), 380-386.

1321 Wolfe, Ralph Haven, and Edgar F. Daniels. "Beneath the Dust of 'Dry September,'" SSF, 1, #2 (Winter, 1964), 158-159.

"ELLY"
(Story, 4 (1934); repr., in Doctor Martino, 1934; and Collected Stories, 1950)

1322 Bokanowski, Hélène, tr. Fontaine, 36 (1944), 54-72.

1323 Bradford, Melvin E. "Faulkner's 'Elly': An Exposé," MissQ, 21 (Summer, 1968), 179-187.

1324 Kerr, Elizabeth M. Yoknapatawpha: Faulkner's "Little Postage Stamp of Native Soil." New York: Fordham U.P., 1969, pp. 214-215, passim.

1325 Malin, Irving. William Faulkner: An Interpretation. Stanford U.P., 1957, pp. 34-35.

1326 Meriwether, James B. The Literary Career of William Faulkner. Columbia: South Carolina U.P., 1971, pp. 83, 172, 175.

1327 Page, Sally R. Faulkner's Women. DeLand, Florida: Everett/Edwards, 1972, pp. 95-96.

1328 Reed, Joseph W., Jr. Faulkner's Narrative. New Haven: Yale U.P., 1973, pp. 55, 278.

"ELMER"
(Cf., Meriwether, James B., 1332 below.)

1329 Gidley, Mich. "One Continuous Force: Notes on Faulkner's Extra-Literary Reading," in William Faulkner: Four Decades of Criticism. Michigan State U.P., 1973, p. 61.

1330 McHaney, Thomas L. "The Elmer Papers: Faulkner's Comic Portraits of the Artist," MissQ, 26 (Summer, 1973), 281-311.

1331 ________. "The Elmer Papers: Faulkner's Comic Portraits of the Artist," A Faulkner Miscellany. James B. Meriwether, ed. Jackson, Miss.: Mississippi U.P., 1974, pp. 37-69. Repr., from MissQ, 26 (1973), 281-311 with additional illustrations.

1332 Meriwether, James B. The Literary Career of William Faulkner. Columbia: South Carolina U.P., 1971, pp. 3, 81.

1333 _______. "A Portrait of Elmer--The Short Fiction of William Faulkner," Proof, 1 (1971), 315-316.

1334 Millgate, Michael. *The Achievement of William Faulkner.* New York: Random House, 1966, pp. 21-22, *passim*.

1335 Richardson, H. Edward. *William Faulkner: The Journey to Self-Discovery.* Columbia: Missouri U. P., 1970, pp. 165, 226-227.

"AN ERROR IN CHEMISTRY"
(Ellery Queen's Mystery Magazine, 7 (1946); repr., in *Knight's Gambit*, 1949)

1336 Hunt, Joel A. "Thomas Mann and Faulkner: Portrait of a Magician," WSCL, 3 (Summer, 1967), 431-436.
Finds echoes of *Mario und der Zauberer* in Faulkner's story.

1337 Meriwether, James B. *The Literary Career of William Faulkner.* Columbia: South Carolina U. P., 1971, pp. 33-34, 77.

1338 _______. "Two Unknown Faulkner Short Stories," RANAM, 4 (1971), 23-30.

A FABLE
(New York: Random House, 1954)

1339 Adams, Richard P. *Faulkner: Myth and Motion.* Princeton: Princeton U. P., 1968, pp. 161-169.

1340 Algren, Nelson. "Faulkner's Thrillers," NYTBR (November 6, 1949), 4.

1341 Anon. "*A Fable*," Booklist (September 1, 1954), 14-15.

1342 Anon. "*A Fable*," Kirkus (July 1, 1954), 402.

1343 Anon. "Faulkner Passion Play," Time (August 2, 1954), 76.

1344 Anon. "Faulkner Wall Plot," Life, 37 (August 9, 1954), 77-78.

1345 Anon. "Fight to the Finish," TLS (June 10, 1955), 313.

1346 Anon. Newsweek (August 2, 1954), 48-52. Review.

1347 Anon. NY, 18 (May 16, 1942), 74. Review.

1348 Anon. "Mr. Faulkner's Fable," Times (June 9, 1955), 11.

1349 Anon. Time, 39 (May 11, 1942), 95. Review.

1350 Anon. Times (London), (October 10, 1942), 497. Review.

1351 Anon. Times (June 9, 1955), 11. Review.

1352 Anon. "The Worldwide Influence of William Faulkner: Reports from Six Capitols," NYTBR, 64 (November 15, 1959), 52-53.

1353 Backman, Melvin. "Faulkner's Sick Heroes," MFS, 2 (Autumn, 1956), 95-108.

1354 Bailey, Dennis Lee. "The Modern Novel in the Presence of Myth," DAI, 35 (Purdue: 1974), 7292A-93A.

1355 Baker, Carlos. "Cry Enough!" Nation, 179 (August 7, 1954), 115-118.

1356 ________. "William Faulkner: The Doomed and the Damned," The Young Rebel in American Literature. Carl Bode, ed. London: Heinemann, 1959; New York: Praeger, 1959, pp. 166-168.

1357 Baldwin, James. "As Much Truth As One Can Bear," NYTBR (January 14, 1962), 1, 38.

1358 Barth, J. Robert. "A Rereading of Faulkner's Fable," America, 92 (October 9, 1954), 44-46.

1359 Bartlett, Phyllis. "Other Countries, Other Wenches," MFS, 3 (Winter, 1957-58), 345-349.
The Jew of Malta as a source.

1360 Bartra, Agusti. Prologo. Una Fabula. Antonio Ribera, tr. Buenos Aires: Jackson, 1956; Ediciones Selectas, 1963.

1361 Basso, Hamilton. "William Faulkner: Man and Writer," SatRL, 45 (July 28, 1962), 11-14.

1362 Bergin, Thomas G. "Una Favola," Dizionario letterario, Appendice opere. Milan: 1964, p. 356.

1363 Berrone, Louis. "A Dickensian Echo in Faulkner," Dickensian, 71, #2 (May, 1975), 100-101.
Notes parallel in "Thursday Night" in Faulkner's A Fable with an incident in Dickens's Somebody's Luggage.

1364 Bianciardi, Luciano, tr. Una favola Romanzo. Milan: Arnoldo Mondadori Editore, 1971.

1365 Blotner, Joseph. "Speaking of Books: Faulkner's *A Fable*," NYTBR (May 25, 1969), 2, 34-39.

1366 Braem, Helmut M. "Das scandalon William Faulkner: Die metaphysische Kampfstatt und ein sadistischer Jehova," DRu, 84, #10 (October, 1958), 944-950.

1367 Breit, Harvey. "In and Out of Books--Word's Worth," NYTBR (September 19, 1954), 8.

1368 _______. "In and Out of Books--Youth," NYTBR (March 20, 1955), 8.

1369 Brumm, Ursula. "Christ and Adam as 'Figures' in American Literature," *American Thought and Religious Typology*. New Brunswick, New Jersey: Rutgers U.P., 1970, pp. 198-221. Tr., of Brumm's *Die religiöese Typologie Amerikanischen Denken*. Leiden: 1963.

1370 _______. "The Figure of Christ in American Literature," PR, 24 (Summer, 1957), 403-413. Rev., and exp., cf., #1369 above.

1371 Brylowski, Walter. *Faulkner's Olympian Laugh*. Detroit: Wayne State U.P., 1968, pp. 183-200.

1372 Butterworth, Abner K., Jr. "A Critical and Textual Study of William Faulkner's *A Fable*," DAI, 31 (South Carolina: 1970), 5390A.

1373 Cabaniss, Allen. *Liturgy and Literature: Selected Essays*. University: Alabama U.P., 1970.

1374 _______. "A Source of Faulkner's *Fable*," UMSE, 6 (1965), 87-89.

1375 Cahoon, Herbert. "*A Fable*," LJ, 79 (August, 1954), 1400.

1376 Carey, Glenn O. "William Faulkner: Man's Fatal Vice," ArQ, 28 (Winter, 1972), 293-300.

1377 Carter, Thomas H. "Dramatization of an Enigma," WR, 10 (Winter, 1955), 147-158.

1378 Chametzky, Jules. "Some Remarks on *A Fable*," FS, 3 (Summer-Autumn, 1954), 39-40.

1379 Cheney, Frances N. "Faulkner's *Fable*," VQR, 30 (Autumn, 1954), 623-626.

1380 Chittick, Kathryn A. "The Fables in William Faulkner's *A Fable*," MissQt, 30, #3 (Summer, 1977), 403-415.

1381 Church, Margaret. "William Faulkner: Myth and Duration," Time and Reality. Chapel Hill: North Carolina U. P., 1963, pp. 248-250.

1382 Collins, Carvel. "War and Peace and Mr. Faulkner," NYTBR (August 1, 1954), 1, 13.

1383 Connolly, Thomas E. "Faulkner's A Fable in the Classroom," CE, 21 (December, 1959), 165-171.

1384 _______. "The Three Plots of A Fable," TCL, 6 (July, 1960), 70-75.

1385 Corke, Hilary. "Bad Conscience," Encounter, 5, #4 (October, 1955), 85-87.

1386 Cottrell, Beekman W. "Faulkner's Cosmic Fable: The Extraordinary Family of Man," Studies in Faulkner. Carnegie Series in English, No. 6. Pittsburgh: Carnegie Institute of Technology, 1961, pp. 17-27.

1387 Coughlan, Robert. "Is A Fable William Faulkner's Masterpiece?" Chicago Sun-Times (August 1, 1954), Sec. II, 1; incorporated into "A Fable," A Private World of William Faulkner. New York: Harper, 1954, pp. 139-151.

1388 Cowley, Malcolm. "Faulkner's Powerful New Novel," NYHTB (August 1, 1954), 1, 8.

1389 Davenport, John. "Faulkner Nods," Observer (June 26, 1955), 19.

1390 Detweiler, Robert. "Christ and the Christ Figure in American Fiction," ChS, 47 (Summer, 1964), 111-124.

1391 Dillistone, F. W. "The Friend Lays Down His Life," The Novelist and the Passion Story. London: Collins, 1960; New York: Sheed and Ward, 1961, pp. 92-118.

1392 Dillon, Richard T. "Some Sources for Faulkner's Version of the First Air War," AL, 44 (January, 1973), 629-637.

1393 Einsiedel, Wolfgang von. "Revolte des Menschenschnes: zu William Faulkners: Eine Legende," Merkur, 10 (March, 1956), 282-290.

1394 Elconin, Victor A. "Faulkner Is Still Brooding," Daily Oklahoman (August 22, 1954), 20.

1395 Emerson, William. "William Faulkner--After Ten Years, A Fable," Newsweek (August 2, 1954), 48-52.

1396 Everett, Walter K. Faulkner's Art and Characters. New York: Barron's Educational Series, 1969, pp. 15-21.

1397 Faulkner, William. "A Note on A Fable," MissQ, 26 (Summer, 1973), 416-417.
A statement by Faulkner concerning A Fable in response to a request by his editor, Saxe Commins, late in 1953 or early in 1954.

1398 "Faulkner Passion Play," Time, 64 (August 2, 1954), 76. Review.

1399 Ficken, Carl. "The Christ Story in A Fable," MissQ, 23 (Summer, 1970), 251-264.

1400 Fiedler, Leslie. "Stone Grotesques," NR, 131 (August 23, 1954), 18-19. Review.

1401 Flint, R. W. "What Price Glory?" HudR, 7 (Winter, 1955), 602-606.

1402 Frady, Marshall. "The Faulkner Place," FurmS, n.s., 13 (November, 1965), 1-6.
A visit to Faulkner's study in his home shows how carefully he plotted his novels, especially A Fable.

1403 Gannett, Lewis. "A Fable," NYHT (August 2, 1954), 13.

1404 Gardiner, Harold C. "William Faulkner's A Fable," America, 91 (August 21, 1954), 502; repr., in In All Conscience. Cambridge: Harvard U.P., 1960, pp. 129-131.

1405 Gay, R. M. Atl, 170 (September, 1942), 136. Review.

1406 Geismar, Maxwell. "Latter-Day Christ Story," SatRL, 37 (July 31, 1954), 11-12.

1407 Gill, Brendan. "Books--Fifth Gospel," NY, 30 (August 28, 1954), 78-80. Review.

1408 Gold, Joseph. "Delusion and Redemption in Faulkner's A Fable," MFS, 7 (Summer, 1961), 145-156.

1409 ________. "A Fable: You'll Put Your Own Ideas in His Mouth," William Faulkner: A Study in Humanism from Metaphor to Discourse. Norman: Oklahoma U.P., 1966, pp. 111-147.

1410 Grutzner, Charles. "Pulitzer Winners: 'A Fable' and 'Cat on Hot Tin Roof,'" NYT (May 31, 1955), 1, 28.

1411 Gwynn, Frederick L., and Joseph L. Blotner, eds. Faulkner in the University. Charlottesville: Virginia U.P., 1959, passim.

1412 Hafley, James Robert. "Faulkner's Fable: A Dream and Transfiguration," Accent, 16 (Winter, 1956), 3-14.

1413 Hamilton, Margaret. "A Rare Gift from the Gods," Daily Worker (July 21, 1955), 2. Review.

1414 Hanoteau, Guillaume. "Faulkner, il s'est battu à Verdun et se souvient," Match (Paris), 474 (May 10, 1958), 14-17.
Faulkner's visit to the Verdun battlefield preparatory to writing A Fable.

1415 Hartt, Julian N. Lost Image of Man. Baton Rouge: Louisiana State U.P., 1963, pp. 110-111.

1416 ______. "Some Reflection on Faulkner's Fable," RelL 24 (Fall, 1955), 601-607.

1417 Hastings, John. "Faulkner's Prose," SatRL, 37 (September 18, 1954), 23. Review.

1418 Hicks, Granville. "Faulkner's Fable Is Powerful, Heroic," New York Post (August 1, 1954), 12-M.

1419 Highet, Gilbert. "Sound and Fury," HarpersM, 209 (September, 1954), 98, 100, 102-104. Review.

1420 Hochstettler, David. "William Faulkner's A Fable: A Fragmented Christ," DAI, 33 (Syracuse: 1972), 5724A-25A.

1421 Hodges, Elizabeth L. "The Bible as Novel: A Comparative Study of Two Modernized Versions of Biblical Stories, Zola's La faute de l'Abbé Mouret and Faulkner's A Fable," DAI, 30 (Georgia: 1969), 5447A.

1422 Hoffman, Frederick J. American Winners of the Nobel Literary Prize. W. G. French and W. E. Kidd, eds. Norman: Oklahoma U.P., 1968, pp. 154-156.

1423 ______. William Faulkner. New York: Twayne's United States Author Series, 1961, pp. 111-115.

1424 Howe, Irving. "A Fable," William Faulkner: A Critical Study. New York: Vintage Books, 1952, pp. 268-281.

1425 ______. "Thirteen Who Mutinied: Faulkner's First World War," Reporter, 11 (September 14, 1954), 43-45.

1426 Howell, Elmo. "William Faulkner and Pro Patria Mori," LaS, 5 (Summer, 1966), 89-96.

1427 Hughes, Riley. "A Fable," CathW, 180 (November, 1954), 150.

1428 Hutten, Robert W. "A Major Revision in Faulkner's A Fable," AL, 45 (May, 1973), 297-299.

1429 Ilacqua, Alma A. "Faulkner's A Fable," NMW, 10 (Spring, 1977), 37-46.

1430 Kenner, Hugh. "A Fable," Shen, 6 (Spring, 1955), 44-53. Review.

1431 King, Roma A., Jr. "Etude sur Une Fable: 'Everyman' et la guerre," RLM, Part I, Nos. 27-29 (1957), 119-130.

1432 ________. "Everyman's Warfare: A Study of Faulkner's Fable," MFS, 2 (Autumn, 1956), 132-138.

1433 ________. "A Fable: Everyman's Warfare," Religious Perspectives in Faulkner's Fiction. J. R. Barth, ed. Notre Dame, Indiana: Notre Dame U.P., 1972, pp. 203-210.

1434 Kirk, Robert W., and Marvin Klotz. Faulkner's People. Berkeley: California U.P., 1963, pp. 147-156.

1435 Kohler, Dayton. "A Fable: The Novel as Myth," CE, 16 (May, 1955), 471-478.

1436 Kunkel, Francis L. "Christ Symbolism in Faulkner: Prevalence of the Human," Renascence, 17 (Spring, 1965), 148-56.

1437 Lambert, J. W. "Fabulous," Sunday Times (June 19, 1955), 5-M.

1438 Lang, Beatrice. "Comparison de Requiem for a Nun et A Fable," RANAM, 9 (1976), 57-72.

1439 Leary, Lewis. "The Last Novels--A Fable," William Faulkner of Yoknapatawpha County. New York: Crowell, 1973, pp. 176-185.

1440 Lewis, R. W. B. "The Loss of Impurity," The Picaresque Saint. Philadelphia: Lippincott, 1959, pp. 209-219.

1441 Littell, Robert. YaleR, 31 (Summer, 1942).

1442 Lytle, Andrew. "The Son of Man: He Will Prevail," SR, 63 (Winter, 1955), 114-137. Also in The Hero with the Private Parts. Baton Rouge: Louisiana State U.P., 1966.

1443 Maclaren-Ross, Julian. "A Cable by W*LL**MF**FKN*R," Punch, 229 (October 5, 1955), 399-401.

1444 ________. "A Fable, by William Faulkner," LondonMag, 2 (November, 1955), 84-87.

1445 Macmillan, Duane J. "The Non-Yoknapatawpha Novels of William Faulkner: An Examination of Soldier's Pay, Mosquitoes, Pylon, The Wild Palms, and A Fable," DAI, 32 (Wisconsin: 1972), 6986A.

1446 Malin, Irving. *William Faulkner: An Interpretation.* Stanford, California: Stanford U. P., 1957, *passim*.

1447 Mercier, Vivian. "A Search for Universality That Led Too Far from Home," Cw, 60 (August 6, 1954), 443-444.

1448 Meriwether, James B., ed. "A Note on *A Fable*," MissQ, 26 (Summer, 1973), 416-417.
The previously unpublished statement by Faulkner on *A Fable*.

1449 Millgate, Michael. "*A Fable*," *The Achievement of William Faulkner*. New York: 1966, pp. 227-234.

1450 Mills, Ralph J., Jr. "Faulkner's Essential Vision: Notes on *A Fable*," ChS, 44 (Fall, 1961), 187-198; revised version in *Germini*, 1 (Autumn, 1957), 60-71.

1451 Milton, John R. "American Fiction and Man," Cresset, 18, #3 (1955), 16-20.

1452 Miner, Ward L. "Faulkner and Christ's Crucifixion," NM, 57 (1956), 260-269.

1453 Mohrt, Michel. "*A Fable*," *Le Nouveau Roman American*. Paris: Gallimard, 1955, pp. 119-123.

1454 Moore, Reginald. "Croix de Guerre," Time and Tide, 36, #25 (June 18, 1955), 806.

1455 Mueller, T. F. "Faulkner Fable," Newsweek, 44 (August 30, 1954), 7.

1456 Novak, Michael. Introduction. *A Fable*. New York: New American Library, 1968.

1457 Oakes, Philip. "*A Fable*," Truth, 155 (July 15, 1955), 903.

1458 Pastore, Philip E. "The Structure and Meaning of William Faulkner's *A Fable*," DAI, 31 (Florida: 1969), 397A-98A.

1459 Paulding, Gouverneur. "A Note in Rejoinder," Reporter, 12 (September 14, 1954), 45-56.

1460 Peckham, Morse. "The Place of Sex in the Work of William Faulkner," STC, 14 (Fall, 1974), 1-20.

1461 Pickrel, Paul. "Outstanding Novels," YR, 44 (Autumn, 1954), viii-xii.

1462 Podhoretz, Norman. "William Faulkner and the Problem of War," Commentary, 18 (September, 1954), 227-232; repr., *Faulkner: A Collection of Critical Essays*. R. P. Warren,

ed. Englewood Cliffs: 1966, pp. 243-250.
Cf., Henry Wasser. "Reply," Commentary, 18 (September, 1954), 569-570.

1463 Portuondo, José Antonio. "The Brush of Faulkner," Américas (January, 1955), 40-41.

1464 ________. "La 'pasión' expresionista de William Faulkner," Américas (November, 1954); Review of A Fable, repr., in El Heroísmo intellectual. México: Fondo de Cultura Económica, 1955, pp. 82-85.

1465 Prescott, Orville. "Books of the Times," NYT (August 2, 1954), 15.

1466 Pritchett, Victor S. "Time Frozen," PR, 21, #5 (September-October, 1954), 557-561; repr., Faulkner: A Collection of Critical Essays. R. P. Warren, ed. Englewood Cliffs: Prentice Hall, 1966, pp. 238-242.

1467 Raimbault, R. N., tr. Parabold [A Fable]. Paris: Gallimard, 1958.

1468 Raisor, Philip. "Up from Adversity: William Faulkner's A Fable," SDR, 11, #3 (1973), 3-15.

1469 Ratner, Marc. "Dualism in Faulkner's A Fable: Humanization versus Dehumanization," Prague Studies in English, 15 (1973), 117-134.

1470 Raymond, Bernard. "A Fable, by William Faulkner," ArQ, 10 (Winter, 1954), 361-363.

1471 Reed, Joseph W., Jr. "Faulkner's Failure: Intruder in the Dust, Requiem for a Nun, and A Fable," Faulkner's Narrative. New Haven: Yale U.P., 1973, pp. 201-217.

1472 Reval, François. "Faulkner, deuxième manière," TM, 10 (November, 1954), 750-754.

1473 Reynolds, Horace. "Dramatizing a Misconception," CSMM (August 5, 1954), 11.

1474 Rice, Philip Blair. "Faulkner's Crucifixion," KR, 16 (Autumn, 1954), 661-670. Repr., in Three Decades of Criticism. Frederick Hoffman and Olga Vickery, eds. East Lansing: Michigan State U.P., 1960, pp. 373-381.

1475 Richardson, Kenneth E. Force and Faith in the Novels of William Faulkner. The Hague: Mouton, 1967, pp. 156-163.

1476 Richardson, Maurice. NS&N, 49 (June 18, 1955), 863-864. Review.

1477 Riedel, F. C. "Faulkner As Stylist," SAQ, 56 (Autumn, 1957), 462-479.

1478 Rinaldi, Nicholas M. "Game Imagery and Game-consciousness in Faulkner's Fiction," TCL, 10 (October, 1964), 108-118 [115-116].

1479 Roberts, Ernest F. "Faulkner," Cw (August 27, 1954), 514.
Letter to the editor about A Fable.

1480 Rolo, Charles J. "Reader's Choice," Atl, 194 (September, 1954), 79-80.

1481 Romanova, Elena. "Anti-War Themes in the Work of William Faulkner," ForLit, 6 (1955), 170-176.

1482 Ros, Armando Lázaro, tr. Una Fabula. Obras escogidas. Vol. II. México: Aguilar, 1960.

1483 Ross, J. Maclaren. Listener, 54, #1376 (July 14, 1955), 75. Review.

1484 ______. LondonMag, 2, #11 (November, 1955), 84-87.

1485 Rousseaux, André. "Parabole de Faulkner," FL, 13 (June 14, 1958), 2.

1486 Samway, Patrick H. "War: A Faulknerian Commentary," ColQ, 18, #4 (Spring, 1970), 370-378.

1487 Sandeen, Ernest. "William Faulkner: His Legend and His Fable," Review of Politics, 18 (January, 1956), 47-68.

1488 Schendler, Sylvan. "William Faulkner's A Fable," DA, 17 (Northwestern: 1957), 366-367.

1489 Schwartz, Delmore. "Faulkner's A Fable," Perspectives, USA, 10 (Winter, 1955), 126-136.

1490 ______. "Faulkner's A Fable," in Selected Essays of Delmore Schwartz. Donald A. Dike and David H. Zucker, eds. Chicago U.P., 1970, pp. 290-304.

1491 ______. "William Faulkner: A Fable," Prospetti, 10 (Winter, 1954), 163-173.

1492 Sebold, Jane. "William Faulkner: The Faulkner Fable: A Reply," AmSch, 27 (Winter, 1957-58), 135.
Letter replying to Walter Fuller Taylor, AmSch 26 (Fall, 1957), 471-477.

1493 Shrapnel, Norman. "Faulkner's Fable," Manchester Guardian (June 21, 1955), 4-F.

1494 Slade, John Howard. "A Study of William Faulkner's A Fable," DAI, 35 (Stanford: 1974), 6160A.

1495 Slatoff, Walter J. "A Fable," Quest for Failure. Ithaca: Cornell U. P., 1960, 2nd pr., 1961, pp. 221-238.

1496 Smith, Julian. "A Source for Faulkner's A Fable," AL, 40 November, 1968), 394-397.
Notes similarity between Humphrey Cobb's Paths of Glory (1935) and Faulkner's A Fable.

1497 Smithey, Robert A. "Faulkner and the Status Quo," CLAJ, 11 (December, 1967), 109-116.

1498 Solomon, Eric. "From Christ in Flanders to Catch-22: An Approach to War Fiction," TSLL, 11 (Spring, 1969), 851-866.

1499 ________. "Joseph Conrad, William Faulkner, and the Nobel Prize Speech," N&Q, 14, #7 (1967), 247-248.
Echoes in the Nobel Prize Speech of A Fable and Joseph Conrad's 1905 essay "Henry James: In Appreciation."

1500 Sowder, William J. "Faulkner and Existentialism: A Note on the Generalissimo," WSCL, 4, #2 (Spring-Summer, 1963), 163-171.

1501 ________. "Lucas Beauchamp as Existential Hero," CE, 25 (November, 1963), 115-127.

1502 Stavrou, Constantine N. "Ambiguity in Faulkner's Affirmation," Person, 40 (Spring, 1959), 169-177.

1503 ________. "William Faulkner's Apologia: Some Notes on A Fable," ColQ, 3 (Spring, 1955), 432-439.

1504 Stein, Randolph Edward. "The World Outside Yoknapatawpha: A Study of Five Novels by William Faulkner," DA, 26 (Ohio: 1965), 2225.

1505 Straumann, Heinrich. "An American Interpretation of Existence: Faulkner's A Fable," Anglia, 73 (1955), 484-515. Also in Four Decades of Criticism. Linda W. Wagner, ed. Michigan State U. P., 1973, pp. 335-357; Three Decades of Criticism. F. J. Hoffman and Olga W. Vickery, eds. East Lansing: Michigan State U. P., 1960, pp. 349-372.

1506 Stuckey, W. J. The Pulitzer Prize Novels: A Critical Backward Look. Norman: Oklahoma U. P., 1966, pp. 170ff.

1507 Swiggart, Peter. The Art of Faulkner's Novels. Austin: Texas U. P., 1962, pp. 184-194.

1508 Tafur, Jose Luis. "Una Fabula de Faulkner," EAm, 12 (August-September, 1956), 153-159.

1509 Tate, Allen. "William Faulkner, 1897-1962," SR, 71 (Winter, 1963), 160-164; repr., from NSt (London), 64 (September 28, 1962), 408.

1510 Taylor, Walter Fuller. "William Faulkner: The Faulkner Fable," AmSch, 26 (Fall, 1957), 471-477.
Cf., Reply by Jane Sebold, AmSch, 27 (1957-58), 135.

1511 Tsagari, Myrto. "A Fable: Faulkner's Message to the World," Nota Bene, 1 (1958), 30-34.

1512 Tuck, Dorothy. Crowell's Handbook of Faulkner. New York: Crowell, 1964, pp. 143-156.

1513 Turaj, Frank. "The Dialectic in Faulkner's A Fable," TSLL, 8 (Spring, 1966), 93-102.

1514 Vallette, Jacques. "Un apologue à la gloire de l'homme," MdF, 325 (October, 1955), 330-334.

1515 Vickery, Olga W. "Culmination and Crisis: A Fable," in The Novels of William Faulkner. Baton Rouge: Louisiana State U.P., 1964, pp. 192-210.

1516 Volpe, Edmond L. A Reader's Guide to William Faulkner. New York: Noonday Press, 1971, pp. 282-304, 396-401.

1517 W., H. "A Fable," AmSch, 24 (Winter, 1955), 125. Review.

1518 Waggoner, Hyatt H. William Faulkner. Lexington: Kentucky U.P., 1959, pp. 225-232.

1519 Wagner, Geoffrey. "Faulkner's Contemporary Passion Play," TC, 156 (December, 1954), 527-538.

1520 Walters, Margaret. "Two Fabulists: Golding and Camus," MCR, 4 (1961), 18-29.
Faulkner's Fable suffers from arbitrary parallels.

1521 Watkins, Floyd C. "Faulkner and His Critics," TSLL, 10 (Summer, 1968), 317-329.

1522 ________. "The Truth Shall Make You Fail," The Flesh and the Word. Nashville: Vanderbilt U.P., 1971, pp. 263-271, passim.

1523 Webb, James W. "Faulkner Writes A Fable," UMSE, 7 (1966), 1-13.

1524 Wegelin, Christof. "'Endure' and 'Prevail': Faulkner's Modification of Conrad," N&Q, 21 (October, 1974), 375-376. Cf., Eric Solomon. "Joseph Conrad, William Faulkner, and the Nobel Prize Speech," N&Q, 14 (July, 1967), 247-248.

1525 Weigel, John A. "Teaching the Modern Novel: From Finnegans Wake to A Fable," CE, 21 (December, 1959), 172-173.

1526 "William Faulkner--After Ten Years, A Fable," Newsweek, 44 (August 2, 1954), 48-52. Review.

1527 Ziolkowski, Theodore. Fictional Transfigurations of Jesus. Princeton: Princeton U.P., 1972, pp. 170-172, 177-178.

"THE FIRE AND THE HEARTH"
(In Go Down, Moses, 1942. Cf., Meriwether, James B., no. 1534 below.)

1528 Arthos, John. "Ritual and Humor in the Writing of William Faulkner," Accent, 9 (Autumn, 1948), 19.

1529 Creighton, Joanne V. "Revisions and Craftsmanship in Faulkner's 'The Fire and the Hearth,'" SSF, 11 (Spring, 1974), 161-172.

1530 Early, James. "The Fire and the Hearth," The Making of 'Go Down, Moses,' Dallas, Texas: Southern Methodist U.P., 1972, pp. 76-85, passim.

1531 Edmonds, Irene C. "Faulkner and the Black Shadow," in Southern Renascence. Louis D. Rubin and Robert Jacobs, eds. Baltimore: Johns Hopkins U.P., 1966, pp. 201-202.

1532 Gregory, Horace. NYTBR (May 10, 1942), 4. Review.

1533 Litz, Walton. "Genealogy as Symbol in Go Down, Moses," FS, 1 (Winter, 1952), 49-50.

1534 Meriwether, James B. The Literary Career of William Faulkner. Columbia: South Carolina U.P., 1971, pp. 73-74.

1535 Mizener, Arthur. A Handbook to Accompany Modern Short Stories. New York: Norton, 1967, pp. 135-142; 3rd ed., pp. 155-160.

1536 O'Connor, William Van. The Tangled Fire of William Faulkner. Minneapolis: Minnesota U.P., 1954, p. 126.

1537 Sandeen, Ernest. "William Faulkner: Tragedian of Yoknapatawpha," in Fifty Years of the American Novel. Harold C. Gardiner. New York: Gordian Press, 1951, 1968, p. 170.

1538 Smithey, Robert A. "Faulkner and the Status Quo," CLAJ, 11 (December, 1967), 109-116.

1539 Starke, Catherine. Black Portraiture in American Fiction: Stock Characters, Archetypes, and Individuals. New York: Basic Books, 1971, pp. 192-194.

1540 Suard, Jean-Marc, with assistance of Zeynab Hafez. "The Fire and the Hearth," Views and Reviews of Modern German Literature. Festschrift für Adolf D. Klarmann. Munchen: Delp, 1974, pp. 143-156.

"FLAGS IN THE DUST"
(For editorial history of this story, see following items.)

1541 Adams, Richard P. "At Long Last, 'Flags in the Dust,'" SoR, 10 (October, 1974), 878-888.

1542 Day, Douglas, ed. Introduction. Flags in the Dust by William Faulkner. New York: Random House, 1973; paper ed., 1974.

1543 Grover, D. C. "Flags in the Dust," ArQ, 32 (Spring, 1976), 74-77.

1544 Hayhoe, George F. "William Faulkner's 'Flags in the Dust,'" MissQ, 28 (Summer, 1975), 370-386.

1545 Hodgin, Katherine C. "Horace Benbow and Bayard Sartoris: Two Romantic Figures in Faulkner's 'Flags in the Dust,'" AL, 50, #4 (January, 1979), 647-652.

1546 Kane, Patricia. "The Narcissa Benbow of Faulkner's 'Flags in the Dust,'" NConL, 4, #4 (1974), 2-3.

1547 McHaney, Thomas L. FCN, 2 (1973), 7-8. Review of "Flags in the Dust." Douglas Day, ed. New York: Random House, 1973.

1548 ________, and Albert Erskine. "Commentary on the Text of 'Flags in the Dust,'" FCN, 3 (May, 1974), 2-4.

1549 McSweeney, Kerry. "The Subjective Intensities of Faulkner's 'Flags in the Dust,'" CRAS, 8 (Fall, 1977), 156-164.

1550 Meriwether, James B. "Faulkner--[Flags in the Dust]," American Literary Scholarship. An Annual/1973. James E. Woodress, ed. Durham: Duke U.P., 1975, p. 135.

1551 Moore, Robert, ed. The Faulkner Concordance Newsletter, # 3 (May, 1974).

1552 Roberts, Melvin Reed. "Faulkner's 'Flags in the Dust' and Sartoris: A Comparative Study of the Typescript and the Originally Published Novel," DAI, 35 (Austin, Texas: 1974), 471A.

"FOOL ABOUT A HORSE"
(Scribner's, 100 (1936); incorporated in The Hamlet, 1934; repr., in Collected Stories, 1950)

1553 Meriwether, James B. The Literary Career of William Faulkner. Columbia: South Carolina U.P., 1971, pp. 69-70, passim.

1554 _______. "The Short Fiction of William Faulkner," Proof, 1 (1971), 301.

1555 Rascoe, Burton. "Faulkner's New York Critics," AmMerc, 50 (June, 1940), 243-247.

"FOX HUNT"
(Harper's, 163 (1931); repr., in Doctor Martino, 1934; Collected Stories, 1950)

1556 Breaden, Dale G. "William Faulkner and the Land," AQ, 10 (Fall, 1978), 354-355.

1557 Meriwether, James B. "The Short Fiction of William Faulkner," Proof, 1 (1971), 301.

1558 Raimbault, R. N., tr. "Chasse au renard," Courtes histoires americaines. Paris: 1948, pp. 141-164.

GO DOWN, MOSES
(New York: Random House, 1942)

1559 Ackerman, R. D. "The Immolation of Isaac McCaslin," TSLL, 16 (Fall, 1974), 557-565.

1560 Adamowski, T. H. "Isaac McCaslin and the Wilderness of the Imagination," CentR, 17 (Winter, 1973), 92-112.

1561 Adams, Richard P. Faulkner. Princeton: Princeton U.P., 1968, pp. 130-154.

1562 _______. "Genetic Faulkner," CEA, 36 (January, 1974), 33-34.

1563 Aguilar, Esperanza. Yoknapatawpha, Propiedad de William Faulkner. Santiago: Chile U. P., 1964, pp. 128-139.

1564 Akin, Warren, IV. "Neither We from Them nor They from Us: An Interpretation of Go Down, Moses," DAI, 36 (Bryn Mawr: 1975), 6094A.

1565 Allingham, Margery. "New Novels," Time and Tide, 23, # 44 (October 31, 1942), 872. Review.

1566 Anon. "Faulkneresque," TLS, # 2123 (October 10, 1942), 497. Review.

1567 Anon. "Go Down, Moses," NY (May 16, 1942), 74. Review.

1568 Anon. "Go Down, Moses," Time (May 11, 1942), 95. Review.

1569 Anon. "South Preoccupies Faulkner," Dallas Morning News, (May 10, 1942), IV, 12.

1570 Backman, Melvin. Faulkner: The Major Years. Bloomington: Indiana U. P., 1966, pp. 160-174.

1571 Barrett, Betty Pratt. "The Tradition of the Coincidentia Oppositorum in Representative Modern Literary Works," DAI, 37 (Emory: 1976), 2856A.

1572 Beck, Warren, IV. "Go Down, Moses," Faulkner: Essays. Madison, Wisconsin: Wisconsin U. P., 1976, pp. 334-582.

1573 Bell, Haney H., Jr. "The Relative Maturity of Lucius Priest and Ike McCaslin," Aegis, 2 (1973), 15-21.

1574 ________. "Sam Fathers and Ike McCaslin and the World in Which Ike Matures," Costerus, 7 (1973), 1-12.

1575 Benert, Annette. "The Four Fathers of Isaac McCaslin," SHR, 9 (Fall, 1975), 423-433.

1576 Beresford, J. D. "New Novels," Manchester Guardian (October 9, 1942), 3.

1577 Bizzarri, Edoardo, tr. Scendi, Mose. Milano: Mondadori, 1947.

1578 Blanchard, Leonard A. "The Failure of the Natural Man: Faulkner's 'Pantaloon in Black,'" NMW, 8 (Spring, 1975), 28-32.

1579 Bond, Christopher James. "I. Sir James Frazer's 'Homeopathy' and 'Contagion' and Structural Principles in William

Faulkner's Go Down, Moses," DAI, 35 (Rutgers: 1974), 3725A.

1580 Bradford, Melvin E. "All the Daughters of Eve: 'Was' and the Unity of Go Down, Moses," ArlQ, 1 (Autumn, 1967), 28-37.

1581 Breaden, Dale G. "William Faulkner and the Land," AQ, 10 (Autumn, 1958), 348-351.

1582 Brocki, Mary D. "Faulkner and Hemingway: Values in a Modern World," MTJ, 11 (Summer, 1962), 5-9, 15.

1583 Brogunier, Joseph. "A Source for the Commissary Entries in Go Down, Moses," TSLL, 14 (Fall, 1972), 545-554.

1584 Brooks, Cleanth. "The Story of the McCaslins--Go Down, Moses," William Faulkner: The Yoknapatawpha Country. New Haven: Yale U. P., 1963, pp. 244-278, 414-420.

1585 Brumm, Ursula. "Wilderness and Civilization: A Note on William Faulkner," PR, 22 (Summer, 1955), 340-350.

1586 Brylowski, Walter. "The Ethical Period," Faulkner's Olympian Laugh. Detroit: Wayne State U. P., 1968, pp. 150-168.

1587 Burdett, Francis. "Fiction: What Environment Can Do," Catholic Herald (January 8, 1943), 3.

1588 Burke, Harry R. "A Mystery of Bloods," St. Louis Globe-Democrat (May 16, 1942), 4-A.

1589 C., C. V. "Black and White," Liverpool Daily Post (November 4, 1942), 2-F.

1590 Campbell, Harry M., and Ruel E. Foster. William Faulkner: A Critical Appraisal. Norman: Oklahoma U. P., 1951, pp. 76-79, 146-158.

1591 Capps, Jack L. "Computer Program Revisions and the Preparation of a Concordance to Go Down, Moses," FCN, 2 (1973), 2-5.

1591a [Capps, Jack L., ed.] Introduction by Michael Millgate. Go Down, Moses, A Concordance to the Novel. West Point, N. Y.: Faulkner Concordance Advisory Board. Ann Arbor, Mich.: Produced and distributed by University Microfilms International, 1977.

1592 Casper, Leonard. "The Square Beatific," America, 103 (1960), 515.

1593 Chapman, Arnold. "Pampas and Big Woods: Heroic Initiation in Güiraldes and Faulkner," CL, 11 (Winter, 1959), 61-77.

1594 Cheney, Frances N. "About New Books," Nashville Banner (May 13, 1942), 4-X.

1595 Church, Margaret. "William Faulkner: Myth and Duration," Time and Reality. Chapel Hill: North Carolina U. P., 1963, pp. 244-247.

1596 Church, Richard. "The Weak and the Strong," John O'London's Weekly, 48, #1194 (November 20, 1942), 73.

1597 Collins, Carvel. "On William Faulkner," Talks with Authors. Carbondale: Southern Illinois U. P., 1968, pp. 40-46, 48-49.

1598 Connolly, Thomas E. Essays on Determinism in American Literature. Sydney Krause, ed. Kent, Ohio: Kent State U. P., 1964, pp. 47-49.

1599 Cowley, Malcolm. "Go Down to Faulkner's Land," NR, 106 (June 29, 1942), 900.

1600 _______. "William Faulkner's Legend of the South," SR, 53 (Summer, 1945), 343-361.

1601 Creighton, Joanne Vanish. "Dubliners and Go Down, Moses: The Short Story Composite," DA, 31 (Michigan: 1969), 1792A-93A.

1602 _______. "Go Down, Moses: Construction of a Short Story Composite," William Faulkner's Craft of Revision. Detroit: Wayne State U. P., 1977, pp. 85-148.

1603 _______. "Revision and Craftsmanship in the Hunting Trilogy of Go Down, Moses," TSLL, 15 (Fall, 1973), 576-592.

1604 Cullen, John B., with Floyd C. Watkins. Old Times in the Faulkner Country. Chapel Hill: North Carolina U. P., 1961, pp. 43-44, passim.

1605 Dabney, Lewis M. "Sam Fathers and Go Down, Moses," The Indians of Yoknapatawpha: A Study in Literature and History. Baton Rouge: Louisiana State U. P., 1974, pp. 118-157.

1606 Danielson, Richard Ely. "Atlantic Bookshelf," Atl, 170 (September, 1942), 136.

1607 Devlin, Albert J. "Faulknerian Chronology: Puzzles and

Games," NMW, 5 (Winter, 1973), 98-101.
Note on inconsistency between Section IV of "The Bear" and the remainder of Go Down, Moses.

1608 ________. "'How Much It Takes to Compound a Man': A Neglected Scene in Go Down, Moses," MwQ, 14 (Summer, 1973), 408-421.

1609 Dewsbury, Ronald. "Go Down, Moses," Life and Letters Today, 35 (December, 1942), 176-177.

1610 Dorsch, Robert L. "An Interpretation of the Central Themes in the Work of William Faulkner," ESRS, 11 (September, 1962), 36-41.

1611 Dussinger, Gloria. "Faulkner's Isaac McCaslin as Romantic Hero Manqué," SAQ, 68 (Summer, 1969), 377-385.

1612 Early, James. The Making of Go Down, Moses. Dallas: Southern Methodist U. P., 1972.
Cf., Jack L. Capps. "Three Faulkner Studies," SLJ, 6 (1973), 117-121.

1613 Eigner, Edwin M. "Faulkner's Isaac and the American Ishmael," JA, 14 (1969), 107-115.

1614 Eisinger, Chester E. "William Faulkner: Southern Archetype," Fiction of the Forties. Chicago U. P., 1963, pp. 179-181.

1615 Engelborghs, M. "Verhalen van William Faulkner," Kultuurleven, 27 (August-September, 1960), 530-532.
Considers the seven stories in Go Down, Moses as Faulkner's best and most representative.

1616 Everett, Walter K. Faulkner's Art and Characters. Woodbury, New York: Barron's Educ Series, 1969, pp. 21-37.

1617 Farnham, James F. "Faulkner's Unsung Hero: Gavin Stevens," ArQ, 21 (Summer, 1965), 115-132.

1618 Fisher, Richard E. "The Wilderness, the Commissary, and the Bedroom: Faulkner's Ike McCaslin as Hero in a Vacuum," ES, 44 (February, 1963), 19-28.

1619 Foronda, Ana María, tr. ¡Desciende, Moisés! Barcelona: Luis de Caralt, 1959.

1620 Gold, Joseph. William Faulkner: A Study in Humanism from Metaphor to Discourse. Norman: Oklahoma U. P., 1966, pp. 49-75.

1621 Graves, John Temple. "Faulkner...," SatRL, 25 (May 2, 1942), 16.

1622 Gregory, Horace. "New Tales by William Faulkner," NYTBR (May 10, 1942), 4.

1623 Guetti, James. The Limits of Metaphor. Ithaca: Cornell U.P., 1967, pp. 158-163.

1624 Gwynn, Frederick L., and Joseph L. Blotner, eds. Faulkner in the University. Charlottesville: Virginia U.P., 1959, passim.

1625 Hamilton, Gary D. "The Past in the Present: A Reading of Go Down, Moses," SHR, 5 (Spring, 1971), 171-181.

1626 Harter, Carol A. C. "The Diaphoric Structure and Unity of William Faulkner's Go Down, Moses," DAI, 31 (S.U.N.Y., Binghamton: 1970), 6057A-58A.

1627 ________. "Recent Faulkner Scholarship: Five More Turns of the Screw," JML, 4 (September, 1974), 139-145.

1628 Hettich, Blaise. "A Bedroom Scene in Faulkner," Renascence, 8 (Spring, 1956), 121-126.

1629 Hochberg, Mark R. "The Unity of Go Down, Moses," TSL, 21 (1976), 58-65.

1630 Hoffman, Frederick J. William Faulkner. Twayne's United States Authors Series. New York: 1961, pp. 111-115.

1631 Hogan, Patrick G., Jr. "Faulkner's 'Female Line': 'Callina' McCaslin," SSF, 1, #1 (Fall, 1963-1964), 63-65.

Carrothers McCaslin's daughter is Callina (Carolina) McCaslin.

1632 ________, Dale A. Myers, and John E. Turner. "Muste's 'Failure of Love' in Faulkner's Go Down, Moses," MFS, 12 (Summer, 1966), 267-270.

A reply to John M. Muste, MFS, 10 (1965), 366-378.

1633 Holmes, Edward M. Faulkner's Twice Told Tales. The Hague: Mouton, 1966, pp. 88-94.

1634 Howe, Irving. William Faulkner: A Critical Study. New York: Vintage, 1952, 1962, pp. 88-92.

1635 Howell, Elmo. "William Faulkner and the Chickasaw Funeral," AL, 36 (January, 1965), 523-535.

States that in the funeral of Sam Fathers, Faulkner confuses Chickasaw and Choctaw customs.

1636 Hunt, John W. William Faulkner: Art in Theological Tension. Syracuse U.P., 1965, pp. 137-168.

1637 Hurt, Lester E. "Mysticism in Go Down, Moses," EngRec, 15 (December, 1964), 17-22.

1638 Hutchison, E. R. "A Footnote to the Gum Tree Scene," CE, 24 (April, 1963), 564-565.

1639 Idei, Yasuko. "Faulkner's Go Down, Moses: An Interrelation Between Content and Structure," KAL, 17 (1976), 29-41.

1640 Ingrasci, H. J. "Strategic Withdrawal or Retreat: Deliverance from Racial Oppression in Kelley's A Different Drummer and Faulkner's Go Down, Moses," SBL, 6 (Fall, 1975), 1-6.

1641 Jacobs, Robert D. "William Faulkner: The Passion and the Penance," South: Modern Southern Literature in Its Cultural Setting. Louis D. Rubin, Jr., and Robert Jacobs, eds. New York: Doubleday, 1961, 171-172.

1642 Josephs, Mary J. "The Hunting Metaphor in Hemingway and Faulkner," DAI, 34 (Michigan State: 1973), 1282A-83A.

1643 Kearful, Frank J. "Tony Last and Ike McCaslin: The Loss of a Usable Past," UWR, 3, ii (Spring, 1968), 45-52.

1644 Kierszys, Zofia, tr. Zstap Mojzeszu. Warszawa: Panstwowy Instytut Wydawniczy, 1966.

1645 Kinney, Arthur F. "Faulkner and the Possibilities for Heroism," SoR, 6 (Autumn, 1970), 1110-1125.

1646 Kirk, Robert W., and Marvin Klotz. Faulkner's People. Berkeley: California U. P., 1963, pp. 236-253.

1647 Klotz, Marvin. "Procrustean Revision in Faulkner's Go Down, Moses," AL, 37 (March, 1965), 1-16.

1648 Korenman, Joan S. "Faulkner's Grecian Urn," SLJ, 7 (Fall, 1974), 3-23.

1649 Kunkel, Francis L. "Christ Symbolism in Faulkner: Prevalence of the Human," Ren, 17 (Spring, 1965), 151-156.

1650 Laverdine, Joëlle. "Go Down, Moses," Views and Reviews of Modern German Literature. Festschrift für Adolf D. Klarmann. Karl S. Weimar, ed. München: Delp, 1974, pp. 211-229.

1651 Lawson, Richard A. "Patterns of Initiation in William Faulkner's Go Down, Moses," DA, 27 (Tulane: 1966), 1372A.

1652 Lewis, R. W. B. The Picaresque Saint. Philadelphia: Lippincott, 1959, pp. 209-219.

1653 Littell, Robert. "Go Down, Moses," YR, 31 (Summer, 1942), viii.

1654 Litz, Walton. "Genealogy As Symbol in Go Down, Moses," FS, 1 (Winter, 1952), 49-53.

1655 ______. "William Faulkner's Moral Vision," SWQ, 37 (Summer, 1952), 200-209.

1656 Longley, John L. The Tragic Mask. Chapel Hill: North Carolina U.P., 1963, pp. 79-101, 105-110.

1657 McHaney, Thomas L. "A Deer Hunt in the Faulkner Country," MissQ, 23 (Summer, 1970), 315-320.

1658 Maguire, Robert Emmett. "The Two Patrimonies of Isaac McCaslin: Responsibilities to Secular and Liminal Time in Faulkner's Go Down, Moses," DAI, 39, #6 (Dallas (Texas): 1977), 3582A.

1659 Makuck, Peter Landers. "Go Down, Moses and Intruder in the Dust, Faulkner Studies in France: 1953-1969," DA, 32 (Kent State: 1971), 3314A.

1660 Malin, Irving. William Faulkner: An Interpretation. Stanford U.P., 1957, p. 74.

1661 Mathiex, Marie-Hélène. "Les négations et le problème racial dans Go Down, Moses," Views and Reviews of Modern German Literature. Festschrift für Adolf D. Klarmann. Karl S. Weimar, ed. München: Delp, 1974, pp. 230-276.

1662 Meeks, E. L. "A Contextual Approach to the Teaching of Two Novels by William Faulkner at College Level," DA, 26 (Houston: 1965), 4505.

1663 Mellard, James M. "The Biblical Rhythm of Go Down, Moses," MissQ, 20 (Summer, 1967), 135-147.

1664 Mendilow, A. A. "Identification and Temporal Transfer," Time and the Novel. London: Peter Nevill, 1952; New York: Humanities Press, 1965, p. 97.

1665 Meriwether, James B. "Go Down, Moses, 1942," The Literary Career of William Faulkner. Columbia: South Carolina U.P., 1971, pp. 30-32.

1666 Michel, Laurence. The Thing Contained: Theory of the Tragic. Bloomington: Indiana U.P., 1970, passim.

1667 Milledge, Luetta U. "Light Eternal: An Analysis of Some Folkloristic Elements in Faulkner's Go Down, Moses, TFSB, 29 (December, 1963), 86-93. Also in AFS, 2 (June, 1964).

1668 Millgate, Michael. "'The Firmament of Man's History': Faulkner's Treatment of the Past," MissQ, 25 (Spring, 1972), 25-35.

1669 ________. "Go Down, Moses," The Achievement of William Faulkner. New York: Random House, 1966, pp. 201-214.

1670 Miner, Ward L. The World of William Faulkner. Durham, North Carolina: Duke U.P., 1952, pp. 148-152, 154-156.

1671 Mizener, Arthur. "The American Hero as Gentleman: Gavin Stevens," The Sense of Life in the Modern Novel. Boston: Houghton Mifflin, 1964, pp. 161-181.

1672 ________. "The Thin Intelligent Face of American Fiction," KR, 17 (Autumn, 1955), 507-519.

1673 Molloy, Robert. "William Faulkner Writes About Deep South He Has Made Familiar," New York Sun (May 15, 1942), 40. Review.

1674 Mukerji, Nirmal. "Ike McCaslin and the Measure of Heroism," PURBA, 5 (1974), 15-21.

1675 Muste, John M. "The Failure of Love in Go Down, Moses," MFS, 10 (Winter, 1964-65), 366-378.
Cf., Patrick G. Hogan, Jr. "Muste's Failure...," MFS, 12 (1966), 267-270.

1676 Nicholson, Norman. "William Faulkner," Man and Literature. London: S.C.M. Press, 1943, pp. 132-137.

1677 Nilon, Charles H. Faulkner and the Negro. New York: Citadel Press, 1965, passim.

1678 O'Brien, Kate. "Go Down, Moses," Spectator, #5966 (October 30, 1942), 418.

1679 O'Connor, William Van. "The Wilderness Theme," Accent, 13 (Winter, 1953), 12-20; repr., with modifications in The Tangled Fire. Minneapolis: Minnesota U.P., 1954, pp. 125-134.

1680 Orloff, Kossia. "Ring Composition: The Structural Unity of William Faulkner's 'Go Down, Moses,'" DAI, 38 (1977), 4184A.

1681 Overly, Dorothy N. The Problem of Character in the Development of Themes in the Novels and Short Stories of William Faulkner. Diss. Chicago University, 1949.

1682 Patterson, Alicia. "Stories from the Southland," New York Sunday News (May 17, 1942), 73. Review.

1683 Pearce, Roy Harvey. Historicism Once More: Problems and Occasions for the American Scholar. New Jersey: Princeton U. P., 1969, pp. 133-136.

1684 Ploegstra, Henry A. William Faulkner's Go Down, Moses: Its Publication, Revisions, Structure, and Reputation. Diss. Chicago University, 1966.

1685 Poirier, Richard. A World Elsewhere: The Place of Style in American Literature. New York: Oxford U. P., 1966, pp. 78-83.

1686 Pritchard, William. "Related Exercises on Joyce and Faulkner," ExEx (November, 1962), 4-5.

1687 Raimbault, R. N., tr. Descends, Moïse. Paris: Gallimard, 1955.

1688 Reed, Joseph W., Jr. "Uncertainties: The Unvanquished and Go Down, Moses," Faulkner's Narrative. New Haven: Yale U. P., 1973, pp. 176-200.

1689 Richardson, Kenneth E. Force and Faith in the Novels of William Faulkner. The Hague: Mouton, 1967, pp. 45-61.

1690 Rinaldi, Nicholas M. "Game Imagery and Game-Consciousness in Faulkner's Fiction," TCL, 10 (October, 1964), 108-118.

1691 Roberts, Ann T. "Introduction," Views and Reviews of Modern German Literature. Festschrift für Adolf D. Klarmann. Karl S. Weimar, ed. München: Delp, 1974, pp. 131-134.

1692 Robinson, Ted. "Go Down, Moses," Plain Dealer (Cleveland), (April 12, 1942), 3.

1693 Rollins, Ronald G. "Ike McCaslin and Chick Mallison: Faulkner's Emerging Southern Hero," WVUPP, 14 (1963), 74-79.

1694 Roth, Russell. "William Faulkner: The Pattern of Pilgrimage," Perspective, 2 (Summer, 1949), 246-254.

1695 Rouberol, Jean. "Les Indiens dans l'oeuvre de Faulkner," EA, 26 (March, 1973), 54-58.

1696 Rugoff, Milton. "The Magic of William Faulkner," NYHTBR, (May 17, 1942), IX, 2.

1697 Ruotolo, Lucio P. "Isaac McCaslin," Six Existential Heroes: The Politics of Faith. Cambridge: Harvard U. P., 1973, pp. 57-78.

1698 Sams, Larry Marshall. "Isaac McCaslin and Keats's 'Ode on a Grecian Urn,'" SoR, 12 (Summer, 1976), 632-639.

1699 Seaver, Edwin. "Books," Direction, 5 (Summer, 1942), 31.

1700 Shattuck, Charles. "*Go Down, Moses*," Accent, 2 (Summer, 1942), 236-237.

1701 Simpson, Lewis P. "Isaac McCaslin and Temple Drake: The Fall of New World Man," *Nine Essays in Modern Literature*. Donald E. Stanford, ed. Baton Rouge: Louisiana State U. P., 1965, pp. 88-106.

1702 Slatoff, Walter J. "*Hamlet*, *Go Down, Moses*, and *Town*," in *Quest for Failure: A Study of William Faulkner*. Ithaca: Cornell U. P., 1960; 2nd pr., 1961, pp. 203-205.

1703 Snell, George. *Shapers of American Fiction*. New York: Dutton, 1947, pp. 102-103.

1704 Sniderman, Stephen L. "The 'Composite' in Twentieth Century American Literature," DAI, 31 (Wisconsin: 1970), 403A.

1705 Sowder, William J. "Lucas Beauchamp as Existential Hero," CE, 25 (November, 1963), 115-127.

1706 Steinberg, Aaron. "Faulkner and the Negro," DA, 27 (N.Y.U., 1966), 1385A.

1707 Stephens, Rosemary. "Ike's Gun and Too Many Novembers," MissQ, 23 (Summer, 1970), 279-288.

1708 Stewart, David H. "The Purpose of Faulkner's Ike," Criticism, 3 (Fall, 1961), 333-342.

1709 Stewart, Randall. *American Literature and Christian Doctrine*. Baton Rouge: Louisiana State U. P., 1958, pp. 136-139.

1710 Stone, William B. "Ike McCaslin and the Grecian Urn," SSF, 10 (Winter, 1973), 93-94.

1711 Sultan, Stanley. "Call Me Ishmael: The Hagiography of Isaac McCaslin," TSLL, 3 (Spring, 1961), 50-66.

1712 Swiggart, Peter. *The Art of Faulkner's Novels*. Austin: Texas U. P., 1962, pp. 175-179.

1713 Swinnerton, Frank. "New Novels," Observer (October 18, 1942), 3.

1714 Taylor, Walter. "Faulkner: Social Commitment and Artistic Temperament," SoR, 6 (Autumn, 1970), 1075-1092.

1715 _______. "Faulkner's Curse," ArQ, 28 (Winter, 1972), 333-338.

1716 _______. "Faulkner's Pantaloon: The Negro Anomaly at the Heart of Go Down, Moses," AL, 44 (November, 1972), 430-444.

1717 _______. "The Freedman in Go Down, Moses: Historical Fact and Imaginative Failure," BSUF, 8 (Winter, 1967), 3-7.

1718 Taylor, Walter F., Jr. "Let My People Go: The White Man's Heritage in Go Down, Moses," SAQ, 58 (Winter, 1959), 20-32.

1719 Thompson, Lawrance. "A Defense of Difficulties in William Faulkner's Art," Carrell, 4 (December, 1963), 7-19.

1720 _______. William Faulkner: An Introduction and Interpretation. 2nd ed. New York: Holt, Rinehart, and Winston, 1967, pp. 81-98.

1721 Thornton, Weldon. "Structure and Theme in Faulkner's Go Down, Moses," Costerus, 3, n.s. (1975), 73-112.

1722 Tick, Stanley. "The Unity of Go Down, Moses, TCL, 8 (July, 1962), 67-73. Repr., William Faulkner: Four Decades of Criticism. Linda Wagner, ed. Michigan State U.P., 1973, pp. 327-334.

1723 TLS, #2123 (October 10, 1942), 497. Review.

1724 Toynbee, Philip. "Go Down, Moses," NS&N, 24 (October 31, 1942), 293.

1725 Trilling, Lionel. "The McCaslins of Mississippi," Nation, 154 (May 30, 1942), 632-633.

1726 Tuck, Dorothy. Crowell's Handbook of Faulkner. New York: Crowell, 1964, pp. 95-106.

1727 Utley, Francis Lee. "Pride and Humility: The Cultural Roots of Ike McCaslin," Bear, Man, and God: Seven Approaches to Faulkner's "The Bear," Francis Lee Utley, Lynn Z. Bloom, and Arthur F. Kinney, eds. New York: Random House, 1963, pp. 233-260.

1728 Vickery, Olga W. "Initiation and Identity: Go Down, Moses, and Intruder in the Dust," The Novels of William Faulkner. Rev. Ed. Baton Rouge: Louisiana State U.P., 1964, pp. 124-134.

1729 Vinson, Audrey L. "Miscegenation and Its Meaning in Go Down, Moses," CLAJ, 14 (December, 1970), 143-155.

1730 Volpe, Edmond L. A Reader's Guide to William Faulkner. New York: Noonday Press, 1971, pp. 230-252, 393-396.

1731 Waggoner, Hyatt H. William Faulkner: From Jefferson to the World. Lexington: Kentucky U.P., 1959, pp. 199-211.

1732 Walter, James. "Expiation and History: Ike McCaslin and the Mystery of Providence," LaS, 10 (Winter, 1971), 263-273.

1733 Walton, Gerald W. "Some Southern Farm Terms in Faulkner's Go Down, Moses," PADS, 47 (April, 1967), 23-29.

1734 _______. "Tennie's Jim and Lucas Beauchamp," AN&Q, 8 (October, 1969), 23-24.

1735 Walton, Litz. "Genealogy as Symbol in Go Down, Moses," FS, 1 (Winter, 1952), 49-50.

1736 Warren, Robert Penn. "Faulkner: The South, the Negro, and Time," SoR, n.s., 1 (July, 1965), 516-518, 520-524.

1737 Watkins, Floyd C. "Faulkner's Inexhaustible Voice," in The Flesh and the Word. Nashville: Vanderbilt U.P., 1971, pp. 234-253.

1738 Weeks, Willis Earl. "Faulkner's Young Males: From Futility to Responsibility," DAI, 34 (Arizona State: 1973), 2663A.

1739 Weiss, Daniel. "William Faulkner and the Runaway Slave," NWR, 6 (Summer, 1963), 71-79.

1740 Wertenbaker, Thomas J., Jr. "Faulkner's Point of View and the Chronicle of Ike McCaslin," CE, 24 (December, 1962), 169-178.

1741 West, Ray B., Jr. "Hemingway and Faulkner," The Short Story in America. Chicago: Henry Regnery, 1951, pp. 101-105.

1742 Wheeler, Otis B. "Faulkner's Wilderness," AL, 31 (May, 1959), 127-136.

1743 Widdows, Margharita. "Literature," Annual Register (1942), Part II, 324.

1744 Winkel, Carol Ann G. "Faulkner's Style and Its Relation to Theme: A Stylistic Study of Two Stories from Go Down, Moses," DAI, 35 (Delaware: 1974), 3017A.

1745 Winn, Harlan Harbour. "Short Story Cycles of Hemingway, Steinbeck, Faulkner, and O'Connor," DAI, 36 (Oregon: 1975), 4500A.

"GOLD IS NOT ALWAYS"
(Atl, 166 (1940), 563-70; revised for Go Down, Moses, 1942)

1746 Meriwether, James B. "The Short Fiction of William Faulkner: A Bibliography," Proof, 1 (1971), 301.

1747 Millgate, Jane. "Short Story into Novel: Faulkner's Reworking of 'Gold Is Not Always,'" ES, 45 (August, 1964), 310-317.

1748 O'Brien, Edward J. "Gold Is Not Always," The Best Short Stories of the Year. Cambridge, Mass.: Houghton, Mifflin, 1941, pp. 83-96.

"GOLDEN LAND"
(AmMerc, 35 (1935), 1-14; repr., in Collected Stories, 1950)

1749 Bradford, M. E. "Escaping Westward: Faulkner's 'Golden Land,'" GaR, 19 (Spring, 1965), 72-76.

1750 Meriwether, James B. "The Short Fiction of William Faulkner," Proof, 1 (1971), 301.

1751 Spatz, Jonas. "Golden Land," Hollywood in Fiction: Some Versions of the American Myth. New York: Humanities Press, 1970, pp. 116-119.

"HAIR"
(AmMerc, 23 (1931), 53-61; revised for These 13, 1931; and repr., in Collected Stories, 1950)

1752 Meriwether, James B. "The Short Fiction of William Faulkner," Proof, 1 (1971), 302.

1753 O'Connor, William Van. The Tangled Fire of William Faulkner. Minneapolis: Minnesota U.P., 1954, p. 68.

1754 Page, Sally. Faulkner's Women. DeLand, Florida: Everett/Edwards, 1972, pp. 176-177.

1755 Reed, Joseph W., Jr. Faulkner's Narrative. New Haven: Yale U.P., 1973, pp. 20, 25-26, 135.

HAMLET--See under THE SNOPES TRILOGY

"HAND UPON THE WATERS"
(Sat. Eve. Post, 212 (1939), passim; repr., in Knight's Gambit, 1949)

1756 Meriwether, James B. The Short Fiction of William Faulkner," Proof, 1 (1971), 302.

1757 O'Connor, William Van. The Tangled Fire of William Faulkner. Minneapolis: Minnesota U. P., 1954, p. 144.

"HELL CREEK CROSSING"
(Sat. Eve. Post, 235 (1962); repr., in The Reivers (1962)

1758 Meriwether, James B. "The Short Fiction of William Faulkner," Proof, 1 (1971), 302.

"HONOR"
(AmMerc, 20 (1930); repr., in Doctor Martino, 1934; Collected Stories, 1950)

1759 Gwynn, Frederick L., and Joseph L. Blotner, eds. Faulkner in the University. Charlottesville: Virginia U. P., 1959, pp. 22-23.

1760 Meriwether, James B. "The Short Fiction of William Faulkner," Proof, 1 (1971), 302.

1761 Millgate, Michael. The Achievement of William Faulkner. New York: Random House, 1965, pp. 35, 138, 274.

1762 O'Connor, William Van. The Tangled Fire of William Faulkner. Minneapolis: Minnesota U. P., 1954, p. 89.

1763 Schiebelhuth, Hans, tr. "Ehre" ["Honor"], Europäische Revue, 11 (August, 1935), 529-538.

"THE HOUND"
(Harper's, 163 (1931); repr., in Doctor Martino, 1934; incorporated in The Hamlet, 1940)

1764 Jones, Leonidas M. "Faulkner's 'The Hound,'" Exp, 15 (March, 1957), Item 37.

1765 Meriwether, James B. "The Short Fiction of William Faulkner," Proof, 1 (1971), 302.

1766 Millgate, Michael. The Achievement of William Faulkner. New York: Random House, 1965, pp. 188-189, passim.

1767 Raimbault, R. N., tr. "Le chien," Table Ronde, Cahier 2 (1945), 107-129.

"IDYLL IN THE DESERT"
(Cf., James B. Meriwether, #1768, below)

1768 Meriwether, James B. The Literary Career of William Faulkner. Columbia: South Carolina U.P., 1971, pp. 177, 178, passim.

1769 ______. The Short Fiction of William Faulkner," Proof, 1 (1971), 302.

1770 Tuck, Dorothy. Crowell's Handbook of Faulkner. New York: Crowell, 1964, pp. 157n, 245.

INTRUDER IN THE DUST
(New York: Random House, 1948)

1771 Adams, Richard P. Faulkner: Myth and Motion. Princeton: Princeton U.P., 1968, pp. 155-156.

1772 Aguilar, Esperanza. Yoknapatawpha, Propiedad de William Faulkner. Santiago de Chile: Editorial Universitaria, 1964, pp. 104-111.

1773 Aisenson, Aida, tr. Intruso en el Polvo. Buenos Aires: Losada, 1951; 2nd ed., 1959.

1774 Allen, Walter. "Mr. Faulkner's Humanity," NS&N, 38, #971 (October 15, 1949), 428-429.

1775 Anderson, Charles R. "Faulkner's Moral Center," EA, 7 (January, 1954), 48-58.

1776 Anon. "Intruder in the Dust," Booklist, 45 (December 1, 1948), 120.

1777 Anon. "Intruder in the Dust," CE, 10 (December, 1948), 178.

1778 Anon. "Intruder in the Dust," Life, 27 (December 12, 1949), 149-153.

1779 Anon. "Intruder in the Dust," Newsweek, (October 4, 1948), 91. Review.

1780 Anon. "Intruder in the Dust," TLS (October 7, 1949), 645. Review.

1781 Anon. Kirkus, 16 (August 1, 1948), 374. Review.

1782 Anon. NYT, 52 (October 4, 1948), 108. Review.

1783 Anon. "A Way Out of the Swamp?" Time, 52 (October 4, 1948), 108, 110, 112. Review.

1784 Baker, Carlos. "William Faulkner: The Doomed and the Damned," The Young Rebel in American Literature. Carl Bode, ed. London: Heinemann, 1959, pp. 145-169; New York: Frederick Praeger, Pubs., 1960, pp. 145-169.

1785 Barzun, Jacques. "New Books," HarperM (December, 1948), 102-108.

1786 Birmingham Post (October, 1949). Review.

1787 Blanzat, Jean. ["Intruder in the Dust"], FL, (juin 7, 1952), 11. Review.

1788 Breit, Harvey. "Faulkner After Eight Years: A Novel of Murder," NYTBR (September 26, 1948), 4. Review.

1789 Brenner, Hans Georg. "Faulkners nobelpreis-Roman," DLD, [333] December 20, 1951), 9.

1790 Brkic, Svetozar, tr. Uljez u prasinu. Sarajevo: Svetjetlost, 1963.

1791 Brooks, Cleanth. "The Community in Action ('Intruder in the Dust')," William Faulkner: The Yoknapatawpha County. New Haven; 1963, 1964. pp. 279-294.

1792 Brylowski, Walter. Faulkner's Olympian Laugh. Detroit: Wayne State U.P., 1968, pp. 168-173.

1793 Bunker, Robert. "Faulkner: A Case for Regionalism," NMQR, 19 (Spring, 1949), 108-115.

1794 Carey, Glenn O. "William Faulkner on the Automobile As Socio-Sexual Symbol," CEA, 36, #2 (January, 1974), 15-17.

1795 Carpenter, David. "Faulkner's 'Intruder in the Dust' Apology for South's Jim Crow," Daily Worker (New York) (October 6, 1948), 13.

1796 Carter, Everett. "The Meaning of, and in, Realism," AntiochR, 12 (March, 1952), 78-94.

1797 Chapman, John. "New Faulkner Novel Expands Prior Ideas," Dallas Morning News (September 26, 1948), VI, 6.

1798 Cheney, Frances N. "Novel Treats Race Problem," Banner (Nashville), (October 1, 1948), 36. Review.

1799 Coffee, Jessie A. "Empty Steeples: Theme, Symbol, and Form in Faulkner's Novels," ArQ, 23 (Autumn, 1967), 197-206.

1800 Cohen, B. Bernard. "Study Aids for Faulkner's 'Intruder in the Dust,'" ExEx, 7 (October, 1959), 12-13.

1801 Connolly, Thomas E. "Fate and 'The Agony of Will': De-

1801 Connolly, Thomas E. "Fate and 'The Agony of Will': Determinism in Some Works of William Faulkner--Intruder in the Dust," Essays on Determinism in American Literature. S. J. Krause, ed. Kent: Kent State U. P., 1964, pp. 49-52.

1802 Conroy, Jack. "William Faulkner's Dixieland Is Getting More Sedate," Sun-Times (Chicago) (September 26, 1948), 8X.

1803 Cooper, Lettice. "Distinguished American Novelists," Yorkshire Post (October 7, 1949). Review.

1804 Cournos, John. "Intruder in the Dust," NY Sun (September 27, 1948), 18. Review.

1805 Cowley, Malcolm. "William Faulkner's Nation," NR, 119 (October 18, 1948), 21-22.

1806 Daniel, Frank. "Yoknapatawpha County Law," AtlJ (October 13, 1948), 35.

1807 Davenport, F. Garvin, Jr. "William Faulkner," The Myth of Southern History. Nashville, Tenn.: Vanderbilt U. P., 1970, pp. 82-130.

1808 Degenfelder, E. Pauline. "The Film Adaptation of Faulkner's Intruder in the Dust," LFQ, 1, #2 (April, 1973), 138-47.

1809 DeJovine, F. Anthony. The Young Hero in American Fiction: A Motif for Teaching Literature. New York: Appleton-Century-Crofts, 1971, pp. 40-41, passim.

1810 De Villier, Mary Anne. "Faulkner's Young Man: As Reflected in the Character of Charles Mallison," LaurelR, 9 (Fall, 1969), 42-49.

1811 Doniol-Valcroze, J. "Faulkner et le cinéma," Observateur (décembre 1, 1950), 23.

1812 Doster, William C. "The Several Faces of Gavin Stevens," MissQ, 11 (1958), 191-195.

1813 Dunlap, Mary M. "The Achievement of Gavin Stevens," DAI, 31 (South Carolina: 1970), 3544A.

1814 Edmonds, Irene C. "Faulkner and the Black Shadow," Southern Renascence: The Literature of the Modern South. Baltimore: Johns Hopkins, 1953, pp. 192-206.

1815 Elconin, Victor. "Hope Rests in the South," Daily Oklahoman (Oklahoma City), (October 31, 1948), 8-D.

1816 Elias, Robert H. "Gavin Stevens--Intruder?" FS, 3 (Summer-Autumn, 1954), 1-4.

1817 Everett, Walter K. Faulkner's Art and Characters. Woodbury, New York: Barrons Educ. Series, 1969, pp. 43-47.

1818 Fadiman, Regina K. "Faulkner's Intruder in the Dust," Novel into Film. Knoxville: Tennessee U. P., 1978.
The screenplay by Ben Maddow as adapted for film by Clarence Brown.

1819 Faulkner, Howard. "The Uses of Tradition: William Melvin Kelley's A Different Drummer," MFS, 21 (Winter, 1975-76), 535-542.
Comparison of characters in A Different Drummer with Lucas Beauchamp in Intruder in the Dust.

1820 "Fiction," Book List (December 1, 1948), 120. Review.

1821 Filler, Louis. "Intruder in the Dust," AntiochR, 8 (December, 1948), 512.

1822 Flowers, Paul. "Faulkner Offers Logic, Not Passion," Commercial Appeal (Memphis) (September 26, 1948), IV, 16.

1823 Frohock, Wilbur M. The Novel of Violence in America. 2nd ed. Dallas: Southern Methodist U. P., 1957, pp. 152-154, passim.

1824 Gannett, Lewis. "Intruder in the Dust," NYHT (September 28, 1948), 21.

1825 Geismar, Maxwell. "Ex-aristocrat's Emotional Education," SatRL, 31 (September 25, 1948), 8-9. Repr., American Moderns. New York: Hill & Wang, 1958, pp. 90-93.

1826 Gerard, Albert. "Justice in Yoknapatawpha County: Some Symbolic Motifs in Faulkner's Later Writings," FS, 2 (Winter, 1954), 49-57.

1827 Gerstenberger, Donna Lorine. "Meaning and Form in Intruder in the Dust," CE, 23 (December, 1961), 223-225.

1828 Giles, Barbara. "Unreconstructed Faulkner," Mass&Main, 1 (November, 1948), 78-81. Review.

1829 Glick, Nathan. "The Novelist as Elder Statesman," Commentary, 7 (May, 1949), 502-504.

1830 Glicksberg, Charles Irving. "Intruder in the Dust," ArQ, 5 (Spring, 1949), 85-88.

1831 Gloster, High M. "Southern Justice," Phylon, 10 (1st Qt., 1949), 93-95. Review.

1832 Gold, Joseph. "Intruder in the Dust: There Is Always Somewhere Someone," in William Faulkner: A Study in Humanism from Metaphor to Discourse. Norman: Oklahoma U. P., 1966, pp. 76-93.

1833 Greer, Dorothy D. "Dilsey and Lucas: Faulkner's Use of the Negro As a Gauge of Moral Character," ESRS, 11 (September, 1962), 54-60.

1834 Gregory, Horace. "Mutations of Belief in the Contemporary Novel," Spiritual Problems in Contemporary Literature. Stanley Romaine Hopper, ed. New York: Harper, 1957, pp. 43-44.

1835 _______. "Regional Novelist of Universal Meaning," NYHTBR (September 26, 1948), 3.

1836 Gwynn, Frederick L., and Joseph L. Blotner, eds. Faulkner in the University. Charlottesville: Virginia U.P., 1959, pp. 141-142, 201.

1837 Hamard, J. LMod (septembre-octobre, 1949), 96. Review.

1838 Hanlon, Frank. "More Light on Race Problems," Sunday Bulletin (Philadelphia) (September 26, 1948), Metro-13.

1839 Hansen, Harry. "Faulkner's New Novel about Negro," World-Telegram (New York) (September 27, 1948), 17. Review.

1840 Hardwick, Elizabeth. "Faulkner and the South Today," PR, 15 (October, 1948), 1130-1135; repr., in Two Decades of Criticism. Frederick Hoffman and Olga Vickery, eds. East Lansing: 1951, pp. 244-250; A Collection of Critical Essays. R. P. Warren, ed. Englewood Cliffs: Prentice-Hall, 1966, pp. 226-230; and "William Faulkner y el sur de hoy," Babel (Santiago), No. 56 (October-December, 1950), 185-191.

1841 Hart, H. W. "Intruder in the Dust," LibraryJ, 73 (August, 1948), 1089. Review.

1842 Hart, John A. "That Not Impossible He: Faulkner's Third-Person Narrator," Studies in Faulkner. Carnegie Series in English No. 6. Pittsburgh: Carnegie Institute of Technology, 1961, pp. 29-41.

1843 Heller, Terry L. "Intruders in the Dust: The Representation of Racial Problems in Faulkner's Novel and the MGM Film Adaptation," CoeR, 8 (1977), 79-90.

1844 Hoffman, Frederick J. William Faulkner. Twayne's United States Authors Series. New York: 1961, pp. 99-101.

1845 Howe, Irving. "The South and Current Literature," AmMerc, 67 (October, 1948), 494-503.

1846 _______. William Faulkner: A Critical Study. 2nd ed. New York: 1962, pp. 98-125.

1847 Howell, Elmo. "William Faulkner's Caledonia: A Note on Intruder in the Dust," SSL, 3 (April, 1966), 248-252.

1848 Hudson, Tommy. "William Faulkner: Mystic and Traditionalist," Perspective, 3 (Autumn, 1950), 227-235.

1849 Hutchinson, D. "The Style of Faulkner's Intruder in the Dust," Theoria, 39 (1973), 33-47.

1850 Jones, Carter Brooke. "Faulkner Novels Shows Radical Change in Style," Sunday Star (Washington), (September 26, 1948), 3.

1851 Kahn, Harry, tr. Griff in den Staub. Zürich: Fretz & Wasmuth Verlag, 1951.

1852 Kane, Patricia. "Only Too Rhetorical Rhetoric: A Reading of Intruder in the Dust," NConL, 4 (May, 1974), 2-3.

1853 Kazin, Alfred. "Faulkner in His Fury," The Inmost Leaf. New York: Harcourt, Brace, 1955, pp. 268-272.

1854 Kearney, J. A. "Paradox in Faulkner's Intruder in the Dust," Theoria, 40 (1973), 55-67.

1855 Kielty, Bernardine. "Undercover Stuff," Ladies Home Journal (October, 1948), 14-21.

1856 Kirk, Robert W., and Marvin Klotz. Faulkner's People. Berkeley: California U.P., 1963, pp. 124-132.

1857 Klein, Francis A. "Faulkner Waves Reformers Away from the South," Globe-Democrat (St. Louis), (September 26, 1948), 7. Review.

1858 Kohler, Dayton. "William Faulkner and the Social Conscience," CE, 11 (December, 1949), 119-127.

1859 Kuhl, Arthur. "Faulkner on a New Tack After Eight-Year Silence," Star-Times (St. Louis), (September 29, 1948), 25.

1860 Lalou, R. NL (mai, 29, 1952), 3. Review.

1861 Lauras, A. Études (novembre, 1952), 278-279. Review.

1862 Laws, Frederick. "New Books," News Chronicle (October 13, 1949), 5. Review.

1863 Leary, Lewis. "The Last Novels--Intruder in the Dust," William Faulkner of Yoknapatawpha County. New York: Crowell, 1973, pp. 171-176.

1864 Lebesque, M. Climats (juin, 1952), 8. Review.

1865 Lewis, Clifford L. "William Faulkner: The Artist As Historian," MASJ, 10, ii (Fall, 1969), 36-48.

1866 Life (December 12, 1949), 149-150. Review of the motion picture of Intruder in the Dust.

1867 Little, Gail B. "Three Novels for Comparative Study in the Twelfth Grade," EJ, 52 (October, 1963), 501-505.

1868 Longley, John L., Jr. The Tragic Mask. Chapel Hill: North Carolina U.P., 1963, pp. 33-41.

1869 Lytle, Andrew Nelson. "Regeneration for the Man," SR, 57 (January-March, 1949), 120-127; repr., in Two Decades of Criticism. Hoffman and Vickery, eds., pp. 251-259.

1870 ________. "Regeneration for the Man," The Hero with the Private Parts. Baton Rouge: Louisiana State U.P., 1966, pp. 129-136.

1871 McCants, Maxine. "From Humanity to Abstraction: Negro Characterization in Intruder in the Dust," NMW, 2 (Winter, 1970), 91-104.

1872 MacLure, Millar. "William Faulkner," QQ, 63 (Autumn, 1956), 336-337.

1873 Magill, Frank N., ed. Masterplots: Combined Edition. New York: Salem Press, 1960, pp. 1449-1451.

1874 Magny, C. E. Samedi Soir (juin 14, 1952), 2. Review.

1875 Makuck, Peter. "Faulkner Studies in France, 1953-1969," DA, 32 (Kent State: 1971), 3314A.

1876 Malin, Irving. William Faulkner: An Interpretation. Stanford U.P., 1957, passim.

1877 Materassi, Mario. "Intruder in the Dust," I romanzi di Faulkner. Roma: Edizioni di Storia e Letteratura, 1968, pp. 277-302.

1878 Maxwell, Desmond E. S. American Fiction: The Intellectual Background. New York: Columbia U.P., 1963, pp. 275-278.

1879 Milano, Paolo. "Faulkner in Crisis," Nation, 167 (October 30, 1948), 496. Review.

1880 Millgate, Michael. "Intruder in the Dust," The Achievement of William Faulkner. New York: Random House, 1965, pp. 215-220.

1881 Millstein, Gilbert. "Faulkner the Mystic Turns Polemicist," New York Star (September 26, 1948), Pleasure Sec., 13.

1882 Mizener, Arthur. "The American Hero As Gentleman: Gavin Stevens," The Sense of Life in the Modern Novel. Boston: Houghton Mifflin, 1964, pp. 161-181.

1883 _______. "The Thin, Intelligent Face of American Fiction," KR, 17 (Autumn, 1955), 507-524.

1884 Mohrt, Michel. Carrefour (édition américaine), (septembre 15, 1949), 7.

1885 Monaghan, David M. "Faulkner's Relationship to Gavin Stevens in Intruder in the Dust," DR, 52 (Autumn, 1972), 449-457.

1886 Moose, Roy C. "Intruder in the Dust," CarQ, 1 (Fall, 1948), 65-67.

1887 Muehl, Lois. "Faulkner's Humor in Three Novels and One 'Play,'" LibChron, 24 (Spring, 1968), 78-93.

1888 Nilon, Charles. "Faulkner and the Negro," UCSLL, 8 (September, 1962), 4-12, 25-30; repr., in Faulkner and the Negro. New York: Citadel, 1965, pp. 1-12, 25-30.

1889 North, Sterling. "Intruder in the Dust," New York Post (September 26, 1948), 15-M.

1890 Norton, Dan S. "This Man's Art and That Man's Scope," VQR, 25 (Winter, 1949), 132-133. Review.

1891 O'Connor, William Fan. "Sectionalism, and the Detective Story," The Tangled Fire of William Faulkner. Minneapolis: Minnesota U.P., 1954, pp. 136-142.

1892 O'Faolain, Sean. Vanishing Hero: Studies in Novelists of the Twenties. Boston: Little, Brown, 1957, pp. 104-106.

1893 Pedrolo, Manuel, tr. Intrus en la pols. Primera edicio. Barcelona: d'Edicions 62, 1969. Translation into Catalan.

1894 Pivano, Fernanda. [Introduction.] "Il Sud di Faulkner," La balena bianca e altri miti. Milano: Mondadori, 1961, pp. 239-287.

1895 Poresky, Louise A. "Joe Christmas: His Tragedy As Victim," HSL, 8 (1976), 209-222.

1896 Poster, William. "Films," Nation, 170 (January 14, 1950), 45.

Review of film of Intruder in the Dust.

1897 Prescott, Orville. "Books of the Times," NYT (September 27, 1948), 21. Review.

1898 _______. "Outstanding Novels," YR, 38 (Winter, 1949), 382. Review.

1899 Prins, A. P. "Faulkner en het negervraagstuk," Critisch Bulletin (Arnheim), (1950), 126-127.

1900 Pritchett, V. S. "The Hill-billies," Books in General. New York: Harcourt, Brace, 1953, passim.

1901 Radomski, James Louis. "Faulkner's Style: A Syntactic Analysis," DAI, 35 (Kent State: 1974), 6154A.

1902 Raimbault, R. N., tr. L'Intrus. Paris: Gallimard, 1952.

1903 Reed, Joseph W., Jr. "Faulkner's Failure: Intruder in the Dust, Requiem for a Nun, and A Fable," in Faulkner's Narrative. New Haven: Yale U. P., 1973, pp. 201-217.

1904 Reynolds, Horace. "The Interior Country of William Faulkner," CSMM (October 7, 1948), 11. Review.

1905 Richardson, Kenneth E. Force and Faith in the Novels of William Faulkner. The Hague: Mouton, 1967, pp. 103-109.

1906 Rigsby, Carol R. "Chick Mallison's Expectations and Intruder in the Dust," MissQ, 29, # 3 (Summer, 1976), 389-399.

1907 Roberts, James L. "The Individual and the Community," Studies in the American Novel. W. F. McNeir and L. B. Levy, eds. Baton Rouge: Louisiana State U. P., 1960, pp. 132-153.

1908 Rogers, W. G. "Lynching Problem Examined Anew in Faulkner's Novel," Plain Dealer (Cleveland), (September 26, 1948), 6. Review.

1909 Rollins, Ronald G. "Ike McCaslin and Chick Mallison: Faulkner's Emerging Southern Hero," WVUPP, 14 (October, 1963), 74-79.

1910 Rolo, Charles J. "Yoknapatawpha County," Atl, 182 (November, 1948), 108-111.

1911 Rubin, Louis D. "Notes on a Rear-Guard Action. The Curious Death of the Novel. Baton Rouge: Louisiana State U. P., 1967, pp. 131-151.

1912 Samway, Patrick H. "Faulkner's Hidden Story in Intruder in the Dust," Delta, 3 (November, 1976), 63-81.

1913 ________. "New Material for Faulkner's Intruder in the Dust," A Faulkner Miscellany. James B. Meriwether, ed. Jackson, Miss.: Miss. U.P., 1974, pp. 107-112.

1914 ________. "A Textual and Critical Evaluation of the Manuscripts and Typescripts of William Faulkner's Intruder in the Dust," DAI, 36 (North Carolina, Chapel Hill: 1974), 328A.

1815 Sequeria, Isaac. "Intruder in the Dust," Bulletin of the Ramakrishna Mission Institute of Culture, 25 (March, 1974), 64-68.

1916 Seypel, Joachim. "Faulkners Dichtung: Der Weg in die Sackgasse: zu seinem Roman Intruder in the Dust," NPZ, 4, #6 (1952), 369-372.

1917 Sherman, Thomas B. "Mob Psychology, Theme of Faulkner's New Novel," St. Louis Post-Dispatch (September 26, 1948), 4-B. Review.

1918 Shrapnel, Norman. "New Novels," Manchester Guardian (October 7, 1949), 4. Review.

1919 Simpson, Lewis P. "Intruder in the Dust," The Dispossessed Garden: Pastoral and History in Southern Literature. Athens, Ga.: University of Ga. Pr., 1975, pp. 71-75, 78-79.

1920 Skerry, Philip J. "The Adventures of Huckleberry Finn and Intruder in the Dust: Two Conflicting Myths of the American Experience," BSUF, 13, i (Winter, 1972), 4-13.

1921 Slatoff, Walter J. "Intruder in the Dust," Quest for Failure. Ithaca: Cornell U.P., 1960; 2nd pr., 1961, pp. 215-220.

1922 Snow, C. P. "Cult of the Atrocious," Sunday Times (October 16, 1949), 3. Review.

1923 Soderbergh, Peter A. "Hollywood and the South, 1930-1960," MissQ, 19 (Winter, 1965-66), 1-12.
Reference to filming of Intruder in the Dust on location in Benoit, Mississippi.

1924 Sowder, William J. "Lucas Beauchamp as Existential Hero," CE, 25 (November, 1963), 115-127.

1925 Starke, Catherine Juanita. Black Portraiture in American Fiction: Stock Characters, Archetypes, and Individuals. New York: Basic Books, 1971, pp. 192-194.

1926 Steinberg, Aaron. "Faulkner and the Negro," DA, 27 (N.Y.U.: 1966), 1385A.

1927 _______. "Intruder in the Dust: Faulkner As Psychologist of the Southern Psyche," L&P, 15 (Spring, 1965), 120-124.

1928 Stephenson, Shelby Dean. "'You Smart Sheriffs and Such': The Function of Local Peace Officers in William Faulkner's Light in August and Intruder in the Dust," DAI, 35 (Wisconsin: 1974), 3012A.

1929 Sullivan, Walter. "Allen Tate, Flem Snopes, and the Last Years of William Faulkner," Death by Melancholy. Baton Rouge: Louisiana State U.P., 1972, pp. 81-83.

1930 Swiggart, Peter. The Art of Faulkner's Novels. Austin: Texas U.P., 1962, pp. 41-48, 131-148.

1931 Taggart, Joseph. "Boy Runaway in a War," Star (October 3, 1949), 9. Review.

1932 Tagliabue, John. "The Different Stages of the Dark Journey in Intruder in the Dust," TsudaR, (Tokyo), No. 3 (November, 1958), 12-14.

1933 TLS, 2488 (October 7, 1949), 645. Review.

1934 Tsurganova, E. A. "Novaya kritika i roman Folknera 'Oskvernitel' prakha," ["The 'New Criticism' and Faulkner's Novel Intruder in the Dust"], VMU, 3 (1969), 16-29.

1935 Tuck, Dorothy. Crowell's Handbook of Faulkner. New York: Crowell, 1964, pp. 46-55.

1936 Van Nostrand, A. D. "The Poetic Dialogues of William Faulkner," Everyman His Own Poet: Romantic Gospels in American Literature. New York: McGraw-Hill, 1968, pp. 177-181.

1937 Vickery, Olga W. "Gavin Stevens: From Rhetoric to Dialectic," FS, 2 (Spring, 1953), 1-4.

1938 _______. "Initiation and Identity: Go Down, Moses and Intruder in the Dust," The Novels of William Faulkner. Baton Rouge: Louisiana State U.P., 1964, pp. 124-144.

1939 Volpe, Edmond L. A Reader's Guide to William Faulkner. New York: Noonday Press, 1964, pp. 253-264.

1940 Waggoner, Hyatt H. William Faulkner: From Jefferson to the World. Lexington: Kentucky U.P., 1959, pp. 212-219.

1941 Warren, Robert Penn. "Faulkner: The South and the Negro," SoR, 1 (July, 1965), 515ff.

1942 Watkins, Floyd C. "The Truth Shall Make You Fail," The

Flesh and the Word. Nashville: Vanderbilt U. P., 1971, pp. 256-259, 263.

1943 "A Way Out of the Swamp?" Time, 52, Part 2 (October 4, 1948), 108-112. Review.

1944 Weeks, Edward. Atl, 182 (November, 1948), 108. Review.

1945 Weidlé, Wladimir. "Notes: Leçons de bien dire et de bien faire," Cahiers de la plêiade (Spring, 1949), 53.

1946 Welty, Eudora. "In Yoknapatawpha," HudR, 1 (Winter, 1949), 596-598.

1947 _______. "William Faulkner's Intruder in the Dust," in The Eye of the Story: Selected Essays and Reviews. New York: Random House, 1978, pp. 207-211.

1948 Wilson, Edmund. "Books," NY, 24 (December 24, 1949), 52-53. Review.

1949 _______. "William Faulkner's Reply to the Civil Rights Program," NY, 24 (October 23, 1948), 106, 109-112. Repr., in Classics and Commercials. New York: Farrar, Straus, 1950, pp. 460-470.

1950 Wyndham, Francis. "New Novels," Observer (October 2, 1949), 7.

1951 Zink, Karl E. "William Faulkner: Form As Experience," SAQ, 53 (July, 1954), 384-403.

"A JUSTICE"
(These 13, 1931; repr., in Collected Stories, 1950)

1952 Bradford, M. E. "That Other Patriarchy: Observations on Faulkner's 'A Justice,'" ModA, 18 (Summer, 1974), 266-271.

1953 Clark, William Bedford. "A Tale of Two Chiefs: William Faulkner's Ikkemotubbe and Washington Irving's Blackbird," WAL, 12, #3 (Fall, 1977), 223-225.

1954 Dabney, Lewis M. "Faulkner, the Red, and the Black," ColuF, 1, #2 (Spring, 1972), 52-54.

1955 _______. "A Justice," The Indians of Yoknapatawpha. Baton Rouge: Louisiana State U. P., 1974, pp. 72-89.

1956 Howell, Elmo. "Sam Fathers: A Note on Faulkner's 'A Justice,'" TSL, 12 (1967), 149-153.

1957 _______. "William Faulkner and the Mississippi Indians," GaR, 21 (December, 1967), 386-396.

1958 Langford, Beverly Young. "History and Legend in William Faulkner's 'Red Leaves,'" NMW, 6 (Spring, 1973), 19-24.

1959 Libby, Anthony P. "Chronicles of Children: William Faulkner's Short Fiction," DA, 30 (Stanford: 1969), 1568A.

1960 Meriwether, James B. "The Short Fiction of William Faulkner," Proof, 1 (1971), 302-303.

1961 O'Nan, Martha. "William Faulkner's 'Du Homme,'" LaurelR, 10, #2 (1970), 26-28.

1962 Rouberol, Jean. "Les Indiens dans l'oeuvre de Faulkner," EA, 26 (March, 1973), 54-58.

"THE KINGDOM OF GOD"
(New Orleans Times-Picayune Sunday Mag. Sec., 1925, p. 2; repr., in New Orleans Sketches)

1963 Meriwether, James B. "The Short Fiction of William Faulkner," Proof, 1 (1971), 303.

1964 Peavy, Charles D. "An Early Casting of Benjy: Faulkner's 'The Kingdom of God,'" SSF, 3 (Spring, 1966), 347-348.

1965 ________. "The Eyes of Innocence: Faulkner's 'The Kingdom of God,'" PLL, 2 (Spring, 1966), 178-182.

KNIGHT'S GAMBIT
(New York: Random House, 1949)

1966 Algren, Nelson. "Faulkner's Thrillers," NYTBR (November 6, 1949), 4.

1967 Anon. "Faulkner's Detective," Newsweek (November 14, 1949), 92-93.

1968 Anon. "Knight's Gambit," Booklist (November 15, 1949), 97.

1969 Anon. "Knight's Gambit," Cw, 51 (December 2, 1949), 246. Review.

1970 Anon. "Knight's Gambit," Kirkus, 17 (September 1, 1949), 485. Review.

1971 Anon. "Yoknapatawpha Sherlock," Time, 54 (November 21, 1949), 118. Review.

1972 Beck, Warren. "Unique Style of Faulkner's Is Still Tops," Chicago Sunday Tribune (November 13, 1949), IV, 3.

1973 Benedetti, Mario. "*Gambito de caballo*," Número, Nos. 13-14 (March-June, 1951), 216-217.

1974 Boucher, Anthony. "Criminals at Large," NYTBR (July 1, 1956), 13.

1975 Bouchet, André, tr. *Le Gambit du Cavalier*. Paris: Gallimard, 1951.
(Un épisode, "Smoke," n'est pas traduit.)

1976 Bradley, Van Allen. "Faulkner at Best in *Gambit*," Chicago Daily News (November 9, 1949), 44.

1977 Chapin, Ruth. "The World of Faulkner," CSMM (December 8, 1949), 20.

1978 Cowley, Malcolm. "Faulkner Stories, in Amiable Mood," NYHTBR (November 6, 1949), 7.

1979 Crume, Paul. "Again Faulkner's Work Has Violence As Theme," Dallas Morning News (November 6, 1949), II, 10.

1980 Doster, William C. "The Several Faces of Gavin Stevens," MissQ, 11 (1958), 191-195.

1981 Dunlap, Mary M. "The Achievement of Gavin Stevens," DAI, 31 (South Carolina: 1970), 3544A.

1982 ________. "William Faulkner's '*Knight's Gambit*' and Gavin Stevens," MissQ, 23 (Summer, 1970), 223-239.

1983 Everett, W. K. *Faulkner's Art and Characters*. Woodbury, New York: Barron's Educ. Series, 1969.

1984 Frondizi, Josefina B. de. "Faulkner: *Gambito de caballo*," Asomante, 7, # 4 (October-December, 1951), 90-91.

1985 Gidley, Mick. "Elements of the Detective Story in William Faulkner's Fiction," JPC, 7 (1973), 97-123.

1986 Greenberg, Martin. "Gambit Declined," Commentary, 9 (January, 1950), 103-104.

1987 Grossman, Joel M. "The Source of Faulkner's 'Less Oft Is Peace,'" AL, 47 (November, 1975), 436-438.

1988 Guerard, Albert. "Justice in Yoknapatawpha County: Some Symbolic Motifs in Faulkner's Later Writing," FS, 2 (Winter, 1954), 49-57.

1989 H., E. "Knight's Gambit," NR, 121 (November 21, 1949), 19. Review.

1990 Harrison, W. K. "Knight's Gambit," LJ, 74 (September 15, 1949), 321.

1991 Howe, Irving. "Minor Faulkner," Nation, 169 (November 12, 1949), 473-474.

1992 Hunt, Joel A. "Thomas Mann and Faulkner: Portrait of a Magician," WSCL, 8 (Summer, 1967), 431-436.
A possible source for one of the stories in Mann's "Mario and the Magician."

1993 Jones, Howard Mumford. "Loyalty in Tiresias of Yoknapatawpha," SatRL, 32 (November 5, 1949), 17.

1994 Justo, Luis. "La antropología de Faulkner," Sur, 206 (December, 1951), 126-130.

1995 Kierszys, Zofia, tr. Gambit. Warszawa: Panstwowy Instytut Wydawniczy, 1964.

1996 Kirk, Robert W., and Marvin Klotz. Faulkner's People. Berkeley: California U. P., 1963, pp. 133-141.

1997 Klinkowitz, Jerome F. "The Thematic Unity of Knight's Gambit," Critique, 11 (1969), 81-100.

1998 Lalou, R. NL, (janvier 10, 1952), 3. Review.

1999 Lebesque, M. Carrefour (decembre 26, 1951), 7.

2000 ______. Climats (janvier, 3-9, 1952), 8.

2001 Macleod, Alison. "The Plundered Land," Daily Worker (April 12, 1951), 2.

2002 Mayoux, Jean-J. "Faulkner et le sens tragique," Combat (March 6, 1952), 7.

2003 Mazars, P. TR (fêvrier, 1952), 8.

2004 Miles, George. "Knight's Gambit," Cw, 51 (December 9, 1949), 275-276.

2005 Millgate, Michael. The Achievement of William Faulkner. New York: Random House, 1965, pp. 267-270.

2006 Mizener, Arthur. "The American Hero As Gentleman: Gavin Stevens," The Sense of Life in the Modern Novel. Boston: Houghton Mifflin, 1964, pp. 161-181, passim.

2007 Muir, Edwin. "The Gadget," Observer (May 6, 1951), 7.

2008 O'Connor, William Van. The Tangled Fire of William Faulkner. Minneapolis: Minnesota U. P., 1954, pp. 142-145.

2009 Olson, Lawrence. "*Knight's Gambit*," Furioso, 5 (Spring, 1950), 86-88.

2010 Parrish, Philip. "New Novels," Tribune, 730 (April 20, 1951), 14.

2001 Peavy, Charles D. "An Early Casting of Benjy: Faulkner's 'The Kingdom of God,'" SSF, 3 (Spring, 1966), 347-348.

2012 Pickrel, Paul. "Outstanding Novels," YR, 39 (Winter, 1950), 382.

2013 Pouillon, Jean. TM, 7 (February, 1952), 1490-1496.

2014 Prescott, Orville. "Books of the Times," NYT (November 8, 1949), 29.

2015 Pritchett, V. S. "Vogue of Faulkner," NS&N, 41 (June 2, 1951), 624, 626.

2016 Queen, Ellery. "*Knight's Gambit*," *Queen's Quorum: A History of the Detective-Crime Short Story*. Boston: Little, Brown, 1951, pp. 107-110.

2017 Rollins, Ronald G. "Ike McCaslin and Chick Mallison: Faulkner's Emerging Southern Hero," WVUPP, 14 (1963), 74-79.

2018 Rolo, Charles J. "Studies in Murder," Atl, 185 (January, 1950), 85-86.

2019 Rovere, Richard. "Faulkner, Mrs. Roosevelt, and Social History," HarperM, 199 (December, 1949), 108-110.

2020 Rubin, Louis D. "Five Southerners: *Knight's Gambit*," by William Faulkner," HopR, 3 (Spring, 1950), 42-45.

2021 Sáenz, Lucrecia Moreno de, tr. *Cambito de caballo*. Buenos Aires: Emecé, 1951, 1962.

2022 Sandrock, Mary. "*Knight's Gambit* by William Faulkner," CathW, 170 (January, 1950), 314-315.

2023 Schmidt, Albert-Marie. "L'esprit et les lettres: Honnêteté américaine," Réforme (février 16, 1952), 7.

2024 Sherman, Thomas B. "Faulkner's Latest--A Set of Short Stories," Post-Dispatch (St. Louis), (November 20, 1949), 4-B.

2025 Smith, Beverly E. "A Note on Faulkner's 'Greenbury Hotel,'" MissQ, 24 (Summer, 1971), 297-298.
Maintains that Faulkner's Greenbury Hotel is modeled on the Hotel Peabody, now the Sheraton Peabody, in Memphis.

2026 Tuck, Dorothy. Crowell's Handbook of Faulkner. New York: Crowell, 1964, pp. 112-114, passim.

2027 Vickery, Olga. "Gavin Stevens: From Rhetoric to Dialectic," FS, 2 (Spring, 1953), 1-4.

2028 ______. The Novels of William Faulkner. Rev. ed. Baton Rouge: Louisiana State U.P. 1964, pp. 251-252.

2029 Visentin, Giovanni. "Considerazioni su un ladro di cavilli," Fle, 6 (June 10, 1951), 1.

2030 Volpe, Edmond L. "Faulkner's Knight's Gambit: Sentimentality and the Creative Imagination," MFS, 24, #2 (Summer, 1978), 232-239.

2031 Wilson, Edmund. "Henley and Faulkner Not at Their Best," NY, 25 (December 24, 1949), 57-59.

2032 Worsley-Gough, Barbara. Spectator, #6409 (April 27, 1951), 566.

LIGHT IN AUGUST
(New York: Smith & Haas, 1932)

2033 Abel, Darrel. "Frozen Movement in Light in August," BUSE, 3 (Spring, 1957), 32-44.

2034 Adamowski, Thomas H. "Joe Christmas: The Tyranny of Childhood," Novel, 4 (Spring, 1971), 240-251.

2035 Adams, J. Donald. "Mr. Faulkner's Astonishing Novel," NYTBR (October 9, 1932), 6, 24.

2036 Adams, John R. "Faulkner Novel, 'Light in August,' Full of Thrills," Union (San Diego), (October 30, 1932), 7.

2037 Adams, Richard P. "The Apprenticeship of William Faulkner," TSE, 12 (1962), 113-156.

2038 ______. Faulkner: Myth and Motion. Princeton: Princeton U.P., 1968, pp. 84-95.

2039 Agar, Herbert. "Some New Novels," EngRev, 56 (February, 1933), 226. Review.

2040 Agate, James. "Mannered," Daily Express (February 9, 1933), 8. Review.

2041 Akasofu, Tetsuji. "Faulkner Hachigatsu no Hikari," EigoS, 117 (1971), 306-307.

2042 Aldington, Richard. "A Crime Novel with Real Characters," Evening Standard (February 2, 1933), 11.

2043 Allen, Charles A. "William Faulkner's Vision of Good and Evil," PacSpec, 10 (Summer, 1956), 236-241.

2044 Anderson, Charles R. "Faulkner's Moral Center," EA, 7 (January, 1954), 48-58.

2045 Anderson, Dianne Luce. "Faulkner's Grimms: His Use of the Name Before Light in August," MissQ, 29, #3 (Summer, 1976), 443.

2046 Anderson, Thomas D. Light in August: Novel; Chamber Theater; Motion Picture--The Role of Point of View in the Adaptation Process. DAI, 34 (Southern Illinois Univ.: 1973), 6161A.

2047 Anon. "Books in Brief--Light in August," Forum, 88 (December, 1932), vi.

2048 Anon. "Fiction: Intellectual Blood and Thunder," Bookman, 75 (December, 1932), 799.

2049 Anon. "Light in August," CamR, (May 26, 1933), 433. Review.

2050 Anon. "Light in August," Life and Letters, 9 (March-May, 1933), 118-120.

2051 Anon. "Light in August," TLS (February 16, 1933), 106.

2052 Anon. "Luce d'agosto," La Parola e il Libro, 22 (April, 1939), 228.

2053 Anon. "Luz de agosto, por William Faulkner," Revista de las Indias, 2d series, No. 50 (February, 1943).

2054 Antrim, Harry T. "Faulkner's Suspended Style," UKCR, 32 (Winter, 1965), 122-128.

2055 Anzilotti, Rolando. "Il realismo nell'epoca contemporanea--Faulkner," Storia della letteratura americana. Milano: Vallardi, 1957, pp. 71-73.

2056 Applewhite, Davis. "The South of Light in August," MissQ, 11 (Fall, 1958), 167-172.

2057 Arland, Marcel. "L'umière d'août," NRF, 45 (October, 1935), 584-586.

2058 Arthos, John. "Ritual and Humor in the Writing of William Faulkner," Accent, 9 (Autumn, 1948), 17-30.

2059 Asals, Frederick. "Faulkner's Light in August," Expl, 26 (May, 1968), Item 74.

2060 Asselineau, Roger. "Faulkner, moraliste puritain," RLM, 5 (Hiver, 1958-1959), 231-249.

2061 Backman, Melvin. Faulkner: The Major Years. Bloomington: Indiana U. P., 1966, pp. 67-87.

2062 _______. "Sickness and Primitivism: A Dominant Pattern in William Faulkner's Work," Accent, 14 (Winter, 1954), 61-73.

2063 Baker, Carlos. "William Faulkner: The Doomed and the Damned," The Young Rebel in American Literature. London: Heinemann, 1955, pp. 143-169.

2064 Baldanza, Frank. "The Structure of Light in August," MFS, 13 (Spring, 1967), 67-78.

2065 Ballew, Steven Early. "Faulkner's Psychology of Individualism: A Fictional Principle and Light in August," DAI, 35 (Indiana: 1974), 6700A.

2066 Barth, J. Robert. "Faulkner and the Calvinist Tradition," Thought, 39 (Spring, 1964), 100-120.

2067 Bauer, Walter. "Hunger in Amerika: Romane der 'Neuen Welt,'" Eckart, 12 (1936), 207ff.

2068 Beach, Joseph Warren. "William Faulkner: The Haunted South--Novels of Social Reference, Caste and Color: Light in August," American Fiction, 1920-1940. New York: Russell & Russell, 1940, pp. 123-169.

2069 Beck, Warren. "William Faulkner's Style," American Prefaces, 6 (Spring, 1941), 195-211; quoted from William Faulkner: Three Decades of Criticism. Frederick Hoffman and Olga Vickery, eds. East Lansing: Michigan State U. P., 1960, pp. 142-156.

2070 Bedell, George C. "Joe Christmas and the Incarnation," Kierkegaard and Faulkner. Baton Rouge: Louisiana State U. P., 1972, pp. 45-63.

2071 Beja, Morris. Epiphany in the Modern Novel. Seattle: Washington U. P., 1971, passim.

2072 _______. "A Flash, a Glare: Faulkner and Time," Ren, 16 (Spring, 1964), 134-137.

2073 Bellman, Samuel I. "Two-Part Harmony: Domestic Relations and Social Vision in the Modern Novel," CEJ, 3 (Winter, 1967), 31-41.

2074 Benson, Carl. "Thematic Design in Light in August," SAQ, 53 (October, 1954), 540-555.

2075 Berland, Alwyn. "Light in August: The Calvinism of William Faulkner," MFS, 8 (Summer, 1962), 159-170.

2076 Bernberg, Raymond E. "Light in August: A Psychological View," MissQ, 11 (Fall, 1958), 173-176.

2077 Berti, Luigi. "Romanzo e mito del Sud," Storia della letteratura. Milano: Instituto Editoriale Italiano, 1961.

2078 Bessie, Alvah C. "Light in August," Scribner's Magazine (December, 1932), 6.

2079 Bigsby, C. W. E. "Hemingway en de Amerikaanse Traditie van de Mens als Christus," [Hemingway and the American Tradition of the Christ Figure], NVT, 22, #8 (October, 1969), Reference to Joe Christmas of Light in August.

2080 Bleikasten, André. "L'espace dans Lumière d'aôut," Bulletin de la Faculté des Lettres de Strasbourg, 46 (December, 1967), 406-420.

2081 ________, and François Pitavy. William Faulkner: As I Lay Dying, Light in August. Introduction by Michel Gresset. Collection U2, Série Etudes anglo-américaines, Dossiers litteraires. Paris: Armand Colin, 1970.

2082 Borden, Caroline. "Characterization in Faulkner's Light in August," L&I, 13 (1972), 41-50.

2083 Boring, Phyllis Z. "Usmail: The Puerto Rican Joe Christmas," CLAJ, 16 (March, 1973), 324-332.

2084 Bowden, Edwin T. "William Faulkner, Light in August," The Dungeon of the Heart: Human Isolation and the American Novel. New York: Macmillan, 1961, pp. 124-138.

2085 Bowling, Lawrence Edward. "William Faulkner: The Importance of Love," DR, 43 (Winter, 1963-1964), 474-482.

2086 Breuil, Roger. "William Faulkner: Lumère d'août," Esprit, 1 (janvier, 1936), 612-614.

2087 Brickell, Herschel. "The Fruits of Diversity," VQR, 9 (January, 1933), 114-119.

2088 ________. "The Literary Landscape," NAR, 234 (December, 1932), 571.

2089 Brooks, Cleanth. "The Community and the Pariah," VQR, 39 (Spring, 1963), 236-253.

2090 ________. "The Community and the Pariah," William Faulkner: The Yoknapatawpha Country. Yale U. P., 1963, pp. 47-74.

2091 ________. "Faulkner's Vision of Good and Evil," MassR, 3 (Summer, 1962), 692-712; repr., in The Hidden God. New Haven: Yale U. P., 1963, pp. 22-43.

2092 ________. The Hidden God: Studies in Hemingway, Faulkner, Yeats, Eliot, and Warren. New Haven: Yale U. P., 1963, pp. 22-43.

2093 ________. Introduction. Light in August. New York: Random House, 1968.

2094 ________. "Notes on Faulkner's Light in August," HA, 135 (November, 1951), 10-11, 27.

2095 ________. "When Did Joanna Burden Die? A Note," SLJ, 6 (Fall, 1973), 43-46.

2096 Brown, Calvin S. "Faulkner's Geography and Topography," PMLA, 77 (December, 1962), 652-659.

2097 ________. "Faulkner's Manhunts: Fact into Fiction," GaR, 20 (Winter, 1966), 388-395.

2098 Brown, William R. "Faulkner's Paradox in Pathology and Salvation: Sanctuary, Light in August, Requiem for a Nun," TSLL, 9 (Autumn, 1967), 429-449.

2099 Brumm, Anne-Marie. "Authoritarianism in William Faulkner's Light in August and Alberto Moravia's Il Conformista," RLMC, 26 (1973), 196-220.

2100 Bryer, Jackson R., ed. Fifteen Modern American Authors. Durham, North Carolina: Duke U. P., 1969.

2101 Brylowski, Walter. Faulkner's Olympian Laugh: Myth in the Novels. Detroit: Wayne State U. P., 1968, pp. 102-117.

2102 Buckley, G. T. "Is Oxford the Original of Jefferson in William Faulkner's Novels?" PMLA, 76 (September, 1961), 447-454.

2103 Burroughs, Franklin G., Jr. "God the Father and Motherless Children: Light in August," TCL, 19 (July, 1973), 189-202.

2104 Busse, Alfred. "Amerikanischer Brief," Die Literatur, 35 (March, 1933), 403.

2105 Butcher, Fanny. "New Faulkner Writing Fits His Material," Daily Tribune (Chicago), (October 8, 1932), 12. Review.

2106 Cabau, Jacques. La Prairie perdue: Histoire du roman américain. Paris: Editions du Seuil, 1966, pp. 214-236.

2107 Campbell, Harry Modean. "Structural Devices in the Work of Faulkner," Perspective, 3 (Autumn, 1950), 209-226.

2108 ________, and Ruel E. Foster. William Faulkner: A Critical Appraisal. Norman: Oklahoma U. P., 1961, pp. 35-37, 68-74, 109-111.

2109 Campbell, Jeff H. Polarity and Paradox: Faulkner's Light in August," CEA, 34 (January, 1972), 26-31.

2110 CamR, 54, #1336 (May 26, 1933), 433. Review.

2111 Canby, Henry Seidel. "Grain of Life," SatRL, 9 (October 9, 1932), 153, 156.

2112 Cannan, Joanna. "A Tragedy of Mixed Blood," Daily Telegraph (February 7, 1933), 15.

2113 Cantwell, Robert. "Fiction," New Outlook (November, 1932), 60.

2114 Carey, Glenn O. "Light in August and Religious Fanaticism," STC, 10 (Fall, 1972), 101-113.

2115 Cestre, Charles. "William Faulkner: Light in August," RAA, 10 (June, 1933), 466-467.

2116 Chase, Richard. The American Novel and Its Tradition. Garden City, New York: Doubleday Anchor Books, 1957, pp. 210-219.

2117 ________. "The Stone and the Crucifixion: Faulkner's Light in August," KR, 10 (Autumn, 1948), 539-551. Repr., in Critiques and Essays on Modern Fiction. John W. Aldridge, ed. New York: Ronald Press, 1952, pp. 190-199; Two Decades of Criticism. Frederick Hoffman and Olga Vickery, eds. East Lansing: Michigan State U. P., 1951, pp. 205-216.

2118 Church, Margaret. "William Faulkner: Myth and Duration," Time and Reality: Studies in Contemporary Fiction. Chapel Hill: University of North Carolina Press, 1963, 227-250.

2119 Clark, Edward Depriest. "Six Grotesques in Three Faulkner Novels," DAI, 33 (Syracuse: 1972), 302A.

2120 Clark, William G. "Faulkner's Light in August," Expl, 26 (March, 1968), Item 54.

The significance of Christmas's search for racial identity.

2121 Clark, William J. "Faulkner's Light in August," Expl, 28 (November, 1969), Item 19.

2122 Coffee, Jessie A. "Empty Steeples: Theme, Symbol and Irony in Faulkner's Novels," ArQ, 23 (Autumn, 1967), 198-201.

2123 Coindreau, Maurice E. "Light in August," NRF, 239 (août 1, 1933), 302-305.

2124 _______, tr. Préface. Lumière d'août: William Faulkner. Paris: Gallimard, 1935.

2125 _______. "Le Puritanisme de William Faulkner," [préface de Lumière d'août], Cahiers du sud, 12 (avril, 1935), 259-267.

2126 _______. The Time of William Faulkner: A French View of Modern American Fiction. George M. Reeves, tr. and ed. Columbia: South Carolina U. P., 1971.

2127 Collins, Robert George. "Four Critical Interpretations in the Modern Novel," DA, 22 (Denver: 1961), 3642.

2128 _______. "The Game of Names: Characterization Device in Light in August," EngRec, 21 (October, 1970), 82-87.

2129 _______. "Light in August: Faulkner's Stained Glass Triptych," Mosaic, 7 (Fall, 1973), 97-157.

2130 Colvert, James B. "Views of Southern Character in Some Northern Novels," MissQ, 18 (1964-1965), 59-68.

2131 Connolly, Thomas E. "Fate and the 'Agony of Will': Determinism in Some Works of William Faulkner--Light in August," Essays in Determinism in American Literature. S. J. Krause, ed. Kent State Studies in Eng., No. 1, Kent State U. P., 1964, pp. 41-45.

2132 Cottrell, Beekman W. "Christian Symbols in Light in August," MFS, 2 (Winter, 1956), 207-213.

2133 _______. "Le symbolisme chrêtien dans Lumière d'août," RLM, 27-29 (1957), 105-108.

2134 Cowley, Malcolm. Introduction. The Portable Faulkner. Rev. and expanded ed. New York: Viking, 1946.

2135 _______. ["The Unity of Light in August"] Letter to William Faulkner, September 17, 1945, in The Faulkner-Cowley File: Letters and Memories. New York: Viking, 1966, pp. 28-29.

2136 Crickmay, Edward. "Fiction for All Tastes," Sunday Referee (January 29, 1933), 7. Review.

2137 Cullen, John B., and Floyd C. Watkins. "Joe Christmas and Nelse Patton," excerpt from Old Times in the Faulkner Country. Chapel Hill: 1961, pp. 8-98 in The Merrill Studies in Light in August. M. Thomas Inge, ed. Columbus, Ohio: Merrill Studies, 1971, pp. 7-14.

2138 Cutler, B. D. "Bright in August (A Faulknereality)," Amer-Spec, 3 (August, 1935), 13-15. A parody.

2139 D'Avanzo, Mario L. "Allusion in the Percy Grimm Episode of Light in August," NMW, 8 (Fall, 1975), 63-68.

2140 _______. "Bobbie Allen and the Ballad Tradition in Light in August," SCR, 8, i (November, 1975), 22-29.

2141 _______. "Doc Hines and Euphues in Light in August," NMW, 9 (Fall, 1976), 101-106.
Faulkner's allusions to John Lyly's work.

2142 _______. "Love's Labors: Byron Bunch and Shakespeare," NMW, 10 (Winter, 1977), 80-86.

2143 Davis, Charles E. William Faulkner's Joe Christmas: A Rage for Order," ArQ, 32 (Spring, 1976), 61-73.

2144 Davis, Elrick B. "And Faulkner 'Does It Again' with Light in August," Cleveland Press (October 8, 1932), p. 5.

2145 Dawson, Margaret Cheney. "A Rich, Sinister and Furious Novel," NYHTB (October 9, 1932), 3. Repr., in Merrill Studies in Light in August. Columbus, Ohio: 1971, p. 19.

2146 Delafield, E. M. "Mr. Faulkner's Landmark in American Fiction," Morning Post (February 7, 1933), 5. Review.

2147 DeVillier, Mary Anne G. "Faulkner's Young Man: As Reflected in the Character of Charles Mallison," LaurelR, 9 (1969), 42-49.

2148 Dorsch, Robert L. "An Interpretation of the Central Themes in the Work of William Faulkner," ESRS, 11 (September, 1962), 5-42.

2149 Doster, William C. "The Several Faces of Gavin Stevens," MissQ, 11 (Fall, 1958), 191-195.

2150 Douglas, Harold J., and Robert Daniel. "Faulkner and the Puritanism of the South," TSL, 2 (1957), 1-13.

2151 Dunn, Richard J. "Faulkner's Light in August, Chapter 5," Expl, 25 (October, 1966), Item 11.

2152 Edmonds, Irene C. "Faulkner and the Black Shadow,"

Southern Renascence: The Literature of the Modern South. Louis D. Rubin, Jr., and Robert D. Jacobs, eds. Baltimore: Johns Hopkins, 1953, pp. 192-206.

2153 Effelberger, Hans. [Light in August] NS, 44 (1936), 154-161.

2154 Einsiedel, Wolfgang von. Europäische Revue, 11 (1935), 707-708.

2155 Emie, L. CS (Octobre, 1936), 707-703. Review.

2156 "Epsalon." "Two Outstanding American Novels." Free Press (Dundee) (March 3, 1933), 5. Review.

2157 Erdmann, Lothar. [Light in August], Das deutsche Wort, 14 (1938), 152-153. Review.

2158 Everett, Walter K. Faulkner's Art and Characters. Woodbury, New York: Barron's Educ. Series, 1969, pp. 47-52.

2159 Everyman, 9, #209 (January 28, 1933), 117. Review.

2160 Ewell, Barbara N. "To Move in Time: A Study of the Structure of Faulkner's As I Lay Dying, Light in August, and Absalom, Absalom!" DAI, 30 (Florida State: 1970), 3940A.

2161 Fadiman, Regina K. Faulkner's Light in August: A Description and Interpretation of the Revisions. Charlottesville: Virginia U.P., 1975.

2162 ________. "Faulkner's Light in August: Sources and Revisions," DAI, 32 (U.C.L.A.: 1970), 427A.

2163 Farnham, James F. "Faulkner's Unsung Hero: Gavin Stevens," ArQ, 21 (1965), 115-132.

2164 Farrell, James T. "The Faulkner Mixture," NYSun (October 7, 1932), 29. Review.

2165 Fazio, Rocco R. "The Fury and the Design: Realms of Being and Knowing in Four Novels of William Faulkner," DA, 25 (Rochester: 1964), 1910.

2166 Fein, Franz, tr. Licht im august, roman. Berlin: E. Rowohlt Verlag, 1935.

2167 Ferreira, Armando, tr. Luz de agosto. Lisboa: Livros do Brasil, 1961?

2168 Ficken, Carl F. W. "A Critical and Textual Study of William Faulkner's Light in August," DAI, 33 (South Carolina: 1972), 4411A-12A.

2169 _______. "The Opening Scene of William Faulkner's Light in August," Proof, 2 (1972), 175-184.

2170 Fiedler, Leslie A. Love and Death in the American Novel. New York: Stein & Day, 1966, passim.

2171 Field, Louise Maunsell. "The American Novelists vs. the Nation," NAR, 235 (June, 1933), 556.

2172 _______. "The Modest Novelists," NAR, 235 (January, 1933), 63-69.

2173 Fischel, Anne. "Student Views of Faulkner II," MoOc, 1, #2 (Winter, 1971), 270-274.

2174 Fletcher, Helen. "New Fiction," Time and Tide, 14, #5 (February 4, 1933), 120, 122. Review.

2175 Flint, R. W. "Faulkner as Elegist," HudR, 7 (Summer, 1954), 246-257.

2176 Ford, Daniel Gordon. "Comments on William Faulkner's Temporal Vision in Sanctuary, The Sound and the Fury, Light in August, Absalom, Absalom!" SoQ, 15 (April 1977), 283-290.

2177 _______. "Uses of Time in Four Novels by William Faulkner," DAI, 35 (Auburn: 1974), 1654A.

2178 Fowler, Doreen F. "Faith As a Unifying Principle in Faulkner's Light in August," TSL, 21 (1976), 49-57.

2179 Franklin, Rosemary F. "Clairvoyance, Vision and Imagination in the Fiction of William Faulkner," DA, 29 (Emory: 1969), 3135A.

2180 Frazier, David L. "Lucas Burch and the Polarity of Light in August," MLN, 73 (June, 1958), 417-419.

2181 Friedman, Alan. "The Closed Novel and the Open Novel," in The Turn of the Novel. New York: Oxford U. P., 1966, p. 20.

2182 Frohock, W. M. "William Faulkner: The Private versus the Public Vision," SWR, 34 (Summer, 1949), 281-294; repr., in The Novel of Violence in America. Dallas: Southern Methodist U. P., 1957, pp. 143-165.

2183 Gavin, Jerome. "Light in August: The Act of Involvement," HA, 135 (November, 1951), 14-15, 34-37.

2184 Geismar, Maxwell. "William Faulkner: The Negro and the Female," Writers in Crisis: The American Novel, 1925-

1940. Boston: Houghton, Mifflin, 1942, pp. 141-183; excerpt, "Sex and Women in Light in August," repr., in Twentieth Century Interpretations of Light in August. David L. Minter, ed. Englewood Cliffs, New Jersey: 1969, pp. 88-89.

2185 Gide, André. Journal (1889-1939), 4 avril, 1936. Bibliothèque de la Plêide. Vol. 54. Paris: Gallimard, 1941, p. 1249.

2186 Glicksberg, Charles I. "William Faulkner and the Negro Problem," Phylon, 10 (June, 1949), 153-160.

2187 _______. "The World of William Faulkner," ArQ, 25 (Spring, 1949), 46-58.

2188 Goethals, Thomas. Light in August: A Critical Commentary. New York: American R. D. M. Corporation, 1965. Study Master 404.

2189 Gold, Joseph. "The Two Worlds of Light in August," MissQ, 16 (Summer, 1963), 160-167.

2190 _______. William Faulkner: A Study in Humanism from Metaphor to Discourse. Norman: Oklahoma U. P., 1966, pp. 38-42.

2191 Golub, Lester S. "Syntactic and Lexical Problems in Reading Faulkner," EJ, 59 (April, 1970), 490-496.

2192 Gossett, Louise Y. Violence in Recent Southern Fiction. Durham: Duke U. P., 1965, pp. 30-31.

2193 Gould, Gerald. "Sinclair Lewis and Others. Observer (January 29, 1933), 6. Also reviewed in News Chronicle (February 9, 1933), 4-M.

2194 Graham, Don, and Barbara Shaw. "Faulkner's Small Debt to Dos Passos: A Source for the Percy Grimm Episode," MissQ, 27 (Summer, 1974), 327-331.

Finds the course of the Percy Grimm episode in Light in August in the "Paul Bunyan" section of Dos Passos's 1919 which had appeared separately late in 1931.

2195 Green, Martin. "Faulkner: The Triumph of Rhetoric," Re-Appraisals: Some Commonsense Readings in American Literature. New York: W. W. Norton Co., 1965, pp. 167-195.

2196 Greenberg, Alvin. "Shaggy Dog in Mississippi," SoF, 29 (September, 1965), 284-287.

2197 Greer, Scott. "Joe Christmas and the 'Social Self,'" MissQ, 11 (Fall, 1958), 160-166.

2198 Gregg, Alvin L. "Style and Dialect in Light in August and Other Works by William Faulkner," DA, 30 (Austin, Texas: 1969), 3009A.

2199 Gresset, Michel, ed. With Introduction. William Faulkner: "As I Lay Dying" [and] "Light in August." Paris: Armand Colin, 1970.

2200 Griffith, Benjamin W. "Faulkner's Archaic Titles and the Second Shepherds' Play," NMW, 4 (Fall, 1971), 62-63.
Cf., M. Thomas Inge. "Faulknerian Light," NMW, 5 (Spring, 1972), 29.

2202 Grimes, George. "A Rival to Popeye in Faulkner's New Novel of the Southland," Sunday World Herald (Omaha) (October 9, 1932), Mag. Sec., 7.

2202. Günther, A. E. Deutsches Volkstum (1936), 211. Review.

2203 Gwynn, Frederick L., and Joseph L. Blotner, eds. Faulkner in the University. Charlottesville: Virginia U.P., 1959, pp. 72-75, passim.

2204 Hammond, Donald. "Faulkner's Levels of Awareness," FlaQ, 1, ii (1967), 73-75.

2205 Hansen, Harry. "William Faulkner's Forlorn People," New York World-Telegram (October 8, 1932), 17.

2206 Harakawa, Kyoichi. "Bride of Quietness and Walking Shadow," Kameron (Kameron Society), No. 6 (June, 1963), 1-31.

2207 Hardy, John Edward. "William Faulkner: The Legend Behind the Legend," Man in the Modern Novel. Seattle: Washington U.P., 1964, pp. 137-158.

2208 Harnack-Fish, Mildred. "William Faulkner--Amerikas Dichter aus grosser Tradition," Die Literatur, 38 (October, 1935), 66.

2209 Hartley, L. P. "The Literary Lounger," The Sketch, 161 #2093 (March 8, 1933), 439. Review.

2210 Hartt, Julian. The Lost Image of Man. Baton Rouge: Louisiana State U.P., 1963, pp. 38-50.

2211 Hayashi, Nokuyuki. "On Light in August," SELL, 7 (September, 1960), 3-20.

2212 Hays, P. L. "More Light on Light in August," PLL, 11 (Fall, 1975), 417-419.

2213 Heimer, Jackson W. "Faulkner's Misogynous Novel: Light in August," BSUF, 14 (Summer, 1973), 11-15.

2214 Heiseler, Bernt von. Deutsche Zeitschrift, 49 (1936), 468.

2215 Hendin, Josephine. "Flannery O'Connor and Southern Fiction," The World of Flannery O'Connor. Bloomington: Indiana U.P., 1970, pp. 131-157.
Murder scenes compared with similar ones in Light in August.

2216 Hesse, Hermann. "Notizen zu neuen Büchern," DNR, 46, 2 (1935), 664-672.

2217 Hickerson, Donna Davis. "Madmen Stalk in Novel," Minneapolis Journal (November 6, 1932), Ed. Sec., 5. Review.

2218 Hirshleifer, Phyllis. "As Whirlwinds in the South: Light in August," Perspective, 2 (Summer, 1949), 225-238.

2219 Hoffman, Frederick J. "The Tangled Web--Light in August," William Faulkner. New York: Twayne Pubs., 1961, pp. 69-74.

2220 ________, and Olga W. Vickery, eds. William Faulkner: Three Decades of Criticism. East Lansing: Michigan State U.P., 1960.

2221 Holman, C. Hugh. "The Unity of Faulkner's Light in August," PMLA, 73 (March, 1958), 155-166.
An expanded version of paper read before the Modern Language Association, December 28, 1956.

2222 ________. "The Unity of Faulkner's Light in August," The Roots of Southern Writing: Essays on the Literature of the American South. Athens, Georgia: Georgia U.P., 1972, pp. 149-167.

2223 Holmes, Edward M. Faulkner's Twice Told Tales: His Re-Use of His Material. The Hague: Mouton, 1966, pp. 19-45.

2224 Howe, Irving. William Faulkner: A Critical Study. 2nd ed., revised and expanded. New York: Vintage Books, 1962, pp. 61-70, 200-214.

2225 Howell, Elmo. "A Note on Faulkner's Emily as a Tragic Heroine," Serif, 3 (September, 1966), 13-15.
Notes parallels between Emily Grierson and Joanna Burden as tragic heroines.

2226 ________. "A Note on Faulkner's Presbyterian Novel," PLL, 2 (Spring, 1966), 182-187.

2227 ________. "Reverend Hightower and the Uses of Southern Adversity," CE, 24 (December, 1962), 183-187.

2228 Hulley, Kathleen. "Disintegration as Symbol of Community: A Study of The Rainbow, Women in Love, Light in August, Prisoner of Grace, Except the Lord, Not Honour More, and Herzog," DAI, 34 (Calif., Davis: 1973), 6643A-44A.

2229 Hunt, John W. William Faulkner: Art in Theological Tension. Syracuse: Syracuse U. P., 1965, pp. 13-16.
The use of Christ symbolism in the novel.

2230 Inge, M. Thomas. "Faulknerian Light," NMW 5 (Spring, 1972), 29.
Cf., B. W. Griffith. "Faulkner's Archaic Titles and the Second Shepherds' Play," NMW, 4 (Fall, 1971), 62-63.

2231 ________, ed. Introduction. Studies in Light in August. Columbus, Ohio: Charles E. Merrill, 1971.

2232 ________. "William Faulkner's Light in August: An Annotated Checklist of Criticism," RALS, 1 (Spring, 1971), 30-57.

2233 Isaacs, J. "Light in August," Annual Register (1933), Part 2, 37. Review.

2234 Jackson, Esther Merle. "The American Negro and the Image of the Absurd," Phylon, 23 (Winter, 1962), 359-371.

2235 Jackson, Joseph Henry. "A Book a Day," Chronicle (San Francisco) (October 19, 1932), 9. Review.

2236 Jacobs, Robert D. "Faulkner and the Tragedy of Isolation," HopR, 6 (Spring-Summer, 1953), 162-183. Repr., in Southern Renascence. Louis D. Rubin, Jr., and Robert D. Jacobs, eds. Baltimore: Johns Hopkins Press, 1953, pp. 170-191.

2237 ________. "William Faulkner: The Passion and the Penance," South: Modern Southern Literature in Its Cultural Setting. Louis D. Rubin, Jr., and Robert D. Jacobs, eds. Garden City: Doubleday Dolphin Books, 1961, pp. 142-176.

2238 James, David L. "Hightower's Name: A Possible Source," AN&Q, 13 (September, 1974), 4-5.

2239 James, Stuart. "Faulkner's Shadowed Land," DenverQ, 6 (Autumn, 1971), 45-61.

2240 Jarrett-Kerr, Martin. William Faulkner: A Critical Essay. Grand Rapids, Michigan: William B. Eerdmans Pub., 1970, pp. 7-9, 38-41, passim.

2241 Jenkins, Lee Clinton. "Faulkner, the Mythic Mind, and the Blacks," L&P, 27, #2 (1977), 74-91.

2242 Johnston, Walter E. "The Shepherdess in the City," CL, 26 (1974), 124-141.

2243 Juhasz, Leslie A. William Faulkner's Light in August (A Critical Commentary). Monarch Notes and Study Guides. New York: Monarch Press, 1965.

2244 Kaiser, Flora. "Faulkner's Latest Novel Morbid, But Has Brighter Side," St. Louis Globe-Democrat (November 6, 1932), 10-B. Review.

2245 Kaplan, Harold D. "The Inert and the Violent: Faulkner's Light in August," The Passive Voice: An Approach to Modern Fiction. Athens: Ohio U.P., 1966, pp. 111-130.

2246 Kazin, Alfred. "The Stillness of Light in August," PR, 24 (Fall, 1957), 519-538. Repr., in Interpretation of American Literature. Chas. Feidelson, ed. New York: Oxford U.P., 1957, pp. 349-368; Twelve Original Essays on Great American Novels. Chas. Shapiro, ed. Wayne State U.P., 1958, pp. 257-283; Three Decades of Criticism. Frederick Hoffman and Olga Vickery, eds. East Lansing: Michigan State U.P., 1960, pp. 247-264.

2247 Kellogg, Gene. "Alienated Man and the Faculty of Categorization," Dark Prophets of Hope: Dostoevsky, Sartre, Camus, Faulkner. Chicago: Loyola U.P., 1975, pp. 136-156.

2248 Kerr, Elizabeth M. Yoknapatawpha: Faulkner's Little Postage Stamp of Native Soil. New York: Fordham U.P., 1969, passim.

2249 Kimmey, John L. "The Good Earth in Light in August," MissQ, 17 (Winter, 1963-1964), 1-8.

2250 King, James. "Turning New Leaves," CanForum, 45 (March, 1966), 281-282.

2251 Kinoian, Vartkis. Review Notes and Study Guide to Faulkner's "Light in August,".... New York: Monarch Press, 1964, pp. 119-122.

2252 Kirk, Robert W. "Faulkner's Lena Grove," GaR, 21 (Spring, 1967), 57-64.

2253 ________, and Marvin Klotz. Faulkner's People. Berkeley: California U.P., 1963, pp. 65-77.

2254 Kobayashi, Kenji. "The Role of Lena Grove in Light in August," SB&AL, No. 10 (March, 1963), 45-54.

2255 Kobler, J. F. "Lena Grove: Faulkner's 'Still Unravish'd Bride of Quietness,'" ArQ, 28 (Winter, 1972), 339-354.
Sees Lena Grove as analogous to the urn in Keats's "Ode on a Grecian Urn."

2256 Krieger, Murray. "The Light-ening of the 'Burden' of History: Light in August," in The Classic Vision: The Retreat from Extremity in Modern Literature. Baltimore: Johns Hopkins Press, 1971, pp. 313-336.

2257 ______. The Tragic Vision: Variations on a Theme in Literary Interpretation. Chicago: Chicago U. P., 1966, pp. 266-268, passim.

2258 Kristensen, Sven Møller, tr. Forløsning i August. København, Gyldendals, 1964.
Translation into Danish.

2259 Kunkel, Francis L. "Christ Symbolism in Faulkner: Prevalence of the Human," Renascence, 17 (Spring, 1965), 148-156.

2260 Lamont, William H. F. "The Chronology of Light in August," MFS, 3 (Winter, 1957-1958), 360-361. Excerpt in Twentieth Century Interpretations of Light in August. David L. Minter, ed. Englewood Cliffs, New Jersey: 1969, pp. 94-95.

2261 Langston, Albert Beach. "The Meaning of Lena Grove and Gail Hightower in Light in August " BUSE, 5 (Spring, 1961), 46-63.
Finds both Christian and Buddhist symbolism in the characters.

2262 Larsen, Eric. "The Barrier of Language: The Irony of Language in Faulkner," MFS, 13 (Spring, 1967), 19-31.

2263 Lass, Abraham, ed. A Student's Guide to 50 American Novels. New York: Washington Square Press, 1966, pp. 206-214.

2264 Leary, Lewis. "Light in August," William Faulkner of Yoknapatawpha County. New York: Crowell, 1973, pp. 78-95.

2265 Leaver, Florence. "Faulkner: The Word as Principle and Power," SAQ, 57 (Autumn, 1958), 464-476.
The techniques of Faulkner's style.

2266 Leavis, Frank R. "Dostoevsky or Dickens?" Scrutiny, 2 (June, 1933), 91-93. Excerpts in Faulkner: A Collection of Critical Essays. R. P. Warren, ed. Englewood Cliffs, New Jersey: Prentice-Hall, 1966, pp. 277-278; Merrill Studies in Light in August. M. Thomas Inge, ed. Columbus, Ohio: Merrill, 1971, pp. 23-25.

2267 Le Breton, M. RAA (juin, 1936), 471-472. Review.

2268 Lecuona, Pedro, tr. Luz de agosto. Buenos Aires: Sur, 1942.

2269 Lein, Clayton D. "Love in the Novels of Faulkner and Hawthorne," Honors College Essays, 1965-1966. William W. Kelly, ed. East Lansing: Michigan State U.P., 1966, pp. 52-61.

2270 Levith, Murray J. "Unity in Faulkner's Light in August," Thoth, 7 (Winter, 1966), 31-34.
The form of the epic and the theme of fertility and sterility.

2271 Lewis, R. W. B. "William Faulkner: The Hero in the New World," The Picaresque Saint: Representative Figures in Contemporary Fiction. Philadelphia: J. B. Lippincott, 1959, pp. 179-219.

2272 "Licht im August," Der Querschnitt, 15 (1935), 404.

2273 ["Light in August"] Life and Letters, 9 (March-May, 1933), 118-120. Review.

2274 "Light in August" by William Faulkner," NR, 72 (October 26, 1932), 300-301. Review.

2275 Lind, Ilse Dusoir. "Apocalyptic Vision as Key to Light in August," SAF, 3 (Autumn, 1975), 131-141.

2276 ________. "The Calvinistic Burden of Light in August," NEQ, 30 (September, 1957), 307-329.

2277 Linn, James Weber, and Houghton Taylor. "Counterpoint: Light in August," A Foreword to Fiction. New York: Appleton-Century-Crofts, 1935, pp. 144-157.

2278 Little, G. Macintyre. "An American Genius," Scots Observer, 7, #332 (February 11, 1933), 11. Review.

2279 Litvin, Rina. "William Faulkner's Light in August," Hasifrut, 1 (1969), 589-598. In Hebrew.

2280 Longley, John Lewis, Jr. "Faulkner's Byron Bunch," GaR, 15 (Summer, 1961), 197-208.

2281 ________. "Joe Christmas: The Hero in the Modern World," VQR, 33 (Spring, 1957), 233-249.

2282 ________. The Tragic Mask: A Study of Faulkner's Heroes. Chapel Hill: North Carolina U.P., 1963, pp. 50-62, 192-205.

2283 Loughrey, Thomas F. "Light in August: Religion and the Agape of Nature," FourQ, 12 (May, 1963), 14-25.

2284 Lutwack, Leonard. Heroic Fiction: The Epic Tradition and

American Novels of the Twentieth Century. London: Feffer & Simons; Carbondale and Edwardsville: Southern Ill. U. P., 1971, pp. 20, 21.
Discusses meaning of the title.

2285 Lützeler, Heinrich. "Licht im August--Neue Romane," Hochland, 33, #1 (1935), 266-270.

2286 M., J. P. Gringoire (October 4, 1935), 4. Review.

2287 _______. "Luce d'agosto," Radio Corriere, 15 (August 20-26, 1939), 38. Review.

2288 McCamy, Edward. "Byron Bunch," Shenandoah, 3 (Spring, 1952), 8-12.

2289 McCormick, John. Catastrophe and Imagination: An Interpretation of the Recent English and American Novel. London: Longmans, Green & Co., 1957, pp. 257-261.

2290 McDonald, Walter R. "Coincidence in the Novel: A Necessary Technique," CE, 29 (February, 1968), 373-388.

2291 McDowell, Alfred. "Attitudes Toward 'Time' in Light in August," Itinerary 3: Criticism. Frank Baldanza, ed. Bowling Green, Ohio: Bowling Green U. P., 1977, pp. 149-158.

2292 McElderry, B. R., Jr. "Appendix: An Outline of the Narrative Structure of Light in August," Twentieth Century Interpretations of The Light in August. David L. Minter, ed. Englewood Cliffs, New Jersey: Prentice-Hall, 1969, pp. 109-110.

2293 _______. "Narrative Structure of Light in August," CE, 19 (February, 1958), 200-207; repr., in MissQ, 11 (Fall, 1958), 177-187.

2294 Mackenzie, Compton. "Prose Gone Bad," Daily Mail (February 9, 1933), 4. Review.

2295 McLuhan, Herbert Marshall. "The Southern Quality," SR, 55 (Summer, 1947), 357-383.
Joe Christmas as a symbol of both the Southern and the universal spiritual condition.

2296 Magill, Frank N., ed. Masterplots: American Fiction Series. New York: Salem Press, 1957, 1964, pp. 345-347.

2297 Maier, Hansgeorg. Deutsche Zukunft, 5 (June 13, 1937), 11.

2298 Malin, Irving. "*Light in August*: The Technique of Opposition," *William Faulkner: An Interpretation*. Stanford, Calif.: Stanford U.P., 1957, pp. 47-64.

2299 Marriott, Charles. "Fitful Gleams," Manchester Guardian (February 10, 1933), 5. Review.

2300 Materassi, Mario. *I romanzi di Faulkner*. Biblioteca di studi Americani, 17. Roma: Edizione di Storia e Letteratura, 1968, pp. 157-181.

2301 Meade, Everard. "A Terrific Story Marching with Violence to a Bloody End," Times Dispatch (Richmond), (October 9, 1932), III, 5.

2302 Meats, Stephen E. "Who Killed Joanna Burden?" MissQ, 24 (Summer, 1971), 271-277.

2303 Melito, Ignatius M. "The Literary Myth-makers--Faulkner's Myth," EJ, 53 (March, 1964), 167-169.

2304 Meriwether, James B. "*Light in August*," in *Fifteen Modern American Authors*. Jackson R. Bryer, ed. North Carolina: Duke U.P., 1969, pp. 175-210.

2305 ________. "*Light in August*," *The Literary Career of William Faulkner*. Columbia: South Carolina U.P., 1971, pp. 22-23, *passim*.

2306 ________. "*Light in August*," *Sixteen Modern American Authors*. Jackson R. Bryer, ed. Durham, North Carolina: Duke U.P., 1974, pp. 246-247, 269-270, *passim*.

2307 Miller, David M. "Faulkner's Women," MFS, 13 (Spring, 1967), 3-17.

2308 Miller, James E. "William Faulkner: Descent into the Vortex," *Quests Surd and Absurd: Essays in American Literature*. Chicago: Chicago U.P., 1967, pp. 50-52, 58-59, 61-64.

2309 Millgate, Michael. "*Light in August*," *The Achievement of William Faulkner*. New York: Random House, 1966, pp. 124-137.

2310 ________. *William Faulkner*. New York: Grove Press, 1961, pp. 44-50.

2311 Miner, Ward L. *The World of William Faulkner*. Durham: Duke U.P., 1952, pp. 141-144.

2312 Minter, David L., ed. Introduction. *Twentieth Century Interpretations of Light in August*. Englewood Cliffs, New Jersey: Prentice-Hall, 1969.

2313 Moran, Helen. "Light in August," London Mercury, 27, #161 (March, 1933), 470.

2314 Morehead, Albert H. Harold J. Blum, et al., eds. 100 Great American Novels. New York: Signet Book, 1966, pp. 232-238.

2315 Morra, Umberto. "Letterature straniere: William Faulkner: Luce d'agosto," Let (Rome), 3 (July, 1939), 173-174.

2316 Morris, Wright. The Territory Ahead: Critical Interpretations in American Literature. New York: Harcourt, Brace & World, 1958, pp. 171-184.

2317 ________. "The Violent Land: Some Observations on the Faulkner Country," MA, 45 (March, 1952), 99-103.
Faulkner's expressionism.

2318 Morrison, Sister Kristin. "Faulkner's Joe Christmas: Character Through Voice," TSLL, 2 (Winter, 1961), 419-443.
Faulkner's use of voice as key to narrative technique and character.

2319 Mosely, Edwin M. "Christ as Social Scapegoat: Faulkner's Light in August," Pseudonyms of Christ in the Modern Novel: Motifs and Methods. Pittsburgh: Pittsburgh U.P., 1962, pp. 135-151.

2320 Moses, W. R. "The Limits of Yoknapatawpha County," GaR, 16 (Fall, 1962), 297-305.

2321 Muehl, Lois. "Form as Seen in Two Early Works by Faulkner," LC, 38 (1972), 147-157.
Notes that Faulkner used five devices repeatedly.

2322 Mulqueen, James E. "Light in August: Motion, Eros, and Death," NMW, 8 (Winter, 1975), 91-93.

2323 Nakamura, Junichi. "A Study of William Faulkner's Light in August," Stud (Kobe College), 9 (June, 1962), 1-20.

2324 Nash, Alan. "Faulkner's Inhumanity to Man Softened by Touch of Sympathy," Times (Buffalo), (October 9, 1932), 6-C.

2325 Nash, Harry C. "Faulkner's 'Furniture Repairer and Dealer': Knitting up Light in August," MFS, 16 (Winter, 1970-71), 529-531.
The concluding chapter restores "a normal continuity and stability ... critical to the novel's knitting-up."

2326 Nemerov, Howard. "Calculation Raised to Mystery: The

Dialectics of Light in August," Poetry and Fiction: Essays. New Brunswick: Rutgers U.P., 1963, pp. 246-259.

2327 Neufeldt, Leonard. "Time and Man's Possibilities in Light in August," GaR, 25 (Spring, 1971), 27-40.

2328 Nicholson, Norman. "William Faulkner," Man and Literature. London: S.C.M. Press, 1943, pp. 122-138.
Light in August shows a developing morality with a new sense of pity for Natural Man.

2329 Nilon, Charles H. Faulkner and the Negro. New York: Citadel, 1965, pp. 73-93.

2330 Noble, David W. "After the Lost Generation: William Faulkner, ..." The Eternal Adam and the New World Garden: The Central Myth in the American Novel Since 1830. New York: Braziller, 1968, pp. 161-193.

2331 North, Sterling. "Magnolias, Madness and Mississippi Mud," Chicago News (October 5, 1932), 16.
"... [O]ne of the best pictures of the decadent South extant...."

2332 O'Connor, William Van. "Protestantism in Yoknapatawpha County," HopR, 5 (Spring, 1952), 26-42. Repr., in Southern Renascence. Louis D. Rubin, Jr., and Robert D. Jacobs, eds. Baltimore: Johns Hopkins, 1953, pp. 153-169.

2333 _______. The Tangled Fire of William Faulkner. Minneapolis: Minnesota U.P., 1954, pp. 72-87. (Revision of "Protestantism in Yoknapatawpha County.")

2334 _______. William Faulkner. Minneapolis: Minnesota U.P., 1956, pp. 19-23.

2335 O'Donnell, George Marion. "Faulkner's Mythology," KR, 1 (Summer, 1939), 285-299. Repr., Two Decades, pp. 49-62, Three Decades, Frederick Hoffman and Olga Vickery, eds. New York: Harcourt, 1963, pp. 82-93.

2336 _______. "Faulkner's New Work More Mature and Broader in Outlook Than His Earlier Novels," Commercial Appeal (Memphis), (October 9, 1932), IV, 4.

2337 O'Faolain, Sean. "William Faulkner, or More Genius Than Talent," The Vanishing Hero: Studies in the Novelists of the Twenties. London: Eyre & Spottiswoode, 1956, pp. 99-134.

2338 Page, Sally R. "The Feminine Ideal of Light in August," Faulkner's Women. DeLand, Florida: 1972, pp. 139-151.

2339 Palmer, William J. "Abelard's Fate: Sexual Politics in Stendhal, Faulkner, and Camus," Mosaic, 7, #3, (Spr., 1974), 29-41.

2340 Patten, Mercury. "Light in August," NS&N, 5 (February 11, 1933), 163.

2341 Pearce, Richard. "Faulkner's One Ring Circus," WSCL, 7 (Autumn, 1966), 270-283.

2342 ______. "Faulkner's One Ring Circus: Light in August," Stages of the Clown: Perspectives on Modern Fiction: Carbondale and Edwardsville: Southern Ill. U. P., 1970, pp. 47-66.

2343 Pearson, Norman Holmes. "Lena Grove," Shenandoah, 3 (Spring, 1952), 3-7. Also in Four Studies. Verona, Italy: Stamperia Valdonega, 1963, pp. 47-55.
References to Keats and the "Ode on a Grecian Urn."

2344 ______. "The American Writer and the Feeling for Community," ES, 43 (October, 1962), 403-412.

2345 ______. "The American Writer and the Feeling for Community," American Studies Inaugural Lecture, Alabama University, March 20, 1962. Excerpted and repr., in Twentieth Century Interpretations of Light in August. David L. Minter, ed. Englewood Cliffs: 1969, pp. 101-103.

2346 Pedrolo, Manuel de. Llum d'Agost. Barcelona: Edicions, 1959, 1967.

2347 Peterson, Richard F. "Faulkner's Light in August," Expl, 30 (December, 1971), Item 35.
The original source of Joe Christmas's guilt-ridden feelings.

2348 Pitavy, François L. Faulkner's Light in August. Bloomington: Indiana U. P., 1973. Rev. and enlarged ed. trans. from French by Gillian E. Cook with collab. of author.

2349 ______. "The Landscape in Light in August," MissQ, 23 (Summer, 1970), 265-272.

2350 Pohl, Gerhard. [Licht im August], Deutsche Zukunst, 4 (March 8, 1936), 18.

2351 Pommer, Henry F. "Light in August: A Letter by Faulkner," ELN, 4 (September, 1966), 47-48.
Faulkner's letter about a possible typographical error in the text.

2352 Porat, Tsfira. "Bubot Shel Nessoret: Goral Tragi Ve-heirut

Comit Be-Or Be-August Le-William Faulkner," Hasifrut, 2 (1971), 767-782.

Tsfira Porat's "Sawdust Dolls: Tragic Fate and Comic Freedom in Faulkner's Light in August."

2353 Poresky, Louise A. "Joe Christmas: His Tragedy As Victim," HSL, 8 (1976), 209-222.

2354 Porter, Carolyn. "The Problem of Time in Light in August," RUS, 61, #1 (1975), 107-125.

2355 Powers, Lyall H. "Hawthorne and Faulkner and the Pearl of Great Price," PMASAL, 52 (1967), 391-401.

2356 Price-Stephens, Gordon. "The British Reception of William Faulkner, 1929-1962," MissQ, 17 (Summer, 1964), 119-200.

2357 Pryse, Marjorie L. "The Marked Character in American Fiction: Essays in Social and Metaphysical Isolation," DAI, 35 (Calif., Santa Cruz: 1974), 1119A-20A.

2358 Pusey, William Webb, III. "William Faulkner's Works in Germany to 1940: Translations and Criticism," GR, 30 (1955), 211-226.

Important for study of German criticism. Notes that the translation of Light in August (1935) "marked the real beginning of Faulkner's critical fame in Germany."

2359 Reed, Joseph W., Jr. "Appendix B--Light in August: Progressive Cognition," Faulkner's Narrative. New Haven: Yale U.P., 1973, pp. 284-285.

2360 ______. "Light in August," Faulkner's Narrative. New Haven: 1973, pp. 112-144.

2361 Reirdon, Suzanne Renshaw. "An Application of Script Analysis to Four of William Faulkner's Women Characters," DAI, 35 (East Texas State: 1974), 4549-A.

2362 Rice, Julian C. "Orpheus and the Hellish Unity in Light in August," CentR, 19 (Winter, 1975), 380-396.

2363 Rice, Philip Blair. "The Art of William Faulkner," Nation, 138 (April 25, 1934), 478.

2364 Richardson, Kenneth E. Force and Faith in the Novels of William Faulkner. (Studies in American Literature, 7). The Hague: Mouton, 1967, pp. 163-171.

2365 "The Right Books for the Right People," Bookman, 75 (December, 1932), 799.

2366 Rinaldi, Nicholas M. "Game Imagery and Game-Consciousness in Faulkner's Fiction," TCL, 10 (October, 1964), 108-118.

2367 Riva, Arturo Sanchez. "William Faulkner: Luz de Agosto," Sur, 12 (November, 1942), 75-77.

2368 Roberts, Cecil. "Books," Sphere, 132, #1725 (February 11, 1933), 200. Review.

2369 Roberts, James L. "The Individual and the Community: Faulkner's Light in August," Studies in American Literature. Waldo F. McNeir, ed. (Louisiana State University Studies, Humanities Series, No. 8). Baton Rouge: Louisiana State U.P., 1960, pp. 132-153.

2370 ________. Light in August Notes. Lincoln: Cliff's Notes, 1964. Rev. ed., 1968.

2371 Robinson, Ted. "Squeamish Critics Cramp Style of Faulkner's New Novel, Light in August," Plain Dealer (Cleveland), (October 9, 1932), Amusement Sec., 11.

2372 Rolle, Andrew F., ed. "William Faulkner: An Inter-disciplinary Examination," MissQ, 11 (Fall, 1958), 157-159.

2373 Routh, Michael P. "The Story of All Things: Faulkner's Yoknapatawpha County Cosmology by Way of Light in August," DAI, 34 (Wisconsin, Madison: 1974), 6657A-58A.

2374 Rovere, Richard. "Faulkner's Light in August," New Leader (September 9, 1950), 22-24. Revised as Introduction to Modern Library Edition, 1950.

2375 ________. Introduction. Light in August. New York: Modern Library, 1950, pp. v-xiv.

2376 Rubin, Louis D., Jr. The Curious Death of the Novel: Essays in American Literature. Baton Rouge: Louisiana State U.P., 1967, pp. 131-151.

2377 ________. The Faraway Country: Writers of the Modern South. Seattle: Washington U.P., 1963, pp. 43-71.

2378 ________. "Notes on a Rear-Guard Action," The Idea of the South. Frank E. Vandiver, ed. Chicago: Chicago U.P., 1964, pp. 27-41.

2379 Ruppersburg, Hugh M. "Byron Bunch and Percy Grimm: Strange Twins of Light in August," MissQt, 30, #3 (Summer, 1977), 441-443.

2380 Sandstrom, Glenn. "Identity Diffusion: Joe Christmas and Quentin Compson," AQ, 19 (Summer, 1967), 207-223.

2381 Sans, Julien. [Lumière d'Août], Climats, (25 août 1948), 5.

2382 Sartre, Jean-Paul. Being and Nothingness: An Essay on Phenomenological Ontology. Tr. by Hazel E. Barnes. New York: Philosophical Library, 1956, pp. 405-406.
"Nobody has better portrayed the power of the victim's look at his torturers than Faulkner has done in the final pages of Light in August."

2383 Schatt, Stanley. "Faulkner's Thematic Use of Time in Light in August," CCTE, 36 (1971), 28-32.

2384 Scherg, Kurt. Klingsor, 13 (1936), 433. Review.

2385 Schlepper, Wolfgang. "Knowledge and Experience in Faulkner's Light in August," JA, 18 (1973), 182-194.

2386 Schönemann, Friedrich. Westermanns Monatsheste, 88 (1934), 71.

2387 Schriftgiesser, Karl. "Bright Spots Are Many Among the Season's Newest Books," Boston Evening Transcript (November 30, 1932), II, 1.

2388 Shanaghan, Malachy Michael. "A Critical Analysis of the Fictional Techniques of William Faulkner," DA, 20 (Notre Dame: 1960), 4663.

2389 Shapiro, Charles, ed. Twelve Original Essays. Detroit: Wayne State U. P., 1958, pp. 257-283.

2390 Shelton, Wilson E. "The Bookshelf," Beverly Hills Call-Bulletin (December 15, 1932).
Unfavorable Review.

2391 Sherwood, John C. "Thirty-Three" (poem). FS, 2 (Summer, 1953), 29.
A satiric poem on Faulkner's several Christ figures.

2392 Shipman, Evan. "Light in August, by William Faulkner," NR, 72 (October 26, 1932), 300-301.

2393 Slabey, Robert M. "Faulkner's Geography and Hightower House," AN&Q, 3 (February, 1965), 85-86.
Cf., Calvin S. Brown. "Faulkner's Geography and Topography," PMLA, 77 (December, 1962), 652-659.

2394 ________. "Joe Christmas: Faulkner's Marginal Man," Phylon, 21 (Fall, 1960), 266-277.
Joe Christmas's story is that of "a man trying to be human in the chaotic, mechanistic, violent modern world."

2395 ________. "Myth and Ritual in Light in August," TSLL, 2 (Autumn, 1960), 328-349.

2396 Slatoff, Walter J. "Light in August," Quest for Failure. Ithaca, New York: Cornell U. P., 1960, pp. 173-198.

2397 Smith, Don N. "The Design of Faulkner's Light in August: A Comprehensive Study," DAI, 31 (Michigan: 1970), 2402A.

2398 Smith, Hallet. "Summary of a Symposium on Light in August," MissQ, 11 (Fall, 1958), 188-190.

2399 Sowder, William J. "Christmas As Existentialist Hero," UR, 30 (June, 1964), 279-284.

2400 Spear, Karen Isabel. "Will and Body: Dualism in Light in August," DAI, 37 (American: 1976), 1557A.

2401 Stein, William Bysshe. "Walden: The Wisdom of the Centaur," Myth and Literature. John B. Vickery, ed. Lincoln: Nebraska U. P., 1966, p. 347.

2402 Steinberg, Aaron. "Faulkner and the Negro," DA, 27 (N. Y. U.: 1966), 1385A.

2403 Stephenson, Shelby Dean. "'You Smart Sheriffs and Such'--The Function of Local Peace Officers in Light in August and Intruder in the Dust," DAI, 35 (Wisconsin: 1974), 3012A.

2404 Sternberg, Meir. "The Compositional Principles of Faulkner's Light in August and the Poetics of the Modern Novel," Hasifrut, 2 (1970), 498-537.
In Hebrew.

2405 ________. "Temporal Ordering, Modes of Expositional Distribution, and Three Models of Rhetorical Control in the Narrative Text: Faulkner, Balzac, and Austen," PTL, 1 (1976), 295-316.
Light in August illustrates "primacy effect" in Faulkner's depiction of Joe Christmas.

2406 Stewart, Jean. ["Light in August"], CamR, 54 (March 10, 1933), 310-312. Review.

2407 Stewart, Randall. "Hawthorne and Faulkner," CE, 17 (February, 1956), 258-262.
Parallels between Joe Christmas and Dimmesdale.

2408 Stone, Geoffrey. "Keeping Up with the Novelists," Bookman, 75 (November, 1932), 736-738.
Unfavorable review.

2409 Straumann, Heinrich. William Faulkner. Frankfurt am Main: Athenäum Verlag, 1968, pp. 145-166.

2410 Strauss, Mary T. "The Fourteenth View: A Study of Ambiguity in William Faulkner's Light in August," DAI, 31 (Pittsburgh: 1970), 6074A.

2411 Strong, L. A. G. "Light in August," Spectator, #5460 (February 17, 1933), 226.

2412 Sullivan, William P. "William Faulkner and the Community," DA, 22 (Columbia: 1962), 4355.

2413 Swan, Addie May. "Mr. Faulkner's New Novel Shows Surer Technique," Daily Times (Davenport, Iowa), (October 22, 1932), 3. Review.

2414 Swiggart, Peter. "The Puritan Sinner: Light in August," The Art of Faulkner's Novels. Austin: Texas U. P., 1962, pp. 131-148.

2415 _______. "Time in Faulkner's Novels," MFS, 1 (May, 1955), 25-29.

2416 Tanaka, Hisao. "The Significance of the Past for Gail Hightower: One Aspect of Light in August," SALit, 8 (1972), 24-38.

2417 Taylor, Walter. "Faulkner: Social Commitment and the Artistic Temperament," SoR, 6 (October, 1970), 1075-1092.

2418 _______. "Faulkner's Curse," ArQ, 28 (Winter, 1972), 333-338.

Notes that Faulkner said in an interview that the "curse is slavery." The "curse" becomes important in certain works such as Light in August.

2419 Thompson, David J. S. "Societal Definitions of Individualism and the Critique of Egotism As a Major Theme in American Fiction," DAI, 33 (Brown: 1973), 4435A.

2420 Thompson, Frederic. "American Decadence," CW, 17 (November 30, 1932), 139.

A theological reading of the novel as catharsis.

2421 Thompson, Lawrance. ["The Unity of Light in August"], William Faulkner: An Introduction and Interpretation. 2nd ed. New York: Holt, Rinehart & Winston, 1967, pp. 84-85.

2422 TLS, #1620 (February 16, 1933), 106. Review.

2423 Tomlinson, T. B. "Faulkner and American Sophistication," MCR, 7 (1964), 92-103.

2423 Tomlinson, T. B. "Faulkner and American Sophistication," MCR, 7 (1964), 92-103.

2424 Tritschler, Donald H. "The Unity of Faulkner's Shaping Vision," MFS, 5 (Winter, 1959-1960), 337-343.
In Light in August sees violence as a method through which meaning is expressed.

2425 ________. "Whorls of Form in Faulkner's Fiction," DA, 17 (Northwestern: 1957), 3025.

2426 Tuck, Dorothy. Crowell's Handbook of Faulkner. New York: Crowell, 1964, pp. 46-55.

2427 ________. "Faulkner, Light in August: The Inwardness of the Understanding," Approaches to the Twentieth Century Novel. John Unterecker, ed. New York: Crowell, 1965, pp. 79-107.

2428 Tyler, Parker. "Book Reviews," The New Act, No. 1 (January, 1933), 36-39.
Unfavorable review.

2429 Uchino, Takako. "The Pattern and Devices in Light in August," Maekawa Shunichi Kyoju Kaureki Kinen-Ronbunshu [Essays and Studies in Commemoration of Prof. Shunichi Maekawa's Sixty-First Birthday]. Tokyo: Eihosha, 1968, pp. 155-163.

2430 Van Doren, Dorothy. "More Light Needed," Nation 135 (October 26, 1932), 402.

2431 Van Vuren, Floyd. "William Faulkner Attains New Maturity in 'Light in August,'" Milwaukee Journal (October 8, 1932), 4.

2432 Vickery, John B., and Olga W. Vickery, eds. Light in August and the Critical Spectrum. Belmont, California: Wadsworth Pub., 1971.

2433 Vickery, Olga W. "Gavin Stevens: From Rhetoric to Dialectic," FS, 2 (Spring, 1953), 1-4.

2434 ________. The Novels of William Faulkner: A Critical Interpretation. Rev. Ed. Baton Rouge: Louisiana State U.P., 1964, pp. 66-83.

2435 ________. "The Shadow and the Mirror: Light in August," Twentieth Century Interpretations of Light in August. David L. Minter, ed. Englewood Cliffs, New Jersey: Prentice-Hall, 1969, pp. 25-41.

2436 Vittorini, Elio, tr. Luce d'agosto. Milan: Arnoldo Mondadori Editore, 1968.

2437 Volpe, Edmond L. A Reader's Guide to William Faulkner. New York: Farrar, Straus, 1964, pp. 151-174.

2438 Von Heiseler, Bernt. ["Light in August"], Deutsche Zeitschrift, 49 (1936), 468-469.

2439 Waggoner, Hyatt H. "Light in August: Outrage and Compassion," William Faulkner: From Jefferson to the World. Lexington: Kentucky U.P., 1959, pp. 100-120. Excerpt in Religious Perspectives in Faulkner's Fiction. J. R. Barth, ed. Notre Dame: Notre Dame U.P., 1972, pp. 121-137.

2440 Wagner, Linda W. "Faulkner's Fiction: Studies in Organic Form," JNT, 1 (January, 1971), 1-14.

2441 Warren, Robert Penn. "Cowley's Faulkner," NR, 115 (August 12, 1946), 176-180; (August 26, 1946), 234-237. Repr., in Two Decades, pp. 82-101; Three Decades, Frederick Hoffman and Olga Vickery, eds. East Lansing: Michigan State U.P., 1960, pp. 109-124.

2442 _______. "Faulkner: The South, the Negro, and Time," SoR, 1, n.s., (July, 1965), 501-529; repr., Faulkner: A Collection of Critical Essays. Englewood Cliffs, New Jersey: Prentice-Hall, 1966, pp. 251-271.

2443 Waters, Maureen Anne. The Role of Women in Faulkner's Yoknapatawpha. Diss. Columbia: 1975.

2444 Watkins, Floyd C. "Faulkner and the Critics," TSLL, 10 (Summer, 1968), 317-329.
Enumeration of textual and factual errors by critics in their reference to Light in August and other novels.

2445 _______. "Language of Irony: Quiet Words and Violent Acts in Light in August," The Flesh and the Word. Nashville: Vanderbilt U.P., 1971, pp. 203-215.

2446 Weeks, Edward. "Atlantic Bookshelf--Light in August," Atl, 151 (January, 1933), 10. Review.

2447 Weisgerber, Jean. Faulkner et Dostoievski: Confluences et influences. Universitê Libre de Bruxelles, Travaux de la Facultê de Philosophie et Lettres, Tome 39. Bruxelles: Presses Universitaires de Bruxelles, 1968, pp. 175-188.
Draws parallels between Christmas and Dostoievski's Raskolnikov in their limited freedom.

2448 _______. "Faulkner's Monomaniacs: Their Indebtedness to Raskolnikov," CLS, 5 (June, 1968), 181-193.

2449 West, Ray B. "Faulkner's Light in August: A View of Tragedy," WSCL, 1, i (Winter, 1960), 5-12.

2450 ________. "Faulkner's *Light in August*: A View of Tragedy," *The Writer in the Room: Selected Essays*. East Lansing: Michigan State U.P., 1968, pp. 175-184.

2451 Whatley, John Thomas. "A Topographical Study of Thomas Hardy and William Faulkner," DAI, 39 (Yale: 1978), 2266A-67A.

2452 Wheeler, Sally P. "Chronology in *Light in August*," SLJ, 6 (Fall, 1973), 20-42.
The chronology reveals Faulkner's use of time.

2453 Widmer, Kingsley. "Naturalism and the American Joe," *The Literary Rebel*. Carbondale: Southern Illinois U.P., 1965, pp. 118-120.

2454 Williams, John S. "'The Final Copper Light of Afternoon': Hightower's Redemption," TCL, 13 (January, 1968), 205-215.

2455 Williams, Sidney. "Wm. Faulkner Laboring in the Deep, Dark South," Inquirer (Philadelphia), (October 8, 1932), 12.
Unfavorable review.

2456 Willson, Robert H. "*Light in August*," Chicago Herald and Examiner (October 8, 1932), 7.
Unfavorable review.

2457 Wilson, Robert Rawdon. "The Pattern of Thought in *Light in August*," BRMMLA, 24 (December, 1970), 155-161.

2458 Woodworth, Stanley D. *William Faulkner en France (1931-1952)*. Paris: M. J. Minard, 1959.

2459 Wynne, Carolyn. "Aspects of Space: John Marin and William Faulkner," AQ, 16 (Spring, 1964), 59-71.
The paintings of John Marin and Faulkner's *Light in August* as examples of the modern concept of space.

2460 Yorks, Samuel A. "Faulkner's Woman: The Peril of Mankind," ArQ, 17 (Summer, 1961), 119-129.

2461 Yoshizaki, Yasuhiro. "The Unified Plot of *Light in August*," *Maekawa Shunichi Kyoju Kaureki Kinen-Ronbunshu [Essays and Stüdies in Commemoration of Prof. Shunichi Maekawa's Sixty-First Birthday]*. Tokyo: Eihosha, 1968, pp. 217-228.
In Japanese.

2462 Young, Glenn. "Struggle and Triumph in *Light in August*," STC, 15 (Spring, 1975), 33-50.

2463 Zindel, Edith. *William Faulkner in den deutschsprachigen Ländern Europas: Untersuchungen zur Aufnahme seiner Werke nach 1945*. Hamburg: Harmut Lüdke Verlag, 1972.

Rev., by Andre Bleikasten, MissQ, 27 (Summer, 1974), 353-356.

2464 Zink, Karl E. "Faulkner's Garden: Woman and the Immemorial Earth," MFS, 2 (Autumn, 1956), 139-149.

2465 ________. "La Femme et la terre immêmoriale," RLM, Part I, Nos. 27-29 (1957), 131-153.

2466 ________. "Flux and the Frozen Moment: The Imagery of Stasis in Faulkner's Prose," PMLA, 71 (June, 1956), 285-301.

2467 ________. "William Faulkner: Form As Experience," SAQ, 53 (July, 1954), 384-403.
Analysis of Faulkner's "technique of accretion," as well as other devices.

"LION"
(Published in Harper's, 172 (December, 1935), 67-77; greatly revised and expanded for Chapter 5, "The Bear," in Go Down, Moses.)

2468 Grenier, Cynthia. "An Interview with William Faulkner," Accent, 16 (Summer, 1956), 174.

2469 Meriwether, James B. "The Short Fiction of William Faulkner," Proof, 1 (1971), 303.

2470 O'Connor, William Van. "The Wilderness Theme in Faulkner's 'The Bear,'" Accent, 13 (Winter, 1953), 17-18; repr., in The Tangled Fire of William Faulkner. Minneapolis: Minnesota U.P., 1954, pp. 131-132.

2471 Rouberol, Jean. "Les Indiens dans l'oeuvre de Faulkner," EA, 26 (March, 1973), 54-58.

"LIZARDS IN JAMSHYD'S COURTYARD"
(Sat. Eve. Post, 204 (1932), passim; extensively revised and incorporated in The Hamlet. See The Hamlet under THE SNOPES TRILOGY.

"LO!"
("Lo!" Story, 5 (November, 1934), 5-21; repr. in Collected Stories, 1950)

2472 Bradford, Melvin E. "Faulkner and the Great White Father," LaS, 3 (Winter, 1964), 323-329.
"Lo!" suggests that the non-acquisitive Indian culture may be more civilized than the white culture.

2473 Dabney, Lewis M. "Lo!" The Indians of Yoknapatawpha. Baton Rouge: Louisiana State U.P., 1974, pp. 43-56.

2474 Howell, Elmo. "William Faulkner and the Mississippi Indians," GaR, 21 (December, 1967), 386-396.

2475 Langford, Beverly Y. "History and Legend in William Faulkner's 'Red Leaves,'" NMW, 6 (Spring, 1973), 19-24.
Finds historical evidence for the existence of Chief Tobbatubby, possibly a partial model for Faulkner's Chickasaw chiefs.

2476 Meriwether, James B. "The Short Fiction of William Faulkner," Proof, 1 (1971), 303.

2477 Rouberol, Jean. "Les Indiens dans l'oeuvre de Faulkner," EA, 26 (March, 1973), 54-58.

"MARIONETTES"
(Cf., James B. Meriwether, #2482 below)

2478 Collins, Carvel. "Faulkner at the University of Mississippi" in William Faulkner: Early Prose and Poetry. Boston: Little, Brown, 1962, pp. 11-13.

2479 "Faulkner Rarity Comes Home," Kansas City Times, 107, #241 (June 16, 1975), 2A.
Purchase by Howard Duvall and Don Newcombe of a fourth copy of "Marionettes," one of six handwritten and illustrated books by William Faulkner.

2480 Kibler, James E., Jr. "William Faulkner and Provincetown Drama, 1920-1922," MissQ, 22 (Summer, 1969), 226-236.
Edna St. Vincent Millay's play, Aria da Capo, as possible source for Faulkner's play.

2481 Leary, Lewis. "Marionettes," William Faulkner of Yoknapatawpha County. New York: Crowell, 1973, p. 9.

2482 Meriwether, James B. "Marionettes," The Literary Career of William Faulkner. Princeton: 1961; Columbia, South Carolina: 1971, pp. 8-9.

2483 Millgate, Michael. The Achievement of William Faulkner. New York: Random House, 1966, pp. 8-9.

2484 Polk, Noel, ed. Introduction. The Marionettes. Charlottesville: Virginia U.P., 1977.

2485 ________. "William Faulkner's 'Marionettes,'" MissQ, 26 (Summer, 1973), 247-280.

The play "of interest to Faulknerians both for the portrait it paints of Faulkner the artist and this very early point in his career...."

2486 _______. "William Faulkner's _Marionettes_," _A Faulkner Miscellany_. James B. Meriwether, ed. Jackson, Miss.: Miss. U.P., 1974, pp. 3-36.

2487 Richardson, H. Edward. "Marionettes," _William Faulkner: The Journey to Self Discovery_. Columbia: Missouri U.P., 1970, _passim_.

2488 Wasson, Ben. "Memories of Marionettes," Oxford, Miss.: Yoknapatawpha Press, 1975. [A limited facsimile edition with Wasson's essay.]

"MISS ZILPHIA GANT"
(Cf., James B. Meriwether, #2489 below)

2489 Meriwether, James B. _The Literary Career of William Faulkner_. Columbia: South Carolina U.P., 1971, pp. 173-174.

2490 _______. "William Faulkner: A Checklist," PULC, 18 (Spring, 1957), 148.

2491 Morell, Giliane. "Prisoners of the Inner World: Mother and Daughter in _Miss Zilphia Gant_," MissQ, 28 (Summer, 1975), 299-305.

2492 O'Connor, William Van. _The Tangled Fire of William Faulkner_. Minneapolis: Minnesota U.P., 1954, pp. 70-71.

2493 Pitavy, François L. "A Forgotten Faulkner Story: 'Miss Zilphia Gant,'" SSF, 9 (Spring, 1972), 131-142.
Finds the story important, not only for itself, but "as a stage in an exploration that culminated in _Light in August_."

2494 Pivano, Fernanda. Preface. _La pallida Zilphia_. Milano: Il Saggiatore, 1959.

2495 Smith, Henry. Preface. _Miss Zilphia Gant_ by William Faulkner. Dallas: The Book Club of Texas, 1932, vii-xi.

2496 Tinkle, Lon. "Faulkner for $325," Dallas Morning News (May 19, 1963), Sec. VII, 2.
Henry Nash Smith and "Miss Zilphia Gant."

"MISTRAL"
(Sat. Eve. Post, June, 1930; Scribner's July 3, 1930; These 13, 1931; Collected Stories, 1950)

2497 Clark, Charles C. "'Mistral': A Study in Human Tempering," MissQ, 21 (Summer, 1968), 195-204.

2498 Meriwether, James B. "The Short Fiction of William Faulkner," Proof, 1 (1971), 304.

2499 O'Connor, William Van. The Tangled Fire of William Faulkner. Minneapolis: Minnesota U.P., 1954, p. 70.

2500 Shepherd, Allen. "Hemingway's An Alpine Idyll and Faulkner's 'Mistral,'" UPortR, 25 (Fall, 1973), 63-68.

"MONK"
(Scribner's, 101 (1937); repr., in Knight's Gambit, 1949)

2501 Guerard, Albert. "Justice in Yoknapatawpha County: Some Symbolic Motifs in Faulkner's Later Writing," FS, 2 (Winter, 1954), 50-52.

2502 Meriwether, James B. "The Short Fiction of William Faulkner: A Bibliography," Proof, 1 (1971), 304.

2503 O'Connor, William Van. The Tangled Fire of William Faulkner. Minneapolis: Minnesota U.P., 1954, pp. 143-144.

MOSQUITOES
(New York: Boni & Liveright, 1927)

2504 Adams, Richard P. Faulkner: Myth and Motion. Princeton: Princeton U.P., 1968, pp. 40-49.

2505 Aiken, Conrad. "Mosquitoes," NYPost (June 11, 1927), 7; repr., Reviewer's ABC. New York: Meridian Press, 1958, pp. 197-207.

2506 Allen, Walter Ernest. "Literary Letter from London," NYTBR (November 15, 1964), 54.
Cf., Richard Hughes. Introduction. Mosquitoes. London: Chatto and Windus, 1964.

2507 Anon. BCLF (novembre, 1948), 788. Review.

2508 Anon. Boston Transcript (July 2, 1927), 8. Review.

2509 Anon. "Faulkner Discourses on Subject of Bores," Milwaukee Journal (June 4, 1927), 3.

2510 Anon. "A Faulknerian Gnat-Bite," TLS (October 22, 1964), 953.

2511 Anon. "Mosquitoes," SatRL, 3 (June 25, 1927), 933.

2512 Anon. "Mosquitoes," Boston Evening Transcript (July 2, 1927), VI, 8.

2513 Anon. Springfield Republican (July 17, 1927), 7. Review.

2514 Arnold, Edwin T., III. "Faulkner and Huxley: A Note on Mosquitoes and Crome Yellow," MissQt, 30, #3 (Summer, 1977), 433-436.
Faulkner's indebtedness to Huxley.

2515 ________. "Freedom and Stasis in Faulkner's Mosquitoes," MissQ, 28 (Summer, 1975), 281-297.

2516 ________. "William Faulkner's Mosquitoes: An Introduction and Annotations to the Novel," DAI, 39 (South Carolina U: 1978), 6125A.

2517 Blanc-Dufour, A. CS, 290 (1948), 185. Review.

2518 Brooks, Cleanth. "Faulkner's Mosquitoes," GaR, 31 (Spring, 1977), 213-234.

2519 Broughton, Panthea Reid. William Faulkner: The Abstract and the Actual. Baton Rouge: Louisiana State U.P., 1974, pp. 25-27, 28-29, 31.

2520 Brylowski, Walter. "The Early Novels--Mosquitoes," Faulkner's Olympian Laugh: Myth in the Novels. Detroit: Wayne State U.P., 1968, pp. 48-51.

2521 C., M. ["Mosquitoes"], LF (19 aôut 1948), 4. Review.

2522 Carey, Glenn O. "Faulkner and Mosquitoes: Writing Himself and His Age," RS, 39 (1971), 271-283.

2523 Cargill, Oscar. "The Primitivists," Intellectual America. New York: Macmillan, 1941, pp. 370-386.

2524 Carnes, Frank F. "On the Aesthetics of Faulkner's Fiction," DA, 29 (Vanderbilt: 1968), 894A-95A.

2525 Cooley, Thomas W. "Faulkner Draws the Long Bow," TCL, 16 (October, 1970), 268-277.

2526 Côrdoba, Jerônimo, tr. Mosquitos. Buenos Aires: Siglo Veinte, 1956.

2527 Daniel, Robert W. "Mosquitoes," A Catalogue of the Writings of William Faulkner. New Haven: Yale U.P., 1942, p. 9.

2528 Davidson, Donald. "The Grotesque," Nashville Tennessean (July 3, 1927), Mag. Sec., 7; repr., in GaR, 20 (Winter, 1966), 458-459.

2529 Desgroupes, Pierre, tr. Moustiques. Paris: Les Éditions de Minuit, 1948.

2530/31 Dunlap, Mary M. "Sex and the Artist in Mosquitoes," MissQ, 22 (Summer, 1969), 190-206.
Shows how Faulkner correlates the sexual with artistic vitality and normality.

2532 Everett, Walter K. Faulkner's Art and Characters. Woodbury, New York: Barrons Educational Series, 1969, pp. 57-65.

2533 Forestier, M. RN (15 janvier 1949), 110. Review.

2534 Franklin, Phyllis. "The Influence of Joseph Hergesheimer upon Mosquitoes," MissQ, 22 (Summer, 1969), 207-213.

2535 Fuller, John. "Novel of the Twenties," NSt (November 27, 1964), 844.

2536 Geismar, Maxwell. "William Faulkner: The Negro and the Female," Writers in Crisis. Boston: Houghton-Mifflin, 1942, pp. 148-150.

2537 Gidley, Mick. "Some Notes on Faulkner's Reading," JAmS, 4 (1970), 91-102.
The possible influence on Mosquitoes of Aldous Huxley's Crome Yellow.

2538 Gold, Joseph. "William Faulkner's 'One Compact Thing,'" TCL, 8 (April, 1962), 3-4.

2539 Gwynn, Frederic L. "Faulkner's Prufrock--and Other Observations," JEGP, 52 (January, 1953), 63-70.
Asserts that Talliaferro in Mosquitoes is modeled on Eliot's Prufrock.

2540 Haight, Ann Lyon. Banned Books. New York: 2nd ed. rev. Bowker, 1955, p. 77.
Account of 1948 raid in Philadelphia in which titles seized included Mosquitoes, Sanctuary and Wild Palms.

2541 Harwick, Robert Duane. "Humor in the Novels of William Faulkner," DA, 26 (Nebraska: 1965), 1646.

2542 Hellman, Lillian F. "Futile Souls Adrift on a Yacht," NYHTB (June 19, 1927), 9.

2543 Hepburn, Kenneth W. "Faulkner's Mosquitoes: A Poetic

Turning Point," TCL, 17 (January, 1971), 19-28.
Believes "that the pivotal point of Faulkner's career is not the somewhat acclaimed Sartoris, but the much disparaged Mosquitoes."

2544 Hoffman, Frederick J. William Faulkner. Twayne's United States Authors Series. New York: Twayne, 1961, 2nd ed., 1966, pp. 42-44.

2545 Hughes, Richard. "Faulkner and Bennett," Encounter, 21, # 3 (September, 1963), 59-61.

2546 ________. Introduction. Mosquitoes. London: Chatto and Windus, 1964.

2547 Kemp, Robert. [Mosquitoes], NL (2 septembre 1948), 2.

2548 Kirk, Robert W., and Marvin Klotz. Faulkner's People. Berkeley: California U.P., 1963, pp. 10-15.

2549 Kreiswirth, Martin. "William Faulkner and Siegfried Sasson: An Allusion in Mosquitoes," MissQ, 29, # 3 (Summer, 1976), 433-434.

2550 Lambert, J. W. "A Ship of Southern Fools," Sunday Times (London), (November 1, 1964), 50.

2551 Lloyd, James Barlow. "Humours Characterization and the Tradition of the Jonsonian Comedy of Manners in William Faulkner's Early Fiction: New Orleans Sketches, Soldiers' Pay, and Mosquitoes," DAI, 36 (Mississippi: 1975), 4493A.

2552 McClure, John. "Literature and Less," Times-Picayune (New Orleans), (July 3, 1927), Sunday Mag. Sec., 4.

2553 McGinnis, John H. "The Southern Novelists Also Produce Literature of Revolt," Dallas Morning News (May 15, 1927), III, 3.

2554 Macmillan, Duane J. "The Non-Yoknapatawpha Novels of William Faulkner: An Examination of Soldier's Pay, Mosquitoes, the Wild Palms, Pylon, and A Fable," DAI, 32 (Wisconsin: 1972), 6986A.

2555 Malin, Irving. William Faulkner: An Interpretation. Stanford U.P., 1957, pp. 32-33.

2556 Meriwether, James B. "Mosquitoes," The Literary Career of William Faulkner. Columbia: South Carolina U.P., 1971, p. 12.

2557 Millgate, Michael. "Mosquitoes," The Achievement of William Faulkner. New York: Random House, 1965, pp. 68-75.

2558 ________. "Mosquitoes," William Faulkner. New York: Grove Press, 1961, revised, 1966; repr., Capricorn Bks., 1971, passim.

2559 Monteiro, George. "Fugitive Comments on Early Faulkner," NMQ, 10 (Winter, 1977), 95-96.
Comments on Faulkner's first two novels, Mosquitoes and Soldiers' Pay.

2560 O'Connor, William Van. The Tangled Fire of William Faulkner. Minneapolis: Minnesota U.P., 1954, pp. 30-33, 160.

2561 Paz, M. Paru (octobre 1948), 42-43. Review.

2562 Price, R. G. G. "New Novels," Punch (November 18, 1964), 784. Review.

2563 Queneau, Raymond. Présenté. Moustiques. Paris: Les Éditions de Minuit, 1948.

2564 Quigly, Isabel. "Doomed Town," Sunday Telegraph (London), (October 25, 1964), 21. Review.

2565 Richardson, H. Edward. "Faulkner, Anderson, and Their Tall Tale," AL, 34 (May, 1962), 287-291.
Cf., W. B. Rideout and J. B. Meriwether. "On the Collaboration of Faulkner and Anderson," AL, 35 (March, 1963), 85-87.

2566 ________. William Faulkner: The Journey to Self-Discovery. Columbia: Missouri U.P., 1969, pp. 134-138.

2567 Rideout, W. B., and J. B. Meriwether. "On the Collaboration of Faulkner and Anderson," AL, 35 (March, 1963), 85-87.
Cf., H. Edward Richardson. "Anderson and Faulkner," AL, 36 (November, 1964), 298-314; and "Faulkner, Anderson, and Their Tall Tale," AL, 34 (May, 1962), 287-291.

2568 Roberts, James L. "Experimental Exercises--Faulkner's Early Writings," Discourse, 6 (Summer, 1963), 191-196.

2569 Séchan, O. [Mosquitoes], NL (8 juillet 1948), 3. Review.
"... le plus grand, le plus puissant, le plus original."

2570 Slabey, Robert M. "Faulkner's Mosquitoes and Joyce's Ulysses," RLV, 28 (September-October, 1962), 435-437.
Influence of Joyce discernible in certain episodes of Mosquitoes. Cf., Joyce W. Warren. "Faulkner's 'Portrait of the Artist,'" MassQ, 19 (Summer, 1966), 121-131.

2571 Smart, George K. "A Selective Concordance: Mosquitoes ...," Religious Elements in Faulkner's Early Novels. Coral Gables, Florida: Miami U.P., 1965.

2572 Stein, Randolph Edward. "The World Outside Yoknapatawpha: A Study of Five Novels by William Faulkner," DA, 26 (Ohio: 1965), 2225.

2573 Stojanović, Jelena, tr. Snobovi, roman. Beograd: Minerva, 1962. Croatian translation.

2574 Suckow, Ruth. "South Wind Blows But Fitfully," NYWorld (June 12, 1927), 7-M.

2575 Tuck, Dorothy. Crowell's Handbook of Faulkner. New York: Crowell, 1964, pp. 129-131.

2576 Vickery, Olga W. "The Apprenticeship: Soldiers' Pay and Mosquitoes," The Novels of William Faulkner. Baton Rouge: Louisiana State U. P., 1964, pp. 1-14.

2577 _______. Faulkner's Mosquitoes," UKCR, 24 (Spring, 1958), 219-224. Repr., in The Novels of William Faulkner (1959), pp. 8-14.

2578 Volpe, Edmond L. A Reader's Guide to William Faulkner. New York: Noonday Press, 1964, pp. 56-66.

2579 Waggoner, Hyatt H. William Faulkner: From Jefferson to the World. Lexington: Kentucky U. P., 1959, pp. 8-19.

2580 Wall, Stephen. "New Fiction," Listener (October 22, 1964), 637.

2581 Wardle, Irving. "Faulkner in Fancy Dress," Observer (London), (October 25, 1964), 27. Review.

2582 Warren, Joyce W. "Faulkner's 'Portrait of the Artist,'" MissQ, 19 (Summer, 1966), 121-131.

2583 Watkins, Floyd C. "The Unbearable and Unknowable Truth in Faulkner's First Three Novels," The Flesh and the Word. Nashville, Tennessee: Vanderbilt U. P., 1971, pp. 169-180.

2584 Wilson, James Southall. "The Changing Novel," VQR, 10 (January, 1934), 42-52.
Notes that Mosquitoes was banned in Boston.

2585 W[ylie], E[linor] H. "Mosquitoes," NR, (July 20, 1927), 236.

"MOUNTAIN VICTORY"

("A Mountain Victory," Sat. Eve. Post, 205 (1932), passim; revised, entitled "Mountain Victory," in Doctor Martino, 1934, and repr., in Collected Stories, 1950)

2586 Hennecke, Hans, tr. Sieg in den Bergen. München, A. Langen, G. Muller, 1956.

2587 Howe, Irving. "A Note on the Stories--'Mountain Victory,'" William Faulkner: A Critical Study. New York: Vintage, 1952, p. 264.

2588 Howell, Elmo. "William Faulkner and Tennessee," THQ, 21 (September, 1962), 251-262.
Particular attention given to "Mountain Victory."

2589 Knieger, Bernard. "Faulkner's 'Mountain Victory,' 'Doctor Martino,' and 'There Was a Queen,'" Expl, 30 (February, 1972), Item 45.
Disagreement with plot summaries.

2590 Leary, Lewis. "Mountain Victory," William Faulkner of Yoknapatawpha County. New York: Crowell, 1973, pp. 136-137.

2591 Meriwether, James B. "'Mountain Victory,' The Short Fiction of William Faulkner," Proof, 1 (1971), 304.

2592 O'Connor, William Van. The Tangled Fire of William Faulkner. Minneapolis: Minnesota U.P., 1954, p. 89.

2593 Reed, Joseph W., Jr. "Mountain Victory," Faulkner's Narrative. New Haven: Yale U.P., 1973, p. 183.

2594 Tuck, Dorothy. Crowell's Handbook of Faulkner. New York: Crowell, 1964, pp. 158, 159, 171.
Cf., Bernard Knieger. "Faulkner's 'Mountain Victory' ...," Expl, 30 (1972), Item 45.

"MR. ACARIUS"--See under "WEEKEND REVISITED")

"MULE IN THE YARD"
(Scribner's, 96 (1934); repr., Collected Stories, 1950)

2595 Casty, Alan. "Mule in the Yard," The Shape of Fiction. Boston: Heath, 1967, pp. 5-6.
Teaching suggestions.

2596 Leary, Lewis. "Mule in the Yard," William Faulkner of Yoknapatawpha County. New York: Crowell, 1973, p. 163.

2597 Meriwether, James B. "The Short Fiction of William Faulkner," Proof, 1 (1971), 304-305.

2598 Page, Sally R. "Mule in the Yard," Faulkner's Women: Characters and Meaning. DeLand, Florida: Everett/Edwards, 1972, p. 165.

2599 Reed, Joseph W., Jr. "Mule in the Yard," Faulkner's Narrative. New Haven: Yale U.P., 1973, pp. 49-50, 218-219, passim.

"MY GRANDMOTHER MILLARD AND GENERAL BEDFORD FORREST AND THE BATTLE OF HARRYKIN CREEK"
(Story, 22 (1943); Collected Stories, 1950)

2600 Howell, Elmo. "William Faulkner's General Forrest and the Uses of History," THQ, 29 (Fall, 1970), 287-294.
Treats Faulkner's depiction of General Forrest in the story.

2601 Longley, John L., Jr. The Tragic Mask: A Study of Faulkner's Heroes. Chapel Hill: North Carolina U.P., 1963, pp. 110-114.

2602 Meriwether, James B. "The Short Fiction of William Faulkner," Proof, 1 (1971), 305.

2603 Millgate, Michael. The Achievement of William Faulkner. New York: Random House, 1966, pp. 273, 274.

2604 Reed, Joseph W., Jr. Faulkner's Narrative. New Haven: Yale U.P., 1973, p. 183.

"A NAME FOR THE CITY"
(Harper's, 201 (1950). Revised, entitled "The Courthouse (A Name for the City)," as narrative prologue to Act I of Requiem for a Nun, 1951.)

2605 Millgate, Michael. The Achievement of William Faulkner. New York: Random House, 1966, pp. 224, 329.

"NOTES ON A HORSE THIEF"
(Greenville, Miss.: Levee Press, 1951; revised and repr., in A Fable, 1954)

2606 Bond, Adrienne. "Eneas Africanus and Faulkner's Fabulous Racehorse," SLJ, 9 (Spring, 1977), 3-15.

2607 Calvert, Elizabeth. Decorations. Notes on a Horsethief. Greenville, Miss.: Levee Press, 1950.

2608 Collins, Carvel. Review. NYHTBR (February 25, 1951), 8.

2609 Hutten, Robert W. "A Major Revision in Faulkner's A Fable," AL, 45 (May, 1973), 297-299.
The climactic speech in "Notes on a Horse Thief" is assigned to a different speaker in the material transferred to A Fable.

2610 Meriwether, James B. "The Short Fiction of William Faulkner," Proof, 1 (1971), 306.

2611 Millgate, Michael. "Notes on a Horsethief," The Achievement of William Faulkner. New York: Random House, 1966, pp. 49, 230.

2612 O'Connor, William Van. The Tangled Fire of William Faulkner. Minneapolis: 1954, p. 153f.

2613 Poore, Charles. NYT (February 8, 1951), 31.

"AN ODOR OF VERBENA"--See THE UNVANQUISHED

"THE OLD MAN"--See also under THE WILD PALMS

2614 Braem, Helmut M., and Elizabeth Kaiser, trs. Der Strom; Roman. Frankfurt a. M. und Hamburg: Fischer Bücherel, 1961.

2615 Broughton, Panthea Reid. ["The Old Man"], William Faulkner: The Abstract and the Actual. Baton Rouge: La. St. U.P., 1974, pp. 42-43, 44, 172.

2616 Feaster, John. "Faulkner's 'Old Man,': A Psychoanalytic Approach," MFS, 13 (Spring, 1967), 89-93.
Suggests that the convict voluntarily returns to prison as a womb-substitute.

2617 Greenberg, Alvin. "Shaggy Dog in Mississippi," SFQ, 29 (1965), 284-287.

2618 Hamalian, Leon, and Edmond L. Volpe. Eleven Modern Short Novels. New York: Putnam's, 1958, pp. 534-538.

2619 Howe, Irving. William Faulkner: A Critical Study. New York: 2nd ed. Vintage, 1962.
Notes parallels between "The Old Man" and The Wild Palms.

2620 Howell, Elmo. "William Faulkner and the Plain People of Yoknapatawpha County," JMissH, 24 (April, 1962), 73-87.

2621 Jewkes, W. T. "Counterpoint in Faulkner's Wild Palms," WSCL, 2 (Winter, 1961), 39-53.
In "The Old Man" and Wild Palms, Faulkner develops complementary issues and emphases.

2622 McElroy, Davis Dunbar. Existentialism and Modern Literature. New York: Greenwood Press, 1968, pp. 24-25.

2623 Mair, John. "New Novels," NS&N (March 18, 1939), 427. Review.

2624 Merton, Thomas. "'Baptism in the Forest': Wisdom and Initiation in William Faulkner," CathW, 207 (June, 1968), 124-130; repr., Mansions of the Spirit. George A. Panichas, ed. New York: Hawthorn, 1967, pp. 17-44.

2625 Miller, James E., and Bernice Slote. Instructor's Manual to The Dimensions of the Short Story. New York: Dodd, Mead, 1964.

2626 Moses, W. R. "Water, Water Everywhere: 'Old Man' and A Farewell to Arms," MFS, 5 (Summer, 1959), 172-174.

2627 Rama Roa, P. G. "Faulkner's 'Old Man': A Critique," IJAS, 1, iv (1971), 43-50.

2628 Rascoe, Lavon. "An Interview with Faulkner," WR, 15 (Summer, 1951), 300-304.

2629 Rebelo, Sousa. Tr. e prefacio. O homem e o rio. Lisboa: Portugalia editors, 1960(?).

2630 Reed, John Q. "Theme and Symbol in Faulkner's 'Old Man,'" EdL, 21 (January, 1958), 25-31.

2631 Richardson, H. Edward. William Faulkner: The Journey to Self Discovery. Columbia: Missouri U.P., 1969, pp. 15, 96.

2632 Springer, Mary Doyle. "Devices of Old Man," Forms of the Modern Novella. Chicago: Chicago U.P., 1975, pp. 37-39, passim.

2633 Stonesifer, Richard J. "Faulkner's 'Old Man' in the Classroom," CE, 17 (February, 1956), 254-257.

2634 Taylor, Nancy Dew. "The River of Faulkner and Mark Twain," MissQ, 16 (Fall, 1963), 191-199.
The Huck Finn influence is examined in relation to "The Old Man."

2635 Tuck, Dorothy. Crowell's Handbook of Faulkner. New York: Crowell, 1964, pp. 137-142.

2636 Vandenbergh, John, tr. De oude man. Hasselt: Uitgeverij Heideland, 1962.

2637 Waggoner, Hyatt H. William Faulkner: From Jefferson to the World. Lexington: Kentucky U.P., 1959, pp. 201-206, 211.

"THE OLD PEOPLE"
(Harper's, 181 (1940); Revised for Go Down, Moses, 1942, and repr., in Big Woods, 1955)

2638 Adamowski, T. H. "Isaac McCaslin and the Wilderness of the Imagination," CentR, 17 (1973), 92-112.

2639 Brown, Calvin S. "Faulkner's Use of the Oral Tradition," GaR, 22 (Summer, 1968), 160-169.
Faulkner's debt to the oral tradition in "The Old People."

2640 Cambon, Glauco. "Faulkner's 'The Old People': The Numen-Engendering Style," SoR, 1 (Winter, 1965), 94-107.
The "sense of Nature's sacredness as a progressively disappearing value to be re-attained through special rituals pervades the style of 'The Old People.'"

2641 Dabney, Lewis M. ["The Old People"] The Indians of Yoknapatawpha: A Study of Literature and History. Baton Rouge: Louisiana U. P., 1974, pp. 122-135, passim.

2642 Davis, Robert Gorham. Instructor's Manual for Ten Modern Masters. New York: Harcourt, 1953, pp. 46-47.

2643 Early, James. "'The Old People' and 'Was,'" The Making of Go Down, Moses. Dallas: Southern Methodist U. P., 1972, pp. 71-73.

2644 Flanagan, John T. "Folklore in Faulkner's Fiction," PLL, 5 (Summer, 1969), 122-123, 125.

2645 Gruffaz-Besingue, Catherine, with assistance of Christine Le Du. "The Old People," Views and Reviews of Modern German Literature. Festschrift für Adolf D. Klarmann. München: Delp, 1974, pp. 167-181.

2646 Kinney, Arthur F. "Faulkner and the Possibilities for Heroism," SoR, 6, n. s. (1970), 1110-1125; repr., Bear, Man, and God. Francis L. Utley, et al., eds. New York: Random House, 1963; rev. ed. 1971, pp. 235-251.

2647 Litz, Walton. "William Faulkner's Moral Vision," SWR, 37 (Summer, 1952), 204-205.

2648 Longley, John Lewis, Jr. The Tragic Mask: A Study of Faulkner's Heroes. Chapel Hill: North Carolina U. P., 1963, pp. 11-12, 85-86.

2649 Meriwether, James B. "The Short Fiction of William Faulkner," Proof, 1 (1971), 306.

2650 Milum, Richard A. "Ikkemotubbe and the Spanish Conspiracy," AL, 46 (November, 1974), 389-391.

2651 O'Nan, Martha. "William Faulkner's 'Du Homme,'" LaurelR, 10, #2 $1970), 26-28.
A study of the derivation of the name "Doom."

2652 Raimbault, R. N., tr. Gens de jadis. Paris: Les Oeuvres libres. Nouv. ser. No. 115 (v. 341), 1955, pp. 3-28.

2653 Rouberol, Jean. "Les Indiens dans l'Oeuvre de Faulkner," EA, 26 (March, 1973), 54-58.

2654 Ruotolo, Lucio P. "Isaac McCaslin--'The Old People,'" in Six Existential Heroes: The Politics of Faith. Cambridge: Harvard U.P., 1973, p. 57f.

2655 Sandeen, Ernest. "William Faulkner: Tragedian of Yoknapatawpha," Fifty Years of the American Novel: A Christian Appraisal. Harold C. Gardiner, ed. New York: Gordian Press, 1951, 1968, p. 181.

2656 Schorer, Mark. The Story: A Critical Anthology. New York: Prentice-Hall, 1950, pp. 418-419.

2657 Thompson, Lawrance. William Faulkner: An Introduction and Interpretation. New York: Barnes & Noble, 1963, pp. 12, 85, 86.

2658 Waggoner, Hyatt H. William Faulkner: From Jefferson to the World. Lexington: Kentucky U.P., 1959, pp. 201-206, 211.

"ONCE ABOARD THE LUGGER"
(Contempo, 1 (February, 1932), 1, 4)

2659 Meriwether, James B. "The Short Fiction of William Faulkner," Proof, 1 (1971), 306.

2660 Millgate, Michael. The Achievement of William Faulkner. New York: Random House, 1966, pp. 15, 300, 305.

2661 Pitavy, Francois. "W. F.: Y'Avait une Fregate," Delta, 3 (November, 1976), 3-7.

"PANTALOON IN BLACK"
(Harper's, 181 (1940), 503-513; revised for Go Down, Moses, 1942)

2662 Alsen, Eberhard. "An Existentialist Reading of Faulkner's 'Pantaloon in Black,'" SSF, 14 (Spring, 1977), 169-178.

2663 Blanchard, Leonard A. "The Failure of the Natural Man: Faulkner's 'Pantaloon in Black,'" NMW, 8 (Spring, 1975), 28-32.

2664 Bond, Christopher James. "I. Sir James Frazer's 'Homeopathy' and 'Contagion' as Archetypal and Structural Principles in William Faulkner's *Go Down, Moses*...," DAI, 35 (Rutgers: 1974), 3725A.

2665 Cleman, John L. "'Pantaloon in Black': Its Place in *Go Down, Moses*," TSL, 22 (1977), 170-181.

2666 Dabney, Lewis M. *The Indians of Yoknapatawpha*. Baton Rouge: Louisiana State U.P., 1974, pp. 72, 137.

2667 Early, James. *The Making of Go Down, Moses*. Dallas: Southern Methodist U.P., 1972, pp. 6, 11-12, 71.

2668 Gross, Theodore, and Norman Kelvin. *An Introduction to Literature: Fiction*. New York: Random House, 1967, pp. 273-279.

2669 Kerr, Elizabeth M. *Yoknapatawpha: Faulkner's Little Postage Stamp of Native Soil*. New York: Fordham U.P., 1969, *passim*.

2670 Laurent, Hélène. "Pantaloon in Black," *Views and Reviews of Modern German Literature. Festschrift für Adolf D. Klarmann*. Karl S. Weimar, ed. München: Delp, 1974, pp. 157-166.

2671 Noble, Donald R. "Faulkner's 'Pantaloon in Black': An Aristotelian Reading," BSUF, 14 (Summer, 1973), 16-19.

2672 O'Connor, William Van. *The Tangled Fire of William Faulkner*. Minneapolis: Minnesota U.P., 1954, p. 125.

2673 Reed, Joseph W., Jr. *Faulkner's Narrative*. New Haven: Yale U.P., 1973, pp. 190-191.

2674 Stephens, Rosemary. "Mythical Elements of 'Pantaloon in Black,'" UMSE, 11 (1970-71), 45-51.

2675 Stoneback, H. R. "Faulkner's Blues: 'Pantaloon in Black,'" MFS, 21 (Summer, 1975), 241-245.

2676 Taylor, Walter. "Faulkner's Pantaloon: The Negro Anomaly at the Heart of *Go Down, Moses*," AL, 44 (November, 1972), 430-444.

2677 Thompson, Lawrance. *William Faulkner: Introduction and Interpretation*. 2nd ed. New York: Barnes & Noble, 1963, pp. 12, 85.

2678 Winkel, Carol A. G. "Faulkner's Style and Its Relation to Theme: A Stylistic Study of Two Stories from *Go Down, Moses*," DAI, 35 (Delaware: 1974), 3017A.

"PENNSYLVANIA STATION"
(AmMerc, 31 (1934), 166-174; repr., in Collected Stories, 1950)

2679 Meriwether, James B. The Literary Career of William Faulkner. Columbia: South Carolina U.P., 1971, pp. 175, 178, 179.

2680 _______. "The Short Fiction of William Faulkner," Proof, 1 (1971), 306-307.

"A POINT OF LAW"
(Collier's, 105 (1940), passim; revised for Go Down, Moses, 1950; see "The Fire and the Hearth")

2681 Early, James. The Making of Go Down, Moses. Dallas: Southern Methodist U.P., 1972, pp. 6, 7, 9, 33.

2682 Meriwether, James B. "The Short Fiction of William Faulkner," Proof, 1 (1971), 307.

PYLON
(New York: Smith & Haas, 1935)

2683 A., M. A. "Of the Air-Earthy," Daily Post (Liverpool), (May 22, 1935), 7.
Found Pylon "unquestionably brilliant."

2684 Adams, Richard P. Faulkner: Myth and Motion. Princeton: Princeton U.P., 1968, pp. 95-102.

2685 Adelberg, Julius. "In a Southern City at Mardi Gras," Boston Transcript (March 30, 1935), 2.

2686 Anon. "Air Circus: The Old Faulkner Characters in a New Setting," Newsweek (March 30, 1935), 40.

2687 Anon. BCLF (juillet-août, 1946), 17. Review.

2688 Anon. "Faulkner Genius," Courier (Camden, N.J.), (March 30, 1935), 12.

2689 Anon. "Faulkner Joins Obscurists' Cult in Newest Novel," Journal (Milwaukee), (April 21, 1935), Ed. Sec., 3.

2690 Anon. "Faulkner Writes Gripping Tale of Air Barnstormers," Star-News (Pasadena), (May 4, 1935), 6. Review.

2691 Anon. "Literature and Less," Times-Picayune (New Orleans), (April 21, 1935), II, 5. Review.

2692 Anon. "Machine and Men in Faulkner's Story," Sunday Union and Republican (Springfield), (May 19, 1935), 5-C. Review.

2693 Anon. "Pylon," AmSpec (August, 1935), 13. Review.

2694 Anon. "Pylon," TLS (April 11, 1935), 242. Review.

2695 Anon. "Two American Novelists," Times (April 5, 1935), 22.

2696 Anon. "Under Cover Work," New Haven Journal-Courier (April 29, 1935), 6. Review.

2697 Anon. "Vivid New Faulkner Opus," Salt Lake Tribune (May 5, 1935), 4.

2698 Baker, James R. "Ideas and Queries," FS, 1 (Fall, 1952), 39-41.
A letter from Walton Litz relating Pylon to "Test Pilot."

2699 Baldus, Alexander. [Pylon] Das deutsche Wort, 13, iii (1937), 157.

2700 Barthelme, Helen Moore. "Pylon: The Doomed Quest. A Critical and Textual Study of William Faulkner's Neglected Allegory," DAI, 38, #7 (Austin, Texas: 1976), 4163A.

2701 Bay, .A. [Pylon], GL (14 septembre 1946), 13. Review.

2702 Beach, Joseph Warren. American Fiction, 1920-1940. New York: Macmillan, 1941, pp. 149-150.

2703 Bedell, George C. Kierkegaard and Faulkner: Modalities of Existence. Baton Rouge: Louisiana State U. P., 1972, pp. 206-212, passim.

2704 Bell, Laurence. "Faulkner's Coming of Age," Scribner's (May, 1935), 8-9.
"A terrific indictment of a generation...."

2705 B[enet], W[illiam] R. "Faulkner Fades," Tennessean (Nashville), (March 31, 1935), Mag. Sec., 15. Review.
Called the novel "an essay in verbal gymnastics."

2706 Bernd, A. B. "Pylon" Macon Telegraph (March 23, 1935).

2707 Blanzat, Jean. [Pylone] Littêraire (24 août 1946), 4.

2708 ________. MondeF, 4 (October, 1946), 316-321.

2709 Bleikasten, André. "Pylon, ou l'Enfer des signes," EA, 29 (July-Sept., 1976), 432-447.

2710 Bowerman, Sarah G. "Pylon," Washington Evening Star, (April 13, 1935), 6-A.

2711 Breit, Harvey. "Neglected Books," AmSch, 25 (Autumn, 1956), 474.
"The most undeservedly neglected book I can think of."

2712 Brickell, Herschel. "Books on Our Table," NYPost (March 30, 1935), 7.

2713 Bridgers, Emily. "William Faulkner in the Air," News and Observer (Raleigh), (March 31, 1935), 5-M.

2714 Brophy, John. "New Fiction," Time and Tide, 16, #15 (April 13, 1935), 555-556.

2715 Brylowski, Walter. Faulkner's Olympian Laugh: Myth in the Novels. Detroit: Wayne State U. P., 1968, pp. 117-120.

2716 Burdett, Osbert. "Pylon," EngRev, 60 (May, 1935), 626. Review.

2717 Cantwell, Robert. "Books," New Outlook, 165 (May, 1935), 60.

2718 Cargill, Oscar. "The Primitivists," Intellectual America. New York: Macmillan, 1941, pp. 370-386.

2719 Chamberlain, John. "Books of the Times," NYTimes (March 25, 1935), 13. Review.

2720 ________. [Pylon] CurrentHist, 42 (May, 1935), xvi.

2721 Church, Richard. "New Books at a Glance," John O'London's Weekly, 33 (April 13, 1935), 56.

2722 Clayton, Robert. "Pylon," Chattanooga Times (April 7, 1935), Mag. Sec., 15.

2723 Connolly, Cyril. "Pylon," NS&N, 9 (April 13, 1935), 525.

2724 Cooper, Sanford L. "William Faulkner Follows Usual Style in New Story," Pittsburgh Press (March 31, 1935), III, 11.

2725 Corley, Pauline. "Inhuman Creatures of the Air," Miami Herald, (March 31, 1935), 2-F.

2726 Cowley, Malcolm. "Faulkner," Think Back on Us ... A Contemporary Chronicle of the 1930's. Ed. with Introd. by Dan Piper. Carbondale and Edwardsville: Southern Ill. U. P., 1967, pp. 268-271.
Reprints Cowley's reviews of Pylon.

2727 ________. "Voodoo Dance," NR, 82 (April 10, 1935), 254-255.

2728 Currie, George. "Passed in Review," Brooklyn Daily Eagle (March 25, 1935), 16.

2729 Degenfelder, E. Pauline. "Sirk's The Tarnished Angels and Pylon Recreated," Lit-Film Qt, 5 (Summer, 1977), 242-251.

2730 Early, James. The Making of Go Down, Moses. Dallas: Southern Methodist U.P., 1972, p. 5.

2731 Everett, Walter K. Faulkner's Art and Characters. Woodbury, New York: Barron's Edu. Ser., 1969, pp. 65-69.

2732 Fadiman, Clifton. "Books: Medley," NY (March 30, 1935), 73-74.

2733 Fauchery, Pierre ["La Mythologie faulknêrienne dans Pylon,"] Action (25 octobre 1946), 15.

2734 ________. "La Mythologie faulknêrienne dans Pylon," Espace (Paris), 3, (June, 1945), 106-112.

2735 Gannett, Lewis. "Books and Things," NYHT (March 25, 1935), 13.

2736 Geismar, Maxwell. "William Faulkner: The Negro and the Female," Writers in Crisis. Boston: Houghton Mifflin, 1942, pp. 143-183.

2737 Gigli, Lorenzo. "Presentazione del volume," Oggi si vola. Milano: Mondadori, 1937, pp. 9-14.

2738 Goyert, Georg, tr. [Pylon]. Wendemarke. Berlin: Rowohlt Verlag, 1936.

2739 Grimes, George. "Faulkner's Tense, Bitter Novel of Flying Men, Seen Through Haze of Drink," Omaha Sunday World Herald (March 31, 1935), 15-E.

2740 Guereschi, Edward. "Ritual and Myth in William Faulkner's Pylon," Thoth, 3 (Spring, 1962), 101-110.

2741 Guilleminault, C. [Pylon] Bataille (21 août 1946), 6.

2742 Guilloux, R. Gazette des Lettres (14 septembre 1946), 12.

2743 Hall, Theodore. "No End of Books: Pylon, William Faulkner's Powerful, Hypnotic Novel about Stunt and Racing Fliers," Post (Washington) (March 26, 1935), 9.

2744 Hansen, Harry. "Strange Tale, Strangely Told," NYWorld-Telegram (March 25, 1935), 17.

2745 Hanson, Grant D. "Pylon," Tribune (Sioux City, Iowa), (June 1, 1935), 4.

2746 Hatcher, Harlan H. "Ultimate Extensions," Creating the Modern American Novel. New York: Russell & Russell, 1965, p. 239.

2747 Hemingway, Ernest. By-Line: Ernest Hemingway. William White, ed. New York: Scribner's, 1967, p. 200.
Hemingway enjoyed the novel when it came out.

2748 Hennecke, Hans. "Amerika und die Tradition," Europäische Revue, 13 (1937), 418-420.

2749 Hicks, Granville. "Melodrama," New Masses (May 14, 1935), 25.

2750 Hippler, W. G. "A Line on Books," Buffalo Evening News (March 23, 1935), II, 3.

2751 Hoch, Henry George. "Mr. Faulkner's Barnstormers," Detroit News (April 21, 1935), Arts, 17.

2752 Hoffman, Frederick J. "The Negro and the Folk: Pylon," William Faulkner. New York: Twayne, 2nd ed., 1966, pp. 80-101.

2753 Horan, Kenneth. "Faulkner Turns to Decent Horror," Chicago Journal of Commerce and LaSalle Street Journal (April 30, 1935), 16.

2754 Howe, Irving. "Pylon," William Faulkner: A Critical Study. New York: Vintage, 1952, pp. 215-220, passim.

2755 Iles, Francis. "An Air-Circus," Daily Telegraph (May 24, 1935), 8.

2756 Isaacs, J. "Pylon," Annual Register (1935), II, 35-36. Review.

2757 Jane-Mansfield, C. "William Faulkner Has Produced a Novel of Social Significance," NYSun (March 27, 1935), 24.

2758 Jarlot, Gerard. "Pylône," Fontaine, 10 (November, 1946), 653-657.

2759 Jones, Howard Mumford. "Social Notes on the South," VQR, 11 (July, 1935), 452-457.

2760 Karant, Max. "Faulkner Cracks Up with Pylon, Reviewer Thinks," News-Index (Evanston, Ill.) (April 25, 1935), 5.

2761 Kierszys, Zofia, tr. Punkt zwrotny. Warszawa: Państwowy Instytut Wydawniczy, 1967.

2762 Kirk, Robert W., and Marvin Klotz. Faulkner's People. Berkeley: California U. P., 1963, pp. 78-83.

2763 Lattimore, Ralston. "Pylon: A Novel by William Faulkner," Savannah Morning News (April 7, 1935), 26.

2764 Le Breton, Maurice. "William Faulkner's Pylon," RAA, 12 (October, 1935), 81-82.
"... [C]'est dans le choix du detail qui arrache le rire ou provoque l'emot on que l'art de Faulkner se revele superieur; l'impression de vie intense jaillit a chaque page de cette succession rapide de notations precises et justes."

2765 Lhamon, W. T., Jr. "Pylon: The Ylimaf and New Valois," WHR, 24 (Summer, 1970), 274-278.
"Ylimaf" = "family" spelled backwards.

2766 Longley, John L., Jr. The Tragic Masks: A Study of Faulkner's Heroes. Chapel Hill: North Carolina U.P., 1963, pp. 133-137.

2767 Lynd, Sylvia. Book Society News (April, 1935). Review.

2768 _______. "Too Noisy a Novel," News Chronicle (April 15, 1935), 4.
Found the book "well-nigh impossible" to read.

2769 Lyons, Richard. Faulkner on Love: A Letter to Marjorie Lyons. Fargo, N.D.: Merrykit, [1974].
A typeset copy of Faulkner's reply in 1950 to a question about the anonymity of the reporter in Pylon.

2770 McElrath, Joseph. "Pylon: The Portrait of a Lady," MissQ, 27 (Summer, 1974), 277-290.

2771 McGill, Ralph. "Faulkner Writes On," Atlanta Constitution (April 7, 1935), Sec. B, 8.

2772 MacMillan, Duane J. "The Non-Yoknapatawpha Novels of William Faulkner: An Examination of Soldiers' Pay, Mosquitoes, Pylon, The Wild Palms, and A Fable," DAI, 32 (Wisconsin: 1974), 6986-A.

2773 _______. "Pylon: From Short Stories to Major Work," Mosaic, 7 (Fall, 1973), 185-212.

2774 Madge, Charles. "Time and Space in America," London Mercury, 32, #187 (May, 1935), 83.

2775 Magny, Claude-Edmonde. [Pylon] SM (23 novembre 1946), 11.

2776 _______. [Pylon] Esprit (1945).
Thought the ending of the novel excellent.

2777 Maier, Hansgeorg. [Pylon], Deutsche Zukunst, 5 (June 13, 1937), 11.

2778 Marvin, John R. "Pylon: The Definition of Sacrifice," FS, 1 (Summer, 1952), 20-23.

2779 Mason, H. A. "Pylon," Scrutiny, 4 (June, 1935), 74-79.

2780 Matthews, T. S. "Eagles Over Mobile, or Three Yairs for Faulkner," AmSpec, (January, 1936), 9, 12.
Parody.

2781 Meriwether, James B. "Pylon," The Literary Career of William Faulkner. Columbia: South Carolina U.P., 1971, pp. 25-26.

2782 _______. "Pylon," William Faulkner: A Checklist," PULC, 18 (Spring, 1957), 139.

2783 Meyer, Luther. "Faulkner, Flying Scribe in New Opus," Call-Bulletin (San Francisco), (March 30, 1935), 8.

2784 Miller, David M. "Faulkner's Women," MFS, 13 (Spring, 1967), 3-17.

2785 Millgate, Michael. "Faulkner and the Air: The Background of Pylon," MichQR, 3 (Winter, 1964), 271-277.

2786 _______. "Pylon," Achievement of William Faulkner. New York: Random House, 1966, pp. 138-149.

2787 _______. "Pylon," William Faulkner. New York: Grove Press, 1961; Rev., 1966; repr., New York: Capricorn Books, 1971, passim.

2788 Monteiro, George. "Bankruptcy in Time: A Reading of Faulkner's Pylon," TCL, 4 (April-July, 1958), 9-20.
Discusses the "failure of communication" as a major theme.

2789 Muir, Edwin. "New Novels," Listener, 13 (April 24, 1935), 720.

2790 N., I. "Not Good Faulkner," Times (Los Angeles), (March 24, 1935), II, 6.

2791 Nadeau, Maurice. [Pylône]. Gavroche (12 septembre 1946), 5.

2792 Nicholson, Norman. "William Faulkner," Man and Literature. London: S.C.M. Press, 1943, pp. 122-138.
Faulkner as a primitivist.

2793 North, Sterling. "Psychopathic Squirming of the White Trash Marks New Faulkner, Caldwell and Wolfe," Chicago Daily News (March 27, 1935), 15.
Unfavorable review.

2794 O'Connor, William Van. William Faulkner, University of Minnesota Pamphlets on American Literature. Minneapolis: Minnesota U. P., 1959; repr., Seven Modern American Novelists. Minneapolis: Minnesota U. P., 1964, pp. 118-152.

2795 ________. The Tangled Fire of William Faulkner. Minneapolis: Minnesota U. P., 1954, pp. 88-93.

2796 O'Donnell, George Marion. "Faulkner and Insensitivity," Direction, 1 (June, 1935), 152-153.

2797 O'Faolain, Sean. "Fiction," Spectator, 154 (April 19, 1935), 668.
Criticizes the brutality.

2798 ________. [Pylon] Springfield Republican (May 19, 1935), 50.

2799 Patterson, Alicia. "The Book of the Week," NYSunday News (March 24, 1935), 70.

2800 Pearce, Richard. "Pylon, Awake and Sing! and the Apocalyptic Imagination of the 30's," Criticism, 13 (Spring, 1971), 131-141.
Thinks that the novel's contradictions, the sexual frenzy, and the meaningless motion link it with Odet's play Awake and Sing! as expression of irrational apocalyptic vision characteristic of the 1930's.

2801 Pouillon, Jean. "William Faulkner, un têmoin (à propos de Pylone)," TM, 1 (October, 1946), 172-178.

2802 Preston, W. E. Hayter. "Pasteboard People in Fiction," Sunday Referee (April 14, 1935), 6.

2803 Price, Reynolds. Introduction. Pylon. New York: New American Library (Signet Modern Classic), 1968.

2804 ________. "Pylon: The Posture of Worship," Shenandoah, 19 (Spring, 1968), 49-61.
Sees the reporter as the central character, not the pilots.

2805 ________. "Pylon," Things Themselves: Essays and Scenes. New York: Atheneum Pubs., 1972, pp. 91-108.

2806 "R. W." [Pylon] Oxford Mail (April 22, 1935). Review.

2807 Raimbault, R. N., tr. ["Trouble," extrait de Pylône] Samedi Soir (10 novembre 1945), 6.

2808 ________, and Mme. G. L. Rousselet, trs. Pylône. Paris: Gallimard, 1946.

2809 Ransom, John Crowe. "Faulkner, South's Most Brilliant but Wayward Talent, Is Spent," Banner (Nashville) (March 24, 1935), 8.

2810 Rauch, Karl. [Pylon] Der Bucherwurm, 22 (1936), 123. Found "bold, figurative language" in the novel.

2811 Redman, Ben Ray. "Flights of Fancy," SatRL, 11 (March 30, 1935), 577, 581.

2812 Reed, Joseph W., Jr. Faulkner's Narrative. New Haven: Yale U.P., 1973, p. 275.

2813 Richardson, H. Edward. "William Faulkner: Journey to Self-Discovery. Columbia: Missouri U.P., 1969, p. 125.

2814 Richardson, Maurice L. [Pylon], "Mr. Faulkner Takes to the Air," Observer (April 7, 1935), 7.

2815 Rivallan, Jean. "Pylône," Paru (octobre 1946), 48-49.

2816 Robinson, Ted. "Faulkner Pens Mighty Tale of Flyers Who Are Gods in the Air, Pigs on Ground," Plain Dealer (Cleveland), (March 24, 1935), Amusement Sec., 15.

2817 R[oueché], B[erton]. "Faulkner's Furious Portrait of the Lost," Kansas City Star (April 13, 1935), 14.

2818 Rousseaux, André. [Pylône], Le Littéraire (19 octobre 1946), 2.

2819 Salpeter, Harry. "Memory and Experience," Literary America, 2 (June, 1935), 418.

2820 Sans, Julien. [Pylône] Climats (17 octobre 1946), 10. "... [L]a plus grande oeuvre contemporaire."

2821 Slatoff, Walter J. "Pylon," Quest for Failure. Ithaca: Cornell U.P., 1960; 2nd pr., 1961, pp. 211-215.

2822 Soskin, William. "William Faulkner's Pylon," New York American (March 25, 1935), 17.

2823 Spring, Howard. "Her 1/--Horse Won the 'National,'" Evening Standard (April 4, 1935), 10.

2824 Stallings, Lawrence. "Gentleman from Mississippi," AmMerc, 34 (April, 1935), 499-501.

2825 Stonier, G. W. "Pylon," Fortnightly, 137 (May, 1935), 640.

2826 Strauss, Harold. "Mr. Faulkner's New Novel Strikes a Fresh Vein," NYTBR (March 24, 1935), 2.

"... It is a book that must not be missed." It "vindicates [Faulkner] from the current suspicion that his genius is limited to themes of violence, horror and the psychopathology of sex...."

2827 Swiggart, Peter. The Art of Faulkner's Novels. Austin: Texas U.P., 1962, pp. 27-29.

2828 Thompson, Lawrance. William Faulkner: An Introduction and Interpretation. New York: Barnes & Noble, 1967, pp. 10-11.

2829 Torchiana, Donald T. "Faulkner's Pylon and the Structure of Modernity," MFS, 3 (Winter, 1957-58), 291-308.
"... [T]he predominant theme in Pylon appears to be the modern inversion of life and eros into death and destruction by means of the cult of the machine, which, in turn, is impelled by the power of money. Yet there is an opposite theme of equal force ... the triumph of life in the self-sacrifice of Shumann, and the affirmation of life by his fellow flyers ... while they all strenuously pursue death...."

2830 ________. "Pylone et la Structure du Monde Moderne," RLM, Part I, Nos. 27-29 (1957), 55-85.

2831 ________. "The Reporter in Faulkner's Pylon," HINL, 4 (Spring, 1958), 33-39.

2832 Toubro, Peter, tr. Pylon. København: Spektrum, 1963. Published earlier under title Trekanten. Danish translation.

2833 Troy, William. "And Tomorrow," Nation, 140 (April 3, 1935), 393.
"... By writing about fliers and flying machines he [Faulkner] has indeed made his subject indistinguishable from the theme of flight into the life of action, which has been one of the three or four dominating themes in contemporary fiction."

2834 Tuck, Dorothy. Crowell's Handbook of Faulkner. New York: Crowell, 1964, pp. 132-135.

2835 Van Doren, Mark. "A Story Written with Ether, Not Ink," NYHTB (March 24, 1935), 3.

2836 Veruly, A. "Vliegerromans," CrB (1935), 313-316.

2837 Vickery, John B. "William Faulkner and Sir Philip Sidney," MLN, 70 (May, 1955), 349-350.
The phrase "Nilebarge clatterfalque" is similar to a phrase in Arcadia.

2838 Vickery, Olga W. "A New World Folklore: Pylon," The Novels of William Faulkner. Rev. ed. Baton Rouge: Louisiana State U.P., 1964, pp. 145-155.

2839 Volpe, Edmond L. A Reader's Guide to William Faulkner. New York: Noonday P., 1964, pp. 174-184.

2840/1 W., R. "Three Notable Novels," Oxford Mail (April 22, 1935), 4.

2842 Waggoner, Hyatt H. William Faulkner: From Jefferson to the World. Lexington: Kentucky U.P., 1959, pp. 121-132, 145-147.

2843 Wagner, Charles A. "Books," New York Mirror (March 25, 1935), 25; (March 24, 1935), 29.

2844 Warwick, Ray. "Pylon," Journal (Atlanta) (April 14, 1935), Mag. Sec., 12. Review.

2845 Weeks, Edward. "Atlantic Bookshelf," Atl, 155 (June, 1935), 16, 18. Review.

2846 W[emer], W[illis]. "Pylon," Union (San Diego), (March 31, 1935), Feature Sec., 7. Review.

2847 W[illiams], S[idney]. "Faulkner's Pylon, and Bishop's 'Act of Darkness,'" Philadelphia Inquirer (March 30, 1935), 11.

"RACE AT MORNING"
(Sat. Eve. Post, 227 (1955), 26-27, passim; revised for Big Woods, 1955)

2848 Bradford, Melvin E. "'The Winding Horn': Hunting and the Making of Men in Faulkner's 'Race at Morning,'" PELL, 1 (Summer, 1965), 272-278.

2849 Meriwether, James B. "The Short Fiction of William Faulkner," Proof, 1 (1971), 307.

2850 Smith, Harrison. ["Race at Morning"], SatRL, 38 (October 29, 1955), 16. Review.

2851 Waggoner, Hyatt H. William Faulkner: From Jefferson to the World. Lexington: Kentucky U.P., 1959, pp. 209, 213, 273.

"RAID"
(Sat. Eve. Post, 207 (1934), 18-19, passim; revised for The Unvanquished, 1938)

2852 Millgate, Michael. The Achievement of William Faulkner. New York: Random House, 1965, pp. 165, 170.

2853 Mizener, Arthur. A Handbook to Modern Short Stories. New York: Norton, 1967, rev. ed., pp. 143-149; 3rd ed., 1971, pp. 163-169.

2854 Muir, Edwin. Listener, 19 (May 25, 1938), 1146. Review.

"RED LEAVES"
(Sat Eve. Post, 203 (1930), 6-7, passim; revised for These 13, 1931; repr., in Collected Stories, 1950; a part revised for Big Woods, 1955)

2855 Beebe, Maurice. "Red Leaves," Criticism of William Faulkner," MFS, 13 (Spring, 1967), 147.

2856 Beidler, Peter G. "A Darwinian Source for Faulkner's Indians in 'Red Leaves,'" SSF, 10 (Fall, 1973), 421-423.
Suggests Darwin's journal of his voyage on the Beagle as source.

2857 Brown, Calvin S. "Faulkner's Manhunts: Fact into Fiction," GaR, 20 (December, 1966), 388-395.

2858 Cowley, Malcolm, ed. "Faulkner: The Yoknapatawpha Story," A Second Flowering: Works and Days of the Lost Generation. New York: Viking, 1973, p. 138.

2859 ________. "Red Leaves," The Portable Faulkner. New York: Viking, 1949, pp. 74-104.

2860 Dabney, Lewis M. "Red Leaves," The Indians of Yoknapatawpha. Baton Rouge: Louisiana State U.P., 1974, pp. 90-117, passim.
"'Red Leaves' ... is a darker vision of the Indian world and of what it means to be a man...."

2861 Early, James. The Making of Go Down, Moses. Dallas: Southern Methodist U.P., 1972, pp. 4, 65.

2862 Flanagan, John T. "Folklore in Faulkner's Fiction," PLL, 5 (Summer, 1969), 133, 134.

2863 Frakes, James B. NYTBR (November 1, 1970), 5.
Sees one of the best scenes of Vance Bourjaily's Brill Among the Ruins as derivative of Faulkner's "Red Leaves."

2864 ________, and Isadore Traschen. Short Fiction: A Critical Collection. Englewood Cliffs, New Jersey: Prentice-Hall, 1969, pp. 40-43.

2865 Funk, Robert W. "Satire and Existentialism in Faulkner's 'Red Leaves,'" MissQ, 25 (Summer, 1972), 339-348.
"... The Satire mutates into an investigation of the far-reaching consequences of slavery by focusing upon an existential concern that affects all men."

2866 Garnett, David. NS&N, 6 (September 30, 1933), 387.
"It is a magnificent, a marvellous story, a work which only a great creative artist could have written."

2867 Gwynn, Frederick, and Joseph L. Blotner, eds. Faulkner in the University. Charlottesville: Virginia U. P., 1959, p. 39.
At Virginia, Faulkner spoke of the meaning of the title: "It was the deciduation of nature which no one could stop that had suffocated, destroyed the Negro ... the red leaves had nothing against him ... they probably liked him, but it was a normal deciduation...."

2868 Howe, Irving. "A Note on the Stories: 'Red Leaves,'" William Faulkner: A Critical Study. New York: Vintage, 1952, p. 266, passim.
"Faulkner's two best stories--the two that may, I think be called 'great'--are 'That Evening Sun' and 'Red Leaves.'"

2869 Howell, Elmo. "William Faulkner and the Mississippi Indians," GaR, 21 (December, 1967), 386-396.

2870 ________. "William Faulkner's Chickasaw Legacy: A Note on 'Red Leaves,'" ArQ, 26 (Winter, 1970), 293-303.
Suggests that Faulkner's aim in 'Red Leaves' was to create a wilderness horror unsoftened by any recognized moral system and also to show that the spectacle of life is joyous.

2871 Kazin, Alfred. ["Red Leaves"], "William Faulkner: More Snopeses," Contemporaries. Boston: Little, Brown, 1962, pp. 156-157.

2872 Kerr, Elizabeth M. Yoknapatawpha: Faulkner's "Little Postage Stamp of Native Soil." New York: Fordham U. P., 1969, passim.

2873 Langford, Beverly Young. "History and Legend in William Faulkner's 'Red Leaves,'" NMW, 6 (Spring, 1973), 19-24.

2874 Leary, Lewis. William Faulkner of Yoknapatawpha County. New York: Crowell, 1973, pp. 30, 133, 134.

2875 Libby, Anthony P. "Chronicles of Children: William Faulkner's Short Fiction," DA, 30 (Stanford: 1969), 1568A.

2876 Meriwether, James B. "The Short Fiction of William Faulkner," Proof, 1 (1971), 307.

2877 Milum, Richard A. "Ikkemotubbe and the Spanish Conspiracy," AL, 46 (November, 1974), 381-391.
Finds probable historical context for the relationship between Faulkner's Ikkemotubbe and the French adventurer Chevalier de Vitry.

2878 [Milum, Richard A.] "The Title of Faulkner's Red Leaves," AN&Q, 13 (1974), 58-59.

2879 Muller, Gilbert H. "The Descent of the Gods: Faulkner's 'Red Leaves' and the Garden of the South," SSF, 11 (Summer, 1974), 243-249.
"... The theological statement of the human predicament in 'Red Leaves' is rendered with a force and a complexity that no other short story by Faulkner matches...."

2880 Nilon, Charles H. Faulkner and the Negro. New York: Citadel Press, 1965, pp. 39-43.

2881 O'Connor, William Van. The Tangled Fire of William Faulkner. Minneapolis: Minnesota U.P., 1954, p. 69, 171.

2882 Pryse, Marjorie L. "Race: Faulkner's 'Red Leaves,'" SSF, 12 (Spring, 1975), 133-138.

2883 Raimbault, R. N., and Ch. P. Vorce, trs. "Feuilles rouges," Europe (15 avril 1936), 512-539.

2884 Rouberol, Jean. "Les Indiens dans l'Oeuvre de Faulkner," EA, 26 (March, 1973), 54-58.

2885 Smith, Henry Nash. "'Writing Right Smart Fun,' Says Faulkner," Dallas Morning News (February 14, 1932), Sec. IV, 2.
When asked about the source of the episode in which Doom has his slaves drag a houseboat twelve miles inland for use as a residence (in "Red Leaves"), Faulkner said the incident had been invented.

2886 Styron, William. NYTBR (May 6, 1973), 10.

2887 Volpe, Edmond L. "Faulkner's 'Red Leaves': The Deciduation of Nature," SAF, 3 (Autumn, 1975), 121-131.

2888 Voss, Arthur. "Red Leaves," The American Short Story. Norman: Oklahoma U.P., 1973, pp. 246-247.

THE REIVERS
(New York: Random House, 1962)

2889 Adams, Martin. "Fiction Chronicle," HudR, 15 (Autumn, 1962), 423-425.

2890 Adams, Richard P. Faulkner: Myth and Motion. Princeton: Princeton U. P., 1968, passim.

2891 Alexander, James E. "Book Choices of the Week," Pittsburgh Post Gazette (June 2, 1962), 19.

2892 Allsop, Kenneth. "Comic," Daily Mail (September 20, 1962), 14.

2893 Anderson, Charles R. "Faulkner in a Lighter Vein," Baltimore Sun (June 10, 1962), 5-A.

2894 Anon. "Are Writers Smarter Than Politicians?" Miami News (June 10, 1962), 6-B.

2895 Anon. "Books," Glamour (August, 1962), 66. Review.

2896 Anon. "Books," McCalls's (June, 1962), 12, 14.

2897 Anon. "The Last of William Faulkner," TLS, #3160 (September 21, 1962), 726.

2898 Anon. "Prospero in Yoknapatawpha," Time, 79 (June 8, 1962), 92.

2899 Anon. "New Novels," Times (September 20, 1962), 15.

2900 Anon. "Picaresque and Puzzling," Newsweek (June 4, 1962), 100.

2901 Anon. "The Reivers," Booklist, 58 (June 1, 1962), 682.

2902 Anon. "The Reivers," Dixie Guide (August, 1962).

2903 Anon. "The Reivers," Negro Digest (October, 1962), 96.

2904 Anon. "The Reivers," Evening Bulletin (Philadelphia), (June 1, 1962).

2905 Anon. "The Reivers," Playboy (August, 1962), 24.

2906 Anon. "The Reivers' Mirrors Faulkner in a Distinctive, Penetrating Way," NatlObs (July 9, 1962), 17.

2907 Anon. "Tale Is Faulkner at Hilarious Best," CathStandard (Washington, D. C.), (July 6, 1962), 7.

2908 Atkinson, Brooks. "Faulkner and Comedy," Tuesdays and Fridays. New York: Random House, 1963, pp. 244-246.

2909 ________. "New Picaresque Novel by Faulkner Gives Academic Theory of Comedy," NYT (June 5, 1962), 38.

2910 Barbosa, Manuel. Tradução e prefácio. Os ratoneiros. Lisboa: Portugália Editora, 1964.

2911 Barklund, Gunnar, tr. Tre rövare. Stockholm: Albert Bonniers Forlag, 1963.

2912 Barley, Rex. "Faulkner's Latest Lacks Early Skill," ArRep (Phoenix), (June 10, 1962), 1-C.

2913 Barrett, William. "Reader's Choice," Atl (July, 1962), 109-110.

2914 Barth, J. Robert, S.J. "Faulkner and the Calvinist Tradition," Religious Perspectives in Faulkner's Fiction: Yoknapatawpha and Beyond. J. Robert Barth, S.J., ed. Notre Dame: Notre Dame U.P., 1972, p. 31.

"... Faulkner's final vision is one of hope: man sinful, but striving for the good; man shackled by bonds within and without him, but struggling to be free."

2915 Beck, Warren. "Told with Gusto," VQR, 38 (Autumn, 1962), 681-685.

2916 ________. "Told with Gusto," Faulkner: Essays by Warren Beck. Wisconsin U.P., 1976, pp. 660-664.

2917 Bell, Haney H., Jr. "The Relative Maturity of Lucius Priest and Ike McCaslin," Aegis, 2 (1973), 15-21.

2918 Blakeston, Oswell. "The Living and the Dead," John o'London's Weekly, 7 (October 4, 1962), 325.

2919 Boštjančič-Turk, Vera, tr. Zlikovci. Roman. Ljubljani: Prešernova Družba, 1968.

Slovenian translation of The Reivers.

2920 Boswell, Margaret. "Slapstick--Can This Be Faulkner?" State Journal-Register (Springfield, Ill.), (June 3, 1962), 8-C.

2921 Bouise, Oscar. "Fiction," Best Sellers (Scranton University), (June 15, 1962), 126-127.

2922 Bracker, Milton. "Reivers Is Pulitzer Novel," NYTimes (May 7, 1963), 1, 35.

2923 Bradbury, Malcolm. "New Novels," Punch, 243 (October 10, 1962), 540.

2924 Bradford, M. C. "What Grandfather Said: The Social

Testimony of Faulkner's The Reivers," Occasional Rev, 1 (February, 1974), 5-15.
The relationship of the form of The Reivers to its social implications.

2925 Bradley, Jack. "Fast-Paced The Reivers Faulkner at His Best," Fort Worth Star-Telegram (June 3, 1962), II, 15.

2926 Bradley, Van Allen. "Ribald Humor in a Faulkner Tale," Chicago Daily News (June 2, 1962), 20.

2927 Brooks, Cleanth. William Faulkner: The Yoknapatawpha County. New Haven: Yale U.P., 1963, 1964, pp. 349-368, 446.

2928 Brown, Calvin S. "Faulkner's Three-in-One Bridge in The Reivers," NConL, 1, #2 (March, 1971), 8-10.
Notes that Faulkner apparently combined details of three actual bridges across the Tallahatchie River in creating the bridge which Boon and companions cross on their way to Mamphis.

2929 Brown, Irby B. "Wit Marks Faulkner's New Book," Times-Dispatch (Richmond, Va.), (July 1, 1962), 8L.

2930 Brusar, Branko, tr. Lupeži, uspomena. Zagreb: Mladost, 1964.
Croatian translation of The Reivers.

2931 Brylowski, Walter. Faulkner's Olympian Laugh: Myth in the Novels. Detroit: Wayne State U.P., 1968, pp. 215-219.

2932 Bungert, Hans. "William Faulkners letzter Roman," NS, 12 (November, 1963), 498-506.
Relates The Reivers to Faulkner's earlier work and also to Huckleberry Finn.

2933 Calder-Marshall, Arthur. "Faulkner's County," Financial Times (September 27, 1962), 22.

2934 Cameron, D. K. "Books and People," Socialist Leader (October 20, 1962), 7.

2935 Campbell, Mary. "Faulkner Characters Return in New Novel," Plain Dealer (Cleveland), (June 3, 1962), 7-H.

2936 Cargill, Oscar. "American Literature: Faulkner," Colliers Encyclopedia 1963 Yearbook. Louis Shores, et al., eds.; Canada Macmillan, 1963; Canada and New York, 1974, p. 68.

2937 Cevasco, George A. "The Reivers," The Sign (Union City, N.J.), (August, 1962), 66-67.

2938 Chamberlain, John. "A Car, a Horse and Virtue," Wall Street Journal (June 4, 1962), 12.

2939 Coindreau, Maurice, and Raymond Girard, trs. Les larrons. Paris: Gallimard, 1964.

2940 Copeland, Edith. "Faulkner Comedy Simply Told," Daily Oklahoman (Oklahoma City), (June 10, 1962), 9-D.

2941 Corke, Hilary. "Faulkner Across the Water," NR, 147 (July 16, 1962), 20-22.

2942 Crawford, William. "The Reivers," El Paso Times (June 17, 1962), 8-C.

2943 Cronin, Mary A. "Mississippi Revisited," Lit, 5 (1964), 11-14.

2944 Culligan, Glendy. "Faulkner Still Tracks the Grail in Southern Accent," Washington Post (June 3, 1962), E-4.

2945 Curley, Thomas F. "Faulkner Smiles," Cw (June 22, 1962), 331-332.

2946 "Daily Book Review: The Reivers," NYHTB (June 4, 1962), 21.

2947 Devlin, Albert J. "The Reivers: Readings in Social Psychology," MissQ, 25 (Summer, 1972), 327-337.

2948 Donnelly, William and Doris. "William Faulkner: In Search of Peace," Personalist, 44 (Autumn 1963), 496-498.

2949 Drake, Robert. "Yoknapatawpha Innocence Lost," NatlRev (July 31, 1962), 70, 72.

2950 Emch, Tom. "Faulkner in Surprise Comic Vein," Houston Chronicle (June 10, 1962), Zest Mag., 13.

2951 Enzenberger, Christian. "Erheiterung in Yoknapatawpha," Die Zeit (April 24, 1964), 25, 26. Review.

2952 Everett, Walter K. Faulkner's Art and Characters. Woodbury, New York: Barron's Educ. Ser., 1969, pp. 69-73.

2953 Fadiman, Clifton. "The Reivers," Book-of-the-Month Club News (July, 1962), (July Selection).

2954 Ferrer-Vidal Turull, Jorge, tr. Los rateros. Barcelona: Plaza & Janis, 1964.

2955 Fiedler, Leslie A. "The Last of William Faulkner," Guardian (September 28, 1962), 6.

2956 First, Helen G. "Curl Up and Read," Seventeen (October, 1962), 18.

2957 Frankel, Chuck. "Faulkner Novel Humorous, Racy," Honolulu Star-Bulletin (June 3, 1962), Hawaiian Life Sec., 16.

2958 G., D. "The Reivers," Record (Kitchener-Waterloo, Ontario), (July 7, 1962), III, 21.

2959 Gardiner, Harold C. "The Reivers," America (June 16, 1962), 405-406.

2960 George, Daniel. "Recent Fiction," Daily Telegraph (September 28, 1962), 17.

2961 Gilmore, Jane L. "Faulkner's New Novel Robust, Earthy, Comic," Omaha Sunday World Herald (June 10, 1962), Mag. Sec., 28.

2962 Girard, Raymond. Préface. Les larrons. Paris: Gallimard, 1964.

2963 Gold, Joseph. "The Reivers: A Gentleman Accepts the Responsibility," William Faulkner: A Study in Humanism from Metaphor to Discourse. Norman: Oklahoma U.P., 1966, pp. 174-187.

2964 Greene, A. C. "Back to Yoknapatawpha," Dallas Times Herald (June 3, 1962), 5-E.

2965 Gresset, Michael. "Les larrons," MdF, 351 (May, 1964), 153-154.

2966 Griffin, Lloyd. "The Reivers," LJ (June 1, 1962), 2156.

2967 Griffith, Benjamin W. "Faulkner's Archaic Titles and the Second Shepherds' Play," NMW, 4 (Fall, 1971), 62-63.

2968 Harwick, Robert Duane. "Humor in the Novels of William Faulkner," DA, 26 (Nebraska: 1965), 1646.
The comedy of The Reivers is "more obvious, more relaxed and more anecdotal than that of most of the earlier novels."

2969 Haseloff, Cynthia. "Formative Elements of Film: A Structural Comparison of Three Novels and Their Adaptations by Irving Ravetch and Harriet Frank, Jr.," DAI, 33, #1 (Missouri (Columbia): 1971), 438A.

2970 Hasley, Louis. "Reivers' Progress," [poem], CEA Critic, 36 (January, 1974), 24-25.

2971 Hatfield, Mary Jo. "The Reivers: Waste of Talent," Catholic Register (Peoria, Ill.), (January, 1963). Review.

2972 Hayes, Ben. "The Reivers," Columbus Citizen-Journal (June 2, 1962), 13. Review.

2973 Hicks, Granville. "Building Blocks of a Gentleman," SatRL, (June 2, 1962), 27.

2974 Hoffman, Frederick J. "The 'Eternal Verities': The Reivers," William Faulkner. New York: 2nd ed., revised, Twayne, 1966, pp. 115-117.

2975 Howe, Irving. "Time Out for Fun in Old Mississippi: William Faulkner's New Novel," NYTBR (June 3, 1962), 1, 24-25.

2976 _______. William Faulkner: A Critical Study. 3rd ed. Chicago: Chicago U.P., 1975.

2977 Howell, Elmo. "In Ole Mississippi: Faulkner's Reminiscence," KM, 30 (1965), 77-81.

2978 _______. "Reverend Hightower and the Uses of Southern Adversity," CE, 24 (December, 1962), 183-187.

2979 Hoyt, Elizabeth N. "William Faulkner Turns to Humor," Cedar Rapids Gazette (June 10, 1962), 2-C, 10-C.

2980 Hughes, Richard. "Faulkner and Bennett," Encounter, 21 (September, 1963), 61.

2981 Hutchens, John K. "The Reivers," NYHTB (June 4, 1962), 21.

2982 Hyman, Stanley. "Taking a Flyer with Faulkner," New Leader (July 9, 1962), 18-19.

2983 Igoe, W. J. "Faulkner's Swan Song," Tablet (November 24, 1962), 1134-1136.

2984 Jay, Leah. "A New 'Huck' by Faulkner," Detroit Free Press (June 10, 1962), Amusement Sec., 5.

2985 Jelliffe, R. A. "Fabulous Tale Has Humor, Wisdom, and Rare Artistry," Chicago Sunday Tribune (June 3, 1962), Mag. of Books, 1-2.

2986 Kane, Patricia. "Adaptable and Free: Faulkner's Ratliff," NConL, 1, # 3 (May, 1971), 9-11.

2987 Kerr, Elizabeth M. "The Reivers: The Golden Book of Yoknapatawpha County," MFS, 13 (Spring 1967), 95-113.
Finds that The Reivers as a conclusion to the Yoknapatawpha saga takes on greater importance for recapitulation of themes and motifs in earlier novels.

2988 Kierszys, Zofia. Prżełozyli. Czerwone liscie; opowiadania. Warszawa: Państwowy Instytut Wydawniczy, 1964.

2989 Kirk, Robert W., and Marvin Klotz. Faulkner's People. Berkeley, California: California U. P., 1963, pp. 203-228.

2990 Knickerbocker, Conrad. "The Blessings of Yoknapatawpha," Kansas City Star (June 3, 1962), 5-E.

2991 Lambert, J. W. "The Old Man and the South," Sunday Times (September 23, 1962), 29.

2992 "The Last of William Faulkner," TLS, 3160 (September 21, 1962), 726.

2993 Leary, Lewis. "The Last Novels--The Reivers," William Faulkner of Yoknapatawpha County. New York: Crowell, 1973, pp. 185-190.

2994 Lerner, Laurence. "New Fiction," Listener, 68, #1747 (September 20, 1962), 449.

2995 Levins, Lynn Gartrell. "The Heroic Ideal," Faulkner's Heroic Design: The Yoknapatawpha Novels. Athens: Georgia U.P., 1976, pp. 174-180.

2996 McCarron, William E. "Shakespeare, Faulkner and Ned William McCaslin," NConL, 7, v (1977), 8-9.

2997 McColgan, Kristin Pruitt. "The World's Slow Stain: The Theme of Initiation in Selected American Novels," DAI, 36 (Chapel Hill, North Carolina: 1974), 279A.

2998 McLellan, Joseph. "The Reivers," Ave Maria (Notre Dame, Ind.), (November 10, 1962), 27-28.

2999 Mellard, J. M. "Faulkner's 'Golden Book': The Reivers as Romantic Comedy," BuR, 13 (December, 1965), 19-31.
Finds that "characters, structure, and themes belong, first, to the mode of comedy generally, and, second, to the form of romantic comedy specifically."

3000 Meriwether, James B. "Faulkner's Gentle Comedy of Rustic Rustlers," Houston Post (July 1, 1962), Now Sec., 30.

3001 _______. "The Novel Faulkner Never Wrote: His Golden Book or Doomsday Book," AL, 42 (March, 1970), 93-96.
"The Compson Appendix, ... appears to fulfill exactly, though on a reduced scale, the conception which Faulkner had described to Cowley as a 'Golden book of my apocryphal county ...: an alphabetical, rambling genealogy of the people.'" Cf., Elizabeth Kerr. "The Reivers: The Golden Book of Yoknapatawpha County," MFS, 13 (1967), 95-113.

3002 Millgate, Michael. "The Reivers," The Achievement of William Faulkner. New York: Random House, 1965, pp. 253-258.

3003 Mitchell, Julian. Spectator, #7004 (September 21, 1962), 409-410.

3004 Monicelli, Giorgio, tr. I saccheggiatori, romanzo. Milano: Arnold Mondadoni, 1963.

3005 Montague, John. "Faulkner's Last Book," Irish Times (November 3, 1962), 7.

3006 Moses, Edwin. "Faulkner's The Reivers: The Art of Acceptance," MissQ, 27 (Summer, 1974), 307-318.

3007 Muehl, Lois. "Faulkner's Humor in Three Novels and One 'Play,'" LC, 34 (1968), 78-93.

3008 Mueller, William R. "The Reivers: William Faulkner's Valediction," ChrC, 80 (September 4, 1963), 1079-1081.

3009 Müller, Christopher. "Zu William Faulkners Roman The Reivers," ZAA, 24 (1976), 258-264.

3010 Nathan, Monique. "Jeunesse de Faulkner," Preuves, 161 (July, 1964), 85-88.
Rev.-art., William Faulkner, Les Larrons; Frederick L. Gwynn and Joseph L. Blotner, Faulkner à l'Université.

3011 Nedelin V. Sovremennaia khudozhestvennaia literatura za rubezhom, No. 9-10 (1962), pp. 61-64.
Review of The Reivers. Russian.

3012 Nelson, Erik C. "Faulkner's Noble Prince," ArizQt, 35 (Summer, 1979), 129-134.

3013 Nordell, Roderick. "A Wild Ride with Faulkner in 1905," CSMM (June 7, 1962), 7; and "Book Report," (June 27, 1962), 9.

3014 Norris, Hoke. "A Comic Spirit Moves Faulkner," Chicago Sunday Sun-Times (June 3, 1962), III, 1.

3015 Nye, Robert. "Faulkner's Frolic," Glasgow Herald (September 20, 1962), 10.

3016 ________. "Faulkner's Last Jest," Tribune (October 19, 1962), 10.

3017 O'Connor, William Van. "Young Boy Discovers the World," Minneapolis Sunday Tribune (August 19, 1962), Home and Hobby Sec., 10.

3018 Owen, B. Evan. "Comic Faulkner Country," Oxford Mail (September 20, 1962), 6.

3019 Plimpton, George. "*The Reivers,*" NYHTB (May 27, 1962), 3.

3020 Prasad, V. R. N. "The Pilgrim and the Picaro: A Study of Faulkner's *The Bear* and *The Reivers,*" *Indian Essays in American Literature: Papers in Honour of Robert E. Spiller.* Sujit Mukherjee, and D. V. K. Raghavacharyulu, eds. Bombay: Popular Prakashan, 1969, pp. 209-221.

3021 Prescott, Orville. "Books of the Times," NYT (June 4, 1962), 27. Review.

3022 Pritchett, V. S. "Autumn Books: That Time and That Wilderness," NSt, 64, #1646 (September 28, 1962), 405-406.

3023 "Prospero in Yoknapatawpha: *The Reivers*--William Faulkner," Time, (June 8, 1962), 92.

3024 Pulitzer Prize posthumously for *The Reivers,* 1963.
Cf., John Hohenberg. *The Pulitzer Prizes.* New York and London: Columbia U.P., 1974, p. 258.

3025 Rossky, William. "*The Reivers* and *Huckleberry Finn:* Faulkner and Twain," HLQ, 28 (August, 1965), 373-387.
A thorough study of parallels between the two works.

3026 ________. "*The Reivers:* Faulkner's *Tempest,*" MissQ, 18 (Spring, 1965), 82-93.

3027 Sandeen, Ernest E. "Books: *The Reivers,*" Critic 20 (June-July, 1962), 62-63.

3028 Schnack, Elisabeth. *Die Spitzbuben; roman.* Zürich: Fretz & Wasmuth, 1965.

3029 Shepherd, Allen. "Code and Comedy in Faulkner's *The Reivers,*" LWU, 6 (1973), 43-51.

3030 Sherman, Thomas B. "Faulkner's New Novel a Pastoral Comedy," St. Louis Post-Dispatch (June 3, 1962), 4-B.

3031 Sickles, Noel. Illustrations. *Hell Creek Crossing: A Condensation from The Reivers.* Pleasantville, New York: Reader's Digest Association, 1963.

3032 Silverira, Breno. *Os desgarrados; tradução.* Rio de Janeiro: Editora Civilização Brasileira, 1963.

3033 Smith, Gerald J. "Medicine Made Palatable: An Aspect of Humor in *The Reivers,*" NMW, 8 (Fall, 1975), 58-62.

3034 Southern, Terry. "Tom Sawyer in the Brothel," Nation, 194 (June 9, 1962), 519-521.

3035 Stafford, William T. "'Some Homer of the Cotton Fields': Faulkner's Use of the Mule Early and Late (Sartoris and The Reivers)," PLL, 5 (Spring, 1969), 190-196.
In both novels "the mule is used by Faulkner as a central symbol of ideal behavior."

3036 Storm, Ole, tr. Røverne. København: Gyldendals Traneboger, 1964.
Danish translation of The Reivers.

3037 Strøm, Leo, tr. Tyvehnektene; et minne. Oslo: Gyldendal Norsk Forlag, 1964.

3038 Swiggart, Peter. "A Note on The Reivers," The Art of Faulkner's Novels. Austin: Texas U.P., 1962, pp. 207-214.

3039 Tanner, Gale. "Sentimentalism and The Reivers: A Reply to Ben Merchant Vorpahl," NMW, 9 (Spring, 1976), 50-58.
Reply to Ben M. Vorpahl. SLJ, 1, (Spring, 1969), 3-26.

3040 Thorpe, Day. "Faulkner's Newest: A Jovial Amalgam," Washington Sunday Star (June 3, 1962), 5-C. Review.

3041 Tinkle, Lon. "New Faulkner Novel Gentle to the Old South," Dallas Morning News (June 3, 1962), V, 9.

3042 Travis, Mildred K. "Echoes of Pierre in The Reivers," NConL, 3, ii [iv] (1973), 11-13.

3043 Tredway, Martha. "The Reivers," St. Louis Review (September 7, 1962), Book Sec., 3.

3044 Tuck, Dorothy. Crowell's Handbook of Faulkner. New York: Crowell, 1964, pp. 121-124.

3045 Valja, Jiri. Přeložil. Pobertovѐ reminiscence. Praha: SNKLU, 1965.
Translation of The Reivers.

3046 Vandenbergh, John. Vertaling. De rovers. Utrecht: A. W. Bruna en Zoon, 1963.

3047 Vickery, Olga. The Novels of William Faulkner: A Critical Interpretation. Revised Edition. Baton Rouge: Louisiana State U.P., 1964, pp. 228-239.
The Reivers as romance was to Faulkner what The Tempest was to Shakespeare.

3048 Volpe, Edmond L. A Reader's Guide to William Faulkner. New York: Noonday Press, 1964, pp. 343-349.

3049 Vorpahl, Ben M. "Moonlight at Ballenbaugh's: Time and Imagination in The Reivers," SLJ, 1, ii (Spring, 1969), 3-26.

Discussion of the sublimation of the actual into the apocryphal, focusing on the image of moonlight, the framework of the recollected story, and the importance of "There is no such thing as was."

3050 Wade, Gerald. "Gentleman Accepts Consequences of His Actions Faulkner Contends," Journal (Beaumont, Texas), (June 1, 1962), 17.

3051 Walker, Gerald. "Faulkner Writes a Comedy," NYPost (June 3, 1962, 11-M.

3052 Weiss, Miriam. "Hell Creek Bottom Is: A Reminiscence," JMissH, 30 (August, 1968), 196-201.

States that Hell Creek Bottom that appears in The Reivers is a "real" place.

3053 White, Ellington. "Throw Out the Paddle and Get a Reactor," KR, 24 (Autumn, 1962), 753-754.

REQUIEM FOR A NUN

(New York: Random House, 1951)

3054 Adams, Richard P. Faulkner: Myth and Motion. Princeton: Princeton U. P., 1968, passim.

3055 Aguilar, Esperanza. Yoknapatawpha, Propiedad de William Faulkner. Santiago de Chile: Editorial Universitaria, 1964, pp. 116-128.

3056 Allen, Walter. [Requiem for a Nun], NS&N, 45, #1146 (February 21, 1953), 214.

3057 Anon. "No Sanctuary," Newsweek (September 24, 1951), 90-92.

3058 Anon. "Le nouveau Faulkner est une suite de 'Sanctuaire,'" Samedi-Soir (29 septembre 1941).

3059 Anon. "Requiem for a Nun," Booklist, 48 (October 1, 1951), 49.

3060 Anon. "Requiem for a Nun," CE, 8 (November, 1951), 128.

3061 Anon. "Requiem for a Nun," Kirkus, 19 (July 15, 1951), 356.

3062 Anon. ["Requiem for a Nun,"] NYTimes (September 27, 1951), 29.

3063 Anon. ["Requiem for a Nun"], Times (June 9, 1955); (November 28, 1957).

3064 Anon. "A Saga of the Deep South," TLS, #2663 (February 13, 1953), 104.

3065 Anon. "Sanctuary Revisited," Time, 58 (September 24, 1951), 114-118.

3066 Arban, Dominque. "En attendant Requiem pour une nonne," FL, #544 (September 22, 1956), 4.

3067 Baker, Carlos. "William Faulkner: The Doomed and the Damned," The Young Rebel in American Literature. Carl Bode, ed. London: Heinemann, 1959, pp. 163-166.

3068 Baker, James R. "Ideas and Queries," FS, 1 (Spring, 1952), 4-7.
Discussion of conflict between mass law and individual conscience.

3069 Beck, Warren. "Mr. Faulkner's New Surprise," Milwaukee Journal (September 23, 1951), V, 4.

3070 ________. "Requiem for a Nun," Faulkner: Essays. Madison: Wisconsin U. P., 1976, pp. 583-635.

3071 Blair, John G. "Camus' Faulkner: Requiem for a Nun," BFLS, 47 (January, 1969), 249-257.
Notes that while Camus is "remarkably faithful" to Faulkner, his position as a "moral absolutist" is in contrast to Faulkner's moral meliorism.

3072 Breit, Harvey. "William Faulkner," Atl, 188 (October, 1951), 53-56.

3073 Brooks, Cleanth. "Discovery of Evil (Sanctuary and Requiem for a Nun)," William Faulkner: The Yoknapatawpha Country. New Haven: Yale U. P., 1963, pp. 116-140.

3074 ________. "Faulkner's Sanctuary, the Discovery of Evil," SR, 71 (Winter, 1963), 1-24.

3075 Broughton, Panthea R. "Requiem for a Nun: No Part in Rationality," SoR, 8, n. s. (Autumn, 1972), 749-762.

3076 Brown, William R. "Faulkner's Paradox in Pathology and Salvation: Sanctuary, Light in August, and Requiem for a Nun," TSLL, 9 (Autumn, 1967), 429-449.

3077 Brylowski, Walter. Faulkner's Olympian Laugh: Myth in the Novels. Detroit: Wayne State U. P., 1968, pp. 173-183.

3078 Bullough, Geoffrey. "New Novels," Birmingham Post (February 24, 1953), 3.

3079 Byam, Milton S. "Requiem for a Nun," LJ, 76 (August, 1951), 1220.

3080 C., J. F. "Faulkner Novel Has Message of Expiation," Arizona Republic (Phoenix), (September 23, 1951), III, 7.

3081 ________. "Temple Drake's Redemption," Columbia Missourian (December 19, 1951), 4.

3082 Camus, Albert. Prêface. Requiem pour une nonne. Tr. by Maurice Coindreau. Paris: Gallimard, 1957.

3083 Cantwell, Robert. "Sequel to 'Sanctuary,'" Freeman (February 11, 1952), 317-318.

3084 Carbonnell, Hortènsia Curell de., tr. Requiem per a una monja. Barcelona: Editorial Vergara, 1967.

3085 Castelli, F. "Tragedia e distruzione dell'uomo nell'opera di William Faulkner," CC, 104 (March 7, 1953), 530-543.

3086 Cêzan, Claude. "Avant Requiem pour une nonne," NL, 1516 (September 20, 1956), 10.
Interview with Albert Camus.

3087 Chapman, John. "Novel by Nobel Prize Winner Faulkner," Dallas Morning News (September 23, 1951), VII, 4.

3088 Clurman, Harold. "The Theatre," Nation, 188 (February 28, 1959), 193-194.

3089 Coindreau, Maurice Edgar. "Requiem for a Nun," France-Amêrique (October 8, 1951). Review.

3090 Collins, Carvel. "Mississippi's Nobel Prize Winner Experiments with Play Form in Middle of His Newest Novel," Delta Democrat-Times (Greenville, Miss.), (September 30, 1951), 15.

3091 Cooper, Lettice. "Novels and Stories," Yorkshire Post and Leeds Mercury (February 13, 1953), 4.

3092 Cowley, Malcolm. "In Which Mr. Faulkner Translates Past into Present," NYHTBR (September 30, 1951), I, 14.

3093 Crane, John Kenny. "The Jefferson Courthouse: An Axis Exsecrabilis Mundi," TCL, 15 (1969), 19-23.

3094 Cullen, John B., with Floyd C. Watkins. Old Times in the Faulkner Country. Chapel Hill: North Carolina U.P., 1961, pp. 74-76.

3095 Cypher, James R. "The Tangled Sexuality of Temple Drake," AI, 19 (1962), 243-252.

3096 D., P. "Faulkner Probes Further into Story of Temple Drake," Corpus Christi Caller-Times (October 21, 1951), 16-C.

3097 Degenfelder, E. Pauline. "The Four Faces of Temple Drake: Faulkner's Sanctuary, Requiem for a Nun, and the Two Film Adaptations," AQ, 28 (1976), 544-560.

3098 DeVries, Peter. "'Requiem for a Noun, or Intruder in the Dusk. (What Can Come of Trying to Read William Faulkner While Minding a Child, or Vice Versa.)" American Literature in Parody. Robert P. Falk, ed. New York: Twayne Publishers, 1955, pp. 271-276; also in Parodies. Dwight MacDonald, ed. New York: Random House, 1960, pp. 242-248.

3099 Doster, William C. "The Several Faces of Gavin Stevens," MissQ, 11 (Fall, 1958), 191-195.

3100 D[ouglas], C[laude] L. "Requiem for a Nun," Fort Worth Press (September 29, 1951), 6.

3101 Edmonds, Irene C. "Faulkner and the Black Shadow," Southern Renascence: The Literature of the Modern South. L. D. Rubins and Robert Jacobs, eds. Baltimore: Johns Hopkins Press, 1953, pp. 202-204.

3102 Elconin, Victor A. "Faulkner Reaffirms Man's Ability to Triumph Over Evil," Daily Oklahoman (Oklahoma City), (September 23, 1951), Magazine Sec., 14.

3103 Elias, Robert H. "Gavin Stevens: Intruder?" FS, 3, #1 (Spring, 1954), 1-4.

3104 English, H. M., Jr. "Requiem for a Nun," Furioso, 7 (Winter, 1952), 60-63.

3105 Everett, Walter K. Faulkner's Art and Characters. Woodbury, New York: Barrons Educ. Ser., 1969, pp. 73-77.

3106 Fadiman, Clifton. "Party of One," Holiday (November, 1951), 8-11.

3107 Fiedler, Leslie A. "Le viol des [sic] Temple: de Richardson à Faulkner," Preuves, 138 (August, 1962), 75-81.

Comments on the excessive role which Gothic fiction has played in the American novel and on the total absence in American literary masterpieces of great love stories.

3108 Gannett, Lewis. "Requiem for a Nun," NYHTB (September 27, 1951), 21.

3109 Gardiner, Harold C. "Two Southern Tales," America (October 6, 1951), 18. Also in In All Conscience: Reflections on Books and Culture. Prentice-Hall, 1962, pp. 128-129.

3110 Gassner, John. "Broadway in Review," ETJ, 11 (May, 1959), 117-126.

3111 Geismar, Maxwell. "Requiem for a Nun," NYPost (September 23, 1951), 12-M.

3112 _______. "Requiem for a Nun," American Moderns: From Rebellion to Conformity. New York: Hill and Wang, 1958, pp. 93-95.

3113 Giermanski, James R. "William Faulkner's Use of the Confessional," Renascence, 21 (Spring, 1969), 119-123, 166.
Explores the method of "expiation through the suffering and penance of sin-telling."

3114 Gold, Joseph. "Requiem for a Nun: The Tragic Life of a Prostitute," William Faulkner: A Study in Humanism from Metaphor to Discourse. Norman: Oklahoma U.P., 1966, pp. 94-110.

3115 Gossett, Louise Y. "The Climate of Violence: Wolfe, Caldwell, Faulkner," Violence in Recent Southern Fiction. Durham, North Carolina: Duke U.P., 1965, pp. 3-47.

3116 Graham, Philip. "Patterns in Faulkner's Sanctuary and Requiem for a Nun," TSL, 8 (1963), 39-46.
"In both books the emphasis is first on the physical, then on the social, and last on Truth--from nature to society to the abstract."

3117 Guerard, Albert. "Requiem for a Nun: An Examination," HA, 135 (November, 1961), 19, 41, 42.

3118 _______. "Requiem for a Nun," Profils litterature, art, musique des Etats-Unis, 1 (October, 1952), 216-218.

3119 _______. "Some Recent Novels," Perspective, 1 (Fall, 1952), 171-172.

3120 _______. "William Faulkner: Requiem for a Nun," Prospetti, 1 (Autumn, 1952), 203-208.

3121 Gwynn, Frederick L. "Requiem for Five Runs: With One Eye on William Faulkner's Latest Novel and the Other on the World Series," Furioso, 7 (Winter, 1952), 51-58. Parody.

3122 _______, and Joseph J. Blotner, eds. Faulkner in the University. Charlottesville: Virginia U.P., 1959, passim.

3123 Hamblen, Abigail Ann. "Faulkner's Pillar of Endurance: Sanctuary and Requiem for a Nun," MwQ, 6 (July, 1965), 369-375.

3124 Hamilton, Edith. "Faulkner: Sorcerer or Slave?" SatRL, 38 (July 12, 1952), 39-41. Also in Saturday Review Gallery. Jerome Beatty, ed. New York: Simon & Schuster, 1959, pp. 419-429.

3125 Hass, Victor P. "Mr. Faulkner--As Before," Omaha World Herald (October 21, 1951), Mag. Sec., 29.

3126 Haugh, Robert F. "Faulkner's Corrupt Temple," ESA, 4 (March, 1961), 7-16.
The "counterpoint between social contract in the origins of the state, and moral responsibility in the individual."

3127 Hawkins, E. O., Jr. "Jane Cook and Cecilia Farmer," MissQ, 18 (Fall, 1965), 248-251.
Historical source of anecdote in Requiem for a Nun.

3128 Heilman, Robert B. "School for Girls," SR, 60 (Spring, 1952), 304-309.

3129 Hicks, Granville. "Faulkner's Sequel to Sanctuary," New Leader (October 22, 1951), 21-23.

3130 Hoch, Henry George. "Evil World of Faulkner," Detroit News (February 10, 1952), Women's Sec., 18.

3131 Hoffman, Frederick J. William Faulkner. New York: Twayne, 1961, 2nd ed., 1966, pp. 108-111.

3132 Holmes, Edward M. Faulkner's Twice Told Tales: His Re-Use of His Material. The Hague: Mouton, 1966, pp. 65-66.

3133 ______. "Requiem for a Scarlet Nun," Costerus, 5 (1972), 35-49.

3134 Howe, Irving. Nation (September 29, 1951), 263-264. Review.

3135 ______. William Faulkner: A Critical Study. New York: Random House, 1952, pp. 105-107.

3136 Howell, Elmo. "The Chickasaw Queen: in William Faulkner's Story," ChronOkla, 49 (1971), 334-339.
Quotes a description of Mohataha, an old Indian queen, from Requiem for a Nun, which indicates the tragedy of the Indians.

3137 Hughes, Riley. Chicago Sunday Tribune (October 7, 1951), 6. Review.

3138 _______. "New Novels," CathWorld, 174 (December, 1951), 232.

3139 Hyman, Stanley Edgar. "Some Trends in the Novel," CE, 20 (October, 1958), 2. Review.

3140 Izard, Barbara, and Clara Hieronymus. Requiem for a Nun: On Stage and Off. Nashville/London: Aurora Publishers, Inc., 1970.

3141 Jacobs, Robert D. "William Faulkner: The Passion and the Penance," South: Modern Southern Literature in Its Cultural Setting. Louis D. Rubin, Jr., and Robert D. Jacobs, eds. Garden City, New York: Doubleday, 1961, pp. 173-174.

3142 Jessup, Lee Cheney. "Faulkner's Most Complex Work," Nashville Banner (November 2, 1951), 30.

3143 Killingsworth, Kay. "Au-delà du déchirement: L'héritage méridional dans l'oeuvre de William Faulkner et d'Albert Camus," Esprit, n.s., No. 31 (September, 1963), 209-234.

3144 Kirby, John Pendy. "Fashions in Sinning," VQR, 28 (Winter, 1952), 126. Review.

3145 Kirk, Robert W., and Marvin Klotz. Faulkner's People. Berkeley: California U.P., 1963, pp. 142-146.

3146 K[lein], F[rancis] A. "Books--What's New," St. Louis Globe-Democrat (October 21, 1951), 3.

3147 Lambert, J. W. "Up to Their Tricks," Sunday Times (February 15, 1953), 5.

3148 Lane, Allen. "Social Problems," CurL (February, 1953), 19.

3149 Lang, Béatrice. "Comparison de Requiem for a Nun and A Fable," RANAM, 9 (1976), 57-72.

3150 Larson, Sixten. "I nobelpristagaren William Faulkners bok Själamässa för en nunna," Planläggning i landskommun. Uppsala: Landskommunernas Förbunds Förlag, 1953, pp. 3-4.

3151 Lehmann, John. "New Novels," Listener, 49 (February 19, 1953), 321.

3152 Lemarchand, Jacques. "Requiem pour une Nonne," NRF, 4 (November, 1956), 896-900.

3153 McGann, George. "Faulkner's New Novel Has Religious Savorings," Dallas Times Herald (September 23, 1951), V, 10.

3154 McHaney, Thomas L. "Faulkner Borrows from the Mississippi Guide," MissQ, 19 (Summer, 1966), 116-120.

3155 Makuck, Peter. "Requiem for a Nun," Faulkner Studies in France, 1953-1969," DAI, 32 (Kent State: 1971), 3314A.

3156 Malin, Irving. William Faulkner: An Interpretation. Stanford: Stanford U. P., 1957, passim.

3157 Match, Richard. "The 'New' Faulkner," NR, 125 (November 5, 1951), 19-20.

Does not estimate Requiem for a Nun as a "major addition" to the body of Faulkner's work, but adds that "... it seems to signal the emergence of a 'new' and mellower Faulkner, who believes that 'good must come out of evil,' that people are 'inherently gentle and compassionate and kind,' and that his trigger-happy Southerners are not 'vicious' after all;...."

3158 Millgate, Michael. "'The Firmament of Man's History': Faulkner's Treatment of the Past," MissQ, 25 (Spring, 1972), Supp., 25-35.

3159 ________. "Requiem for a Nun," The Achievement of William Faulkner. New York: Random House, 1966, pp. 221-226.

3160 ________. William Faulkner. New York: Grove Press, 1961; Revised, 1966; Repr., Capricorn Bks, 1971, passim.

3161 Minot, George E. "Requiem for a Nun," Boston Sunday Herald, 211 (September 30, 1951), III, 4. Review.

3162 Morel, Jacques. " 'Requiem pour une nonne,' " Etudes, 291 (December, 1956), 204-410.

3163 Morgan, Frederick. "Seven Novels," HudR, 5 (Spring, 1952), 154-160.

3164 Moritsugu, Frank. "Yoknapatawpha Revisited," Varsity (Toronto Univ.), (October 16, 1951).

3165 Morrissy, W. B. "Return Ticket to Sanctuary," Montreal Gazette (September 29, 1951), 29.

3166 Murphree, Alex. "New Faulkner Novel Neither Detracts, Adds to Stature," Denver Post (September 23, 1951), 6-E.

3167 Nicolson, Nigel. "New Books," Manchester Daily Dispatch (February 13, 1953), 6.

3168 Nores, Dominique. "Contre un théâtre d'effraction. À propos de Requiem pour une nonne," RT, 36 (1958), 46-52.

3169 North, Sterling. "Sequel to Sanctuary," NY World-Telegram and Sun (September 24, 1951), 22.

3170 Ocampo, Victoria, tr. Rêquiem para una reclusa; pieza en dos partes y siete cuadros tomada de la novela de William Faulkner. Buenos Aires: Sur, 1957.

3171 O'Connor, William Van. The Tangled Fire of William Faulkner. Minneapolis: Minnesota U. P., 1954, pp. 157-159, passim.

3172 O'Neill, Frank. "New Faulkner Novel Is Story-Drama Headed for Broadway This Fall," Cleveland News (September 25, 1951), 9.

3173 Onimus, Jean. "Camus adapte à la scène Faulkner et Dostoievski," RSH, 104 (October-December, 1961), 607-621.

3174 Otten, Terry. "Faulkner's Use of the Past: A Comment," Renascence, 20 (Summer, 1968), 198-207, 214.

3175 Palievskii, P. "Afterword on Faulkner and Albert Camus to the Russian Translation of Camus' Translation of Requiem for a Nun," InL, 9 (1970), 177-218.

3176 Patrick, Corbin. "Faulkner's Latest Work Is Play-Novel," Indianapolis Star (September 23, 1951), VI, 8.

3177 Paul, David. "The Faulkner Stammer," Observer (February 15, 1953), 9.

3178 Peckham, Morse. "The Place of Sex in the Work of William Faulkner," STC, 14 (Fall, 1974), 1-20.

3179 Perkin, Robert L. "Faulkner Better Than Ever," Rocky Mountain News (Denver), (September 23, 1951), 6-A.

3180 Pfaff, William. "The Future That Is Already Here," Cw, 54 (September, 1951), 601.

3181 Pivano, Fernanda, tr. Requiem per una monaca. Milano: Mondadori, 1955, 1966.

3182 Polk, Noel. "Alec Holston's Lock and the Founding of Jefferson," MissQ, 24 (Summer, 1971), 247-269.

3183 ________. "Faulkner's 'The Jail' and the Meaning of Cecilia Farmer," MissQ, 25 (Summer, 1972), 305-325.

3184 ________. "A Textual and Critical Study of William Faulkner's Requiem for a Nun," DAI, 32 (South Carolina: 1971), 980A.

3185 ________. "The Textual History of Faulkner's Requiem for a Nun," Proof, 4 (1975), 109-128.

3186 Pooley, E. M. "Requiem for a Nun," El Paso Herald Post (September 29, 1951), 4.

3187 Poore, Charles. "New Books: New Works from Old Hands," HarperM, 203 (October, 1951), 102.
"He [Faulkner] always has a story to tell that illuminates the squalor and splendor of life...."

3188 Poster, Herbert. "Faulkner's Folly," AmMerc, 73 (December, 1951), 106-112.

3189 Powers, Clare. "Requiem for a Nun," The Sign (November, 1951), 73-74.

3190 Prescott, Orville. "Books of the Times," NYTimes (September 27, 1951), 29.

3191 Presley, Delma Eugene. "Is Reverend Whitfield a Hypocrite?" RS, 36 (March, 1968), 57-61.

3192 Price, Emerson. "Tragic Faulkner Novel Has Spiritual Message," Cleveland Press (September 25, 1951), 10.

3193 Raven, Simon. "New Novels," Time and Tide, 34 (February 21, 1953), 250-251.
"... [D]ime-novel level...."

3194 Rebelo, Sousa, tr. and preface. Requiem por uma freira. Lisboa: Minerva, 1958.

3195 Reed, Joseph W., Jr. "Faulkner's Failure: Intruder in the Dust, Requiem for a Nun, and A Fable," Faulkner's Narrative. New Haven: Yale U.P., 1973, pp. 201-217.

3196 "Requiem for a Nun," SatRL, 39 (October 30, 1956), 58.

3197 "Requiem for a Nun," ThArts, 35 (October, 1951).
Review of the novel, but prediction of the play.

3198 Richards, Robert. "The Value of Faith Comes to Us Again in Faulkner Book," Press-Scimitar (Memphis), (October 13, 1951), 6.
Reviewer says that few ministers can preach as eloquent a sermon.

3199 Richardson, Kenneth E. Force and Faith in the Novels of William Faulkner. The Hague: Mouton, 1967, passim.

3200 Ridgely, Joseph V. "A Moral Play," HopR, 5 (Spring, 1952), 81-83.
Review of the book.

3201 Rubin, Louis D., Jr. "Thomas Wolfe in Time and Space," Southern Renascence. Louis D. Rubin and Robt. D. Jacobs, eds. Baltimore: Johns Hopkins, 1953, pp. 293-294.
"Faulkner's Requiem for a Nun is full of ... awareness of the omnipresence of the past...."

3202 Ruppersburg, Hugh Michael. "The Narrative Structure of Faulkner's Requiem for a Nun," MissQ, 31, #3 (Summer, 1978), 387-406.

3203 Savelli, Giovanni. "Paràbola di Faulkner," LitM, 4 (May-June, 1953), 337-342.

3204 Schnorr, Robert, tr. Requiem für eine Nonne. Zürich: Fretz & Wasmuth, 1956.

3205 Schott, Webster. "Faulkner's Experiment--a Play in a Novel," Kansas City Star (October 13, 1951), 16.

3206 Schulberg, Budd. "Requiem for a Nun: William Faulkner Wrote Like an Angel About His Particular Vision of Hell," TVGuide, 23, #5 (February 1, 1975), 31-32.

3207 Shaw, John Bennett. "Faulkner Both Good, Bad in Requiem for a Nun," Daily World (Tulsa, Oklahoma), (November 4, 1951), V, 9.

3208 Sherman, Thomas B. "Faulkner's New Novel a Departure in Form," St. Louis Post-Dispatch (September 30, 1951), 4-C.

3209 Simpson, Lewis P. "Isaac McCaslin and Temple Drake: The Fall of the New World Man," Nine Essays in Modern Literature. Donald E. Stanford, ed. Baton Rouge: Louisiana State U.P., 1965, pp. 88-106.

3210 Slatoff, Walter J. "Requiem for a Nun," Quest for Failure. Ithaca: Cornell U.P., 1960, 2nd pr., 1961, pp. 208-210.

3211 Smith, Harrison. "Purification by Sacrifice," SatRL, 34 (September 29, 1951), 12.

3212 Spain, Nancy. "Deep in the Heart of Faulkner," Daily Express (February 19, 1953), 4.

3213 Swiggart, Peter. The Art of Faulkner's Novels. Austin: Texas U.P., 1962, 181-184.

3214 ________. "Time in Faulkner's Novels," MFS, 1 (May, 1955), 25-29.

3215 Thompson, Lawrance. William Faulkner: An Introduction and Interpretation. New York: Barnes & Noble, 1963, pp. 117-132.

3216 TLS, #2663 (February 13, 1953), 104. Review.

3217 Truax, Charles. "Newest Faulkner 'Novel' Sequel to Earlier Book," Dayton News (October 7, 1951), II, 8.

3218 Tuck, Dorothy. Crowell's Handbook of Faulkner. New York: Crowell, 1964, pp. 115-120.

3219 Ulrey, Pamela Anne. "Faulkner's Sanctuary and Requiem for a Nun: Songs of Innocence and Experience," DA, 24 (Cornell: 1963), 2043-44.

3220 Vickery, Olga W. "Gavin Stevens: From Rhetoric to Dialectic," FS, 2 (Spring, 1953), 1-4.

3221 ________. "Sanctuary, and Requiem for a Nun," The Novels of William Faulkner. Revised ed. Baton Rouge: Louisiana State U.P., 1964, pp. 114-123.

3222 Volpe, Edmond L. A Reader's Guide to William Faulkner. New York: Noonday Press, 1969, pp. 265-281.

3223 Waggoner, Hyatt H. "William Faulkner's Passion Week of the Heart," The Tragic Vision and the Christian Faith. Nathan A. Scott, Jr., ed. New York: Association Press, 1957, pp. 306-323; revised for William Faulkner: From Jefferson to the World. Lexington: Kentucky U.P., 1959, pp. 238-266.

3224 Wagner, Geoffrey. "Faulkner's Contemporary Passion Play," TC, 156 (December, 1954), 527-538.

3225 Warren, Robert Penn. "The Redemption of Temple Drake," NYTBR (September 30, 1951), 1, 31.

3226 Watkins, Floyd C. "The Truth Shall Make You Fail," The Flesh and the Word. Nashville: Vanderbilt U.P., 1971, pp. 260-262, 263-264.

3227 West, Anthony. "Requiem for a Dramatist," NY, 27 (September 22, 1951), 109-112.

3228 West, Ray B., Jr. "William Faulkner: Artist and Moralist," WR, 16 (Winter, 1952), 162-167.

3229 Worsley, T. "Redemption," NSt, 54 (December 7, 1957), 773.

3230 Zalamea, Jorge, tr. Réquiem para una mujer. Buenos Aires: Emecé Editores, 1952; 5th ed., 1963.

Dramatic Production of Requiem for a Nun

3231 Anderson, Michael, et al. Crowell's Handbook of Contemporary Drama. New York: Crowell, 1971, p. 146.

3232 Anon. "New Plays in Manhattan: Requiem for a Nun," Time, 73 (February 9, 1959), 70.

3233 Anon. "Plans for Faulkner's Play," NYHTB (October 26, 1951).

3234 Anon. "Requiem for a Nun," America (February 21, 1959), 614.

3235 Atkinson, Brooks. "Theatre: Faulkner's Play," NYTimes (January 31, 1959), 13.

3236 Barjon, R. P., et al. "Faulkner et Camus: Requiem pour une nonne (dêbat du 15/1/1957)," Recherches et dêbats du Centre Catholique des Intellectuels Français, No. 20 (September, 1957), 133-156.

3237 Beaumont, Paule de. "Paris Diary," Rêalitês, No. 74 (January, 1957), 5.
Comment on Camus' version of Requiem for a Nun.

3238 Behrman, Daniel and Lida. "Catherine Sellers: France's Greatest Young Tragedienne," Rêalitês, No. 136 (March, 1962), 46-51.
Note on the French actress who played Temple Drake in the Paris production.

3239 Betjeman, John. ["Requiem for a Nun"], Daily Telegraph (February 13, 1953).
Thought the prologue too long.

3240 [Brecht, Bertolt]. Neues Osterreich (Zurich), (June 2, 1962).
Quotes Bertolt Brecht, who, after seeing a dress rehearsal, is said to have remarked, "This is excellent."

3241 Bree, Germaine. Camus. New Brunswick, New Jersey: Revised Edition, Harcourt, 1964, pp. 162-165, passim.

3242 Bullough, Geoffrey. ["Requiem for a Nun"]. Birmingham Post (February 24, 1953).
Thought the prologue unnecessary.

3243 Calta, Louis. "Customers Wanted," NYTimes (March 4, 1959), 34.

3244 Camus, Albert. Requiem pour une nonne, pièce en deux parties et sept tableaux d'après William Faulkner. Paris:

Gallimard, 1956.
Rev., by Hugh W. Treadwell, Books Abroad, 31 (1957-58), 141.

3245 ________. "William Faulkner: Foreword to Requiem for a Nun," Lyrical and Critical Essays. Ed. with Notes by Philip Thody; translated from French by Ellen C. Kennedy. New York: Knopf, 1968, pp. 311-320.

3246 Capron, Marcell. ["Requiem for a Nun"], Combat (May 1957).
Noted differences between Camus' version and Robert Schnorr and Edwin Piscator's German version.

3247 Chapman, John. "Faulkner's Requiem for a Nun Is About As Confusing As He Is," NYDaily News (January 31, 1959), 21.

3248 Clurman, Harold. Lies Like Truth. New York: Macmillan, 1958, pp. 239-240.

3249 ________. "The Theatre," Nation, 188 (February 28, 1959), 193-194.
"... [F]or all its serious shortcomings Requiem involved me far more than many a glibber piece...."

3250 Coindreau, M. R., tr. Requiem pour une nonne. Paris: Gallimard, 1957.

3251 Coleman, Robert. "Requiem for a Nun Is Sordid," NYMirror (January 31, 1959), 27.

3252 Couch, John Philip. "Camus and Faulkner: The Search for the Language of Modern Tragedy," YFS, 25 (Spring, 1960), 120-125.

3253 ________. "Camus' Dramatic Adaptations and Translations," FR, 33 (October, 1959), 27-36.

3254 Driver, Tom F. "Faulkner's Faith with Corruption," NR, 140 (March 9, 1959), 22.

3255 Ford, Jesse Hill, Jr. "Intricate Faulkner Work Symbolizes Destruction," Nashville Tennessean (September 30, 1951), C, 18.

3256 Ford, Ruth. Requiem for a Nun: A Play from the Novel by William Faulkner. Adapted to the Stage by Ruth Ford. New York: Random House, 1959.

3257 French Cultural Services. Quarterly Letter to Teachers, 1, #2 (October, 1956).
Recounts the "enthusiastic reception" of Requiem, adapted

by Albert Camus from Faulkner's novel, and presented in Paris at the Théâtre des Mathurins on September 30th.

3258 Funke, Lewis. "News and Gossip on the Rialto," NYTimes (October 19, 1952), II, 1.

3259 ________. "Rialto Gossip," NYTimes (March 8, 1959), II, 1.

3260 Gassner, John. "Broadway in Review," Educ. Theatre Journal, 11 (May, 1959), 117-126.

3261 ________. Theatre at the Crossroads: Plays and Playwrights of the Mid-Century American Stage. New York: Holt, Rinehart & Winston, 1960, pp. 165-167, 290.

3262 Golden, John. "Requiem for a Nun," CathWorld, 189 (April, 1959), 61.

3263 Greek Reviews of the Play, Requiem for a Nun: Ethnos (March 11, 1957); "Theater's Premiere," Kathimerini (March 10, 1957); Estia (March 11, 1957).

3264 Gruen, John. "Ruth Ford: A Tomorrow Kind of Woman," Status/Diplomat (June/July, 1967), 54-57, 73.

3265 Guérard, Albert. "Requiem for a Nun: An Examination," HA, 135 (November, 1951), 19, 41-42.

3266 Hamelin, Jean. "Le Requiem pour une nonne de Faulkner," Montreal DeVoir (March 3, 1962), 9.
Review of the Camus version of the play.

3267 Hewes, Henry. "Faulkner and the Fallen Idle," SatRL, 42 (February 14, 1959), 32.

3268 ________. "O'Neill and Faulkner via the Abroad Way: Criticism," SatRL, 39 (October 20, 1956), 59.

3269 Howe, Irving. "Faulkner: An Experiment in Drama," Nation, 173 (September 29, 1951), 263-264.

3270 Izard, Barbara, and Clara Hieronymus. Requiem for a Nun: Onstage and Off. Nashville and London: Aurora, 1970.
An extensive study of the play, the author's intent, and its reception at home and abroad.

3271 Josset, André. "The Season in Paris," The Best Plays for 1956-57. Louis Kronenberger, ed. New York: Dodd, Mead & Co., 1957, p. 47.

3272 Kerr, Walter. "First Night Report: Requiem for a Nun," NYHTB (January 31, 1959), 7.

3273 Kronenberger, Louis, ed. "Requiem for a Nun: A Play in Three Acts," The Best Plays of 1958-59. New York: Dodd, Mead and Co., 1959, pp. 189-208.

3274 Lambert, J. W. [Requiem for a Nun], The Sunday Times (February 15, 1953).

3275 Lazere, Donald. The Unique Creation of Albert Camus. London and New Haven: Yale U. P., 1973, pp. 231-232.

3276 Lebesque, Morvan. Camus par lui-même. Paris: Écrivains de Toujours, Éditions du Seuil, 1963, 1966, pp. 150-151.

3277 Lehmann, John. ["Requiem for a Nun"], Listener, 49 (February 19, 1953), 321.

3278 Lyons, Leonard. "The Lyons Den," NYPost (January 30, 1959), 37.

3279 McClain, John. "Stark Drama by Faulkner Too Complex," NY Journal-American (January 31, 1959), 14.

3280 McCord, Bert. "Plans for Faulkner's Play," NYHTB (October 26, 1951), 12.

3281 McLaughlin, Richard. "Requiem for Temple Drake--A Nobel Prize Winner Comes to Broadway," ThA, 35 (October, 1951), 50, 77.

3282 Millstein, Gilbert. "An Actress Who Got Her Wish," NY Times (January 25, 1959), II, 1.

3283 Morel, Jacques. "Requiem pour une nonne au Théâtre des Mathurins," Etudes (Paris), No. 291 (December 19, 1956), 402-410.

3284 Mullen, Phil. ["Requiem for a Nun"], Oxford Eagle (October 25, 1951).

3285 "The Murkier Depths," Newsweek, 53 (February 9, 1959), 56.

3286 "New Plays in Manhattan: Requiem for a Nun," Time, 73 (February 9, 1959), 70.

3287 "No Sanctuary," Newsweek (September 24, 1951), 90-91. Review.

3288 O'Connor, William Van. "Faulkner on Broadway," KR, 21 (Spring, 1959), 334-336.

3289 Piscator, Maria Ley. The Piscator Experiment. New York: James H. Heineman, 1967, p. 283.

3290 Polk, Noel. "The Staging of Requiem for a Nun," MissQ, 24 (Summer, 1971), 299-314.

3291 "Requiem for a Nun," ThA, 43 (April, 1959), 23, 67.

3292 Ryan, Jack. "The Lady of the Dakota," Delta Rev. 2 (July-August, 1965), 44-45.
An interview with Ruth Ford.

3293 Schneider, Marcel. "Une nonne americaine," Cahiers des saisons, 9 (February-March, 1957), 232-233.
Review of the Faulkner play as presented in the Camus adaptation.

3294 Schumach, Murray. The Face on the Cutting Room Floor. New York: William Morrow, 1964, p. 145.
Note on film of Sanctuary and Requiem.

3295 Talley, Rhea. "A Southerner in New York," Commercial Appeal (Memphis), (March 22, 1953), VI, 12.

3296 Taylor, Nancy Dew. "The Dramatic Productions of Requiem for a Nun," MissQ, 20 (Summer, 1967), 123-134.
Deals with the adaptation by Faulkner and Ruth Ford, and also with the French version by Albert Camus.

3297 Thody, Philip, ed. "William Faulkner: Foreword to Requiem for a Nun," Albert Camus, Lyrical and Critical Essays. Tr. from French by Ellen C. Kennedy. New York: Knopf, 1968, pp. 311-320.

3298 Troy, William. "Faulkner in Hollywood," Nation, 136 (May 24, 1933), 594-595.
Paramount's offering of a "truly extraordinary version" of Faulkner's Sanctuary in "The Story of Temple Drake."

3299 Tynan, Kenneth. "At the Theatre," NY, 34 (February 7, 1959), 83-84.

3300 _______. "Requiem for a Nun," Curtains: Selections from the Drama Criticism and Related Writings. New York: Atheneum, 1961, pp. 276-278, 299-301.

3301 Watt, David. "Down South Again," Spectator, 199 (December 6, 1957), 791, 793.

3302 Watts, Richard. "Play by William Faulkner Adapted from His Novel," NYPost (February 1, 1959), 14.

3303 West, Anthony. "Requiem for a Dramatist," NY, 27 (September 22, 1951), 109-114.

3304 West, Ray B., Jr. "William Faulkner: Artist and Moralist," WR (1952), 162-167.

3305 Worsley, T. C. "Redemption," NS&N (December 7, 1957), 773.

3306 Zolotow, Samuel. "Faulkner Script Names Ruth Ford," NYTimes (January 30, 1959), 32.

"RETREAT"
(Published in SatEP, 207 (October 13, 1934), 16-17, passim; revised for The Unvanquished)

3307 Early, James. "Retreat," The Making of Go Down, Moses. Dallas: Southern Methodist U.P., 1972, pp. 17, 32.

3308 Kerr, Elizabeth M. "Retreat," Yoknapatawpha: Faulkner's Little Postage Stamp of Native Soil." New York: Fordham U.P., 1969, pp. 95, 98, 99.

3309 Tuck, Dorothy. "Retreat," Crowell's Handbook of Faulkner. New York: Crowell, 1964, pp. 67-68.

"RIPOSTE IN TERTIO"
(Entitled "The Unvanquished" in SatEP, 209 (November 14, 1936), 12-13, passim; revised and entitled "Riposte in Tertio" for The Unvanquished, 1938.)

3310 Early, James. "Riposte in Tertio," The Making of Go Down, Moses. Dallas: Southern Methodist U.P., 1972, p. 17.

3311 Tuck, Dorothy. "Riposte in Tertio," Crowell's Handbook of Faulkner. New York: Crowell, 1964, pp. 68, 181.

"A ROSE FOR EMILY"
(Pub., in Forum, 83 (April, 1930), 233-238; slightly revised for These 13, 1931; repr., in Collected Stories, 1950.)

3312 Allen, Charles. "William Faulkner: Comedy and the Purpose of Humor," ArQ, 16 (Spring, 1960), 59-69.

3313 Barber, Marion. "The Two Emilys: A Ransom Suggestion to Faulkner?" NMW, 6 (Winter, 1973), 103-105.
John Crowe Ransom's poem, "Emily Hardcastle, Spinster," suggested as a source for Faulkner's story.

3314 Barnes, Daniel R. "Faulkner's Miss Emily and Hawthorne's Old Maid," SSF, 9 (Fall, 1972), 373-377.
Suggests Hawthorne's "The White Old Maid" as a possible source for Faulkner's story.

3315 Bartra, Agusti, tr. "Una rosa para Emily," Cuentos policíacos y de misterio. México: Novelas Atlante, 1955, pp. 442-451.

3316 Bride, Sister Mary, O. P. "Faulkner's 'A Rose for Emily,' " Expl, 20 (May, 1962), Item 78.

3317 Brooks, Cleanth, and Robert Penn Warren. "On Faulkner's 'A Rose for Emily,' " Understanding Fiction. New York: Appleton-Century-Crofts, 1959, pp. 350-354.

3318 Campbell, Harry M., and Ruel E. Foster. William Faulkner: A Critical Appraisal. Norman: Oklahoma U. P., 1951, pp. 99-100.

3319 Clements, Arthur L. "Faulkner's 'A Rose for Emily,' " Expl, 20 (May, 1962), Item 78.
Cf., Elmo Howell. "Faulkner's 'A Rose for Emily,' " Expl, 19 (January, 1961), 26.

3320 Coindreau, Maurice Edgar, tr. "Une Rose pour Emilie," Commerce, 29 (hiver, 1932), 110-137.

3321 ________. "Une Rose pour Emilie," NRF, 38 (January, 1932), 49-65.

3322 Collmer, Robert G. "The Displaced Person in the Novels of Gabriel Casaccia," Re: A&L, 3 (Spring, 1970), 37-45.

3323 Cullen, John B., with Floyd C. Watkins. Old Times in the Faulkner Country. Chapel Hill: North Carolina U. P., 1961, pp. 70-71.

3324 Davis, W. V. "Another Flower for Faulkner's Bouquet: Theme and Structure in 'A Rose for Emily,' " NMW, 7 (Fall, 1974), 34-38.
Analysis in terms of time.

3325 Deegan, Dorothy Yost. The Stereotype of the Single Woman in American Novels: A Social Study with Implications for the Education of Women. New York: Octagon Books, 1969, p. 8.

3326 Edwards, C. H., Jr. "Three Literary Parallels to Faulkner's 'A Rose for Emily,' " NMW, 7 (Spring, 1974), 21-25.
Possible parallels in Dickens's Great Expectations, Browning's "Porphyria's Lover," and Poe's "To Helen."

3327 Fenson, Harry, and Hildreth Kritzer. Reading, Understanding, and Writing About Short Stories. New York: Free Press, 1966, passim.

3328 Going, William T. "Chronology in Teaching 'A Rose for Emily,' " ExEx, 5 (February, 1958), 8-11.

3329 ________. "Faulkner's 'A Rose for Emily,' " Expl, 16 (February, 1958), Item 27.

3330 Gwynn, Frederick L., and Joseph L. Blotner, eds. *Faulkner in the University*. Charlottesville: Virginia U.P., 1959, *passim*.

3331 Hagopian, John V., and Martin Dolch. "Faulkner's 'A Rose for Emily,' " Expl, 22 (April, 1964), Item 68.

3332 ______, ______. "A Rose for Emily," *Insight I: Analyses of American Literature*. Frankfurt am Main: Hirschgraben-Verlag, 1962, pp. 42-50.

3333 Happel, Nikolaus. "William Faulkner's 'A Rose for Emily,' " NS, 9 (August, 1962), 396-404.

3334 Heiney, Donald W. *Recent American Literature*. Great Neck, New York: Barron's Educ. Ser., 1958, pp. 224-225.

3335 Heller, Terry. "The Telltale Hair: A Critical Study of William Faulkner's 'A Rose for Emily,' " ArQ, 28 (Winter, 1972), 301-318.

3336 Hendricks, William O. "'A Rose for Emily': A Syntagmatic Analysis," PTL, 2 (April, 1977), 257-295.
A study of plot structure.

3337 Holland, Norman N. "Fantasy and Defense in Faulkner's 'A Rose for Emily,'" HSL, 4 (1972), 1-35.

3338 Howe, Irving. "A Note on the Stories: 'A Rose for Emily,' " *William Faulkner: A Critical Study*. New York: Vintage, 1952, p. 262-265.

3339 Howell, Elmo. "Faulkner's 'A Rose for Emily,' " Expl, 19 (January, 1961), Item 26.

3340 ______. "A Note on Faulkner's Emily As a Tragic Heroine," Serif, 3 (September, 1966), 13-15.

3341 Hutchens, E. N. "Towards a Poetics of Fiction: 5 'The Novel as Chronomorph,'" Novel, 5 (Spring, 1972), 215-224.
"A Rose for Emily" and *The Sound and the Fury* both indicate the importance of time in shaping narratives.

3342 Inge, M. Thomas, ed. *William Faulkner: A Rose for Emily*. Columbus, Ohio: Charles E. Merrill, 1970.

3343 Jäger, Dietrich. "Der 'verheimlichte Raum' in Faulkners 'A Rose for Emily' und Brittings 'Der Schneckenweg,' " LWU, 1 (1968), 108-116.

3344 Johnson, C. W. M. "Faulkner's 'A Rose for Emily,'" Expl, 6 (May, 1948), Item 45.

3345 Kazin, Alfred. "William Faulkner: The Short Stories--'A Rose for Emily,' " Contemporaries. Boston: Little, Brown, 1962, pp. 155-156.

3346 Kempton, Kenneth P. The Short Story. Cambridge: Harvard U. P., 1947, pp. 104-106.

3347 Kerr, Elizabeth M. Yoknapatawpha: Faulkner's "Little Postage Stamp of Native Soil." New York: Fordham U. P., 1969, pp. 108, 159, 214.

3348 Kierszys, Zofia i Jan Zakrzewski, trs. Róza dla Emilil. Opowiadania. Warszawa: Ksiazka i Wiedza, 1967.

3349 Kobler, J. F. "Faulkner's 'A Rose for Emily,' " Exp. 32 (April, 1974), Item 65.

3350 Levitt, Paul. "An Analogue for Faulkner's 'A Rose for Emily,' " PLL, 9 (Winter, 1973), 91-94.
John Crowe Ransom's poem, "Emily Hardcastle, Spinster," suggested as analogue for Faulkner's story.

3351 Lopez Landeira, Ricardo. "Aura, The Aspern Papers, 'A Rose for Emily': A Literary Relationship," JSSTC, 3 (1975), 125-143.
Similarities of structure.

3352 McGlynn, Paul D. "The Chronology of 'A Rose for Emily,' " SSF, 6 (Summer, 1969), 461-462.

3353 Magalaner, Marvin, and Edmond L. Volpe, eds. Teachers' Manual: Twelve Short Stories. New York: Macmillan, 1961, pp. 143-148.

3354 Malin, Irving. William Faulkner: An Interpretation. Stanford: Stanford U. P., 1957, pp. 37-38.

3355 Marcus, Fred H. Instructor's Manual: Perception and Pleasure: Stories for Analysis. Boston: Heath, 1967.

3356 Mathieu-Higginbotham, Corina. "Faulkner y Onetti: una visión de la realidad a travês de Jefferson y Santa Maria," Hispanofila, 61 (September, 1977), 51-60.

3357 Millgate, Michael. The Achievement of William Faulkner. New York: Random House, 1965, pp. 263-264.

3358 Muller, Gil. "Faulkner's 'A Rose for Emily,'" Expl, 33, # 9 (1975), Item 79.

3359 Nebeker, Helen E. "Chronology Revised," SSF, 8 (Summer, 1971), 471-473.
Cf., Paul D. McGlynn. "The Chronology of 'A Rose for

Emily,' " SSF, 6 (1969), 461-462; G. R. Wilson, Jr. "The Chronology of Faulkner's 'A Rose for Emily,' Again," NMW, 5 (1972), 44, 56, 58-62.

3360 ________. "Emily's Rose of Love: A Postscript," BRMMLA, 24 (December, 1970), 190-191.
Emendation: The date 1894 is the time when Emily's taxes were remitted, not the date of her father's death. Her birth date was about 1854, and her lover disappeared about 1886.

3361 ________. "Emily's Rose of Love: Thematic Implications of Point of View in Faulkner's 'A Rose for Emily,' " BRMMLA, 24 (March, 1970), 3-13.

3362 O'Connor, William Van. "The State of Faulkner Criticism," SR, 60 (Winter, 1952), 183-184.

3363 ________. The Tangled Fire of William Faulkner. Minneapolis: Minnesota U. P., 1954, pp. 68-69.

3364 Page, Sally R. Faulkner's Women. DeLand, Florida: Everett-Edwards, 1972, pp. 99-103.

3365 Ross, Danforth. The American Short Story. Minneapolis: Minnesota U. P., 1961, pp. 36-37.

3366 Sale, William M., Jr., and James Hall, Martin Steinmann, Jr. Critical Discussions for Teachers Using "Short Stories: Tradition and Direction." Norfolk: New Directions, 1949, pp. 37-40.

3367 Skaggs, Calvin, and Merrill Maguire Skaggs. Instructor's Manual for Mark Schorer's Galaxy: Literary Modes and Genres. New York: Harcourt, 1967, pp. 37-39.

3368 Snell, George. "The Fury of William Faulkner," WR, 11 (Autumn, 1946), 35-37; repr., in Shapers of American Fiction. New York: Cooper Square Pubs., 1961, pp. 96-99.

3369 Stafford, T. J. "Tobe's Significance in 'A Rose for Emily,' " MFS, 14 (Winter, 1968-69), 451-453.

3370 Stevens, Aretta J. (Sister Mary Dominic Stevens). "Faulkner and 'Helen': A Further Note," PoeN, 1 (October, 1968), 31.
Comparison of Emily posed statue-like before her window and Poe's "Helen."

3371 Stewart, James Tate. "Miss Havisham and Miss Grierson," FurmS, 6 (Fall, 1958), 21-23.
Comparison of Great Expectations and "A Rose for Emily."

3372 Stone, Edward. A Certain Morbidness: A View of American Literature. London: Feffer & Simons; Carbondale and Edwardsville: So. Ill. U. P., 1969, pp. 85-100.

3373 _______. "Usher, Poquelin, and Miss Emily: The Progress of Southern Gothic," GaR, 14 (Winter, 1960), 433-443.

3374 Stronks, James. "A Poe Source for Faulkner? 'To Helen' and 'A Rose for Emily,' " PoeN, 1 (April, 1968), 11.

3375 Sullivan, Ruth. "The Narrator in 'A Rose for Emily,' " JNT, 1 (September, 1971), 159-178.
Cf., Helen Nebeker. "Chronology Revised," SSF, 8 (1971), 471-473.

3376 _______. "Some Variations on the Oedipal Theme in Three Pieces of Fiction: 'A Rose for Emily,' Three Hours After Marriage, and 'Christabel,' " DAI, 33 (Tufts: 1973), 4366A.

3377 Tate, Allen. "Miss Emily and the Bibliographer," Reason in Madness. New York: Putnam's, 1941, pp. 101-116. Also in Allen Tate, Collected Essays. Denver: Alan Swallow, 1959, pp. 49-61.

3378 Tatsunokuchi, Naotarō, ed., with Notes. A Rose for Emily and Other Stories. Tokyo: Nan'un-do, 1957.

3379 Tefs, Wayne. A. "Norman N. Holland and 'A Rose for Emily': Some Questions Concerning Psychoanalytic Criticism," Sphinx, 2 (1974), 50-57.

3380 Timko, Michael, and Clinton F. Oliver. Instructor's Manual to 38 Short Stories: An Introductory Anthology. New York: Knopf, 1968.

3381 Trilling, Lionel. "Mr. Faulkner's World," Nation, 133 (November 4, 1931), 491-492.

3382 Warren, Robert Penn. "Not Local Color," VQR, 8 (January, 1932), 160.

3383 Watkins, Floyd C. "The Structure of 'A Rose for Emily,' " MLN, 69 (November, 1954), 508-510.

3384 West, Ray B. "Atmosphere and Theme in Faulkner's 'A Rose for Emily,' " Perspective, 2 (Summer, 1949), 329-345. Repr., in Two Decades of Criticism. Frederick Hoffman and Olga Vickery, eds. East Lansing: Michigan State U. P., 1951, pp. 259-268; William Faulkner: Four Decades of Criticism. Linda W. Wagner, ed. Michigan State U. P., 192-198.

3385 _______. "Faulkner's 'A Rose for Emily,' " Expl, 7 (October, 1948), Item 8.

3386 ________. Reading the Short Story. New York: Crowell, 1968, pp. 79-85.

3387 ________. The Short Story in American, 1900-1950. Chicago: H. Regnery, 1952, pp. 93-94.

3388 ________, and R. W. Stallman. "Theme Through Atmosphere," The Art of Modern Fiction. New York: Rinehart, 1949, pp. 270-275.

3389 Wilson, G. R., Jr. "The Chronology of Faulkner's 'A Rose for Emily' Again," NMW, 5 (Fall, 1972), 44, 56, 58-62.
Cf., Paul D. McGlynn. "The Chronology of 'A Rose for Emily,' " SSF, 6 (1969), 461-462; Helen E. Nebeker. "Chronology Revised," SSF, 8 (1971), 471-473; Helen E. Nebeker. "Emily's Rose of Love: A Postscript," BRMMLA, 24 (1970), 190-191.

3390 Woodward, Robert H. "The Chronology of 'A Rose for Emily,' " ExEx, 13 (March, 1966), 17-19.

3391 Zmora, Zvi. "Hirhurim al-'Vered le-Emily,' " Shdemot, 56 (1975), 150-152.

"ROSE OF LEBANON"
(Cf., James B. Meriwether, # 3392 below)

3392 Meriwether, James B. The Literary Career of William Faulkner. Columbia: South Carolina U. P., 1971, pp. 87, 175.

3393 Millgate, Michael. The Achievement of William Faulkner. New York: Random House, 1966, pp. 130, 131.

SANCTUARY
(New York: Cape & Smith, 1931)

3394 Aalberse, Han B., and Mar Van Keulen, trs. Het meisje Temple Drake. 's Gravenhage: Uitgeverij Oisterwijk, 1969.
Dutch translation.

3395 Adamowski, T. H. "Faulkner's Popeye: The 'Other' As Self," CRAS, 8 (Spring, 1977), 36-51.

3396 Adams, Richard P. Faulkner: Myth and Motion. Princeton: Princeton U. P., 1968, pp. 59-71.

3397 Angelius, Judith Wood. "Temple's Provocative Quest: Or, What Really Happened at the Old Frenchman Place," NMW, 10 (Winter, 1977), 74-79.

3398 Anon. "Books Banned in Utica," NYTimes (October 24, 1954), 81.

3399 Anon. "Sanctuary," AmMerc, 23 (June, 1931), xviii.

3400 Anon. "Sanctuary," Forum, 85 (April, 1931), xviii.

3401 Anon. "Sanctuary," London TLS (September 24, 1931), 327.

3402 Anon. "Sanctuary," Time (February 16, 1931), 55-56.

3403 Arthos, John. "Ritual and Humor in William Faulkner," Accent, 19 (Autumn, 1948), 17-30. Also in Hoffman and Vickery, eds. Two Decades of Criticism, pp. 116-118.

3404 Backman, Melvin. Faulkner: The Major Years. Bloomington: Indiana U.P., 1966, pp. 41-49.

3405 Beck, Warren. "Faulkner: A Preface and a Letter," YR, 52 (Autumn, 1962), 157-160.
On the Preface with quotations from a letter by Faulkner.

3406 Bergel, Lienhard. "Faulkner's Sanctuary," Expl, 6 (December, 1947), Item 20.

3407 Bertin, Celia. "From Paris," NYTBR (November 15, 1959), 52-53.

3408 Bixler, Paul H. "In 'Sanctuary' Wm. Faulkner Plumbs the Depths of Horror," Cleveland Plain Dealer (February 7, 1932), Amusement Sec., 16.

3409 Bleikasten, André. "La terreur et la nausée, ou le langage des corps dans Sanctuaire," Sud, 14 (1975), 81-116.

3410 Borgström, Greta I. "The Roaring Twenties and William Faulkner's Sanctuary," MSprak, 62 (1968), 237-248.
Sees the novel as an attack on the sterility and decay of the flapper era of the 1920's.

3411 Bowling, Lawrence Edward. "William Faulkner: The Importance of Love," DR, 43 (Winter, 1963-64), 474-482.

3412 Brickell, Herschel. "The Literary Landscape," NAR, 233 (April, 1932), 376-377.

3413 Britt, George. [Sanctuary], NYTel (February 17, 1931).

3414 Brodin, Pierre. Le roman régionaliste américain. Préface de Maurice E. Coindreau. Paris: 1937.

3415 Brooks, Cleanth. "Faulkner's Sanctuary: The Discovery of Evil," SR, 71 (Spring, 1963), 1-24. Repr., William Faulkner. Yale U.P., 1963, pp. 116-140, 387-398.

3416 _______. "Faulkner's Vision of Good and Evil," MassR, 3 (Summer, 1962), 692-712.
A revised version of "Faulkner's _Sanctuary_: The Discovery of Evil," SR, 71 (1963), 1-24.

3417 _______. _The Hidden God_. New Haven: Yale U. P., 1963, pp. 22-43.

3418 _______. "William Faulkner: Vision of Good and Evil," _Religion and Modern Literature_. G. B. Tennyson and E. E. Ericson, Jr., eds. Grand Rapids, Mich.: Wm. B. Eerdmans, 1975, pp. 310-315.

3419 _______. _William Faulkner: The Yoknapatawpha County_. New Haven: Yale U. P., 1963, pp. 116-140.

3420 Brooks, Van Wyck. "From a Critic and Biographer," SatRL, 11 (November 10, 1934), 272.

3421 Brown, Calvin S. "_Sanctuary_: From Confrontation to Peaceful Void," Mosaic, 7 (Fall, 1973), 75-95.

3422 Brown, James. "Shaping the World of _Sanctuary_," UKCR, 25 (December, 1958), 137-142.

3423 Brown, William R. "Faulkner's Paradox in Pathology and Salvation: _Sanctuary_, _Light in August_, _Requiem for a Nun_," TSLL, 9 (Autumn, 1967), 429-449.

3424 Brylowski, Walter. "A Demonic World," _Faulkner's Olympian Laugh_. Detroit: Wayne State U. P., 1968, pp. 97-102.

3425 Burgum, Edwin Berry. "William Faulkner's Patterns of American Decadence," _The Novel and the World's Dilemma_. New York: Oxford U. P., 1947, pp. 217-220.

3426 Busse, A. "Amerikanischer Brief," Die Literature, 34 (1932), 340.

3427 Calvo, Lino Novâs, tr. _Santuario_. Buenos Aires: Espasa Calpe, 1945.

3428 Campbell, Harry Modean, and Ruel E. Foster. _William Faulkner: A Critical Appraisal_. Norman: Oklahoma U. P., 1951, pp. 61-62, _passim_.

3429 _______, and James Penn Pilkinton. "Faulkner's Sanctuary," Expl, 4 (June, 1946), Item 61.

3430 Camus, Albert. [Letter dated May 30, 1951]. HA, 135 (November, 1951), 21.
"_Sanctuaire_ et _Pylône_ sont des chefs-d'oeuvre."

3431 Canby, Henry Seidel. "The Literature of Horror," SatRL, 11 (October 20, 1934), 217-218.
Cf., Lawrence S. Kubie. "William Faulkner's *Sanctuary*," SatRL, 11 (October 20, 1934), 224-226.

3432 _______. "The School of Cruelty," SatRL, 7 (March 21, 1931), 673-674. Repr., in *Seven Years Harvest*. New York: Farrar & Rinehart, 1934, pp. 77-83.
Cf., Alan R. Thompson. "The Cult of Cruelty," Bookman, 74 (January-February, 1932), 477-487.

3433 Cantwell, Robert. "Faulkner's 'Popeye,'" Nation, 186 (February 15, 1958), 140-141, 148.
Suggested source for the character "Popeye."

3434 Carey, Glenn O. "Faulkner and His Carpenter's Hammer," ArQ, 32 (Spring, 1976), 5-15.

3435 _______. "William Faulkner on the Automobile as Socio-Sexual Symbol," CEA Critic, 36 (January, 1974), 15-17.

3436 Cargill, Oscar. "The Primitivists," *Intellectual America*. New York: Macmillan, 1941, pp. 370-386.

3437 Castille, Philip. "'There Was a Queen' and Faulkner's Narcissa Sartoris," MissQ, 28 (Summer, 1975), 307-315.

3438 Cecchi, Emilio. "William Faulkner," Pan, 2 (May, 1934), 64-70. A revised version of the article, "Note su William Faulkner" in *William Faulkner: venti anni di critica*. Frederick J. Hoffman, and Olga W. Vickery, eds. Parma: Guanda, 1957, pp. 102-110; also in Emilio Cecchi, *Scrittori inglesi e americani: saggi, note e versioni*, II, 4th ed., rev. Milano: Il Saggiatore, 1964, pp. 196-203.

3439 Cestre, C. [*Sanctuary*]. RAA (avril, 1933), 371-372. Édition anglaise.

3440 Chamberlain, John. "Dostoyefsky's Shadow in the Deep South," NYTBR (February 15, 1931), 9.

3441 Chapple, Richard L. "Character Parallels in *Crime and Punishment* and *Sanctuary*," GSlav, 2, i (1976), 5-14.

3442 Chase, Richard. "*Sanctuary* and *The Turn of the Screw*," Appendix I, *The American Novel and Its Tradition*, Garden City, New York: Doubleday Anchor Books, 1957, pp. 237-241.

3443 Church, Margeret. "William Faulkner: Myth and Duration," *Time and Reality: Studies in Contemporary Fiction*. Chapel Hill: North Carolina U.P., 1963, pp. 237-238.

3444 Coindreau, Maurice Edgar. Prêface. Le roman rêgionaliste amêricain by Pierre Brodin. Paris: G. P. Maisonneuve, 1937.

3445 Cole, Douglas. "Faulkner's Sanctuary: Retreat from Responsibility," WHR, 14 (Summer, 1960), 291-298.

3446 Collins, Carvel. "Nathanael West's The Day of the Locust and Sanctuary," FS, 2 (Summer, 1953), 23-24.

3447 ______. "A Note on Sanctuary," HA, 135 (November, 1951), 16. Condensation repr., Faulkner: A Collection of Critical Essays. Robert Penn Warren, ed. Englewood Cliffs, New Jersey: Prentice-Hall, 1966, pp. 290-291.

3448 Cook, Richard M. "Popeye, Flem, and Sutpen: The Faulknerian Villain As Grotesque," SAF, 3 (Spring, 1975), 3-14.

3449 Covarrubias, Miguel, illustrator. In the Worst Possible Taste by Corey Ford. New York: Scribner, 1932.
Drawing by Miguel Covarrubias of Faulkner as a popeyed boy standing in a bin of corncobs.

3450 Cowley, Malcolm. "An Introduction to William Faulkner," Critiques and Essays on Modern Fiction. John W. Aldridge, ed. New York: Ronald Press, 1952, pp. 427-446.

3451 ______. "Sanctuary," NR, 97 (January 25, 1939), 349.

3452 ______. "William Faulkner's Human Comedy," NYTBR (October 29, 1944), 4.

3453 Creighton, Joanne V. "Self-Destructive Evil in Sanctuary," TCL, 18 (October, 1972), 259-270.
"The allegorical truth that Sanctuary conclusively demonstrates is ... the inherent self-destruction of evil," a central theme in Faulkner's fiction.

3454 Cullen, John B., with Floyd C. Watkins. Old Times in the Faulkner Country. Chapel Hill: North Carolina U. P., 1961, pp. 65-66, 80-83.

3455 Cypher, James R. "The Tangled Sexuality of Temple Drake," AI, 19 (Fall, 1962), 243-252.

3456 Dabit, Eugene. Sanctuaire, Europe (15 avril 1934), 599-600.

3457 Dawson, Margaret Cheney. "Power and Horror," NYHTB (February 15, 1931), 3.

3458 Degenfelder, E. Pauline. "The Four Faces of Temple Drake: Faulkner's Sanctuary, Requiem for a Nun, and the Two Film Adaptations," AQ, 28 (1976), 544-560.

3459 Derycke, G. [Sanctuaire], CS (octobre 1935), 697-698.

3460 Dickinson, Asa Don. The Best Books of the Decade: 1926-1935. New York: H. W. Wilson, 1937, p. 61.
The Faulkner choice is Sanctuary.

3461 Edlund, Marten, tr. Det allra heligaste. Stockholm, Bokforlaget: Aldus Bonniers, 1961.

3462 Eshelman, William R. "Faulkner's Sanctuary," Expl, 4 (June, 1946), Item 61. Replies: Cf., H. M. Campbell and James P. Pilkington, Expl, 4 (June, 1946), Item 61; Lienhard Bergel, Expl, 6 (December, 1947), Item 20.

3463 Esslinger, Pat M. "No Spinach in Sanctuary," MFS, 18 (Winter, 1972-73), 555-558.
An examination of Faulkner's use of comic strip humor in the novel.

3464 Everett, Walter K. Faulkner's Art and Characters. Woodbury, New York: Barron's Edu. Ser., 1969, pp. 77-83.

3465 Fadiman, Clifton P., "The World of William Faulkner," Nation, 132 (April 15, 1931), 422-423.

3466 Fiedler, Leslie. The Collected Essays of Leslie Fiedler. New York: Stein & Day, 1971, I, pp. 333-334, passim; II, passim.

3467 ________. An End to Innocence: Essays on Culture and Politics. Boston: Beacon Press, 1955, p. 95.
"...[O]ut of the ravaged landscapes of Sanctuary and Winesburg, Ohio, the Italians have contrived a utopia. Imagine the wit and desperation necessary to such a conceit!"

3468 ________. "From Clarissa to Temple Drake," Encounter, 8 (March, 1957), 14-20; trans., "Le viol des Temple: De Richardson à Faulkner," Preuves, 138 (1962), 75-81.

3469 ________. Love and Death in the American Novel. New York: Criterion Books, 1960, pp. 311-313.

3470 ________. No! in Thunder: Essays on Myth and Literature. Boston: Beacon Press, 1960, pp. 113-114, passim.

3471 ________. Waiting for the End: The Crisis in American Culture and a Portrait of Twentieth Century American Literature. New York: Dell Pub. Co., 1964, pp. 139, 143.

3472 Fingerit, Julio. "Los 'frankestein' [sic] de William Faulkner," La Nación (Buenos Aires) (June 24, 1934), Sec. 2, 2.

3473 Fisher, A. E. "Mr. Faulkner Is Visited by the Muse," Bookman, 75, #7 (1931), 697.
A caricature depicting Faulkner having a dream.

3474 Fletcher, Helen. "New Fiction," Time and Tide, 12 (September 19, 1931), 1094.

3475 Flynn, Robert. "The Dialectic of Sanctuary," MFS, 2 (Autumn, 1956), 109-113; trans., "La dialectique de Sanctuary," RLM, 4, Nos. 27-29 (June, 1957), 32-40.

3476 Ford, Corey [Pseud. John Ridell]. In the Worst Possible Taste. New York: Scribner, 1932, pp. 84-99.
Cf., Illustration by Miguel Covarrubias.

3477 Ford, Daniel Gordon. "Comments on William Faulkner's Temporal Vision in Sanctuary, The Sound and the Fury, Light in August, Absalom, Absalom!" SoQ, 15 (April, 1977), 283-290.

3478 ________. "Uses of Time in Four Novels by William Faulkner," DAI, 35 (Auburn: 1974), 1654A.

3479 Foster, Ruel E. "Dream as Symbolic Act in Faulkner," Perspective, 2 (Summer, 1949), 179.

3480 Fowler, Albert. "Source Books of Violence," Trace, 21 (April, 1957), 11-18.

3481 Franklin, Malcolm A. "A Christmas in Columbus," MissQ, 27 (Summer, 1974), 319-322.
As excerpt from the book of reminiscences of William Faulkner's stepfather: "Columbus did not feel towards Bill's book Sanctuary as did Oxford. After Sanctuary he was shunned by many he knew in Oxford...."

3482 Frazier, David Lowell. "Gothicism in Sanctuary: The Black Pall and the Crap Table," MFS, 2 (Autumn, 1956), 114-124; trans., "L'utilisation du 'gothique' dans Sanctuary," RLM, 4, Nos. 27-29, (1957), 86-104.

3483 Frohock, W. M. "William Faulkner: The Private Vision," The Novel of Violence in America. 2nd ed. Dallas: Southern Methodist U.P., 1957, pp. 148-151.

3484 Fuller, Edmund. Man in Modern Fiction: Some Minority Opinions on Contemporary American Writing. New York: Random House, 1958, p. 105.
"... With his sequel [Requiem] Faulkner did unmistakably lift Sanctuary to a different level and category, ..."

3485 Fuller, Timothy. "The Story of Jack and Jill," SatRL, 15 (December 19, 1936), 10.

A parody of Sanctuary: the ways Alexander Woollcott, P. G. Wodehouse, and Faulkner would treat the story of Jack and Jill.

3486 Geismar, Maxwell. "William Faulkner: The Negro and the Female," Writers in Crisis. Boston: Houghton Mifflin, 1942, pp. 143-183.

3487 Glicksberg, Charles I. "The World of William Faulkner," ArQ, 5 (Spring, 1949), 46-58.

3488 Gold, Joseph. "No Refuge: Faulkner's Sanctuary," UKCR, 33 (December, 1966), 129-135.

3489 Gossett, Louise Y. Violence in Recent Southern Fiction. Durham, North Carolina: Duke U. P., 1965, pp. 27, 34-35.

3490 Gould, Gerald. "A Ghastly Plot," News Chronicle (September 14, 1931), 4.

3491 _______. ["Sanctuary"] Observer (September 20, 1931), 6.

3492 Graham, Bessie. The Bookman's Manual. New York: R. R. Bowker, 1935, passim.

3493 Graham, Philip. "Patterns in Faulkner's Sanctuary and Requiem for a Nun," TSL, 8 (1963), 39-46.

3494 Green, A. Wigfall. "William Faulkner at Home," SR, 40 (Summer, 1932), 304.

"Sanctuary ... is probably the most local of Faulkner's novels...."

3495 Grella, George. "The Gangster Novel: The Urban Pastoral," Tough Guy Writers of the Thirties. David Madden, ed. Carbondale and Edwardsville: Southern Ill. U. P., 1968, pp. 194-195.

3496 Grossman, Joel M. "The Source of Faulkner's 'Less Oft Is Peace,'" AL, 47 (1975), 436-438.

The phrase quoted in Sanctuary and Knight's Gambit is borrowed from a poem by Shelley, "To Jane: The Recollection."

3497 Guerard, Albert J. "The Misogynous Vision as High Art: Faulkner's Sanctuary," SoR, 12 (April, 1976), 215-231.

3498 _______. "Sanctuary," The Triumph of the Novel: Dickens, Dostoevsky, Faulkner. New York: Oxford U. P., 1976, pp. 120-135.

3499 Gwynn, Frederick L., and Joseph L. Blotner, eds. Faulkner in the University. Charlottesville: Virginia U. P., 1959, passim.

3500 Györgу, Dêry, tr. Szentêly. Budapest: Magvetô, 1968.

3501 Hamblen, Abigail Ann. "Faulkner's Pillar of Endurance: Sanctuary and Requiem for a Nun," MwQ, 6 (July, 1965), 369-375.

3502 Hansen, Harry. "The First Reader," NYWorld (February 10, 1931), 13.

3503 Hashiguchi, Yasuo. "Popeye Extenuated," KAL, No. 5 (April, 1962), 1-9.

3504 Haugh, Robert F. "Faulkner's Corrupt Temple," ESA, 4 (March, 1961), 7-16.

3505 Heflin, Martin. "Faulkner's Book Full of Horror and Realism," Daily Oklahoman (Oklahoma City), (April 5, 1931), 9-C.

3506 Herbert, Alice. "Novels of the Week," Yorkshire Post (September 16, 1931), 8.

3507 Hoffman, Frederick J. "The Tangled Web: Sanctuary," William Faulkner. New York: Twayne, 1966, pp. 66-74.

3508 Horvath, Violet, tr. "Preface by Andrê Malraux to William Faulkner's Sanctuary," SoR, 10 (October, 1974), 889-891.

3509 Howe, Irving. "Sanctuary," William Faulkner: A Critical Study. New York: Vintage, 1962, pp. 192-199.

3510 Howell, Elmo. "The Quality of Evil in Faulkner's Sanctuary," TSL, 4 (1959), 99-107.
Terms Sanctuary "a supremely moral book."

3511 Hume, Robert D. "Gothic versus Romantic: A Revaluation of the Gothic Novel," PMLA, 84 (March, 1969), 282-290.

3512 Isaacs, J. "Sanctuary," Annual Register (1931), II, 35.

3513 J. K. W. B. "Literature and Less," New Orleans Times-Picayune (April 26, 1931), 26.

3514 Jacobs, Robert D. "Faulkner's Humor," The Comic Imagination in American Literature. Louis D. Rubin, Jr., ed. New Brunswick, New Jersey: Rutgers U. P., 1973, pp. 305-318.
"One of the functions of the comic episodes in Sanctuary is to serve as relief from the horror of murder, rape, and lynching; but they are also thematic...."

3515 Johnson, Gerald W. "The Horrible South," VQR, 11 (April, 1935), 214-215.

3516 Johnson, Oakley. "Sanctuary," ModQ, 6 (Winter, 1931-1932), 122-123.

3517 Jones, E. B. C. "Sanctuary," Adelphi, 3 (November, 1931), 133.

3518 Junius, Junior (pseud.). Pseudo-Realists. New York: Outsider Press, 1931. [Attributed to Samuel E. Wells]
A brochure on Sanctuary.

3519 Kauffman, Linda. "The Madam and the Midwife: Reba Rivers and Sairey Gamp," MissQ, 30 (Summer, 1977), 395-401.
Sairey Gamp of Martin Chuzzlewit suggested as model for Reba Rivers of Sanctuary.

3520 Keefer, Frederick T. "William Faulkner's Sanctuary: A Myth Examined," TCL, 15 (July, 1969), 97-104.

3521 Kinoian, Vartkis. Review Notes and Study Guide to Faulkner's "Sanctuary,".... New York: Monarch Press, 1964, pp. 114-118.

3522 Kirk, Robert W., and Marvin Klotz. Faulkner's People. Berkeley: California U.P., 1963, pp. 58-64.

3523 Kubie, Lawrence S. "William Faulkner's Sanctuary: An Analysis," SatRL, 11 (October 20, 1934), 218; SatRL, 11 (November 10, 1934), 272.
See the latter particularly for responses.

3524 Langford, Gerald. Faulkner's Revision of Sanctuary. Austin: Texas U.P., 1972.
Revs., Jack L. Capps, SLJ, 6 (1973), 117-121; Terry Heller, ArQ, 29 (1973), 365-366; Noel Polk, MissQ, 26 (1973), 458-465.

3525 Larbaud, Valery. "Un roman de William Faulkner," Ce Vice Impuni, La Lecture Domaine Anglais. Paris: Gallimard, 1925; revised and enlarged, 1936, repub., 1951, as Vol. III of Larbaud's complete works, pp. 218-222.

3526 Levinson, André. [Sanctuaire. Édition anglaise], NL (25 juin 1932), 6.
"Ce livre est atroce. Il est celui d'un poëte."

3527 Lewis, Wyndham. "A Moralist with a Corncob," Life and Letters, 10 (June, 1934), 312-328; repr., Men without Art. London: Cassell, 1934, 42-64; New York: Harcourt, Brace, 1934, pp. 42-64; Russell & Russell, 1964, pp. 477-487.
"... William Faulkner is not an artist: he is a satirist with the shears of Atropos more or less: and he is a very considerable moralist--a moralist with a corn-cob!"

3528 Lisca, Peter. "Some New Light on Faulkner's Sanctuary," FS, 2 (Spring, 1953), 5-9.
Temple's motivation.

3529 Litz, Walton. "William Faulkner's Moral Vision," SWR, 37 (Summer, 1952), 200-209.

3530 Longley, John L., Jr. The Tragic Mask: A Study of Faulkner's Heroes. Chapel Hill: North Carolina U. P., 1963, pp. 27-29, 142-144.

3531 McHaney, Thomas L. "Sanctuary and Frazer's Slain Kings," MissQ, 24 (Summer, 1971), 223-245.
Notes Faulkner's successful adaptation of primitive myth and ritual.

3532 Maclaren-Ross, Julian. Memoirs of the Forties. London: Alan Ross, 1965, p. 10.

3533 McLaughlin, Richard. "Requiem for Temple Drake," ThA, 25 (October, 1951), 50.

3534 Magill, Frank N., ed. Masterplots: First Series. New York: Salem Press, 1957, pp. 862-864.

3535 Malin, Irving. William Faulkner: An Interpretation. Stanford: Stanford U. P., 1956, passim.

3536 Malraux, André. "Prêface à Sanctuaire de William Faulkner," NRF, 41 (November 1, 1933), 744-777; trans., and repr., YFS, 10 (Fall, 1952), 92-94; repr., Sanctuaire. Prefacê d'Andrê Malraux. Traduit de l'anglais par R. N. Raimbault et Henri Delgove. Paris: Gallimard, 1934; trans., by Violet M. Horvath, SoR, 10 (October, 1974), 889-891.

3537 Marichalar, Antonio. "William Faulkner," RdO (Madrid), 42 (October, 1933), 78-86.

3538 Mason, Robert L. "A Defense of Faulkner's Sanctuary," GaR, 21 (Winter, 1967), 430-438.
Stresses Temple's fascination with evil.

3539 Massey, Linton Reynolds. "Notes on the Unrevised Galleys of Faulkner's Sanctuary," SB, 8 (1956), 195-208.
Comparison of the published version with the theretofore unknown early version reveals major changes in style, plot, and point of view.

3540 Maxence, J. [Sanctuaire] Gringoire (29 dêcembre 1933), 4.

3541 Mayoux, Jean-Jacques. "La crêation du rêel chez William Faulkner," EA, 5 (February, 1952), 25-39; repr., in Three

Decades of Criticism, Frederick Hoffman and Olga Vickery, eds. East Lansing: Michigan State U.P., 1960, 1966, pp. 156-172.

3542 Meriwether, James B. The Literary Career of William Faulkner. Columbia: South Carolina U.P., 1971, pp. 18-20, passim.

3543 _______. "Some Notes on the Text of Faulkner's Sanctuary," PBSA, 55 (3rd Qt., 1961), 192-206.

3544 _______. "The Text of Faulkner's Books: An Introduction and Some Notes," MFS, 9 (Summer, 1963), 159-170.

3545 Mihajlović, Milica. Prevela. Svetilište; roman. Beogard: Kultura, 1963.
Croatian translation.

3546 Miller, David M. "Faulkner's Women," MFS, 13 (Spring, 1967), 3-17.

3547 Miller, James E. "Sanctuary: Yoknapatawpha's Waste Land," Individual and Community: Variations on a Theme in American Fiction. Kenneth H. Baldwin and David K. Kirby, eds. Durham, North Carolina: Duke U.P., 1975, pp. 137-159.

3548 _______. "Sanctuary: Yoknapatawpha's Waste Land," The Twenties: Fiction, Poetry, Drama. Warren G. French, ed. DeLand, Florida: Everett/Edwards, 1975, pp. 249-267.

3549 _______. "William Faulkner: Descent into the Vortex," Quests Surd and Absurd: Essays in American Literature. Chicago: Chicago U.P., 1967, pp. 58-61, 63.

3550 Millgate, Michael. The Achievement of William Faulkner. New York: Random House, 1965, pp. 113-123.

3551 _______. " 'A Fair Job': A Study of Faulkner's Sanctuary," REL, 4 (October, 1963), 47-62.
Discusses revisions of the earlier version and calls the novel Faulkner's Measure for Measure.

3552 _______. William Faulkner. New York: Grove Press, 1966, Repr., New York: Capricorn, 1971, passim.

3553 Miner, Ward L. The World of William Faulkner. Durham, North Carolina: Duke U.P., 1952, pp. 107-108, 126-128.

3554 Monicelli, Giorgio, Fernanda Pivano, Eleana Vivante, trs. La famiglia Stevens: Santuario.... Milano: Arnoldo Mondadori, 1963.

3555 Monteiro, George. "Initiation and the Moral Sense in Faulkner's Sanctuary," MLN, 73 (November, 1958), 500-504.
"... Popeye and Temple clearly fail to develop a moral sense through initiation.... It is Temple's indifference, her irresponsibility, which is the true tragedy of Sanctuary."

3556 Morell, Giliane. "The Last Scene of Sanctuary," MissQ, 25 (Summer, 1972), 351-355.

3557 Munson, Gorham B. "Our Post-War Novel," Bookman, 74 (October, 1931), 141-144. Trans., Louis and Renée Guillox. "Le roman d'après guerre aux Etats-Unis," Europe, 29 (1932), 39f.

3558 Mutis, Alvaro. "Santuario, William Faulkner (Colección Austral-Espasa-Calpe)," Revista de las Indias, 17 (January, 1946), 154-155.

3559 Nicholson, Norman. "William Faulkner," Man and Literature. London: S. C. M. Press, 1943, pp. 122-128.

3560 Nishiyama, Tamotsu. "What Really Happens in Sanctuary?" SELit, 42 (March, 1966), 235-243.

3561 "No Sanctuary," Newsweek, 38 (September 24, 1951), 90.

3562 O'Connor, William Van. "Faulkner on Broadway," KR, 21 (Spring, 1959), 334-336.

3563 ________. "A Short View of Faulkner's Sanctuary," FS, 1 (Fall, 1952), 33-39.

3564 ________. The Tangled Fire of William Faulkner. Minneapolis: Minnesota U.P., 1954, pp. 55-64.

3565 O'Donnell, George Marion. "Faulkner's Mythology," KR, 1 (Summer, 1939), 285-299; repr., in Three Decades, pp. 82-93.
Sees Sanctuary as "a kind of allegory."

3566 Ojetti, Paola, tr. Santuario; romanzo. Verona: Mondadori, 1958.

3567 Orvis, Mary. The Art of Writing Fiction. New York: Prentice-Hall, 1948, pp. 101-103.

3568 Page, Sally R. "The Ideal of Motherhood: Sanctuary," Faulkner's Women. DeLand, Florida: Everett/Edwards, 1972, pp. 71-90.

3569 Pavese, Cesare. "Faulkner, cattivo allievo di Anderson," La Cultura (April, 1934); repr., "Un angelo senza cura d'anime," La letteratura americana e altri saggi. 2nd ed. Torino: Einaudi, 1953, pp. 167-170.

3570 Pedrolo, Me. de, tr. Pròleg de Joaquim Marco. Santuari. Barcelona: Edicions Proa, 1970.

3571 "People Are Talking about ... Yves Montant," Vogue (October 1, 1960), 151.
On the motion picture of Sanctuary.

3572 Perry, J. Douglas, Jr. "Gothic as Vortex: The Form of Horror in Capote, Faulkner, and Styron," MFS, 19 (1973), 153-167.

3573 Phillips, Gene. "Faulkner and the Film: Two Versions of Sanctuary," LFQ, 1 (July, 1973), 263-273.

3574 Pilkington, James Penn. "Faulkner's Sanctuary," Expl, 4 (June, 1946), Item 61.

3575 Polk, Noel. "Alec Holston's Lock and the Founding of Jefferson," MissQ, 24, iii (1971), 247-269.

3576 Praz, Mario. "William Faulkner," La Stampa (December 4, 1931); repr., Cronache letterarie anglosassoni. Roma: Edizioni di Storia e Letteratura, 1951, II, 246-256.

3577 Raimbault, R. N., et Henri Delgove, trs. Sanctuaire. Préface, André Malraux. Paris: Gallimard, 1933.

3578 Rascoe, Lavon. "An Interview with William Faulkner," WestR, 15 (Summer, 1951), 300-304.

3579 Reed, Joseph W., Jr. "Sanctuary," Faulkner's Narrative. New Haven: Yale U. P., 1973, pp. 58-73.

3580 Richardson, Kenneth F. Force and Faith in the Novels of William Faulkner. The Hague: Mouton, 1967, pp. 77-80, 116-117, 132-134.

3581 Riddell, John. (Pseud. for Corey Ford). "Popeye the Pooh," Vanity Fair, 38 (March, 1932), 49, 66; repr., In the Worst Possible Taste. New York: Scribners, 1932, pp. 84-99.
A parody.

3582 Rinaldi, Nicholas M. "Game Imagery and Game-Consciousness in Faulkner's Fiction," TCL, 10 (October, 1964), 114-115.

3583 Robbins, Frances L. "Sanctuary," Outlook and Independent, 157 (March 11, 1931), 375.

3584 Roberts, Kenneth. I Wanted to Write. Garden City: Doubleday, 1949, 236-237.

3585 Rogers, Katherine M. The Troublesome Helpmate: A History of Misogyny in Literature. Seattle: Washington U. P., 1966, pp. 252-257.

3586 "Les romans horribles de M. William Faulkner," Le mois (November, 1931), 165-169.
"Le Sanctuaire est composé comme une sorte d'énigme psychologique;... et ce n'est qu'à la fin du livre que le lecteur commen ce à entrevoir les mobiles cachés de l'intrigue."

3587 Rossky, William. "The Pattern of Nightmare in Sanctuary; or, Miss Reba's Dogs," MFS, 15 (Winter, 1969-70), 503-515.
Studies the images of nightmare in the novel which depict "the universal dream-horror of existence."

3588 Saint-Jean, Robert de. "Sanctuaire," Revue Hebdomadaire, 43 (April 21, 1934) 487-491.

3589 "Sanctuary, by William Faulkner," AmMerc, 23 (June, 1931), xviii. Review.

3590 "Sanctuary Revisited," Time, 58 (September 24, 1951), 114. Review.

3591 Schmuhl, Robert. "Faulkner's Sanctuary: The Last Laugh of Innocence," NMW, 6 (Winter, 1974), 73-80.
Analysis of Tommy's role.

3592 Schumach, Murray. The Face on the Cutting Room Floor. New York: William Morrow, 1964, p. 145.
Note on the film of Sanctuary and Requiem for a Nun.

3593 Scott, McNair. "Sanctuary," EngRev, 53 (October, 1931), 639-640.

3594 Scribners Present the Modern Library in First Editions. New York: Scribner's Rare Books, 1938, p. 85.
Mention of the first Modern Library edition of Sanctuary.

3595 Seaver, Edwin. "A Chamber of Horrors," NYSun (February 13, 1931), 31.

3596 Sherwood, Robert. "Spring List: Sanctuary," Scribner's Mag, 89 (April, 1931), 13.

3597 Shipman, Evan. "Violent People," NR, 66 (March 4, 1931), 78-79.

3598 Simon, John K. "Faulkner and Sartre: Metamorphosis and the Obscene," CL, 15 (1963), 216-225.
Comparison of La Nausée with Sanctuary and As I Lay Dying.

3599 Simpson, Lewis P. "Ike McCaslin and Temple Drake: The Fall of the New World Man," Nine Essays in Modern Literature. Donald E. Stanford, ed. Baton Rouge: Louisiana U.P., 1965, pp. 88-106.

3600 Slabey, Robert M. "Faulkner's Sanctuary," Expl, 21 (January, 1963), Item 45.
Associates Popeye with Hermes and Miss Reba's house with Hades.

3601 Slatoff, Walter J. "Sanctuary," Quest for Failure: A Study of William Faulkner. Ithaca: Cornell U.P., 1960; 2nd pr., 1961, pp. 210-211.

3602 Stein, William Bysshe. "The Wake in Faulkner's Sanctuary," MLN, 75 (January, 1960), 28-29.

3603 Strong, L. A. G. "Books of Last Year," Observer (January 3, 1932), 4.

3604 _______. "Sanctuary," Spectator, 5386 (September 19, 1931), 362, 364. Review.

3605 Swiggart, Peter. The Art of Faulkner's Novels. Austin: Texas U.P., 1962, pp. 29-31.

3606 Talbot, Francis. "More on Smut," America (February 25, 1933), 500-501.

3607 Tate, Allen. "Faulkner's Sanctuary and the Southern Myth," VQR, 44 (Summer, 1968), 418-427.

3608 _______. Faulkner's Sanctuary and the Southern Myth," Memoirs and Opinions: 1926-1974. Chicago: Swallow Press, 1975, pp. 144-154.

3609 _______. Introduction. Sanctuary. New York: New American Library, 1968.

3610 _______. "The State of Letters: William Faulkner, 1897-1962," NSt (London), 64 (September 28, 1962), 108; repr., SR, 71 (Winter, 1963), 161.
Ranked Sanctuary among Faulkner's five masterpieces.

3611 Thompson, Alan Reynolds. "The Cult of Cruelty," Bookman, 74 (January-February, 1932), 477-487.
Cf., Henry Seidel Canby. "The School of Cruelty," SatRL, 7 (1931), 673-674.

3612 ________. "Sanctuary," Bookman, 73 (April, 1931), 188-189.

3613 Thompson, Lawrance. William Faulkner: An Introduction and Interpretation. New York: 2nd ed. Holt, Rinehart & Winston, 1967, pp. 99-116.

3614 Thompson, Ralph. "In and Out of Books," NYTBR (November 7, 1948), 8.

3615 TLS, No. 1547 (September 24, 1931), 732. Review.

3616 Toles, George Edward, Jr. "The Darkening Window: Four Problematic American Novels," DAI, 37 (Virginia: 1977), 4378A.

3617 Tomlinson, T. B. "Faulkner and American Sophistication," MCR, 7 (1964), 92-103.

3618 Trintzius, René. [Sanctuaire], L'Intransigeant (8 janvier 1934), 6.

3619 Troy, William. "Faulkner in Hollywood," Nation (May 24, 1933), 594-595.

3620 Tuck, Dorothy. Crowell's Handbook of Faulkner. New York: Crowell, 1964, pp. 40-45.

3621 Ulrey, Pamela Anne. "Faulkner's Sanctuary and Requiem for a Nun: Songs of Innocence and Experience," DA, 24 (Cornell: 1963), 2043-44.

3622 Uzzell, Thomas H. The Technique of the Novel. New York: Lippincott, 1947, pp. 235-238.

3623 Vickery, Olga W. "Crime and Punishment: Sanctuary and Requiem for a Nun," The Novels of William Faulkner. Baton Rouge: Louisiana State U. P., 1964, 103-123.

3624 Volpe, Edmond L. A Reader's Guide to William Faulkner. New York: Noonday Press, 1964, pp. 140-151, 383-387.

3625 Waggoner, Hyatt H. William Faulkner: From Jefferson to the World. Lexington: Kentucky U. P., 1959, pp. 88-100, 118-120.

3626 Ward, Alfred Charles. American Literature, 1880-1930. New York: Dial Press, 1932, pp. 153ff.

3627 Wasiolek, Edward. "Dostoevsky and Sanctuary," MLN, 74 (February, 1959), 114-117.

3628 Watkins, Floyd C. "The Word and the Deed in Faulkner's

First Great Novels," The Flesh and the Word. Nashville: Vanderbilt U. P., 1971, pp. 181-202.

3629 Way, Brian. "William Faulkner," CritQ, 3 (Spring, 1961), 44-47.

3630 West, Rebecca. "Literary Poses," Daily Telegraph (October 2, 1931), 18.

3631 Wheelwright, Philip E. "Sanctuary," Symposium, 2 (April, 1931), 276-281.

3632 "William Faulkner's Sanctuary...," PubW, 120 (October 3, 1931), 1622.

3633 Williams, Aubrey. "William Faulkner's 'Temple' of Innocence," RiceIP, 47 (October, 1960), 51-67.

3634 Wilson, Colin. The Strength to Dream: Literature and the Imagination. Boston: Houghton Mifflin, 1962, pp. 36-38.

3635 Yonce, Margaret. " 'His True Penelope Was Flaubert': Madame Bovary and Sanctuary," MissQ, 29, #3 (Summer, 1976), 439-442.

3636 Zink, Karl E. "Flux and the Frozen Moment: The Imagery of Stasis in Faulkner's Prose," PMLA, 71 (June, 1956), 285-301.

SARTORIS

(New York: Harcourt, Brace, 1929)

3637 "A. N. M." [Sartoris], Manchester Guardian (March 4, 1932).

3638 Adamowski, T. H. "Bayard Sartoris: Mourning and Melancholia," L&P, 23 (1973), 149-158.

3639 Adams, Richard P. Faulkner: Myth and Motion. Princeton: Princeton U. P., 1968, pp. 49-56.

3640 Anon. "Other Novels of the Week," Everyman (March 3, 1932), 181.

3641 Anon. [Sartoris], NYTimes (October 20, 1951), 13.

3642 Anon. "A Southern Family," NYTBR (March 3, 1929), 8.

3643 Anon. "The Whole and the Parts," NS&N (April 2, 1932), 428, 430.

3644 Arnold, Lilian. [Sartoris], John O'London's Weekly, 26 (March 5, 1932), 870.

3645 "B." "Dressing Down," The Granta, 41 (February 26, 1932), 320.

3646 Backman, Melvin Faulkner: The Major Years. A Critical Study. Bloomington: Indiana U.P., 1966, pp. 3-12.

3647 _______. "Faulkner's Sick Heroes: Bayard Sartoris and Quentin Compson," MFS, 2 (1956), 95-108; "Bayard Sartoris et Quentin Compson, hêros malades de William Faulkner," RLM, 4, Nos. 27-29 (June, 1957), 7-31.

3648 _______, and P. Rozenberg. "William Faulkner: De 'Sartoris' à 'Descends, Moïse.' " Paris: Minard, 1968.

3649 Bell, Haney H. "A Reading of Faulkner's Sartoris and There Was a Queen," Forum (Texas), 4 (Fall-Winter, 1965), 23-26.

3650 Blair, John G. "Camus' Faulkner: Requiem for a Nun," BFLS, 47 (January, 1969), 249-257.

3651 Blotner, Joseph. "William Faulkner's Essay on the Composition of Sartoris," YULG, 47 (1972), 121-124.

3652 Brickell, Herschel. "Books," NYHTB (February 24, 1929), 5.

3653 _______. "A Wild Southern Family," NAR 227 (April, 1929).

3654 Brooks, Cleanth. "The Waste Land: Southern Exposure (Sartoris)," William Faulkner: The Yoknapatawpha Country. New Haven: 1963, pp. 100-115.

3655 Brown, Calvin S. "Faulkner's Idiot Boy: The Source of Simile in Sartoris," AL, 44 (November, 1972), 474-476.
Suggests that Harris Dickson's The House of Luck (1916) may have influenced Faulkner's treatment of the idiot in Sartoris.

3656 Bruccoli, Matthew. "A Source for Sartoris?" MissQ, 20 (Summer, 1967), 163.
A possible source for the name Sartoris may have been a play of the 1920's called Two Little Girls in Blue.

3657 Brylowski, Walter. Faulkner's Olympian Laugh: Myth in the Novels. Detroit: Wayne State U.P., 1968, pp. 51-58.

3658 Buckley, G. T. "Is Oxford the Original of Jefferson in William Faulkner's Novels?" PMLA, 76 (September, 1961), 448-450.

3659 Campbell, Harry Modean, and Ruel E. Foster. William

Faulkner: A Critical Appraisal. Norman: Oklahoma U. P., 1951, pp. 25-26, 121-123.

3660 Cantwell, Robert. "Le Colonel Falkner: Sartoris," LetN, No. 10 (December, 1953), 1304-1314.
Colonel Falkner, Father's great-grandfather may have been the prototype of Col. Sartoris.

3661 ________. Introduction. Sartoris. New York: New American Library, Signet Books, 1953, pp. vii-xxv.

3662 Carey, Glenn O. "William Faulkner on the Automobile as Socio-Sexual Symbol," CEA, 36 (January, 1974), 15-17.

3663 Cargill, Oscar. "The Primitivists," Intellectual America. New York: Macmillan, 1941, pp. 340-386.

3664 Carpenter, Richard C. "Faulkner's Sartoris," Expl, 14 (April, 1956), Item 41.
The conclusion indicates that the novel is an "exploration of the Christian myth of sin, guilt, and redemption."

3665 Castille, Philip. " 'There Was a Queen' and Faulkner's Narcissa Sartoris," MissQ, 28 (Summer, 1975), 307-315.

3666 Charensol, Georges. [Sartoris], NL (8 janvier 1938), 5.

3667 Church, Margaret. "William Faulkner: Myth and Duration," Time and Reality: Studies in Contemporary Fiction. Chapel Hill: North Carolina U. P., 1963, pp. 232-233.

3668 Collins, Carvel E. "Are These Mandalas?" L&P, 3 (November, 1953), 3-6.
Discussion of passages in Sartoris and "The Bear."

3669 Connolly, Thomas E. "Fate and 'the Agony of Will': Determinism in Some Works of William Faulkner--Sartoris," Essays on Determinism in American Literature. Sidney J. Krause, ed. Kent: Kent State U. P., 1964, pp. 37-39.

3670 Cook, Richard M. "Popeye, Flem, and Sutpen: The Faulknerian Villain As Grotesque," SAF, 3 (Spring, 1975), 3-14.

3671 Corrington, John W. "Escape into Myth: The Long Dying of Bayard Sartoris," RANAM, 4 (1971), 31-47.

3672 Cosgrove, William. "The 'Soundless Moiling' of Bayard Sartoris," ArizQt, 35 (Summer, 1979), 165-169.

3673 Crickmay, Edward. "William Faulkner's New Novel," Sunday Referee (March 6, 1932), 6.

3674 Davidson, Donald. "Two Mississippi Novels," Tennessean (Nashville), (April 14, 1929), 7.

3675 Day, Douglas, ed. Introduction. Flags in the Dust. New York: Random House, 1973.
An uncut version first published in 1929 under title Sartoris.

3676 Dennis, Stephen N. "The Making of Sartoris: A Description and Discussion of the Manuscript and Composite Typescript of William Faulkner's Third Novel," DAI, 31 (Cornell, 1970), 384A.
Provides information about the manuscript and typescript of Flags in the Dust, the early, uncut version of Sartoris.

3677 Devlin, Albert J. "Sartoris: Rereading the MacCullum Episode," TCL, 17 (April, 1971), 83-90.
The MacCallums "in no sense [represent] normality."

3678 Dillon, Richard T. "Some Sources for Faulkner's Version of the First Air War," AL, 44 (January, 1973), 629-637.
Suggests that Faulkner may have borrowed material from Elliott White Springs and James Warner Bellah.

3679 Engle, Paul. "Sartoris," Sunday Tribune (Chicago), (October 28, 1951), Mag. of Books, 6.

3680 Everett, Walter K. Faulkner's Art and Characters. Woodbury, New York: Barrons Educ. Ser., 1969, pp. 83-94.

3681 Faulkner, William. "Colonel Sartoris Snopes and Faulkner's Aristocrats," CarQ, 11 (Summer, 1959), 13-19.

3682 Fletcher, Helen. "Sartoris," Time and Tide, 13 (February 27, 1932), 230.

3683 Foster, Ruel E. "Social Order and Disorder in Faulkner's Fiction," Approach, 55 (Spring, 1965), 21-22.

3684 Geismar, Maxwell. "William Faulkner: The Negro and the Female," Writers in Crisis. Boston: Houghton Mifflin, 1942, pp. 150-154.

3685 Gold, Joseph. William Faulkner: A Study in Humanism from Metaphor to Discourse. Norman: Oklahoma U.P., 1966, pp. 45-48.

3686 ________. "William Faulkner's 'One Compact Thing,'" TCL, 8 (April, 1962), 7-9.

3687 Govan, Gilbert E. "Roaming the Book World," Chattanooga Times (October 13, 1935), Mag. Sec., 15.
Sartoris, a "grand book."

3688 Grigs, Mary. "The Growing Pains of Youth," Evening News (March 16, 1932), 10.

3689 Grözinger, Wolfgang. "Faulkner, William. Sartoris," Hochland, 53 (1961), 572. Review.

3690 Gwynn, Frederick L., and Joseph L. Blotner. Faulkner in the University. Charlottesville: Virginia U. P., 1959, passim.

3691 Hale, Nancy. "Colonel Sartoris and Mr. Snopes," Vogue, 142 (August 1, 1963), 112, 113, 135, 136, 138, 139.

3692 Henss, Herbert. William Faulkners Roman "Sartoris" als literarisches Kunstwerk. Munich: Max Hueber Verlag, 1964.
Revs., Bungert, Hans. JbAS, 11 (1966), 355-357; Holst, Gunther, ZAA, 14 (1966), 403-404; Meriwether, James B., AL, 38 (1966), 414.

3693 _______. William Faulkners Sartoris als literarisches Kunstwerk. Diss. Mainz, 1964.

3694 Hoffman, Frederick J. William Faulkner. New York: Twayne, 1961, 2nd ed., 1966, pp. 44-48.

3695 Howe, Irving. William Faulkner. 2nd ed. New York: Vintage Books, 1962, pp. 33-41.

3696 Howell, Elmo. "Faulkner's Sartoris," Expl, 17 (February, 1959), Item 33.

3697 _______. "Faulkner's 'Sartoris' and the Mississippi Country People," SFQ, 25 (June, 1961), 136-146.

3698 _______. "William Faulkner and the New Deal," MwQ, 5 (July, 1964), 323-332.

3699 _______. "William Faulkner and the Plain People of Yoknapatawpha County," JMissH, 24 (April, 1962), 73-87.

3700 Jacobs, Robert D. "William Faulkner: The Passion and the Penace," South: Modern Southern Literature in Its Cultural Setting. L. D. Rubin, Jr., and Robt. D. Jacobs, eds. New York: Doubleday, 1961, pp. 144-146.

3701 Jaloux, Edmond. [Sartoris], NL (17 septembre 1938), 4.
Faulkner "... le plus original que nous a donné l'après-guerre, avec Franz Kafka et Mrs. Virginia Woolf."

3702 Jones, E. B. C. "Sartoris," Adelphi, 4 (May, 1932), 564-566.

3703 Keiser, Merle Wallace. "Faulkner's Sartoris: A Comprehensive Study," DAI, 38 (New York: 1977), 7333A-34A.

3704 Kibler, James E. "The Making of Sartoris," MissQ, 24 (1971), 315-319.
A review of doctoral dissertation by Stephen Neal Dennis.

3705 Kirk, Robert W., and Marvin Klotz. Faulkner's People. Berkeley: California U. P., 1963, pp. 83-94.

3706 Le Breton, Maurice. [Sartoris], ÉA (octobre-décembre 1938), 441-442.

3707 Lewis, Wyndham. "The Moralist with a Corn-cob: A Study of William Faulkner," Life and Letters, 10 (June, 1934), 312-328; repr., Men without Art. London: Cassell, 1934, pp. 42-64.

3708 "The Literary Editor," Oxford Mail (March 8, 1932). Review.

3709 McDonald, Walter R. "Sartoris: The Dauntless Hero in Modern American Fiction," Proceedings of the Comparative Literature Symposium, Vol. 5; Modern American Fiction: Insights and Foreign Lights. Wolodymyr T. Zyla and Wendell M. Aycock, eds. Committee on Comp. Lit., Texas Tech U., 1972, pp. 107-120.

3710 McGinnis, Wayne D. "Faulkner's Use of the Mule: Symbol of Endurance and Derision," NMW, 10 (Spring, 1977), 19-26.

3711 Malin, Irving. William Faulkner: An Interpretation. Stanford U. P., 1957, passim.

3712 Martin, Carter. "Faulkner's Sartoris: The Tailor Re-Tailored," SCR, 6 (April, 1974), 56-59.

3713 Matton, Collin Gilles. "The Role of Women in Three of Faulkner's Families," DAI, 35 (Marquette: 1974), 2283-A.

3714 Meriwether, James B. "Sartoris," The Literary Career of William Faulkner. Columbia: South Carolina U. P., 1971, pp. 14-16, passim.

3715 ________. "Sartoris and Snopes: An Early Notice," LCUT, 7 (Summer, 1962), 36-39.
A notice by Phil Stone containing references to Sartoris and to an uncompleted manuscript about the Snopes family.

3716 Miller, Douglas T. "Faulkner and the Civil War: Myth and Reality," AQ, 15 (Summer, 1963), 201-202, passim.

3717 Miller, William. "Hardy, Falls, and Faulkner," MissQ, 29, # 3 (Summer, 1976), 435-436.

3718 Millgate, Michael. The Achievement of William Faulkner. New York: Random House, 1965, pp. 76-85.

3719 ________. William Faulkner. New York: Capricorn Bks., 1971, passim.

3720 Morris, Lawrence S. "Sartoris," Bookman, 69 (May, 1929), 310-311.
"...[T]he Sartorises seemed melodramatic rather than dramatic."

3721 Muehl, Lois. "Faulkner's Humor in Three Novels and One 'Play,'" LibChron, 24 (Spring, 1968), 78-93.

3722 ________. "Form as Seen in Two Early Works by Faulkner," LibChron, 38 (1972), 147-157.

3723 ________. "Word Choice and Choice Words in Faulkner's Sartoris," LibChron, 35 (Winter-Spring, 1969), 58-63.

3724 Muir, Edward H. "A Footnote on Sartoris and Some Speculation," JML, 1 (1971), 389-393.
The plane in which young Bayard Sartoris is killed seems based on an actual airplane designed by W. W. Christmas.

3725 Nathan, Monique. "Un Sartoris chez les Snopes," Critique, 16 (March, 1960), 222-227.

3726 Nilon, Charles H. Faulkner and the Negro. New York: Citadel Press, 1965, pp. 70-73.

3727 Nishiyama, Tamotsu. "Sartoris," KAL, No. 2 (May, 1959), 28-32.

3728 NSt&N, 3 (April 2, 1932), 428, 430. Review.

3729 O'Connor, William Van. The Tangled Fire of William Faulkner. Minneapolis: Minnesota U.P., 1954, passim.

3730 O'Donnell, George Marion. "Faulkner's Mythology," KR, 1 (Summer, 1939), 285-299; repr., Three Decades of Criticism. Frederick J. Hoffman and Olga Vickery, eds. East Lansing: Michigan U.P., 1960, pp. 82-93.

3731 O'Faolain, Sean. "William Faulkner," The Vanishing Hero: Studies in Novelists of the Twenties. London: Eyre and Spottiswoode, 1956, pp. 106-112.

3732 Page, Ralph. "John Sartoris: Friend or Foe," ArQ, 23 (Spring, 1967), 27-33.
Thinks the relationship between the two brothers is that of Cain and Abel.

3733 Peden, William. "Sartoris, Snopes and Everyman," SatRL, 33 (August 26, 1950), 12.

3734 Putzel, Max. "Evolution of Two Characters in Faulkner's Early and Unpublished Fiction," SLJ, 5 (Spring, 1973), 47-63.

Faulkner's early stories and sketches show the evolution of Bayard Sartoris and Caddy Compson.

3735 Raimbault, R. N., and Henri Delgove, trs. Sartoris. Paris: Gallimard, 1937.

3736 Richardson, H. Edward. "Anderson and Faulkner," AL, 36 (November, 1964), 298-314.

3737 ________. "Sartoris: Home Again," William Faulkner: Journey to Self-Discovery. Columbia: Missouri U. P., 1969, pp. 164-184.

3738 ________. "William Faulkner: From Past to Self-Discovery: A Study of His Life and Work through Sartoris," DA, 24 (So. California: 1964), 3756.

3739 Richardson, Kenneth E. Force and Faith in the Novels of William Faulkner. (Studies in American Literature, Vol. 7). The Hague: Mouton, 1967, pp. 20-25.

3740 Roberts, Melvin Reed. "Faulkner's 'Flags in the Dust' and 'Sartoris': A Comparative Study of the Typescript and the Originally Published Novel," DAI, 35 (Austin, Texas: 1974), 471A.

3741 Sartre, Jean-Paul. "Sartoris par William Faulkner," NRF, 26 (février 1938), 323-328; repr., YFR, 10 (1952), 95-99; Literary and Philosophical Essays. Annette Michelson, tr. London: Rider, 1955, New York: Criterion Books, 1955, pp. 73-78; Situations I. Paris: Gallimard, 1947, pp. 7-13.

3742 Scholes, Robert. "Myth and Manners in Sartoris," GaR, 16 (Summer, 1962), 195-201.

3743 Smart, George. "A Selective Concordance: ... Sartoris," Religious Elements in Faulkner's Early Novels. Coral Gables, Florida: Miami U. P., 1965, passim.

3744 Smith, Bernard. "More Talent Than Theme," NYSun (February 5, 1929), 10.

3745 Smith, Henry [Nash]. "In His New Novel William Faulkner Broadens His Art," Dallas Morning News (February 17, 1929), Amusement Sec., 3.

3746 Sorenson, Dale A. "Structure in William Faulkner's Sartoris: The Contrast between Psychological and Natural Time," ArQ, 25 (Autumn, 1969), 263-270.

3747 Spinella, Maria. "Sartoris Nelle Vita Degli U. S. A.," FLe, 3 (July 13, 1947), 31.

3748 Stafford, William T. "Some Homer of the Cotton Fields': Faulkner's Use of the Mule Early and Late. (Sartoris and The Reivers)," PLL, 5 (Spring, 1969), 190-196.

3749 Stevens, Lauren R. "Sartoris: Germ of the Apocalypse," DR, 49 (Spring, 1969), 80-87.
Comparison of the novel with Shakespeare's Hamlet.

3750 Stone, Edward. "William Faulkner's Two Little Confederates, OUR, 4 (1962), 5-18.

3751 Strong, L. A. G. "Fiction," Spectator, #5409 (February 27, 1932), 296, 298.

3752 Swiggart, Peter. The Art of Faulkner's Novels. Austin: Texas U.P., 1962, pp. 34-37, passim.

3753 Tasker, J. Dana. "Sartoris," Outlook and Independent, 151 (February 20, 1929), 311.

3754 Thompson, Lawrance. Afterword. Sartoris. New York: Signet Books, 1964.

3755 Thorp, Willard. "And the Novel? Four Times and Out?" Scrutiny, 1 (September, 1932), 172-173.
Implied that Sartoris was Faulkner's fourth novel; it was the third to be written but in England was the fourth in order of publication.

3756 Tuck, Dorothy. Crowell's Handbook of Faulkner. New York: Crowell, 1964, pp. 16-21.

3757 Vickery, Olga W. "The Making of a Myth: 'Sartoris,'" WR, 22 (Spring, 1958), 209-219.

3758 ________. "The Making of a Myth: Sartoris," The Novels of William Faulkner: A Critical Interpretation. Rev. ed. Baton Rouge: Louisiana State U.P., 1964, pp. 15-27.

3759 Vieira, Carlos, tr. Sartoris. Prefácio de Robert Cantwell. Lisboa: Ulisseia, 1958.

3760 Volpe, Edmond L. A Reader's Guide to William Faulkner. New York: Noonday Press, 1964, pp. 66-76.

3761 Waggoner, Hyatt H. William Faulkner: From Jefferson to the World. Lexington: Kentucky U.P., 1959, pp. 20-33.

3762 Walker, Ronald G. "Death in the Sound of Their Name: Character Motivation in Faulkner's Sartoris," SHR, 7 (Summer, 1973), 271-278.

3763 Warren, Robert Penn. "Faulkner: The South, the Negro,

and Time," SoR, n.s., 1 (July, 1965), 506; repr., in Faulkner: A Collection of Critical Essays. Englewood Cliffs, New Jersey: Prentice-Hall, 1966, pp. 251-271.

3764 Watkins, Floyd C. "The Unbearable and Unknowable Truth in Faulkner's First Three Novels," The Flesh and the Word. Nashville: Vanderbilt U.P., 1971, pp. 169-180.

3765 Watson, James G. "'The Germ of My Apocrypha': Sartoris and the Search for Form," Mosaic, 7 (Fall, 1973), 15-33.

3766 Way, Brian. "William Faulkner," CritQ, 3 (Spring, 1961), 43-44.

3767 Weisgerber, Jean. Faulkner and Dostoevsky: Influence and Confluence. Dean McWilliams, tr. Presses Universitaires de Bruxelles, 1968; Athens, Ohio: Ohio U.P., 1973, passim.

3768 West, Rebecca. "The Oddities of Our Modern Novelists: Cleverness Is Not Enough," Daily Telegraph (March 4, 1932), 6.

"SEPULTURE SOUTH: GASLIGHT"
(Harper's Bazaar, 88 (1954), 84-85, passim)

3769 Meriwether, James B. "The Short Fiction of William Faulkner," Proof, 1 (1971), 307-308.

3770 _______. "Two Unknown Faulkner Short Stories," RANAM, 4 (1971), 23-30.

"SHALL NOT PERISH"
(Story, 23 (1943), 40-47; repr., in Collected Stories, 1950)

3771 Bradford, Melvin E. "Faulkner and the Jeffersonian Dream: Nationalism in 'Two Soldiers' and 'Shall Not Perish,'" MissQ, 18 (Spring, 1965), 94-100.

3772 Cullen, John B., with Floyd C. Watkins. Old Times in the Faulkner Country. Chapel Hill: North Carolina U.P., 1961, pp. 64-65.

3773 Kerr, Elizabeth M. Yoknapatawpha: Faulkner's "Little Postage Stamp of Native Soil." New York: Fordham U.P., 1969, pp. 35, 45, 153.

3774 Meriwether, James B. "The Short Fiction of William Faulkner," Proof, 1 (1971), 308-324.

3775 Millgate, Michael. The Achievement of William Faulkner. New York: Random House, 1966, pp. 271-272.

3776 Tuck, Dorothy. Crowell's Handbook of Faulkner. New York: Crowell, 1964, pp. 175-176, 210.

"SHINGLES FOR THE LORD"
(Sat. Eve. Post, 215 (1943); repr., in Collected Stories, 1950)

3777 Breaden, Dale G. "William Faulkner and the Land," AQ, 10 (Fall, 1958), 353-354.

3778 Davis, Robert Gorham. Instructor's Manual for Ten Modern Masters. 2nd ed. New York: Harcourt, Brace, 1959, pp. 33-34.

3779 Hardy, John Edward. "William Faulkner: 'Shingles for the Lord,'" Commentaries on Five Modern American Short Stories. Frankfurt: Verlag Moritz Diesterweg, 1963, pp. 20-23.

3780 Howell, Elmo. "Faulkner's Country Church: A Note on 'Shingles for the Lord,'" MissQ, 21 (Summer, 1968), 205-210.
Felt Faulkner was not able to view the country church correctly.

3781 Kerr, Elizabeth M. Yoknapatawpha: Faulkner's "Little Postage Stamp of Native Soil." New York: Fordham U. P., 1969, pp. 152, 153, 179.

3782 Lêon, Abel, tr. "Un toit pour le seigneur," LF (2 mai 1947), 3.

3783 Longley, John L., Jr. The Tragic Mask: A Study of Faulkner's Heroes. Chapel Hill: North Carolina U. P., 1963, pp. 120-122.

3784 Meriwether, James B. "The Short Fiction of William Faulkner," Proof, 1 (1971), 308, 324.

3785 Millgate, Michael. The Achievement of William Faulkner. New York: Random House, 1966, p. 271.

3786 Myres, William V. "Faulkner's Parable of Poetic Justice," LaS, 8 (Fall, 1969), 224-230.
"Poetic justice" is the central theme.

3787 Tuck, Dorothy. Crowell's Handbook of Faulkner. New York: Crowell, 1964, pp. 176, 227, 229.

"SKIRMISH AT SARTORIS"
(Scribner's, 97 (1935), 193-200; revised for The Unvanquished, 1938).

3788 Meriwether, James B. "The Short Fiction of William Faulkner," Proof, 1 (1971), 308, 323.

3789 Millgate, Michael. The Achievement of William Faulkner. New York: Random House, 1966, pp. 165, 168, 169.

3790 Tuck, Dorothy. Crowell's Handbook of Faulkner. New York: Crowell, 1964, pp. 69, 176.

"SMOKE"
(Harper's, 164 (1932); repr., in Doctor Martino, 1934; and Knight's Gambit, 1949)

3791 Meriwether, James B. "The Short Fiction of William Faulkner," Proof, 1 (1971), 308, passim.

3792 O'Connor, William Van. The Tangled Fire of William Faulkner. Minneapolis: Minnesota U.P., 1954, pp. 142-143.

THE SNOPES TRILOGY
(See also under The Hamlet, The Town, and The Mansion, all following.)

3793 Adams, Percy G. "Humor As Structure and Theme in Faulkner's Trilogy," WSCL, 5 (Autumn, 1964), 205-212.

3794 Adams, Richard P. Faulkner: Myth and Motion. Princeton: Princeton U.P., 1968, pp. 158-161.

3795 Allen, Charles. "William Faulkner: Comedy and the Purpose of Humor," ArQ, 16 (Spring, 1960), 64-69.

3796 Allen, Walter Ernest. "Snopes on the March," NSt (February 1, 1958), 143.

3797 Anon. "Faulkner's Curse," TLS (February 7, 1958), 74.
On the Snopes family saga and on Faulkner's method.

3798 Arpad, Joseph J. "William Faulkner's Legendary Novels: The Snopes Trilogy," MissQ, 22 (Summer, 1969), 214-225.

3799 Arthos, John. "Ritual and Humor in Faulkner," Accent, 9 (Autumn, 1948), 17-30; repr., in Two Decades of Criticism. Hoffman and Vickery, eds., pp. 101-118.

3800 Backman, Melvin. Faulkner: The Major Years. A Critical Study. Bloomington: Indiana U.P., 1966, pp. 139-159.

3801 Barth, J. Robert. "Faulkner and the Snopes Trilogy," America, 102 (February 27, 1960), 638-640.

3802 Beck, Warren. Man in Motion: Faulkner's Trilogy. Madison: Wisconsin U. P., 1961.

Cf., Michel Gresset. "Faulkneriana," LMod, 59 (January-February), 1965).

Rev., by Warren Beck. GaR, 16 (Spring, 1962), 106-108.

3803 ______. "William Faulkner's Style," American Prefaces, 6 (Spring, 1941), 195-211; repr., Two Decades of Criticism. Hoffman and Vickery, pp. 142-156; Robert Penn Warren, ed. Faulkner. Englewood Cliffs, New Jersey, 1966, pp. 53-65.

3804 Benêt, Stephen. "Flem Snopes and His Kin," SatRL, 21 (April 6, 1940), 7.

3805 Bigelow, Gordon E. "Faulkner's Snopes Saga," EJ, 49 (December, 1960), 595-605.

Sees Faulkner's use of the Snopes saga as a protest against "the sterilization and dehumanization of man."

3806 Bowling, Lawrence Edward. "William Faulkner: The Importance of Love," DR, 43 (Winter, 1963-64), 479-480.

3807 Boyle, Karen Paden. [Snopes Trilogy], MissQ, 25 (Summer, 1972), 380-385.

Reviews of dissertations which treat the Snopes trilogy as a whole.

3808 Brooks, Cleanth. "Faulkner's Revengers' Tragedy: Discrepancies among the Three Novels in the Trilogy," William Faulkner: The Yoknapatawpha Country. New Haven: Yale U. P., 1963, pp. 167-243.

3809 Brown, Calvin S. "Faulkner's Use of the Oral Tradition," GaR, 22 (Summer, 1968), 160-169.

3810 Buckley, G. T. "Is Oxford the Original of Jefferson in William Faulkner's Novels?" PMLA, 76 (September, 1961), 450.

3811 Campbell, Harry Modean, and Ruel E. Foster. William Faulkner: A Critical Appraisal. Norman: Oklahoma U. P., 1951, pp. 15-17, 79-81, 102-106, passim.

3812 Carey, Glenn O. "William Faulkner: The Rise of the Snopeses," STC, 8 (Fall, 1971), 37-64.

3813 Cecil, Moffitt L. "A Rhetoric for Benjy," SLJ, 3 (Fall, 1970), 32-46.

3814 Cowley, Malcolm. "Flem Snopes Gets His Come-Uppance," NYTBR, 64 (November 15, 1959), 1, 18.

3815 Crawford, John W. "Bred and Bawn in a Briar Patch--Deception in the Making," SCB, 34 (Winter, 1974), 149-150.

3816 Creighton, Joanne V. *William Faulkner's Craft of Revision: The Snopes Trilogy, "The Unvanquished" and "Go Down, Moses." William Faulkner's Craft of Revision.* Detroit: Wayne State U.P., 1977.

3817 Cullen, John B., and Floyd C. Watkins. *Old Times in the Faulkner Country.* Chapel Hill: North Carolina U.P., 1961, 99-127.

3818 Davis, Roger Lewis. "William Faulkner, V. K. Ratcliff, and the Snopes Saga (1925-1940)," DAI, 32 (U.C.L.A.: 1971), 3300A.

3819 Dirksen, Sherland N. "The First of the Snopeses--William Faulkner's Snopes Family," ESRS, 11 (December, 1962), 12-22.

3820 Eby, Cecil D. "Faulkner and the Southwestern Humorists," Shenandoan, 11 (Autumn, 1959), 13-21.

3821 Eisinger, Chester E. "William Faulkner: Southern Archetype," *Fiction of the Forties.* Chicago: Chicago U.P., 1963, pp. 182-184.

3822 Farmer, Norman, Jr. "The Love Theme: A Principal Source of Thematic Unity in Faulkner's Snopes Trilogy," TCL, 8 (October, 1962-January, 1963), 111-123.

3823 Farnham, James F. "Faulkner's Unsung Hero: Gavin Stevens," ArQ, 21 (Summer, 1965), 115-132.

3824 Foster, Ruel E. "Social Order and Disorder in Faulkner's Fiction," Approach, No. 55 (Spring, 1965), 20-27.

3825 French, Warren G. "The Background of Snopesism in Mississippi Politics," MASJ, 5 (Fall, 1964), 3-17; revised and repr., as "A Troubled Section," *The Social Novel at End of an Era.* Carbondale and Edwardsville: So. Illinois U.P., 1966, pp. 18-41.

3826 Friedman, Alan Warren. "Faulkner's Snopes Trilogy: Omniscience as Impressionism," Delta, 3 (November, 1976), 125-157.

3827 Gernes, Sonia Grace. "The Relationship of Storyteller to Community in the Tales of the Southwest Humorists, Mark Twain and William Faulkner," DAI, 36 (Washington: 1975), 3685A-86A.

3828 Gold, Joseph. "The 'Normality' of Snopesism," WSCL, 3 (Winter, 1962), 25-34; repr., in *William Faulkner: Four Decades of Criticism.* Linda Wagner, ed. Michigan State U.P., 1973, pp. 318-327.

Sees the Snopeses not as unique, but as an eruption of certain characteristics of the normal citizens of Frenchman's Bend.

3829 ________. William Faulkner: A Study in Humanism from Metaphor to Discourse. Norman: Oklahoma U. P., 1966, pp. 148-173.

3830 Gossett, Louise Y. Violence in Recent Southern Fiction. Durham, North Carolina: Duke U. P., 1965, pp. 42-45.

3831 Gresset, Michel. "Homofaunie," Delta, 3 (November, 1976), 85-93.
Labove and Ike Snopes are perhaps Faulkner's "last faunesque figures."

3832 Gwynn, Frederick L., and Joseph L. Blotner, eds. Faulkner in the University. Charlottesville: Virginia U. P., 1959, pp. 29-34, passim.

3833 Hale, Nancy. "Colonel Sartoris and Mr. Snopes," Vogue (August, 1963), 112-113, 135-139.
Cf., responses in Charlottesville Daily Progress (August 2), 4; (August 6), 4; (August 12), 4; (August 14), 4.

3834 Harder, Kelsie B. "Proverbial Snopeslore," TFSB, 24 (September, 1958), 89-95.

3835 Hartt, Julian N. The Lost Image of Man. Baton Rouge: Louisiana State U. P., 1963, pp. 89-92.

3836 Hayes, Ann L. "The World of The Hamlet," Carnegie Series in English, No. 6. Pittsburgh, Pa.: Carnegie Institute of Technology, 1961, pp. 3-16.

3837 Hicks, Granville. "At Home with the Snopeses," SatRL, 46 (December 7, 1963), 37-38.

3838 ________. "Last of the Snopses," SatRL, 42 (November 14, 1959), 20-21.

3839 Hoffman, Frederick J. William Faulkner. Twayne's United States Authors Series. New York: 1961, pp. 85-95.

3840 Holmes, Edward M. Faulkner's Twice-Told Tales: His Re-Use of His Material. The Hague: Mouton, 1966, pp. 19-45.

3841 Howe, Irving. "Faulkner: End of a Road," NR, 141 (December 7, 1959), 17-21.
Analysis of the Snopes trilogy.

3842 ________. William Faulkner: A Critical Study. 2nd ed. New York: Vintage Books, 1962, pp. 107-115, 282-294.

3843 Howell, Elmo. "Colonel Sartoris Snopes and Faulkner's Aristocrats," CarQ, 2 (Summer, 1959), 13-19.
Cf., Phillis Franklin. "Sarty Snopes and 'Barn Burning,'" MissQ, 21 (Summer, 1968), 189-193.

3844 _______. "The Meaning of Snopesism," SSJ, 31 (Spring, 1966), 223-225.

3845 _______. "Mink Snopes and Faulkner's Moral Conclusions," SAQ, 67 (Winter, 1968), 13-22.

3846 _______. "William Faulkner and the Plain People of Yoknapatawpha County," JMissH, 24 (April, 1962), 73-87.

3847 Hyman, Stanley E. "Snopeslore," New Leader (December 7, 1964), 13-14.

3848 _______. "Snopeslore," Hyman's Standards: A Chronicle of Books for Our Time. New York: Horizon Press, 1966, pp. 259-263.

3849 Inge, M. Thomas. "William Faulkner and George Washington Harris: In the Tradition of Southwestern Humor," TSL, 7 (1962), 49-53.

3850 Jacobs, Robert D. "Faulkner's Humor," The Comic Imagination in American Literature. Louis D. Rubin, Jr., ed. New Brunswick, New Jersey, 1973, pp. 305-318.

3851 _______. "William Faulkner: The Passion and the Penance," South: Modern Southern Literature in Its Cultural Setting. Louis D. Rubin, Jr., and Robt. D. Jacobs, eds. Garden City, New York: Doubleday, 1961, pp. 169-171, 174-176.

3852 Kane, Patricia. "Adaptable and Free: Faulkner's Ratliff," NConL, 1 (May, 1971), 9-11.

3853 Kazin, Alfred. "Mr. Faulkner's Friends, the Snopses," NYTBR (May 5, 1957), 1, 24.

3854 _______. "William Faulkner: More Snopeses," Contemporaries. Boston: Little, Brown, 1962, pp. 150-154.

3855 Kerr, Elizabeth M. "Snopes," WSCL, 1 (Spring-Summer, 1960), 66-84.

3856 Kulseth, Leonard I. "Cincinnatus among the Snopeses: The Role of Gavin Stevens," BSUF, 10 (Winter, 1969), 28-34.

3857 Labatt, Blair Plowman. "Faulkner the Storyteller," DAI, 34 (Virginia: 1974), 7761A.

3858 Lawson, Lewis. "The Grotesque-Comic in the Snopes Trilogy," L&P, 15 (Spring, 1965), 107-119; repr., in Hidden Patterns: Studies in Psychoanalytic Literary Criticism. Leonard Falk and Eleanor B. Manheim, eds. New York: Macmillan, 1966, pp. 243-258.

3859 Leaf, Mark. "William Faulkner's Snopes Trilogy: The South Evolves," The Fifties: Fiction, Poetry, Drama. Warren French, ed. DeLand, Florida: Everett/Edwards, 1970, pp. 51-62.

3860 Leary, Lewis. "Snopes Saga," William Faulkner of Yoknapatawpha County. New York: Thos. Y. Crowell, 1973, pp. 150-170.

3861 Leibowitz, Herbert A. "The Snopes Dilemma and the South," UKCR, 28 (June, 1962), 273-284.

3862 Lemay, Harding. "Faulkner and His Snopes Family Reach the End of Their Trilogy," NYHTBR (November 15, 1959), 1, 14.

3863 Lêtargez, Joseph. "William Faulkner's Snopes Trilogy," RLV, 27 (September-October, 1961), 446-451.

3864 Levine, Paul. "Love and Money in the Snopes Trilogy," CE, 23 (December, 1961), 196-199.

3865 Longley, John L., Jr. "Galahad Gavin and a Garland of Snopeses," VQR, 33 (Autumn, 1957), 623-628.

3866 ________. The Tragic Mask: A Study of Faulkner's Heroes. Chapel Hill: North Carolina U.P., 1963, pp. 63-78, 150-164.

3867 Lytle, Andrew. "The Town: Helen's Last Stand," SR, 65 (July-September, 1957), 475-484.

3868 McCormick, John. "The United Snopes Information Service," KR, 24 (Spring, 1962), 330-350.

3869 McDowell, Richard David. "Faulkner's Trilogy: A Revaluation," DAI, 38 (Tulane: 1977), 5481A-82A.

3870 McFarland, Holly. The Mask Not Tragic ... Just Damned: The Women in Faulkner's Trilogy," BSUF, 18, ii (Spring, 1977), 27-50.

3871 McIlwaine, Shields. "Faulkner Begins a Trilogy about the Snopes Family," Memphis Commercial Appeal (April 14, 1940), IV, 10.

3872 MacLure, Millar. "Snopes: A Faulkner Myth," CanForum, 39 (February, 1960), 245-250.
A review of the mythic elements in the Snopes trilogy.

3873 Maddocks, Gladys. "William Faulkner and the Evolution of V. K. Ratliff," CCTE, 33 (September, 1968), 24-28.

3874 Marcus, Steven. "Snopes Revisited," PR, 24 (Summer, 1957), 432-441; repr., in Three Decades of Criticism. Frederick Hoffman and Olga Vickery, eds. East Lansing: Michigan State U. P., 1960, pp. 382-392.

3875 _______. "Snopes Revisited," Representations: Essays on Literature and Society. New York: Random House, 1975, pp. 28-40.

3876 Matton, Collin Gilles. "The Role of Women in Three of Faulkner's Families," DAI, 35 (Marquette: 1974), 2283A. The Compson, Sartoris, and Snopes families.

3877 Meriwether, James B. "Sartoris and Snopes: An Early Notice," LCUT, 7 (Summer, 1962), 36-39.

3878 _______. "The Snopes Revisited," SatRL, 40 (April 27, 1957), 12-13.

3879 _______. "The Snopes Trilogy Completed," CarQ, 12 (Winter, 1959), 30-34.

3880 Millgate, Michael. The Achievement of William Faulkner. New York: Random House, 1965, pp. 180-200, 235-252.

3881 _______. William Faulkner. New York: Grove Press, 1961; revised, 1966; repr., Capricorn Bks., 1971, pp. 82-93.

3882 Moses, W. R. "The Limits of Yoknapatawpha County," GaR, 16 (fall, 1962), 302-305, passim.

3883 Müller, Christopher. "On William Faulkner's Manner of Narration," KN, 25 (1978), 201-212.

3884 Nathan, Monique. "Un Sartoris chez les Snopes," Critique, 16 (March, 1960), 222-227.

3885 Norris, Nancy. "The Hamlet, The Town, and The Mansion: A Psychological Reading of the Snopes Trilogy," Mosaic, 7 (Fall, 1973), 213-235.

3886 _______. "William Faulkner's Trilogy," DAI, 32 (Pennsylvania: 1971), 6994A.

3887 O'Connor, William Van. The Tangled Fire of William Faulkner. Minneapolis: Minnesota U. P., 1954, pp. 111-124.

3888 _______. "William Faulkner," Seven Modern American Novelists. Minneapolis: Minnesota U. P., 1964, pp. 144-146.

3889 Page, Sally R. "The Male and the Female Principles: The Snopes Trilogy," Faulkner's Women. DeLand, Florida: 1972, pp. 153-173.

3890 Palmer, William J. "The Mechanistic World of Snopes," MissQ, 20 (Fall, 1967), 185-194.
The symbolic pattern unifying the trilogy is the machine.

3891 Payne, Ladell. "The Trilogy: Faulkner's Comic Epic in Prose," SNNTS, 1 (Spring, 1969), 27-37.
Applies Fielding's assertion that a novel is a "comic epic poem in prose" to Faulkner's trilogy.

3892 Petesch, Donald A. "Theme and Characterization in Faulkner's Snopes Trilogy," DA, 29 (Texas, Austin: 1969), 3618A-19A.
Rev., by Karen P. Boyle, MissQ, 25 (1972), 380ff.

3893 Podhoretz, Norman. "Faulkner in the 50's: Snopesishness," Doings and Undoings. New York: Farrar, Straus, 1964, pp. 13-24, 24-29.

3894 ________. "Snopesishness and Faulknerishness," NY, 33 (June 1, 1957), 110-116.

3895 Powell, Irma Anne. "Man in His Struggle: Structure, Technique, and Theme in Faulkner's Snopes Trilogy," DAI, 31 (Florida State: 1969), 1287-8A.
Rev., by Karen P. Boyle, MissQ, 25 (1972), 380ff.

3896 Rait-Kovaleva, Rita, Victor Hinkis, and Simon Markish, trs. Snopes Trilogy: Hamlet, Town, Mansion. Khudozhestvennaya Literatura Publishing House, 1965.

3897 Reed, Joseph W., Jr. "Snopes," Faulkner's Narrative. New Haven: Yale U.P., 1973, pp. 218-257.

3898 Rice, Michael. "Myth and Legend: The Snopes Trilogy: The Hamlet, The Town and The Mansion," UES, 14, i (1976), 18-22.

3899 Richardson, Kenneth E. Force and Faith in the Novels of William Faulkner. The Hague: Mouton, 1967, pp. 113-129.
"... [A] predatory amorality" cloaked by respectability.

3900 Rinaldi, Nicholas M. "Game Imagery and Game-Consciousness in Faulkner's Fiction," TCL, 10 (October, 1964), 108-118.

3901 Roberts, James L. "Snopeslore: The Hamlet, The Town, The Mansion," UKCR, 28 (Autumn, 1961), 65-71.

3902 Rubin, Louis D. "Snopeslore," WR, 22 (Autumn, 1957), 73-76.

3903 Sharma, P. P. "The Snopes Theme in Faulkner's Larger Context," IJAS, 1, iv (1971), 33-41.

3904 Slatoff, Walter J. Quest for Failure: A Study of William Faulkner. Ithaca, New York: Cornell U.P., 1960, pp. 203-205, passim.

3905 Smith, Gerald. "A Note on the Origin of Flem Snopes," NMW, 6 (Fall, 1973), 56-57.

3906 Sullivan, Walter. "Allen Tate, Flem Snopes and the Last Years of William Faulkner," Death by Melancholy: Essays on Modern Southern Fiction. Baton Rouge: Louisiana State U.P., 1972, pp. 3-21.

3907 Swiggart, Peter. The Art of Faulkner's Novels. Austin: Texas U.P., 1962, pp. 48-51, 195-206.

3908 ________. "The Snopes Trilogy," SR, 68 (Summer, 1960), 319-325; repr., in Modern American Fiction: Essays in Criticism, Walton Litz, ed. New York: Oxford U.P., 1963, pp. 194-200.

3909 Thompson, Lawrance. William Faulkner: An Introduction and Interpretation. 2nd ed. New York: Holt, Rinehart & Winston, 1967, pp. 133-158.

3910 Trimmer, Joseph F. "V. K. Ratliff: A Portrait of the Artist in Motion," MFS, 20 (Winter, 1974-75), 451-467.

3911 Turner, Decherd. "Faulkner's Greatest Work Completes the 'Design,'" Dallas Times Herald (July 28, 1957), 18.

3912 ________. "Rise and Victory of Flem Snopes," Dallas Times Herald (November 15, 1959), Roundup Sec., 13.

3913 ________. "Some More Snipping at Snopesism Suggesting Chance at Salvation," Dallas Times Herald (July 21, 1957), 22.

3914 Vickery, Olga. The Novels of William Faulkner: A Critical Interpretation. Rev. ed. Baton Rouge: Louisiana State U.P., 1964, pp. 168-208, passim.

3915 Volpe, Edmond L. A Reader's Guide to William Faulkner. New York: Noonday Press, 1964, pp. 304-343, 401-403.

3916 Waggoner, Hyatt H. William Faulkner: From Jefferson to the World. Lexington: Kentucky U.P., 1959, pp. 183-193, 232-237.

3917 Warren, Robert Penn. "The Snopes World," KR, 3 (Spring, 1941), 253-257.

3918 Watson, James G. The Snopes Dilemma: Faulkner's Trilogy. Coral Gables, Florida: Miami U. P., 1970.
Rev. by John V. Hagopian, AL, 43 (1971), 304-306; Elmo Howell, SAQ, 70 (1971), 430-431.

3919 ________. "'The Snopes Dilemma': Morality and Amorality in Faulkner's Snopes Trilogy," DA, 29 (Pittsburgh: 1969), 1237A-38A.

3920 Weisgerber, Jean. Faulkner and Dostoevsky. Dean McWilliams, tr. Athens, Ohio: Ohio U. P., 1974, passim.

3921 West, Anthony. "A Dying Fall," NY, 35 (December 5, 1959), 236-243.

3922 Wheeler, Otis. "Some Uses of Folk Humor," MissQ, 17 (Spring, 1964), 107-122.

3923 Whitbread, Thomas. "The Snopes Trilogy: The Setting of The Mansion," Six Contemporary Novels. William O. S. Sutherland, ed. Austin: Texas U. P., 1962, pp. 76-88.

3924 White, John O. "The Existential Absurd in Faulkner's Snopes Trilogy," DAI, 32 (Arizona State: 1971), 3336A.

3925 Wills, Arthur. "A Study of Faulkner's Revisions," ExEx, 10 (March, 1963), 14-16.

3926 Wills, Garry. "The Thin World of the Snopeses," NatlR, 7 (November 21, 1959), 498-499.

3927 Young, Thomas D., and Floyd C. Watkins. "Faulkner's Snopeses," MissQ, 11 (Fall, 1958), 196-200.
"... [T]he Snopeses are materialistic, immoral, and debased, but there are gradations of morality, even among the Snopeses."

The Hamlet
(New York: Random House, 1940)

3928 Adams, Percy G. "Humor As Structure and Theme in Faulkner's Trilogy," WSCL, 5 (Autumn, 1964).
The Hamlet demonstrates the variety and purpose of Faulkner's humor.

3929 Adams, Richard P. Faulkner: Myth and Motion. Princeton: Princeton U. P., 1968, pp. 115-129.

3930 Aguilar, Esperanza. Yoknapatawpha, Propiedad de William Faulkner. Santiago de Chile: Editorial Universitaria, 1964, 87-95.

3931 Allen, Charles A. "William Faulkner's Comedy and the Purpose of Humor," ArQ, 16 (Spring, 1960), 59-69.

3932 ________. "William Faulkner's Vision of Good and Evil," PacS, 10 (Summer, 1956), 236-241.

3933 Anastasjew, N. "Faulkners Weg zum Roman 'Das Dorf,'" KuL, 19 [1970?], 956-974; reported as a translation of the author's "Folkner: Put'k'Derevuvske," VLit, 14, xi [1970], 122-141.

3934 Anon. "Genius-á-la-King," Time (April 1, 1940), 73.

3935 Anon. "New Novels: Queer Fish," Glasgow Herald (September 12, 1940), 3.

3936 Anon. "Rural Scum: Faulkner Pens Tale of an Ornery Tribe Given to Lust and Homicide," Newsweek (April 1, 1940), 32.

3937 Anon. "Village Napoleon," TLS (London), (September 21, 1940), 481.

3938 Anon. "William Faulkner Etches Acid Vignettes of South," Milwaukee Evening Post (April 6, 1940), 5.

3939 Anon. "William Faulkner's World Is Enlarged by New Novel," Dallas Morning News (April 21, 1940), IV, 10.

3940 Backman, Melvin. Faulkner: The Major Years. Bloomington: Indiana U.P., 1966, pp. 139-159.

3941 Barnett, Suzanne B. "Faulkner's Relation to the Humor of the Old Southwest," JOFS, 2 (Winter, 1967), 149-165.
Comparison of Hamlet with Harris' Sut Lovingood's Yarns.

3942 Beach, Joseph Warren. American Fiction, 1920-1940. New York: Macmillan, 1941, pp. 123-169.

3943 Beck, Warren. Man in Motion: Faulkner's Trilogy. Madison: Wisconsin U.P., 1961, passim.

3944 ________. "A Note on Faulkner's Style," RockyMR, 6 (Spring-Summer, 1942), 5-6. 14; repr., in Faulkner: A Collection of Critical Essays. Robert Penn Warren, ed. Englewood Cliffs, New Jersey: Prentice-Hall, 1966, pp. 53-65.

3945 ________. "William Faulkner's Style," American Prefaces, 6 (Spring, 1941), 195-211; repr., in Three Decades of Criticism. Hoffman and Vickery, eds. East Lansing: Michigan State U.P., 1960, pp. 142-156.

3946 Benêt, Stephen Vincent. "Flem Snopes and His Kin," SatRL, 21 (April 6, 1940), 7.

3947 Berger, Yves. "Prêsence et signification chez William Faulkner," NRF, 15 (May, 1960), 951-960.

3948 Bowling, Lawrence E. "William Faulkner: The Importance of Love," DR, 43 (Winter, 1963), 479-480.

3949 Brighouse, Harold. "New Novels," Manchester Guardian (September 20, 1940), 7.

3950 Brooks, Cleanth. "Faulkner's Savage Arcadia: Frenchman's Bend," VQR, 39 (Autumn, 1963), 598-611; repr., *William Faulkner: The Yoknapatawpha County*. New Haven: Yale U.P., 1963, pp. 167-191.

3951 Broughton, Panthea R. "Masculinity and Menfolk in *The Hamlet*," MissQ, 22 (Summer, 1969), 181-189.

3952 Bruss, Elizabeth W. "The Game of Literature and Some Literary Games," New Lit Hist, 8 (Autumn, 1977), 153-172. *The Hamlet* as a literary game.

3953 Brylowski, Walter. *Faulkner's Olympian Laugh: Myth in the Novels*. Detroit: Wayne State U.P., 1968, pp. 139-149.

3954 Buckley, G. T. "Is Oxford the Original of Jefferson in William Faulkner's Novels?" PMLA, 76 (September, 1961), 450.

3955 Burgum, Edwin Berry. "William Faulkner's Patterns of American Decadence," *The Novel and the World's Dilemma*. New York: Oxford U.P., 1947, pp. 220-221.

3956 Butcher, Fanny. "Another by Faulkner," Chicago Daily Tribune (April 3, 1940), 14.

3957 Călinescu, Matei. "La o lectură a 'Cătunului' lui W. Faulkner," *Eseuri despre literatura modernă*. [*Essays on modern literature*.] Bucarest: Editura Eminescu, 1970, pp. 314-320.

3958 Cameron, May. "William Faulkner's *The Hamlet* Casts a Spell," NYPost (April 1, 1940), 9.

3959 Campbell, Harry Modean, and Ruel E. Foster. *William Faulkner: A Critical Appraisal*. Norman: Oklahoma U.P., 1951, pp. 15-17, 19-21, 66-67, 79-81, 102-106, *passim*.

3960 Chapdelaine, Annick. "Perversion As Comedy in *The Hamlet*," Delta, 3 (November, 1976), 95-104.

3961 Church, Richard. "New Novels to Read," JO'LW, 43 (September 20, 1940), 663.

3962 Clayton, Charles C. "Faulkner Writes Novel of Decay in the Old South," St. Louis Globe-Democrat (April 13, 1940), 1-B.

3963 Collins, Carvel. "Faulkner and Certain Earlier Southern Fiction," CE, 16 (November, 1954), 92-97.
Concerns Southwestern humor and Southern romanticism.

3964 Cook, Richard M. "Popeye, Flem, and Sutpen: The Faulknerian Villain As Grotesque," SAF, 3 (Spring, 1975), 3-14.

3965 Cowley, Malcolm. "Faulkner by Daylight," NR, 102 (April 15, 1940), 510; repr., Think Back on Us ... A Contemporary Chronicle of the 1930's. Henry Dan Piper, ed. Carbondale: Southern Ill. U.P., 1967, pp. 358-360.

3966 Creighton, Joanne V. "Surratt to Ratliff: A Genetic Approach to Hamlet," MichA, 6 (Summer, 1973), 101-112.

3967 Cross, Richard K. "The Humor of The Hamlet," TCL, 12 (January, 1967), 203-215.

3968 Cullen, John B., with Floyd C. Watkins. Old Times in the Faulkner Country. Chapel Hill: North Carolina U.P., 1961, pp. 99-127.

3969 Dillingham, William B. "William Faulkner and the 'Tragic Condition,'" Edda, 53 (1966), 322-335.

3970 Dirksen, Sherland N. "William Faulkner's Snopes Family: The Hamlet, The Town, and The Mansion," ESRS, 11 (December, 1962), 5-45.

3971 Dupee, F. W. "William Faulkner's Anger at Humanity Puts Forth Another Bitter Flower," NYSun (April 2, 1940), 40.

3972 Eby, Cecil D. "Faulkner and the Southwestern Humorists," Shenandoah, 11 (Autumn, 1959), 13-21.
Hamlet's South "is the less familiar wasteland of the early regionalists ... rather than the well-known plantation settings of the romantic novelist...."

3973 ________. "Ichabod Crane in Yoknapatawpha," GaR, 16 (Winter, 1962), 465-469.

3974 Edwards, Duane. "Flem Snopes and Thomas Sutpen: Two Versions of Respectability," DR, 51 (1971-72), 559-570.

3975 Eisinger, Chester E. "William Faulkner: Southern Archetype," Fiction of the Forties. Chicago: Chicago U.P., 1963, pp. 178-186.

3976 Everett, Walter K. Faulkner's Art and Characters. Woodberry, New York: Barron's Edu. Series, 1969, pp. 37-43.

3977 Fadiman, Clifton. "Horrors, Charm, Fun," NY, 16 (April 16, 1940), 73.

3978 Farmer, Norman J., Jr. "The Love Theme: A Principal Source of Thematic Unity in Faulkner's Snopes Trilogy," TCL, 8 (October, 1962), 111-123.

3979 "Faulkner Bought for Film," NYTimes (March 15, 1957), L-21.
The purchase of Hamlet for the production of The Long, Hot Summer.

3980 Flanagan, John Theodore. "Folklore in American Literature: Faulkner's The Hamlet," The Family Saga. Mody C. Boatright, ed. Urbana, Illinois: Illinois U.P., 1958, pp. 61-63.

3981 Foster, Ruel E. "Social Order and Disorder in Faulkner's Fiction," Approach, No. 55 (Spring, 1965), 20-28.

3982 French, Warren G. "The Background of Snopesism in Mississippi Politics," MASJ, 5 (Fall, 1964), 3-17.
"The Hamlet is thus, while not a mirror of Mississippi politics, a revelation of the inner workings of the culture that produced these politics...."

3983 ________. "A Troubled Section: 'A Little Sweetening for the Chaps,'" The Social Novel at the End of an Era. Carbondale: Southern Illinois U.P., 1966, pp. 18-41.

3984 Gates, Allen. "The Old Frenchman Place: Symbol of a Lost Civilization," IEY, 13 (Fall, 1968), 44-50.

3985 Geismar, Maxwell. "The Meaning of Faulkner's Humor," American Moderns: From Rebellion to Conformity. New York: Hill & Wang, 1958, pp. 101-106.

3986 ________. "William Faulkner: The Negro and the Female," Writers in Crisis. Boston: Houghton Mifflin, 1942, pp. 141-183.

3987 Glasgow Herald (September 12, 1940).

3988 Gold, Joseph. "The 'Normality' of Snopesism: Universal Themes in Faulkner's The Hamlet," WSCL, 3 (Winter, 1962), 25-34; repr., in William Faulkner: Four Decades of Criticism. L. W. Wagner, ed. East Lansing: Michigan State U.P., 1973, pp. 318-327.

3989 Gossett, Louise Y. "The Climate of Violence," Violence in Recent Southern Fiction. Durham: North Carolina U.P., 1965, pp. 42-45.

3990 Graham, Bessie. The Bookman's Manual. New York: R. R. Bowker Co., 1941.

3991 Greet, T. Y. "The Theme and Structure of Faulkner's The Hamlet," PMLA, 72 (September, 1957), 775-790; repr., William Faulkner: Three Decades of Criticism. Hoffman and Vickery eds., pp. 330-347; William Faulkner: Four Decades of Criticism. L. W. Wagner, ed. East Lansing: Michigan State U.P., 1973, pp. 302-318.

3992 Guerard, Albert. "Snopes Family Devour Village," Boston Evening Transcript (April 13, 1940), V. 1.

3993 Gwynn, Frederick L., and Joseph L. Blotner, eds. Faulkner in the University. Charlottesville: Virginia U.P., 1959, pp. 29-34, passim.

3994 Hall, James. "Play, the Fractured Self, and American Angry Comedy: from Faulkner to Salinger," The Lunatic Giant in the Drawing Room: The British and American Novel Since 1930. Bloomington: Indiana U.P., 1968, pp. 57-59, 62-74, 131.

3995 _______. "Play, the Training Camp, and American Angry Comedy," HAB, 15 (Spring, 1964), 7-9.

3996 Hansen, Harry. "The Hamlet, by William Faulkner, and The Crazy Hunter, by Kay Boyle, Are Characteristic of Their Best Work," NYWorld-Telegram (April 3, 1940), 27.

3997 Harakawa, Kyoichi. "Faulkner and The Hamlet," Kam, No. 4 (Spring, 1962), 26-46. In Japanese.

On tragic elements in The Hamlet.

3998 Harder, Kelsie B. "Proverbial Snopeslore," TFSB, 24 (September, 1958), 89-95.

Folklore in The Hamlet and The Town.

3999 Harkness, Bruce. "Faulkner and Scott," MissQ, 20 (Summer, 1967), 164.

Faulkner's use of Scott in The Hamlet.

4000 Harrison, Sally. "New Faulkner Novel," Brooklyn Citizen (March 29, 1940).

4001 Hartt, Julian N. The Lost Image of Man. Baton Rouge: Louisiana State U.P., 1963, pp. 89-92.

4002 Harwick, Robert Duane. "Humor in the Novels of William Faulkner," DA, 26 (Nebraska: 1965), 1646.

"The Hamlet is a virtuoso performance in which Faulkner displays his complete mastery of manifold fictional elements, both serious and comic."

4003 Hatcher, Harlan. "Faulkner's The Hamlet Is 'Exercise in

Horror,'" Columbus Citizen (April 28, 1940), Mag. Sec., 4.

4004 Hawkins, Desmond. "The Hamlet," NS&N, 20 (September 28, 1940), 312-314.

4005 Hayes, Ann L. "The World of Hamlet," Studies in Faulkner. Carnegie Series in English No. 6. Pittsburgh: Carnegie Institute of Technology, 1961, pp. 3-16.

4006 Heald, William F. "Morality in 'Spotted Horses,'" MissQ, 15 (Spring, 1962), 85-91.

4007 Hodgart, Patricia. [The Hamlet], Manchester Guardian (February 11, 1958), 4.

4008 Hoffman, Frederick J. William Faulkner. Twayne's United States Author Series. New York: Twayne, 1961, pp. 85-95.

4009 Holmes, Edward Morris. "Faulkner's Twice-Told Tales: His Re-Use of His Material," DA, 23 (Brown: 1963), 2527.

4010 Hopkins, Viola. "William Faulkner's The Hamlet: A Study in Meaning and Form," Accent, 15 (Spring, 1955), 125-144.
An analysis indicating "how symbolism, characterization, and humor contribute" to unity.

4011 Hopper, Vincent. "Faulkner's Paradise Lost," VQR, 23 (Summer, 1947), 405-420.

4012 Houghton, Donald E. "Whores and Horses in Faulkner's 'Spotted Horses,'" MidQ, 11 (Summer, 1970), 361-369.
Explains how the revised story as it appears in The Hamlet improves upon the original.

4013 Howard, Alan B. "Huck Finn in the House of Usher: The Comic and Grotesque World of The Hamlet," SoRA, 5 (June, 1972), 125-146.
The interplay of frontier humor and grotesque terror.

4014 Howe, Irving. "End of a Road," NR, 141 (December, 1959), 17-21.

4015 ________. "The Hamlet," William Faulkner: A Critical Study. New York: Vintage, 1952, pp. 243-252.

4016 Howell, Elmo. "Mink Snopes and Faulkner's Moral Conclusions," SAQ, 67 (Winter, 1968), 13-22.

4017 ________. "William Faulkner and the Plain People of Yoknapatawpha County," JMissH, 24 (April, 1962), 73-87.

4018 Inge, M. Thomas. "William Faulkner and George Washington

Harris: In the Tradition of Southwestern Humor," TSL, 7 (1962), 47-59.

4019 Jackson, Joseph Henry. "Faulkner Again Writes Strongly About Extremely Nasty People," San Francisco Chronicle (April 8, 1940), 15.

4020 Jacobs, Robert D. "Faulkner's Humor," The Comic Imagination in American Literature. New Brunswick: Rutgers U.P., 1973, pp. 305-318.

4021 ________. "William Faulkner: The Passion and the Penance," South: Modern Southern Literature in Its Cultural Setting. Louis D. Rubin and Robert D. Jacobs, eds. Garden City: Doubleday, 1961, pp. 142-176.

4022 Jarrett, David W. "Eustacia Vye and Eula Verner, Olympians: The Worlds of Thomas Hardy and William Faulkner," Novel, 6 (Winter, 1973), 163-174.
Similarities between the two characters and also between The Return of the Native and The Hamlet.

4023 Johnston, Esther. "The Hamlet," LibJ, 65 (April 1, 1940), 300.

4024 Kane, Patricia. "Adaptable and Free: Faulkner's Ratliff," NConL, 1, #3 (May, 1971), 9-11.

4025 Kibler, James E., Jr. "A Study of the Text of William Faulkner's The Hamlet," DAI, 31 (South Carolina: 1970), 5407A.

4026 Kinoian, Vartkis. Review Notes and Study Guide to Faulkner's "The Hamlet".... New York: Monarch Press, 1964, pp. 128-132.

4027 Kirk, Robert W., and Marvin Klotz. Faulkner's People. Berkeley: California U.P., 1963, pp. 109-123.

4028 Kronenberger, Louis. "The World of William Faulkner," Nation, 150 (April 13, 1940), 481-482.

4029 Lawson, John Howard. "William Faulkner," [The Hamlet], IL, No. 9 (September, 1961), 178-186.
In Russian.

4030 Lawson, Lewis A. "The Grotesque-Comic in the Snopes Trilogy," L&P, 15 (1965), 107-119; repr., in Hidden Patterns. Leonard F. Manheim and Eleanor B. Manheim, eds. New York: Macmillan, 1966, pp. 243-258.

4031 Lawson, Strang. "Faulkner's The Hamlet," CEA Critic, 10 (December, 1948), 3.

The Hamlet a "four-movement semi-comic rhapsody in purple."

4032 Leaver, Florence. "The Structure of The Hamlet," TCL, 1 (July, 1955), 77-84.

4033 Leibowitz, Herbert A. "The Snopes Dilemma and the South," UKCR, 28 (1962), 273-284.

4034 Levit, Donald Jay. William Faulkner's The Hamlet: Its Revisions and Structure. Diss. Chicago: 1969.

4035 Lisca, Peter. "The Hamlet: Genesis and Revisions," FS, 3 (Spring, 1954), 5-13.

4036 Littell, Robert. "The Hamlet," YR, 29 (Summer, 1940), viii.

4037 Longley, John L. The Tragic Mask: A Study of Faulkner's Heroes. Chapel Hill: North Carolina U.P., 1963, passim.

4038 Lupan, Radu. Prefata. Cǎtunul. In romǎneste de Eugen Barbu si Andrei Ion Deleanu. Bucuresti: Editura Pentri Literatura Universala, 1967.

4039 McClennen, Joshua. "Why Read Faulkner," MAQR, 62 (Summer, 1956), 342-345.

4040 McDonald, W. U., Jr. "The Time-Scheme of The Hamlet," MidR, 5 (1963), 22-29.

4041 McIlwaine, Shields. "Faulkner Begins a Trilogy about the Snopes Family," Memphis Commercial Appeal (April 14, 1940), IV, 10.

4042 MacLure, Millar. "Snopes: A Faulkner Myth," CanForum, 39 (February 1960), 245-260.

4043 Magill, Frank N., ed. Masterplots: Combined Edition. New York: Salem Press, 1960, pp. 1204-1206.

4044 Mann, E. L. "Turning the Pages," Concinnati Times-Star (April 2, 1940), 7.

4045 Mercer, Caroline and Susan J. Turner. "Restoring Life to Faulkner's The Hamlet," CEA Critic, 21 (December, 1959), 1, 4-5.

4046 Merino, Santos, tr. El villorrio, novella. Buenos Aires: Compañía General Fabril Editora, 1962.

4047 Michel, Laurence. The Thing Contained: Theory of the Tragic. Bloomington: Indiana U.P., 1970, passim.

4048 Millgate, Michael. "The Hamlet," The Achievement of William Faulkner. New York: Random House, 1965, pp. 180-200.

4049 _______. William Faulkner. Writers and Critics Series. New York: Grove Press, 1961, pp. 84-90.

4050 Millum, Richard A. "'The Horns of Dawn': Faulkner and Metaphor," AN&Q. 11 (May, 1973), 134.

4051 Moses, Edwin. "Faulkner's The Hamlet: The Passionate Humanity of V. K. Ratliff," NDEJ, 8 (Spring, 1973), 98-109.

4052 Murray, D[onald] M. "Faulkner, the Silent Comedies, and the Animated Cartoon," SHR, 9 (1975), 241-257.

4053 Nathan, Monique. "Un Sartoris chez les Snopes," Critique, 16, #154 (March, 1960), 222-227.
A critical study of The Hamlet.

4054 Norris, Nancy. "The Hamlet, The Town, and The Mansion: A Psychological Reading of the Snopes Trilogy," Mosaic, 7 (Fall, 1973), 213-235.

4055 North, Sterling. "Darker Than the Moody Dane," Chicago Daily News (April 3, 1940), 16.

4056 O'Connor, William Van. "Frenchman's Bend and the Folk Tradition," [The Hamlet], The Tangled Fire of William Faulkner. Minneapolis: Minnesota U.P., 1954, pp. 111-124.

4057 _______. William Faulkner. Minnesota University Pamphlets on American Literature. Minneapolis: Minnesota U.P., 1959, pp. 31-34; repr., Seven Modern American Novelists. W. V. O'Connor, ed. Minneapolis: Minnesota U.P., 1964, pp. 144-146.

4058 O'Donnell, George Marion. "Not Pleasant, but Truthful," Nashville Banner (August 21, 1940), 4X.

4059 Orwell, George. "Fiction and Life," Time and Tide, 21, #45 (November 9, 1940), 1097.

4060 Patterson, Alicia. "The Shocking Snopes," NYSunday News (March 31, 1940), 72.

4061 Pfeiffer, Andrew. "'No Wiser Spot on Earth': Community and the Country Store in Faulkner's The Hamlet," NMW, 6 (Fall, 1973), 45-52.
The "community" as theme and main character.

4062 Pierle, Robert C. "Snopesism in Faulkner's The Hamlet," ES, 52 (June, 1971), 246-252.

4063 Pisani, Assunta Sarnacchiaro. "The Raging Impotence: Humor in the Novels of Dostoevsky, Faulkner, and Beckett," DAI, 38 (Brown: 1976), 248A.

4064 Porteus, Clark. "Faulkner's Hamlet Like Bridge Hand," Memphis Press-Scimitar (April 11, 1940), 11.

4065 Prior, Linda T. "Theme, Imagery, and Structure in The Hamlet," MissQ, 22 (Summer, 1969), 237-256.

4066 "Proshchainie so Snoupsami" [A farewell to the Snopes], Literaturnaia gazeta (December 17, 1959).
Russian criticism.

4067 Pruvot, Monique. "Le Sacre de la vache," Delta, 3 (November, 1976), 105-123.
The significance of the cow in The Hamlet.

4068 Ramsey, William Currie. "Coordinate Structure in Four Faulkner Novels," DAI, 33 (Chapel Hill: 1971), 283A-84A.
The Hamlet is one of the novels studied.

4069 Rascoe, Burton. "Faulkner's New York Critics," AmMerc, 50 (June, 1940), 243-247.
The critics mostly unfavorable.

4070 Richardson, Kenneth E. Force and Faith in the Novels of William Faulkner. The Hague: Mouton, 1967, pp. 118-125.

4071 Rinaldi, Nicholas M. "Game-Consciousness and Game-Metaphor in the Work of William Faulkner," DA, 24 (Fordham: 1964), 4196-97.

4072 Roberts, James L. "Snopeslore: The Hamlet, The Town, The Mansion," UKCR, 28 (Autumn, 1961), 65-71.

4073 Robinson, Ted. "The Hamlet," Cleveland Plain Dealer (April 14, 1940), Feature Sec., 3.

4074 Robson, W. W. [The Hamlet], Spec (February 14, 1958).

4075 Rogers, Katharine M. The Troublesome Helpmate: A History of Misogyny in Literature. Seattle: Washington U.P., 1966, pp. 252-257.

4076 Roth, Russell. "The Centaur and the Pear Tree," WR, 16 (Spring, 1952), 199-205.

4077 R[oueché], B[erton]. "Faulkner Fills His Gallery," Kansas City Star (April 6, 1940), 14.

4078 Rousseaux, André. "Le monde infernal de Faulkner," FL, 15 (January 16, 1960), 2.

4079 Rubens, Philip M. "St. Elmo and the Barn Burners," NMW, 7 (Winter, 1975), 86-90.
St. Elmo Snope's name in The Hamlet.

4080 Rubin, Louis D., Jr. "The Great American Joke," SAQ, 72 (Winter, 1973), 82-94.
Comparison of The Hamlet, Faulkner's "comic masterpiece," with other humorous novels.

4081 ________. Introduction: "The Great American Joke," The Comic Imagination in American Literature. New Brunswick: Rutgers U.P., 1973, pp. 3-15.

4082 Rugoff, Milton. "Out of Faulkner's Bog," NYHTB (March 31, 1940), 4.
Cf., Burton Rascoe. "Faulkner's New York Critics," AmMerc, 50 (1940), 243-247.

4083 Sampaio, Jorge, tr. A aldeia, romance. Lisboa: Arcádia, 1965(?)

4084 Serruya, Barbara Booth. "The Evolution of an Artist: A Genetic Study of William Faulkner's The Hamlet," DAI, 35 (Los Angeles: 1974), 2298-A.

4085 Shanaghan, Malachy M., O.S.B. "A Critical Analysis of the Fictional Techniques of William Faulkner," DA, 20 (Notre Dame: 1960), 4663.
Remarks that in Hamlet, Faulkner chose the point of view of "omniscient narration."

4086 Showett, H. K. "Faulkner and Scott: Addendum," MissQ, 22 (Spring, 1969), 152-153.
Cf., Bruce Harkness. "Faulkner and Scott," MissQ, 20 (1967), 164.

4087 Skaggs, Merrill Maguire. "The Tradition in the Twentieth Century," The Folk of Southern Fiction. Athens: Georgia U.P., 1972, pp. 225-230.

4088 Slatoff, Walter J. "Hamlet," Quest for Failure. Ithaca: Cornell U.P., 1960, 2nd pr., 1961, pp. 203-205.

4089 Smith, Gerald J. "A Note on the Origin of Flem Snopes," NMW, 6 (1973), 56-57.

4090 Smith, Janet A. "New Novels," Spectator, 165 (September 27, 1940), 324; also, Time, 35 (April 1, 1940), 73.

4091 Stanford, Don. "The Beloved Returns and Other Recent Fiction," SoR, 6 (Winter, 1941), 619-620.
An attack on The Hamlet.

4092 Stegner, Wallace. "The New Novels," VQR, 16 (Summer, 1940), 464.

4093 Stein, William Bysshe. "Faulkner's Devil," MLN, 76 (December, 1961), 731-732.

4094 Stevens, Aretta J. "Faulkner and 'Helen'"--A Further Note," PoeN, 1 (October, 1968), 31.

4095 Stineback, David C. "'The price had been necessity': William Faulkner's The Hamlet," Shifting World: Social Change and Nostalgia in the American Novel. Lewisburg, Ohio: Bucknell U. P., 1976, pp. 142-155.

4096 Stone, Edward. A Certain Morbidness: A View of American Literature. Carbondale: Southern Ill. U. P., 1969, pp. 110-120.

4097 Stonesifer, Richard J. "Faulkner's The Hamlet in the Classroom," CE, 20 (November, 1958), 71-77.

4098 Strauss, Harold. "Mr. Faulkner's Family of Poor Whites," NYTBR (April 7, 1940), 2.

4099 Sullivan, Walter. "Allen Tate, Flem Snopes, and the Last Years of William Faulkner," Death by Melancholy: Essays on Modern Southern Fiction. Baton Rouge: Louisiana State U. P., 1972, pp. 3-21.

4100 ________. "The Decline of Regionalism in Southern Fiction," GaR, 18 (Fall, 1964), 300-308.

4101 Swiggart, Peter. The Art of Faulkner's Novels. Austin: Texas U. P., 1962, pp. 49-51.

4102 ________. "The Snopes Trilogy," SR, 68 (Spring, 1960), 319-325. Repr., in Modern American Fiction: Essays in Criticism. A. Walton Litz, ed. New York: Oxford U. P., 1963, pp. 194-200.

4103 Swinnerton, Frank. "Tests of Quality," Observer (September 22, 1940), 5.
Found little to commend in Hamlet.

4104 Thompson, Lawrance. William Faulkner: An Introduction and Interpretation. New York: Holt, Rinehart, & Winston, 1967, passim.

4105 Thompson, Ralph. "Books of the Times," NYTimes (April 1, 1940), 17.

4106 Thonon, Robert. "William Faulkner: From The Hamlet to The Town," ESA, 2 (September, 1959), 190-202.

4107 Times Literary Supplement, No. 2016 (September 21, 1940), 481; also (February 7, 1958), 74.

4108 Trimmer, Joseph F. "V. K. Ratliff: A Portrait of the Artist in Motion," MFS, 20 (Winter, 1974-75), 451-467.

4109 Tuck, Dorothy. Crowell's Handbook of Faulkner. New York: Crowell, 1964, pp. 74-81.

4110 Vickery, Olga W. The Novels of William Faulkner. Rev. ed. Baton Rouge: Louisiana State U. P., 1964, pp. 167-191.

4111 Vorpahl, Ben M. "Such Stuff as Dreams Are Made On: History, Myth and the Comic Vision of Mark Twain and William Faulkner," DA, 28 (Wisconsin: 1967), 698A.
The Hamlet and Huckleberry Finn examined as to the failure of the frontier myth when confronted with human reality.

4112 Waggoner, Hyatt H. William Faulkner: From Jefferson to the World. Lexington: Kentucky U. P., 1959, pp. 183-193.

4113 Wagner, Linda W. "Faulkner's Fiction: Studies in Organic Form," JNT, 1 (January, 1971), 1-14.

4114 Wall, Carey. "Drama and Technique in Faulkner's The Hamlet," TCL, 14 (April, 1968), 17-23.

4115 Walton, Eda Lou. "The Snopeses Move Up," New Masses (April 16, 1940), 27.

4116 Walton, Gerald W. "A Word List of Southern Farm Terms from Faulkner's The Hamlet," MissFR, 6 (1972), 60-75.

4117 Warren, Robert Penn. "The Snopes World," KR, 3 (Spring, 1941), 253-257.

4118 Watkins, Floyd C., and Thomas Daniel Young. "Revisions of Style in Faulkner's The Hamlet," MFS, 5 (Winter, 1959-60), 327-336.

4119 Watson, James Gray. Faulkner's Trilogy. Coral Gables, Florida: Miami U. P., 1970, pp. 147-221.

4120 Wilson, Edmund. "Books--Horrors, Charm, Fun," NY (April 6, 1940), 73.

4121 Wojciechowska, Kalina, tr. Zaścianek. Warsaw: Czytelnik, 1964.
Polish translation of The Hamlet.

4122 Yonce, Margaret. "Faulkner's 'Atthis' and 'Attis': Some Sources of Myth," MissQ, 23 (1970), 289-298.

The Town
(New York: Random House, 1957)

4123 Adams, Percy G. "Humor as Structure and Theme in Faulkner's Trilogy," WSCL, 5 (Autumn, 1964), 205-212.

4124 Allen, Walter. "Snopes on the March," NSt, 55 (February 1, 1958), 143.

4125 Anon. "Faulkner's Snopeses Revisited," Denver Post (May 12, 1957), Roundup Sec., 8.

4126 Anon. "Faulkner's 'The Town' Rewarding," NYMirror (May 26, 1957), Home Ed., 7.

4127 Anon. "The Snopeses," Time (May 6, 1957), 110.

4128 Anon. "The Town," Booklist (July 1, 1957), 500.

4129 Anon. [The Town], Newsweek (May 6, 1957), 116-117.

4130 Anon. "The Town," South Bend Tribune (February 2, 1958), 10.

4131 Antonini, Giacomo. "Ritorno di William Faulkner," FLe, No. 25 (June 23, 1957), 6.

4132 Beck, Warren. Man in Motion: Faulkner's Trilogy. Madison: Wisconsin U.P., 1961, passim.

4133 "Books of the Week," Socialist Leader, 50 (March 1, 1958), 7.

4134 Borgal, Clément. "William Faulkner: La ville, traduit de l'anglais par J. et L. Bréant," TR, 183 (April, 1963), 140-141.

4135 Bradley, Van Allen. "His Finest Hour," Chicago Daily News, n.d. (May, 1957), 16.

4136 Breaden, Dale G. "William Faulkner and the Land," AmQt, 1 (Fall, 1958), 344-357.

4137 Bréant, J. and L., trs. La ville. Paris: Gallimard, 1962.

4138 Brett, David. Manchester Evening News (February 8, 1958), 2.

4139 Brooks, Cleanth. "Passion, Marriage and Bourgeois Respectability (The Town)," William Faulkner: The Yoknapatawpha County. New Haven: Yale U.P., 1964, pp. 192-218.

4140 Bruccoli, M. J. "Faulkner Continues the Snopes' Story," Richmond News Leader (July 2, 1957), 13.

4141 Brusar, Branko. "Humor Williama Faulknera Na Primjerima iz Romana 'Grad,'" Republika (Zagreb), 15 (July-August, 1959), 32.

4142 Brylowski, Walter. "Yoknapatawpha Revisited," Faulkner's Olympian Laugh: Myth in the Novels. Detroit: Wayne State U.P., 1968, pp. 201-216.

4143 Burlingame, Robert. "The Town," El Paso Herald Post (May 4, 1957), 4.

4144 Butler, G. Paul. "Faulkner's Novel Tops," NYMirror (May 5, 1957), 32.

4145 Copeland, Edith. "Bitter Smile Is Provoked," Daily Oklahoman (Oklahoma City), (May 12, 1957), Mag. Sec., 30.

4146 Cullen, John B., and Floyd C. Watkins. Old Times in the Faulkner Country. Chapel Hill: North Carolina U.P., 1961, pp. 108-115.

4147 DeCillier, Mary Anne G. "Faulkner's Young Man: As Reflected in the Character of Charles Mallison," Laurel R, 9, #2 (1969), 42-49.

4148 Dirksen, Sherland N. "William Faulkner's Snopes Family: The Hamlet, The Town, and The Mansion," ESRS, 11 (December, 1962), 5-45.

4149 Dolbier, Maurice. "The Town," NYHTBR (May 1, 1957), 21.

4150 Doster, William C. "The Several Faces of Gavin Stevens," MissQ, 11 (1958), 191-195.

4151 Durston, J. H. "Come, Come, William Faulkner," House and Garden (June, 1957), 16-17.

4152 Edwards, Duane. "Flem Snopes and Thomas Sutpen: Two Versions of Respectability," DR, 51 (1971-72), 559-570.

4153 Elliott, George P. "Fiction Chronicle," HudR, 10 (Summer, 1957), 292-293.

4154 Ellman, Richard. "Faulkner Genius Shines in New Novel," Chicago Sun-Times (May 5, 1957), III, 1.

4155 Engle, Paul. "New Faulkner Is Richly Rewarding," Chicago Sunday Tribune (May 5, 1957), IV, 4.

4156 Everett, Walter K. Faulkner's Art and Characters. Woodbury, New York: Barron's Educ. Ser., 1969, pp. 115-119.

4157 Farnham, James F. "Faulkner's Unsung Hero: Gavin Stevens," ArQ, 21 (Summer, 1965), 115-132.

4158 "Faulkner's Curse," TLS (February 7, 1958), 74.

4159 "Faulkner's Old Spell in a New Novel of Yoknapatawpha," NYHTB (May 5, 1957), 1.

4160 Fecher, Charles A. "The Town," Books on Trial (June-July, 1957), 448.

4161 Fersch, Ellsworth A. "The Town," YLM (May, 1957), 23.

4162 Fretz, Gene. "Snopeses Take Over Yoknapatawpha as Faulkner Resumes Story-telling," Arkansas Gazette (Little Rock), (April 28, 1957), 6-F.

4163 Frost, Derland. "Yoknapatawphians in New Faulkner Novel," Houston Post (May 5, 1957), Now Sec., 37.

4164 Gold, Joseph. "The Town: All People Learn a Little More," William Faulkner: A Study in Humanism from Metaphor to Discourse. Norman: Oklahoma U.P., 1966, pp. 148-161.

4165 _______. "Truth or Consequences: Faulkner's The Town," MissQ, 13 (Summer, 1960), 112-116.

4166 Green, Peter. "Faulkner's Small-town Anecdotes," Daily Telegraph and Morning Post," (February 7, 1958), 13.

4167 Gregory, Eileen. "Faulkner's Typescripts of The Town," MissQ, 26 (Summer, 1973), 361-386.

4168 _______. "Faulkner's Typescripts of The Town," A Faulkner Miscellany. James B. Meriwether, ed. Jackson, Miss.: Mississippi U.P., 1974, pp. 113-138.

4169 _______. "A Study of the Early Version of Faulkner's The Town and The Mansion," DAI, 36 (South Carolina: 1975), 3686A-87A.

4170 Hanscom, Leslie. "Faulkner's Latest Snopesish Humor," New York World-Telegram & Sun (May 1, 1957), 31.

4171 Harder, Kelsie B. "Proverbial Snopeslore," TFSB, 24 (September, 1958), 89-95.
Folklore in The Town and The Hamlet.

4172 Harrington, Michael. "Uneven Addition to a Magnificent Whole," Cw, 66 (June 21, 1957), 306.

4173 Haselmayer, Louis. "The Town," Hawkeye-Gazette (Burlington, Iowa), (July 15, 1957), 2.

4174 Hass, Victor P. "From a Bookman's Notebook," Omaha World Herald (May 19, 1957), Mag. Sec., 30-G.

4175 Hicks, Granville. "The Question of William Faulkner: His New Novel, The Town, As Test," NewL (May, 1957), 6-8.

4176 Hoffman, Frederick J. "The Snopes Balance: 1940 and 1957," Progressive (September, 1957), 33-35.

4177 Holmes, Edward Morris. Faulkner's Twice Told Tales: His Re-Use of His Material. The Hague: Mouton, 1966, pp. 19-45.

4178 Howe, Irving. "Faulkner: End of a Road," NR, 141 (December 7, 1959), 17-21.

4179 ________. "The Town and The Mansion," William Faulkner: A Critical Study. New York: Vintage, 1952, pp. 282-294.

4180 Howell, Elmo. "Mink Snopes and Faulkner's Moral Conclusions," SAQ, 67 (Winter, 1968), 13-22.

4181 Jacobs, Robert D. "Faulkner's Humor," The Comic Imagination in American Literature. Louis D. Rubin, Jr., ed. New Brunswick, New Jersey: Rutgers U.P., 1973, pp. 305-318.

4182 Jarrett, David. "Eustacia Vye and Eula Varner, Olympians: The Worlds of Thomas Hardy and William Faulkner," Novel, 6 (Winter, 1973), 163-174.

4183 Kane, Patricia. "Adaptable and Free: Faulkner's Ratliff," NConL, 1 (May, 1971), 9-11.

4184 Kazin, Alfred. "Mr. Faulkner's Friends, the Snopeses," NYTBR (May 5, 1957), 1, 24.

4185 Keister, Don A. "Faulkner's Evil Hero Top Dog in a New Tale," Plain Dealer (Cleveland), (May 5, 1957), 16-G.

4186 Kempton, Murray. "Another Day in the Creation of a World," NYPost (May 5, 1957), 11-M.

4187 Kindrick, Robert L. "Lizzie Dahlberg and Eula Varner: Two Modern Perspectives on the Earth Mother," Midamerica, 2 (1975), 93-111.

4188 Kirk, Robert W., and Marvin Klotz. Faulkner's People. Berkeley: California U.P., 1963, pp. 157-177.

4189 Klein, Francis A. "The Town," St. Louis Globe-Democrat (May 12, 1957), 4-F.

4190 Korg, Jacob. "Buckboard to Model T," Nation, 184 (June 8, 1957), 503-504.

4191 Lambert, J. W. "Faulkner's World," Sunday Times (London) (February 2, 1958), 7.

4192 Las Vergnas, Raymond. "Deux morts, deux vivants: Lettres amêricaines, William Faulkner, La ville," NL (January 31, 1963), 5.

4193 Lawson, John Howard. "William Faulkner," IL, No. 9 (September, 1961), 178-186.

4194 Lawson, Lewis. "The Grotesque-Comic in the Snopes Trilogy," L&P, 15 (1963), 107-119.

4195 Levine, Paul. "Love and Money in the Snopes Trilogy," CE, 23 (December, 1961), 196-203.

4196 Lombardo, Agostino. "The Town di William Faulkner," Criterio, 2 (February-March, 1958), 132-139.

4197 Long, Ulman E. "Faulkner's South Is Study in Contrast," Daily Times (Wichita Falls, Texas), (May 12, 1957), 3-D.

4198 Longley, John. "Galahad Gavin and a Garland of Snopeses," VQR, 33 (Autumn, 1957), 623-628.

4199 Lytle, Andrew. "The Town: Helen's Last Stand," SR, 65 (Summer, 1957), 475-484.

4200 ________. "The Town: Helen's Last Stand," and "The Son of Man: He Will Prevail," in The Hero with the Private Parts: Essays by Andrew Lytle. Foreword by Allen Tate. Baton Rouge: Louisiana State U. P., 1966, 137-147, 103-128.

4201 "M. P." Eastern Daily Press (January 31, 1958).

4202 McLaren, Moray. "Meandering in William Faulkner's Town," Scotsman (January 30, 1958), 4.

4203 Magill, Frank N., ed. Masterplots: Combined Edition. New York: Salem Press, 1960, pp. 3171-3173.

4204 Mais, S. P. B. "Taking the Lid off the Town," Oxford Mail (January 30, 1958), 6.

4205 Malcolm, Donald. "Faulkner Returns to Yoknapatawpha," NR, 136 (May 27, 1957), 20-21.

4206 Marcus, Steven. "Faulkner's Town: Mythology as History," PR, 24 (Summer, 1957), 432-441. Repr., in Three Decades of Criticism. Frederick Hoffman and Olga Vickery, eds. East Lansing: Michigan State U. P., 1960, pp. 382-399.

4207 ________. "The Town: Snopes Revisited," Representations: Essays on Literature and Society. New York: Random House, 1975, pp. 28-40.

4208 Meriwether, James B. "The Snopes Revisited," SatRL, 40 (April 27, 1957), 12-13.

4209 Millgate, Michael. "The Town," The Achievement of William Faulkner. New York: Random House, 1966, pp. 235-244.

4210 Mizener, Arthur. "The Town by William Faulkner," KR, 19 (Summer, 1957), 484-488.

4211 Mooney, Stephen L. "Faulkner's 'The Town': A Question of Voices," MissQ, 13 (Summer, 1960), 117-122.

4212 Muir, Edwin. "Life in the South," Observer (February 9, 1958), 15.

4213 Nelson, Stan. "Second in Faulkner's Trilogy Holds Interest," Fort Worth Star-Telegram (May 12, 1957), II, 8.

4214 Norris, Nancy. "The Hamlet, The Town and The Mansion: A Psychological Reading of the Snopes Trilogy," Mosaic, 7 (Fall, 1973), 213-235.

4215 "Novyi roman Folknera [Faulkner's new novel]. (The Town). Literaturnaia gazeta (June 15, 1957).
Russian criticism.

4216 O'Leary, Theodore M. "Faulkner at His Best in His Latest Novel," Kansas City Star (May 11, 1957), 6.

4217 O'Neill, Frank. "Faulkner at Peak," Cleveland News (May 1, 1957), 17.

4218 Paulding, Gouverneur. "Book Notes: Many Souths," Reporter (September 19, 1957), 47-48.

4219 Pickrel, Paul. "The New Books," Harper'sM (June, 1957), 85-86.

4220 Podhoretz, Norman. "Books: Snopesishness and Faulknerishness," NY, 33 (June 1, 1957), 110-116.

4221 Prescott, Orville. "Books of the Times," NYTimes (May 1, 1957), 39M.

4222 Priestley, J. B. "I'm Tired of Deep South Decadence," Reynolds News (February 9, 1958), 4.

4223 Reynolds, Horace. "The Snopes Story Continues," CSMM (May 2, 1957), 7.

4224 Richardson, Kenneth E. Force and Faith in the Novels of William Faulkner. The Hague: Mouton, 1967, passim.

4225 Richardson, Maurice. "Well, the Backgrounds Are Real," Evening Standard (February 4, 1958), 10.

4226 Roberts, James L. "Snopeslore: The Hamlet, The Town, The Mansion," UKCR, 38 (October, 1961), 65-71.

4227 Robson, W. W. "William Faulkner," Spectator, 6764 (February 14, 1958), 206.

4228 Rogers, Thomas H. "Farce and Anecdote--The Town," Chicago Review, 6 (Autumn, 1957), 110-114.

4229 Rolo, Charles J. "Reader's Choice," Atl, 199 (May, 1957), 80, 82. See also reviews by C. J. Rolo in Booklist, 53 (June 1, 1957), 500; Bookmark, 16 (June, 1957), 214.

4230 Rubin, Louis D. "Faulkner's Newest," Evening Sun (Baltimore), (May 30, 1957), 28; also "Snopeslore: Or, Faulkner Clears the Deck," WR, 22 (Autumn, 1957), 73-76.

4231 Rugoff, Milton. "Faulkner's Old Spell in a New Novel of Yoknapatawpha," NYHTBR (May 5, 1957), 1.

4232 Scott, Nathan A., Jr. "The Vision of William Faulkner," ChrC, 74 (September 11, 1957), 1104-1106.

4233 Sender, Ramon. "La última novela de Faulkner," Diario de Nueva York (June 9, 1957).

4234 Shanaghan, Malachy M. "A Critical Analysis of the Fictional Techniques of William Faulkner," DA, 20 (Notre Dame: 1960), 4663.

4235 Sherman, Thomas B. "Faulkner Continues Saga of Yoknapatawpha County," St. Louis Post-Dispatch (May 5, 1957), 4-C.

4236 Slatoff, Walter J. "Hamlet, Go Down, Moses, Town," Quest for Failure. Ithaca: Cornell U.P., 1960, 2nd pr., 1961, pp. 203-205.

4237 "The Snopeses," Time (May 6, 1957), 110.

4238 Stein, Jean. "William Faulkner," Writers at Work. Malcolm Cowley, ed. New York: Viking, 1958, pp. 119-141.

4239 Stephens, R. C. "Faulkner's Roots in the Deep South," Belfast Telegraph (February 1, 1958), 4.

4240 Sullivan, William Patrick. "William Faulkner and the Community," DA, 22 (Columbia, 1961), 4355.
The Town, Chapter 5.

4241 "The Superb Story-Teller," Newsweek (May 6, 1957), 6.

4242 Thompson, Lawrance R. William Faulkner. 2nd ed. New York: Holt, Rinehart, and Winston, 1967, pp. 148-158.

4243 Thompson, Ralph. "The Town," Book-of-the-Month Club News (May, 1957).

4244 Thonon, Robert. "William Faulkner: From The Hamlet to The Town," ESA, 2 (September, 1959), 190-202.

4245 Tinkle, Lon. "Of Snopes and Sin in Faulkner Country," Dallas Morning News, (May 5, 1957), VII, 5.

4246 Trimmer, Joseph F. "V. K. Ratliff: A Portrait of the Artist in Motion," MFS, 20 (1974-75), 451-467.

4247 Trotter, Margaret G. "The Town," GaR, 12 (Summer, 1958), 226-228.

4248 Tuck, Dorothy. Crowell's Handbook of Faulkner. New York: Crowell, 1964, pp. 81-85.

4249 "Uneven Addition to a Magnificent Whole," Cw (June 21, 1957), 306-307.

4250 Urquhart, Fred. "New Novels," Time and Tide, 39, #7 (February 15, 1958), 202-204.

4251 Vickery, Olga W. "The Profit and the Loss: The Hamlet and The Town," The Novels of William Faulkner. Rev. ed. Baton Rouge: Louisiana State U.P., 1964, pp. 167-191.

4252 Volpe, Edmond L. A Reader's Guide to William Faulkner. New York: Noonday Press, 1964, pp. 317-331.

4253 Waggoner, Hyatt H. William Faulkner: From Jefferson to the World. Lexington: Kentucky U.P., 1959, pp. 232-237.

4254 Watson, James Gray. "The Town," The Snopes Dilemma: Faulkner's Trilogy. Coral Gables, Florida: Miami U.P., 1968, pp. 17-74.

4255 Watts, Richard. "Random Notes on This and That," NYPost (May 7, 1957), 44.

4256 Wheeler, Otis B. "Some Uses of Folk Humor by Faulkner," MissQ, 17 (Spring, 1964), 107-122.

4257 Willingham, John R. "The Town," LibJ, 82 (May 15, 1957), 1319-1320.

The Mansion
(New York: Random House, 1959)

4258 Adams, Percy G. "Humor as Structure and Theme in Faulkner's Trilogy," WSCL, 5 (Autumn, 1964), 205-212.

4259 Anissimov, I. "The Middle of the Century," IL, No. 7 (July, 1962), 178-188.

4260 Anon. "Enthralling to the End," Newsweek (November 16, 1959), 119-120.

4261 Anon. "Flem Snopes Is Dead," TLS (January 13, 1961), 21.

4262 Anon. "The Mansion," Booklist (January 1, 1960), 266.

4263 Anon. "Round off the Annals of Yoknapatawpha County," Times (January 12, 1961), 15.

4264 Anon. "Saga's End," Time (November 2, 1959), 90.

4265 Barth, J. Robert. "Faulkner and the Snopes Trilogy," America (February 27, 1960), 638-640.

4266 Beck, Warren. "Faulkner in The Mansion," VQR, 36 (Spring, 1960), 272-292. Repr., Faulkner: Essays by Warren Beck. 1976, pp. 639-659.

4267 _______. Man in Motion: Faulkner's Trilogy. Madison: Wisconsin U.P., 1961, passim.

4268 Bianciardi, Luciano, tr. Il palazzo; romanzo della famiglia Snopes. Torino: Carlo Frassinelli, 1963.

4269 Bradley, Van Allen. "Faulkner Completes a Great Trilogy," Chicago Daily News (November 15, 1959), 8.

4270 Brooke-Rose, Christine. "The Mansion," London Magazine (March, 1961), 67-68.

4271 Brooks, Cleanth. "Faulkner's Revenger's Tragedy (The Mansion)," William Faulkner: The Yoknapatawpha Country. New Haven: Yale U.P., 1963, pp. 219-243, 412-414.

4272 _______. "Faulkner's Savage Arcadia: Frenchman's Bend," VQR, 39 (Autumn, 1963), 598-611.

4273 Brylowski, Walter. Faulkner's Olympian Laugh. Detroit: Wayne State U. P., 1968, pp. 206-215,

4274 Butcher, Fanny. "Faulkner's 'Final' Snopes Novel by Far the Best in the Trilogy," Chicago Sunday Tribune (November 1959), Mag. of Books, 3.

4275 Cambon, Glauco. "L'ultimo Faulkner," FLe, 15 (January 3, 1960), 1-2.

4276 Carter, Thomas H. [The Mansion]. Shenandoah, 11 (Winter, 1960), 64-69.

4277 Casper, Leonard. "Reviews of Books," SWR, 45 (Spring, 1960), viii-x, 186.

4278 Cevasco, George A. "The Mansion," The Sign (February, 1960), 77-78.

4279 Charles, Gerda. "New Novels," NSt, 61 (January 13, 1961), 54.

4280 Chase, Richard. "The Snopeses at an End," Commentary, 29 (February, 1960), 179-181.

4281 Chugunov, Konstantin. "Faulkner's Mansion in the U. S. S. R.," SovL, No. 2 (1962), 171-172.

4282 Copeland, Edith. "Books in Orbit," Daily Oklahoman (Oklahoma City), (November 29, 1959), Mag. Sec., 26.

4283 Cowley, Malcolm. "Flem Snopes Gets His Come-Uppance," NYTBR (November 15, 1959), 1, 18.

4284 Creighton, Joanne V. "The Dilemma of the Human Heart in The Mansion," Renascence, 25 (Autumn, 1972), 35-45.

4285 Cullen, John B. "The Mansion," Old Times in the Faulkner Country. Chapel Hill: North Carolina U. P., 1961, pp. 116-127.

4286 DeMott, Benjamin. "Monge and Other Destinations," HudR, 12 (Winter, 1960), 618-620.

4287 Dirksen, Sherland N. "William Faulkner's Snopes Family: The Hamlet, The Town, and The Mansion," ESRS, 11 (December, 1962), 33-40.

4288 Dolbier, Maurice. "The Mansion," NYHTB (November 14, 1959), 6.

4289 Donnelly, Tom. "Wild Bill's Yonder in the Cornfield," Washington Daily News (November 13, 1959), 41.

4290 Edwards, Duane. "Flem Snopes and Thomas Sutpen: Two Versions of Respectability," DR, 51 (Winter, 1971-72), 559-570.

4291 Everett, Walter K. Faulkner's Art and Characters. Woodbury, New York: Barron's Educ. Series, 1969, pp. 52-57.

4292 Fadiman, Clifton. "Reading I've Liked," Holiday (January, 1960), 23.

4293 Farmer, Norman J., Jr. "The Love Theme: A Principal Source of Thematic Unity in Faulkner's Snopes Trilogy," TCL, 8 (October, 1962), 111-123.

4294 Farnham, James F. "Faulkner's Unsung Hero: Gavin Stevens," ArQ, 21 (Summer, 1965), 114-132.

4295 "Faulkner's Discrepancies," PubW (October 26, 1959), 16.
Points out discrepancies between the new book and its predecessors.

4296 "Flem Snopes Is Dead," TLS, #3072 (January 13, 1961), 21.

4297 Fletcher, Raymond. "Faulkner's Contradictions," Tribune (January 13, 1961), 11.

4298 Gold, Joseph. "The Mansion: To Trust in God Without Depending on Him," William Faulkner: A Study in Humanism from Metaphor to Discourse. Norman, Oklahoma U. P., 1966, pp. 162-173.

4299 Greene, Theodore M. "The Philosophy of Life Implicit in Faulkner's The Mansion," TSLL, 2 (Winter, 1961), 401-418.

4300 Gregory, Eileen. "Faulkner's Typescript of The Town," MissQ, 26 (Summer, 1973), 361-386.
Also refers to The Mansion.

4301 ________. "A Study of the Early Versions of Faulkner's The Town and The Mansion," DAI, 36 (South Carolina: 1975), 3686A-87A.

4302 ________. "The Temerity to Revolt: Mink Snopes and the Dispossessed in The Mansion," MissQ, 29, #3 (Summer, 1976), 401-421.

4303 Harding, D. W. "Revenger's Tragedy," Spectator, 206 (January 27, 1961), 110-111.

4304 H[ass], V[ictor] P. "Tiresome Faulkner Ends Tiresome Trilogy," Sunday World Herald (Omaha), (November 15, 1959), Mag. Sec., 29.

4305 Hicks, Granville. "The Last of the Snopeses," SatRL, 42 (November 14, 1959), 20-21.

4306 Hilleret, René, tr. Le domaine. Paris: Gallimard, 1962.

4307 Hoffman, Frederick J. "This Is the End of Flem Snopes," Progressive (March, 1960), 55-57.

4308 Holmes, Edward Morris. "Faulkner's Twice-Told Tales: His Re-Use of His Material," DA, 23 (Brown: 1963), 2527.

4309 Holroyd, Stuart. "Fate and the Snopeses," JO'L, 4 (January 12, 1961), 33.

4310 Howe, Irving. "End of a Road," NR, 141 (December 7, 1959), 17-21.

4311 _______. "The Town and The Mansion," William Faulkner: A Critical Study. New York: Vintage, 1952, pp. 282-294.

4312 Howell, Elmo. "Mink Snopes and Faulkner's Moral Conclusions," SAQ, 67 (Winter, 1968), 13-22.

4313 Hunt, Joel A. "Reply," ConL, 11 (Spring, 1970), 311-312.
Cf., Henry A. Pochmann and Joel A. Hunt. "Faulkner and His Sources," ConL, 11 (Spring, 1970), 310-312.

4314 _______. "William Faulkner and Rabelais: The Dog Story," ConL, 10 (Summer, 1969), 383-388.
Suggests Rabelais' Pantagruel, (Chaps. XXI and XXII of the second book) as source for the dog episode in Chapter 13 of The Mansion.

4315 Jacobs, Robert D. "Faulkner's Humor," The Comic Imagination in American Literature. Louis D. Rubin, Jr., ed. New Brunswick: Rutgers U.P., 1973, pp. 305-318.

4316 Jennings, Elizabeth. "The Mansion," Listener (January 19, 1961), 151.

4317 Jessup, Lee Cheney. "Chronicle of Snopes Clan Comes to Close," Banner (Nashville), (November 13, 1959), 32.

4318 Kane, Patricia. "Adaptable and Free: Faulkner's Ratliff," NConL, 1 (May, 1971), 9-11.

4319 Keister, Don A. "Faulkner Saga Ends on Note of Optimism," Cleveland Plain Dealer (November 15, 1959), 10-F.

4320 Kempton, Murray. "Here Lies Snopes," NYPost (November 15, 1959), 10-M.

4321 Kirk, Robert W., and Marvin Klotz. Faulkner's People. Berkeley: California U. P., 1963, pp. 178-202.

4322 Klein, Francis A. "Faulkner Winds Up Trilogy," St. Louis Globe-Democrat (November 15, 1959), 4-F.

4323 Lawson, John Howard. "William Faulkner," IL, No. 9 (September, 1961), 178-186.

4324 Lawson, Lewis. "The Grotesque-Comic in the Snopes Trilogy," L&P, 15 (1963), 107-119; repr., in Hidden Patterns. Leonard Falk and Eleanor B. Manheim, eds. New York: Macmillan, 1966, pp. 244-245, 248-249. 250-251.

4325 Leibowitz, Herbert A. "The Snopes Dilemma and the South," UKCR, 28 (Summer, 1962), 273-284.

4326 Lemay, Harding. "Faulkner and His Snopes Family Reach the End of Their Trilogy," NYHTBR (November 15, 1959), Sec. 6, 1, 14.

4327 Levidova, Inna. "Saga of a Gloomy Dynasty," Novy Mir, No. 7 (1962), 265-269.

4328 Levine, Paul. "Love and Money in the Snopes Trilogy," CE 23 (December, 1961), 196-203.

4329 MacLure, Millar. "Snopes: A Faulkner Myth," CanForum, 39 (February, 1960), 245-260.

4330 Marks, Laurence. [The Mansion]. Evening Standard (January 24, 1961), 11.

4331 Masterman, John. "Faulkner Concludes Era of Flem Snopes," Daily News (Amarillo, Texas), (November 15, 1959), I, 16.

4332 Meriwether, James B. "Flem Snopes Gets His Come-uppance," Houston Post (November 15, 1959), Now Sec., 36, 38.

4333 ________. "The Snopes Trilogy Completed," CarQ, 12 (Fall-Winter, 1959), 30-34.

4334 Millgate, Michael. "The Mansion," The Achievement of William Faulkner. New York: Random House, 1965, pp. 245-252.

4335 Moore, Geoffrey. "Mink Agonistes," KR, 22 (Summer, 1960), 519-522.

4336 Moses, W. R. "The Limits of Yoknapatawpha County," GaR, 16 (Fall, 1962), 297-305.

Calls The Mansion Faulkner's "Doomsday Book," which ties up the "loose ends" of the Yoknapatawpha epic.

4337 Mosley, Nicholas. "William Faulkner's Universe," Time and Tide, 42, #2 (January 13, 1961), 61-63.

4338 Nelson, Stan. "Mansion Wraps Up Snopes Saga," Fort Worth Star Telegram, (November 15, 1959), II, 11.

4339 Nordell, Rod. "Faulkner Trilogy Complete," CSMM (November 12, 1959), 15.

4340 Norman, Jerry. "Faulkner Writes End to Snopeses," Standard Times (San Angelo, Texas), (November 15, 1959), 10-B.

4341 Norris, Hoke. "Faulkner Kills, Destroys, Demolishes Snopes," Chicago Sunday Times (November 15, 1959), III, 1.

4342 Norris, Nancy. "The Hamlet, The Town, and The Mansion: A Psychological Reading of the Snopes Trilogy," Mosaic, 7 (Fall, 1973), 213-235.

4343 O'Connor, William Van. "Best in Faulkner Comes Out Again," Sunday Tribune (Minneapolis), (November 15, 1959), Home and Hobby Sec., 12.

4344 _______. "The Old Master, The Sole Proprietor," VQR, 36 (Winter, 1960), 147-151.

4345 _______. The Tangled Fire of William Faulkner. Minneapolis: Minnesota U.P., 1954, passim.

4346 O'Neill, Frank. "The Mansion," Cleveland News (May 20, 1959), 9.

4347 Owens, Patrick J. "Mansion Is Final Faulkner Snopes Story," Arkansas Gazette (Little Rock), (November 8, 1959), 6-E.

4348 Paulding, Gouverneur. "Right Wind, Right Rain," Reporter, (November 26, 1959), 41-44.

4349 Peckham, Stanton. "William Faulkner Completes a Great Trilogy," Sunday Denver Post (November 8, 1959), 9.

4350 Pickrel, Paul. "The New Books," Harper'sM (November 1959), 102, 104.

4351 Pochmann, Henry A., and Joel A. Hunt. "Faulkner and His Sources," ConL, 11 (Spring, 1970), 310-312.
Cf., Joel A. Hunt. "William Faulkner and Rabelais: The Dog Story," ConL, 10 (Summer, 1969), 383-388,

and "Reply," by Joel A. Hunt, ConL, 11 (Spring, 1970), 311-312.

4352 Prescott, Orville. "Books of the Times," NYTimes (November 13, 1959), 27.

4353 Price, Emerson. "William Faulkner," Cleveland Press (November 17, 1959), 22.

4354 Price, Martin. "Dreams and Doubts: Some Recent Fiction," YR, 49 (December, 1959), 278-280.

4355 Price, R. G. G. "New Fiction," Punch (January 11, 1961), 117.

4356 Regan, Stephen P. "The Mansion," Best Sellers (November 15, 1959), 278.

4357 Richardson, Kenneth E. Force and Faith in the Novels of William Faulkner. The Hague: Mouton, 1967, pp. 163-171.

4358 Roberts, James L. "Snopeslore: The Hamlet, The Town, The Mansion," UKCR, 38 (October, 1961), 65-71.

4359 Rolo, Charles. "Reader's Choice," Atl, 204 (November, 1959), 170-171.

4360 Rossky, William. "Faulkner: The Image of the Child in The Mansion," MissQ, 15 (Winter, 1961-62), 17-20.

4361 Rowland, Stanley J., Jr. "End of a House," ChrC (December 23, 1959), 1503.

4362 Rubin, Louis D. "The Trilogy of the Snopes Family Complete," Evening Sun (Baltimore), (November 27, 1959), 26.

4363 Rubinstein, Annette T. "Poorly Furnished," Mainstream (January, 1960), 60-61.

4364 Ryan, Stephen P. "The Mansion," Ave Maria (March 19, 1960), 27-28.

4365 "Saga's End," Time (November 2, 1959), 90.

4366 Schnack, Elizabeth, tr. Das Haus. Roman. Zürich: Fretz & Wasmuth, 1960.

4367 Schott, Webster. "The Snopes Era Is Now Brought to Conclusion," Kansas City Star (November 21, 1959), 7.

4368 Serebnick, Judith. "The Mansion," LibJ (November 15, 1959), 3586.

4369 Sherman, Thomas B. "Continued Chronicle of the Snopes Family," St. Louis Post-Dispatch (November 8, 1959), 4-B.

4370 Shrapnel, Norman. "Tedium as an Art Form," Manchester Guardian (January 13, 1961), 6.

4371 Singer, Burns. "The Face of Evil," Encounter, 16 (March, 1961), 82-85.

4372 Slatoff, Walter J. "*The Mansion*," Epoch, 10 (Winter, 1960), 124-125.

4373 Startsev, Abel. Znakomstvo s Folknerom [An acquaintance with Faulkner]. (Osobniak [*The Mansion*]). Literaturnaia gazeta (March 13, 1962).
Russian criticism.

4374 Sutherland, W. O. S., ed. *Six Contemporary Novels*. Austin, Texas: Texas U.P., 1962, *passim*.

4375 Swiggart, Peter. "The Snopes Trilogy," SR, 68 (Spring, 1960), 319-325; repr., *The Art of Faulkner's Novels*. Austin: Texas U.P., 1962, pp. 195-206.

4376 Tinkle, Lon. "In Faulkner Country with Sinful Snopes," Dallas Morning News (November 15, 1959), V, 8.

4377 Tuck, Dorothy. *Crowell's Handbook of Faulkner*. New York: Crowell, 1964, pp. 86-94.

4378 Turner, Decherd. "Rise and Victory of Flem Snopes," Dallas Times Herald (November 15, 1959), Roundup Sec., 13.

4379 Vickery, Olga W. *The Novels of William Faulkner*. 2nd ed. Baton Rouge: Louisiana State U.P., 1964, pp. 191-208.

4380 Volpe, Edmond L. *A Reader's Guide to William Faulkner*. New York: Noonday Press, 1964, pp. 331-343, 401-403.

4381 Watson, James Gray. "The Town," *The Snopes Dilemma: Faulkner's Trilogy*. Coral Gables, Florida: Miami U.P., 1968, pp. 75-146.

4382 Watts, Richard. "Random Notes on This and That," NYPost (November 18, 1959), 77.

4383 West, Anthony. "A Dying Fall," NY, 35 (December 5, 1959), 228, 230, 232, 234-235.

4384 Whitbread, Thomas. "The Snopes Trilogy: The Setting of *The Mansion*," *Six Contemporary Novels*. William O. S. Sutherland, Jr., ed. Austin: Texas U.P., 1962, pp. 76-88.

4385 Williams, George. "The Mansion," NEA Journal (February, 1960), 71.

4386 Wills, Garry. "The Thin World of the Snopeses," NatlR (November 21, 1959), 498-499.

4387 Wyndham, Francis. "The Snopes Saga," Observer (January 15, 1961), 29.

4388 Young, Thomas Daniel. "Book Reviews," JMissH, 22 (July, 1960), 208-211.

"SNOW"

4389 Cantrell, Frank. "An Unpublished Faulkner Short Story: 'Snow,'" MissQ, 26 (Summer, 1973), 325-330.

4390 Meriwether, James B. "'Snow': The Short Fiction of William Faulkner," Proof, 1 (1971), 316.

SOLDIERS' PAY
(New York: Boni & Liveright, 1926)

4391 Adams, Richard P. Faulkner: Myth and Motion. Princeton: Princeton U.P., 1968, pp. 34-40.

4392 Angoff, Allan, ed. "Soldiers' Pay," American Writing Today: Its Independence and Vigor. New York: New York U.P., 1957, pp. 372-374.

4393 Anon. "The Bookman's Guide to Fiction," Bookman, 63 (June, 1926), 472.

4394 Anon. "Books in Vogue," Vogue, 76 (July 23, 1930), 66.

4395 Anon. "Genius from America," Everyman (July 3, 1930), 719.

4396 Anon. "The New Books at a Glance," JO'L (July 26, 1930), 582.

4397 Anon. "New Novel," Times (London), (June 24, 1930), 19.

4398 Anon. Republican (Springfield), (April 4, 1926), 7.

4399 Anon. TLS (London), #1483 (July 3, 1930), 552.

4400 Anon. "War's Aftermath," Times (New York), (April 11, 1926), 8.

4401 Arthos, John. "Ritual and Humor in the Writing of William Faulkner," Accent, 9 (Autumn, 1948), 17-30.

4402 Barth, J. Robert. "Religion and Literature: Soldiers' Pay," Religious Perspectives in Faulkner's Fiction. J. Robert Barth, ed. Notre Dame: Notre Dame U.P., 1972, p. 16.

4403 Beach, Joseph Warren. American Fiction, 1920-1940. New York: Macmillan, 1941, pp. 125-126.

4404 Beatty, Richard Croom. "A Personal Memoir of the Agrarians," Shenandoah, 3 (Summer, 1952), 11.

4405 Beckwith, E. C. "Soldiers' Return Theme of New Novel Called One of Biting Power," NY Evening Post Literary Review (April 3, 1926), 2.

4406 Beidler, Peter G. "The Decadence in Faulkner's First Novel: The Faun, the Worm, and the Tower," EA, No. 3 (1968), 225-242.

4407 Bennett, Arnold. "American Authors 'Made' in England," Evening Standard (June 26, 1930), 7.

4408 Blondel, J. [Soldiers' Pay], Réforme (21 août 1948), 7.

4409 "The Book Taster," Liverpool Post and Mercury (July 2, 1930).

4410 Bosha, Francis John. "The Textual History and Definitive Textual Apparatus for Soldiers' Pay: A Bibliographic Study of Faulkner's First Novel," DAI, 39, #9 (Marquette: 1978), 5509A.

4411 Boyd, Thomas. "Honest But Slap-Dash," SatRL, 2 (April 24, 1926), 736.

4412 Brooks, Cleanth. "Faulkner's First Novel," SoR, 6 (October, 1970), 1056-1074.

4413 Bross, Addison. "Soldiers' Pay and the Art of Aubrey Beardsley," AQ, 19, #1 (Spring, 1967), 3-23.

4414 Brylowski, Walter. "The Early Novels," Faulkner's Olympian Laugh: Myth in the Novels. Detroit: Wayne State U.P., 1968, pp. 43-51.

4415 C., M. [Monnaie de singe], LF (19 août 1948), 4.

4416 Campbell, Harry Modean, and Ruel E. Foster. William Faulkner: A Critical Appraisal. Norman: Oklahoma U.P., 1951, pp. 17-18, 24, 119.

4417 Carey, Glenn O. "William Faulkner: Man's Fatal Vice," ArQ, 28 (Winter, 1972), 293-300.

4418 Cargill, Oscar. "The Primitivists," Intellectual America. New York: Macmillan, 1941, pp. 370-386.

4419 Church, Margaret. "William Faulkner: Myth and Duration," Time and Reality: Studies in Contemporary Fiction. Chapel Hill: North Carolina U. P., 1963, pp. 231-232.

4420 Coffee, Jessie A. "Empty Steeples: Theme Symbols, and Irony in Faulkner's Novels," ArQ, 23 (Autumn, 1967), 197-206.

4421 Collins, Carvel, and Salvatore Quasimodo. Faulkner: Naturalismo Tragedia. Colleccion Estar al dia. Buenos Aires: Carlos Perez, 1968.

4422 Cooperman, Stanley. "A World Withdrawn: Mahon and Hicks," World War I and the American Novel. Baltimore: Johns Hopkins Press, 1967, pp. 159-166.

4423 Dalgarno, Emily. "Soldiers' Pay and Virginia Woolf," MissQ, 29, #3 (Summer, 1976), 339-346.

4424 Daniel, Robert W. "Soldiers' Pay," A Catalogue of the Writings of William Faulkner. New Haven: Yale U. P., 1942, pp. 8-10.

4425 Davidson, Donald. "William Faulkner," Nashville Tennessean (April 11, 1926), Mag. Sec., 6; repr., in GaR, 20 (Winter, 1966), 456-458.

4426 d'Houville, G. [Monnaie de singe] RDM (15 août 1948), 757.

4427 Ditsky, John M. "'Dark, Darker Than Fire': Thematic Parallels in Lawrence and Faulkner," SHR, 8 (Fall, 1974), 497-505.

4428 Duesberg, Jacques. "Monnaie de singe," MN (July 9, 1951), 58-59.

4429 Ehnmark, Anders. "Rebels in American Literature," WR, 23 (Autumn, 1958), 43-56.

4430 Everett, Walter K. Faulkner's Art and Characters. Woodbury, New York: Barrons Educ. Series, 1969, pp. 94-101.

4431 Forestier, M. [Monnaie de singe] RN (15 novembre 1949), 473.

4432 Fraser, Aidan. "Not a War Book," Scots Observer (June 19, 1930), 19.

4433 Frederick, John T. "Anticipation and Achievement in Faulkner's Soldiers' Pay," ArQ, 23 (Autumn, 1967), 243-249.

4434 Gaucher, Maxime, tr. "Monnaie de singe," (extrait du roman). GLet (26 juin 1948), 13, 14.

4435 ________, tr. and préf. Monnaie de Singe. Grenoble et Paris: Arthaud, 1948; Paris: Seghers, 1968.

4436 Geismar, Maxwell. "William Faulkner: The Negro and the Female," Writers in Crisis. Boston: Houghton Mifflin, 1942, pp. 146-148.

4437 Gold, Joseph. "William Faulkner's 'One Compact Thing,'" TCL, 8 (April, 1962), 3-9.

4438 Goodway, Hilda. "Two New American Authors," Daily Telegraph (July 1, 1930), 6.

4439 Gould, Gerald. "Fantasy and Effort," Observer (July 13, 1930), 6.

4440 Grattan, C. Hartley. "A Book of Hatred," NYSun (April 3, 1926), 8.

4441 Gurza, Francisco, tr. La paga de los soldados. Buenos Aires: Editorial Schapire, 1953, 1959.

4442 Hepburn, Kenneth W. "Soldiers' Pay to The Sound and the Fury: Development of Poetic in the Early Novels of William Faulkner," DA, 29 (Washington: 1969), 2263A.

4443 Hoffman, Frederick J. William Faulkner. Twayne's Authors Series. New York: Twayne Pubs., 1961, pp. 40-42; revised 1966.

4444 Howe, Irving. William Faulkner: A Critical Study. New York: Random House, 1952; 2nd ed., 1962, passim.

4445 Hughes, Richard. "Faulkner and Bennett," Encounter, 21 (September, 1963), 59-61.
Concerns Arnold Bennett's introduction of Faulkner to English readers.

4446 ________. Introduction. Soldiers' Pay. London: Chatto & Windus, 1930.

4447 Illustrated London News, 177, #4762 (July 26, 1930), 175.

4448 JO'L, 23, #588 (July 26, 1930), 582.

4449 Kemp, R. [Monnaie de singe]. NL (2 septembre 1948), 2.

4450 Kierszys, Zofia, tr. Żołnierska zapłata. Warszawa: Państwowy Instytut Wydawniczy, 1965.

4451 Kirk, Robert W., and Marvin Klotz. Faulkner's People. Berkeley: California U.P., 1963, pp. 3-9.

4452 Kronenberger, Louis. "Soldiers' Pay," LitD, 4 (July, 1926), 518-519.

4453 L., M. A. "An American Novelist," Guardian (Manchester), (July 11, 1930), 7.

4454 Las Vergnas, R. [Monnaie de singe] HM (août 1948), 677-681.

4455 Le Breton, Maurice. "Technique et psychologie chez William Faulkner," EA, 1 (September 1937), 418-438.

4456 Lloyd, James Barlow. "Humours Characterization and the Tradition of the Jonsonian Comedy of Manners in William Faulkner's Early Fiction: New Orleans Sketches, Soldiers' Pay, and Mosquitoes," DAI, 36 (Mississippi: 1975), 4493A.

4457 Longley, John L., Jr. The Tragic Mask: A Study of Faulkner's Heroes. Chapel Hill: North Carolina U.P., 1963, pp. 26-27.

4458 Macauley, Robie. Introduction. Soldiers' Pay. New York: Signet, 1968.

4459 McClure, John. "Literature and Less," Times-Picayune (New Orleans), (April 11, 1926), Mag. Sec., 4.

4460 Macmillan, Duane J. "The Non-Yoknapatawpha Novels of William Faulkner: An Examination of Soldiers' Pay, Mosquitoes, Pylon, The Wild Palms, and A Fable," DAI, 32 (Wisconsin: 1972), 6986A.

4461 Malin, Irving. William Faulkner: An Interpretation. Stanford: Stanford U.P., 1957, pp. 31-32, 42-43.

4462 Materassi, Mario. "Le Immagini in Soldiers' Pay," SA, 9 (1964), 353-370.

4463 Mellard, James M. "Soldiers' Pay and the Growth of Faulkner's Comedy," American Humor: Essays Presented to John C. Gerber. O. M. Brack, Jr., ed. Scottsdale, AZ: Arete, 1977.

4464 Meriwether, James B. "Soldiers' Pay," The Literary Career of William Faulkner. Princeton: Princeton U.P., 1961, p. 12.

4465 Millgate, Michael. "Soldiers' Pay," The Achievement of William Faulkner. New York: Random House, 1966, pp. 61-67.

4466 ________. "Starting Out in the Twenties: Reflections on Soldiers' Pay," Mosaic, 7 (Fall, 1973), 1-14.

4467 ________. William Faulkner. New York: Grove Press, 1961; Rev., 1966; repr., Capricorn Books, 1971, passim.

4468 Mills, Martin. "Novels of the Week," Yorkshire Post (June 25, 1930), 8.

4469 Monteiro, George. "Fugitive Comments on Early Faulkner," NMW, 10 (Winter, 1977), 95-96.
Early comments on Faulkner's Mosquitoes and Soldiers' Pay.

4470 Morris, Lawrence S. "Flame and Ash," NY, 47 (June 23, 1926), 147, 148.

4471 Nicholson, Norman. "William Faulkner," Man and Literature. London: S.C.M. Press, 1943, pp. 123-125.

4472 Nicolson, Harold. "A Very Mixed Lot of Books This Week," Daily Express, (July 18, 1930), 6.

4473 Nilon, Charles H. Faulkner and the Negro. New York: Citadel Press, 1965, pp. 67-70.

4474 O'Connor, William Van. The Tangled Fire of William Faulkner. Minneapolis: Minnesota U.P., 1954, pp. 28-29, passim.

4475 O'Donnell, George Marian. "Faulkner's Mythology," KR, 1 (Summer, 1939), 52.

4476 Praz, Mario. "William Faulkner," La Stampa (December 4, 1931); also in Cronache letterarie anglosassoni. Roma: Edizioni di Storia e Letteratura, 1951, II, 246-256.

4477 Price-Stephens, Gordon. "Faulkner and the Royal Air Force," MissQ, 17 (Summer, 1964), 123-128.

4478 Pritchett, Victor S. "Vogue of Faulkner, Soldiers' Pay," NS&N, 41 (June 2, 1951), 624-626.

4479 Proteus. "Soldiers' Pay," NSt, 35 (June 28, 1930), 369.

4480 Quasimodo, Salvatore. "La paga del soldato," L'Unità, 31 (February 23, 1954), 3; repr., as "L'epica del Faulkner maggiore," in Il poeta e il politico, e altri suggi. Milano: Schwartz, 1960, pp. 149-152.

4481 Richardson, H. Edward. "Anderson and Faulkner," AL, 36 (November, 1964), 308-309.

4482 ________. "The Decadence in Faulkner's First Novel: The Faun, the Worm, and the Tower," EA, 21 (July-September, 1968), 225-235.

Traces the decadent influence of the French Symbolists in Soldiers' Pay.

4483 _______. "Soldiers' Pay: Detour Through Decadence," William Faulkner: Journey to Self-Discovery. Columbia: Missouri U.P., 1969, pp. 139-163.

4484 Roberts, James L. "Experimental Exercises--Faulkner's Early Writings," Discourse, 6 (Summer, 1963), 183-197.

4485 Sans, J. [Monnaie de Singe] Cl (25 août 1948), 5.

4486 _______ [Monnaie de Singe] Sem (25 août 1948), 5.

4487 Schevill, James. Sherwood Anderson. Denver: Denver U.P., 1951, pp. 194, 195, passim.
Describes Anderson's success in placing Faulkner's first novel, Soldiers' Pay.

4488 Sigaux, G. [Monnaie de Singe], TR (décembre 1948), 2056.

4489 Slabey, Robert M. "Soldiers' Pay: Faulkner's First Novel," RLV, 30 (May-June, 1964), 234-243.

4490 Smart, George K. "A Selective Concordance: Soldiers' Pay, ..." Religious Elements in Faulkner's Early Novels. Coral Gables: Miami U.P., 1965, pp. 1-127.

4491 Smith, Stella P. "The Evolution of Patterns of Characterization from Faulkner's Soldiers' Pay (1926) Through Absalom, Absalom!" DAI, 37 (1976), 2881A.

4492 Stonier, G. W. "Soldiers' Pay," Fortnightly Review, 128 (August, 1930), 285-286.

4493 Swiggart, Peter. The Art of Faulkner's Novels. Austin: Texas U.P., 1962, pp. 31-32.

4494 Thompson, Lawrance. William Faulkner: An Introduction and Interpretation. 2nd ed. New York: Holt, Rinehart & Winston, 1967, passim.

4495 Tomlinson, Kathleen C. "New Novels," Nation & Athenaeum, 47, #15 (July 12, 1930), 477.

4496 Tuck, Dorothy. Crowell's Handbook of Faulkner. New York: Crowell, pp. 125-128.

4497 Vickery, Olga W. "The Apprenticeship: Soldiers' Pay and Mosquitoes," The Novels of William Faulkner. Rev. ed. Baton Rouge: Louisiana State U.P., 1964, pp. 1-14.

4498 _______. "Faulkner's First Novel," WHR, 11 (Summer,

1957), 251-256; repr., in The Novels of William Faulkner (1959), pp. 1-8.

4499 _______. "A Selective Bibliography: Soldiers' Pay," William Faulkner: Three Decades of Criticism. Frederick Hoffman and Olga Vickery, eds. New York: Harcourt, Brace, 1963, p. 422.

4500 Volpe, Edmond L. A Reader's Guide to William Faulkner. New York: Noonday Press, 1964, pp. 49-56.

4501 Waggoner, Hyatt H. William Faulkner: From Jefferson to the World. Lexington: Kentucky U.P., 1959, pp. 1-19.

4502 Wallis, Donald desG. "Soldiers' Pay: Faulkner's First Myth," The Bulletin of the West Virginia Association of College English Teachers (Marshall University), 1, ii (1974), 15-21.

4503 Watkins, Floyd C. "The Unbearable and Unknowable Truth in Faulkner's First Three Novels," The Flesh and the Word. Nashville: Vanderbilt U.P., 1971, pp. 169-180.

4504 Yonce, Margaret. "Faulkner's 'Atthis' and 'Attis': Some Sources of Myth," MissQ, 23 (Summer, 1970), 289-298.
Notes that Januarius Jones's reference to Attis in Soldiers' Pay does not have its source in Ovid's Metamorphoses, but in Poem 17 from Faulkner's Green Bough.

4505 _______. "Soldiers' Pay: A Critical Study of William Faulkner's First Novel," DAI, 32 (South Carolina: 1971), 991A.

THE SOUND AND THE FURY
(New York: Cape and Smith, 1929)

4506 Absalom, H. P. "Order and Disorder in The Sound and the Fury," DUJ, 58 (December, 1965), 30-39.
On Benjy and Faulkner's uses of time.

4507 Adams, Richard P. "The Apprenticeship of William Faulkner," TSE, 12 (1962), 137-140, passim.

4508 _______. "Work: The Sound and the Fury," Faulkner: Myth and Motion. Princeton, New Jersey: Princeton U.P., 1968, pp. 215-248.

4509 Adams, Robert M. "Poetry in the Novel: or Faulkner Esemplastic," VQR, 29 (Summer, 1953), 419-434.
Stresses the mood of cosmic pessimism.

4510 _______. Proteus, His Lies, His Truth: Discussions of

Literary Translation. New York: W. W. Norton, 1973, pp. xi, 23-28, 33, 156.

4511 _______. "William Faulkner's Sound and Fury," Strains of Discord. Ithaca, New York: Cornell U.P., 1958, pp. 190-198.

4512 Aguilar, Esperanza. Yoknapatawpha, Propiedad de William Faulkner. Santiago de Chile: Editorial Universitaria, 1964, pp. 36-42.

4513 Aiken, Conrad. "William Faulkner: The Novel As Form," Atl, 164 (November, 1939), 650-654.

4514 Aiken, David Hubert. "Joyce, Faulkner, O'Connor: Conceptual Approaches to Major Characters," DAI, 36 (New York State, Stony Brook: 1975), 3680A-81A.

4515 _______. "The 'Sojer Face' Defiance of Jason Compson," Thought, 52 (June, 1977), 188-203.
The Easter morning sermon as key to understanding the conflict and its resolution.

4516 Albert, Theodore Gibbs. "1. The Law vs. Clarissa Harlowe. 2. The Pastoral Argument of The Sound and the Fury. 3. Melville's Savages," DAI, 37 (Rutgers: 1976), 3601A.

4517 Allen, Walter E. The Modern Novel in Britain and the United States. New York: E. P. Dutton, 1964, pp. 116-118.

4518 _______. Tradition and Dream. London: Phoenix House, 1964, pp. 108-137, passim.

4519 Alpert, Hollis. "Old Times There Are Not Forgotten," SatRL, 42 (March 7, 1959), 28.
On the film of The Sound and the Fury.

4520 Anderson, Charles R. "Faulkner's Moral Center," EA, 7 (January, 1954), 48-58.

4521 Anon. Boston Transcript (October 23, 1929), 2.

4522 Anon. "Decayed Gentility," NYTBR (November 10, 1929), 28.

4523 Anon. "New Novels: Macabre, Fantastic, and Real," Glasgow Herald (April 16, 1931), 4.

4524 Anon. "Readers' Reports: The Sound and the Fury," Life and Letters Today, 7 (July, 1931), 67-68.

4525 Anon. "The Sound and the Fury," TLS (May 14, 1931), 386.

4526 Arthos, John. "Ritual and Humor in the Writing of William Faulkner," Accent, 9 (Autumn, 1948), 17-30.

4527 Aswell, Duncan. "The Recollection and the Blood: Jason's Role in The Sound and the Fury," MissQ, 21 (Summer, 1968), 211-218.
Jason is as incompetent and obsessed as his brothers.

4528 Auer, Michael J. "Caddy, Benjy, and the Acts of the Apostles: A Note on The Sound and the Fury," SNNTS, 6 (Winter, 1974), 475-476.

4529 Backman, Melvin. "Bayard Sartoris et Quentin Compson, hêros malades de William Faulkner," RLM, I, Nos. 27-29 (1957), 7-31.

4530 ________. Faulkner: The Major Years. Bloomington: Indiana U.P., 1966, pp. 13-40.

4531 ________. "Faulkner's Sick Heroes: Bayard Sartoris and Quentin Compson," MFS, 2 (Autumn, 1956), 95-108.

4532 ________. "The Pilgrimage of William Faulkner: A Study of Faulkner's Fiction, 1929-1942," DA, 21 (Columbia: 1960), 193-194.

4533 ________. "Sickness and Primitivism: A Dominant Pattern in William Faulkner's Work," Accent, 14 (Winter, 1954), 61-73.

4534 Backus, J. M. "Each in Its Ordered Place: Structure and Narrative in Benjy's Section of The Sound and the Fury," AL, 29 (January, 1958), 440-456.

4535 ________. "Names of Characters in Faulkner's The Sound and the Fury," Names, 6 (December, 1958), 226-233.

4536 Baker, Carlos. "William Faulkner: The Doomed and the Damned," The Young Rebel in American Literature: Seven Lectures. Carl Bode, ed. London: William Heinemann, 1959, pp. 145-169.
Jason is one of the damned, Quentin one of the doomed.

4537 Baker, James R. "The Symbolic Extension of Yoknapatawpha County," ArQ, 7 (Autumn, 1952), 223-228.

4538 Baldanza, Frank. "Faulkner's 1699-1945: The Compsons," Expl, 19 (May, 1961), Item 59.
Cf., H. A. Simpson, Expl, 21 (1962), Item 27.

4539 Baquirin, Josephina Q. "Themes, Style, and Symbolism in The Sound and the Fury," SLURJ, 4 (December, 1973), 658-672.

4540 Barklung, Gunnar. Översättning. Stormen och vreden; roman. Stockholm: Bonniers, 1964.

4541 Barrett, William. Irrational Man: A Study in Existential Philosophy. New York: Doubleday, 1958, pp. 50-53, passim.

4542 Barth, J. Robert. "Faulkner and the Calvinist Tradition," Thought, 39 (March, 1964), 100-120.

4543 ________, ed. Religious Perspectives in Faulkner's Fiction: Yoknapatawpha and Beyond. Notre Dame: Notre Dame U.P., 1972, passim.

4544 Bass, Eben. "Meaningful Images in The Sound and the Fury," MLN, 76 (December, 1961), 728-731.

4545 Bassan, Maurice. "Benyi at the Monument," ELN, 2 (September, 1964), 46-50.

4546 Bassett, J. E. "William Faulkner's The Sound and the Fury: An Annotated Checklist of Criticism," RALS, 1 (Autumn, 1971), 217-246.

4547 Basso, Hamilton. "Thomas Wolfe," After the Genteel Tradition: American Writers Since 1910. Malcolm Cowley, ed. New York: Norton & Co., 1937, pp. 209-210.

4548 Baum, Catherine B. "'The Beautiful One': Caddy Compson as Heroine of The Sound and the Fury," MFS, 13 (Spring, 1967), 33-44.

4549 Beach, Joseph Warren. "William Faulkner: The Haunted South: Novels of Social Reference--The Sound and the Fury," American Fiction, 1920-1940. New York: Macmillan, 1942, pp. 123-143.

4550 Beauvoir, Simone de. The Prime of Life. Peter Green, tr. Cleveland: World, 1962, pp. 149-150.

States that in 1936 she and Sartre read and admired As I Lay Dying and The Sound and the Fury.

4551 Bedell, George C. Kierkegaard and Faulkner: Modalities of Existence. Baton Rouge: Louisiana State U.P., 1972, pp. 134-137, 184-190, 198-203, passim.

4552 Beebe, Maurice. "Criticism of William Faulkner: A Selected Checklist,..." MFS, 2 (Autumn, 1956), 150-164.

4553 ________. "Criticism of William Faulkner: A Selected Checklist," MFS, 13 (Spring, 1967), 154-158.

4554 Beja, Morris. "It Must be Important: Negroes in Contem-

porary American Fiction," AntiochR, 24 (Fall, 1964), 323-336.
Description of Negroes in the South who are treated in fiction without reference to race as in The Sound and Fury.

4555 Bennett, Arnold. "Books and Persons: A Christmas Lament of Some Bookish Men," Evening Standard (December 19, 1929), 9.

4556 Benson, Jackson J. "Quentin Compson: Self-Portrait of a Young Artist's Emotions," TCL, 17 (July, 1971), 143-159.

4557 _______. "Quentin's Responsibility for Caddy's Downfall," NMW, 5 (Fall, 1972), 63-64.
Quentin is guiltless.

4558 Berets, Ralph Adolph. "The Irrational Narrator in Virginia Woolf's The Waves, William Faulkner's The Sound and the Fury, and Gunter Grass's The Tin Drum," DAI, 31 (Michigan: 1969), 751A.

4559 Blanchard, Margaret. "The Rhetoric of Communion: Voice in The Sound and the Fury," AL, 41 (January, 1970), 555-565.
A study of the narrator of the fourth section of The Sound and the Fury.

4560 Bleikasten, André. The Most Splendid Failure: Faulkner's The Sound and the Fury. Bloomington: Indiana U. P., 1976.
Rev. by Gail Moore Morrison, MissQt, 30 (Summer, 1977), 477-482.

4561 _______. "Noces noires, noces blanches: Le jeu du désir et de la mort dans le monologue de Quentin Compson (The Sound and the Fury)," RANAM, 6 (1973), 14.

4562 _______. "The Sound and the Fury: Du Désir à l'Oeuvre," RANAM, 9 (1976), 18-34.

4563 Booth, Wayne C. The Rhetoric of Fiction. Chicago: Chicago U. P., 1961, pp. 306-308.

4564 Bowlin, Karla J. "The Brother and Sister Theme in Post-Romantic Fiction," DAI, 34 (Auburn: 1973), 1232A.

4565 Bowling, Laurence E. "Faulkner and the Theme of Innocence," KR, 20 (Summer, 1958), 466-487.
Analysis of The Sound and the Fury as an exploration of the idea of innocence.

4566 _______. "Faulkner and the Theme of Isolation," GaR, 18 (Spring, 1964), 50-66.

4567 ________. "Faulkner: The Technique of The Sound and the Fury," KR, 10 (Autumn, 1948), 552-566; repr., in Two Decades of Criticism. Frederick Hoffman and Olga Vickery, eds. East Lansing: Michigan U. P., 1951, pp. 165-179.

4568 ________. "Faulkner: The Theme of Pride in The Sound and the Fury," MFS, 11 (Summer, 1965), 129-139.

4569 ________. "What Is the Stream of Consciousness Technique?" PMLA, 65 (June, 195), 333-345.

4570 ________. "William Faulkner: The Importance of Love," DR, 43 (Winter, 1963), 474-482.

4571 Brannon, Lil. "Psychic Distance in the Quentin Section of The Sound and the Fury," PAPA, 2, ii (1976), 11-18.

4572 Breaden, Dale G. "William Faulkner and the Land," AmQ, 1 (Fall, 1958), 344-357.

4573 Bridges, Jean Bolen. "Similarities Between The Waste Land and The Sound and the Fury," NConL, 7 (January, 1977), 10-13.

4574 Broderick, John C. "Faulkner's The Sound and the Fury," Expl, 19 (November, 1960), Item 12.

4575 Brogunier, Joseph. "A Housman Source in The Sound and the Fury," MFS, 18 (Summer, 1972), 220-225.

4576 Brooks, Cleanth. "Faulkner's Vision of Good and Evil," MassR, 3 (Summer, 1962), 692-712.

4577 ________. The Hidden God: Studies in Hemingway, Faulkner, Yeats, Eliot, and Warren. New Haven: Yale U. P., 1963, pp. 40-43.

4578 ________. "Man, Time, and Eternity: The Sound and the Fury," William Faulkner: The Yoknapatawpha Country. New Haven: Yale U. P., 1963, pp. 325-348.

4579 ________. "Primitivism in The Sound and the Fury," English Institute Essays, 1952. New York: Columbia U. P., 1954, pp. 5-28.

4580 Brophy, Brigid, et al. Fifty Works of English and American Literature We Could Do Without. London: Rapp & Carroll, 1967, pp. 145-146.

4581 Brown, Calvin S. "Dilsey: From Faulkner to Homer," Proceedings of the Comparative Literature Symposium. Vol. IV. William Faulkner: Prevailing Verities and World Literature. Zyla, Wolodymr T., and Wendell M. Aycock, eds. Lubbock: Interdept. Comm. on Comp. Lit. Texas Tech U., 1973, pp. 57-75.

4582 ________. "Faulkner's Idiot Boy: The Source of a Simile in Sartoris," AL, 44 (November, 1972), 474-476.

4583 Brown, May Cameron. "Quentin Compson As Narrative Voice in the Works of William Faulkner," DAI, 36, #8 (Georgia State: 1975), 5291A-92A.

4584 Brylowski, Walter. "The Dark Vision: Myth in The Sound and the Fury," Faulkner's Olympian Laugh. Detroit: Wayne State U.P., 1968, pp. 59-85, passim. Repr., in Studies in The Sound and the Fury. James B. Meriwether, comp. Columbus, Ohio: Chas. E. Merrill, 1970, pp. 33-58.

4585 Burgum, Edwin Berry. The Novel and the World's Dilemma. New York: Oxford U.P., 1947, pp. 205-215.

4586 Burton, Dolores M. "Intonation Patterns of Sermons in Seven Novels," LangS, 3 (1970), 205-218.
The Sound and the Fury one of the novels studied.

4587 Campbell, Harry M. "Experiment and Achievement: As I Lay Dying and The Sound and the Fury," SR, 51 (Spring, 1943), 305-320.
Cf., George M. O'Donnell. "Reply," SR, 51 (July, 1943), 446-447.

4588 ________, and Ruel E. Foster. William Faulkner: A Critical Appraisal. Norman: Oklahoma U.P., 1951, pp. 50-60, 125-130.

4589 Cargill, Oscar. Intellectual America. New York: Macmillan, 1941, pp. 373-376.

4590 Caro-Radenez, Joëlle, and Philippe Radenez. "The Sound and the Fury," Views and Reviews of Modern German Literature: Festschrift für Adolf D. Klarmann. Karl S. Weimar, ed. München: Delp, 1974, pp. 277-291.

4591 Castelli, F. "Tragedia e distruzione dell 'uomo nell' opera di William Faulkner," La Civilità Cattolica, 104 (March 7, 1953), 530-543.

4592 Cecchi, Emilio. "William Faulkner," Pan, 2 (May, 1934), 64-70; revised and repr., in William Faulkner: Venti anni critica. Frederick Hoffman and Olga Vickery, eds. Parma: Guanda, 1957, pp. 102-110; also in E. Cecchi. Scrittori inglesi e americani: saggi, note e versioni. II, 4th ed., rev. Milano: Il Saggiatore, 1964, pp. 196-203.
In the original version of the article, the statement was made that "works such as The Sound and the Fury... not

even an ostrich could stomach; the statement was deleted in revised versions.

4593 Cecil, L. Moffitt. "A Rhetoric for Benjy," SLJ, 3 (Fall, 1970), 32-46.

4594 Chappell, Fred. "The Comic Structure of The Sound and the Fury," MissQ, 31, #3 (Summer, 1978), 381-386.

4595 Chase, Richard. "Faulkner--The Great Years: The Sound and the Fury," The American Novel and Its Tradition. Garden City, New York: Doubleday Anchor, 1957, pp. 219-236.

4596 Chastel, André. [The Sound and the Fury] CS (mars 1940), 196-197.

4597 Chisholm, William Sherman. "Sentence Patterns in The Sound and the Fury," DA, 25 (Michigan: 1965), 7254-55.

4598 Church, Margaret. "William Faulkner: Myth and Duration," Time and Reality: Studies in Contemporary Fiction. Chapel Hill: North Carolina U. P., 1963, pp. 233-235.

4599 Clark, Edward D., Sr. "Private Truth in The Sound and the Fury," CLAJ, 19 (1976), 513-523.

4600 Clark, Edward Depriest. "Six Grotesques in Three Faulkner Novels," DAI, 33 (Syracuse: 1972), 302A.

4601 Clerc, Charles. "Faulkner's The Sound and the Fury," Expl, 24 (November, 1965), Item 29.
References to St. Francis of Assisi.

4602 Cobau, William W. "Jason Compson and the Costs of Speculation," MissQ, 22 (Summer, 1969), 257-261.
Notes inaccuracies in description of cotton market.

4603 Coffee, Jessie A. "Empty Steeples: Theme, Symbol, and Irony in Faulkner's Novels," ArQ, 23 (Autumn, 1967), 197-206.

4604 ________. "Faulkner's The Sound and the Fury," Expl, 24 (October, 1965), Item 21.
Believes that Nancy was a large animal, probably a cow.

4605 Coindreau, Maurice E. "Preface to The Sound and the Fury," tr. by George M. Reeves. MissQ, 19 (Summer, 1966), 107-115; also in The Time of William Faulkner: A French View of Modern American Fiction. George M. Reeves, ed., and tr. Columbia: South Carolina U. P., 1971, pp. 41-50.

4606 ________. Traduction et préface. Le Bruit et la fureur. Paris: Gallimard, 1938.

4607 Collins, Carvel. "A Conscious Literary Use of Freud?" L&P, 3 (June, 1953), 2-4.

4608 ________. "Faulkner's Reputation and the Contemporary Novel," Literature and the Modern World. William J. Griffin, ed. Nashville, Tennessee: George Peabody College for Teachers, 1954, pp. 67-69.

4609 ________. "Faulkner's The Sound and the Fury," Expl, 17 (December, 1958), Item 19.
On Quentin Compson and Quentin Durward, Scott's character.

4610 ________. "The Interior Monologues of The Sound and the Fury," English Institute Essays. New York: Columbia U.P., 1952, pp. 29-56; repr., as Massachusetts Institute of Technology Publications in Humanities, No. 6, 1954; revised and repr., in Psychoanalysis and American Fiction. Irving Malin, ed. New York: Dutton, 1965; further revised and repr., in Studies in The Sound and Fury. James B. Meriwether, comp. Columbus, Ohio: Charles E. Merrill, 1970, pp. 59-79.

4611 ________. "Miss Quentin's Paternity Again," TSLL, 2 (Autumn, 1960), 253-269; revised and repr., in The Merrill Studies in The Sound and the Fury. James B. Meriwether, comp. Columbus, Ohio: Chas. E. Merrill, 1970, pp. 80-88.

4612 ________. "The Pairing of The Sound and the Fury and As I Lay Dying," PULC, 18 (Spring, 1957), 114-123; repr., "Christian and Freudian Structures," in Twentieth Century Interpretations. Michael Cowan, ed. Englewood Cliffs, 1968, pp. 71-74.
The theme of the failure of love in a family.

4613 ________. "William Faulkner, The Sound and the Fury," The American Novel from James Fenimore Cooper to William Faulkner. Wallace Stegner, ed. New York: Basic Books, 1965, pp. 219-228.

4614 ________, and Salvatore Quasimodo. Faulkner: naturalismo tragedia. Coleccion Estar al dia. Buenos Aires: Carlos Perez, 1968.
Contains two essays on the naturalistic elements in Faulkner's work--The Sound and the Fury and Soldiers' Pay.

4615 Connolly, Thomas E. "Fate and the 'Agony of Will': Determinism in Some Works of William Faulkner," Essays on Determinism in American Literature. Sidney J. Krause, ed. Kent, Ohio: Kent State U.P., 1964, pp. 36-52.

4616 Cook, Albert S. "Plot as Discovery," The Meaning of Fiction. Detroit: Wayne State U.P., 1960, pp. 232-241.
Faulkner's relation of characters to their past and their traditions.

4617 Cowan, J. C. "Dream-Work in the Quentin Section of The Sound and the Fury," L&P, 24, #3 (1974), 91-98.

4618 Cowan, Michael H., ed. Introduction. Twentieth Century Interpretations of The Sound and the Fury: A Collection of Critical Essays. Englewood Cliffs, New Jersey: Prentice-Hall, 1968, pp. 1-13.

4619 Crickmay, Edward. "Recent Fiction," Sunday Referee (April 26, 1931), 9.

4620 Cross, Barbara M. "The Sound and the Fury: The Pattern of Sacrifice," ArQ, 16 (Spring, 1960), 5-16.

4621 Cullen, John B., and Floyd C. Watkins. Old Times in the Faulkner Country. Chapel Hill: North Carolina U.P., 1961, pp. 78-80.
Callie Barr Clark suggested as the model for Dilsey.

4622 Dauner, Louise. "Quentin and the Walking Shadow: The Dilemma of Nature and Culture," ArQ, 21 (Summer, 1965), 159-171.

4623 ________. "Quentin and the Walking Shadow," Twentieth Century Interpretations of The Sound and the Fury. Michael H. Cowan, ed. Englewood Cliffs, New Jersey: Prentice-Hall, 1968, pp. 75-80.

4624 Davenport, Basil. "Tragic Frustration," SatRL, 6 (December 28, 1929), 601-602.

4625 Davidson, Donald. "The 43 Best Southern Novels for Readers and Collectors," PubW, 127 (April 27, 1935), 1675-1676.
The Sound and the Fury (1929) and As I Lay Dying (1930) listed. Cf., M. Thomas Inge. MissQ, 24 (Spring, 1971), 155-158.

4626 Davis, Boyd. "Caddy Compson's Eden," MissQ, 30 (Summer, 1977), 381-394.
The significance of "the imagery of a Biblical Eden."

4627 Davis, Thadious M. "The Other Family and Luster in The Sound and the Fury," CLAJ, 20 (December, 1976), 245-261.

4628 Davis, William V. "Quentin's Death Ritual: Further Christian Allusions in The Sound and the Fury," NMW, 6 (Spring, 1973), 27-32.
Cf., Carvel Collins. "The Pairing of The Sound and the Fury and As I Lay Dying," PULC, 18 (1957), 115-116.

4629 ________. "The Sound and the Fury: A Note on Benjy's Name," SNNTS, 4 (Spring, 1972), 60-61.
Comments on the Hebrew meanings of Benjamin.

4630 Dean, Sharon W. "Lost Ladies: The Isolated Heroine in the Fiction of Hawthorne, James, Fitzgerald, Hemingway, and Faulkner," DAI, 34 (New Hampshire: 1973), 2616A.

4631 Delay, Florence, and Jacqueline de Labriolle. "Marquez est-il le Faulkner colombien?" RLC, 47 (1973), 88-123.

4632 Despain, Norma LaRene. "Stream of Consciousness Narration in Faulkner: A Redefinition," DAI, 37 (Conn.: 1976), 306A-07A.
The Sound and the Fury and As I Lay Dying.

4633 DeVoto, Bernard. "Witchcraft in Mississippi," SatRL, 15 (October 31, 1936), 3-4; repr., in Minority Report. Boston: Little, Brown, 1940, pp. 209-218.

4634 ________. The World of Fiction. Boston: Houghton Mifflin, 1950, pp. 288-289.

4635 Dickerson, Mary Jane. "'The Magician's Wand': Faulkner's Compson Appendix," MissQ, 28 (Summer, 1975), 317-337.

4636 Dillingham, William B. "William Faulkner and the 'Tragic Condition,'" Edda, 53 (1966), 322-335.

4637 Dorsch, Robert L. "An Interpretation of the Central Themes in the Work of William Faulkner," ESRS, 11 (September, 1962), 21-26.

4638 Dove, George N. "Shadow and Paradox: Imagery in The Sound and the Fury," Essays in Memory of Christine Burleson in Language and Literature. T. G. Burton, ed. Johnson City: East Tenn. State University, 1969, pp. 89-95.

4639 Downer, Alan S., ed. [The Sound and the Fury] English Institute Essays. 1952. New York: Columbia U.P., 1954, passim.

4640 Duesberg, Jacques. "Le bruit et le tumulte de William Faulkner," RG, 72 (decembre 15, 1939), 834-841.

4641 Dukes, Thomas. "Christianity as Curse and Salvation in The Sound and the Fury," ArizQt, 35 (Summer, 1979), 170-182.

4642 Eberley. Ralph Dunbar. Immediacy, Suspense, and Meaning in William Faulkner's "The Sound and the Fury": An Experiment in Critical Analysis. Diss. Michigan: 1953.

4643 Edel, Leon. "How to Read The Sound and the Fury," Varieties of Literary Experience. Eighteen Essays in World Literature. Stanley Burnshaw, ed. New York: New York U. P., 1962, pp. 241-257.

4644 _______. The Psychological Novel: 1900-1950. New York: Lippincott, 1955, pp. 147-154.

4645 Edgar, Pelham. The Art of the Novel. New York: Macmillan, 1933, pp. 347-352.
An early analysis of the novel's structure and tragedy.

4646 Edmonds, Irene C. "Faulkner and the Black Shadow," Southern Renascence: The Literature of the Modern South. Louis D. Rubin and R. D. Jacobs, ed. Baltimore: Johns Hopkins Press, 1953, pp. 192-206.

4647 Edward, Sister Ann. "Three Views on Blacks: The Black Woman in American Literature," CEA Critic, 37 (May, 1975), 14-16.
Dilsey in The Sound and the Fury.

4648 England, Martha W. "Quentin's Story: Chronology and Explication," CE, 22 (January, 1961), 228-235.

4649 _______. "Teaching The Sound and the Fury," CE, 18 (January, 1957), 220-224.

4650 Everett, Walter K. Faulkner's Art and Characters. Woodbury, New York: Barron's Educ. Ser., 1969, pp. 101-114.

4651 F., H. I. A. "The Sound and the Fury," Manchester Guardian (May 15, 1931), 7.

4652 Faber, M. D. "Faulkner's The Sound and the Fury: Object Relations and Narrative Structure," AI, 34 (Winter, 1977), 327-350.

4653 Fadiman, Clifton. "Hardly Worth While," Nation, 130 (January 15, 1930), 74-75.

4654 Fasel, Ida. "A 'Conversation' Between Faulkner and Eliot," MissQ, 20 (Fall, 1967), 195-206.
Influence of The Wasteland on The Sound and the Fury.

4655 _______. "Spatial Form and Spatial Time," WHR, 16 (Summer, 1962), 223-234.
The Bergsonian space-time structure.

4656 Faulkner, William. "Appendix: The Sound and the Fury," The Modern Library. New York: Random House, 1946.

4657 _______. "Discussions at the University of Virginia, 1957-58," Faulkner in the University. Frederick L. Gwynn and

Joseph L. Blotner, eds. Charlottesville: Virginia U. P., 1959.

4658 _______. "An Introduction for The Sound and the Fury," ed. with Introduction by James B. Meriwether, SoR, 8 (Autumn, 1972), 705-710.

4659 _______. "An Introduction to The Sound and the Fury," MissQ, 26 (Summer, 1973), 410-415.

4660 "Faulkner Novel Bought for Film," NYTimes (August 30, 1956), 19.
Film rights to The Sound and the Fury sold to Jerry Wald.

4661 Fazio, Rocco Roberto. "The Fury and the Design: Realms of Being and Knowing in Four Novels of William Faulkner," DA, 25 (Rochester: 1964), 1910.

4662 Fetz, Howard W. "Of Time and the Novel," XUS, 8 (Summer, 1969), 1-17.
Conrad's Lord Jim as predecessor of techniques used by Faulkner in The Sound and the Fury.

4663 Fischel, Anne. "Student Views of Faulkner II," MoOc, 1, #2 (Winter, 1971), 270-274.

4664 Fitts, Dudley. "Two Aspects of Telemachus," H&H, 3 (April-June, 1930), 445-450.

4665 Ford, Corey. "Popeye the Pooh," In the Worst Possible Taste. New York: Scribner's, 1932, pp. 84-99.

4666 Ford, Daniel Gordon. "Comments on William Faulkner's Temporal Vision in Sanctuary, The Sound and the Fury, Light in August, Absalom, Absalom!" SoQ, 15 (April, 1977), 283-290.

4667 _______. "Uses of Time in Four Novels by William Faulkner," DAI, 35 (Auburn: 1974), 1654A.

4668 Foster, Ruel E. "Dream as Symbolic Act in Faulkner," Perspective, 2 (Summer, 1949), 179-194.

4669 _______. "Social Order and Disorder in Faulkner's Fiction," Approach, 55 (Spring, 1965), 20-28.

4670 Fredrickson, Michael A. "A Note on 'The Idiot Boy' as a Probable Source for The Sound and the Fury," MinnR, 6, #4 (1966), 368-370.

4671 Freedman, William A. "The Technique of Isolation in The Sound and the Fury," MissQ, 15 (Winter, 1961-62), 21-26.
Isolation and confinement as image, symbol, and mood.

4672 Fridy, Will. "'Ichthus': An Exercise in Synthetic Suggestion," SAB, 39 (May, 1974), 95-101.
Analysis of the fish symbol in the Quentin section of The Sound and the Fury.

4673 Friedling, Sheila. "Problems of Perception in the Modern Novel: The Representation of Consciousness in Works of Henry James, Gertrude Stein, and William Faulkner," DAI, 34 (Wisconsin: 1973), 3391A.

4674 Frye, Northrop. Anatomy of Criticism. Princeton, New Jersey: Princeton U.P., 1957, pp. 98, 238.
"... [T]he romantic presenter or Prospero figure is parodied in the Benjy of The Sound and the Fury whose idiot mind contains, without comprehending, the whole action of the novel...."

4675 Garmon, Gerald M. "Faulkner's The Sound and the Fury," Expl, 25 (September, 1966), Item 2.
The sparrow scene.
Cf., Norwood J. Pratt. "Faulkner's The Sound and the Fury," Exp, 23 (1965), Item 37.

4676 ______. "Mirror Imagery in The Sound and the Fury," NMW, 2 (Spring, 1969), 13-24.

4677 Gatlin, Jesse C., Jr. "Of Time and Character in The Sound and the Fury," HAB, 17 (Autumn, 1966), 27-35.

4678 Geffen, Arthur. "Profane Time, Sacred Time, and Confederate Time in The Sound and the Fury," SAF, 2 (1974), 175-197.

4679 Geismar, Maxwell. Writers in Crisis. Boston: Houghton Mifflin, 1942, pp. 154-159.

4680 Gibbons, Kathryn Gibbs. "Quentin's Shadow," L&P, 12 (Winter, 1962), 16-24.
Analysis of the repetition of the shadow image in terms of Frazer and Jung.

4681 Gibson, William M. "Faulkner's The Sound and the Fury," Expl, 22 (January, 1964), Item 33.
Quentin Compson's motivation.

4682 Gill, Linda Gerson. "Faulkner's Narrative Voices in The Sound and the Fury," DAI, 36 (California, San Diego: 1975), 4489A.

4683 Glicksberg, Charles I. "William Faulkner and the Negro Problem," Phylon, 10 (June, 1949), 153-160.

4684 ______. "The World of William Faulkner," ArQ, 5 (Spring, 1949), 46-58.

4685 Godden, Richard. "So That's What Frightens Them Under the Tree?" JAmS, 11 (December, 1977), 371-377.

4686 Gold, Joseph. "Faulkner's The Sound and the Fury," Expl, 19 (February, 1961), Item 29.
The final scene at the monument.

4687 ______. William Faulkner: A Study in Humanism from Metaphor to Discourse. Norman: Oklahoma U. P., 1966, pp. 25-30.

4688 Goldberg, Gerald J. "'The Interior Monologues,'" FS, 3, # 3 (1954), 58-59.
Cf., Carvel Collins. "The Interior Monologues of The Sound and the Fury," EIE, 1952. Alan Downer, ed. New York: Columbia U. P., 1954, pp. 29-56.

4689 Gordon, L. G. "Meaning and Myth in The Sound and the Fury and The Waste Land," The Twenties: Fiction, Poetry, Drama. Warren G. French, ed. DeLand, Florida: Everett/Edwards, 1975, pp. 269-302.

4690 Gorlier, Claudio. "William Faulkner, la genesi e la redenzione," L'Approdo Letterario, No. 20 (nuova serie), 8 (October-December, 1962), 42-68.

4691 Gossett, Louise Y. "The Climate of Violence," Violence in Recent Southern Fiction. Durham: Duke U. P., 1965, pp. 29-47.

4692 Gould, Gerald. "The Peaceful Tumblers," Observer (April 19, 1931), 6.

4693 Gould, Jack. "TV: Faulkner's 'Sound and Fury,'" NYTimes (December 7, 1955), 79.

4694 Grant, William E. "Benjy's Branch: Symbolic Method in Part I of The Sound and the Fury," TSLL, 13 (Winter, 1972), 705-710.

4695 Graves, T. W., Jr. "A Portrait of Benjy." William and Mary Review, 2 (Winter, 1964), 53-57.

4696 Green, Martin. "Faulkner: The Triumph of Rhetoric," Re-Appraisals: Some Commonsense Readings in American Literature. New York: Norton: 1965, pp. 167-195.

4697 Greer, Dorothy D. "Dilsey and Lucas: Faulkner's Use of the Negro as a Gauge of Moral Character," ESRS, 11 (September, 1962), 43-61.

4698 Gregory, Eileen. "Caddy Compson's World," Studies in "The Sound and the Fury," James B. Meriwether, ed. Columbus: Charles E. Merrill, 1970, pp. 89-101.

4699 Grenier, Cynthia. "The Art of Fiction: An Interview with William Faulkner, September, 1955," Accent, 16 (Summer, 1956), 167-177. Excerpt, "Faulkner Discusses The Sound and the Fury," repr., in Twentieth Century Interpretations of The Sound and the Fury. Michael H. Cowan, ed. Englewood Cliffs, New Jersey: Prentice-Hall, 1968, pp. 14-15.

4700 Gresset, Michel. "Psychological Aspects of Evil in The Sound and the Fury," MissQ, 19 (Summer, 1966), 143-153; revised and repr., in Studies in The Sound and the Fury. James B. Meriwether, comp. Chas. E. Merrill, Columbus, Ohio: 1970, pp. 114-124.

4701 Griffin, Robert J. "Ethical Point of View in The Sound and the Fury," SSH, #1 (1963), 55-64; repr., in Essays in Modern American Literature. Richard Langford, ed. DeLand, Florida: Stetson U.P., 1963, pp. 55-64.

4702 Groden, Michael. "Criticism in New Composition: Ulysses and The Sound and the Fury," TCL, 21 (October, 1975), 265-277.

4703 Gross, Beverly. "Form and Fulfillment in The Sound and the Fury," MLQ, 29 (December, 1968), 439-449.
Considers the last scene as "the novel's most intense depiction of sound and fury."

4704 Guetti, James. The Limits of Metaphor: A Study of Melville, Conrad, and Faulkner. Ithaca: Cornell U.P., 1967, pp. 148-153.

4705 Gunter, Richard. "Style and Language in The Sound and the Fury," MissQ, 22 (Summer, 1969), 264-279; repr., in Studies in The Sound and the Fury. James B. Meriwether, comp. Columbus, Ohio: Chas. E. Merrill, 1970, pp. 140-156.

4706 Gwynn, Frederick L. "Faulkner's Raskolnikov," MFS, 4 (Summer, 1958), 169-172.
Quentin in The Sound and the Fury compared with the protagonist in Crime and Punishment.

4707 ________, and Joseph L. Blotner, eds. Faulkner in the University. Charlottesville: Virginia U.P., 1959, passim.

4708 Hagopian, John V. "Nihilism in Faulkner's The Sound and the Fury," MFS, 13 (Spring, 1967), 45-55.

4709 Handy, William J. "The Sound and the Fury: A Formalist Approach," NDQ, 44, iii (Summer, 1976), 71-83.

4710 Hansen, Harry. "The First Reader," NYWorld (October 9, 1929), 16.

4711 Hardy, John Edward. "William Faulkner: The Legend Behind the Legend," *Man in the Modern Novel*. Seattle: Washington U.P., 1964, pp. 137-158.
Miss Quentin and Benjy as Christ figures.

4712 Harnack-Fish, Mildred. "William Faulkner: Amerikas Dichter aus grosser Tradition," Die Literatur, 38 (October, 1935), 66.

4713 Harris, Wendell V. "Faulkner's *The Sound and the Fury*," Expl, 21 (March, 1963), Item 54.

4714 ________. "Of Time and the Novel," BuR, 16 (March, 1968), 114-129.
Comparison of *The Sound and the Fury* with *David Copperfield* and *Nostromo*.

4715 Haseloff, Cynthia. "Formative Elements of Film: A Structural Comparison of Three Novels and Their Adaptations by Irving Ravetch and Harriet Frank, Jr.," DAI, 33, #1 (Missouri (Columbia): 1971), 438A.

4716 Hashiguchi, Yasuo. "Popeye Extenuated," KAL, No. 5 (April, 1962), 1-9.
Popeye as a symbol of "amoral modernism."

4717 Hassan, Ihab. *Radical Innocence: Studies in the Contemporary American Novel*. Princeton: Princeton U.P., 1961, p. 57.

4718 Hatcher, Harlan. *Creating the Modern American Novel*. New York: Farrar and Rinehart, 1935, pp. 237-238.

4719 Hathaway, Baxter. "The Meanings of Faulkner's Structures," EngRec, 15 (December, 1964), 22-27.
Faulkner's use of counterpoint.

4720 Hepburn, Kenneth W. "*Soldiers' Pay* to *The Sound and the Fury*: Development of Poetic in the Early Novels of William Faulkner," DA, 29 (Washington: 1969), 2263A.

4721 Hewitt, Douglas. *The Approach to Fiction: Good and Bad Readings of Novels*. Totowa, New Jersey: Rowman & Littlefield, 1972, pp. 75-76, *passim*.

4722 Hicks, Granville. "The Past and Future of William Faulkner," Bookman, 74 (September, 1931), 17-24.

4723 Highet, Gilbert. "*The Sound and Fury*," Harpers, 209 (September, 1954), 98.

4724 Hill, Douglas B., Jr. "Faulkner's Caddy," CRAS, 7 (Spring, 1976), 26-38.

4725 Hinkle, Diane L. "The Mystery of Significance and the Enigma of Time: An Analysis of the Thematic Structures of Faulkner's The Sound and the Fury and Claude Simon's L'herbe," DAI, 32 (North Carolina at Chapel Hill: 1971), 2689A-90A.

4726 Hoffman, Frederick. Freudianism and the Literary Mind. Baton Rouge: Louisiana State U.P., 2nd ed., 1957, pp. 129-130.

4727 _______. The Modern Novel in America. Chicago: Regnery, 1956, pp. 178-179.

4728 _______. "The Original Talent--The Sound and the Fury," William Faulkner. 2nd ed., revised. New York: Twayne, 1966, 49-60.

4729 _______. The Twenties: American Writing in the Post War Decade. New York: Viking, 1955, pp. 213-216, passim.
Faulkner's use of the subconscious.

4730 Hornback, Vernon T., Jr. "The Uses of Time in Faulkner's The Sound and the Fury," PELL, 1 (Winter, 1965), 50-58.

4731 Howe, Irving. "In Search of a Moral Style," NR, 145 (September 25, 1961), 26-27.
"... [W]hen Faulkner composed his despairing estimate of social loss in The Sound and the Fury he was also portraying some of the central disabilities of modern civilization...."

4732 _______. "The Sound and the Fury," William Faulkner: A Critical Study. New York: 2nd ed., Vintage Books, 1962, pp. 46-52, 157-174.

4733 _______. "William Faulkner and the Negroes," Commentary, 12 (October, 1951), 359-368.

4734 Howell, Elmo. "A Note on Faulkner's Negro Characters," MissQ, 11 (Fall, 1958), 201-203.
Faulkner has "perhaps more than any other American writer treated the Negro as a human being and not merely as the member of a race."

4735 _______. "William Faulkner's 'Christmas Gift!'" KFR, 13 (April-June, 1967), 37-40.
Explains background of the greeting "Christmas Gift!" used in lieu of "Merry Christmas" in The Sound and the Fury.

4736 Howell, John M. "Hemingway and Fitzgerald in The Sound and the Fury," PLL, 2 (Summer, 1966), 234-242.

Notes how Faulkner parodied "the romantic despair and cynicism" of Hemingway and Fitzgerald.

4737 Hughes, Richard. Preface. The Sound and the Fury. London: Chatto and Windus, 1931.

4738 Humphrey, Robert. "Form and Function of the Stream of Consciousness in William Faulkner's The Sound and the Fury," UKCR, 19 (Autumn, 1952), 34-40; revised for Stream of Consciousness in the Modern Novel. Berkeley: California U.P., 1954, pp. 17-21, 64-70, 104-111.

4739 Hunt, John W. "The Locus and Status of Meaning," William Faulkner: Art in Theological Tension. Syracuse, New York: Syracuse U.P., 1965, pp. 35-99; repr., in Twentieth Century Interpretations of The Sound and the Fury. Michael Cowan, ed. Englewood Cliffs: Prentice-Hall, 1968, pp. 83-92.

4740 Hutchens, E. N. "Toward a Poetics of Fiction: 5 'The Novel as Chronomorph,'" Novel, 5 (Spring, 1972), 215-224.

4741 Inge, M. Thomas. "Donald Davidson Selects the Best Southern Novels," MissQ, 24 (Spring, 1971), 155-158.

Reprints 1935 article in which Davidson included The Sound and the Fury and As I Lay Dying among the best Southern novels.

4742 Irwin, John T. Doubling and Incest, Repetition and Revenge: A Speculative Reading of Faulkner. Baltimore and London: Johns Hopkins U.P., 1975.

4743 Isaacs, J. "The Sound and the Fury," Annual Register, 1931, Part II, 35.

4744 Iser, W. "Self-Reduction: Perception, Temporality, and Action as Modes of Subjectivity," The Implied Reader: Patterns of Communication from Bunyan to Beckett. Baltimore: Johns Hopkins U.P., 1974, pp. 136-152.

4745 Ivănescu, Mircea. "Dostoievski si Faulkner," SXX, 12, #iv (1969), 209-212.

4746 ________, tr. Zgomotul si furia in românește. București: Univers, 1971.

4747 Ivasheva, V. Review: [The Sound and the Fury], Literaturnaia gazeta (September 11, 1933).

4748 Izsak, Emily K. "The Manuscript of The Sound and the Fury: The Revisions in the First Section," SB, 20 (1967), 189-202.

4749 J. K. W. B. "Literature and Less," New Orleans Times-Picayune (June 26, 1930), 23.

4750 Jacobs, Robert D. "Faulkner and the Tragedy of Isolation," HopkinsR, 6 (Spring-Summer, 1953), 163-183.

4751 ________. "How Do You Read Faulkner?" Provincial, 1 (Spring, 1957), 3-5.

4752 ________. "William Faulkner: The Passion and the Penance," South: Modern Southern Literature in Its Cultural Setting. Louis D. Rubin and Robt. D. Jacobs, eds. Garden City, New York: Doubleday, 1961, pp. 146-153.

4753 Jelliffe, Robert A., ed. "Faulkner Discusses The Sound and the Fury," excerpt from Faulkner at Nagano, Tokyo, 1956, repr., in Twentieth Century Interpretations of The Sound and the Fury. Michael Cowan, ed. Englewood Cliffs: Prentice-Hall, 1968, pp. 162ff.

4754 Kaluza, Irena. The Functioning of Sentence Structure in the Stream-of-Consciousness Technique of William Faulkner's The Sound and the Fury: A Study in Linguistic Stylistics. Krakow: Nakladem Uniwersytetu Jagiellonskiego, 1967.

4755 Kaplan, Harold. The Passive Voice: An Approach to Modern Fiction. Athens, Ohio: 1966, pp. 112-113, passim.

4756 Kartiganer, Donald M. "The Sound and the Fury and Faulkner's Quest for Form," ELH, 37 (December, 1970), 613-639.

4757 Kawin, Bruce F. "The Sound and the Fury," Faulkner and Film. New York: Ungar Pub. Co., 1977, pp. 14-29.

4758 Kazin, Alfred, Perry Miller, and George D. Crothers. "The Sound and the Fury," Invitation to Learning: English and American Novels. New York: Basic Books, 1966, pp. 349-356.

4759 Kellogg, Jean D. "William Faulkner and the Tyranny of Linear Consciousness," [The Sound and the Fury], Dark Prophets of Hope: Dostoevsky, Sartre, Camus, Faulkner. Chicago: Loyola U.P., 1975, pp. 123-135.

4760 Kelly, H. A. "Consciousness in the Monologues of Ulysses," MLQ, 24 (March, 1963), 3-12.

4761 Kelly, Jimmy Lee. "The Artist in Shadow: Quentin Compson in William Faulkner's The Sound and the Fury," DAI, 39, #1 (N. Carolina, Chapel Hill: 1977), 279A-80A.

4762 Kendon, Frank. "The New Books at a Glance," JO'LW (May 2, 1931), 130.

4763 Kenner, Hugh. "The Last Novelist," A Homemade World: The American Modernist Writers. New York: Knopf, 1975, pp. 194-210.

4764 Kermenli, Leyla. "William Faulkner's The Sound and the Fury," Litera, 8 (1965), 99-115.

4765 King, Frances H. "Benjamin Compson--Flower Child," CEA Critic, 31 (January, 1969), 10.

4766 Kinoian, Vartkis. Review Notes and Study Guide to Faulkner's "The Sound and the Fury,".... New York: Monarch Press, 1964, pp. 9-109.

4767 Kirk, Robert W., and Marvin Klotz. Faulkner's People. Berkeley: California U.P., 1963, pp. 28-49.

4768 Klotz, Marvin. "The Triumph Over Time: Narrative Form in William Faulkner and William Styron," MissQ, 17 (Winter, 1963-64), 9-20.

4769 Kopoor, Kapil. "Faulkner's The Sound and the Fury: A Note on Form and Meaning," JSL, 3, ii (1975-76), 85-91.

4770 Korg, Jacob. "The Literary Esthetics of Dada," Works, 1, #3 (Spring, 1968), 43-54.

4771 Kraus, Richard. "Archetypes and the Trilogy Structure--A Study of Joyce Cary's Fiction," DA, 27 (Stanford: 1967), 3430A.

Comparison of Cary's narrative technique with that in The Sound and the Fury.

4772 L., R. N. "Told by an Idiot," Scribner's, 36 (December 1929), 42, 46.

4773 Labatt, Blair Plowman. "Faulkner the Storyteller," DAI, 34 (Virginia: 1974), 7761A.

4774 Labor, Earle. "Faulkner's The Sound and the Fury," Expl, 17 (January, 1959), Item 30.

4775 Laporte, Roger. "L'impossible rêpêtition," Quinzaine Littêraire, #270 (January 15, 1978), 8.

4776 Lavalle, F. E., tr. El sonido y la furia; novela. Buenos Aires: Talleres Graficos de la Compania General Fabril Financiera, S. A., 1961.

4777 Layman, Lewis M. "Fourteen Ways of Looking at a Blackbird: Point of View in The Sound and the Fury," DAI, 34 (British Columbia: 1974), 7763A.

4778 Leary, Lewis. "The Sound and the Fury," William Faulkner of Yoknapatawpha County. New York: Crowell, 1973, pp. 41-62.

4779 Lebesque, Morvan. [Le Bruit et la Fureur] Carrefour (26 dêcembre 1951), 7.

4780 LeBreton, Maurice. "Technique et psychologie chez William Faulkner," EA, 1 (septembre 1937), 418.

4781 Lee, Edward B. "A Note on the Ordonnance of The Sound and the Fury," FS, 3 (Summer-Autumn, 1954), 37-39.
Relationships between narrative and dream structures.

4782 Lehan, Richard. "William Faulkner: The Sound and the Fury," A Dangerous Crossing: French Literary Existentialism and the Modern Novel. London: Feffer & Simons, 1973, pp. 74-75.

4783 "The Leisure Arts," Outlook and Independent (New York), (October 16, 1929), 268.

4784 Lilly, Paul, Jr. "Caddy and Addie: Speakers of Faulkner's Impeccable Language," JNT, 3 (September, 1973), 170-182.

4785 Lind, Ilse Dusior. "The Teachable Faulkner," CE, 16 (February, 1955), 284-287, 302.
The Sound and the Fury "probably" most often selected for class study.

4786 Litz, Walton. "William Faulkner's Moral Vision," SWR, 37 (Summer, 1952), 200-209.

4787 Logan, John. "Nota sobre el personaje balbuciente como hêroe," Sur, 332 (1970), 148-154.

4788 Longley, John L., Jr. The Tragic Mask: A Study of Faulkner's Heroes. Chapel Hill: North Carolina U.P., 1963, pp. 144-150, 211-223.

4789 ________. "'Who Never Had a Sister': A Reading of The Sound and the Fury," Mosaic, 7 (Fall, 1973), 35-53.

4790 Lowrey, Perrin. "Concepts of Time in The Sound and the Fury," English Institute Essays, 1952. New York: Columbia U.P., 1954, pp. 57-82.

4791 Luedtke, Carol L. "The Sound and the Fury and Lie Down in Darkness: Some Comparisons," LWU, 4 (1971), 45-51.
Comparison of the novels by Faulkner and Styron which includes the geographical and social setting of the Old South.

4792 McGann, Mary E. "The Waste Land and The Sound and the Fury: To Apprehend the Human Process Moving in Time," SLJ, 9 Fall, 1976), 13-21.

4793 McHaney, Thomas L. "Robinson Jeffers' Tamar and The Sound and the Fury," MissQ, 22 (Summer, 1969), 261-263.
The incest theme in The Sound and the Fury has an analogue in Jeffers' long poem.

4794 Mackenzie, Orgill. "The Sound and the Fury," Adelphi, 2 (July, 1931), 365-366.

4795 Magill, Frank N., ed. Masterplots: First Series. New York: Salem Press, 1957, pp. 917-919.

4796 Magny, Claude Edmond. Les Sandales d'Empedocle. Neuchatel, Switzerland: Editions de la Baconniere, 1945.

4797 Malin, Irving. William Faulkner: An Interpretation. Stanford: Stanford U.P., 1957, pp. 16-18, passim.

4798 Manley, Justine M. "The Function of Stock Humor and Grotesque Humor in Faulkner's Major Novels," DAI, 35 (Loyola, Chicago: 1974), 1111A.
"The Sound and the Fury is not a predominantly humorous novel although there is a lot of stock humor in the characters of the Negroes ... of Mrs. Compson and of Jason; the stock humor is linked to the theme of the novel concerning the fall of a family and of the South."

4799 Marshall, Howard. "Modern Experimenters in the Art of Novel Writing," Daily Telegraph (April 21, 1931), 17.

4800 Marshall, Leonore. "The Power of Words," SatRL, 45 (July 28, 1962), 16-17.
A former reader for Cape & Smith speaks of a "severely battered manuscript" which had been rejected by thirteen publishers.

4801 Martin, Abbott. "Faulkner's Difficult Novel Has Sin and Decay as Theme," Tennessean (Nashville), (November 17, 1929), 6.

4802 ________. "Signifying Nothing," SR, 38 (January, 1930), 115-116.

4803 Materassi, Mario. "Il primo grande romanzo di Faulkner: The Sound and the Fury," Convivium, 35 (May-June, 1967), 303-324.

4804 Matton, Collin Gilles. "The Role of Women in Three of Faulkner's Families," DAI, 35 (Marquette: 1974), 2283A.

4805 Maurice, Martin. "La Vie est un Conte Plein de Bruit et de Fureur," Lumière (5 novembre 1938).

4806 Mayoux, Jean-Jacques. "La Creation du Reel Chez William Faulkner," EA, 5 (February, 1952), 25-39; repr., in Three Decades of Criticism. Frederick Hoffman and Olga Vickery, eds. East Lansing: Michigan State U.P., 1960, pp. 156-172.

4807 Meeks, Elizabeth Lorraine. "A Contextual Approach to the Teaching of Two Novels by William Faulkner at College Level," DA, 26 Houston: 1965), 4505.

4808 Mellard, James M. "Caliban as Prospero: Benjy and The Sound and the Fury," Novel, 3 (Spring, 1970), 233-248.

4809 ________. "Faulkner's Jason and the Tradition of Oral Narrative," JPC, 2 (Fall, 1968), 195-210.

4810 ________. "Jason Compson: Humor, Hostility and the Rhetoric of Aggression," SHR, (Summer, 1969), 259-267.

4811 ________. "The Sound and the Fury: Quentin Compson and Faulkner's 'Tragedy of Passion,'" SNNTS, 2 (Spring, 1970), 61-75.

4812 ________. "Type and Archetype: Jason Compson As Satirist," Genre, 4 (June, 1971), 173-188.

4813 Meriwether, James B. "Faulkner, Lost and Found," NYTBR (November 5, 1972), 6-7.

4814 ________, ed. "An Introduction for The Sound and the Fury," SoR, 8 (October, 1972), 705-710.

The full text of the Introduction written by Faulkner for a projected new edition of The Sound and the Fury by Random House in 1933, but never published.

4815 ________, ed. "An Introduction to The Sound and the Fury," MissQ, 26 (Summer, 1973), 410-415.

The 1933 Introduction written by Faulkner is longer than that originally published with the novel.

4816 ________. The Literary Career of William Faulkner. Columbia: South Carolina U.P., pp. 16-17, passim.

4817 ________. "Notes on the Textual History of The Sound and the Fury," PBSA, 56 (3rd Qt., 1962), 285-316; revised and repr., "The Textual History of The Sound and the Fury in Studies in the Sound and the Fury. James B. Meriwether, ed. Columbus, Ohio: Chas. E. Merrill, 1961, pp. 1-32; also repr., in Art and Error: Modern Textual Editing. R. Gottesman and S. Bennett, eds. Bloomington: Indiana U.P., 1970, pp. 219-253.

4818 ________. "A Prefatory Note by Faulkner for the Compson Appendix," AL, 43 (May, 1971), 281-284.
The first publication of a brief note apparently intended to preface the reprinting of the Compson Appendix in the 1946 Modern Library double volume of *The Sound and the Fury* and *As I Lay Dying*.

4819 ________, ed. *Studies in The Sound and the Fury*. (Merrill Studies.) Columbus, Ohio: Chas. E. Merrill, 1970.

4820 Messerli, Douglas. "The Problem of Time in *The Sound and the Fury*: A Critical Reassessment and Reinterpretation," SLJ, 6 (Spring, 1974), 19-41.

4821 Millgate, Jane. "Quentin Compson as Poor Player: Verbal and Social Clichês in *The Sound and the Fury*," RLV (Brussels), 34 (No. 1, 1968), 40-49.

4822 Millgate, Michael. "Faulkner and Lanier: A Note on the Name Jason," MissQ, 25 (Summer, 1972), 349-350.

4823 ________. "*The Sound and the Fury*," *The Achievement of William Faulkner*. New York: Random House, 1966, pp. 86-103. Repr., in *Faulkner: A Collection of Critical Essays*. Robert Penn Warren, ed. Englewood Cliffs: Prentice-Hall, 1966, pp. 94-108.

4824 ________. "William Faulkner: The Problem of Point of View," *Patterns of Commitment in American Literature*. Marston LaFrance, ed. Toronto: Toronto U.P., 1967, pp. 181-192; repr., in *Studies in The Sound and the Fury*. James B. Meriwether, ed. Columbus, Ohio: Merrill, 1970, pp. 125-139.

4825 Millichap, Joseph R. "Distorted Matter and Disjunctive Forms: The Grotesque as Modernist Genre," ArQ, 33 (1977), 339-347.

4826 Milliner, Gladys. "The Third Eve: Caddy Compson," MidwQ, 16 (Spring, 1975), 268-275.

4827 Miner, Ward L. "Faulkner and Christ's Crucifixion," NM, 57 (1956), 260-269.

4828 ________. *The World of William Faulkner*. Durham, North Carolina: Duke U.P., 1952, pp. 138-141.

4829 Mizener, Arthur. "William Faulkner: *The Sound and the Fury*," *Twelve Great American Novels*. New York: New American Library, 1967, pp. 142-159.

4830 Moloney, Michael F. "The Enigma of Time: Proust, Virginia Woolf, and Faulkner," Thought, 32 (Spring, 1957), 69-85.

4831 Morillo, Marvin. "Faulkner's The Sound and the Fury," Expl, 24 (February, 1966), No. 50.

4832 Morrison, Gail Moore. "'Time, Tide, and Twilight': Mayday and Faulkner's Quest Toward The Sound and the Fury," MissQ, 31, # 3 (Summer, 1978), 337-357.

4833 Mueller, William R. "The Theme of Suffering: William Faulkner's The Sound and the Fury," The Prophetic Voice in Modern Fiction. New York: Association Press, 1959, pp. 110-135.

4834 Müller, Knud, tr. Brølet og vreden. København: Gyldendals Bekkasinboger, 1968.

4835 Murphy, Denis. "The Sound and the Fury and Dante's Inferno: Fire and Ice," MarkR, 4 (October, 1974), 71-78.

4836 Myers, Walter L. "Make-Beliefs," VQR, 6 (January, 1930), 140-141.

4837 Naples, Diane C. "Eliot's 'Tradition' and The Sound and the Fury," MFS, 20 (Summer, 1974), 214-217.
Faulkner's novel and Eliot's "mythic" method.

4838 Neidhardt, Frances Elam. "Verbal-Visual Simultaneity in Faulkner's The Sound and the Fury: A Literary Montage Filmscript for Quentin," DAI, 39, # 3 (East Texas State: 1978), 1165A.

4839 Neville, Helen. "The Sound and the Fury," PR, 5 (June, 1938), 53-55.

4840 Nicolson, Harold. "Chirping of a Tom-Boy Princess," Evening Standard (April 16, 1931), 21.
Thought the novel would have been incomprehensible without the Introduction by Richard Hughes to the 1931 edition.

4841 Nilon, Charles H. Faulkner and the Negro. New York: Citadel Press, 1965, pp. 101-104.

4842 O'Connor, William Van. "Protestantism in Yoknapatawpha County," HopR, 5 (Spring, 1952), 26-42; repr., in The Tangled Fire of William Faulkner. Minneapolis: Minnesota U.P., 1954, pp. 72-87.

4843 ________. "The Sound and the Fury and the Impressionist Novel," NorthR, 6 (June-July, 1953), 17-22; repr., in The Tangled Fire of William Faulkner. Minneapolis: Minnesota U.P., 1954, pp. 37-45.

4844 ________. William Faulkner. Minnesota University Pamphlets on American Literature. Minneapolis: Minnesota

U.P., 1959; repr., in Seven Modern American Novelists. Wm. Van O'Connor, ed. Minneapolis: 1964, pp. 125-128.

4845 O'Donnell, George Marion. "Faulkner's Mythology," KR, 1 (Summer, 1939), 285-299.

4846 ________. "Reply," SR, 51 (July, 1943), 446-447.
Cf., Harry M. Campbell. "Experiment and Achievement: As I Lay Dying and The Sound and the Fury," SR, 51 (April, 1943), 305-320.

4847 O'Faolain, Sean. "William Faulkner: Or More Genius Than Talent," The Vanishing Hero: Studies in Novelists of the Twenties. London: Eyre & Spottiswoode, 1956; Boston, 1957, pp. 119-124.

4848 O'Nan, Martha. "William Faulkner's Benjy: Hysteria," The Role of Mind in Hugo, Faulkner, Beckett, and Grass. New York: Philosophical Library, 1969, pp. 13-22.
Comments on Benjy with reference to theories of Freud, Pierre Janet, and Pierre Briquet.

4849 Page, Sally R. "The Ideal of Motherhood: The Sound and the Fury," Faulkner's Women. DeLand, Florida: Everett/Edwards, 1972, pp. 45-70.

4850 Parr, Susan Dale Resneck. "'And by Bergson, Obviously,' Faulkner's The Sound and the Fury, As I Lay Dying, and Absalom, Absalom!" DAI, 32 (Wisconsin: 1972), 6996A.

4851 Pate, Willard. "Benjy's Names in the Compson Household," FurmS, 15 (May, 1968), 37-38.
Attitudes toward Benjy revealed by names used.

4852 Patmore, Derek. "Modern American Writers," NineC, 109 (January, 1931), 103-114.

4853 Pearson, Theresa Lee. "The Sound and the Fury: An Archetypal Reading," DAI, 37, #10 (New Mexico: 1976), 6487A.

4854 Peary, Gerald, and Roger Shatzkin, eds. The Classic American Novel and the Movies. New York: Frederick Ungar, 1977.

4855 Peavy, Charles D. "'Did You Ever Have a Sister?' Holden, Quentin, and Sexual Innocence," FQ, 1 (Winter, 1968), 82-95.

4856 ________. "An Early Casting of Benjy: Faulkner's 'The Kingdom of God,'" SSF, 3 (Spring, 1966), 347-348.

4857 ________. "The Eyes of Innocence: Faulkner's 'The Kingdom of God,'" PLL, 2 (Spring, 1966), 178-182.
Similar commentary to some ideas in "An Early Casting of

Benjy: Faulkner's 'The Kingdom of God,'" SSF, 3 (1966), 347-348.

4858 ________. "Faulkner's Use of Folklore in The Sound and the Fury," JAF, 79 (April, 1966), 437-447.

4859 ________. "'If I Just Had a Mother': Faulkner's Quentin Compson," L&P, 23, #3 (1973), 114-121.

4860 ________. "Jason Compson's Paranoid Pseudocommunity," HSL, 2, #2 (1970), 151-156.

4861 ________. "A Note on the 'Suicide Pact' in The Sound and the Fury," ELN, 5 (March, 1968), 207-209.

4862 Peyre, Henri. "American Literature Through French Eyes," VQR, 23 (Summer, 1947), 421-438.
Called the first part of The Sound and Fury a "locus classicus" of French criticism.

4863 Picon, Gaëtan, "L'agnoisse et le désordre," NL, 40 (12 juillet 1962), 3.

4864 Pitavy, François. "Quentin Compson, ou le regard du poète," Sud, 14 (1975), 62-80.

4865 Powell, Sumner C. "William Faulkner Celebrates Easter, 1928," Perspective, 2 (Summer, 1949), 195-218.
Emphasizes Christian symbolism in The Sound and the Fury.

4866 Powers, Lyall H. "Hawthorne and Faulkner and the Pearl of Great Price," PMASAL, 52 (1967), 391-401.
Relationship between The Scarlet Letter and The Sound and the Fury.

4867 Prasad, Thakur Guru. "Nihilism in The Sound and the Fury," PURBA, 3, i (1972), 35-43.

4868 Pratt, J. Norwood. "Faulkner's The Sound and the Fury," Expl, 23 (January, 1965), Item 37.
The sparrow scene. Cf., Gerald Garmon, Expl, 25 (1966), Item 2.

4869 Praz, Mario. "William Faulkner," La Stampa (December 4, 1931), included in Cronache letterarie anglosassoni. Roma: Edizioni di Storia e Letteratura, 1951, II, 246-256.

4870 Putzel, Max. "Evolution of Two Characters in Faulkner's Early and Unpublished Fiction," SLJ, 5 (Spring, 1973), 47-63.
In Faulkner's early stories and sketches we see the evolution of Bayard Sartoris and Caddy Compson.

4871 Rabi. "Faulkner et la génération de l'exil," Espace, 9 (January, 1951), 47; Esprit (Paris), 175 (January, 1951), 47-65; repr., in Three Decades of Criticism. Frederick Hoffman and Olga Vickery, eds. East Lansing: Michigan State U.P., 1956, pp. 118-138.

4872 Ramsey, Roger. "Faulkner's The Sound and the Fury," Expl, 30 (April, 1972), Item 70.
Discusses why Benjy is said to "smell" death.

4873 ________. "Light Imagery in The Sound and the Fury: April 7, 1928," JNT, 6 (Winter, 1976), 41-50.
Study of both literary and psychological use of light imagery in the novel.

4874 Ramsey, William Currie. "Coordinate Structure in Four Faulkner Novels," DAI, 33 (North Carolina, Chapel Hill: 1971), 283A-284A.

4875 Rantavaara, Irma. "William Faulkner in The Sound and the Fury," Parnasso (Helsinki), 9 (1958), 281-285.
In Finnish.

4876 Rascoe, Lavon. "An Interview with William Faulkner," WR, 15 (August, 1951), 300-304.
Faulkner's statements about The Sound and the Fury. Cf., "Classroom Statements at the University of Mississippi," in Lion in the Garden. James B. Meriwether and Michael Millgate, eds. New York: Random House, 1968, pp. 52-58.

4877 Rebelo, Luis de Sousa. Prefacio. O som e a fúria. Traduzido do inglês por Mario Henrique Leiria e H. Santos Cervalho. Lisboa: Portugalia Editora, 1960.

4878 Reed, Joseph W., Jr. "The Sound and the Fury," Faulkner's Narrative. New Haven: Yale U.P., 1973, pp. 74-83.

4879 Reirdon, Suzanne Renshaw. "An Application of Script Analysis to Four of William Faulkner's Women Characters," DAI, 35 (East Texas State: 1974), 4549A.

4880 Rhynsburger, Mark. "Student Views of William Faulkner," MoOc, I, #2 (Winter, 1971), 264-269.

4881 Richardson, Kenneth E. Force and Faith in the Novels of William Faulkner. The Hague: Mouton, 1967, pp. 24-29, 70-73, 100-103.

4882 Rinald, Nicholas M. "Game Imagery and Game-Consciousness in Faulkner's Fiction," TCL, 10 (October, 1964), 109-118.

4883 Robbins, Frances L. "Novels of the Week," Outlook, 153 (October 16, 1929), 268.

4884 Roberts, James L. The Sound and the Fury: Notes. Lincoln, Nebraska: Cliff's Notes, 1963.

4885 Robinson, Ted. "Full of Sound and Fury, Horror Tale Sinks Spurs into Snorting Nightmare," Plain Dealer (Cleveland), (October 13, 1929), Amusement Sec., 6.

4886 Rodrigues, Eusebio L. "Time and Technique in The Sound and the Fury," LCrit, 6 (Summer, 1965), 61-67.

4887 Rosenberg, Bruce A. "The Oral Quality of Rev. Shegog's Sermon in William Faulkner's The Sound and the Fury," LWU, 2 (1969), 73-88.
Believes that Faulkner has here "created one of the very few, and certainly the best, spontaneously composed oral sermons in fiction."

4888 Ross, Stephen M. "Jason Compson and Sut Lovingood: Southwestern Humor as Stream of Consciousness," SNNT, 8 (Fall, 1976), 278-290.

4889 ________. "The 'Loud World' of Quentin Compson," SNNTS, 7 (Summer, 1975), 245-257.

4890 Rothkopf, Carol Z., Series Consultant. A Critical Commentary: The Sound and the Fury. New York: American R. D. M. Corp., 1964.

4891 Rubel, Warren G. "The Structural Function of the Christ Figure in the Fiction of William Faulkner," DA, 25 (Arkansas: 1964), 5941.

4892 Rubin, Louis D., Jr. "Chronicles of Yoknapatawpha: The Dynasties of William Faulkner," The Faraway Country: Writers of the Modern South. Seattle: Washington U. P., 1963, pp. 43-71.

4893 ________, and Robert D. Jacobs. "Faulkner's Tragedy of Isolation," Southern Renaissance: Literature of the Modern South. Baltimore: Johns Hopkins, 1953, pp. 170-191.

4894 Ruiz Ruiz, Jose M. "El sentido de la vida y de la muerte en The Sound and the Fury, de W. Faulkner," FMod, 13 (1973), 117-138.

4895 Ruppel, James Robert. "Narcissus Observed: The Pastoral Elegiac in Woolf, Faulkner, Fitzgerald, and Graeme Gibson," DAI, 39, #7 (Toronto, Canada: 1977), 4249A.

4896 Ryan, Marjorie. "The Shakespearean Symbolism in The Sound and the Fury," FS, 2 (Autumn, 1953), 40-44.
On Quentin and Hamlet.

4897 S., M. L. "The Tumult in a Southern Family," Boston Evening Transcript (October 23, 1929), III, 2.

4898 Sandeen, Ernest. "William Faulkner: Tragedian of Yoknapatawpha," Fifty Years of the American Novel. Harold C. Gardiner, ed. New York: Scribners, 1952, pp. 165-182.
Discussion of the family curse.

4899 Sandstrom, Glenn. "Identity Diffusion: Joe Christmas and Quentin Compson, AQ, 19 (Summer, 1967), 207-223.
Use of Erik Erikson's theory of identity.

4900 Sartre, Jean-Paul. "A Propos de 'Le Bruit et la Fureur': La Temporalitê chez Faulkner," NRF, 52 (June, 1939), 1057-1061; continued, NRF, 53 (July, 1939), 147-151. Trans. by Martine Darmon, repr., in Faulkner: Three Decades of Criticism. Frederick Hoffman and Olga Vickery, ed. East Lansing: Michigan State U.P., 1960, pp. 225-232. Also repr., in Situations I. Paris: Gallimard, 1947, pp. 70-81.

4901 Saxon, Lyle. "A Family Breaks Up," NYHTB (October 13, 1929), XII, 3.

4902 Schwerner, Armond, and Jerome Neibrief. "The Sound and the Fury," A Critical Commentary. New York: American R. D. M., 1964.

4903 Scott, Evelyn. On William Faulkner's The Sound and the Fury. New York: Cape and Smith, 1929, pp. 3-10.
Ten-page pamphlet, limited edition. Excerpted in Twentieth Century Interpretations. Michael Cowan, ed. Englewood Cliffs, New Jersey: 1968, pp. 25-29.

4904 ________. "On William Faulkner's The Sound and the Fury," PubW, 116 (September 21, 1929), 1138.
"His [Faulkner's idiot] is better than Dostoevsky's."

4905 S[cott], W[infield] T[ownley]. "The Waning South," Providence Sunday Journal (October 20, 1929), Mag. Sec., 27.

4906 Shaw, Joy Farmer. "The South in Motley: A Study of the Fool Tradition in Selected Works by Faulkner, McCullers, and O'Connor," DAI, 38, #7 (Virginia: 1977), 4162A.

4907 Simonsen, Helge. Oversatt. Larmen og vreden. Oslo: Gyldendal Norsk Forlag, 1967.

4908 Simpson, Hassell A. "Faulkner's The Sound and the Fury, Appendix," Expl, 21 (December, 1962), Item 27.
Cf., Frank Baldanza. Expl, 19 (1961), Item 59.

4909 Sims, Barbara B. "Jaybirds as Portents of Hell in Percy and Faulkner," NMW, 9 (Spring, 1976), 24-27.
On The Moviegoer and The Sound and the Fury.

4910 Slabey, Robert M. "Quentin As Romantic," Twentieth Century Interpretations of The Sound and the Fury. Michael H. Cowan, ed. Englewood Cliffs, New Jersey: Prentice-Hall, 1968, pp. 81-82.

4911 ______. "Quentin Compson's 'Lost Childhood,'" SSF, 1 (Spring, 1964), 173-183.

4912 ______. "The 'Romanticism of The Sound and the Fury," MissQ, 16 (Summer, 1963), 146-159.

4913 Slater, Judith. "Quentin's Tunnel Vision: Modes of Perception and Their Stylistic Realization in The Sound and the Fury," L&P, 27, #1 (1977), 4-15.

4914 Slatoff, Walter J. "The Edge of Order: The Pattern of Faulkner's Rhetoric," TCL, 3 (1957), 107-127; excerpt, "Unresolved Tensions," repr., in Twentieth Century Interpretations of The Sound and the Fury. Michael Cowan, ed. Englewood Cliffs: Prentice-Hall, 1968, pp. 93-96.

4915 ______. "The Sound and the Fury," Quest for Failure: A Study of William Faulkner. Ithaca: Cornell U.P., 1960, pp. 149-158.

4916 Smith, Henry Nash. "Notes on Recent Novels," SoR, 2 (1936-37), 583f.

4917 ______. "Three Southern Novels: The Sound and the Fury," SWR, 15 (Autumn, 1929), iii-iv.

4918 "The Sound and the Fury," Photoplay, 55 (April, 1959).
Review of the motion picture.

4919 Spiegel, Alan. "A Theory of the Grotesque in Southern Fiction," GaR, 26 (Winter, 1972), 426-437.

4920 Spilka, Mark. "Quentin Compson's Universal Grief," ConL, 11 (Autumn, 1970), 451-469.

4921 Stafford, T. J. "Tobe's Significance in 'A Rose for Emily,'" MFS, 14 (Winter, 1968-69), 451-453.
Comparison of Tobe's function with that of Dilsey in The Sound and the Fury.

4922 Steege, M. Ted. "Dilsey's Negation of Nihilism: Meaning in The Sound and the Fury," RS, 38 (1970), 266-275.

4923 Stein, Jean. "Interview with Faulkner," ParisR, 12 (Spring, 1956), 28-53; excerpt repr., in Twentieth Century Interpretations of The Sound and the Fury. Michael Cowan, ed. Englewood Cliffs: Prentice-Hall, 1968, pp. 16-17.
Faulkner describes his efforts in writing The Sound and the Fury.

4924 Steinberg, Aaron. "Faulkner and the Negro," DA, 27 (N. Y. U.: 1966), 1385A.

4925 Stewart, George R., and J. M. Backus. "'Each in Its Ordered Place': Structure and Narrative in 'Benjy's Section' of The Sound and the Fury," AL, 29 (January, 1958), 440-456.

4926 Stonier, G. W. "Selected Fiction," Fortnightly Review, 129 (June, 1931), 842-843.

4927 Strandberg, Victor. "Faulkner's Poor Parson and the Technique of Inversion (or William Faulkner: An Epitaph)," SR, 73 (April-June, 1965), 181-190.

4928 Strong, L. A. G. "Mr. Faulkner Again," Spectator, #5365 (April 25, 1931), 674.

4929 Stuckey, W. J. The Pulitzer Prize Novels: A Critical Backward Look. Norman: Oklahoma U. P., 1966, p. 86.
"... What makes the authorities' neglect of The Sound and the Fury especially ironic is that ... Faulkner's concern here ... is ultimately a moral one...."

4930 Styron, William. "This Quiet Dust," HarperM, 230, Special Supp. (April, 1965), 137.
Dilsey "comes richly alive."

4931 Swanson, William J. "William Faulkner and William Styron: Notes on Religion," CimR, 7 (March, 1969), 45-52.
Contrasts Faulkner's optimistic treatment of religion in The Sound and the Fury with Styron's pessimistic one in Lie Down in Darkness.

4932 Swiggart, Peter. "Faulkner's The Sound and the Fury," Expl, 22 (December, 1963), Item 31.
Reference to "Byron's wish" traced to Don Juan.

4933 _______. "Moral and Temporal Order in The Sound and the Fury," SR, 61 (April-June, 1953), 221-237.

4934 _______. "Rage against Time: The Sound and the Fury," The Art of Faulkner's Novels. Austin: Texas U. P., 1962, pp. 87-107.

4935 _______. "Time in Faulkner's Novels," MFS, 1 (February, 1955), 25-29.
"Faulkner's novels ... have as a central theme the reconciliation of past and present...."

4936 Swinnerton, Frank. "Writers Who Know Life," Evening News (May 15, 1931), 8.

4937 Thompson, Lawrance. "Faulkner's The Sound and the Fury," English Institute Essays, 1952. New York: Columbia U. P., 1954, pp. 3-4.

4938 _______. "Mirror Analogues in The Sound and the Fury," English Institute Essays, 1952. New York: Columbia U. P., 1952, pp. 83-106; repr., in Three Decades of Criticism. Frederick Hoffman and Olga Vickery, eds. East Lansing: Michigan State U. P., 1960; William Faulkner: Four Decades of Criticism. Linda Wagner, ed. Michigan State U. P., 1973, pp. 199-212.

4939 _______. William Faulkner: An Introduction and Interpretation. New York: Barnes & Noble 1963; 2nd ed. Holt, Rinehart & Winston, 1967, pp. 29-52.

4940 Thornton, Patricia Elizabeth. "The Prison of Gender: Sexual Roles in Major American Novels of the 1920's," DAI, 37 (New Brunswick, Canada: 1976), 7133A-34A.

4941 Thornton, Welden. "A Note on the Source of Faulkner's Jason," SNNTS, 1 (Fall, 1969), 370-372.
The Hebrew high priest names Jason in II Maccabees a more likely source than Josephus (Antiquities of the Jews).

4942 Tilley, Winthrop. "The Idiot Boy in Mississippi: Faulkner's The Sound and the Fury," AJMD, 53 (January, 1955), 374-377.
Expresses scientific doubt as to characterization of Benjy.

4943 Tomlinson, T. B. "Faulkner and American Sophistication," MCR, 7 (1964), 92-103.

4944 Traschen, Isadore. "The Tragic Form of The Sound and the Fury," SoR, 12 (Autumn, 1976), 798-813.

4945 Trilling, Lionel. "Tragedy and Three Novels," Symposium, 1 (January, 1930), 112-114.

4946 Tuck, Dorothy. Crowell's Handbook of Faulkner. New York: Crowell, 1964, pp. 22-33.

4947 Underwood, Henry J., Jr. "Sartre on The Sound and the Fury: Some Errors," MFS, 12 (Winter, 1966-67), 447-479.

4948 Vahanian, Gabriel. "William Faulkner: Rendezvous with Existence," Wait Without Idols. New York: Braziller, 1964, pp. 93-116.
Through Gilsey Faulkner affirms the "possibility of a new beginning."

4949 Vandenbergy, John, tr. Het geraas en gebral. Utrecht: A. W. Bruna & Zoon, 1965.

4950 Van Nostrand, A. D. "The Poetic Dialogues of William Faulkner," Everyman His Own Poet. New York: McGraw-Hill, 1968, pp. 175-176.

4951 Vickery, Olga W. "The Sound and the Fury: A Study in Perspective," PMLA, 69 (December, 1954), 1017-1037; condensed and repr., as "Worlds in Counterpoint," in The Novels of William Faulkner. Baton Rouge: Louisiana State U.P., 1959, rev. ed., 1964, pp. 28-49.

4952 Volpe, Edmond L. "Chronology and Scene Shifts in Benjy's and Quentin's Sections," A Reader's Guide to William Faulkner. New York: Noonday Press, 1964, pp. 363-365, 373-377; repr., as "Appendix," in Twentieth Century Interpretations of The Sound and the Fury. Michael Cowan, ed. Englewood Cliffs: Prentice-Hall, 1968, pp. 103-108.

4953 Waggoner, Hyatt. "Form, Solidity, Color," William Faulkner: From Jefferson to the World. Lexington: Kentucky U.P., 1959; repr., in Twentieth Century Interpretations. Michael Cowan, ed. Englewood Cliffs: Prentice-Hall, 1968, pp. 97-101.

4954 ________. "William Faulkner's Passion Week of the Heart," The Tragic Vision and the Christian Faith. Nathan A. Scott, Jr., ed. New York: Association Press, 1957, pp. 306-323; revised for William Faulkner. 1959, pp. 238-266.

4955 Wagner, Linda W. "Faulkner's Fiction: Studies in Organic Form," JNT, 1 (January, 1971), 1-14.

4956 ________. "Jason Compson: The Demands of Honor," SR, 79 (Autumn, 1971), 554-575.

4957 Wald, Jerry. "From Faulkner to Film," SatRL, 42 (March 7, 1959), 16, 42.
On Wald's production of The Sound and the Fury. Cf., Hollis Alpert. SatRL, 42 (March 7, 1959), 28.

4958 Wall, Carey. "The Sound and the Fury: The Emotional Center," MidQ, 11 (Summer, 1970), 371-387.
Examination of the monologues and voice styles.

4959 Walters, Paul S. "Theory and Practice in Faulkner: The Sound and Fury," ESA, 10 (March, 1967), 22-39.

4960 Warren, Joyce W. "Faulkner's 'Portrait of the Artist,'" MissQ, 19 (Summer, 1966), 121-131.
Joyce's influence on Faulkner's The Sound and the Fury.

4961 Warren, Robert Penn. "Faulkner: The South, the Negro, and Time," SoR, n.s., 1 (July, 1965), 506-510, 512-513; repr., in Faulkner: A Collection of Critical Essays.

Englewood Cliffs, New Jersey: Prentice-Hall, 1966, pp. 251-271.

4962 Watkins, Floyd C. "The Word and the Deed in Faulkner's First Great Novels," The Flesh and the Word. Nashville: Vanderbilt U.P., 1971, pp. 181-202.

4963 Way, Brian. "William Faulkner," CritQ, 3 (Spring, 1961), 42-53.

4964 Weatherby, H. L. "Sutpen's Garden," GaR, 21 (Fall, 1967), 354-369.

4965 Weber, Robert W. Die Aussage der Form: Zur Textur und Struktur des Bewusstseinsromans. Dargestellt an W. Faulkners The Sound and the Fury. Heidelberg: Carl Winter, 1969.

The importance of form in The Sound and the Fury.

4966 ________. "Die Aussage der Form [The Message of Form. Texture and Structure of the Stream-of-Consciousness Novel. Illustrated with William Faulkner's The Sound and the Fury.]," Mon/BZJA, 27 (1969), 1-104.

4967 Weinstein, Arnold L. "Vision as Feeling: Bernanos and Faulkner," Vision and Response in Modern Fiction. Ithaca, New York: Cornell U.P., 1974, pp. 91-153.

4968 Weinstein, Philip M. "Caddy Disparue: Exploring an Episode Common to Proust and Faulkner," CLS, 14 (March, 1977), 38-52.

4969 Weisgerber, Jean. "Faulkner et Dostoievski," RLC, 39 (July-September, 1965), 406-421.

4970 ________. "Faulkner's Monomaniacs: Their Indebtedness to Raskolnikov," CLS, 5 (June, 1968), 181-193.

4971 West, Ray B., Jr. "The Modern Writer," CE, 15 (January, 1954), 207-215.

Discusses allusion to Macbeth in The Sound and the Fury.

4972 Westbrook, Wayne W. "Jason Compson and the Costs of Speculation--A Second Look," MissQt, 30, #3 (Summer, 1977), 437-440.

Cf., William W. Cobau. "Jason Compson and the Costs of Speculation," MissQt, 22 (Summer, 1969), 257-261.

4973 Whicher, Stephen E. "The Compsons' Nancies: A Note on The Sound and the Fury and 'That Evening Sun,'" AL, 26 (May, 1954), 253-255.

Believes the corpse in the ditch is that of a horse, not the character from the short story.

4974 Wilder, Amos N. "Faulkner and Vestigial Moralities," *Theology and Modern Literature*. Cambridge: Harvard U.P., 1958, pp. 113-131; repr., in *Religious Perspectives in Faulkner's Fiction*. J. R. Barth, ed. Notre Dame: Notre Dame U.P., 1972, pp. 91-102.

4975 Woodward, Robert H. "Poe's Raven, Faulkner's Sparrow, and Another Window," PoeN, 2 (1969), 37-38.

4976 Wynne, Carolyn. "Aspects of Space: John Marin and William Faulkner," AQ, 16 (Spring, 1964), 59-71.

4977 Young, Calvin Eugene. "A Critical Explication of Irony as a Thematic Structure," DA, 30 (Indiana: 1969), 5007A-8A.
The Sound and the Fury is one of the novels "thematically explicated as novels of ironic failure...."

4978 Young, James Dean. "Quentin's Maundy Thursday," TSE, 10 (1960), 143-151.
A search for Christian symbolism.

4979 Zink, Karl E. "Flux and the Frozen Moment: The Imagery of Stasis in Faulkner's Prose," PMLA, 71 (June, 1956), 285-301.

4980 Ziolkowski, Theodore. "The Discordant Clocks," *Dimensions of the Modern Novel: German Texts and European Contexts*. Princeton: Princeton U.P., 1969, pp. 185-186, *passim*.

"SPOTTED HORSES"

(Published in Scribner's, 89 (June, 1931), 585-597; revised to become the spotted-horse episode in *The Hamlet*.)

4981 Backman, Melvin. *Faulkner: The Major Years*. Bloomington: Indiana U.P., 1966, pp. 139-140.

4982 Bradford, Melvin E. "'Spotted Horses' and the Short Cut to Paradise: A Note on the Endurance Theme in Faulkner," LaS, 4 (Winter, 1965), 324-331.

4983 Campbell, Harry M. "Mr. Roth's Centaur and Faulkner's Symbolism," WR, 16 (Summer, 1952), 320-321.

4984 Cowley, Malcolm. *The Faulkner-Cowley File: Letters and Memories, 1944-1962*. New York: Viking, 1966, *passim*.

4985 D'Agostino, Nemi. Introduzione. *Ambuscade, Spotted Horses, by William Faulkner*. Milano: Mursia, 1965, pp. 5-19.

4986 Dashiell, Alfred. "Spotted Horses," *Editor's Choice*. New York: G. P. Putnam's, 1934, pp. 133-154.

4987 Felheim, Marvin, Franklin Newman, and William Steinhoff. Study Aids for Teachers for Modern Short Stories. New York: Oxford U.P., 1951, pp. 17-19.

4988 Flanagan, John T. "Folklore in Faulkner's Fiction," PLL, 5 (Summer, 1969), 124.

4989 Gardner, John, and Lennis Dunlap. The Forms of Fiction. New York: Random House, 1962, pp. 108-112.

4990 Gordon, Caroline. "Notes on Faulkner and Flaubert," HudR, 1 (Summer, 1948), 222-231; revised and repr., in The House of Fiction. Caroline Gordon and Allen Tate, eds. New York: Scribner's, 1950, pp. 531-534; 2nd ed., 1960, pp. 289-331, 331-334.

4991 Greiner, Donald J. "Universal Snopesism: The Significance of 'Spotted Horses,'" EJ, 57 (November, 1968), 1133-1137.
Faulkner in his story showed greed as a universal human trait.

4992 Gwynn, Frederick L., and Joseph L. Blotner, eds. Faulkner in the University. Charlottesville: Virginia U.P., 1959, passim.

4993 Heald, William F. "Morality in 'Spotted Horses,'" MissQ, 15 (Spring, 1962), 85-91.

4994 Houghton, Donald E. "Whores and Horses in Faulkner's 'Spotted Horses,'" MidQ, 11 (Summer, 1970), 361-369.

4995 Ilacqua, Alma A. "An Artistic Vision of Election in Spotted Horses," Cithara, 15, ii (1976), 33-45.

4996 Ludwig, Jack Barry, and W. Richard Poirier. Instructor's Manual to Accompany Stories: British and American. Boston: Houghton-Mifflin, 1953, pp. 10-11.

4997 Meriwether, James B. The Literary Career of William Faulkner. Columbia: South Carolina U.P., 1971, passim.

4998 ________. "The Short Fiction of William Faulkner: A Bibliography," Proof, 1 (1971), 308.

4999 Millgate, Michael. The Achievement of William Faulkner. New York: Random House, 1966, pp. 182-183, passim.

5000 O'Connor, William Van. The Tangled Fire of William Faulkner. Minneapolis: Minnesota U.P., 1954, pp. 122-124.

5001 Page, Sally R. Faulkner's Women. DeLand, Florida: Everett/Edwards, 1972, pp. 158-160, passim.

5002 Rea, Joy. "Faulkner's 'Spotted Horses,'" HSL, 2 (1970), 157-164.
Links the horses with the mythological Pegasus.

5003 Richardson, H. Edward. William Faulkner: The Journey to Self-Discovery. Columbia: Missouri U. P., 1969, passim.

5004 Roth, Russell. "The Centaur and the Pear Tree," WR, 16 (Spring, 1952), 199-205.

5005 Sanderson, James L. "'Spotted Horses' and the Theme of Social Evil," EJ, 57 (May, 1968), 700-704.
Views the horses as symbolic of the evil propagated by Flem Snopes.

5006 Springer, Mary Doyle. "Larger than Life: Spotted Horses," Forms of the Modern Novella. Chicago: Univ. of Chicago Pr., 1975, pp. 32-37, 45-46, passim.

5007 Swiggart, Peter. The Art of Faulkner's Novels. Austin: Texas U. P., 1962, pp. 50-51, passim.

5008 Thompson, Lawrance. William Faulkner: An Introduction and Interpretation. New York: Barnes & Noble, 1967, pp. 199-200.

5009 Tuck, Dorothy. Crowell's Handbook of Faulkner. New York: Crowell, 1964, pp. 157, 176.

5010 Waggoner, Hyatt H. William Faulkner: From Jefferson to the World. Lexington: Kentucky U. P., 1959, p. 211.
"... [T]he comedy of "Spotted Horses' has as one of its integral elements an awareness of man's situation as precarious."

5011 Welty, Eudora. ["Spotted Horses"] Place in Fiction. New York: House of Books, 1957. (No pagination.)

"THE TALL MEN"
(Sat. Eve. Post, 213 (1941); repr., in Collected Stories, 1950)

5012 Bradford, Melvin E. "Faulkner's 'Tall Men,'" SAQ, 61 (Winter, 1962), 29-39.

5013 Hashiguchi, Yasuo. "The 'Tall' in William Faulkner's 'The Tall Men,'" KAL, No. 6 (1963), 8-12.

5014 Howell, Elmo. "William Faulkner and the New Deal," MwQ, 5 (Summer, 1964), 323-332.
Sees Faulkner as attacking the social policies of the New Deal in "The Tall Men."

5015 ________. "William Faulkner and the Plain People of Yoknapatawpha County," JMissH, 24 (April, 1962), 80-82.

5016 Kazin, Alfred. "William Faulkner: The Short Story 'The Tall Men,'" Contemporaries. Boston: Little, Brown & Co., 1962, pp. 157-158.

5017 Kerr, Elizabeth. "The Tall Men," Yoknapatawpha: Faulkner's "Little Postage Stamp of Native Soil." New York: Fordham U.P., 1969, passim.

5018 Meriwether, James B. "The Short Fiction of William Faulkner," Proof, 1 (1971), 308.

"THE EVENING SUN GO DOWN"
(Published in AmMerc, 22 (March, 1931), 257-267; revised and entitled "That Evening Sun" in These 13, a version repr., in Collected Stories, 1950)

5019 Barth, J. Robert. "Faulkner and the Calvinist Tradition," Religious Perspectives in Faulkner's Fiction, Notre Dame U.P., 1972, p. 24.
"... Nancy sits waiting for a fate she cannot escape ... 'Putting it off wont do no good.'"

5020 Bethea, Sally. "Further Thoughts on Racial Implications in Faulkner's 'That Evening Sun,'" NMW, 6 (Winter, 1974), 87-92.

5021 Bradford, Melvin E. "Faulkner's 'That Evening Sun,'" CEA, 28 (June, 1966), 1-3.
Cf., Patrick Hogan. "Faulkner: A Rejoinder," CEA, 28 (June, 1966), 3.

5022 Brooks, Cleanth. "Faulkner's Treatment of the Racial Problem: Typical Examples," A Shaping Joy: Studies in the Writer's Craft. New York: Harcourt Brace Jovanovich, 1972.

5023 Brown, May Cameron. "Voice in 'That Evening Sun': A Study of Quentin Compson," MissQ, 29, #3 (Summer, 1976), 347-359.

5024 Cantwell, Robert. "Faulkner's Thirteen Stories," NR, 68 (October 21, 1931), 271.

5025 Coburn, Mark D. "Nancy's Blues: Faulkner's 'That Evening Sun,'" Per, 17, iii (1974), 207-216.

5026 Coindreau, M. E., tr. "Soleil couchant," Europe (15 janvier 1936), 37-60.

5027 Cowley, Malcolm, ed. "That Evening Sun," The Portable Faulkner. New York: Viking, 1966, pp. 22, 28, 50, 55, 158.

5028 Cullen, John B., with Floyd C. Watkins. Old Times in the Faulkner Country. Chapel Hill: North Carolina U. P., 1961, pp. 72-73.

5029 Dabney, Lewis M. The Indians of Yoknapatawpha. Baton Rouge: Louisiana State U. P., 1974, pp. 73, 89.

5030 Davis, Scottie. "Faulkner's Nancy: Racial Implications in 'That Evening Sun,'" NMW, 5 (Spring, 1972), 30-32.
Cf., S. Bethea, NMW, 6 (1974), 87-92.

5031 Edward, Sister Ann. "Three Views on Blacks: The Black Woman in American Literature," CEA Critic, 37 (May, 1975), 14-16.
Nancy in "That Evening Sun."

5032 Fisher, Marvin. "The World of Faulkner's Children," UKCR, 27 (Autumn, 1960), 13-18.

5033 Franzen, Erich, tr. Abendsonne; drei Erzählungen. München: R. Piper, 1956. Translation of "That Evening Sun" and other stories.

5034 Frey, Leonard H. "Irony and Point of View in 'That Evening Sun,'" FS, 2 (Autumn, 1953), 33-40.

5035 Garrison, Joseph M., Jr. "The Past and the Present in 'That Evening Sun,'" SSF, 13 (Summer, 1976), 371-373.

5036 Gwynn, Frederick L., and Joseph L. Blotner, eds. Faulkner in the University. Charlottesville: Virginia U. P., 1959, pp. 21, 79.

5037 Hagopian, John V., and Martin Dolch. Insight I: Analyses of American Literature. Frankfurt am Main: Hirschgraben-Verlag, 1962, pp. 50-55.

5038 Harrington, Evans B. "Technical Aspects of William Faulkner's 'That Evening Sun,'" FS, 1 (Winter, 1952), 54-59.

5039 Heilman, Robert B. Modern Short Stories. New York: Harcourt, Brace, 1950, pp. 80-81.

5040 Hermann, John. "Faulkner's Heart's Darling in 'That Evening Sun,'" SSF, 7 (Spring, 1970), 320-323.

5041 Hogan, Patrick G., Jr. "Faulkner: A Rejoinder," CEA, 28 (June, 1966), 3.
Cf., M. E. Bradford. "'That Evening Sun,'" CEA, 28 (June, 1966), 1-3.

5042 Howe, Irving. "A Note on the Stories: 'That Evening Sun,'" William Faulkner: A Critical Study. New York: Vintage, 1952, pp. 266-267.

5043 Johnston, K. G. "Year of Jubilee: Faulkner's 'That Evening Sun,'" AL, 46 (March, 1974), 93-100.

5044 Kazin, Alfred. "William Faulkner: The Short Stories--'That Evening Sun,'" Contemporaries. Boston: Little, Brown & Co., 1962, p. 156.

5045 Kempton, Kenneth. The Short Story. Cambridge: Harvard U.P., 1947, pp. 8-10.

5046 Kerr, Elizabeth. "That Evening Sun," Yoknapatawpha: Faulkner's "Little Postage Stamp of Native Soil." New York: Fordham U.P., 1969, pp. 204, 213, 234.

5047 Leary, Lewis. "That Evening Sun," William Faulkner of Yoknapatawpha County. New York: Crowell, 1973, pp. 48-49, passim.

5048 Lee, Jim. "The Problem of Nancy in Faulkner's 'That Evening Sun,'" SCB, 21 (Winter, 1961), 49-50.

5049 Magny, Claude-Edmonde. "Faulkner's Inverse Theology," Cross Currents, 4 (Spring-Summer, 1954), 218.

5050 Manglaviti, Leo J. M. "Faulkner's 'That Evening Sun' and Mencken's 'Best Editorial Judgment,'" AL, 43 (January, 1972), 649-654.

Discussion of Faulkner's modification of the story, at Mencken's prompting, prior to its publication in American Mercury in 1931.

5051 Meriwether, James B. "The Short Fiction of William Faulkner," Proof 1, (1971), 308.

5052 Momberger, Philip. "Faulkner's The Village and That Evening Sun: The Tale in Context," SLJ, 11, #1 (Fall, 1978), 20-31.

5053 Muir, Edwin. "That Evening Sun," in Review of These Thirteen, Listener, 10 (October-December, 1933), 519.

5054 Nilon, Charles. Faulkner and the Negro. New York: Citadel Press, 1962, pp. 44-47.

5055 O'Brien, Edward J. The Short Story Case Book. New York: West, Richard, 1935, pp. 324-361.

5056 Orvis, Mary. The Art of Writing Fiction. New York: Prentice-Hall, 1948, pp. 104-105.

5057 Pearson, Norman Holmes. "Faulkner's Three 'Evening Suns,'" YULG, 29 (October, 1954), 61-70.
Comparison of the manuscript and the two printed versions.

5058 Reed, Joseph W., Jr. "That Evening Sun," Faulkner's Narrative. New Haven and London: Yale U.P., 1973, pp. 30-34, 45-46, passim.

5059 Rubel, Warren G. "The Structural Function of the Christ Figure in the Fiction of William Faulkner," DA, 25 (Arkansas: 1964), 5941.

5060 Sakai, K., ed. Introduction and Notes. The Tall Men and Other Stories. Kyoto: Apollonsha, 1962.

5061 Sanders, Barry. "Faulkner's Fire Imagery in 'That Evening Sun,'" SSF, 5 (Fall, 1967), 69-71.

5062 Silver, James W. Mississippi: The Closed Society. New York: Harcourt, Brace & World, 1970, passim.

5063 Singleton, Ralph H. Instructor's Manual for Two and Twenty: A Collection of Short Stories. New York: St. Martin's Press, 1962, pp. 11-12.

5064 Slabey, Robert M. "Quentin Compson's 'Lost Childhood,'" SSF, 1 (Spring, 1964), 173-183.
Mostly on "That Evening Sun."

5065 Snell, George. "The Fury of William Faulkner," WR, 11 (Autumn, 1946), 37-39; repr., in Shapers of American Fiction. New York: Dutton, 1947, pp. 99-102.

5066 Toole, William B., III. "Faulkner's 'That Evening Sun,'" Expl, 21 (February, 1963), Item 52.

5067 Waggoner, Hyatt H. William Faulkner: From Jefferson to the World. Lexington: Kentucky U.P., 1959, p. 194.

5068 West, Ray B., Jr. The Short Story in America, 1900-1950. Chicago: Regnery, 1952, pp. 98-99.
Compares "That Evening Sun" with Hemingway's "The Killers."

5069 Whicher, Stephen E. "The Compsons' Nancies: A Note on The Sound and the Fury and 'That Evening Sun,'" AL, 26 (May, 1954), 253-255.

"THAT WILL BE FINE"
("That Will Be Fine," AmMerc, 35 (July, 1935), 264-276; repr., in Collected Stories, 1950.)

5070 Kerr, Elizabeth. Yoknapatawpha: Faulkner's "Little Postage Stamp of Native Soil." New York: Fordham U.P., 1969, p. 67.
Suggests that Water Valley, county seat of Yalobusha County, fits the details given for the location of Mottstown in "That Will Be Fine."

5071 Moering, Richard. ["That Will Be Fine"] Die neue Rundschau, 49 (1938), 312.
Comments that the narrator in "That Will Be Fine" was both the seven-year-old boy and the poet.

5072 Reed, Joseph W., Jr. "That Will Be Fine," Faulkner's Narrative. New Haven and London: Yale U.P., 1973, 34-35, 37-39, passim.

5073 Rubel, Warren G. "The Structural Function of the Christ Figure in the Fiction of William Faulkner," DA, 25 (Arkansas, 1964), 5941.

5074 Stresau, Herman, tr. "Morgen Kinder, wird's was geben," ["That Will Be Fine"], Neu Amerika [A Collection of Present-Day American Writers], Robert W. Ullrich, ed. Berlin: S. Fischer, 1937, pp. 108-134.

"THERE WAS A QUEEN"
("There Was a Queen," Scribner's, 93 (January, 1933), 10-16; repr., in Doctor Martino, 1934; and in Collected Stories, 1950.)

5075 Bell, Haney H. "A Reading of Faulkner's Sartoris and 'There Was a Queen,'" Forum (Texas), 4, #8 (Fall-Winter, 1965), 23-26.

5076 Bradford, Melvin E. "Certain Ladies of Quality: Faulkner's View of Women and the Evidence of 'There Was a Queen,'" ArlQ, 1 (Winter, 1967-68), 106-134.
Suggests Miss Jenny as a type of Faulkner's "natural" women.

5077 Castille, Philip. "'There Was a Queen' and Faulkner's Narcissa Sartoris," MissQ, 28 (Summer, 1975), 307-315.

5078 Coindreau, M. E., tr. "Il Était une reine," NRF (août 1933), 213-233.

5079 Howe, Irving. "A Note on the Stories: 'There Was a Queen,'" William Faulkner: A Critical Study. New York: Vintage, 1952, pp. 70, 262.

5080 Kerr, Elizabeth. "There Was a Queen," Yoknapatawpha: Faulkner's "Little Postage Stamp of Native Soil." New York: Fordham U.P., 1969, passim.

5081 Knieger, Bernard. "Faulkner's 'Mountain Victory,' 'Doctor Martino,' and 'There Was a Queen,'" Expl, 30 (February, 1972), Item 45.

5082 Malin, Irving. William Faulkner: An Interpretation. Stanford U.P., 1957, p. 39.

5083 Meriwether, James B. "There Was a Queen," The Literary Career of William Faulkner. Columbia: South Carolina U.P., 1971, passim.

5084 Millgate, Michael. The Achievement of William Faulkner. New York: Random House, 1966, p. 273.

5085 Nilon, Charles H. Faulkner and the Negro. New York: Citadel Press, 1962, pp. 104-105.

5086 O'Connor, William Van. "There Was a Queen," The Tangled Fire of William Faulkner. Minneapolis: Minnesota U.P., 1954, p. 89.

5087 O'Donnell, George Marion. "Faulkner's Mythology," KR, 1 (Summer, 1939), 287-288.

5088 Page, Sally R. Faulkner's Women. DeLand, Florida: Everett/Edwards, 1972, p. 38.

5089 Rodewald-Grebin, Vivian, tr. "Eine Königin," ["There Was a Queen"] Die neue Rundschau, 44 (1933), 527-541.

5090 Tuck, Dorothy. Crowell's Handbook of Faulkner. New York: Crowell, 1964, pp. 178-179.

THESE THIRTEEN

(New York: Cape and Smith, 1931)

5091 Anon. These 13. AmMerc, 25 (January, 1932), xxiv. Review.

5092 Anon. These 13. Booklist, 28 (January, 1932), 201. Review.

5093 Anon. These 13. NYTBR (September 27, 1931), 7.

5094 "A. P. D." These Thirteen. London: Chatto & Windus, 1958.

5095 Bernárdez, Aurora, tr. Estos trece. Buenos Aires: Losada, 1956.

5096 "C. F." [These Thirteen] Oxford Mail (October 9, 1933). Review.

5097 Cantwell. "Faulkner's Thirteen Stories." NR, 68 (October 21, 1931), 271.

5098 Cestre, C. [These Thirteen] (édition anglaise), RAA (décembre 1933), 176.

5099 Cleeve, Tristram. [These Thirteen] Time & Tide, 14 (October 14, 1933), 1234, 1236.

5100 Cowley, Malcolm, ed. Introduction and Notes. The Portable Faulkner. New York: Viking, 1946.

5101 Crigler, John Peyton, III. "Faulkner's Early Short Story Career," DAI, 37 (Yale: 1976), 4352A.

5102 Cushing, Edward. "A Collection of Studies," SatRL, 8 (October 17, 1931), 201.

5103 Day, Douglas Turner. "The War Stories of William Faulkner," GaR, 15 (Winter, 1961), 385-394.

5104 Espinouze. "Six Drawings for Faulkner's These Thirteen," ParisR, 2 (Summer, 1953), 72-78.

5105 Gannett, Lewis. These Thirteen, NYHT (September 22, 1931).

5106 Garnett, David. "Current Literature," NS&N, 6 (September 30, 1933), 387.

5107 Gillett, Eric. These Thirteen. FnR, 134 (November, 1933), 636-637.

5108 Gould, Gerald. [These Thirteen] Observer (October 22, 1933).

5109 H. K. L. CamR, 55 (October 27, 1933), 52.

5110 Hartley, L. P. These Thirteen. Week-End Review, 8 (September 23, 1933), 302-306.

5111 Howe, Irving. "A Note on the Stories," William Faulkner: A Critical Study. New York: Vintage, 1952, pp. 260-267.

5112 ________. "Thirteen Who Mutinied: Faulkner's First World War," Reporter, 11 (September 14, 1954), 43-46.

5113 Leary, Lewis. "The Short Stories: 'These Thirteen,'" William Faulkner: of Yoknapatawpha County. New York: Crowell, 1973, pp. 133-134.

5114 Leibowitz, Rene. "L'art tragique de William Faulkner," Cahiers du Sud, 17 (November, 1940), 502-508.

5115 Life and Letters, 9 (December, 1933-February, 1934), 496-498.

5116 Little, G. Mcintyre. [These Thirteen] Scots Observer, 7, #365 (September 23, 1933), 11.

5117 Maxence, J. [Treize histoires] Gringoire (27 juillet 1939), 4.

5118 Meriwether, James B. "These 13, 1931," The Literary Career of William Faulkner: Columbia: South Carolina U.P., 1971, pp. 20-21.

5119 Miner, Ward. "These Thirteen," The World of William Faulkner. Durham, North Carolina: Duke U.P., 1952, pp. 14, 111.

5120 Montague, John. [These Thirteen] The Irish Times (November 15, 1958).

5121 Muir, Edwin. These Thirteen, Listener, 10 (October 4, 1933), 519.

5122 "O. M." [These Thirteen] Punch, 235 (September 24, 1958), 415-416.

5123 O'Connor, William Van. "These Thirteen and Other Stories," The Tangled Fire of William Faulkner. Minneapolis: Minnesota U.P., 1954, pp. 65-71.

5124 Paulding, Gouverneur. "Thirteen Who Mutinied: Faulkner's First World War," Reporter, 11 (September 14, 1954), 43-46.

Cf., Irving Howe. "Note in Rejoinder," Reporter, 11 (September 14, 1954), 43-46.

5125 Pearson, Norman Holmes. "Faulkner's Three Evening Suns," YULG, 29 (October, 1954), 61-70.

Compares the story, "That Evening Sun," as it appeared in American Mercury, March, 1931, and the story as it appeared in These 13.

5126 Picon, Gaëtan. "Treize histoires par William Faulkner," Cahiers du Sud (February, 1940), 133-136.

5127 Raimbault, R. N., and Ch. P. Vorce in collaboration with M. E. Coindreau, trs. Preface by R. N. Raimbault. Treize histoires. Paris: Gallimard, 1939.

5128 Schwartz, Delmore. "The Fiction of William Faulkner," Selected Essays of Delmore Schwartz. Donald A. Dike and David H. Zucker, eds. Chicago U.P., 1970, pp. 274-289.

5129 Showett, H. K. "A Note on Faulkner's Title, These Thirteen," NMW, 9 (Fall, 1976), 120-122.

5130 Skei, Hans H. Bold and Tragical and Austere: William Faulkner's These Thirteen. Dept. of Literature, University of Oslo. [1977?]

5131 Stallings, Lawrence. [These Thirteen] NYSun (September 22, 1931), 29.

5132 Thompson, Lawrance. "These Thirteen," William Faulkner: An Introduction and Interpretation. New York: Barnes & Noble, 1967, p. 10.

5133 Toynbee, Philip. [These Thirteen] Observer (February 1, 1959).

5134 Trilling, Lionel. "Mr. Faulkner's World," Nation, 133 (November 4, 1931), 491-492.

5135 Tuck, Dorothy. Crowell's Handbook of Faulkner. New York: Crowell 1964, passim.

5136 Vernon, Grenville. "Fallen Angel?" Cw, 15 (January 20, 1932), 332-333.

5137 Warren, Robert Penn. "Not Local Color," VQR, 8 (January, 1932), 160.

5138 Watkins, Floyd C. The Flesh and the Word. Nashville: Vanderbilt U. P., 1971, passim.

"THRIFT"
("Thrift," Sat. Eve. Post, 203 (September 6, 1930), 16-17, 76, 82.)

5139 Meriwether, James B. "The Short Fiction of William Faulkner," Proof, 1 (1971), 309.

5140 Williams, Blanche Colton, ed. O. Henry Memorial Award Prize Stories of 1931. New York: Doubleday, Doran, 1931, pp. 153-169.

"TOMORROW"
("Tomorrow," Sat. Eve. Post, 213 (November 23, 1940), 22-23, 32, 35, 37, 38, 39; repr., in Knight's Gambit, 1949.)

5141 Bakal, Sid. "Television Review," NYHT (March 8, 1960), 28.
"Tomorrow" adapted for TV.

5142 Bradford, M. E. "Faulkner's 'Tomorrow' and the Plain

People," SSF, 2 (Spring, 1965), 235-240.
"Though it has obvious merit as an independent work of fiction, 'Tomorrow' should be approached as a part of Faulkner's admiring study of the plain people of Yoknapatawpha County, ... "

5143 Canby, Vincent. "The Screen: 'Tomorrow,'" NYTimes (April 10, 1972), 44.
Faulkner's story adapted to cinema.

5144 Foote, Horton. "Tomorrow": A Play Adapted from a Story by William Faulkner. [Rev. Acting ed.] New York: Dramatists Play Service, 1963.

5145 Howell, Elmo. "Faulkner's Enveloping Sense of History: A Note on 'Tomorrow,'" NConL, 3, ii (1973), 5-6.

5146 Meriwether, James B. "'Tomorrow,' The Short Fiction of William Faulkner," Proof, 1 (1971), 309.

5147 Tuck, Dorothy. "Tomorrow," Crowell's Handbook of Faulkner. New York: Crowell, 1964, passim.

"TURN ABOUT"
("Turn About," Sat. Eve. Post, 204 (March 5, 1932); revised for Doctor Martino (1934); that version, entitled "Turnabout," repr., in Collected Stories, (1950); adapted for the screen by Faulkner as "Today We Live" (1950).

5148 Benson, Warren R. "Faulkner for the High School: 'Turnabout,'" EJ, 55 (October, 1966), 867-869, 874.

5149 Butterfield, Roger P. (Stories selected by). "Turn About," The Saturday Evening Post Treasury. New York: Simon & Schuster, 1954, pp. 204-216.

5150 Day, Douglas. "The War Stories of William Faulkner," GaR, 15 (Winter, 1961), 385-394.

5151 Leary, Lewis. "Turn About," William Faulkner of Yoknapatawpha County. New York: Crowell, 1973, p. 31.

5152 Meriwether, James B. The Literary Career of William Faulkner. Columbia: South Carolina U. P., 1971, pp. 156-157, passim.

5153 Millgate, Michael. The Achievement of William Faulkner. New York: Random House, 1966, pp. 33, 273; film based on, 35.

5154 O'Connor, William Van. The Tangled Fire of William Faulkner. Minneapolis: Minnesota U. P., 1954, p. 89.

5155 Raimbault, R. N., tr. "Chacun son tour," Samedi Soir (27 avril 1946), 6; 4 mai, p. 6; 11 mai, p. 6.

5156 Richardson, H. Edward. William Faulkner: The Journey to Self-Discovery. Columbia: Missouri U.P., 1969, p. 45.
Says that "All the Dead Pilots" (1931) and "Turn About" (1932) are related pieces."

5157 Tuck, Dorothy. Crowell's Handbook of Faulkner. New York: Crowell, 1964, pp. 158, 179-180, 241.

"TWO DOLLAR WIFE"
("Two Dollar Wife," College Life, 18 (January, 1936), 8-10, 85, 86, 88, 90.)

5158 Meriwether, James B. "The Short Fiction of William Faulkner," Proof, 1 (1971), 309.

5159 _______. "Two Unknown Faulkner Short Stories," RANAM, 4 (1971), 23-30.
The two stories discussed are "Two Dollar Wife" and "Sepulture South."

"TWO SOLDIERS"
(Sat. Eve. Post, 214 (March 28, 1942), 9-11ff; repr., in Collected Stories, 1950.)

5160 Bradford, M. E. "Faulkner and the Jeffersonian Dream: Nationalism in 'Two Soldiers' and 'Shall Not Perish,'" MissQ, 18 (Spring, 1965), 94-100.

5161 Coindreau, Maurice Edgar, tr. "Deux soldats," William Faulkner, Sélections du Livre. Paris: Gallimard, 1955, pp. 11-135.

5162 Kerr, Elizabeth. "Two Soldiers," Yoknapatawpha: Faulkner's "Little Postage Stamp of Native Soil." New York: Fordham U.P., 1969, passim.

5163 Leary, Lewis. William Faulkner of Yoknapatawpha County. New York: Crowell, 1973, p. 136.

5164 Millgate, Michael. The Achievement of William Faulkner. New York: Random House, 1966, p. 271.

5165 Raimbault, R. N., tr. "Deux Soldats," Écrit aux U.S.A.: anthologie des prosateurs amercains du XXe siècle. Paris: 1947, pp. 227-255; ce conte a aussi paru dans Samedi Soir (27 décembre 1947), 8.

5166 Reed, Joseph W., Jr. "Two Soldiers," Faulkner's Narrative. New Haven: Yale U.P., 1973, pp. 35-37.

5167 Tuck, Dorothy. Crowell's Handbook of Faulkner. New York: Crowell, 1964, p. 180.

"UNCLE WILLY"
(AmMerc, 36 (October, 1935), 156-168; repr., in Collected Stories, 1950.)

5168 O'Connor, William Van. "Protestantism in Yoknapatawpha County," in Southern Renascence. Louis D. Rubin and Robt. D. Jacobs, eds. Baltimore: Johns Hopkins, 1953, pp. 153-154.

5169 Page, Sally R. "Minor Figures and Major Motifs," Faulkner's Women. DeLand, Florida: Everett/Edwards, 1972, p. 184.

5170 Reed, Joseph W., Jr. Faulkner's Narrative. New Haven: Yale U.P., 1973, pp. 39-41, 190, 262.

5171 Tuck, Dorothy. Crowell's Handbook of Faulkner. New York: Crowell, 1964, pp. 180-181, 190.

THE UNVANQUISHED
(The story, "The Unvanquished," Sat. Eve. Post, 209 (November 14, 1936); revised and entitled "Riposte in Tertio" in The Unvanquished, 1938)

5172 Aaron, Daniel. The Unwritten War: American Writers and the Civil War. New York: Knopf, 1973.
Deals primarily with The Unvanquished in his examination of Faulkner's Civil War material.

5173 Adamowski, T. H. "Bayard Sartoris: Mourning and Melancholia," L&P, 23 (1973), 149-158.

5174 Anderson, Charles R. "Faulkner's Moral Center," EA, 7 (January, 1954), 48-58.

5175 Anderson, Hilton. "Two Possible Sources for Faulkner's Drusilla Hawk," NMW, 3 (Winter, 1971), 108-110.

5176 Anon. "Four Americans," Times (May 13, 1938), 10.

5177 Anon. "Town-A-Building," Time, 31 (February 21, 1938), 79.

5178 Anon. "The Unvanquished," Booklist, 34 (March 15, 1938), 266.

5179 Anon. "The Unvanquished," ChrC, 55 (March 9, 1938), 306.

5180 Anon. [The Unvanquished] Lettres Francaises (25 aôut 1949), 3.

5181 Anon. "The Unvanquished," London Mercury, 38 (July, 1938), 288.

5182 Anon. "War in Tennessee," TLS (London), (May 14, 1938), 333.

5183 Backman, Melvin. Faulkner: The Major Years. Bloomington: Indiana U. P., 1966, pp. 113-126.

5184 _______. "Faulkner's 'An Odor of Verbena': Dissent from the South," CE, 22 (January, 1961), 253-256.
Points out the conflict between Christian morality and a code of violence.

5185 Barth, J. Robert, ed. "The Unvanquished," Religious Perspectives in Faulkner's Fiction. Notre Dame: Notre Dame U. P., 1974, pp. 146-147, 149-150, passim.

5186 Beatty, Richard Croom. "Vitality of a Code," Banner (Nashville), (April 23, 1938), Mag., 2.

5187 Beauchamp, G. "The Unvanquished: Faulkner's Oresteia," William Faulkner: Four Decades of Criticism. Linda Wagner, ed. East Lansing: Michigan State U. P., 1973, pp. 298-302.

5188 _______. "The Unvanquished: Faulkner's Oresteia," MissQ, 23 (Summer, 1970), 273-277.

5189 Bentley, Phyllis. "Among the New Books," Yorkshire Post (May 18, 1938), 8.

5190 Beresford, J. D. "Harmony and Disharmony," Manchester Guardian (May 13, 1938), 7.

5191 Bianchi, Ruggero. "Faulkner e The Unvanquished," SA, 8 (1962), 129-150.

5192 Birney, Earle. "The Two William Faulkners," CanForum, 18 (June, 1938), 84-85.

5193 Blakeston, Oswell. "Novels," Life and Letters Today, 19 (September, 1938), 125-126.

5194 Blanzat, Jean. [The Unvanquished] FL (6 août 1949), 5.

5195 Bledsoe, A. S. "Colonel John Sartoris' Library," NMW, 7 (Spring, 1974), 26-29.
Analysis of contents of Sartoris' library as indicated in The Unvanquished.

5196 Boutang, Pierre. "L'Invaincu," Aspects de la France (21 juillet 1949), 3.

5197 Boyle, Kay. "Tattered Banners," NR, 94 (March 9, 1938), 136-137.
"There are two Faulkners...: the one who stayed down South and the one who went to war in France and mixed with foreigners and aviators...."

5198 ________. "The Unvanquished," The Critic as Artist: Essays on Books, 1920-1970. Gilbert A. Harrison, ed. New York: Liveright, 1972, pp. 38-41.

5199 Bradford, M. E. "Faulkner's The Unvanquished: The High Costs of Survival," SoR, 14, #3 (July, 1978), 428-437.

5200 Bradley, Van Allen. "A Faulkner Rarity," Chicago Daily News (October 9, 1965), 11.
The value of a first edition.

5201 Braspart, M. [L'Invaincu] Réforme (13 août 1949), 7.

5202 Brickell, Herschel. "William Faulkner Returns to the Sartorises in The Unvanquished," NYPost (February 18, 1938), 19.

5203 Brooks, Cleanth. "Faulkner's Vision of Good and Evil," MassR, 3 (Summer, 1962), 692-712; repr., in The Hidden God. New Haven: Yale U.P., 1963, pp. 22-43.

5204 ________. "The Language of Poetry: Some Problem Cases," Archiv, #6 (April, 1967), 401-414.

5205 ________. "The Old Order: The Unvanquished as an Account of the Disintegration of Society," William Faulkner: The Yoknapatawpha County. New Haven: Yale U.P., 1963, pp. 382-383.

5206 Brylowski, Walter. Faulkner's Olympian Laugh: Myth in the Novels. Detroit: Wayne State U.P., 1968, pp. 121-126.

5207 Butcher, Fanny. "Faulkner Uses Softer Touch in His Writing," Chicago Daily Tribune (February 26, 1938), 8.

5208 "C. H. H." [The Unvanquished] Oxford Times (May 27, 1938).

5209 Calverton, Victor F. "William Faulkner: Southerner at Large," ModQ, 10 (March, 1938), 11-12.

5210 Cargill, Oscar. "The Primitivists," Intellectual America. New York: Macmillan, 1941, pp. 370-386.

5211 Carrouges, M. [L'Invaincu] MN-P (mars 1950), 43.

5212 Chamberlain, John. "Books," ScribnerM (May, 1938), 82-83.

5213 Chauffeteau, J. [L'Invaincu] Arts et Lettres (n° 16, 1949), 58.

5214 Clayton, Charles C. "Vivid Vignettes of War in the Deep South," St. Louis Globe-Democrat (February 19, 1938), 2-B.

5215 Coindreau, Maurice E. "La guerra civil y la novela norteamericana," La Nación (November 20, 1938), Sec. 2, p. 1.

5216 Collins, Carvel, ed. Introduction. The Unvanquished. New York: New American Library (Signet), 1959, pp. vii-xii.

5217 Cournos, John. "The Spirit of the South in the Civil War Lives in Faulkner's The Unvanquished," NYSun (February 16, 1938), 23.

5218 Cowley, Malcolm. "An Odor of Verbena," [The Unvanquished], in The Portable Faulkner. New York: Viking, 1946.

5219 Creighton, Joanne V. "The Unvanquished: Revision, Retrospection, and Race," William Faulkner's Craft of Revision. Detroit: Wayne State U.P., 1977, pp. 73-84.

5220 Cullen, John B., with Floyd C. Watkins. Old Times in the Faulkner Country. Chapel Hill: North Carolina U.P., 1961, pp. 66-68.

5221 Davidson, Donald. "The South Today: Report on Southern Literature," Dallas Times Herald (July 17, 1938), Sec. I, 6.

5222 Davis, Bennett. "Books of the Week in Review," Buffalo Courier-Express (February 20, 1938), Sec. V, 6.

5223 DeVoto, Bernard. "Faulkner's South," SatRL, 17 (February 19, 1938), 5.

5224 Everett, Walter K. Faulkner's Art and Characters. Woodbury, New York: Barron's Educ. Ser., 1969, pp. 119-123.

5225 Fadiman, Clifton. "An Old Hand and Two New Ones," NY (February 19, 1938), 60-61.

5226 Fischer, Walther. Beiblatt zur Anglia, LI (1940), 283-284.

5227 Fuerbringer, Otto. "Fails to Excite One Reader," St. Louis Post-Dispatch (March 6, 1938), 4-B.

5228 Glicksberg, Charles I. "William Faulkner and the Negro Problem," Phylon, 10 (June, 1949), 153-160.

5229 Gold, Joseph. "The Unvanquished," William Faulkner: A

Study in Humanism from Metaphor to Discourse. Norman: Oklahoma U. P., 1966, pp. 42-45.

5230 _______. "William Faulkner's 'One Compact Thing,'" TCL, 8 (April, 1962), 3-9.

5231 Gwynn, Frederick L., and Joseph L. Blotner. Faulkner in the University. Charlottesville: Virginia U. P., 1959, pp. 252-256.

5232 Hawkins, Desmond. Crit, 18 (October, 1938), 85-86.

5233 _______. "The Unvanquished," Fortnightly, 144 (July, 1938), 117.

5234 Hawkins, E. O., Jr. "Jane Cook and Cecilia Farmer," MissQ, 18 (Fall, 1965), 248-251.

5235 Hicks, Granville. "Confederate Heroism," New Masses (February 22, 1938), 24.

5236 Hoffman, Frederick J. "The Negro and the Folk: The Unvanquished," William Faulkner. New York: Twayne Pubs., 1961, 2nd ed. rev., 1966, pp. 80-101.

5237 Holmes, Edward Morris. "Faulkner's Twice-Told Tales: His Re-Use of His Material," DA, 23 (Brown: 1963), 25-27.

5238 Howard, Brian. "New Novels," NS&N, 15 (May 14, 1938), 844, 846.

5239 Howe, Irving. William Faulkner: A Critical Study. 2nd ed. New York: Vintage Bks, 1962, pp. 41-45.

5240 Howell, Elmo. "William Faulkner and the Concept of Honor," NWR, 5 (Summer, 1962), 51-59.

5241 _______. "Faulkner and Scott and the Legacy of the Lost Cause," GaR, 26 (Fall, 1972), 314-325.
Particular attention given to The Unvanquished.

5242 _______. "William Faulkner and the Andrews Raid in Georgia, 1862," GHQ, 49 (June, 1965), 187-192.
Discussion of the fictional treatment of the Andrews raid in The Unvanquished.

5243 _______. "William Faulkner's General Forrest and the Uses of History," THQ, 29 (Fall, 1970), 287-294.

5244 Ingram, Forrest L. "William Faulkner: The Unvanquished," Representative Short Story Cycles in the Twentieth Century. The Hague: Mouton, 1971, pp. 106-142.

5245 Isaacs, J. "The Unvanquished," Annual Register, Part II (1938), 347-348.

5246 "J. S." The Times (May 13, 1938).
Gave attention to the scene called "Raid."

5247 Johnson, Robert. "Faulkner Retains Ability as Craftsman in New Book," Press-Scimitar (Memphis), (February 16, 1938), 7.

5248 Jour, Jean. "William Faulkner: L'Invaincu," Synthèses, 18 (May, 1963), 71-75.

5249 Kazin, Alfred. "In the Shadow of the South's Last Stand," NYHTB (February 20, 1938), 5.

5250 Kerr, Elizabeth M. "The Unvanquished," Yoknapatawpha: Faulkner's "Little Postage Stamp of Native Soil." New York: Fordham U. P., 1969, passim.

5251 Kibler, James E., Jr. "A Possible Source in Ariosto for Drusilla," MissQ, 23 (Summer, 1970), 321-322.

5252 Kirk, Robert W., and Marvin Klotz. Faulkner's People. Berkeley: California U. P., 1963, pp. 94-102.

5253 Knoll, Robert E. "The Unvanquished for a Start," CE, 19 (May, 1958), 338-343.
Cf., Isle Dusoir Lind, CE, 16 (February, 1955), 284-287.

5254 Krey, Laura. "Southern Selections," SR, 46 (July-September, 1938), 365-374.

5255 Kronenberger, Louis. "Faulkner's Dismal Swamp," Nation, 146 (February 19, 1938), 212-214.

5256 Lalou, R. [L'Invaincu] NL (1 septembre 1949), 3.

5257 Lean, Tangye. "William Faulkner's Civil War," News Chronicle (May 16, 1938), 4.

5258 Leary, Lewis. "The Unvanquished," William Faulkner of Yoknapatawpha Country. New York: Crowell, 1973, pp. 137-143.

5259 Lebesque, M. [L'Invaincu] Climats (5 août 1949), 8.

5260 LeBreton, Maurice. "William Faulkner: The Unvanquished and The Wild Palms," EA, 3 (July-September, 1939), 313-314.

5261 Lockhart, Jack. "Faulkner's New Book, The Unvanquished, Will Make Southern Hearts Beat Stronger," Memphis Commercial Appeal (February 27, 1938), IV, 9.

5262 Longley, John L., Jr. The Tragic Mask: A Study of Faulkner's Heroes. Chapel Hill: North Carolina U.P., 1963, pp. 177-191.

5263 Lytle, Andrew. "The Son of Man: He Will Prevail," SR, 63 (1955), 114-137.

5264 Malin, Irving. "An Odor of Verbena," William Faulkner: An Interpretation. Stanford U.P., 1957, passim.

5265 Memmott, A. James. "Sartoris Ludens: The Play Element in The Unvanquished," MissQ, 29, #3 (Summer, 1976), 375-387.

5266 Meriwether, James B. "Faulkner and the South," The Dilemma of The Southern Writer. R. K. Meeker, ed. Farmville, Virginia: Longwood College, Inst. of So. Culture, 1961, pp. 143-163.

5267 _______. The Literary Career of William Faulkner. Columbia: South Carolina U.P., 1971, passim.

5268 _______. "The Place of The Unvanquished in William Faulkner's Yoknapatawpha Series," DA, 19 (Princeton: 1959), 2957.

5269 _______. "A Source in Balzac for The Unvanquished," MissQ, 20 (Summer, 1967), 165-166.

5270 Miller, Douglas T. "Faulkner and the Civil War: Myth and Reality," AmQ, 15 (Summer, 1963), 206-208, passim.

5271 Millgate, Michael. "The Unvanquished," The Achievement of William Faulkner. New York: Random House, 1966, pp. 165-170.

5272 _______. William Faulkner. New York: Grove Press, 1961; revised, 1966; repr., Capricorn Bks, 1971, passim.

5273 Milum, Richard A. "Faulkner, Scott, and Another Source for Drusilla," MissQ, 31, #3 (Summer, 1978), 425-428.
Diana Vernon of Sir Walter Scott's Rob Roy (1817), a possible source.

5274 Mizener, Arthur. Modern Short Stories: The Uses of Imagination. New York: Rev. ed., Norton, 1967.

5275 Muir, Edwin. "New Novels," Listener, 19 (May 25, 1938), 146.

5276 Müller, Knud, tr. Drommen og daden. København: Glydendal, 1969.

5277 Nakajima, Toykiya, and Hisashi Saito, eds. with Notes. [The Unvanquished]. Tokyo: Asahi Press, 1968.

5278 Neville, Helen. "The Sound and the Fury," PR, 5 (June, 1938), 53-55.
See also as to The Unvanquished.

5279 Nilon, Charles H. Faulkner and the Negro. New York: Citadel Press, 1965, pp. 59-66.

5280 O'Brien, Edward J. The Short Story Case Book. New York: West, Richard, 1935, pp. 324-361.

5281 O'Brien, Kate. "Action," Spectator (May 20, 1938), 928.

5282 O'Brien, Matthew C. "A Note on Faulkner's Civil War Women," NMW, 1 (Fall, 1968), 56-63.
Analysis of actions of Rosa Millard and Drusilla Hawk in The Unvanquished, and, as well, certain characters in Absalom, Absalom!

5283 O'Connor, William Van. "Faulkner's Legend of the Old South," WHR, 7 (Fall, 1953), 293-301; revised for The Tangled Fire of William Faulkner. Minneapolis: Minnesota U.P., 1954, pp. 94-100.

5284 _______. "William Faulkner," Seven Modern American Novelists. Wm. Van O'Connor, ed. Minneapolis: Minnesota U.P., 1964, pp. 140-141.

5285 O'Donnell, George Marion. "Faulkner's Mythology," KR, 1 (Summer, 1939), 285-299; repr., Frederick Hoffman and Olga Vickery, eds. William Faulkner: Three Decades of Criticism. East Lansing: Michigan State U.P., 1960, pp. 83-84.

5286 O'Faolain, Sean. "New Novels to Read," John O'London's, 39 (May 20, 1938), 270.

5287 Organ, Dennis. "The Morality of Rosa Millard: Inversion in Faulkner's The Unvanquished," Pubs. Arkansas Philol. Assn., 1, ii (1975), 37-41.

5288 Orvis, Mary. The Art of Writing Fiction. New York: Prentice-Hall, 1948, pp. 104-105.

5289 Otten, Terry. "Faulkner's Use of the Past: A Comment," Renascence, 20 (Summer, 1968), 198-207, 214.

5290 Patterson, Alicia. "The Book of the Week," NYSunday News (February 20, 1938), 56.

5291 Pavese, Cesare. [The Unvanquished], Lettere, 1924-1944. Lorenzo Mondo, ed. 3rd ed. Torino: Einaudi, 1966, 326.

5292 Peraile, Esteban and Lorenzo. "Una lectura de Los invictos," CHA, 291 (1974), 692-701.

5293 Powell, Dilys. "Mr. Faulkner's Second Best," Sunday Times (June 12, 1938), 11.

5294 Raimbault, R. N., and Ch. P. Vorce, trs. L'Invaincu. Paris: Gallimard, 1949.

5295 Ramsey, William C. "Coordinate Structure in Four Faulkner Novels," DAI, 33 (North Carolina, Chapel Hill: 1971), 283A-84A.

5296 Reed, Joseph W., Jr. "Uncertainties: The Unvanquished and Go Down, Moses," Faulkner's Narrative. New Haven: Yale U.P., 1973, pp. 176-200.

5297 Roberts, John J., and R. Leon Scott, Jr. "Faulkner's The Unvanquished," Expl, 34 (March, 1976), Item 49.

5298 Robinson, Ted. "The Unvanquished," Cleveland Plain Dealer (February 20, 1938), All Feature Sec., 2.

5299 R[oueché], B[erton]. "Humor and a Heroine to Faulkner's Rescue," Kansas City Star (February 19, 1938), 14.

5300 S., M. W. "The Unvanquished," CSMM (February 16, 1938), 16.

5301 Schönemann, Friedrich. [The Unvanquished], Zeitschrift für neusprachlichen Unterricht, 35 (1936), 282; and 38 (1939), 120-121.

5302 Schwarz, Josef. Přelozil. Nepřemozeni. Praha: Naše Vojsko, 1958.

5303 Scott, R. Leon, and John J. Roberts. "Faulkner's The Unvanquished," Expl, 35, #2 (Winter, 1976), Item 3.
Explanation of the frozen water-moccasin in The Unvanquished," "Vendée."

5304 Shenton, Edward. Drawings. The Unvanquished. New York: Random House, 1938; reproduction, 1965.

5305 Sigaux, G. [L'Invaincu], Gazette de Lettres (1 octobre 1949), 7.

5306 Spring, Howard. "New Books," Evening Standard (May 19, 1938), 11.

5307 Strauss, Harold. "The Unvanquished," NYTBR (February, 1938), 6.

5308 Sullivan, Walter. "Southern Novelists and the Civil War," Southern Renascence. L. D. Rubin and Robert Jacobs, eds. Baltimore: Johns Hopkins Press, 1966, pp. 123-125.

5309 Swiggart, Peter. The Art of Faulkner's Novels. Austin: Texas U. P., 1962, pp. 36-37.

5310 Swinnerton, Frank. "Black and White," Observer (May 15, 1938), 6.

5311 Thompson, Ralph. "Books of the Times," NYTimes (February 15, 1938), 23.

5312 TLS, #1893 (May 14, 1938), 333.

5313 "Town-A-Building," Time, 31 (February 21, 1938), 79.

5314 Trimmer, Joseph Francis. "The Unvanquished: The Teller and the Tale," BSUF, 10 (Winter, 1969), 35-42.

5315 Tuck, Dorothy. Crowell's Handbook of Faulkner. New York: Crowell, 1964, pp. 67-71.

5316 Tucker, Edward L. "Faulkner's Drusilla and Ibsen's Hedda," ModD, 16 (September, 1973), 157-161.
Comparison of Drusilla in The Unvanquished with Hedda Gabler.

5317 Vallette, J. [L'Invaincu] MdF (novembre 1949), 532.

5318 Vandenbergh, John. Vertaling. Onoverwinnelijk. Utrecht: A. W. Bruna & Zoon, 1964.

5319 Volpe, Edmond L. A Reader's Guide to William Faulkner. New York: Noonday Press, 1964, pp. 76-87.

5320 Waggoner, Hyatt. William Faulkner: From Jefferson to the World. Lexington: Kentucky U. P., 1959, pp. 170-183.

5321 Walker, William E. "The Unvanquished: The Restoration of Tradition," Reality and Myth: Essays in American Literature in Memory of Richmond Croom Beatty. William E. Walker and Robert L. Welker, eds. Nashville, Tenn.: Vanderbilt U. P., 1964, pp. 275-297.

5322 Watkins, Floyd C. The Flesh and the Word. Nashville: Vanderbilt U. P., 1971, passim.

5323 Zycieńska, Ewa, tr. Niepokonana. Warszawa: Państwowy Instytut Wydawniczy, 1969.

"VENDEE"
(Sat. Eve. Post, 209 (December 5, 1936), 16-17, passim; revised for The Unvanquished, 1938)

5324 Meriwether, James B. "'Vendee,' The Short Fiction of William Faulkner," Proof, 1 (1971), 309.

5325 Tuck, Dorothy. Crowell's Handbook of Faulkner. New York: Crowell, 1964, pp. 68-69, 181, 204.

"VICTORY"
(These 13 (1931); repr., in Collected Stories (1950)

5326 Day, Douglas. "'Victory,' The War Stories of William Faulkner," GaR, 15 (Winter, 1961), 391-392.

5327 Meriwether, James B. "'Victory,' The Short Fiction of William Faulkner," Proof, 1 (1971), 310.

5328 Millgate, Michael. "Victory," The Achievement of William Faulkner. New York: Random House, 1966, pp. 260, 261, 273.

5329 Reed, Joseph W., Jr. "Victory," Faulkner's Narrative. New Haven: Yale U.P., 1973, p. 55.

5330 Smith, Raleigh W., Jr. "Faulkner's 'Victory': The Plain People of Clydebank," MissQ, 23 (Summer, 1970), 241-249.
The sin of pride causes Alec Gray to reject family ties.

5331 Trilling, Lionel. "Mr. Faulkner's World," Nation, 133 (November 4, 1931), 491-492.

5332 Tuck, Dorothy. "Victory," Crowell's Handbook of Faulkner. New York: Crowell, 1964, p. 181.

"THE WAIFS"
(Sat. Eve. Post, 229 (May 4, 1957); included in The Town as the story of Byron Snopes's four half-Indian children.)

5333 Meriwether, James B. The Literary Career of William Faulkner. Columbia: South Carolina U.P., 1971, p. 44.

5334 Millgate, Michael. The Achievement of William Faulkner. New York: Random House, 1966, pp. 236, 329.

5335 Tuck, Dorothy. "The Waifs," Crowell's Handbook of Faulkner. New York: Crowell, 1964, p. 181.

"WAS"

("Was," Go Down, Moses, 1942. Cf., Russell Roth, Perspective, 2 (1949)

5336 Bradford, Melvin E. "All the Daughters of Eve: 'Was' and the Unity of Go Down, Moses," ArlQ, 1 (Autumn, 1967), 28-37.

5337 Brown, Calvin S. "Faulkner's Manhunts: Fact into Fiction," GaR, 20 (Winter, 1966), 388-395.

5338 Brumm, Ursula. "William Faulkner, 'Was,' (1942)," Die amerikanische Short Story der Gegenwart: Interpretationen. Peter Freese, ed. Berlin: Schmidt, 1976, pp. 30-38.

5339 Brunel, Elisabeth. "Was," Views and Reviews of Modern German Literature: Festschrift für Adolf D. Klarmann. Karl S. Weimar, ed. München: Delp, 1974, pp. 135-142.

5340 Cowley, Malcolm, ed. "Was," The Faulkner-Cowley File. New York: Viking, 1966, pp. 22, 28.

5341 Dabney, Lewis M. "'Was': Faulkner's Classic Comedy of the Frontier," SoR, 8, n.s. (October, 1972), 736-749.

5342 Davis, Robert Gorham. Instructor's Manual for Ten Modern Masters. New York: Harcourt, 1953, pp. 45-46.

5343 Early, James. "'The Old People' and 'Was,'" The Making of Go Down, Moses. Dallas: So. Methodist U.P., 1972, pp. 71-73.

5344 Kerr, Elizabeth M. Yoknapatawpha: Faulkner's "Little Postage Stamp of Native Soil." New York: Fordham U.P., 1969, pp. 217, 243, passim.

5345 Malbone, Raymond G. "Promissory Poker in Faulkner's 'Was,'" EngRec, 22 (Fall, 1971), 23-25.

5346 Meriwether, James B. "The Short Fiction of William Faulkner," Proof, 1 (1971), 310.

5347 Millett, Fred B. Reading Fiction: A Method of Analysis with Selections for Study. New York: Harpers, 1950, pp. 222-224.

5348 Millgate, Michael. The Achievement of William Faulkner. New York: Random House, 1966, passim.

5349 Roth, Russell. "The Brennan Papers," Perspective, 2 (Summer, 1949), 219-224.
The "shifting of the point of narration" noted as to the opening story "Was" of Go Down, Moses.

5350 Taylor, Walter. "Horror and Nostalgia: The Double Perspective of Faulkner's 'Was,'" SHR, 8 (Winter, 1974), 74-84.
"Was" demonstrates "the presentness of the past through the simultaneous application of the tragic and comic moods."

5351 Tuck, Dorothy. Crowell's Handbook of Faulkner. New York: Crowell, 1964, passim.

5352 Waggoner, Hyatt. William Faulkner: From Jefferson to the World. Lexington: Kentucky U.P., 1959, pp. 199-201, passim.

5353 Walters, Thomas N. "On Teaching William Faulkner's 'Was,'" EJ, 55 (February, 1966), 182-188.

5354 Weiss, Daniel. "William Faulkner and the Runaway Slave," NwRev, 6 (Summer, 1963), 71-79.
On the Negro in "Was" and "Dry September."

5355 Zender, Karl F. "A Hand of Poker: Game and Ritual in Faulkner's 'Was,'" SSF, 11 (Winter, 1974), 53-60.
The denouement of "Was," showing "clearly and compactly the dual formal requirements of games and of rituals," is "tipped in favor of ritual."

"WASH"
("Wash," Harper's, 168 (February, 1934), 258-266; repr., in Dr. Martino (1934); revised in Absalom, Absalom! (1936); Dr. Martino version repr., in Collected Stories (1950).

5356 Breaden, Dale G. "William Faulkner and the Land," AQ, 10 (Fall, 1958), 355-356.

5357 Callen, Shirley. "Planter and Poor White in Absalom, Absalom! 'Wash,' and The Mind of the South," SCB, 23 (1963), 24-36.

5358 Cowley, Malcolm, ed. The Faulkner-Cowley File. New York: Viking, 1966, passim.

5359 Gettmann, Royal A., and Bruce Harkness. Teacher's Manual for A Book of Stories. New York: Rinehart, 1955, pp. 13-16.

5360 Howe, Irving. "A Note on the Stories: 'Wash,'" William Faulkner: A Critical Study. New York: Vintage, 1952, pp. 265-267.

5361 Howell, Elmo. "Faulkner's Wash Jones and the Southern Poor White," BSUF, 8 (Winter, 1967), 8-12.

The story shows the intricate social relationships of the old South, and, as well, serves as an indictment of the aristocracy.

5362 Isaacs, Neil D. "Götterdämmerung in Yoknapatawpha," TSL, 8 (1963), 47-55.
"Wash" as a miniature of Absalom, Absalom!

5363 Kerr, Elizabeth. Yoknapatawpha: Faulkner's "Little Postage Stamp of Native Soil." New York: Fordham U. P., 1969, p. 215

5364 Leary, Lewis. William Faulkner of Yoknapatawpha County. New York: Crowell, 1973, p. 134.

5365 Meriwether, James B. "'Wash,' The Short Fiction of William Faulkner," Proof, 1 (1971), 310.

5366 Millgate, Michael. The Achievement of William Faulkner. New York: Random House, 1965, pp. 262, 265, passim.

5367 Miner, Ward L. The World of William Faulkner. New York: Grove Press, 1959, p. 134.

5368 O'Connor, William Van. The Tangled Fire of William Faulkner. Minneapolis: Minnesota U. P., 1954, p. 89, passim.

5369 Raimbault, R. N., tr. "Wash," Arbalète, 9 (automne, 1944), 125-136.

5370 Stewart, Jack F. "Apotheosis and Apocalypse in Faulkner's 'Wash,'" SSF, 6 (Fall, 1969), 586-600.
Sees Wash Jones as the "apocalyptic figure of the man with the scythe, the silent, self-destroying prophet of social revolution."

5371 Tuck, Dorothy. Crowell's Handbook of Faulkner. New York: Crowell, 1964, pp. 181-182, passim.

5372 Tuso, Joseph F. "Faulkner's 'Wash,'" Expl, 27 (November, 1968), Item 17.
Thinks that the mare Griselda's role is that of a foil for the young mother Milly.

5373 Waggoner, Hyatt. William Faulkner: From Jefferson to the World. Lexington: Kentucky U. P., 1959, p. 195.
Calls "Wash" a story "unsurpassed of its kind."

"WEEKEND REVISITED"
(The first of Faulkner's unpublished stories to appear posthumously, "Mr. Acarius," in Sat. Eve. Post, 238 (October 9, 1965), 26-31; but apparently two typescripts are extant, one entitled "Mr. Acarius," the other "Weekend Revisited.")

5374 Gresset, Michel. "Weekend, Lost and Revisited," MissQ, 21 (Summer, 1968), 173-178.
Sees the story, "Weekend Revisited," as an allusion to Charles R. Jackson's popular post-war novel, The Lost Weekend.

5375 Meriwether, James B. "The Short Fiction of William Faulkner," Proof, 1 (1971), 304-305.

THE WILD PALMS
(New York: Random House, 1939)

5376 A., A. M. "Passion and Petrification," Daily Post (Liverpool), (April 19, 1939), 7.

5379 Adams, Richard P. Faulkner: Myth and Motion. Princeton: Princeton U.P., 1968, pp. 111-114.

5378 Aiken, Conrad. "William Faulkner: The Novel as Form," Atl, 164 (November, 1939), 650-654.
"... [I]t is difficult to choose between The Sound and the Fury and The Wild Palms, with Absalom, Absalom! a very close third...."

5379 Anon. "Mississippi Tragedy," TLS (London), (March 18, 1939), 161.

5380 Anon. "New Faulkner Novel Lacks Organization," Observer (Charlotte), (January 29, 1939), IV, 7.

5381 Anon. "When the Dam Breaks," Time, 33 (January 23, 1939), 45-46, 48.

5382 Anon. [Les Palmiers sauvages], BCLF (juillet-août 1952), 501-502.

5383 Anon. "The Wild Palms," ChrC (March 22, 1939), 387.

5384 Anon. "Wild Palms and Ripe Olives," SatRL, 19 (February 11, 1939), 8.

5385 Aury, Dominique. [Les Palmiers sauvages], Arts (10-16 avril 1952), 5.

5386 Backman, Melvin. Faulkner: The Major Years. Bloomington: Indiana U.P., 1966, pp. 127-138.

5387 ________. "Faulkner's The Wild Palms: Civilization Against Nature," UKCR, 28 (March, 1962), 199-204.
States that the novel's thesis is "that civilization is suicidally alienated from nature...."

5388 _______. "Sickness and Primitivism: A Dominant Pattern in William Faulkner's Work," Accent, 14 (Winter, 1954), 61-73.

5389 Baker, Carlos. "William Faulkner: The Doomed and the Damned," The Young Rebel in American Literature. Carl Bode, ed. London: Heinemann, 1959, pp. 159-163.

5390 Banning, Margaret C. "Changing Moral Standards in Fiction," SatRL, 20 (July 1, 1939), 4-5, 14.

5391 Barth, J. Robert. "Faulkner and the Calvinist Tradition," Thought, 39 (March, 1964), 100-120.

5392 Bauer, Ljubica. Prevela. Divlje palme. Geograd: Prosveta, 1961.

5393 Beach, Joseph Warren. "William Faulkner, Virtuoso," American Fiction, 1920-1940. New York: Macmillan, 1941, pp. 147-169.

5394 Blakeston, Oswell. "The Wild Palms," Life and Letters Today, 21 (June, 1939), 141-142.

5395 Blanc-Dufour, A. [Les Palmiers sauvages] Cahiers du Sud (1er semestre 1952, no 311), 166.

5396 Blanzat, J. [Les Palmiers sauvages] FL (1 mars 1952), 9.

5397 Boynton, Percy H. American in Contemporary Fiction. Chicago: Chicago U.P., 1940, pp. 106-112.

5398 Brooks, Cleanth. "The Tradition of Romantic Love and The Wild Palms," MissQ, 25 (Summer, 1972), 265-287.
The article incorporates an edited transcript of a discussion as to various aspects of the novel by Cleanth Brooks and others, among them Morse Peckham, James B. Meriwether, and Thomas L. McHaney.

5399 Brophy, John. "A Queer Mixture," Daily Telegraph and Morning Post (March 17, 1939), 8.

5400 Brylowski, Walter. "Toward Romance," Faulkner's Olympian Laugh. Detroit: Wayne State U.P., 1968, pp. 127-139.

5401 Burgum, Edwin Berry. "Faulkner's New Novel," New Masses (February 7, 1939), 23-24.

5402 [Cantwell, Robert.] "When the Dam Breaks," Time, 33 (January 23, 1939), 45-46, 48.

5403 Cargill, Oscar. "The Primitivists," Intellectual America. New York: Macmillan, 1941, pp. 370-386.

5404 Cassill, R. V. Introduction. The Wild Palms. New York: New American Library, 1968.

5405 Chamberlain, John. "The New Books," HarperM, 178 (February, 1939), Advertising pages.

5406 Childers, J[ames] S. "Mr. Faulkner Once Again Produces An Exciting Novel," Birmingham News (February 5, 1939), Mag. Sec., 7.

5407 Church, Margaret. "William Faulkner: Myth and Duration," Time and Reality: Studies in Contemporary Fiction. Chapel Hill: North Carolina U.P., 1963, pp. 243-244.

5408 Church, Richard. "Two Parallel Themes in William Faulkner's New Book," JO'L, 40 (March 24, 1939), 969.

5409 Clayton, Charles C. "William Faulkner's New Novel Is Study in Passion," St. Louis Globe-Democrat (January 21, 1939), 1-B.

5410 Coindreau, Maurice. Préface. Les Palmiers sauvages. Paris: Gallimard, 1952, pp. i-xiv. Repr., in The Time of William Faulkner. George M. Reeves, ed., tr. by George M. Reeves and Thomas McHaney. Columbia: South Carolina U.P., 1971, pp. 51-63.

5411 _______. "Preface aux Palmiers sauvages," TM, 7 (January, 1952), 1187-1196.

5412 Colson, Theodore. "Analogues of Faulkner's The Wild Palms and Hawthorne's 'The Birthmark,'" DR, 56 (Autumn, 1976), 510-518.

5413 Cowley, Malcolm. "Sanctuary," NY, 97 (January 25, 1939), 349.
Essay-review of The Wild Palms.

5414 DeVoto, Bernard. "American Novels: 1939," Atl, 165 (January, 1940), 73-74.
"Another of the tours de force expected of him."

5415 Everett, Walter K. Faulkner's Art and Characters. Woodbury, New York: Barron's Educ. Ser., 1969, pp. 124-129.

5416 Fadiman, Clifton. "Mississippi Frankenstein," NY, 14 (January 21, 1939), 60-61.

5417 Feaster, John. "Faulkner's Old Man: A Psychoanalytic Approach," MFS, 13 (Spring, 1967), 89-93.

5418 Fitzhugh, Eleanor. "Turns with Bookworms," News (Jackson, Miss.) February 6, 1939), 5.

5419 Galharn, Carl. "Faulkner's Faith: Roots from The Wild Palms," TCL, 1 (October, 1955), 139-160.

5420 Gándara, Carmen. "Al margen de la última novela de Faulkner," La Nación (October 15, 1939), Sec. 2, 1.

5421 Gannett, Lewis. "Books and Things." Washington Post (January 20, 1939), 11.

5422 Gibson, Wilfrid. "Four New Novels," Manchester Guardian (April 6, 1939), 5.

5423 Greenberg, Alvin. "Shaggy Dog in Mississippi," SFQ, 29 (December, 1965), 284-287.

5424 Grimes, George. "Faulkner Tale Shocks: Shows Man in Flight," Sunday World Herald (Omaha), (February 12, 1939), 8-C.

5425 Guerard, Albert. "Faulkner's Two Jobs in One; His Best in Ten Years," Boston Evening Transcript (January 28, 1939), Bk. Revs., 1.

5426 Gwynn, Frederick L., and Joseph L. Blotner, eds. Faulkner in the University. Charlottesville: Virginia U.P., 1959, pp. 171-182, passim.

5427 Haavardsholm, Espen. "The Wild Palms," Vinduet, 20 (1966), 172-176.

5428 Hamalian, Leo, and Edmond L. Volpe. Eleven Modern Short Novels. New York: Putnam's, 1958, pp. 534-538.

5429 Hanley, James. "New Novels," New English Weekly, 15 (June 8, 1939), 127-128.

5430 Hansen, Harry. "The Wild Palms," by William Faulkner, Is a Fantastically Absorbing Novel," NYWorld-Telegram (January 19, 1939), 19.

5431 Hart, Henry. "Books," Direction (March-April, 1939), 21-22.

5432 Hoffman, Frederick J. "The Negro and the Folk--Wild Palms," William Faulkner. New York: Twayne, 2nd ed. rev., 1966, pp. 80-101.

5433 Hoole, William Stanley. "William Faulkner's New Novel Is Bible of Disintegration," Dallas Morning News (January 22, 1939), III, 15.

5434 Howe, Irving. William Faulkner: A Critical Study. New York: Vintage, 1962, pp. 233-241.
Thematic parallels between "Old Man" and Wild Palms.

5435 _______. "William Faulkner and the Quest for Freedom," Tomorrow, 9 (December, 1949), 54-56.
An analysis of structure and discussion of themes.

5436 Howell, Elmo. "William Faulkner and the New Deal," MidQ, 5 (July, 1964), 323-332.
Comment on Faulkner's fear of government infringement on individual freedom.

5437 _______. "William Faulkner and the Plain People of Yoknapatawpha County," JMH, 24 (April, 1962), 82-85.

5438 Jack, Peter Monro. "Mr. Faulkner's Clearest Novel," NYTBR (January 22, 1939), 2.

5439 Jewkes, W. T. "Counterpoint in Faulkner's The Wild Palms," WSCL, 2 (Winter, 1961), 39-53.
Notes that complementary themes, etc., resemble the technique of counterpoint in music.

5440 Kanters, R. [Les Palmiers sauvages] AN (mars 1952), 98-100.

5441 Kazin, Alfred. "A Study in Conscience," NYHTB (January 22, 1939), IX, 2.

5442 Kirk, Robert W., and Marvin Klotz. Faulkner's People. Berkeley: California U.P., 1963, pp. 103-108.

5443 Lalou, René. [Les Palmiers sauvages] NL (20 mars 1952), 3.
"Un hommage a la complexité d'un chef-d'oeuvre."

5444 Las Vergnas, R. [Les Palmiers sauvages] Hommes et Mondes (mars 1952), 469-471.

5445 LeBreton, Maurice. "William Faulkner: The Unvanquished and The Wild Palms," EA, 3 (July-September, 1939), 313-314.

5446 Longley, John L., Jr. The Tragic Mask. Chapel Hill: North Carolina U.P., 1963, pp. 29-33.

5447 Lovett, Robert M. "Ferocious Faulkner," Nation, 148 (February 4, 1939), 153.

5448 McElroy, Davis Dunbar. Existentialism and Modern Literature. Philosophical Library, 1963; repr., New York: Greenwood, 1968, pp. 24-28.

5449 McFee, William. "In Which a Writer with a Talent Outrages the Intelligence of His Readers," NYSun (January 23, 1939), 10.

5450 McHaney, Thomas L. "Anderson, Hemingway, and Faulkner's The Wild Palms," PMLA, 87 (May, 1972), 465-474.
Allusions and comparisons.

5451 _______. "Jeffers' 'Tamar' and Faulkner's The Wild Plums," RJefN1, 29 (August, 1971), 16-18.

5452 _______. "William Faulkner's The Wild Palms: A Textual and Critical Study," DAI, 30 (South Carolina: 1969), 2540A-41A.

5453 _______. William Faulkner's The Wild Palms: A Study. Jackson: Mississippi U. P., 1975.

5454 Macmillan, Duane J. "The Non-Yoknapatawpha Novels of William Faulkner: An Examination of Soldier's Pay, Mosquitos, The Wild Palms, Pylon, and A Fable," DAI, 32 (Wisconsin: 1972), 6986A.

5455 Magny, Claude-Edmonde. [Les Palmiers sauvages] Samedi Soir (6 octobre 1951), 2.

5456 Mair, John. [The Wild Palms], NS&N, 17 (March 18, 1939), 427.

5457 Malin, Irving. William Faulkner: An Interpretation. Stanford U. P., 1957, passim.

5458 Marceau, Félicien. "Les lettres americains--Etrange Amerique," TR, No. 54 (juin 1952), 152-156.

5459 Maxwell, Allen. "The Wild Palms," SWR, 24 (April, 1939), 357-360.

5460 Mayoux, Jean-Jacques. [Les Palmiers sauvages] Combat (6 mars 1952), 7.
Faulkner et le sens tragique.

5461 Merton, Thomas. "'Baptism in the Forest'": Wisdom and Initiation in William Faulkner," Mansions of the Spirit: Essays in Literature and Religion. George A. Panichas, ed. New York: Hawthorn, 1967, pp. 17-44. A portion of the essay appeared in CathW, 207 (January, 1968), 124-130.

5462 Miller, James E., and Bernice Slote. Instructor's Manual to The Dimensions of the Short Story. New York: Dodd, Mead, 1964.

5463 Millgate, Michael. "The Wild Palms," The Achievement of William Faulkner. New York: Random House, 1966, pp. 171-179.

5464 _______. William Faulkner. New York: Capricorn, 1971, passim.

5465 Moht, Michel. "Les Prisonniers du Temps," TR, No. 59 (novembre 1952), 160-165.

5466 Moldenhauer, Joseph J. "Unity of Theme and Structure in The Wild Palms," William Faulkner: Three Decades of Criticism. Frederick Hoffman and Olga Vickery, eds. East Lansing: Michigan State U.P., 1960, pp. 305-322.

5467 Monroe, Elizabeth. "Contemporary Fiction and Society," SoLM, 2 (June, 1940), 364-365.

5468 Monteiro, George. "'Between Grief and Nothing': Hemingway and Faulkner," HemN, 1 (Spring, 1971), 13-15.

5469 ______. "Hemingway and Spain: A Response to Woodward," HemN, 2 (Fall, 1972), 16-17.
Cf., Robert H. Woodward. "Robert Jordan's Wedding/Funeral Sermon," HemN, 2 (Spring, 1972), 7-8.

5470 ______. "The Limits of Professionalism: A Sociological Approach to Faulkner, Fitzgerald and Hemingway," Criticism, 15 (Spring, 1973), 145-155.

5471 Moses, W. R. "Les Palmiers sauvages: Structure et unité du roman," RLM, Part I, Nos. 27-29 (1957), 41-53.

5472 ______. "The Unity of The Wild Palms," MFS, 2 (Autumn, 1956), 125-131.

5473 ______. "Water, Water Everywhere: 'Old Man' and A Farewell to Arms," MFS, 5 (Summer, 1959), 172-174.
Cf., H. Edward Richardson. "The 'Hemingwaves' in Faulkner's Wild Palms," MFS, 4 (1959), 357-360.

5474 Muir, Edwin. "New Novels," Listener, 21 (March 30, 1939), 701.

5475 Myers, Bill. "The Wild Palms," Dayton Daily News (January 22, 1939), Soc. Sec., 7.

5476 Nicholson, Louis. "William Faulkner," Man in Literature. London: S.C.M. Press, 1943, pp. 122-138.

5477 O'Brien, Kate. "Fiction," Spectator, 162 (April 14, 1939), 645-646.

5478 O'Connor, William Van. "Faulkner, Hemingway, and the 1920's," The Twenties: Poetry and Prose. Richard E. Langland and Wm. E. Taylor, eds. DeLand, Florida: Everett/Edwards, 1966, pp. 97-98.

5479 ______. "Faulkner's One-Sided 'Dialogue' with Hemingway," CE, 24 (December, 1962), 208-215.
Includes comment on The Wild Palms.

5480 ________. The Tangled Fire of William Faulkner. Minneapolis: Minnesota U.P., 1954, pp. 104-110.

5481 ________. "William Faulkner," Seven Modern American Novelists. Minneapolis: Minnesota U.P., 1964, pp. 142-144.

5482 O'Donnell, George Marion. "Faulkner's Mythology," KR, 1 (Summer, 1939), 285-299.

5483 O'Faolain, Sean. "William Faulkner," The Vanishing Hero: Studies in Novelists of the Twenties. London: Eyre and Spottiswoode, 1956, pp. 113-115.

5484 Page, Sally R. "The Female Idealist: As I Lay Dying and The Wild Palms," Faulkner's Women. DeLand, Florida: Everett/Edwards, 1972, pp. 111-135.

5485 Patterson, Alicia. "The Book of the Week," NYSunday News (January 22, 1939), 65.

5486 Peckham, Morse. "The Place of Sex in the Work of Wilian Faulkner," STC, 14 (Fall, 1974), 1-20.
Discussion of the tension between idealism and biology in A Fable, Requiem, and The Wild Palms.

5487 Ramsey, William Currie. "Coordinate Structure in Four Faulkner Novels," DA, 33 (Chapel Hill, North Carolina: 1971), 283A-84A.

5488 Rascoe, Burton. "Faulkner's Latest," Newsweek, 13 (January 16, 1939), 34.

5489 Rascoe, Lavon. "An Interview with Faulkner," WestR, 15 (Summer, 1951), 300-305.
Faulkner explained the purpose of the chapter arrangement in The Wild Palms.

5490 Redman, Ben Ray. "Faulkner's Double Novel," SatRL, 19 (January 21, 1939), 1, 5.
"... Faulkner's style has seldom served him better than it has in many passages of this novel."

5491 Reed, John Q. "Theme and Symbol in Faulkner's 'Old Man,'" Educational Leader, 21, #3 (January, 1958), 25-31.

5492 Reeves, Carolyn H. "The Wild Palms: Faulkner's Chaotic Cosmos," MissQ, 20 (Summer, 1967), 148-157.
Feels that the imagery of the novel creates a timeless, chaotic world.

5493 Richards, Lewis. "Sex Under The Wild Palms and a Moral Question," ArQ, 28 (Winter, 1972), 326-332.

5494 Richardson, H. Edward. "The 'Hemingwaves' in Faulkner's Wild Palms," MFS, 4 (Winter, 1958-59), 357-360.
Cf., W. R. Moses. "'Water, Water Everywhere': 'Old Man' and A Farewell to Arms," MFS, 5 (1959), 172-174.

5495 Richardson, Kenneth E. Force and Faith in the Novels of William Faulkner. The Hague: Mouton, 1967, pp. 67-70, 96-99, 117-118.

5496 Richardson, Maurice. "The Wild Palms," Books of the Month, 9 (April, 1939), 23.

5497 Riedel, F. C. "Faulkner as Stylist," SAQ, 56 (Autumn, 1957), 462-479.

5498 Robinson, Ted. "Some of Faulkner's Best and Worst Found in The Wild Palms," Cleveland Plain Dealer (January 22, 1939), All Feature Sec., 2.

5499 R[oueche], B[erton]. "Faulkner's Desperate Love Story," Kansas City Star (January 21, 1939), 14.

5500 Rower, Ann Doniger. "Work in Counterpoint: The Wild Palms," DAI, 35 (Columbia: 1974), 6731A.

5501 Scott-James, Marie. "Highbrow Melodrama," London Mercury, 39 (April, 1939), 647.

5502 Selby, John. "Wild Palms," Ohio State Journal (Columbus), (January 29, 1939), 2-B.

5503 Silhol, Robert. "Interrogation sur la constitution de The Wild Palms," RANAM, 9 (1976), 35-56.

5504 Slatoff, Walter J. "Wild Palms," Quest for Failure. Ithaca: Cornell U.P., 1960; 2nd pr., 1961, pp. 205-208.

5505 Snelling, Paula. "Out of the Gulf Stream," NGR, 4 (Spring, 1939), 24-25.

5506 Spencer, Benjamin T. "Wherefore This Southern Fiction?" SR, 47 (October-December, 1939), 500-513.

5507 Spring, Howard. "Young Doctor in a Woman's Toils," Evening Standard (March 23, 1939), 17.

5508 Stegner, Wallace. "Conductivity in Fiction," VQR, 15 (Summer, 1939), 446-447.

5509 Stein, R. E. "The World Outside Yoknapatawpha: A Study of Five Novels by William Faulkner," DA, 26 (Ohio: 1965), 2225.

5510 Stevens, George. "Wild Palms and Ripe Olives," SatRL, 19 (February 11, 1939), 8.

5511 Stone, Edward. *Voices of Despair: Four Motifs in American Literature.* Athens: Ohio U.P., 1966, pp. 69-72.

5512 Stonesifer, Richard J. "Faulkner's 'Old Man' in the Classroom," CE, 17 (February, 1956), 254-257.

5513 Straumann, Heinrich. "Dialektik der Zeitlosigheit: Zu Faulkners Roman *The Wild Palms*," NZZ (April 3, 1966).

5514 Swiggart, Peter. *The Art of Faulkner's Novels.* Austin: Texas U.P., 1962, pp. 51-59.

5515 Swinnerton, Frank. "Right Proportions," Observer (March 19, 1939), 6.

5516 Taylor, Nancy Dew. "The River of Faulkner and Mark Twain," MissQ, 16 (Fall, 1963), 191-199.
Notes parallels with earlier writings on the Mississippi River.

5517 Thompson, Ralph. "Books of the Times," NYTimes (January 19, 1939), 15.

5518 Tuck, Dorothy. *Crowell's Handbook of Faulkner.* New York: Crowell; 1964, pp. 136-142.

5519 Van Doren, Carl. "Fiction," Scribner'sM, (March, 1939), 55-56.

5520 Van Liew, James. "*The Wild Palms*," Prairie Schooner, 14 (Spring, 1940), 68-69.

5521 Vickery, Olga W. "The Odyssey of Time: *The Wild Palms*," *The Novels of William Faulkner: A Critical Interpretation.* Rev. Ed. Baton Rouge, 1964, pp. 156-165.

5522 Volpe, Edmond L. *A Reader's Guide to William Faulkner.* New York: Noonday Press, 1964, pp. 212-230.

5523 Waggoner, Hyatt H. *William Faulkner: From Jefferson to the World.* Lexington: Kentucky U.P., 1959, pp. 132-147.

5524 Watkins, Floyd C. "Faulkner's Inexhaustible Voice," *The Flesh and the Word.* Nashville: Vanderbilt U.P., 1971, pp. 234-253.

5525 ________. "William Faulkner, the Individual and the World," GaR, 14 (Fall, 1960), 238-247.

5526 Way, Brian. "William Faulkner," CritQ, 3 (Spring, 1961),

42-53.
Declares The Wild Palms "probably Faulkner's finest novel."

5527 Weigle, Edith. "There's Nothing Cheery in New Faulkner Novel," Chicago Daily Tribune (January 21, 1939), 10.

5528 "When the Dam Breaks," Time, 33 (January 23, 1939), 45-56.
"Central figure in any investigation of Southern literary life is William Faulkner."

5529 Widdows, Margharita. [The Wild Palms], The Annual Register (1939), Part II, 349.

5530 Woodward, Robert H. "Robert Jordan's Wedding/Funeral Sermon," HemN, 2 (Spring, 1972), 7-8.
Cf. George Monteiro. "Between Grief and Nothing," HemN, 1 (Spring, 1971), 13-15; and "Hemingway and Spain: A Response to Woodward," HemN, 2 (Fall, 1972), 16-17.

"THE WISHING TREE"
("The Wishing Tree," Sat. Eve. Post, 235 (April 8, 1967), 48-49, passim; repr., New York: Random House, 1967.)

5531 Adams, Phoebe. "The Wishing Tree," Atl, 220 (July, 1967), 114.
"'The Wishing Tree' is a pretty gesture which just happened to be made by William Faulkner."

5532 Anon. "Sea Changes," TLS, 66 (November 30, 1967), 1133.
Faulkner's "first and only children's book," with--"the last thing one would expect from him--a kind of sweet Victorian moral;...."

5533 Bassett, John. William Faulkner: An Annotated Checklist. New York: David Lewis, 1972, p. 315.
See for list of reviews.

5534 Bevington, Helen. "A Present for Victoria," NYTBR (May 7, 1967), Pt. 2, p. 38.

5535 Blotner, Joseph. William Faulkner: A Biography. 2 Vols. New York: Random House, 1974, I, 541-542, passim; II, 1718-1719, passim.

5536 Bolognese, Don, Illustrator. The Wishing Tree. New York: Random House, 1967; London: Chatto & Windus, 1968.

5537 ________. Illus. The Wishing Tree. Zürich: Fretz & Wasmuth. 1969.

5538 Cayton, R. F. "The Wishing Tree," LibJ, 92 (March 15, 1967), 1176.

5539 Ciardi, John. "Faulkner and Child, Faulkner and Negro," HarperM, 234 (May, 1967), 114.

5540 Coindreau, Maurice Edgar, tr. L'Arbre aux souhaits. Paris: Gallimard, 1969.

5541 Collins, Carvel, ed. New Orleans Sketches. New Brunswick, New Jersey: Rutgers U.P., 1958, p. 29.

5542 ______. William Faulkner: Early Prose and Poetry. Boston: Little, Brown & Co., 1962, p. 18.

5543 Derksen, Jan H. Vertaling. De Wensboom. Utrecht: A. Bruna, 1969.

5544 Fremont-Smith, Eliot. "Books for the Times: Questing for the Mellomax," NYTBR (April 27, 1967), 43.

5545 Gresset, Michel. "Un Faulkner feerique," NRF, 17 (September, 1969), 437-440.

5546 Jennings, Elizabeth. "Full of Magic," Spectator, 219 (November 3, 1967), 541-542.

"... Faulkner fans and the very young will gather much from this enchanting story."

5547 Lanes, S. G. "The Wishing Tree," BookW (Spring Children's Issue), (May 7, 1967), 38.

5548 LaRocque, Geraldine E. "Book Marks," EJ, 57 (May, 1968), 752.

5549 Malcolm, Janet. "The Wishing Tree," NY, 43 (December 16, 1967), 178-181.

5550 Meriwether, James B. "The Literary Career of William Faulkner. Columbia, South Carolina: South Carolina U.P., 1971, pp. 35, 87.

5551 ______. "'The Wishing Tree': The Short Fiction of William Faulkner," Proof, 1 (1971), 310.

5552 Millgate, Michael. The Achievement of William Faulkner. New York: Random House, 1966, pp. 11, 62, 298.

5553 Sullivan, Mary. "Short and Long," Listener, (October 19, 1967), 508.

5554 Sutherland, Zena. "The Wishing Tree," SatRL, 50 (May 13, 1967), 61.

"WITH CAUTION AND DISPATCH"
(Unpublished Story)

5555 Meriwether, James B. The Literary Career of William Faulkner. Columbia: South Carolina U.P., 1971, pp. 35, 87-88.

5556 _______. "'With Caution and Dispatch': The Short Fiction of William Faulkner," Proof, 1 (1971), 316-317.

5557 Putzel, Max. "Evolution of Two Characters in Faulkner's Early and Unpublished Fiction," SLJ, 5 (1973), 47-63.
Suggests that the unpublished story, "With Caution and Dispatch," was abandoned when Faulkner wrote Sartoris, although Faulkner stated that he wrote it later.

ARTICLES, ESSAYS, SKETCHES (LETTERS, POETRY, SPEECHES)

MIRRORS OF CHARTRES STREET and NEW ORLEANS SKETCHES

5558 Allen, Walter. "William Faulkner: New Orleans Sketches," NSt, 58 (August 22, 1959), 226-227.

5559 Baumwoll, Dorothy. "William Faulkner: New Orleans Sketches," BA, 32 (Summer, 1958), 260.

5560 Brooks, Cleanth. "A Note on Faulkner's Early Attempts at the Short Story," SSF, 10 (Fall, 1973), 381-388.
Considers the literary influences to be found in Faulkner's early sketches.

5561 Campbell, Harry Modean. [New Orleans Sketches], SAQ, 57 (1957-58), 518-519.

5562 Collins, Carvel, ed. Introduction. New Orleans Sketches. New Brunswick, New Jersey: Rutgers U.P., 1958; revised ed. New York: Random House, 1968.

5563 _______. Mirrors of Chartres Street. Review. NYTBR (February 7, 1954), 4.

5564 _______. "Nota," New Orleans. Milano: Il Saggiatore, 1959, pp. 7-12.
Excerpt from preface to New Orleans Sketches.

5565 Corbett, Edward P. J. [New Orleans Sketches], America (September 28, 1957-58), 261-263. Review.

5566 "Early Faulkner," Newsweek, 50, Part 2 (December 30, 1957), 70.

5567 Fane, Vernon. [New Orleans Sketches], Sphere, 237, #3087 (May 30, 1959), 337.

5568 Garrett, George Palmer. "The Earliest Faulkner," PrS, 32 (Fall, 1958), 159-160.

5569 _______. "William Faulkner: New Orleans Sketches," GaR, 14 (Summer, 1960), 215-216.

5570 Giannitrapani, Angela Minssi. "La New Orleans e la Louisian del Faulkner," Annali Instituto Universitario Orientale, 2 (1959), 265-339.

5571 Greacen, Robert. [New Orleans Sketches], Daily Telegraph (May 29, 1959).

5572 Howell, Elmo. "William Faulkner's New Orleans," LaHist, 7 (Summer, 1966), 229-240.

5573 Kane, Harnette T. "Faulkner's Early Work Gave Hints," Washington Post (August 10, 1958), E-7.

5574 Kazin, Alfred. "Faulkner Forecast," NYTBR (March 2, 1958), 4-5.

5575 Lloyd, James Barlow. "Humours Characterization and the Tradition of the Jonsonian Comedy of Manners in William Faulkner's Early Fiction: New Orleans Sketches, Soldiers' Pay and Mosquitoes," DAI, 36 (Mississippi: 1975), 4493A.

5576 Lombardo, Agostino. "William Faulkner. Mirrors of Chartres Street," Lo Spettatore Italiano, 8 (September, 1955), 374-375. (A modified version of this article included in "Il primo e l'ultimo Faulkner," Realismo e simbolismo. Roma: Edizioni di Storia e Letteraturea, 1957, pp. 207-221.)

5577 Meriwether, James B. The Literary Career of William Faulkner. Columbia: South Carolina U.P., 1971, pp. 115-116, passim.

5578 _______. "William Faulkner: A Checklist," PULC, 18 (Spring, 1957), 143-144.

5579 Miller, Karl. "Creole Mumbo," Spectator, #6831 (May 29, 1959), 785.

5580 Nishizaki, Ichiro, ed. Notes. New Orleans Sketches. Tokyo: Hokuseido Press, 1956.

5581 O'Connor, William Van. Introduction. Mirrors of Chartres Street. Minneapolis: Minnesota U.P., 1953.

5582 Phillips, Eric. [New Orleans Sketches], The Writer (August, 1959), 37-38.

5583 Polk, Noel. "'Hong Li' and Royal Street: The New Orleans Sketches in Manuscript," MissQ, 26 (Summer, 1973), 394-395.
Provides the text of a brief piece, "Hong Li," which Faulkner added to the copy he made in 1926 of the sketches entitled "New Orleans," which he had published in the Double Dealer in 1925.

5584 ________. "'Hong Li' and Royal Street: The New Orleans Sketches in Manuscript," A Faulkner Miscellany. James B. Meriwether, ed. Jackson, Miss.: Mississippi U.P., 1974, pp. 143-144.

5585 Poore, Charles. "Books of the Times," NYTimes (April 1, 1958), C-29.

5586 Ridgely, Joseph V. [New Orleans Sketches], MLN, 74 (February, 1959), 175-176.

5587 Ross, J. Maclaren. [New Orleans Sketches], Punch, 237 (August 26, 1959), 86-87.

5588 Salmaggi, Cesare, tr. New Orleans. Milano: Il Saggiatore, 1959.

5589 Schmidt, Arno, tr. New Orleans; Skizzen und Erzählungen. Stuttgart: Henry Goverts Verlag, 1962.

5590 Smart, George K. "Appendix C: Mirrors of Chartres Street," Religious Elements in Faulkner's Early Novels. Coral Gables: Miami U.P., 1965, pp. 139-144.

5591 TLS, [New Orleans Sketches], #2993 (July 10, 1959), 408.

5592 Urquhart, Fred. Time and Tide, 40, #27 (July 4, 1959), 749.

5593 Ziolkowski, Theodore. Fictional Transfigurations of Jesus. Princeton: Princeton U.P., 1972, p. 170.

SALMAGUNDI

5594 Romaine, Paul, ed. Introduction. Salmagundi. Milwaukee: Casanova Press, 1932.
Contained essays and poems by Faulkner which had previously appeared in magazines.

"THE HILL"

("The Hill," Mississippian (March 10, 1922), 1, 2.)

5595 Adams, Richard P. ["The Hill"] Faulkner: Myth and Motion. Princeton: Princeton U.P., 1968, pp. 23-24.

5596 Collins, Carvel, ed. William Faulkner: Early Prose and Poetry. Boston: Little, Brown & Co., 1962, pp. 90-92, 131-132.

5597 Gresset, Michel. "Faulkner's 'The Hill,'" SLJ, 6 (Spring, 1974), 3-18.
Considers "The Hill," one of Faulkner's first publications, as the germ of many of his stories.

5598 Meriwether, James B., ed. "Nympholepsy," MissQ, 26 (Summer, 1973), 403-409.
Faulkner's expansion of "The Hill," published in The Mississippian, undergraduate newspaper at Mississippi University.

5599 _______. "The Short Fiction of William Faulkner," Proof, 1 (1971), 302.

5600 Millgate, Michael. The Achievement of William Faulkner. New York: Random House, 1966, p. 12.

5601 Momberger, Philip. "A Reading of Faulkner's 'The Hill,'" SLJ, 9 (Spring, 1977), 16-29.

5602 Richardson, H. Edward. William Faulkner: The Journey to Self-Discovery. Columbia: Missouri U.P., 2nd pr., 1970, pp. 99-103, 111-112.

"MISSISSIPPI"
("Mississippi," Holiday, 15 (April, 1954), 33-47; revised for prelude to "Race at Morning" in Big Woods, 1955.)

5603 Ehrlich, Arnold, ed. "Mississippi," The Beautiful Country. New York: Viking, 1970, pp. 36-38.
Excerpt from "Mississippi" in Holiday version.

5604 Fadiman, Clifton. Introduction. "Mississippi," Ten Years of Holiday. New York: Simon & Schuster, 1956, pp. 368-389.

5605 Hicks, Granville. "Faulkner on Faulkner," SatRL, 49 (January 8, 1966), 77-78.
Considers "Mississippi" as "a piece of writing that is as good as anything Faulkner did in the last two decades of his life."

5606 Meriwether, James B. "Faulkner's 'Mississippi,'" MissQ, 25 (Spring, 1972), Supplement, 15-23.
Calls "Mississippi" an "undeservedly neglected little masterpiece."

5607 _______, ed. "Mississippi," Essays, Speeches, and Public

Letters by William Faulkner. New York: Random House, 1966, p. 37.

5608 _______. "'Mississippi,' The Short Fiction of William Faulkner," Proof, 1 (1971), 304.

5609 Millgate, Michael. The Achievement of William Faulkner. New York: Random House, 1966, pp. 15, 39, 213, 253, 300.

5610 "Mississippi," American Panorama East of the Mississippi. A Holiday Magazine Book. Garden City: Doubleday. 1961, pp. 443-465.

5611 Smith, Beverley E. "A Note on Faulkner's 'Greenbury Hotel,'" MissQ, 24 (Summer, 1971), 297-298.
Notes that "Mississippi" opens with the statement that Mississippi begins in the lobby of a Memphis, Tennessee, hotel, and suggests the analogy to the "Greenbury Hotel" in a passage in Knight's Gambit.

OTHER SKETCHES

5612 Anon. "Topics of the Time," NYTimes (August 10, 1955), 24.

5613 Collins, Carvel. Early Prose and Poetry. Boston: Little, Brown & Co., 1962, passim.

5614 Commins, Saxe, ed. The Faulkner Reader. New York: Random House, 1954, passim.

5615 Fadiman, Clifton. "Party of One," Holiday, 18 (December, 1955), 6-19.

5616 Gresset, Michel. "Faulkner Essayiste," NRF, 15 (1967), 309-313.

5617 "Growing Myth," Time, 87 (February 11, 1966), 90f.

5618 Meriwether, James B., ed. "And Now What's To Do," MissQ, 26 (Summer, 1973), 399-402.
Copy of two-page manuscript of unfinished piece by Faulkner found in 1970 at Rowanoak.

5619 _______. "Early Notices of Faulkner by Phil Stone and Louis Cochran," MissQ, 17 (Summer, 1964), 136-164.

5620 _______, ed. Essays, Speeches and Public Letters of William Faulkner. New York: Random House, 1965. Traduit de l'anglais par J. et L. Breant. Paris: Gallimard, 1969.

5621 Millgate, Michael. "Faulkner on the Literature of the First World War," MissQ, 26 (Summer, 1973), 387-393.

5622 Runyan, Harry. "Faulkner's Non-Fiction Prose," FS, 3 (Winter, 1954), 67-69.

AWARDS

NOBEL PRIZE

(Speech of Acceptance upon the Award of the Nobel Prize for Literature, Delivered in Stockholm on December 10, 1950.)

5623 Adams, J. Donald. "Speaking of Books," NYTBR (February 18, 1951), 2.

5624 Alexander, Sidney. "The Nobel Prize Comes to Mississippi: How Yoknapatawpha County Sees Its Author," Commentary 12 (Summer, 1951), 176-180.

5625 Anderson, Charles. "Faulkner's Moral Center," EA, 7 (January, 1954), 48-58.
Finds the principles announced by Faulkner in his Nobel Prize acceptance speech are the moral center of his major novels.

5626 Anon. "Controversy Has Been Stirred Often by Words of New Nobel Prize Winners," Kansas City Star (November 13, 1950), 22.

5627 Anon. "Faulkner Back from Sweden," NYTimes (December 18, 1950), 33.

5628 Anon. "Faulkner Off for Nobel Prize," NYTimes (December 9, 1950), 9.

5629 Anon. "Faulkner to Use Prize for Welfare of South," NYTimes (December 4, 1950), 26.

5630 Anon. "Faulkner's Rating by Critics Is High," NYTimes (November 11, 1950), 10.

5631 Anon. "Foreign News," Time (November 20, 1950), 29.

5632 Anon. "Four Americans Get Their Nobel Prizes," NYTimes (December 11, 1950), 10.

5633 Anon. "Honored," Newsweek (November 20, 1950), 64.

5634 Anon. "Off to Receive the Nobel Peace Prize," NYTimes (November 28, 1950), 10.

5635 Anon. "The Winner," Newsweek, 36 (December 11, 1950), 96.

5636 Archer, H. Richard. "The Writings of William Faulkner: A Challenge to the Bibliographer," PBSA, 50 (3rd Qt., 1956), 229-242.
Gives an account of the differing versions of the Nobel Prize Speech.

5637 Axelsson, George. "Faulkner Gets Nobel Prize," NYTimes (November 11, 1950), 1, 10.

5638 Barger, James. William Faulkner, Modern American Novelist and Nobel Prize Winner. D. Steve Rahmas, ed. (Outstanding Personalities Series, #63) Charlotteville, N.Y.: SamHar Press, 1973.

5639 Beck, Warren. "Faulkner Versus Hemingway," Milwaukee Journal (December 24, 1950), V, 4.

5640 Bookwright. "Nobel Prize Winner and Some Ghosts," NYHTB (December 3, 1950), 52.

5641 Breit, Harvey. "Faulkner Uneasy in His Nobel Role," NYTimes (December 8, 1950), 27.

5642 Brion, Marcel. "Les prix Nobel: Bertrand Russell et William Faulkner," RDM (1 decembre 1950), 529.

5643 Cerf, Bennett. "Trade Winds: In Case You Missed," SatRL, 34 (February 3, 1951), 4-5.
Reprint of Nobel Prize Speech as given in NYHTB, January 14, 1951.

5644 Clêment, Danielle. "Faulkner, prix Nobel," TH, No. 2 (fevrier 1951), 122.

5645 Coindreau, Maurice E. "Deux prix Nobel: Faulkner, Mauriac," Bulletin de la societê des professeurs français en Amêrique (janvier 1953), 11-15.

5646 ________. "William Faulkner: prix Nobel de littêrature," France-Amêrique, 236 (26 novembre 1950), 9.

5647 Coughlan, Robert. "The Nobel Prize," The Private World of William Faulkner. New York: Harper, 1954, pp. 131-138.

5648 Downing, Francis. "An Eloquent Man," Cw (December 15, 1950), 255-258.

5649 Duffield, Marcus. "Nobel Literature Prizes," NYHTB (November 12, 1950), II, 1.

5650 Edwards, C. H. "A Hawthorne Echo in Faulkner's Nobel Prize Acceptance Speech," NConL, 1 (March, 1971), 4-5.

5651 Erval, François. "Faulkner après le Prix Nobel," TM, 8 (June, 1953), 2024-2030.

5652 "Faulkner and Russell Win Nobel Prizes," PubW, 158 (November 18, 1950), 2207.

5653 Faulkner, William. "I Decline to Accept the End of Man," NYHTB (January 14, 1951), 5.
H. Richard Archer, (PBSA, 50 (1956), 237), said this was the earliest printing of the acceptance speech which he had seen.

5654 _______. "Man Will Prevail," Great Essays by Nobel Prize Winners. Leo Hamalian and E. L. Volpe, eds. New York: Noonday, 1960, pp. 84-85.

5655 French, Warren G., and Walter E. Kidd, eds. Introduction. American Winners of the Nobel Literary Prize. Norman: Oklahoma U.P., 1968, pp. 3-15.

5656 Geismar, Maxwell. "William Faulkner: Before and After the Nobel Prize," American Moderns: From Rebellion to Conformity. New York: Hill & Wang, 1958, pp. 91-106.

5657 Goldstein, Melvin. "A Source for Faulkner's 'Nobel Prize Speech of Acceptance': or, Two Versions of a Single Manifesto," BSTCF, 4 (Spring, 1963), 78-80.
Finds parellels in Dylan Thomas's "In My Craft and Sullen Art."

5658 Grenzmann, Wilhelm. Nobelpreisträger William Faulkner: sein Weg und seine Dichtung," Universitas, 14 (September, 1959), 909-920.

5659 Hellstrom, Gustaf. "Nobelpriset i litteratur för år 1949," Le Prix Nobel en 1950. Stockholm: P. A. Norstedt & Söner, 1951, pp. 47-50; translation, pp. 51-53.

5660 Hoffman, Frederick J. "Part Two: The Nobel Prize and the Achievement of Status," William Faulkner: Three Decades of Criticism. Frederick J. Hoffman and Olga Vickery, eds. East Lansing: Michigan State U.P., 1960, pp. 26-50.

5661 _______. "William Faulkner," American Winners of the Nobel Literary Prize. Warren G. French and Walter E. Kidd, eds. Norman: Oklahoma U.P., 1968, pp. 138-157.

5662 Hunter, Marjorie. "49 Nobel Prize Winners Honored at White House," NYTimes (April 30, 1962), 1, L-19.

5663 Hutchens, John K. "Nobel Matters," NYHTBR (November 26, 1950), 3.

5664 Jacoël, L., tr. "Je me refuse à admettre la fin de l'homme," Profils, 1 (octobre 1952), 239-240.

5665 LaGanipote. "Les prix Nobel," LF (16 novembre 1950), 3.

5666 Lalou, René. "Les gêmeaux du Nobel," NL (16 novembre 1950), 1.

5667 Lebesque, Morvan. "William Faulkner, prix Nobel de littêrature," Carrefour (14 novembre 1950), 9; Climats (23 novembre 1950), 8.

5668 MacLeish, Archibald. "Faulkner and the Responsibility of the Artist," HA, 135 (November, 1951), 18-43.
Notes the positive response to Faulkner's Nobel Prize speech.

5669 ________. "Faulkner at Stockholm," _A Continuing Journey._ Boston: Houghton Mifflin, 1968, pp. 163-167.

5670 Meriwether, James B. "A. E. Housman and Faulkner's Nobel Prize Speech: A Note," JAmS, 4 (February, 1971), 247-248.
"Faulkner's image of griefs, ... is not only bolder than Housman's grieving flesh; he chose to leave it ambiguous."

5671 ________. _Essays, Speeches and Public Letters of William Faulkner._ New York: Random House, 1966, _passim_.

5672 Merwin, William S. "William Faulkner." _Nobel Prize Winners._ London: Arco, 1957, pp. 43-60.

5673 "Nobel Prize Acceptance Speech," Writer, 64 (June, 1951), 180.

5674 O'Connor, William Van. "The Right of Responsibility," _The Tangled Fire of William Faulkner._ Minneapolis: Minnesota U.P., 1954, pp. 146-149.

5675 Poore, Charles J. "Books of the Times," NYTimes (November 16, 1950), 29.

5676 Rosenfeld, Isaac. "On the Nobel Novelist," NR, 127 (August 4, 1952), 10-19.

5677 Smith, Harrison. "The Nobel Winners," SatRL, 33 (November 25, 1950), 20-21.

5678 Solomon, Eric. "Joseph Conrad, William Faulkner, and the Nobel Prize Speech," N&Q, 14 (July, 1967), 247-248.

5679 Stavrou, Constantine Nicholas. "Ambiguity in Faulkner's Affirmation," Personalist, 40 (Spring, 1959), 166-177.

5680 "Sweden's Nobel Prize Awards," Time, 56 (November 20, 1950), 29.

5681 "La voix du poète," [discourse Nobel], Liberté de l'Esprit (mars 1951), 68.

5682 Wegelin, Christof. "'Endure' and 'Prevail': Faulkner's Modification of Conrad," N&Q, 21 (October, 1974), 375-376.

5683 William, Cecil B. "William Faulkner and the Nobel Prize Awards," FS, 1 (Summer, 1952), 17-19.

5684 "William Faulkner, Prix Nobel de Littérature," Aspects de la France (11 novembre 1950), 2.

OTHER AWARDS

5685 Anon. "Academy Elects 4 to Membership," NYTimes (November 24, 1948), 44. [American Academy of Arts and Letters]

5686 Anon. "Book Group is Honored," NYTimes (May 12, 1954), 37.

5687 Anon. "Faulkner and Morison Are Lauded," NYTimes (February 27, 1962), 24.
Faulkner and Samuel Eliot Morison given medals of the National Institute of Arts and Letters.

5688 Anon. "Faulkner, Arvin, Stevens Honored by Publishers as Best U.S. Authors," NYTimes (March 7, 1951), 30.
The National Book Award.

5689 Anon. "Faulkner Honored in Athens," NYTimes (March 19, 1957), 19.

5690 Anon. "Faulkner to Receive the Howells Medal," NYTimes (April 26, 1950), 27.

5691 Anon. "Faulkner Wins O. Henry Prize," PubW (December 2, 1939), 2074.

5692 Anon. "National Book Award," NYTimes (January 26, 1955), 24.

5693 Anon. "O. Henry Award Winners," PubW (November 19, 1949), 2142.

5694 Anon. "Pulitzer Prizes," NYTimes (May 3, 1955), 30.

5695 Anon. "Three Literary Awards," NYTimes (March 14, 1951), 32.

5696 Archer, H. Richard. "The Writings of William Faulkner: A Challenge to the Bibliographer," PBSA, 50 (3rd Qt., 1956), 229-242.

5697 Bond, Alice Dixon. "National Book Awards," Boston Sunday Herald (February 6, 1955), I, 6.

5698 Coindreau, Maurice E. "Les Prix Pulitzer," Larousse mensuel, 43° année, Tome XII, Numéro 429 (mai 1950).

5699 Hohenberg, John. The Pulitzer Prizes: A History of Awards in Books, Drama, Music, and Journalism, Based on the Private Files over Six Decades. New York and London: Columbia U.P., 1974, pp. 258-259, passim.

5700 "National Book Award Address," SatRL, 45 (July 28, 1962), 25.

5701 North, Sterling. "Faulkner Gets Howells Medal," NY World-Telegram & Sun (May 5, 1950), 30.

5702 Schott, Webster. "Pulitzer Award to Faulkner Brings Comment, Right Writer, Wrong Book," Kansas City Star (May 19, 1955), 40.

5703 Smith, Henry. "More Gold Medals," SatRL, 34 (March 17, 1951), 22-23.
Faulkner's reception of the National Book Award for The Collected Stories (1950).

5704 Stuckey, William Joseph. The Pulitzer Prize Novels: A Critical Backward Look. Norman: Oklahoma U.P., 1966, passim.

COLLECTIONS OF MANUSCRIPTS AND MATERIALS

5705 Anon. "Blotner Publishes Book Cataloging Faulkner's Prize-Winning Library," Cavalier Daily (February 10, 1965).

5706 Anon. "Exhibit Opens at Princeton," Charlottesville Daily Progress (May 10, 1957), 13.

5707 Anon. "Faulkner Catalogue Is Planned," Richmond Times-Dispatch (December 10, 1959).

5708 Anon. "University of Virginia to Get Faulkner's Literary Papers," NYTimes (August 4, 1962), 19.

5709 Archer, H. Richard. "Collecting Faulkner Today," FS, 1 (Fall, 1952), 42-43.

5710 Capps, Jack L. "West Point's William Faulkner Room," GaR, 20 (Spring, 1966), 3-8.

5711 ________, ed. The William Faulkner Collection at West Point and the Faulkner Concordances. West Point, New York: U.S. Military Academy, 1974.

5712 Cofield, Jack. William Faulkner: The Cofield Collection. Lawrence Wells, ed. Introduction by Carvel Collins. Oxford, Miss.: Yoknapatawpha Pr., 1978.

5713 Gribbin, Daniel V. "Stories and Articles by William Faulkner in the Rare Book Room Collection of the University of North Carolina Library," Bookmark, n.v. (September, 1972), 23-27.

5714 Langford, Gerald. "Insights into the Creative Process: The Faulkner Collection at the University of Texas," Proceedings of the Comparative Literature Symposium. Vol. IV. William Faulkner: Prevailing Verities and World Literature. Wolodymyr T. Zyla and Wendell M. Aycock, eds. Lubbock: Interdept. Comm. on Comp. Lit. Texas Tech U., 1973, pp. 115-133.

5715 Massey, Linton R. William Faulkner, "Man Working;" 1919-1962: A Catalogue of the William Faulkner Collections at the University of Virginia. Charlottesville: Virginia U.P., 1968.

Lists extensive Faulkner material housed at the University of Virginia.

5716 Meriwether, James B. "Awards and Public Career," The Literary Career of William Faulkner. Princeton, New Jersey: Princeton University Library, 1961; Columbia: South Carolina U P., 1971, pp. 49-54.

5717 ________. "The Literary Career of William Faulkner: Catalogue of an Exhibition," PULC, 21 (Spring, 1960), 111-164.

Includes twenty-one plates showing some of the important pieces in the 1957 Princeton University Library exhibition.

5718 ________, comp. William Faulkner: An Exhibition of Manuscripts. Austin: Texas University, October 15, 1959.

Catalogue of rare Faulkner material at the Research Center of the University.

5719 ________. "William Faulkner's Own Collection of His Books in 1959," A Faulkner Miscellany. James B. Meriwether, ed. Jackson, Mississippi: Mississippi U.P., 1974, pp. 139-141.

5720 Millgate, Michael. The Achievement of William Faulkner. New York: Random House, 1966, passim.
Many references to various collections.

5721 "New and Notable: The William Faulkner Collection," PULC, 18 (1957), 166-167.

5722 Nichols, Lewis. "Foundation," NYTBR (January 29, 1961), 8.

5723 Petersen, Carl. Each in Its Ordered Place: A Faulkner Collector's Notebook. Ann Arbor: Ardis Publisher, 1975.
Catalogues and describes the results of twenty-five years of collecting Faulkneriana.

5724 Polk, Noel. "'Hong Li' and Royal Street: The New Orleans Sketches in Manuscript," MissQ, 26 (Summer, 1973), 394-395.

5725 Pruett, D. F. "Papers of John Faulkner," MVC Bul, 3 (Fall, 1970), 81-84.
Papers of the author of My Brother Bill are now in the Mississippi Valley Collection of the Brister Library at Memphis State University.

5726 Szladits, Lola L. New in the Berg Collection, 1970-1972. New York: New York Public Library, 1973.

5727 Watterson, John. "Faulkner Exhibit Staged in Alderman Library," Cavalier Daily (October 21, 1959), 1, 4.

5728 "William Faulkner," Wilson Library Bulletin, 4 (February, 1930), 252.

5729 "The William Faulkner Collection," Serif (October 1, 1964), 31.

INTERVIEWS

5730 Anon. "Doom," NY, 29 (February 28, 1953), 18-20.

5731 Anon. "A Novelist on His Art," TLS (June 1, 1956), 329.
On Jean Stein's interview.

5732 Anon. "Oxford Man," NY (November 28, 1931).

5733 Anon. "Slavery Better for the Negro, Says Faulkner," NYHT (November 14, 1931).

5734 Arban, Dominique. "Interview de William Faulkner," FL, [5-6] (December 16, 1950), 1.

5735 Ashraf, S. A. "Faulkner in '57," Venture, 1, (March, 1960), 13-17.
While living in Charlottesville, Faulkner was interviewed on various topics.

5736 Baker, John F., ed. "Interview: Author of Faulkner Biography," PubW, 205 (April 1, 1974), 6-7.
Interview of Joseph Blotner, author of the two-volume Faulkner biography.

5737 Beale, Betty. "William Faulkner and Senator Mundt Attend A. Burks Summers' Big Party," Washington Evening Star (June 14, 1954), 3-B.

5738 Bouvard, Loïc. "Conversation with William Faulkner," MFS, 5 (Winter, 1959-60), 361-364, tr. by Henry Dan Piper.
Interview originally appeared in Bulletin de l'association amicale France-Amerique (January, 1954), 23-29.

5739 Breit, Harvey. Interview. NYTB (May 6, 1956), 8.

5740 ________. [Interview with Faulkner] NYTBR (January 30, 1955), 4, 12; repr., The Writer Observed. Cleveland, New York: World, 1956.

5741 Brennan, Dan. "Faulkner Revisited," WriterD, 48 (February, 1968), 50f.

5742 ________. "Journey South," UKCR, 22 (Autumn, 1955), 11-16.
Memoir of a visit to Faulkner in 1940.
Cf., Russell Roth. "The Brennan Papers," Perspective, 2 (Summer, 1949), 47.

5743 Brière, Annie. "Dernière rencontre avec Faulkner," NL, 40 (12 juillet 1962), 3.

5744 ________. "Faulkner parle," NL, No. 1466 (October 6, 1955), 1, 6.

5745 [Cantwell, Robert] "When the Dam Breaks," Time, 33 (January 23, 1939), 45-48.

5746 Chapsal, Madeleine. "A Lion in the Garden," Reporter, 13 (November 3, 1955), 40.
An account of Faulkner at a Gallimard cocktail party in Paris.

5747 Chaze, Elliott. "Visit to a Two-Finger Typist," Life, 51 (July 14, 1961), 11-12.
Cf., "Letters to the Editor," Life, 52 (August 4, 1961),--containing comments on "Visit to a Two-Finger Typist."

5748 Claxton, Simon. "William Faulkner: An Interview," Cate Review (June, 1962), 6.
Simon Claxton, an English boy studying at the Cate School in California, interviewed Faulkner in Oxford, March 23, 1962.

5749 Collins, Carvel. "On William Faulkner," Talks with Authors. Charles F. Madden, ed. Carbondale: Southern Ill. U.P., 1968, pp. 39-55.
Transcription of a telephone interview.

5750 Cowley, Malcolm, ed. "The Cosmos of the Artist," SatRL, 45 (July 28, 1962), 18-21.
Viking Press gave permission to reprint excerpts from the interview which were included in Writers at Work.

5751 _______, ed. Writers at Work: The Paris Review Interviews. New York: Viking Press, 1957, 1958, 1967, pp. 139-140.

5752 Crisler, B. R. "Film Gossip of the Week," NYTimes (August 2, 1936), X, 3.
Reports Nunnally Johnson's account of Faulkner's interview with Mr. Zanuck.

5753 Dominicis, A. M. "An Interview with Faulkner," FS, 3 (Summer-Autumn, 1954), 33-37; Elizabeth Nissen, tr.

5754 _______. "Scrivo perchè mi piace, dice William Faulkner," FLe, 9 (February 14, 1954), 1-2.

5755 Emerson, O. B. "Faulkner and His Friend: An Interview with Emily W. Stone," Comment, 10 (Spring, 1971), 31-37.

5756 Fasel, Ida. "A 'Conversation' Between Faulkner and Eliot," MissQ, 20 (Fall, 1968), 195-206.

5757 Faulkner, William. "Mr. Faulkner Writes," Reporter 14 (April 19, 1956), 7.
Cf., Russell Warren Howe, Reporter 14 (March 22, 1956), 18-20; and 14 (April 19, 1956), 7. In Faulkner's letter concerning the Howe interview, he states: "The South is not armed to resist the United States that I know of, because the United States is neither going to force the South nor permit the South to resist or recede either."

5758 "Faulkner in Manila," Report of Interview. "Faulkner on Truth and Freedom. [A Pamphlet]. Published by Philippine Writers Association, 1956.

5759 Ferris, William R., Jr. "William Faulkner and Phil Stone: An Interview with Emily Stone," SAQ, 68 (Autumn, 1969), 536-542.

An interview with Stone's widow who discusses her husband's friendship with Faulkner.

5760 Geduld, Harry M., ed. Authors on Film. Bloomington: Indiana U. P., 1972, pp. 198-199, 203-205.
Excerpts from the Paris Review as to Faulkner's Hollywood experiences.

5761 Grenier, Cynthia. "The Art of Fiction: An Interview with William Faulkner--September, 1955," Accent, 16 (Summer, 1956), 167-177.

5762 ________. "Dialogue de William Faulkner avec Cynthia Greiner," TR, (January, 1957), 34-36.
An earlier version of the article in Accent, 16 (1956), 167-177. Cf., Mario Picchi. "William Faulkner si confessa," FLe, #3 (January 20, 1957), 3.

5763 Guth, Paul. "En Remontant avec Faulkner les chemins de la vie et ceux de l'écriture," FL, 10 (October 8, 1955), 3.

5764 Gwynn, Frederick L., and Joseph L. Blotner, eds. Faulkner in the University: Class Conferences at the University of Virginia, 1957-1958. Charlottesville: Virginia U. P., 1959.

5765 ________. "Faulkner in the University," CE, 19 (October, 1957), 1-6.

5766 ________. "William Faulkner on Dialect," UVM, 2, i (Winter, 1958), 32-37.

5767 Heuvel, Jean Stein Vanden. "The Art of Fiction," Paris Review, 12 (Spring, 1956).
Slightly enlarged version in Writers at Work. Malcolm Cowley, ed. New York: 1958.

5768 Hilleret, René. "Colloques en Virginie avec William Faulkner," RdP, 2 (February, 1964).

5769 Howard, Edwin. "Foot-note on Faulkner," DeltaR, 2 (July-August, 1965), 37, 80.
Interview with Shelby Foote.

5770 Howard, Leon. Literature and the American Tradition. New York: Doubleday, 1960, passim.

5771 Howe, Russell Warren. "Letter," NSt, (November 30, 1962), 776.

5772 ________. "Nobel Prizeman on Crisis in the Deep South," Sunday Times (March 4, 1956).
Faulkner was interviewed on February 21, 1956, in the New York offices of his publishers by Russell Warren

Howe, then New York correspondent for the London Sunday Times. A longer and somewhat different version appeared in Reporter, March 22, 1956.

5773 ______. "A Talk with William Faulkner," Reporter, 14 (March 22, 1956), 18-20.

5774 ______. [Letter relative to the interview above], Reporter 14 (April 19, 1956), 7.
Cf., William Faulkner's letter relative to the interview, Reporter 14 (April 19, 1956), 7. Also, Howe's statement as to interview in Time, 67 (April 23, 1956), 12.

5775 Hutchens, John K. "On the Books," NYHTBR (October 31, 1948), 6.

5776 Jelliffe, Robert A., ed. Preface. Faulkner at Nagano. Tokyo: Kenkyusha, Ltd., 1956.
Transcript of Faulkner's interviews, colloquies, and statements during his visit to Japan, August, 1955.

5777 La Capria, Raffaele. "Faulkner raccontato da lui stesso," Tempo Presente, 6 (January, 1961), 21-39.
Mario Materassi calls this "a well documented collage of Faulkner's recorded interviews." Faulkner Criticism in Italy," Italian Q, 57 (1971), 76.

5778 Lambert, J. W. [Interview]. Sunday Times (July 8, 1962); see also (March 1, 1956), 7.

5779 Longstreet, Stephen. We All Went to Paris: Americans in the City of Light, 1776-1971. New York: Macmillan, 1972.
Contains an interview with Faulkner.

5780 Lopez, Guido. "Faulkner and the Horses," YR, 64 (March, 1975), 468-476; translated from Italian by Ruth Feldman.
Faulkner's visit to Italy, the interview, and Faulkner's visit to the stables of thoroughbred horses.

5781 Marcovic, Vida. "Interview with Faulkner," TSLL, 5 (Winter, 1964), 463-466.

5782 "Meet the Author--and His Editor," Books from the U.S.A., 1 (November, 1957), 504-506, 508.
An interview with Saxe Commins, executive editor, Random House.

5783 Meriwether, James B., and Michael Millgate, eds. Lion in the Garden: Interviews with William Faulkner, 1926-1962. New York: Random House, 1968.
A most valuable collection of interviews.

5784 Mok, Michael. "The Squire of Oxford," NYPost (October 17, 1939), 9.

5785 Nauman, Hilda. "How Faulkner Went His Way and I Went Mine," Esquire, 68 (December, 1967), 173-175.

5786 "A Novelist on His Art," TLS (June 1, 1956), 329.
Comment on Stein interview.

5787 Paris Review, Spring Issue, 1956, devoted to Faulkner interviews.

5788 Peavy, Charles D. "Faulkner and the Howe Interview," CLAJ, 11 (December, 1967), 117-123.
Notes the occasions Faulkner tried to correct the impression of what were taken to be racially biased statements recorded in the interview for London Sunday Times (March 4, 1956) by Russell Howe.

5789 Picchi, Mario. "William Faulkner si confessa," FLe, 3 (January 20, 1957), 3.
Cf., Cynthia Grenier. "Dialogue de William Faulkner avec Cynthia Grenier," TR (January, 1957), 34-36.

5790 Rascoe, Lavon. "An Interview with William Faulkner," WR, 15 (Summer, 1951), 300-304.

5791 Roth, Russell. "The Brennan Papers," Perspective, 2 (Summer, 1949), 47.
Cf., Dan Brennan. "Journey South," UKCR, 22 (Autumn, 1955), 11-16.

5792 Samuels, Charles Thomas. "The Lion at Bay," NR, 159 (August 31, 1968), 27-28.

5793 Saporta, Marc. "Avec Faulkner," Informations et documents (Faulkner Issue) (August 1, 1970), 30-33.

5794 Smith, Harrison. "William Faulkner vs. the Literary Conference," SatRL, 39 (July 7, 1956), 16.

5795 Smith, Henry Nash. "Writing Right Smart Fun, Says Faulkner," Dallas Morning News (February 14, 1932), IV, 2.
An account of Smith's visit in Faulkner's home.

5796 Smith, Marshall J. "Faulkner of Mississippi," Bookman, 74 (December, 1931), 411-417.

5797 ________. "Faulkner of Mississippi," Bookman, 74 (December, 1931), 411-417; a revision of "Faulkner in Seclusion, Writing Movie Script," Memphis Press-Scimitar (July 10, 1931).

5798 Stein, Jean. "The Cosmos of the Artist," SatRL, 45 (July 28, 1962), 18-21.

5799 ________. "An Interview with William Faulkner," ParisR, 12 (Spring, 1956), 28-52. Repr., in Writers at Work. New York: 1958; Three Decades. East Lansing: 1960; Lion in the Garden. 1968.

5800 ________. "William Faulkner," Writers at Work: The Paris Review Interviews. Malcolm Cowley, ed. New York: Viking, 1958, pp. 122-141.

5801 "Talker," Time, 67 (May 28, 1956), 104.
Faulkner reported to have said, "The writer's only responsibility is to his art...."

5802 Thompson, Howard. "Through Faulkner's View-Finder," NYTimes (March 16, 1958), II, 7.
Interview at Princeton.

5803 Thompson, Ralph. "In and Out of Books," NYTBR (November 7, 1948), 8.

5804 Trêdant, Paul. [Interview], NL (14 decembre 1950), 1.
Le rêcit de l'interview accordêe à Paul Trêdant à New York.

5805 "Visit with the Author," Newsweek, 53 (February 9, 1959), 58.
An interview with Faulkner and a reference to the play Faulkner had "fashioned" for Ruth Ford whom he had first known "back in the 30's."

5806 Welty, Eudora. "The Art of Fiction, XLVII," ParisR, 14 (Fall, 1972), 72-97.
Report of interview containing references to Faulkner.

LETTERS

(Although the aim is to present secondary bibliography, a few Faulkner letters are listed below.)

5807 Abel, Lionel. "Lettera da New York," Tempo Presente, 1 (April, 1956), 76-78.
Reply to Faulkner's "Letter to the North."

5808 Anon. "Mr. Faulkner Exhausts the Future," Nation, 185 (October 26, 1957), 274-275.

5809 Anon. "A Note on Faulkner Letter," NYTimes (October 7, 1967), 26.

5810 Beck, Warren. "Faulkner: A Preface and a Letter," YR, 52 (Autumn, 1962), 157-160.

5811 Blotner, Joseph, ed. Selected Letters of William Faulkner. New York: Random House, 1977.
The letters cover the period 1918 to 1962.

5812 Bungert, Hans. "William Faulkner on Moby-Dick: An Early Letter," SA, 9 (1964), 371-375.
Reprints a letter by Faulkner to Fanny Butcher who published it in the Chicago Tribune (July 6, 1972), in which Faulkner stated that Moby-Dick was the book he would rather have written than any other.

5813 Coindreau, Maurice E. "Lettres étrangères: William Faulkner," NRF, 36 (June, 1931), 926-930.

5814 Collins, Wesley. "Letter to the Editor," Reporter, 14 (April 19, 1956), 7.
Concerns Russell Howe interview.

5815 Cowley, Malcolm, ed. The Faulkner-Cowley File: Letters and Memories, 1944-1962. New York: Viking, 1966.

5816 Faulkner, William. "Beyond the Machine: Man's Good Judgment," Time, 65 (January 3, 1955), 19.

5817 _______. "Faulkner's 'Ode to the Louver,'" MissQ, 27 (Summer, 1974), 333-335.
Reprint of a comic poem and letter signed "Ernest V. Simms" sent by Faulkner to Phil Stone from Paris, 1925.

5818 _______. "Letter to the North," Life, 40 (March 5, 1956), 51-52; (March 26, 1956), 19; also Reader's Digest, 68 (May, 1956), 75-78.
An important statement by Faulkner on the race problem.

5819 _______. "Mr. Faulkner Writes," Reporter, 14 (April 19, 1956), 7.
Faulkner's letter relative to the Russell Howe interview.

5820 _______. "To Unite for Freedom," NYTimes (October 13, 1957), 10-B.
"We ... may have to be the rallying point for all men, no matter what color they are or what tongue they speak, willing to federate into a community dedicated to the proposition that a community of individual free men not merely must endure, but can endure."

5821 Franklin, Malcolm. Appendix. Bitterweeds: Life with William Faulkner at Rowan Oak. Irving, Texas: Society for Study of Traditional Culture, 1977.
Contains twelve letters from Faulkner to Malcolm Franklin, 1942 to 1959.

5822 Gregory, Eileen. "Faulkner's Typescripts of The Town,"

MissQ, 26 (Summer, 1973), 361-386.
Contains reprint of Faulkner letters.

5823 Handler, M. S. "Faulkner, in Letter to Ex-Butler, Said Negro Must Learn Equality," NYTimes (August 3, 1967), 15.

5824 Hilburn, Lincoln C. "Letter to Editor," Reporter, 14 (April 19, 1956), 5-6.

5825 Krash, Otto. "Instruments and Intuition," NYTimes (January 9, 1955), IV, 8.

5826 Lerner, Max. "Scattered Gunshot, NYPost (March 16, 1956), 42.
Relative to Faulkner's "Letter to the North."

5827 Lippmann, Walter. "Mr. Faulkner's Letter," NYHT (March 8, 1956), 18.

5828 ________. "Mr. Faulkner's Letter: The Middle Road He Urges Has Not Yet Been Charted." Daily Progress (Charlottesville, Va.), (March 9, 1956), 4.
On "Letter to the North."

5829 Lyons, Richard. Faulkner on Love: A Letter to Marjorie Lyons. Fargo, N.D.: Merrykit, [1974].

5830 Mahler, Michael D. "Faulkner vs. Kunen," NYTBR (June 29, 1969), 20.

5831 Meriwether, James B. "Early Notices of Faulkner by Phil Stone and Louis Cochran," MissQ, 17 (Summer, 1964), 136-164.

5832 ________. Essays, Speeches and Public Letters of William Faulkner. New York: Random House, 1965, passim.

5833 ________. "Faulkner's Correspondence with Scribner's Magazine," Proof, 3 (1973), 253-282.
Provides letters which give important information concerning a number of Faulkner's stories in the period 1928-35.

5834 ________. "Faulkner's Correspondence with Scribner's Magazine," Proof: The Yearbook of American Bibliographical and Textual Studies. Vol. 3. Joseph Katz, ed. Columbia: South Carolina U.P., 1973, pp. 253-282.

5835 ________. "Faulkner's Correspondence with The Saturday Evening Post," MissQ, 30 (Summer, 1977), 461-475.
Letters, 1927-1931.

5836 Monaghan, William E. "Faulkner and the South," Reporter, 14 (April 19, 1956), 5.
Concerns the Russell Howe interview.

5837 O'Brien, Matthew C. "Faulkner, General Chalmers, and the Burning of Oxford," AN&Q, 12 (February, 1974), 87-88.
In a letter to the editor of the Oxford Eagle, Faulkner mistakenly blamed Chalmers whom he called a Yankee. A Confederate brigadier of the same name had apparently been an enemy of Col. William C. Falkner, William Faulkner's great-grandfather.

5838 O'Connor, William Van. The Tangled Fire of William Faulkner. Minneapolis: Minnesota U. P., 1954, p. 141.

5839 Pozner, Vladimir. "Lettre à William Faulkner et à quelques autres," Lettres Françaises (31 août 1950), 1.

5840 Richardson, Wendell A. "Letter to Editor," Reporter, 14 (April 19, 1956), 6.
Concerns the Russell Howe interview.

5841 Schweitzer, Mrs. Robert Newby. [Letter to the Editor], Reporter, 14 (April 19, 1956), 5.

5842 Steinbeck, Elaine, and Robert Wallsten, eds. A Life in Letters. New York: Viking, 1976, pp. 564-565.
Contains excerpt from a letter which Faulkner wrote to Steinbeck in response to Steinbeck's question as to how he should "comport" himself in Japan.

5843 Webb, Constance. Richard Wright: A Biography. New York: Putnam's, 1968, pp. 208-209.
Reprints excerpts from Faulkner's letter to Richard Wright relative to Native Son.

5844 Westfeldt, Gustaf R. [Letter to Editor,] Reporter, 14 (April 19, 1956), 6-7.

POETRY

A GREEN BOUGH
(New York: Smith & Haas, 1933)

5845 Anon. A Green Bough. Nation, 136 (May 17, 1933), 565.

5846 Benét, William R. [A Green Bough], SatRL, 9 (April 29, 1933), 565.

5847 Deutsch, Babett. "Poetry Out of Chaos," VQR, 8 (1932), 620.

5848 Garrett, George P. "An Examination of the Poetry of William Faulkner," William Faulkner: Four Decades of Criticism. Linda Wagner, ed. East Lansing: Michigan St. U.P., 1973, pp. 44-54.

5849 Jack, Peter Monro. A Green Bough. NYTimes (May 14, 1933), 2.

5850 Meriwether, James B. "A Green Bough," The Literary Career of William Faulkner. Columbia: South Carolina U.P., 1971, pp. 23-24.

5851 Richardson, H. Edward. "Intermezzo: A Green Bough," William Faulkner: A Journey to Self-Discovery. Columbia: Missouri U.P., 1969, pp. 104-115.

5852 Schappes, Morris U. "Faulkner as Poet: A Green Bough, by William Faulkner," Poetry, 43 (October, 1933), 48-52.

5853 Stone, Phil. Introduction. The Marble Faun and A Green Bough. Boston: The Four Seas Co., 1924, pp. 6-8.

5854 Walton, Eda Lou. Review of A Green Bough, NYHTB (April 30, 1933), 2.

THE MARBLE FAUN
(Boston: The Four Seas Co., 1924.)

5855 Anon. "The Marble Faun," Time, 86 (November 26, 1965), 110.

5856 Anon. "Notes on Rare Books," NYTimes (May 29, 1932), IV, 20.

5857 Bassett, John, ed. William Faulkner: The Critical Heritage. Boston: Routledge & Kegan Paul, 1975.
Contains reviews of The Marble Faun.

5858 Boozer, William. William Faulkner's First Book: "The Marble Faun" Fifty Years Later. Memphis: The Pigeon Roost Press, 1974.

5859 Brooks, Cleanth. "Faulkner as Poet," SLJ, 1 (December, 1968), 5-19.

5860 Daniel, Robert W. A Catalogue of the Writings of William Faulkner. New Haven: Yale U. Library, 1942, p. 7.

5861 Garrett, George P. "An Examination of the Poetry of William Faulkner," William Faulkner: Four Decades of Criticism. Linda Wagner, ed. East Lansing: Michigan State U.P., 1973, pp. 44-54.

5862 McClure, John. Review of The Marble Faun, New Orleans

Times-Picayune (January 25, 1925), Mag. Sec., p. 6; repr., in William Faulkner: The Critical Heritage. John Bassett, ed. London; Boston: Routledge & Kegan Paul, 1975, pp. 49-51.

Bassett suggests this as "most likely the first book review ever written on Faulkner."

5863 "The Marble Faun," NYTBR (January 9, 1966), 12.

5864 "The Marble Faun," SatRL (March 7, 1925), 587.

5865 "The Marble Faun," Time, 86 (November 26, 1965), 110.

5866 Meriwether, James B. "The Marble Faun," The Literary Career of William Faulkner. Columbia: South Carolina U.P., 1971, pp. 9-10, passim.

5867 _______. "Review of William Faulkner's First Book: The Marble Faun Fifty Years Later," MissQ, 28 (Summer, 1975), 393-395.

5868 Mulqueen, James E. "Horace Benbow: Avatar of Faulkner's Marbel [sic] Faun," NMW, 9 (Fall, 1976), 88-96.

5869 O'Connor, William Van. The Tangled Fire of William Faulkner. Minneapolis: Minnesota U.P., 1954, passim.

5870 Richardson, H. Edward. William Faulkner: The Journey to Self-Discovery. Columbia: Missouri U.P., 1969, pp. 47-60, passim.

5871 Stone, Phil. Introduction. The Marble Faun by William Faulkner. Boston: The Four Seas Co., 1924, pp. 6-8.

5872 Vanden Heuvel, Jean. "Faulkner's Views on South," NYTimes (October 16, 1962), 38.

OTHER POEMS

5873 Anon. "Current Poetry," LitD, 115 (March 11, 1933), 32.

5874 Anon. "William Faulkner as Poet," TLS (May 18, 1967), 420.

5875 Bassett, John, ed. William Faulkner: The Critical Heritage. Boston: Routledge & Kegan Paul, 1975.

Provides a record of contemporary response to Faulkner's prose and poetry.

5876 Benêt, William Rose. "Faulkner as Poet," SatRL, 9 (April 29, 1933), 565.

5877 Brooks, Cleanth. "Faulkner as a Poet," SLJ, 1 (December, 1968), 5-19; Shaping Joy: Studies in the Writer's Craft. New York: Harcourt, 1971, pp. 247-269.

5878 ______. "Faulkner's Poetry," William Faulkner: Toward Yoknapatawpha and Beyond. New Haven: Yale U. P., 1978, pp. 1-31.

5879 Butterworth, Keen. "A Census of Manuscripts and Typescripts of William Faulkner's Poetry," MissQ, 26 (Summer, 1973), 333-359.

5880 ______. "A Census of Manuscripts and Typescripts of William Faulkner's Poetry," A Faulkner Miscellany. James B. Meriwether, ed. Jackson, Miss.: Mississippi U. P., 1974, pp. 70-97.

5881 Collins, Carvel, ed. Introduction. William Faulkner: Early Prose and Poetry. Boston: Little, Brown & Co., 1962. Traduction et préface par Henri Thomas. Paris: Gallimard, 1966.

5882 Garrett, George P., Jr. "An Examination of the Poetry of William Faulkner," PULC, 18 (Spring, 1957), 124-135. Repr., in William Faulkner: Four Decades of Criticism. Linda Wagner, ed. East Lansing: Michigan State U. P., 1973, pp. 44-54.

5883 Hills, Rust. "The Big Trend in Little Magazines," SR, 42 (May 9, 1959), 10-11, 50.
Cf., Gerald H. Strauss. "Faulkner's First Appearance," SatRL, 42 (May 30, 1959), 25. Corrects statement of Hills as to date and title of Faulkner's first publication.

5884 Meriwether, James B., ed. "Faulkner's 'Ode to the Louver,'" MissQ, 27 (Summer, 1974), 333-335.

5885 ______. The Literary Career of William Faulkner. Columbia: South Carolina U. P., 1971, passim.

5886 Millum, Richard A. "'The Horns of Dawn': Faulkner and Metaphor," AN&Q, 11 (May, 1973), 134.
Notes that the metaphor of a cow, used for the paramour of Ike Snopes in The Hamlet, had appeared in Faulkner's last published poem, "The Flowers That Died," Contempo, 3 (June 25, 1933), 1.

5887 Peskin, S. G. "William Faulkner: A 'Failed' Poet," Unisa English Studies, 2 (May, 1969), 39-45.
Considers the influence of Wilde and Swinburne in Faulkner's poetry.

5888 Pitavy, François L. "Faulkner Poète," EA, 29 (July-September, 1976), 456-467.

5889 Raimbault, R. N. Trad. et commentaire. "Point de nymphe aux seins tumescents pour troubler." "Un jour sur une montagne adolescente," TR (janvier 1951), 38-40.

5890 Romaine, Paul. Preface. Salmagundi. Milwaukee: Casonova Pr., 1932.

5891 Runyan, Harry. "Faulkner's Poetry," FS, 3 (Summer-Autumn, 1954), 23-29.

5892 Shapiro, Karl. "Classicists All," NYTBR (January 9, 1966), 12, 14.

5893 Strauss, Gerald H. "Faulkner's First Appearance," SatRL, 42 (May 30, 1959), 25.
Says that first publication of anything by Faulkner was "L'Apres Midi d'un Faune," NR, 20 (August 6, 1919), 24. Cf., Rust Hills, SR, 42 (May 9, 1959), 10-11.

5894 Tolliver, Kenneth R. "Truth and the Poet," DeltaR, 2 (July-August, 1965), 48, 67-69.

5895 Vance, Eleanor Graham. "William Faulkner," SatRL, 32 (January 22, 1949), 30.

5896 Yonce, Margaret. "'Shot Down Last Spring': The Wounded Aviators of Faulkner's Wasteland," MissQ, 31 (Summer, 1978), 359-368.

SPEECHES

5897 Anon. "John Dos Passos Receives Gold Medal for Fiction," NYTimes (May 23, 1957), 39.
Faulkner spoke.

5898 Bradford, M. E. "Faulkner's Last Words and 'The American Dilemma,'" ModA, 16 (Winter, 1972), 77-82.
Analysis of Faulkner's "Gold Medal" speech of May 24, 1962.

5899 Colvert, James B. Review of Essays, Speeches and Public Letters by James B. Meriwether. MissQ, 19 (Summer, 1966), 154-155.

5900 Daniel, Bradford. "Faulkner on Race," Ramparts, 2 (Winter, 1963), 43-49.

5901 Grimwood, Michael. "The Self-Parodic Context of Faulkner's Nobel Prize Speech," SoR, 15 (April, 1979), 366-375.

5902 Harvard Advocate ("William Faulkner Issue"), 135 (November, 1951).
Contains Faulkner speeches.

5903 Meriwether, James B., ed. Essays, Speeches and Public Letters. New York: Random House, 1965.

5904 _______, ed. "Faulkner's Speech at the Teatro Municipal, Caracas, in 1961," MissQ, 27 (Summer, 1974), 337.
Text and explanatory note on a previously unpublished Faulkner speech.

III. GENERAL CRITICISM

5905 Aaron, Daniel. "The South in American History," The South and Faulkner's Yoknapatawpha: The Actual and the Apocryphal. Evans Harrington and Ann J. Abadie, eds. Jackson, Miss.: U.P., 1977, pp. 3-21.

5906 _______. "William Faulkner," The Unwritten War: American Writers and the Civil War. New York: Alfred A. Knopf, 1973, pp. 310-326.

5907 Abramson, Doris E. The Negro Playwrights in the American Theatre, 1925-1929. New York: Columbia U.P., 1969, passim.
Notes that the Negro image has been projected by Faulkner and others.

5908 Adamowski, Thomas H. "The Dickens World and Yoknapatawpha County: A Study of Character and Society in Dickens and Faulkner," DAI, 30 (Indiana: 1969), 2995A-96A.

5909 Adams, James Donald. "It Is a Nightmare World, Wearing a Mask of Reality," The Idea of an American Novel. Louis D. Rubin, Jr., and John Rees Moore, eds. New York: Crowell, 1961, pp. 352-254.

5910 _______. "William Faulkner," The Shape of Books to Come. New York: Viking, 1944, pp. 91-95.

5911 Adams, Percy G. "Faulkner, French Literature, and 'Eternal Verities,'" Proceedings of the Comparative Literature Symposium. Vol. 4. William Faulkner: Prevailing Verities and World Literature. Wolodymyr T. Zyla, and Wendell M. Aycock, eds. Lubbock: Interdept. Comm. on Comp. Lit. Texas Tech U., 1973, pp. 7-24.

5912 _______. "The Franco-American Faulkner," TSL, 5 (1960), 1-13.

5913 Adams, Richard P. "The Apprenticeship of William Faulkner," TSE, 12 (1962), 113-155; repr., in William Faulkner: Four Decades of Criticism. Linda W. Wagner, ed. Michigan State U.P., 1973, pp. 7-44.

5914 _______. "Faulkner and the Myth of the South," MissQ, 14 (Summer, 1961), 131-137.

5915 ________. Faulkner: Myth and Motion. Princeton: Princeton U. P., 1968.

5916 ________. "Faulkner: The European Roots," Faulkner: Fifty Years after the Marble Faun. George H. Wolfe, ed. University: Alabama U. P., 1976, pp. 21-41.

5917 ________. "The Franco-American Faulkner," TSL, 5 (1960), 1-13.

5918 ________. "Permutations of American Romanticism," SIR, 9 (Fall, 1970), 249-268.

5919 ________. "Some Key Words in Faulkner," TSE, 16 (1968), 135-148.
Notes the context of words like "doom," "terrible."

5920 Adams, Robert M. "Poetry in the Novel; or Faulkner Esemplastic," VQR, 29 (Spring, 1953), 419-434.

5921 ________. Strains of Discord: Studies in Literary Openness. Ithaca: Cornell U. P., 1958, passim.

5922 Addison, Bill Kaler. "The Past in the Works of William Faulkner," DAI, 32 (Minnesota: 1971), 2669A-70A.

5923 Aguilar, Esperanza. Yoknapatawpha, Propiedad de William Faulkner. Santiago de Chile: Editorial Universitaria, 1964.

5924 Aiken, Conrad Potter. "Inventiveness of the Richest Possible Sort," The Idea of an American Novel. Louis D. Rubin, Jr., and John Rees Moore, eds. New York: Crowell, 1961, pp. 354-359.

5925 ________. "William Faulkner: The Novel as Form," Atl, 164 (November, 1939), 650-654. Also in Aiken, Conrad. ABC: Collected Criticism from 1916 to the Present. New York: Meridian, 1958, pp. 200-207; HA, 135 (November, 1951), 13, 24-26; William Faulkner: Three Decades of Criticism. Frederick J. Hoffman and Olga Vickery, eds. East Lansing: Michigan State U. P., 1960; William Faulkner: Four Decades of Criticism. Linda W. Wagner, ed. Michigan State U. P., 1973, pp. 134-140.

5926 ________. "William Faulkner," A Reviewer's ABC. New York: Meridian Books, 1958, pp. 197-207.

5927 ________. "The Writer in Perspective," SatRL, 45 (July 28, 1962), 23.

5928 Aiken, David Hubert. "Joyce, Faulkner, O'Connor: Conceptual Approaches to Major Characters," DAI, 36 (State U. of New York at Stony Brook: 1975), 3680A-81A.

5929 Ainsa, Fernando. "En el santuario de William Faulkner," CHA, 269 (1972), 232-243.

5930 Akai, Yasumitsu. "A Study of the Negro English in William Faulkner's Works," Anglica, 4 (January, 1961), 72-90; 4 (September, 1961), 44-56.

5931 Akasofu, Tetsuji. *Kotoba to Fudo--"Shin-Hihyoka" no Faulkner ron o meguru Hihyo no Mondai.* [Language and Criticism: A Study of Faulkner] Tokyo: Kaibunsha, 1969.

5932 Albérès, R. M. "Aux sources du 'nouveau roman': L'impressionnisme anglais," RdP, 69 (May, 1962), 74-86.

5933 Aldridge, John W., ed. *Critiques and Essays on Modern Fiction, 1920-1951.* New York: Ronald Press, 1952, *passim.*

5934 _______. "The Death of the Lions," *The Devil in the Fire: Retrospective Essays on American Literature and Culture, 1951-1971.* New York: Harper's Magazine Press, 1972, pp. 142-152.

5935 _______. *In Search of Heresy.* New York: McGraw-Hill, 1956, pp. 106-107, 140-143, *passim.*

5936 _______. *Time to Murder and Create: The Contemporary Novel in Crisis.* New York: David McKay Co., 1966, *passim.*

5937 Alexander, Margaret Walker. "Faulkner and Race," in *The Maker and the Myth: Faulkner and Yoknapatawpha, 1977.* Evans Harrington and Ann J. Abadie, eds. Jackson: University Press of Miss., 1978, pp. 105-121.

5938 Alexandrescu, Sorin. "A Project in the Semantic Analysis of the Characters in William Faulkner's Work," Semiotica, 4 (1971), 37-51.

5939 _______. "Unele aspecte ale relatiilor lui W. Faulkner cu literatura europeană." [Some aspects of Faulkner's relations with European literature.] Unpub. doctoral diss., Univ. of Bucharest, 1972.

5940 _______. *William Faulkner.* Bucharest: Editura Pentru Literatura Universala, 1969.

5941 _______. "William Faulkner and the Greek Tragedy," RoR, 24 iii (1970), 102-110.

5942 Allen, Charles A. "William Faulkner: Comedy and the Purpose of Humor," ArQ, 16 (Spring, 1960), 59-69.

5943 _______. "William Faulkner's Vision of Good and Evil," PS, 10 (Summer, 1956), 236-241.
Sees Faulkner's subject as "Everyman's good and evil."

5944 Allen, Gay Wilson. "With Faulkner in Japan," AmSch, 31 (Autumn, 1962), 566-571.

5945 Allen, Michael. "Some Examples of Faulknerian Rhetoric in Ellison's Invisible Man," The Black American Writer. C. W. E. Bigsby, ed. DeLand, Florida: Everett-Edwards, 1969, I, 143-151.

5946 Allen, Walter. "Mr. Faulkner's Humanity," NS&N, 38 (October 15, 1949), 428-429.

5947 _______. The Modern Novel: In Britain and the United States. New York: E. P. Dutton, 1964, passim.

5948 _______. "The Southern Novel Between the Wars," The Novel Today. New York: Longmans, Green, 1960; Tradition and Dream. London: Phoenix House, 1964, pp. 108-137, passim.

5949 _______. "Uncle Tom's Cabin Revisited," Listener, 76 (August 11, 1966), 197-200.
Finds "raw material" of Faulkner and other novelists in Uncle Tom's Cabin.

5950 _______. The Urgent West: The American Dream and the Modern Man. New York: E. P. Dutton, 1969, passim.

5951 _______. "The Worldwide Influence of William Faulkner: Reports from Six Capitals," NYTBR (November 15, 1959), 52-53.

5952 Alpert, Hollis. "Old Times There Are Not Forgotten," SatRL, 42 (March 7, 1959), 28.

5953 Alter, Jean V. "Faulkner, Sartre, and the 'Nouveau Roman,'" Symposium, 20 (Summer, 1966), 101-112.

5954 Alter, Robert. "The New American Novel," Commentary, 60 (November, 1975), 44-51.

5955 Alvarez, Alfred. "The Difficulty of Being South African," NSt, 59 (June 4, 1960), 827-828.
Compares Dan Jacobson and Faulkner in their treatment of race.

5956 Amette, Jacques-Pierre. "Le premier grand romancier de l'inconscient," Sud, 14 (1975), 7-11.

5957 Anastas'ev, N. "Folkner: Put'k 'Derevuske,'" VLit, 14, ix (1970), 122-141.

5958 _______. ["The Necessity of Faulkner,"] SovLit, #8 (1977), 180-183.

5959 Anderson, Carl L. The Swedish Acceptance of American Literature. Philadelphia: Penn. U.P., 1957, p. 150.
Faulkner's standing in Swedish libraries.

5960 Anderson, Charles. "Faulkner's Moral Center," ES, 7 (January, 1954), 48-58.

5961 _______. "William Faulkner and the Condition of Man," JHopM, 14 (February, 1963), 16-18, 24-27.

5962 Anderson, Dianne Luce. "Jehlen, Class and Character in Faulkner's South," MissQt, 30, #3 (Summer, 1977), 493-497.
Rev.-art of Jehlen's Class and Character in Faulkner's South.

5963 Anderson, Don[ald]. "Comic Modes in Modern American Fiction," SoRA, 8 (1975), 152-165.

5964 Anderson, Hilton. "Colonel Falkner's Preface to The Siege of Monterey," NMW, 3 (Spring, 1970), 36-40.
Perhaps helpful for the study of William Faulkner's Colonel Sartoris.

5965 _______. "'The White Rose of Memphis': A Clarification," NMW, 1 (Fall, 1968), 64-67.

5966 Anderson, LaVere. "Mr. Faulkner's Ambition," Tulsa Sunday World (July 31, 1955), Mag. Sec., 22.

5967 Anderson, Sherwood. Letters of Sherwood Anderson. Sel. and ed., with Introduction and Notes by Howard Mumford Jones in association with Walter B. Rideout. Boston: Little, Brown, & Co., 1953, passim.

5968 _______. "A Meeting South," Dial, 78 (April, 1925), 269-279.
Anderson's first impressions of Faulkner are said to be suggested by the character David in the above story.

5969 _______. Memoirs. Ray Lewis White, ed. Chapel Hill: North Carolina U.P., 1942; 1969, pp. 462-466, passim.

5970 _______. "They Come Bearing Gifts," AmMerc, 21 (October, 1930), 129-137.

5971 _______. "William Faulkner," We Moderns. New York: Gotham Book Mart, 1940, p. 29.

5972 Angoff, Allan, ed. American Writing Today: Its Independence and Vigor. New York: New York U.P., 1957, passim.

5972a Anon. "A propos d'une phrase de Faulkner," Preuves, 2 (June, 1952), I, 2.

5972b Anon. "A propósito de la última novela publicada por William Faulkner," Nación (15 marzo 1936).

5973 Anon. "Air Circus," Newsweek, 5 (March 30, 1935), 40.

5974 Anon. "American Writing Today," TLS (September 17, 1954), Spec. Sec.; American Writing Today. New York: New York U.P., 1957.

5975 Anon. "Book Marks for Today," NYWorld-Telegram (October 17, 1939), 19.

5976 Anon. "Books--Authors," NYTimes (January 1, 1946), 25.

5977 Anon. "The Bridges Still Stand, TLS, 17 (March, 1961), 161-162.

5978 Anon. "Cartes d'identité," GLet (14 septembre 1946), 4-5, 15.

5979 Anon. "The Curse and the Hope," Time (July 17, 1964), 44-48.

5980 Anon. "Une discussion sur Faulkner chez les étudiants communistes américains," La Nouvelle Critique, 1 (July-August, 1949), 87-96.

5981 Anon. "Faulkner," Stud. Cur. Eng. (Tokyo), 10 (October, 1955), 42-43.
Faulkner in Japan.

5982 Anon. "Faulkner Accepts U. of Virginia Post," NYTimes (January 11, 1959), 10.

5983 Anon. "Faulkner Advises at Princeton," NYTimes (March 4, 1958), 31.

5984 Anon. "Faulkner Arrives in Munich," NYTimes (September 18, 1955), 74.

5985 Anon. "Faulkner Believes the South Would Fight," NYTimes (March 15, 1956), 17.

5986 Anon. "Faulkner Calls Self 'Peasant,'" NYTimes (August 29, 1955), 17.

5987 Anon. "Faulkner Concordance," PMLA, 86 (May, 1971), 492.

5988 Anon. "Faulkner Disputed on Civil Rights Views," NYTimes (March 23, 1956), 28.

5989 Anon. "Faulkner Hails Mankind's Spirit," NYTimes (October 3, 1959), 3.

5990 Anon. "Faulkner Visiting Iceland," NYTimes (October 13, 1955), 27.

5991 Anon. "Faulkner Wall Plot," Life (August 9, 1954), 77-78.

5992 Anon. "Faulkner's Curse," TLS (February 7, 1958), 74.

5993 Anon. "He Will Prevail," Time (July 13, 1962), 85-86.

5994 Anon. "Juvenilia," TLS (January 16, 1964), 41.

5995 Anon. "Lecturer Off to Japan," NYTimes (July 17, 1955), 6.

5996 Anon. "Lifting the Hollywood Fog," Vanity Fair (May, 1933), 40.

5997 Anon. "A Memory of William Faulkner," SatEP (October 9, 1965), 88.

5998 Anon. "Mississippi Musings," America (March 29, 1958), 742.

5999 Anon. "Mr. Faulkner's Creed," NYTimes (October 4, 1959), IV, 8.

6000 Anon. "New and Notable: The William Faulkner Collection," PULC, 18 (1957), 166-167.

6001 Anon. "Random House," PubW (May 27, 1950), 2284.

6002 Anon. "Le roman américain à l'étranger," Arts (20 septembre 1946), 2.

6003 Anon. "A Saga of the Deep South," TLS (February 13, 1953), 104.

6004 Anon. "Texas Topics and Gossip," Dallas Morning News (August 5, 1962), VII, 9.

6005 Anon. "This Is William Faulkner's Homeland People ... and World," Newsweek (May 6, 1957), 116-117.

6006 Anon. "William Faulkner," NYTimes (May 3, 1955), 28.

6007 Anon. "The Writer in Critical Perspective," SatRL (July 28, 1962), 22-26.

6008 Anon. "Yoknapatawpha Possum," Newsweek (April 30, 1962), 58.

6009 Ansermoz-Dubois, Felix. L'interprétation française de la littérature américaine d'entre-deux guerres (1919-1939). Lausanne: Imprimerie la Concorde, 1944.

6010 Antoniadis, Roxandra I. "The Dream as Design in Balzac and Faulkner," Zagadnienia rodzajów literackich, 17, #2 (1974), 45-58.

6011 _______. "Faulkner and Balzac: The Poetic Web," CLS, 9 (September, 1972), 303-325.

6012 _______. "The Human Comedies of Honore de Balzac and William Faulkner: Similarities and Differences," DAI, 31 (Colorado: 1970), 4753A.

6013 Antonini, Giacomo. "Faulkner e lo zio Gavin," Fle, 8 (October 4, 1953), 5.

6014 _______. "Ritorno di William Faulkner," FLe, No. 25 (June 23, 1957), 6.

6015 Antrim, Harry T. "Faulkner's Suspended Style," UR, 32 (December, 1965), 122-128.

6016 Appel, Alfred Jr. "Powerhouse's Blues," SSF, 2 (Spring, 1965), 221-234.
A brief comparison of Eudora Welty's treatment of the Negro in fiction with that of Faulkner.

6017 Archer, H. Richard. "Collecting Faulkner Today," FS, 1 (Fall, 1952), 42-43.

6018 Archer, Lewis F. "Coleridge's Definition of the Poet and the Works of Herman Melville and William Faulkner," DA, 28 (Drew: 1967), 1810A-1811A.

6019 Armour, Richard. American Lit Relit. New York: McGraw-Hill, 1964, pp. 154-158.

6020 Arnavon, Cyrille. "Les deux derniers Faulkner," Europe, No. 425 [52] (September, 1964), 136-143.

6021 _______. Histoire littéraire des États-Unis. Paris: Librairie Hachette, 1953, pp. 311-312, 340-343.

6022 Arthos, John. "Ritual and Humor in the Writing of William Faulkner," Accent, 9 (Autumn, 1948), 17-30; repr., in William Faulkner: Two Decades of Criticism. Frederick Hoffman and Olga Vickery, eds. East Lansing: Michigan St. U.P., 1951, pp. 101-118.

6023 Arthur, Christopher Edward. "Possibilities of Place: The Fiction of Place: The Fiction of William Faulkner," DAI, 38, #3 (Cornell: 1976), 1383A-84A.

6024 "Artists and Thinkers," Cw, 67 (October 25, 1957), 86.

6025 Arvin, Newton. "The New American Writers," HarpB, 81 (March, 1947), 196-299.

6026 Asselineau, Roger. "William Faulkner, moraliste puritain," RLM, 5 (Nos. 40-42), (Winter, 1958-59), 231-249.

6027 Astre, Georges Albert. "L'apport amêricain au roman contemporain," Age nouveau, No. 68 (December, 1951), 29-32.

6028 _______. "L'oeuvre close de William Faulkner," Critique (Paris), 20 (March, 1964), 284-286.

6029 Atkinson, Justin Brooks. "Faulkner and Comedy," Tuesdays and Fridays. New York: Random House, 1963, pp. 244-246.

6030 _______. [William Faulkner], NYTimes (February 8, 1959).

6031 Aury, Dominique. "William Faulkner," NRF, 10 (August, 1962), 315-316.

6032 Avni, Abraham. "The Influence of the Bible on American Literature: A Review of Research from 1955 to 1965," BB, 27 (October-December, 1970), 101-106.

6033 Aymê, Marcel. "What French Readers Find in William Faulkner's Fiction," NYTBR (December 17, 1950), 4; repr., Highlights of Modern Literature. Francis Brown, ed. New York: Mentor, 1954, pp. 103-106.

6034 Aytür, Necla. "Faulkner in Turkish," Proceedings of the Comparative Literature Symposium. Vol. IV. William Faulkner: Prevailing Verities and World Literature. Wolodymyr T. Zyla and Wendell M. Aycock, eds. Lubbock: Interdept. Comm. on Comp. Lit., Texas Tech. U., 1973, pp. 25-39.

6035 Baacke, Margareta. William Faulkners Menschen: Charakterdarstellung der Weissen aus Yoknapatawpha County. Diss. Phillips University: Marburg, Germany, 1953.

6036 Backman, Melvin. Faulkner, The Major Years: A Critical Study. Bloomington, Indiana: Indiana U.P., 1966.

6037 _______. "The Pilgrimage of William Faulkner: A Study of Faulkner's Fiction, 1929-1942," DA, 21 (Columbia: 1960), 193-194.

6038 _______. "Sickness and Primitivism: A Dominant Pattern in William Faulkner's Work," Accent, 14 (Winter, 1954), 61-73.

6039 Backvis, Claude. "Faulkner versus Dostoevsky," Revue de l'Universitê Libre de Bruxelles, 1970-73, 205-32.

6040 Baiwir, Albert. "William Faulkner," Abrégé de l'histoire du roman américain, Collection Savoire. Manteau, Brussels, 1946, pp. 81-83.

6041 _______. "William Faulkner," Le déclin de l'individualisme chez les romanciers américains contemporains. Paris: Société d'Edition les Belles Lettres, 1943, pp. 313-332.

6042 Baker, Carlos. Ernest Hemingway: A Life Story. New York: Scribner's, 1969.
References to Hemingway's attitude toward Faulkner.

6043 _______, et al. "Ernest Hemingway Memorial Number," ETJ, 11 (Summer, 1962), 1-19.

6044 _______. "William Faulkner: The Doomed and the Damned," The Young Rebel in American Literature: Seven Lectures. Carl Bode, ed. London: Heinemann, 1959, pp. 145-169; New York: Frederick A. Praeger, 1959, pp. 145-169.

6045 Baker, Ernest A., and James Packman. A Guide to the Best Fiction, English and American. London: Routledge, 1932; new and enl. ed. New York: Barnes & Noble, 1967, p. 170.

6046 Baker, Howard. "In Praise of the Novel," SoR, 5 (Spring, 1940), 778-800.

6047 Baker, James R. "Ideas and Queries," FS, 1 (Spring, 1952), 4-7.

6048 _______. "The Symbolic Extension of Yoknapatawpha County," ArQ, 8 (Autumn, 1952), 223-228.

6049 Baker, Russell. "White House Literary Blacklist," Kansas City Star, Vol. 95, #348 (August 31, 1975), 2B.
Faulkner among the writers listed as unsuitable to visit the White House.

6050 Baldanza, Frank. "Faulkner and Stein: A Study in Stylistic Intransigence," GaR, 13 (Fall, 1959), 274-286.

6051 Baldwin, James. "As Much Truth as One Can Bear," NYTBR (January 14, 1962), 1, 38.
Praises Faulkner's major fiction.

6052 _______. "Faulkner and Desegregation," PR, 23 (Fall, 1956), 568-573.

6053 Ballinger, Sara E. The Reception of the American Novel in German Periodicals, 1945-1957. Diss. Indiana: 1959.

6054 Balotă, Nicolae. "Increderea în Faulkner," RoLit, 17 (August, 1972), 13.

6055 ________. "Lumini si umbre faulkneriene," RoLit, 29 (November, 1973), 15.

6056 ________. "O fraza despre Faulkner," RoLit, 6 (March, 1975), 19.

6057 Baltzer, Peter. "Blicke hinter die Kulissen: Gespräche mit Faulkner," Züricher Woche (December 15, 1961), 11.

6058 Bamberg, Robert D. Plantation and Frontier: A View of Southern Fiction. Diss. Cornell: 1961.

6059 Barberet, Gene J. "A Remembered Talk with Roger Martin du Gard," BA, 32 (Autumn, 1958), 379-381.
Quotes du Gard's praise of Faulkner.

6060 Barbezat, Marc. "Nouvelle revue française," Confluences, 5 (November, 1941), 678-679.

6061 Barbour, Brian M. "Faulkner's Decline," DAI, 30 (Kent State: 1970), 5436A-37A.

6062 Barjon, Louis. "Retour aux enfers de Faulkner," Etudes (Paris), 279 (November, 1953), 225-236.

6063 Barklund, Gunnar. "I Faulkners Oxford," Dagens Nyheter (Stockholm) (March 28, 1964), 3.

6064 Barksdale, Richard K. "White Tragedy--Black Comedy: A Literary Approach to Southern Race Relations," Phylon, 22 (1961), 226-233.

6065 Barrault, Jean Louis. "Ce Qu'ils Pensent de Faulkner," Carrefour (November 14, 1950), 9.

6066 ________. "Le Roman adapté au théâtre," CRB, 91 (1976), 27-58.

6067 Barrett, George. "Faulkner Finds Cadets Knowing," NYTimes (April 21, 1962), 21.

6068 Barrett, William. "Backward Toward the Earth," Time of Need: Forms of Imagination in the Twentieth Century. New York: Harper & Row, 1972, pp. 96-129.

6069 Barricklow, Gary Edwin. "Kenneth Burke's Structuralism: A Structural Description of Narrative and Technique in Faulkner's Fiction of the Southern Aristocracy," DAI, 37 (New Mexico: 1976), 2856A-57A.

6070 Barth, J. Robert. "Faulkner and the Calvinist Tradition," Thought, 39 (Spring, 1964), 100-120.

6071 ________, ed. Religious Perspectives in Faulkner's Fiction: Yoknapatawpha and Beyond. Notre Dame: Notre Dame U.P., 1972.

6072 Bartlett, Phyllis. "Other Countries, Other Wenches," MFS, 3 (Winter, 1957-58), 345-349.

6073 Barucca, Primo. "L'aristocratico del Sud," Persona, 4, i (1963), 14-15.

6074 ________. "La citta di Faulkner," FLe, 17 (February 11, 1962), 5.

6075 ________. "Faulkner e i negri," FLe, 16 (April 9, 1961), 5.

6076 ________. "Il Sud di William Faulkner," Italia che scrive, 44 (April, 1961), 59-60.

6077 Bassett, John E. "Faulkner's Readers: Crosscurrents in American Reviews and Criticism, 1926-1962," DAI, 32 (Rochester: 1970), 1502A.

6078 ________, ed. Introduction. William Faulkner: The Critical Heritage. Boston: Routledge & Kegan Paul, 1975, pp. 1-46.

6079 Basso, Hamilton. "Letters in the South," NR, 83 (June 19, 1935), 161-163.

6080 ________. "William Faulkner: Man and Writer," SatRL, 45 (July 28, 1962), 11-14.

6081 Batâri, Gyula. "William Faulkner ês az amerikai Dêl," [William Faulkner and the American South], VF, 9 (1963), 272-275.

6082 Bates, Herbert Ernest. The Modern Short Story: A Critical Survey. London and New York: T. Nelson, 1941, pp. 180-183.
Notes similarities between Faulkner and Conrad.

6083 Bates, Ophelia. "Faulkner: Assessment," Books and Bookmen (London), (September, 1962), 16-17.

6084 Beach, Joseph W. "American Letters Between Wars," CE, 3 (October, 1941), 1-12.

6085 ________. "Eight Novelists Between Wars," SatRL, 23 (March 29, 1941), 3-4, 17-19.

6086 ________. The Twentieth Century Novel: Studies in Technique. New York: Century Co., 1932, pp. 520-522, passim.

6087 ________. "William Faulkner: The Haunted South," and "William Faulkner: Virtuoso," American Fiction, 1920-1940. New York: Macmillan, 1942; Russell & Russell, 1960, pp. 123-143, 147-169.

6088 Beards, Richard. "Parody as Tribute: William Melvin Kelley's A Different Drummer and Faulkner," SBL, 5, iii (1974), 25-28.

6089 Beasley, William Madison. "The New South and Five Southern Novelists, 1920-1950," DA, 18 (Vanderbilt: 1957), 210-211.

6090 Beatty, Richard Croom, Floyd C. Watkins, and Thomas Daniel Young. The Literature of the South. Chicago: Scott, Foresman, 1952, passim.

6091 Beauchamp, Fay Elizabeth. "William Faulkner's Use of the Tragic Mulatto Myth," DAI, 36 (Pennsylvania: 1974), 297A.

6092 Beaver, Howard L. American Critical Essays. New York: Oxford U.P., 1961, pp. 211-233.

6093 Beck, Warren. "Faulkner and the South," AntiochR, 1 (Spring, 1941), 82-94.

6094 ________. "Faulkner et le sud," RLM, Part II, Nos. 40-42, (1958-59), 271-291.

6095 ________. "Faulkner's Point of View," CE, 2 (May, 1941), 736-749; also CE, 22 (November, 1960), 86-93.

6096 ________. "A Note on Faulkner's Style," Rocky Mt. Review, 6 (Spring-Summer, 1942), 5-6, 14.

6097 ________. "Le Style des William Faulkner," RLM, No. 40-42 (1957), 365-384.

6098 ________. William Faulkner: Essays. Madison: Wisconsin U.P., 1976.

6099 ________. "William Faulkner's Style," American Prefaces, 6 (Spring, 1941), 195-211; repr., in William Faulkner: Four Decades of Criticism. Linda W. Wagner, ed. Michigan State U.P., 1973, pp. 141-154.

6100 Bedell, George Chester. "Kierkegaard and Faulkner: Modalities of Existence," DAI, 30 (Duke: 1969), 5056A-57A.

6101 ________. Kierkegaard and Faulkner: Modalities of Existence. Baton Rouge: Louisiana State U.P., 1972.

6102 Beebe, Maurice. "Critique faulknérienne de langue anglaise," RLM, I, Part IV, Nos. 27-29 (June, 1957), 154-177.

6103 Beidler, Philip Douglas. "The Parabolic Design: Self-Conscious Form in American Narrative," DAI, 35, #7 (Virginia: 1974), 4498A.

6104 Beja, Morris. "A Flash, a Glare: Faulkner and Time" Renascence, 16 (Spring, 1964), 133-141, 145.

6105 _______. "William Faulkner: A Flash, A Glare," Epiphany in the Modern Novel. Seattle: Washington U. P., 1971, pp. 182-210.

6106 Bellman, Samuel I. "Hemingway, Faulkner, and Wolfe ... and the Common Reader," SoR, 4 (Summer, 1968), 834-849.

6107 Bellue, John Vernon. "William Faulkner as a Literary Naturalist," DAI, 36 (Wayne State: 1975), 7417A.

6108 Benedetti, Mario. "William Faulkner, un novelista de la fatalidad," Numero, 2 (September-December, 1950), 63-571.

6109 Benêt, William Rose, and Norman Holmes Pearson, eds. The Oxford Anthology of American Literature. New York: Oxford U. P., 1938, pp. 1640-1641.

6110 Benson, Jackson J. "Quentin Compson: Self-Portrait of a Young Artist's Emotions," TCL, 17 (July, 1971), 143-159.

6111 Bentley, Frederick. "A Curtain of Green: Themes and Attitudes," American Prefaces, 7 (Spring, 1942), 241-251.

6112 Bentley, Phyllis. "I Look at American Fiction," SatRL, 20 (May 13, 1939), 3-4, 14-15.

6113 Berger, Yves. "Prêsence et Signification chez William Faulkner," NRF, 15 (May, 1960), 951-960.

6114 Bergman, Alix and M. L. Becker. "Les êcrivains amêricains et leurs oeuvres depuis 1939," Paru (avril 1945), 7-16.

6115 Beringause, A. F. "Faulkner's Yoknapatawpha Register," BuR, 11 (May, 1963), 71-82.
Faulkner's use of names.

6116 Berk, Lynn M. L. "The Barrier of Words: A Study of William Faulkner's Distrust of Language," DAI, 33 (Purdue: 1973), 5163A-64A.

6117 Bernackaja, V. "Raspavšijsja projadok (O pisatel'skoj individual'nosti Folknera)," VLit, 18, iii (1974), 85-100.

6118 Bernard, Harry. "William Faulkner," Le roman rêgionaliste aux États-Unis, 1913-1940. Montreal: Fides, 1949, pp. 121-123.

6119 Berner, Robert Leslie. "The Theme of Responsibility in the Later Fiction of William Faulkner," DA, 21 (Washington: 1960), 1561.

6120 Berrone, Louis. "A Dickensian Echo in Faulkner," Dickensian, 71 (1975), 100-101.

6121 Berry, Thomas E. A History of the Recent Translations of the American Novel into Spanish. Diss. Pittsburgh: 1949.

6122 Berti, Luigi. "Interpretazione per Faulkner," Boccaporto secondo. Firenze: Parenti, 1944, pp. 264-268.

6123 _______. "Romanzo e mito del Sud," Storia della letteratura americana. Milano: Istituto Editoriale Italiano, 1961, pp. 500-521.

6124 Bertin, Celia. "The Worldwide Influence of William Faulkner: Reports from Six Capitals," NYTBR (November 15, 1959), 52-53.

6125 Bickerstaff, Thomas A. "Mr. Burleson, the Bold Mouse," William Faulkner of Oxford. J. W. Webb and A. W. Green, eds. Louisiana State U. P., 1965, pp. 60-62.

6126 Bickham, Robert S. "The Origins and Importance of the Initiation Story in Twentieth Century British and American Fiction," DA, 22 (New Mexico: 1961), 2790.

6127 Bier, Jesse. The Rise and Fall of American Humor. New York: Holt, Rinehart & Winston, 1968, passim.

6128 _______. "The Romantic Coordinates of American Literature," BuR, 18 (Fall, 1970), 16-33.

6129 Bihalji-Merin, Oto. "William Faulkner: Mythos der Zeit," Sinn und Form, 16 (1964), 752-770.

6130 Binder, David. "The U. S. Professor Explains Faulkner to Rumanians," NYTimes (November 24, 1964), 11.

6131 Birney, Earle. "The Two William Faulkners," CanForum, 18 (June, 1938), 84-85.

6123 Bishop, John Peale. "Myth and Modern Literature," SatRL, 22 (July 22, 1939), 14.

6133 _______. "The South and Tradition," VQR, 9 (April, 1933), 161-174.

6134 Blackley, Charles. "William Faulkner's County: A Chronological Guide to Yoknapatawpha," TAIUS (Texas A&I), 4 (1971), 73-86.

6135 Blackwell, Louise. "Faulkner and the Womenfolk," KM, 35 (1967), 73-77.

6136 Blair, Arthur Hadfield. "Faulkner's Military World," DAI, 36 (North Carolina, Chapel Hill: 1975), 6679A.

6137 Blake, Nelson M. "The Decay of Yoknapatawpha County," Novelists' America: Fiction as History, 1910-1940. Syracuse, New York: Syracuse U. P., 1969, pp. 75-109.

6138 Blanc-Dufour, A. "A propos de romans amêricains," CS (premier semestre, 1949), 291.

6139 Blanchot, Maurice. "D'un art sans avenir," NRF, 5e annêe, No. 51 (March, 1957), 488-498.

6140 Blanzat, Jean. "Les lettres," MonF, 3 (novembre-dêcembre 1945), 131-136; 4 (octobre, 1946), 316-321.

6141 _______. "Les romans," Poêsie, 43 (octobre-novembre 1943), 75-82.

6142 _______. "Romans policiers," FL (28 août 1948), 5.

6143 Bleikasten, Andrê. "Faulkner et le nouveau roman," LanM, 60, #4 (July-August, 1966), 422-432.

6144 _______. "Modernitê de Faulkner," Delta, 3 (November, 1976), 155-172.

6145 Blöcker, Günter. "William Faulkner," Die Neuen Wirklichkeiten. Trans., Jacqueline Merriam. Berlin: Argon Verlag, 1958, pp. 112-123.

6146 Blom, T. E. "Anita Loos and Sexual Economics: Gentlemen Prefer Blondes," CRevAS, 7 (1976), 39-47.

6147 Blonski, Jan. "Americans in Poland," KR, 23 (Winter, 1961), 32-51.

6148 Blotner, Joseph. "The Achievement of Maurice Edgar Coindreau," SLJ, 4 (Fall, 1971), 95-96.

6149 _______. "Faulkner in Hollywood," Man and the Movies. W. R. Robinson, ed. Baton Rouge: Louisiana State U. P., 1967, pp. 261-303.

6150 _______. The Modern American Political Novel, 1900-1960. Austin: Texas U. P., 1966, pp. 204-205, passim.

6151 _______. "The Region Can Be Universal," NYTBR (October 25, 1964), 55.

6152 ______. "Romantic Elements in Faulkner," Romantic and Modern: Revaluation of Literary Tradition. George Bornstein, ed. Pittsburgh: U. of Pittsburgh Pr., 1977, pp. 207-21.

6153 ______. "The Sole Owner and Proprietor," Faulkner: Fifty Years After the Marble Faun. George Wolfe, ed. (University, Ala.: Ala. U.P., 1976, pp. 1-20.

6153a [______.] "Uncollected Stories of William Faulkner," Time, 114, #19 (November 5, 1979), 105-106.

6153b ______. "William Faulkner: Committee Chairman," Themes and Directions in American Literature. Ray B. Browne and Donald Pizer, eds. Lafayette, Indiana: Purdue U.P., 1969, pp. 200-219.

6154 ______. "William Faulkner, Roving Ambassador," International Educational and Cultural Exchange. (U.S. Advisory Commission on International Educational and Cultural Affairs), (Summer, 1966), 1-22.

6155 ______. William Faulkner's Library: A Catalogue. Charlottesville: Virginia U.P., 1964.

6156 ______. "William Faulkner's Name Was in the Books He Loved Best," NYTBR (December 8, 1963), 4-5, 45.
Faulkner's library at "Rowan Oak."

6157 Bluestein, Gene. "The Blues as a Literary Theme," MassR, 8, #4 (1967), 593-617.
Finds Faulkner "incredibly accurate in his description of what the music sounded like...."

6158 Blumenberg, Hans. "Mythos und Ethos Amerikas im Werk William Faulkner," Hochland, 50 (February, 1958), 234-250.

6159 Bode, Carl, ed. The Young Rebel in American Literature. London: Heinemann, 1959, pp. 143-169.

6160 Bompard, Paola. "Non si scava nella polvere," FLe, 19 (October 14, 1951), 1-2.

6161 Bongartz, Roy. "Faulkner Bars Debate," NYTimes (April 18, 1956), 29.

6162 ______. "Faulkner Challenged," NYTimes (April 16, 1956), 8.

6163 ______. "Faulkner Disputed on Civil Rights View," NYTimes (March 23, 1956), 28.

6164 ______. "Give Them Time: Reflections on Faulkner," Nation, 182 (March 31, 1956), 259.

6165 ______. "Go Slow Now," Life, 40 (March 12, 1956), 37.

6166 Booth, Wayne C. The Rhetoric of Fiction. Chicago: Chicago U.P., 1961), pp. 306-308.

6167 Boring, Phyllis Zatlin. "Faulkner in Spain: The Case of Elena Quiroga," CLS, 14 (June, 1977), 166-176.
Faulkner's influence.

6168 Borowsky, Alexandre S. "Faulkner's Fictional Children: A Study of Their Narrative Stances. Diss. North Carolina, Chapel Hill, 1971.

6169 Bosquet, Alain. "William Faulkner: un visionnaire boroque," Combat (Paris), No. 5, 608 (July 7-8, 1962), 1.

6170 Boswell, George W. "Folkways in Faulkner," MissFR, 1, #3 (Fall, 1967), 83-90.

6171 _______. "The Legendary Background of Faulkner's Work," TFSB, 36 (September, 1970), 53-65.

6172 _______. "Notes on the Surnames of Faulkner's Characters," TFSB, 34 (September, 1970), 64-66.

6173 _______. "Picturesque Faulknerisms," UMSE, 9 (1968), 47 ff.

6174 _______. "Superstition and Belief in Faulkner," Costerus, 6 (1972), 1-26.

6175 _______. "Traditional Verse and Music Influence in Faulkner," NMW, 1 (Spring, 1968), 23-31.

6176 Boussard, Leon. "William Faulkner," RDM (August 1, 1962), 424-430.

6177 Bowen, Catherine Drinker. "Harold Ober, Literary Agent," Atl, 206 (July, 1960), 35-40.

6178 Bowen, Elizabeth. "A Matter of Inspiration," SatRL 34 (October 13, 1951), 27-28, 64.

6179 Bowling, Lawrence E. "Faulkner and the Theme of Innocence," KR, 20 (Summer, 1958), 466-487.

6180 _______. "Faulkner and the Theme of Isolation," GaR, 18 (Spring, 1964), 50-66.

6181 _______. "William Faulkner: The Importance of Love," DR, 43 (1963), 474-482; repr., in William Faulkner: Four Decades of Criticism. Linda W. Wagner, ed. Michigan State U.P., 1973, pp. 109-117.

6182 Boyd, G. N., and L. A. Boyd. Religion in Contemporary Fiction: Criticism from 1945 to the Present. San Antonio, Texas: Trinity U.P., 1973.

6183 Boyle, Anthony Joseph. "Modernism, Radical Humanism, and the Contemporary Novel," DAI, 36, #3 (New York at Buffalo: 1975), 1498A.

6184 Boynton, Percy Holmes. Literature and American Life. Boston: Ginn & Co., 1936, pp. 862-863.

6185 _______. "William Faulkner of Mississippi: The Retrospective South," American in Contemporary Fiction. Chicago: Chicago U.P., 1940, pp. 103-112.

6186 Brace, Marjorie. "Thematic Problems of the American Novelist," Accent, 6 (Autumn, 1945), 44-53.

6187 Brack, O. M., Jr., ed. American Humor: Essays Presented to John C. Gerber. Scottsdale, Arizona: Arete Publications, 1977.

6188 Bradbury, John M. Renaissance in the South: A Critical History of the Literature, 1920-1960. Chapel Hill: North Carolina U.P., 1963, pp. 50-57, passim.

6189 Bradbury, Malcolm. Possibilities: Essays on the State of the Novel. New York: Oxford U.P., 1973, passim.

6190 Bradford, Melvin E. "Faulkner Among the Puritans," SR, 72 (January-March, 1964), 146-150.

6191 _______. "Faulkner and the Great White Father," LaS, 3 (Winter, 1964), 323-329.

6192 _______. "Faulkner and the Jefferson Dream," MissQ, 18 (Spring, 1965), 94-100.

6193 _______. "Faulkner, James Baldwin, and the South," GaR, 20 (December, 1966), 431-443.

6194 _______. "Faulkner's Doctrine of Nature: A Study of the 'Endurance' Theme in the Yoknapatawpha Fiction," DA, 29 (Vanderbilt: 1969), 3999A.

6195 _______. Faulkner's Tall Men," SaQ, 61 (Winter, 1962), 29-39.

6196 _______. "On the Importance of Discovering God: Faulkner and Hemingway's The Old Man and the Sea," MissQ, 20 (Summer, 1967), 158-162.

6197 _______. "Spring Paradigm: Faulkner's Living Legacy," Forum, 6 (Spring, 1968), 4-7.
Faulkner's concept of "endurance."

6198 Bradford, Roark. "The Private World of William Faulkner," '48, the Magazine of the Year, 2 (May, 1948), 83-90.

6199 Brady, Emily Kuempel. "The Literary Faulkner: His Indebtedness to Conrad, Lawrence, Hemingway, and Other Modern Novelists," DA, 23 (Brown: 1962), 2131-32.

6200 Brady, Ruth Annette H. H. "The Reality of Gothic Terror in Faulkner," DAI, 32 (Texas (Austin): 1971), 5774A-75A.

6201 Braem, Helmut. "Das scandalon William Faulkner: Die metaphysische Kampfstatt und ein sadistischer Jehova," Deutsche Rundschau, 10 (October, 1958), 944-950.

6202 Brand, David. "Tribute to William Faulkner," Humanist (London), 78 (February, 1963), 46-47.

6203 Brasil, Assis. _Faulkner e a têcnica do romance_. Rio de Janeiro: Editora Leitura, 1964.

6204 Braspart, Michel. "Autant n'en emportera pas le vent," Rêforme, (16 fêvrier 1952), 7.

6205 Breaden, Dale G. "William Faulkner and the Land," AQ, 10 (Fall, 1958), 344-357.

6206 Breit, Harvey. "At Home and Abroad," NYTBR, 61 (October 14, 1956), 8.

6207 ________. "Faulkner: sfida alla critica," FLe, 36 (September 7, 1952), 4.

6208 ________. "In and Out of Books," NYTBR (January 30, 1955), 8. Also: (March 22, 1953), 8; (October 14, 1956), 8.

6209 ________. "Repeat Performances," NYTBR (May 8, 1955).

6210 ________. "A Sense of Faulkner," PR, 18 (January-February, 1951), 88-94.

6211 ________. "A Walk with Faulkner," NYTBR (January 30, 1955), 4.
Repr., in _Writer Observed_. Cleveland: World Pub. Co., 1956, pp. 281-284.

6212 ________. "William Faulkner," Atl, 188 (October, 1951), 53-56.

6213 ________. "Word's Worth," NYTBR (March 20, 1955), 8.

6214 ________. "Youth," NYTBR (September 19, 1954), 8.

6215 Brennan, Dan. "Journey South," UKCR, 22 (Autumn, 1955), 11-16.

6216 Brennan, Joseph X., and Seymour L. Gross. "The Problem

of Moral Values in Conrad and Faulkner," Personalist, 41 (Winter, 1960), 60-70.

6217 Breuil, Roger. "William Faulkner," Esprit, 1 (January, 1936), 612-614.

6218 Breyer, Bernard R. "A Diagnosis of Violence in Recent Southern Fiction," MissQ, 14 (Spring, 1961), 59-67.

6219 Brickell, Herschel. "The Literary Awakening in the South," Bookman, 76 (October, 1927), 138-143.

6220 Bricker, Emil Stanley. "Duality in the Novels of William Faulkner and Fyodor Dostoevsky," DAI, 32 (Michigan: 1971), 6413A-14A.

6221 "The Bridges Still Stand," TLS (March 17, 1961), 161-162.

6222 Brien, Delores E. "William Faulkner and the Myth of Woman," RS, 35 (June, 1967), 132-140.

6223 Brière, Annie. "Dernière rencontre avec Faulkner," NL, 40 (July 12, 1962), 3.

6224 ________. "Faulkner Parle," NL, 43 (October 6, 1955), 1, 6.

6225 Brion, Marcel. "William Faulkner," LM, 19 (July 9, 1962), 1, 13.

6226 Brite, Jerrold. "A True-Blue Hunter," William Faulkner of Oxford. James W. Webb and A. Wigfall Green, eds. Baton Rouge: Louisiana State U.P., 1965, pp. 154-161.

6227 Brocki, Mary D. "Faulkner and Hemingway: Values in a Modern World," MTJ, 11 (Summer, 1962), 5-9, 15.

6228 Brodin, Pierre. Présences contemporaines: Courants et thèmes principaux de la littérature française contemporaine. Paris: Debresse, 1957, passim.

6229 ________. "William Faulkner," Les écrivains américains de l'entre-deux guerres. Paris: Horizons de France, 1946, pp. 145-170.

6230 Brogunier, Joseph E. "The Jefferson Urn: Faulkner's Literary Sources and Influences," DAI, 31 (Minnesota: 1970), 2375A.

6231 Brooks, Cleanth. "The American 'Innocence': In James, Fitzgerald, and Faulkner," Shenandoah, 16 (Autumn, 1964), 21-37.

6232 ________. "The British Reception of Faulkner's Work," Proceedings of the Comparative Literature Symposium. Vol. IV. William Faulkner: Prevailing Verities and World Literature. Wolodymyr T. Zyla, and Wendell M. Aycock, eds. Lubbock: Interdept. Comm. on Comp. Lit. Texas Tech U. P., 1973, pp. 41-55.

6233 ________. "The Community and the Pariah," VQR, 39 (Spring, 1963), 236-253.

6234 ________. "Faulkner, William," The Reader's Encyclopedia of American Literature. Max J. Herzberg, ed. New York: Crowell, 1962, pp. 325-329.

6235 ________. "Faulkner and History," MissQ, 25 (Spring, 1972), 3-14.

6236 ________. "Faulkner and the Muse of History," MissQ, 28 (Summer, 1975), 265-279.

6237 ________. "Faulkner's Criticism of Modern America," VQR, 51 (Spring, 1975), 294-308.

6238 ________. "Faulkner's Savage Arcadia: Frenchman's Bend," VQR, 39 (Autumn, 1963), 598-611.

6239 ________. "Faulkner's Treatment of the Racial Problem: Typical Examples," A Shaping Joy: Studies in the Writer's Craft. New York: Harcourt Brace, 1972, pp. 239-246.

6240 ________. "Faulkner's Vision of Good and Evil," MassR, 3 (Summer, 1962), 692-712; repr., in The Hidden God. New Haven: Yale U. P., 1963, pp. 22-43.

6241 ________. "The Image of Helen Baird in Faulkner's Early Poetry and Fiction," SR, 85 (Spring, 1977), 218-234.

6242 ________. "A Note on Faulkner's Early Attempts at the Short Story," SSF, 10 (1973), 381-388.

6243 ________. "Southern Literature: The Wellsprings of Its Vitality," GaR, 16 (Fall, 1962), 238-253.

6244 ________. "What Deep South Literature Needs," SatRL, 25 (September, 19, 1942), 8, 9-29, 30.

6245 ________. "William Faulkner and William Butler Yeats: Parallels and Affinities," Faulkner: Fifty Years After The Marble Faun. University, Ala.: Ala. U. P., 1976, pp. 139-158.

6246 ________. William Faulkner: The Yoknapatawpha Country. New Haven; London: Yale U. P., 1963; 2nd pr., 1964.

6247 _______. William Faulkner: Toward Yoknapatawpha and Beyond. New Haven: Yale U. P., 1978.
Rev. by John W. Hunt, MissQ, 31 (Summer, 1978), 465-476.

6248 _______, and Robert Penn Warren. Understanding Fiction. New York: Appleton, Century, Crofts, 1944, pp. 409-414.

6249 Brooks, Peter. "In the Laboratory of the Novel," Daedalus, 92 (Spring, 1963), 265-280.

6250 Brooks, Van Wyck. "Fashions in Defeatism," SatRL, 23 (March 22, 1941), 3-4, 14; repr., in On Literature Today. New York: Dutton, 1941.

6251 _______. Opinions of Oliver Allston. New York: Dutton, 1941, passim.

6252 _______. The Writer in America. New York: Dutton, 1953, passim.

6253 Broughton, Panthea Reid. "Abstraction and Insularity in the Fiction of William Faulkner," DAI, 32 (North Carolina, Chapel Hill: 1971), 5220A.

6254 _______. "Faulkner As Carpenter," SoR, 11 (July, 1975), 681-684.

6255 _______. William Faulkner: The Abstract and the Actual. Baton Rouge: Louisiana State U. P., 1974.

6256 Brown, Calvin S. "A Dim View of Faulkner's Country," GaR, 23 (Winter, 1969), 501-511.
Essay-review of Elizabeth Kerr's Yoknapatawpha: Faulkner's 'Little Postage Stamp of Native Soil.'

6257 _______. "Faulkner's Geography and Topography," PMLA, 77 (December, 1962), 652-659.

6258 _______. "Faulkner's Localism," in The Maker and the Myth. Evans Harrington and Ann J. Abadie, eds. Jackson: Miss U. P., 1978, pp. 3-24.

6259 _______. "Faulkner's Manhunts: Facts into Fiction," GaR, 20 (Winter, 1966), 388-395.

6260 [Brown, Calvin S.] "Faulkner's Universality," in The Maker and the Myth. Evans Harrington and Ann J. Abadie, eds. Jackson: 1978, pp. 146-169.

6261 _______. "Faulkner's Use of the Oral Tradition," GaR, 22 (Summer, 1968), 160-169.

6262 ________. A Glossary of Faulkner's South. New Haven: Yale U.P., 1976.
Rev., by Leland H. Cox, MissQt, 30, #3 (Summer, 1977).

6263 ________, gen. ed. The Reader's Companion to World Literature. New York: New American Library, 1956, p. 162-3.

6264 Brown, John. "Les lettres américaines en 1944," Esprit (mars 1945), 598-602.

6265 ________. "Tendences du roman américain moderne," CLM, (décembre 1946), 275-285.

6266 Brown, John L. "William Faulkner," Panorama de la littérature contemporaine aux États-Unis. Paris: Point du Jour, 1954, pp. 179-201.

6267 ________. "William Faulkner, gigante solitario," Mondo Occidentale, 9 (July-August, 1962), 27-38.

6268 Brown, John Mason. The Worlds of Robert E. Sherwood. New York: Harper & Row, 1965, pp. 281, 284.

6269 Brown, Maud Morrow. "William C. Falkner, Man of Legends," GaR, 10 (Winter, 1956), 421-438.

6270 Brown, May Cameron. "Quentin Compson as Narrative Voice in the Works of William Faulkner," DAI, 36 (Georgia State: 1975), 5291A-92A.

6271 Brown, Sterling A. "A Century of Negro Portraiture in American Literature," MassR, 7 (Winter, 1966), 73-96.

6272 ________. "William Faulkner," The Negro in American Fiction. Washington, D.C.: Associates in Negro Folk Education, 1937, repr., 1957, pp. 177-179.

6273 Brown, William Richard. "William Faulkner's Use of the Material of Abnormal Psychology in Characterization," DA, 26 (Arkansas: 1965), 1036-37.

6274 Brumm, Ursula. "Christ and Adam as 'Figures' in American Literature," excerpt from "American Thought and Religious Typology," in The American Puritan Imagination. S. Bercovitch, ed. Cambridge: Cambridge U.P., 1974, pp. 196-212.

6275 ________. "Forms and Functions of History in the Novels of William Faulkner," Archiv, 209 (1972), 43-56.

6276 ________. "The Historical Novel and Historicist Criticism: Notes on the Critical Reception of Scott and Faulkner," Geschichte und Gesellschaft in der amerikanischen Literatur. Schubert and Muller-Richter, eds. Heidelberg: Quelle & Meyer, 1975.

6277 ________. "Thoughts on History and the Novel," CLS, 6 (September, 1969), 317-329.
Discusses Faulkner as an example of use of history in the novel.

6278 ________. Die Religiöse Typologie im Amerikanischen Dencken: Ihre Bedeutung für die Amerikanische literature - und Geistesgeschichte. Studien zur Amerikanischen Literature und Geschichte, Vol. II. Leiden: E. J. Brill, 1963.

6279 ________. "Wilderness and Civilization," PR, 22 (Summer, 1955), 340-350; repr., in William Faulkner: Three Decades of Criticism. Frederick Hoffman and Olga Vickery, eds. East Lansing: Michigan State U. P., 1960, pp. 125-134.

6280 ________. "William Faulkner:--Im Alten Süden," Welt-Stimmen (Stuttgart) 19 (May, 1950), 374-380.

6281 Bruneau, Jean. "Existentialism and the American Novel," YFS, 1, #1 (Spring-Summer, 1948), 66-72.
Comparison of Faulkner with the French existentialists.

6282 Brusar, Branko. "Humor William Faulkner na primjerima iz Romana 'Grad,'" Republika, 15 (July-August, 1959), 32.

6283 Brylowski, Walter. Faulkner's Olympian Laugh: Myth in the Novels. Detroit: Wayne State U. P., 1968.

6284 ________. "Man's Enduring Chronicle: A Study of Myth in the Novels of William Faulkner," DA, 25 (Michigan: 1965), 6617-6618.

6285 Bubeníková, Libušě. "Obraz americkêho Jihu u Williama Faulknera," Neodpočivej v pokoji. Prague: Naše Vojske, 1958, pp. 172-177.

6286 Buchanan, Harriette Cuttino. "Southern Writing in 1929," DAI, 36 (North Carolina, Chapel Hill: 1974), 301.

6287 Büchler, Franz. Wasserscheide zweier Zeitalter: Essais. (PuW, 12) Heidelberg: Stiehm, 1970.

6288 Buck, Lynn Dillon. "The Demonic Paradox: Studies in Faulkner's Imagery," DAI, 37 (Stony Brook, New York: 1976), 3620A.

6289 Buckler, William E., and Arnold B. Sklare, eds. Stories from Six Authors. New York: McGraw-Hill, 1960.

6290 Buckley, G. T. "Is Oxford the Original of Jefferson in William Faulkner's Novels?" PMLA, 76 (September, 1961), 447-454.

6291 Buice, Joe C. "The Rise and Decline of Aristocratic Families in Yoknapatawpha County," DAI, 31 (E. Texas State: 1970), 2375A-76A.

6292 Bungert, Hans, ed. Die Amerikanische Short Story: Theorie und Entwicklung. Darmstadt: Wissenschaftliche Buchgesellschaft, 1972.

6293 ______. "William Faulkner on Moby Dick," SA, 9 (1964), 371-375.

6294 ______. William Faulkner und die humoristische Tradition des amerikanischen Südens. Heidelberg: Carl Winter, 1971. Cf., #7461.

6295 ______. "William Faulkners letzter Roman," NS, 12 (1963), 498-506.

6296 Bunker, Robert. "Faulkner: A Case for Regionalism," NMQR, 19 (Spring, 1949), 108-115.

6297 Burger, Nash K. "A Story to Tell: Agee, Wolfe, Faulkner," SAQ, 63 (Winter, 1964), 32-43.

6298 Burgess, Anthony. The Novel Now: A Guide to Contemporary Fiction. New York: Norton, 1967, pp. 89-91, passim.

6299 ______. "The Post-War American Novel: A View from the Periphery," AmSch, 35 (Winter, 1966), 150-156.

6300 Burgum, Edwin Berry. "William Faulkner's Patterns of American Decadence," The Novel and the World's Dilemma. New York: Oxford U.P., 1947, pp. 205-222.

6301 Burke, Kenneth. "Formalist Criticism: Its Principles and Limits," Language as Symbolic Action: Essays on Life, Literature, and Method. Berkeley, California: California U.P., 1966, pp. 480-506, passim.

6302 Burnham, James. "Trying to Say," Symposium, 2 (January, 1931), 51-59.
Defense of Faulkner's style.

6303 Burns, Mattie Ann. "The Development of Women Characters in the Works of William Faulkner," DAI, 35 (Auburn: 1974), 4502A-03A.

6304 Burrows, Robert N. "Institutional Christianity As Reflected in the Works of William Faulkner," MissQ, 14 (Summer, 1961), 138-147.

6305 Busch, Günther. "Zum Tode William Faulkners," Merkur, 16 (1962), 897-899.

6306 Butcher, Fanny. "The Literary Spotlight," Chicago Sunday Tribune (September 12, 1948), Mag. of Books, 2.

6307 _______. "The Other Day," Chicago Tribune (October 18, 1939), 22.

6308 Butor, Michel. "Les relations de parenté dans l'Ours de William Faulkner," LetN, 4 (May, 1956), 734-745.

6309 _______. "Son pays a mis longtemps à le comprendre," FL (July 14, 1962).

6310 Butterfield, Roger, and Roland Gelatt. "From Babbitt to the Bomb," SatRL, 32 (August 6, 1949), 99-122.

6311 Buttitta, Anthony. "William Faulkner: That Writin' Man of Oxford," SatRL, 18 (May 21, 1938), 6-8.

6312 Byrne, Mary Ellen. "An Exploration of the Literary Relationship between Sherwood Anderson and William Faulkner," DAI, 36 (Temple: 1976), 8055A.

6313 Byrne, Sister Mary Enda. "From Tradition to Technique: Development of Character in Joyce and Faulkner," DA, 29 (So. Mississippi: 1969), 3091A.

6314 Cady, Edwin Harrison. "William Faulkner," The Growth of American Literature. New York: American Book Co., 1956, pp. 593-596.

6315 Cahen, Jacques. "Du roman américain," Le Divan, 267 (July, September, 1948), 393-406; 268 (October-December, 1948), 455-469.

6316 _______. "William Faulkner," La littérature américaine. Paris: Presses Universitarie de France, 1958, pp. 110-113.

6317 Cain, Kathleen Shine. "Beyond the Meaning of History: The Quest for a Southern Myth in Faulkner's Characters," DAI, 39, #9 (Marquette: 1978), 5509A-10A.

6318 Calhoun, Richard James. "Southern Writing: The Unifying Strand," MissQ, 27 (Winter, 1973-74), 106.

6319 Călinescu, Matei. "Faulkner cătunul," Gazeta Literara, 18 (May, 1967), 8.

6320 Callen, Shirley Parker. "Bergsonian Dynamism in the Writings of William Faulkner," DA, 23 (Tulane: 1963), 2521.

6321 Calverton, Victor Francis. The Liberation of American Literature. New York: Scribner's, 1932, p. 111.

6322 _______. "Pathology in Contemporary Literature," Thinker, 4 (December, 1931), 7-16.

6323 _______. "Steinbeck, Hemingway and Faulkner," ModQ, 11 (Fall, 1939), 36-44.

6324 Calvo, Lino Novás. "El demonio de Faulkner," Revista de occidente, 39 (January, 1933), 98-103.

6325 Cambon, Glauco. "Il commiato di Faulkner," FLe, 17 (September 16, 1962), 3, 5.

6326 _______. "Il commiato di Faulkner," Verri, 6 (1962), iii, 59-62.

6327 _______. "Faulkner fa scuola," FLe, 9 (March 7, 1954), 5.

6328 _______. La lotta con Proteo. Milano: Bompiani, 1963, passim.

6329 _______. Proceedings of the Comparative Literature Symposium. Vol. IV. William Faulkner: Prevailing Verities and World Literature. Wolodymyr T. Zyla, and Wendell M. Aycock, eds. Lubbock: Interdept. Comm. on Comp. Lit. Texas Tech U., 1973, pp. 77-93.

6330 _______. "Stile e percezione del numinoso in un racconto di Faulkner," SA, 7 (1961), 147-162.

6331 _______. "L'ultimo Faulkner," FLe, 15 (January 3, 1960), 1-2.

6332 Camerino, Aldo. "Novità di William Faulkner," Scrittori di lingua inglese. Milano, Napoli: Ricciardi, 1968, pp. 208-215.

6333 Cameron, May. "An Interview with Thomas Wolfe," Press Time--A Book of Post Classics. New York: Books, Inc., 1936, pp. 247-252.

6334 Camillucci, Marcello. "Faulkner nel romanzo americano," Persona, 4 (1963), 15-16.

6335 Camino, Ioana. "Coordonate mitologice ale lumii 'faulkneriene,'" (Mythological co-ordinates of the Faulknerian world), Contemporanul, No. 28 (July 14, 1967), 2.

6336 Campbell, Harry Modean. "Faulkner's Philosophy Again: A Reply to Michel, Gresset," MissQ, 23 (Winter, 1969-70), 64-66.
Cf., Michel Gresset, MissQ, 20 (Summer, 1967), 177-181.

6337 _______. "Mr. Roth's Centaur and Faulkner's Symbolism,"

WR, 16 (Summer, 1952), 320-321.
Cf., Russell Roth. "The Centaur and the Pear Tree," WR, 16 (Spring, 1952), 199-205.

6338 _______. "Structural Devices in the Works of Faulkner," Perspective, 3 (Autumn, 1950), 209-226.

6339 _______, and Ruel E. Foster. "An Answer to Cleanth Brooks' Attack," FS, 3 (Summer-Autumn, 1954), 40-42.

6340 _______, and _______. William Faulkner: A Critical Appraisal. Norman, Oklahoma: Oklahoma U. P., 1951.

6341 _______, et al. "William Faulkner: A New Look," MissQ, 14 (Summer, 1961), 115-116.

6342 Camus, Albert. Letter. HA, 135 (November, 1951), 21.
"He [Faulkner] is, in my opinion, your greatest writer...."

6343 _______. "Illuminating Answers to Searching Questions," NYHTBR (February 21, 1960), 1.

6344 Canby, Henry Seidel. "Fiction Tells All," Harper'sM, 171 (August, 1935), 308-315.

6345 _______. "Introductory Essay: The Literature of Horror," SatRL, 11 (October 20, 1934), 217-218.

6346 _______. "The School of Cruelty," SatRL, 7 (March 21, 1931), 673-674; repr., in Seven Years Harvest. New York: Farrar & Rinehart, 1936, pp. 77-83; Designed for Reading. New York: Macmillan, 1934, pp. 42-47.

6347 Cannon, Gerard. Basic Facts to Improve Your Grades in American Literature. New York: Collier Bks., 1964, pp. 51, 52.

6348 Cantrell, William F. "Faulkner's Late Short Fiction," DAI, 31 (South Carolina: 1970), 5391A.

6349 Cantrill, Dante Kenneth. "Told by an Idiot: Toward an Understanding of Modern Fiction Through an Analysis of the Works of William Faulkner and John Barth," DAI, 35 (Washington: 1974), 4505A.

6350 Cantwell, Robert. "Le Colonel Faulkner," LetN, 10 (1953), 1304-14.

6351 _______. Introduction. The White Rose of Memphis. New York: Coley Taylor, 1953, pp. v-xxvii.

6352 Capps, Jack L. "Auxiliary Faulkner: Six New Volumes, 1976-1977," SLJ, 10, 1 (1977), 106-114.

6353 _______. "Three Faulkner Studies," SoLJ, 6 (Fall, 1973), 117-121.

6354 _______. "West Point's William Faulkner Room," GaR, 20 (Spring, 1966), 3-8.

6355 Caraceni, Augusto. "William Faulkner," Aretusa, 2 (November, 1945), 23-29.

6356 Carey, Glenn O. "Faulkner and His Carpenter's Hammer," ArQ, 32 (Spring, 1976), 5-15.

6357 _______. "William Faulkner as a Critic of Society," ArQ, 21 (Summer, 1965), 101-108.

6358 _______. "William Faulkner: Critic of Society," DA, 23 (Illinois: 1962), 2522.

6359 _______. "William Faulkner: Man's Fatal Vice," ArQ, 28 (Winter, 1972), 293-300.
War is Faulkner's symbol for man's fatal vice.

6360 _______. "William Faulkner on the Automobile As Socio-Sexual Symbol," CEA Critic, 36 (January, 1974), 15-17.

6361 Cargill, Oscar. "The Primitivists," Intellectual America: Ideas on the March. New York: Macmillan, 1941, pp. 370-386.

6362 _______. Toward a Pluralistic Criticism. Carbondale: Southern Ill. U. P., 1965, pp. 139, 190.

6363 _______. "Yoknapatawpha Conundrums," SatRL, 43 (September 3, 1960), 24.

6364 Carlock, Mary Sue. "Kaleidoscopic Views of Motion," Proceedings of the Comparative Literature Symposium. Vol. IV. William Faulkner: Prevailing Verities and World Literature. Wolodymyr T. Zyla, and Wendell M. Aycock, eds. Lubbock: Interdept. Comm. on Comp. Lit. Texas Tech U., 1973, pp. 95-113.

6365 Carnes, Frank F. "On the Aesthetics of Faulkner's Fiction," DA, 29 (Vanderbilt: 1968), 894A-95A.

6366 Carothers, James B. "Faulkner Criticism: Footprints and Monuments," CEA, 36, ii (1974), 38-40.

6367 _______. "William Faulkner's Short Stories," DAI, 31 (Virginia: 1970), 4757A.

6368 Carpenter, Frederic I. "'The American Myth': Paradise (To Be) Regained," PMLA, 74 (December, 1959), 599-606.

6369 Carpenter, Robert A. "Faulkner 'Discovered,'" Delta Review, 2 (July-August, 1965), 27-29.

6370 Carpenter, Thomas P. The Material of Abnormal Psychology in Some Contemporary English and American Novels. Diss. Stanford: 1947.

6371 Carrouges, Michel. "Faulkner le voyant," Monde nouveau paru, 75 (January, 1954), 74-79.

6372 Carruth, Hayden. "Yoknapatawpha County," Nation, 175 (October 11, 1952), 331-332.

6373 Carter, Hodding. "Faulkner and His Folk," PULC, 18 (Spring, 1957), 95-107; repr., in First Person Rural. Garden City: Doubleday, 1963, pp. 71-85.

6374 _______. "Faulkner, Fish, Fowl and Financiers," Where Main Street Meets the River. New York: Rinehart, 1953, pp. 199-213.

6375 _______. "The Forgiven Faulkner," JI-AmS, 7 (April, 1965), 137-147.

6376 _______. "Looking at the South," Delta Democrat Times (August 27, 1950), 4.

6377 _______. "The Unvarnished Faulkner," Americas, 17 (October, 1965), 30-33.

6378 _______. "William Faulkner: The Man, the Writer, the Legend," NYHTB (July 8, 1962), 1-3.

6379 Carter, Thomas H. "Dramatization of an Enigma," WR, 19 (Winter, 1955), 147-158.

6380 _______. "William Faulkner: A Critical Study, by Irving Howe," Shenandoah, 3 (Autumn, 1952), 62-63.

6381 Cash, W. J. "Literature and the South," SatRL, 23 (December 28, 1940), 3-4, 18-19.

6382 _______. The Mind of the South: Its Origin and Development in the Old South. New York: Knopf, 1941, pp. 376-379, 419.

6383 Castelli, F., S.J. "Tragedia e distruzione dell'uomo nell'opera di William Faulkner," Civiltà cattolica, 104 (March 7, 1953), 530-543.

6384 Castiglione, Luigi. "Conversazione con Faulkner," FLe, 17 (July 22, 1962), 1-2.

6385 Castille, Philip Dubuisson. "Faulkner's Early Heroines," DAI, 38, #4 (Tulane: 1977), 2121A.

6386 Cater, Althea C. "Myth and the Contemporary Southern Novelist," MwJ, 2 (Winter, 1949), 1-8.

6387 _______. Social Attitudes in Five Contemporary Southern Novelists: Erskine Caldwell, William Faulkner, Ellen Glasgow, Caroline Gordon, and T. S. Stribling. Diss. Michigan, 1946.

6388 Cavanaugh, Hilayne E. "Faulkner, Stasis, and Keats's 'Ode on a Grecian Urn,'" DAI, 38 (Nebraska, Lincoln: 1977), 2783A-84A.

6389 Cecchi, Emilio. "Introduzione," Americana: raccolta di narratori dalle origini ai nostri giorni. Elio Vittorini, ed. Milano: Bompiani, 1943, p. xvi.

6390 _______. "Note su William Faulkner," Prospetti, 7 (Spring, 1954), 80-93.

6391 _______. "Ricordo di Faulkner," Paragone, 13 (October, 1962), 3-10.

6392 _______. "William Faulkner," Pan, 2 (May, 1934), 64-70; a revised version, "Note su William Faulkner" in William Faulkner: venti anni di critica. Frederick J. Hoffman and Olga Vickery, eds. Parma: Guanda, 1957, pp. 102-110; also, in E. Cecchi, Scrittori inglesi e americani: saggi, note e versioni, II, 4th ed., rev. Milano: Il Saggiatore, 1964, pp. 196-203.

6393 _______. "The Worldwide Influence of William Faulkner: Reports from Six Capitals," NYTBR (November 15, 1959), 53.

6394 Cela, Camilo J. "Faulkner," PSA, 26 (August, 1962), 115-118.

6395 Cerf, Bennett A. "Author, Author," This Week Magazine (February 27, 1955), 4.

6396 _______. "The Cerfboard: William Faulkner," This Week Mag. (October 25, 1953), 5.

6397 _______. "A Distinguished Commuter," SatRL, 34 (June 9, 1951), 4.

6398 _______. "From William Faulkner's Publisher," SatRL, 45 (July 28, 1962), 12.

6399 _______. "The Literary Scene," SatRL, 27 (September 23, 1944), 18.

6400 ________. "Trade Winds," SatRL, 36 (December 26, 1953), 4.

6401 Cestre, Charles. "William Faulkner," La littérature américaine. Paris: Librairie Armand Colin, 1945, pp. 172-173.

6402 ________. "William Faulkner in France," YFS, 10 (1953), 85-91.
A review of the outstanding French critics of Faulkner.

6403 Cézan, Claude. "'Faulkner est le plus grand écrivain contemporain,' nous dit Albert Camus," NL (September 20, 1956), 10.

6404 Chamberlain, John. "American Writers," Life (September 1, 1949), 82-92.

6405 ________. "Dostoefsky's Shadow in the Deep South," NYTBR (February 15, 1931), 9.

6406 ________. "Literature," America Now. Harold Stearns, ed. New York: Scribner's, 1938, p. 47.

6407 Chapman, Arnold. "The Darkening Stream: William Faulkner: The Demonic Novel," The Spanish-American Reception of United States Fiction, 1920-1940. Berkeley: California U.P., 1966, pp. 127-150.
Contains bibliography of Spanish-American items on Faulkner.

6408 Chase, Richard. "Faulkner: The Great Years," The American Novel and Its Tradition. Garden City, New York: Doubleday, 1957, pp. 205-236.

6409 Chavkin, Allan Richard. "The Secular Imagination: The Continuity of the Secular Romantic Tradition of Wordsworth and Keats in Stevens, Faulkner, Roethke, and Bellow," DAI, 38 (Illinois at Urbana-Champaign: 1977), 6129A.

6410 Chaze, Elliott. "Visit to a Two-Finger Typist," Life, 51 (July 14, 1961), 11-12.

6411 Chen, Yüan-yin. "Heng-ri yu Wei-erh-po-ssu chik chien--Lun Hai-ming-wei yü Fu-ko-na," [Henry Versus Melbourne--A Comparative Study of Hemingway and Faulkner], TkJ, 11 (1973), 217-224.

6412 Chitragupta. "The World of Books: Multiple Focus on Faulkner," Thought, 26 (March 30, 1974), 15-16.
Description of a Faulkner seminar in Delhi, February 1974, in which American and Indian scholars participated.

6413 Christadler, Martin. "Natur und Geschichte im Werk von William Faulkner," JA, 8 (1962), 1-200.

6414 ________. Natur und Geschichte im Werk von William Faulkner. Diss. Tubingen, 1959.

6415 ________. Natur und Geschichte im Werk von William Faulkner. Heidelberg: Carl Winter, 1962.

6416 Chung, Hae-Ja Kim. "Point of View As a Mode of Thematic Definition in Conrad and Faulkner," DAI, 35 (Michigan: 1974), 442A.

6417 Church, Margaret. "William Faulkner: Myth and Duration," Time and Reality: Studies in Contemporary Fiction. Chapel Hill: North Carolina U.P., 1963, pp. 227-250.

6418 Church, Richard. JO'LW, 40 (March 24, 1939), 969.

6419 Ciancio, Ralph A. "Faulkner's Existentialist Affinities," Studies in Faulkner. Carnegie Series in English, No. 6. Pittsburgh: Carnegie Institute of Tech., 1961, pp. 70-91.

6420 ________. "The Grotesque in Modern American Fiction: An Existential Theory," DA, 26 (Pittsburgh: 1964), 365-366.

6421 Clark, A. F. B. "Jean-Paul Sartre: Philosopher and Novelist," CanForum, 37 (March, 1958), 269-271.

6422 Clark, Anderson Aubrey. "Courtly Love in the Writings of William Faulkner," DAI, 36 (Vanderbilt: 1975), 4482A-83A.

6423 Clark, Emily. "A Week-End at Mr. Jefferson's University," NYHTB (November 8, 1931), 1-2.

6424 Clark, John Abbott. "Whither American Literature?--A Symposium (IV)," American Prefaces, 1 (March, 1936), 96.

6425 Clark, William Bedford. "The Serpent of Lust in the Southern Garden: The Theme of Miscegenation in Cable, Twain, Faulkner, and Warren," DAI, 34 (Louisiana State: 1974), 5958A-59A.

6426 Clark, Wm. G. "Is King David a Racist?" UKCR, 34 (1967), 121-126.

6427 Clark, Winifred. "The Religious Symbolism in Faulkner's Novels," DAI, 32 (Tulsa: 1971), 1506A.

6428 Cleaton, Irene. "William Faulkner," Books and Battles. Boston: Houghton Mifflin, 1937, pp. 244-246.

6429 Clifford, Paula M. "The American Novel and the French Nouveau Roman: Some Linguistic and Stylistic Comparisons," CLS, 13 (December, 1976), 348-358.
Similarities in the works of Claude Simon and Faulkner.

6430 Clouard, Henri. "Faulkner, Dos Passos, Maupassant, Flaubert," TR, 34 (October, 1950), 152-156.

6431 _______. "Littérature," RF (avril 1950), 46-48.

6432 Clough, Wilson O. The Necessary Earth: Nature and Solitude in American Literature. Austin: Texas U.P., 1964, pp. 180-183.

6433 Coale, Samuel C., V. "The Role of the South in the Fiction of William Faulkner, Carson McCullers, Flannery O'Connor, and William Styron," DAI, 31 (Brown: 1970), 6596A-97A.

6434 Coan, Otis W., and Richard G. Lillard. America in Fiction. Stanford: Stanford U.P., Rev. ed., 1945, pp. 39, 45, 89.

6435 Cochran, Louis. "William Faulkner, Literary Tyro of Mississippi," Commercial Appeal (November 6, 1932), Part 4; also in James B. Meriwether's "Early Notices ...," MissQ, 17 (1964), 136-164.

6436 Coffee, Jessie A. "Empty Steeples: Theme, Symbol, and Irony in Faulkner's Novels," ArQ, 23 (Autumn, 1967), 197-206.

6437 _______. "Faulkner's Un-Christlike Christians: Biblical Allusions in the Novels," DAI, 32 (Nevada: 1971), 1506A.

6438 Cohen, Hennig, ed. Landmarks of American Writing. New York: Basic Books, 1969.

6439 Coindreau, Maurice Edgar. "L'Art de William Faulkner," France-Amérique, 237 (3 décembre 1950), 9-10.

6440 _______. "Los Campesinos vistos por William Faulkner," La Nación, 9 (agosto 1940), 62-65.

6441 _______. "Extraits," Jefferson, Mississippi. Paris: Gallimard, 1956, pp. 15-48; 230-248; 248-294; 294-310; 435-445; 446-458.

6442 _______. "The Faulkner I Knew," Shenandoah, 16 (Winter, 1965), 27-35.

6443 _______. "Faulkner tel que je l'ai connu," Preuves, 144 (February, 1963), 9-14.

6444 _______. "From Bill Cody to Bill Faulkner," PULC, 17 (Summer, 1956), 185-190.

6445 _______. "Lettres étrangères: William Faulkner," NRF, 236 (1 juin 1931), 926-931.

Apparently the first article in French on Faulkner. Cf., YFS, 10 (Fall, 1942), 85-91.

6446 ________. "On Translating Faulkner," PULC, 18 (Spring, 1957), 108-113.

6447 ________. "Panorama de la actual literatura joven norte-americana," Sur (Buenos Aires), 7 (March, 1937), 49-65.

6448 ________. "Les principaux Romans de William Faulkner," Aperçus de Littérature américaine. Paris: Gallimard, 1946, pp. 111-146.

6449 ________. "A propósito de la última novela publicada por William Faulkner," La Nación (March 3, 1935), Sec. 2, 2.

6450 ________. "Le Puritanisme de William Faulkner," CS, 22 (April, 1935), 266-267.

6451 ________. "Quadrille américain," Les Oeuvres Nouvelles. New York: Editions de la Maison Française, 1942, pp. 139-164.

6452 ________. The Time of William Faulkner: A French View of Modern American Fiction. George M. Reeves, ed., and tr. Columbia: South Carolina U.P., 1971.

6453 ________. "William Faulkner in France," YFS, 10 (Fall, 1952), 85-91.

6454 ________. "William Faulkner: Translated from the English," University (Princeton), 4 (Spring, 1966), 25-26.

6455 ________. "William Faulkner y su último gran libro," La Nación, Sec. 2 (13 diciembre 1936), 1.

6456 Cole, Hunter McKelva. "Elizabeth Spencer at Sycamore Fair," NMW, 6 (Winter, 1974), 81-86.
Transcript of interview with Elizabeth Spencer in which she described her acquaintance with Faulkner.

6457 ________. "Welty on Faulkner," NMW, 9 (Spring, 1976), 23-49.
A list of Welty's comments on Faulkner.

6458 Collins, Carvel. "A Conscious Literary Use of Freud?" L&P, 3 (November, 1953), 2-6.

6459 ________. "Faulkner and Certain Earlier Southern Fiction," CE, 16 (November, 1954), 92-97.

6460 ________. "Faulkner and Certain Earlier Southern Fiction," The Frontier Humorists: Critical Views. M. Thomas

Inge, ed. Hamden, Conn.: Shoestring Press, 1975, pp. 259-265.

6461 _______. "Faulkner's Reputation and the Contemporary Novel," Literature in the Modern World. William Griffin, ed. Nashville: Peabody College, 1954, pp. 65-71.

6462 _______. "A Fourth Book Review by Faulkner," MissQ, 28 (Summer, 1975), 339-346.

6463 _______. "War and Peace and Mr. Faulkner," NYTBR (August 1, 1954), 1, 13.

6464 _______, comp. William Faulkner: Early Prose and Poetry. Tokyo: Kenkyusha, 1962; Boston: Little, Brown & Co., 1962.

6465 Collins, Norman. The Facts of Fiction. New York: Dutton, 1933, pp. 281, 282-283.

6466 Collins, R. G., and Kenneth McRobbie, eds. The Novels of William Faulkner. Winnipeg: Manitoba U. P., 1973.
Contains essays from a special number of Mosaic, No. 7 (Fall, 1973).

6467 "Colloques en Virginie avec William Faulkner," RdP (February, 1964), 5-14.

6468 Colson, Theodore L. "The Characters of Hawthorne and Faulkner: A Typology of Sinners," DA, 28 (Michigan: 1967), 2204A-05A.

6469 Commager, Henry Steele. The American Mind. New Haven: Yale U. P., 1950, pp. 120-125, 249.

6470 Commins, Saxe, ed. The Faulkner Reader. New York: Random House, 1954.

6471 Comşa, Ioan. "Faulkner: Un inovator al artei narrative," RevBib, 25, ix (1972), 456-457.

6472 "Configuration critique de William Faulkner," Part I: RLM, IV, Nos. 27-29 (1957); Part II: RLM, V, Nos. 40-42 (1958-1959).

6473 Conley, Timothy K. "Beardsley and Faulkner," JML, 5 (September, 1976), 339-356.

6474 _______. "Shakespeare and Faulkner: A Study in Influence," DAI, 39, #8 (Pennsylvania State: 1978), 4945A.

6475 Connelly, Marc. Voices Offstage: A Book of Memoirs. New York: Holt, Rinehart & Winston, 1968, pp. 215-216.

6476 Connolly, Thomas E. "Fate and 'the Agony of Will': Determinism in Some Works of William Faulkner," KSE, 1 (1964), 36-52.

6477 _______. "Fate and 'the Agony of Will': Determinism in Some Works of William Faulkner," Essays on Determinism in American Literature. Sydney J. Krause, ed. (Kent Studies in English, No. 1). Kent, Ohio: Kent State U.P., 1964, pp. 36-52.

6478 Cook, Albert. "Plot As Discovery: Conrad, Dostoevsky, and Faulkner," The Meaning of Fiction. Detroit: Wayne State U.P., 1960, pp. 232-241, passim.

6479 Cook, Bruce. "New Faces in Faulkner Country," SatR (September 4, 1976), 39-41.

6480 Cook, Richard M. "Popeye, Flem, and Sutpen: The Faulknerian Villain as Grotesque," SAF, 3, #1 (Spring, 1975), 3-14.

6481 Cook, Sylvia Jenkins. "Faulkner's Celebration of the Poor White Paradox," From Tobacco Road to Route 66: The Southern Poor White in Fiction. Chapel Hill: North Carolina U.P., 1976, pp. 39-63.

6482 _______. "The Literary Treatment of the Southern Poor White in the 1930's," DAI, 34, #4 (Michigan: 1973), 1899A.

6483 Cooke, Alistair. "William Faulkner's Road to Stockholm," GW (Manchester), (April 5, 1951), 13.

6484 Cooley, John Ryder. "Modes of Primitivism: Black Portraits by White Writers in Twentieth Century American Literature," DAI, 31 (MA: 1970), 2377A-78A.

6485 Cooley, Thomas W., Jr. "Faulkner Draws the Long Bow," TCL, 16 (October, 1970), 268-277.

6486 Cooper, Gerald Hurst. "Furious Motion: Metamorphosis and Change in the Works of William Faulkner," DAI, 39, #8 (Washington: 1978), 4946A.

6487 Cooperman, Stanley. "A World Withdrawn: Mahon and Hicks (William Faulkner, Thomas Boyd)," World War I and the American Novel. London and Baltimore: Johns Hopkins Press, 1970, pp. 159-165.

6488 Core, George, ed. Southern Fiction Today: Renascence and Beyond. Athens: Georgia U.P., 1969, pp. 58-59, 69-70, 82-85, passim.

6489 Cormeau, Nelly. "Éthique de la littérature française d'aujourd'hui," Synthèses, 1 (mai 1946), 63; et juin, 60-73.

6490 Corridori, Edward L. "The Quest for Sacred Space: Setting in the Novels of William Faulkner," DAI, 32 (Kent State: 1971), 5224A.

6491 Corsini, Gianfranco. "Faulkner e la critica," Contemp, 5 (1963), 42-47.

6492 Corwin, Ronald Lloyd. "The Development of Narrative Technique in the Apprenticeship Fiction of William Faulkner," DAI, 37 (Brandeis: 1976), 2869A.

6493 Couch, John Philip. "Camus and Faulkner: The Search for the Language of Modern Tragedy," YFS, 25 (Spring, 1960), 120-125.

6494 _______. "Camus' Dramatic Adaptations and Translations," FR, 33 (October, 1959), 27-36.

6495 Couch, W. T., ed. Culture in the South. Chapel Hill: North Carolina U.P., 1934, pp. 193, 205-207, 386-387.

6496 Coughlan, Robert. "The Man Behind the Faulkner Myth," Life, 35 (October 5, 1953), 55-58.

6497 _______. "The Private World of William Faulkner," Life, 35 (September 28, 1953), 118-136.

6498 _______. The Private World of William Faulkner. New York: Harper & Bros., 1954.

6499 Coulombe, Michael Joseph. "The Trilogy of Form in Modern American Fiction," DA, 31 (Purdue: 1970), 1792A.

6500 Courtney, Winifred F., ed. The Reader's Adviser. New York and London: R. R. Bowker, 1968, passim.

6501 Cowley, Malcolm. "Afterthoughts on William Faulkner," Critic, 25 (October-November, 1966), 90-92.

6502 _______. "Après la guerre finie," Horizon, 10 (Winter, 1968), 113-119.

6503 _______. "The Etiology of Faulkner's Art," SoR, 13 (Winter, 1977), 83-95.

Cf., Malcolm Cowley's "Faulkner: The Etiology of His Art," in--And I Worked at the Writer's Trade: Chapters of Literary History, 1918-1978. New York: Viking, 1978, pp. 214-230.

6504 _______. The Faulkner-Cowley File: Letters and Memories. London: Chatto & Windus, 1966; New York: Viking, 1966.

6505 _______. "Faulkner: The Yoknapatawpha Story," A Second Flowering: Works and Days of the Lost Generation. New York: Viking, 1973, pp. 130-155, passim.

6506 _______. "Faulkner: Voodoo Dance," and "Faulkner by Daylight," Think Back on Us: A Contemporary Chronicle on the 1930's. Carbondale and Edwardsville: Southern Ill. U.P., 1967, pp. 268-271, 358-360.

6507 _______. "A Fresh Look at Faulkner," SatRL, 49 (June 11, 1966), 22-26.

6508 _______. "The Generation That Wasn't Lost," CE, 5 (February, 1944), 233-239.

6509 _______, ed. Introduction. The Portable Faulkner. New York: Viking, 1946; Sixth Printing, 1959.

6510 _______. "An Introduction to William Faulkner," Critiques and Essays on Modern Fiction. John W. Aldridge, ed. New York: Ronald Press, 1952, 427-446; also in A Southern Vanguard, Allen Tate, ed. New York: Prentice-Hall, 1947, pp. 13-27.

6511 _______. The Literary Situation. New York: Viking, 1947, 1954, passim.

6512 _______. A Many Windowed House: Collected Essays on American Writers and American Writing. Dan Piper, ed. Carbondale and Edwardsville: Southern Ill. U.P., 1944, 1970, passim.

6513 _______. "Sherwood Anderson's Epiphanies," LonM, 7 (July, 1960), 61-66.

6514 _______. "The Solitude of William Faulkner," Atl, 217 (June, 1966), 97-115.

6515 _______. "Twenty-five Years After: The Lost Generation Today," SatRL, 34 (June 2, 1951), 6-7, 33-34.

6516 _______. "Who's to Take the Place of Hemingway and Faulkner?" NYTBR (October 7, 1962), 4, 26.
Responses in NYTBR (October 28, 1962), 48.

6517 _______. "William Faulkner," ARund, 3 (July, 1947), 31-40.

6518 _______. "William Faulkner e la leggenda del Sud," Pensiero Critico, 2 (March, 1952), 46-59.

6519 _______. "William Faulkner, et la lêgende du Sud," Revue Internationale (mars 1946), 263.

6520 ________. "William Faulkner Revisited," SatRL, 28 (April 14, 1945), 13-16.

6521 ________. "William Faulkner's Human Comedy," NYTBR (October 29, 1944), 4.

6522 ________. "William Faulkner's Legend of the South," SR, 53 (Summer, 1945), 343-361; revised and repr., in Introduction, The Portable Faulkner. New York: Viking, 1946, pp. 94-109; repr., in Southern Vanguard. New York: Prentice-Hall, 1947, pp. 13-27; also in Ray B. West's Essays in Modern Criticism. New York: Holt, Rinehart, & Winston, 1952, pp. 513-526.

6523 ________. "The Writer in Critical Perspective," SatRL, 45 (July 28, 1962), 22.

6524 ________. "William Faulkner," Writers at Work. New York: Viking, 1959, pp. 119-141.

6525 Cox, Leland Holcombe, Jr. "Sinbad in New Orleans: Early Short Fiction by William Faulkner: An Annotated Edition," DAI, 38 (South Carolina: 1977), 2122A.

6526 Crane, Joan St. C. "Rare or Seldom-Seen Dust Jackets of American First Editions: IV," Serif, 8 (March, 1971), 21-23.

6527 Crane, John K. "The Jefferson Courthouse: An Axis Exsecrabilis Mundi," TCL, 15 (April, 1969), 19-23.

6528 Creighton, Joanne V. William Faulkner's Craft of Revision. Detroit, Michigan: Wayne State U.P., 1977.

6529 Crichton, Kyle S. "William Faulkner," Total Recoil. Garden City: Doubleday, 1960, pp. 173-175.

6530 Crisler, B. R. "Film Gossip of the Week," NYTimes (August 2, 1936), X, 3.
Faulkner in Hollywood.

6531 Crow, Peter Glenn. "Faulkner's Vitalistic Vision: A Close Study of Eight Novels," DAI, 34 (Duke: 1973), 764A-65A.

6532 Cruickshank, John. Albert Camus and the Literature of Revolt. New York: Oxford U.P., 1960. A Galaxy Book, passim.

6533 Cullen, John B., and Floyd C. Watkins. Old Times in the Faulkner Country. Chapel Hill: North Carolina U.P., 1961.

6534 Culley, Margaret M. M. "Eschatological Thought in Faulkner's Yoknapatawpha Novels," DAI, 33 (Michigan: 1973), 5167A.

6535 ________. "Judgment in Yoknapatawpha Fiction," Renascence, 28 (Winter, 1976), 59-70.
Biblical mythology in the novels.

6536 Cunliffe, Marcus. "William Faulkner," TLS (February 20, 1953), 121.

6537 ________. "William Faulkner," The Literature of the United States. London: Penguin, 1954, pp. 284-288; rev. and enlarged, 1959.

6538 "The Curse and the Hope," Time, 84 (July 17, 1964), 44-48.
Faulkner and the South.

6539 Curto, Joseph J. An Analysis of William Faulkner's Major Techniques of Comedy. Diss. Florida State: 1969.

6540 Dabney, Lewis M. "Faulkner, the Red, and the Black," ColuF, 1 (Spring, 1972), 52-54.

6541 ________. The Indians of Yoknapatawpha: A Study in Literature and History. Baton Rouge: Louisiana State U.P., 1974.

6542 D'Agostino, Nemi. "Faulkner," Par, 9 (1958), 71-79.

6543 ________. "William Faulkner," SA, 1 (1955), 257-308.

6544 Dahl, James. "A Faulkner Reminiscence: Conversations with Mrs. Maude Faulkner," JML, 3 (April, 1974), 1026-1030.
Personal impressions of Faulkner's mother.

6545 ________. "William Faulkner on Individualism," WGCR, 6 (1973), 3-9.

6546 Dahlberg, Edward. Epitaphs of Our Times. New York: Braziller, 1967, passim.

6547 Dain, Martin J. "Faulkner Country," Life, 55 (August 2, 1963), 46B-53.
A photographic essay.

6548 ________. Faulkner's County: Yoknapatawpha. New York: Random House, 1964.
Scenes and people in Faulkner's environment.

6549 Daniel, Bradford. "Faulkner on Race," Ramparts, 2 (Winter, 1963), 43-49.

6550 ________. "William Faulkner and the Southern Quest for Freedom," Black, White and Gray: Twenty-one Points of View on the Race Question. Bradford Daniel, ed. New York: Sheed and Ward, 1964, pp. 291-308.

6551 Daniel, Robert. "The World of Eudora Welty," Southern Renascence. Louis D. Rubin, Jr., and Robert D. Jacobs, eds. Baltimore: Johns Hopkins, 1953; 2nd pr., 1954, pp. 306-315.

6552 Dardis, Tom. "William Faulkner," Some Time in the Sun: The Hollywood Years of Fitzgerald, Faulkner, Nathanael West, Aldous Huxley, and James Agee. New York: Scribner's, 1976, pp. 78-149.

6553 Darnell, Donald G. "Cooper and Faulkner: Land, Legacy, and the Tragic Vision," SAB, 34 (March, 1969), 3-5.

6554 Davenport, F. Garvin. "The Myth of Southern History," DA, 28 (Minnesota: 1968), 3666A.

6555 ________. "William Faulkner," The Myth of Southern History: Historical Consciousness in Twentieth-Century Southern Literature. Nashville: Vanderbilt U.P., 1970, pp. 82-130.

6556 Davenport, Guy. "The Top Is a New Bottom," NatlR, 17 (July 27, 1965), 658-659.

6557 Davidson, Donald. "A Meeting of Southern Writers," Bookman, 74 (January-February, 1932), 494-496.
Cf., M. Thomas Inge, ed. "Donald Davidson on Faulkner: An Early Recognition," GaR, 20 (1966), 456-462.

6558 ________. "The South Today: Report on Southern Literature," Dallas Times Herald (July 17, 1938), I, 6.

6559 ________. "Southern Literature--1931," Creative Reading, 6 (December 1, 1931), 1229-1234.

6560 ________. "The Trend of Literature: A Partisan View," Culture in the South. W. T. Couch, ed. Chapel Hill: North Carolina U.P., 1935; repr., Westport, Conn.: Negro Universities Press, 1970, p. 193.

6561 ________. "Why the South Has a Great Literature," Still Rebels, Still Yankees, and Other Essays. Baton Rouge: Louisiana State U.P., 1957, pp. 162-179.

6562 Davidson, Marshall B. The American Heritage: History of the Writers' America. New York: American Heritage Pub. Co., 1973, pp. 340-341, passim.

6563 Davis, Richard Beale. "Spadework, American Literature

and the Southern Mind: Opportunities," SAB, 31 (March, 1966), 1-4.

6564 ________. "The Works of William Faulkner," AmRep (New Delhi), 7 (October 9, 1957), 7.

6565 Day, Douglas. "The War Stories of William Faulkner," GaR, 15 (Winter, 1961), 385-394.

6566 Dean, Charles Wilbur. "William Faulkner's Romantic Heritage: Beyond America," DAI, 36 (Mass.: 1975), 885A-86A.

6567 Dean, Elizabeth Muriel Lewis. "The Contours of Eros: Landscape in Twentieth Century Art and Literature," DAI, 38 (Emory: 1977), 3455a-56A.

6568 Dean, Sharon Welch. "Lost Ladies: The Isolated Heroine in the Fiction of Hawthorne, James, Fitzgerald, Hemingway, and Faulkner," DAI, 34 (New Hampshire: 1973), 2616A.

6569 De Dominicis, A. M. "Scrivo perchè mi piace, dice William Faulkner," FLe, 9 (February 14, 1954), 1-2.

6570 Degenfelder, E. Pauline. "Essays on Faulkner: Style, Use of History, Film Adaptations on His Fiction," DAI, 33 (Case Western Reserve: 1973), 5169A.

6571 DeGroot, Elizabeth M. "Archetypes in the Major Novels of Thomas Hardy and Their Literary Application," DA, 28 (N. Y. U.: 1967), 1048A.
Compares Wessex to Yoknapatawpha because both are "beset by change."

6572 Delay, Florence, and Jacqueline de Labriolle. "Márquez est-il le Faulkner colombien?" RLC, 47 (1973), 88-123.

6573 Delgado, Feliciano. "El mundo complejo de William Faulkner," Rasón y fe (Madrid), 160 (1959), 323-334.

6574 Denny, Margaret, and William H. Gilman, eds. The American Writer and the European Tradition. Minneapolis: Minnesota U. P., 1950, passim.

6575 Denoreaz, Michel. "William Faulkner ou le parti pris de la fausse réalité," NCr, 3 (January, 1951), 74-84.

6576 de Onis, Harriet. "William Faulkner," La Torre, 3 (October-December, 1955), 11-26.

6577 ________. "William Faulkner y su Mundo," Sur (Argentina), No. 202 (1951), 24-33.

6578 Dêry, György, and I. Kristó Nagy. Faulkner. Budapest: Gondolat, 1966.

6579 Desmond, John Francis. "Christian Historical Analogues in the Fiction of William Faulkner and Flannery O'Connor," DAI, 32 (Oklahoma: 1971), 3994A-95A.

6580 Despain, Norma Larene. "Stream of Consciousness Narration in Faulkner: A Redefinition," DAI, 37 (Connecticut: 1975), 306A-307A.

6581 Desternes, Jean. ["Faulkner"] Litterature prolétarienne aux Etats-Unis. Paris: Editions Nouvelles, 1948, pp. 22-23.

6582 Dettelbach, Cynthia G. In the Driver's Seat: The Automobile in American Literature and Popular Culture. Westport, Connecticut: Greenwood Press, 1976.

6583 Detweiler, Robert. "The Moment of Death in Modern Fiction," CL, 13 (Summer, 1972), 269-294.

6584 Devlin, Albert J. "Faulknerian Chronology: Puzzles and Games," NMW, 6 (1973), 98-101.

6585 ________. "Parent-Child Relationships in the Works of William Faulkner," DAI, 31 (Kansas: 1970), 2910A.

6586 Dickerson, Mary Jane. "Faulkner's Golden Steed," MissQ, 31, #3 (Summer, 1978), 369-380.
Faulkner's use of horse imagery throughout his works.

6587 Dietz, Thomas S. "Living in the Machine Age," NYTimes (January 16, 1955), IV, 10.

6588 Dike, Donald A. "The World of Faulkner's Imagination," DA, 15 (Syracuse: 1955), 265.

6589 Dillingham, William B. "William Faulkner and the 'Tragic Condition,'" Edda, 53 (1966), 322-335.

6590 Dillistone, Frederick William. The Novelist and the Passion Story. London: Collins, 1960.

6591 "Une discussion sur Faulkner chez les étudiants communistes americains," NCr, 1 (juillet-août 1949), 87-96.

6592 Ditsky, John M. "'Dark, Darker Than Fire': Thematic Parallels in Lawrence and Faulkner," SHR, 8 (Fall, 1974), 497-505.

6593 ________. "Faulkner Land and Steinbeck Country," Mon/Or (1971), 11-23.

6594 ________. "Faulkner Land and Steinbeck Country," Steinbeck: The Man and His Work. Richard Astro and T. Hayashi, eds. Corvallis: Oregon State U.P., 1971, pp. 11-23.

6595 ________. "Faulkner's Harrykin Creek: A Note," UWR, 12, 1 (Fall-Winter, 1976), 88-89.

6596 ________. "From Oxford to Salinas: Comparing Faulkner and Steinbeck," SteinbeckQ, 2 (Fall, 1969), 51-55.

6597 ________. "Land-Nostalgia in the Novels of Faulkner, Cather, and Steinbeck," DA, 28 (N.Y.U.: 1967), 1072A.

6598 ________. "Uprooted Trees: Dynasty and the Land in Faulkner's Novels," TSL, 17 (1972), 151-158.

6599 ________. ["William Faulkner"] Steinbeck's Literary Dimension: A Guide to Comparative Studies. Tetsumaro Hayashi, ed. Metuchen, New Jersey: Scarecrow Press, 1973.

6600 Djankov, Krastan. "Zamislenijat genij ot Joknapatofa," [The meditative genius from Yoknapatawpha], Uiljam Fornăr. Izbrani razkazi [Selected Short Stories]. Plovdiv: H. G. Danov, 1970, pp. 7-29.

6601 Dodds, John Lloyd. "The Fatal Arc: The Evolution of Tragic Image and Idea in Three Novels by William Faulkner," DAI, 38, #11 (Loyola U. of Chicago: 1978), 6722A-6723A.
The three novels are Absalom, Absalom!, Light in August, and Sartoris.

6602 Dodds, John W. "The Mediocre American," HLQ, 22 (May, 1959), 163-177.
Faulkner and others have created a concept of the "mediocre American" of the 50's.

6603 Doderer, Hans von. "Zur Technik des modernen amerikanischen Romans," NS, 6 (1958), 275-284.

6604 Dolbier, Maurice. "Faulkneriana," NYHTB (December 9, 1962, 2.
Anecdotes of Cowley and Collins.

6605 Dollon, R. T. "Some Sources of Faulkner's Version of the First Air War," AL, 44 (January, 1973), 629-637.
Elliott White Springs and James Warner Bellah as possible sources.

6606 Doniol-Valcroze, J. "Faulkner et le cinêma," Observateur (7 dêcembre 1950), 23.

6607 Donnelly, William and Doris. "William Faulkner: In Search of Peace," Personalist, 44 (Autumn, 1963), 490-498.

6608 Doody, Terrence Arthur. "The Limited Narrator and the Heroic Character," DA, 31 (Cornell: 1970), 6513A.

6609 "Doom," NY, 29 (February 28, 1953), 18-20.
A reminiscence about Faulkner in the office of Saxe Commins, and Faulkner's remark that "Ah wish mah doom would lift or come on."

6610 Doran, Leonard. "Form and the Story Teller," HA, 135 (November, 1951), 12, 38-41.

6611 Dorsch, Robert L. "An Interpretation of the Central Themes in the Work of William Faulkner," ESRS, 11 (September, 1962), 5-42.

6612 Dos Passos, John. "Faulkner," NatlR, 14 (January 15, 1963), 11.

6613 _______. "Faulkner," Occasions and Protests. Chicago: Henry Regnery, 1964, pp. 275-277.

6614 Doster, William C. "The Several Faces of Gavin Stephens," MissQ, 11 (Fall, 1958), 191-195.

6615 _______. "William Faulkner and the Negro," DA, 20 (Florida: 1959), 1094.

6616 Douglas, Harold J. and Robert Daniel. "Faulkner and the Puritanism of the South," TSL, 2 (1957), 1-13.

6617 _______, and _______. "Faulkner's Southern Puritanism," Religious Perspectives in Faulkner's Fiction. J. R. Barth, ed. Notre Dame: Notre Dame U.P., 1972, pp. 37-51.

6618 Dowell, Bobby Ray. "Faulkner's Comic Spirit," DA, 23 (Denver: 1963), 4355.

6619 Downey, Elizabeth Ann. "Faulkner's Sense of History: Criticism of the Magnolia Myth in the Novels of William Faulkner," DAI, 33 (Denver: 1972), 3534A.

6620 Downing, Francis. "An Eloquent Man," Cw, 53 (December 15, 1950), 255-258.

6621 Doyle, Charles. "The Moral World of Faulkner," Renascence, 19 (Fall, 1966), 3-12.

6622 Drake, Robert. "The Pieties of the Fiction Writer, I," CEA Critic, 32 (October, 1969), 3-4.
Faulkner an example of a writer "less concerned--or enmeshed--in a personal past."

6623 Droit, Michel. "Ecartons l'homme pour apprecier l'ecrivain," FL, 17 (July 14, 1967), 8.

6624 Duclos, D. P. "Son of Sorrow: The Life, Works, and Influence of Colonel William C. Falkner, 1825-1889," DA, 23 (Michigan: 1962), 233.
Conclusions are that a number of characters and themes in William Faulkner's work may be directly traced to his relationship with his own family.

6625 Duesberg, Jacques. "Un createur de mythes," Syntheses, 3 (decembre 1948), 342-354.

6626 ________. "Sur Faulkner," Syn, 8 (August-September, 1953), 84-86.

6627 Duncan, Alastair B. "Claude Simon and William Faulkner," FMLS, 9 (1973), 235-252.

6628 Durant, Ariel and Will. "William Faulkner," Interpretations of Life: A Survey of Contemporary Literature. New York: Simon & Schuster, 1970, pp. 11-27.

6629 Durham, Frank. "Not According to the Book: Materialism and the American Novel," GaR, 20 (Spring, 1966), 97.

6630 ________. "The Southern Literary Tradition: Shadow or Substance?" SAQ, 67 (Summer, 1968), 455-468.

6631 Durham, Philip. "William Faulknerin asema kirjallisuudessa," Aikamme, No. 12 (December, 1955), 30.

6632 Durrett, Frances Bowen. "The New Orleans Double Dealer," Reality and Myth. W. E. Walker and R. L. Welker, eds. Nashville: Vanderbilt U.P., 1964, pp. 212-236.

6633 Durston, J. H. "Come, Come, William Faulkner," House and Garden, 3 (June, 1957), 16-17.

6634 Dusenbery, Peter F. The Self-Creating Narrator and His Hero. Diss. Washington: 1972.

6635 Eaglin, Patrick Gerald. William Faulkner: The Search for Reality. Diss. Harvard: 1977.

6636 "Early Faulkner," Newsweek, 50 (December 30, 1957), 70.

6637 Eastman, Richard M. A Guide to the Novel. San Francisco: Chandler, 1965, passim.

6638 Eby, Cecil D. "Faulkner and the Southwestern Humorists," Shenandoah, 11 (Autumn, 1959), 13-21.

6639 ________. "Ichabod Crane in Yoknapatawpha," GaR, 16 (Winter, 1962), 465-469.

6640 Edel, Leon. The Modern Psychological Novel. New York: Grosset & Dunlap, 1964, passim.

6641 ________. "William Faulkner," Masters of American Literature. Boston: Houghton Mifflin, 1959. Shorter Edition, pp. 1310-1384.

6642 Edgar, Pelham. "Four American Writers: Anderson, Hemingway, Dos Passos, Faulkner," The Art of the Novel. New York: Macmillan, 1934; reissued, Russell & Russell, 1966, pp. 338-351.

6643 Edminston, Susan, and Linda D. Cirino. Literary New York: A History and Guide. Boston: Houghton Mifflin Co., 1976.
Discussion of Faulkner and other Southern writers.

6644 Edmonds, Irene C. "Faulkner and the Black Shadow," Southern Renascence: The Literature of the Modern South. Louis D. Rubin and R. D. Jacobs, eds. Baltimore: Johns Hopkins Press, 1953, pp. 192-206.

6645 Effelberger, Hans. "Neue Entwicklungstendenzen in der amerikanischen Literatur der Gegenwart," NS (1936), 154-161.

6646 ________. [William Faulkner] Umrisse der Amerikanischen Kultur und Kunst. Frankfurt/Main: Diesterweg, 1937.

6647 Egolf, Robert H. "Faulkner's Men and Women: A Critical Study of Male-Female Relationships in His Early Yoknapatawpha County Novels," DAI, 39, #8 (Lehigh: 1978), 4946A-47A.

6648 Egor, Gvozden. "Roman kao moralitet: Pasija po Fokneru," Knji, 56 (1973), 342-351.

6649 Ehrenbourg, Illya. "Les mains sales, Faulkner et Sartre vus par un écrivain soviétique," LF (10 février 1949), 1.

6650 Einsiedel, Wolfgang von. "William Faulkner," Europaische Revue, XI (1935), 707-708.

6651 Eisinger, Chester E. Fiction of the Forties. Chicago: Chicago U.P., 1963, pp. 178-186, passim.

6652 Eitner, Walter H. "The Aristoi of Yoknapatawpha County," NConL, 7, #4 (1977), 10-11.

6653 Elder, John C. "Towards a New Objectivity: Essays on the Body and Nature in Faulkner, Lawrence, and Mann," DAI, 34 (Yale: 1974), 7228A.

6654 Elias, Robert. "Gavin Stevens--Intruder?" FS, 3 (Summer-Autumn, 1954), 1-4.

6655 ________, ed. Letters of Theodore Dreiser. Philadelphia: Pennsylvania U. P., 1959, II, 624.

6656 Elkin, Stanley Lawrence. "Religious Themes and Symbolism in the Novels of William Faulkner," DA, 22 (Illinois: 1961), 3659-60.

6657 Ellison, Ralph. "I negri americani nella letteratura da Mark Twain a Faulkner," Communità, 11 (October, 1957), 48-55.

6658 ________. Shadow & Act. New York: Random House, 1964, pp. 41-44.

6659 ________. "Twentieth-Century and the Black Mask of Humanity," Confluence, 2 (December, 1953), 3-21.

6660 ________. "Twentieth-Century Fiction and the Black Mask of Humanity," Images of the Negro in American Literature. Seymour L. Gross, and John E. Hardy, eds. Chicago: Chicago U. P., 1966, pp. 121-131.

6661 ________. "'A Very Stern Discipline': An Interview with Ralph Ellison," HarpersM, 234 (March, 1967), 76-95.

6662 Elsen, Claude. "Faulkner et le roman noir," Rêforme, (16 fevrier 1952), 7.

6663 Emerson, O. B. "Faulkner and His Bibliographers," BB, 30 (1973), 90-92.

6664 ________. "Faulkner and His Friend: An Interview with Emily W. Stone," Comment, 10 (Spring, 1971), 31-37.
Discussion of the relationship between Faulkner and Phil Stone.

6665 ________. "Faulkner, the Mule, and the South," DeltaR, 6 (November-December, 1969), 108-110.

6666 ________. "Prophet Next Door," Reality and Myth: Essays in American Literature in Memory of Richmond Croom Beatty. William E. Walker and Robert L. Welker, eds. Nashville, Tenn.: Vanderbilt U. P., 1964, pp. 237-274.

6667 ________. "William Faulkner's Literary Reputation in America," DA, 23 (Vanderbilt: 1962), 631.

6668 ________. "William Faulkner's Nemesis--Major Frederick Sullens," JMissH, 36 (May, 1974), 161-164.

6669 Emerson, William. "A Faulkner Fable," Newsweek, 44 (August 30, 1954), 7.
A personal anecdote.

6670 Emmanuel, Pierre. "Faulkner and the Sense of Sin," HA, 135 (November, 1951), 20.

6671 ________. "Romanciers et poètes américains," TP (20 avril 1945), 5.

6672 Engelborghs, M. "Verhalen van William Faulkner," Kultuurleven, 27 (August-September, 1960), 530-532.

6673 England, Kenneth. "The Decline of the Southern Gentleman Character As He Is Illustrated in Novels by Present-Day Southern Novelists," DA, 17 (Vanderbilt: 1941), 2594.

6674 Engle, Paul. "Faulkner's Rhetoric," Chicago Sunday Tribune (August 29, 1954), Mag. of Bks., 7.

6675 Enos, Bertram. "William Faulkner," SatRL, 8 (December 19, 1931), 398.
Censures reviewers for their inaccurate estimate of Faulkner.

6676 Erskine, Albert. "Authors and Editors: William Faulkner at Random House," U.S. Military Academy Library Occasional Papers, No. 2 (1974), 14-19.

6677 ________. "Authors and Editors: William Faulkner at Random House," Die deutsche Literatur in der Weimarer Republik. Wolfgang Rothe, ed. Stuttgart: Reclam, 1974, pp. 14-19.

6678 Erval, François. "Le double Faulkner," Express (Paris), No. 578 (July 12, 1962), 23.

6679 ________. "Faulkner après le prix Nobel," TM, 8 (June, 1953), 2024-2030.

6680 ________. "Faulkner, deuxième manière," TM, 10 (November, 1954), 750-754.

6681 Eschliman, Herbert R. "Francis Christensen in Yoknapatawpha County," UR, 37 (March, 1971), 232-239.
Analysis of Faulkner's use of the cumulative sentence.

6682 Evans, Medford. "Oxford, Mississippi," SWR, 15 (Autumn, 1929), 46-63.

6683 Evans, Walter. "Faulkner's Mississippi," Vogue, 112 (October 1, 1948), 144-149.
Photographic.

6684 Everett, Walter K. Faulkner's Art and Characters. Woodbury, New York: Barron's Educational Series, 1969.
Plot summaries of novels and stories and dictionary of characters.

6685 "An Ex-German," SatRL, 20 (August 26, 1939), 8.
States that the names of Thomas Wolfe and William Faulkner meant less in the United States than in Germany.

6686 F., J. "Faulkner parle pour la liberté," FL (7 juin 1952), 1.

6687 Fabre, Michel. "Bayonne ou le Yoknapatawpha d'Ernest Gaines," RANAM, 9 (1975-76), 208-22.

6688 ________. "The Time of William Faulkner," *Essays by M. E. Coindreau*, George M. Reeves, ed., and tr. CL, 25 (Spring, 1973), 189-190.

6689 Fadiman, Clifton. "Clerihews," SatRL, 11 (June 1, 1957), 23.

6690 ________. "Faulkner, Extra-Special, Double-Distilled," NY, (October 31, 1936), 78-80.

6691 ________. "Mississippi Frankenstein," NY, 14 (January 21, 1939), 60-62.

6692 ________. "Reading I've Liked," Holiday, 27 (January, 1960), 23.

6693 ________. "William Faulkner," *Party of One*. Cleveland: World Pub. Co., 1955, pp. 98-125.

6694 Fagin, N. Bryllion. *America Through the Short Story*. Boston: Little, Brown, 1936, p. 284.

6695 Farnham, James F. "A Note on One Aspect of Faulkner's Style," Lang&S, 2 (1969), 190-192.
Style reflects character.

6696 ________. *They Who Endure and Prevail: Characters in the Fiction of William Faulkner*. Diss. Western Reserve: 1962.

6697 Fasel, Ida. "A 'Conversation' between Faulkner and Eliot," MissQ, 20 (Fall, 1967), 195-206.

6698 ________. "Spatial Form and Spatial Time," WHR, 16 (Summer, 1962), 223-234.
The Bergsonian space-time structure.

6699 "Faulkner Appraised," Newsweek, 40 (July 14, 1952), 93-94.

6700 "Faulkner, William (Harrison) [sic]." *Encyclopedia Americana*. (1954), XI, 63.

6701 "Faulkner: As Seen by Different Artists," SatRL, 45 (July 28, 1962), 15.

Drawings of Faulkner by Ed Beardon, D. Parrot, and Arthur Hawkins.

6702 "Faulkner au cinéma," Gazette des Lettres (15 décembre 1950), 109.

6703 "Faulkner Country," Life, 55 (August 2, 1963), 46B-53.

6704 "Faulkner Fund," Newsweek, 43 (April 26, 1954), 57.

6705 "Faulkner Has Nightmare About the South in Civil War Days," Newsweek, 8 (October 31, 1936), 26.

6706 "Faulkner in Japan," Esquire, 50 (December, 1958), 139, 141-142.

6707 "Faulkner Legacy," Life, 53 (July 20, 1962), 4.

6708/9 "Faulkner l'universal," FL, 17 (July 14, 1962), 8.

6710 The Faulkner Reader. New York: Random House, 1954.

6711 "Faulkner, Soldati and America," Living Age, 351 (September, 1936), 71-72.

6712 "Faulkner Wall Plot," Life, 37 (August 9, 1954), 77-78.

6713 Fäy, Bernard. "L'école de l'infortune," RdP, 44 (August, 1937), 644-665.

6714 Fazio, Rocco Roberto. "The Fury and the Design: Realms of Being and Knowing in Four Novels of William Faulkner," DA, 25 (Michigan: 1964), 1910.

6715 Feibleman, James K. "Literary New Orleans between World Wars," SoR, n.s., 1 (Summer, 1965), 702-719.

6716 _______. The Way of a Man: An Autobiography. New York: Horizon Press, 1969, pp. 268-277.
Memoir of Faulkner in New Orleans.

6717 Fenton, Charles A. Stephen Vincent Benét. New Haven: Yale U.P., 1958, passim.

6718 Ferguson, Robert C. "The Grotesque in the Fiction of William Faulkner," DAI, 32 (Case Western Reserve: 1971), 1508A.

6719 Fetz, Howard W. "Of Time and the Novel," XUS, 8 (Summer, 1969), 1-17.

6720 Fiedler, Leslie A. "The Anti-War Novel and the Good Soldier Schweik," Ramparts, 1 (January, 1963), 43-48.

6721 ________. "The Blackness of Darkness: The Negro and the Development of American Gothic," Images of the Negro in American Literature. Seymour L. Gross, and John E. Hardy, eds. Chicago: Chicago U.P., 1966, pp. 101-105.

6722 ________. The Collected Essays of Leslie Fiedler. New York: Stein & Day, 1971, 2 vols., passim.

6723 ________. "The Death of the Old Men," A&S (Winter, 1963-64), 1-5.

6724 ________. "Development and Frustration," Love and Death in the American Novel. New York: Criterion Books, 1960, pp. 309-315.

6725 ________. An End to Innocence: Essays on Culture and Politics. Boston: Beacon Press, 1955.

6726 ________. The Return of the Vanishing American. New York: Stein and Day, 1968, passim.

6727 ________. "Le viol des Temple: De Richardson à Faulkner," Preuves, 138 (August, 1962), 75-81.

6728 ________. Waiting for the End. New York: Dell Pub. Co., 1965, passim.

6729 ________. "William Faulkner: An American Dickens," Commentary, 10 (October, 1950), 384-387.

6730 ________. "William Faulkner, Highbrows' Lowbrow," No, in Thunder! Essays on Myth and Literature. Boston: Beacon Press, 1960, pp. 111-118.

6731 Field, Louise M. "American Novelists vs. the Nation," NAR, 235 (June, 1933), 552-560.

6732 ________. "Heroines Back at the Hearth," NAR, 236 (August, 1933), 176-183.

6733 Finkelstein, Sidney. "Conflict between Humanization and Alienation: William Faulkner," Existentialism and Alienation in American Literature. New York: Internatl. Pubs., 1965, pp. 184-197.

6734 ________. "Six Ways of Looking at Reality," Mainstream, 13 (December, 1960), 31-42.

6735 ________. "William Faulkner," Mainstream, 15 (August, 1962), 3-6.

6736 Finley, Katherine P., and Paul T. Nolan. "Mississippi Drama Between Wars, 1870-1916: A Checklist and an Argument, Part II," JMissH, 26 (November, 1964), 299-306.

6737 Fisher, Marvin. "The World of Faulkner's Children," UKCR, 27 (October, 1960), 13-18.

6738 Fiskin, A. M. I. "Harvard Advocates," FS, 1 (Fall, 1952), 44-46.

6739 Fitzgerald, James Randolph. "William Faulkner's Literary Reputation in Britain, with a Checklist of Criticism, 1929-1972," DAI, 34 (Georgia: 1973), 5965A-66A.

6740 Flanagan, John T. "Faulkner's Favorite Word," GaR, 17 (Winter, 1963), 429-434.
Finds that no word appears more frequently or with more impact than "implacable."

6741 ________. "Folklore in Faulkner's Fiction," PLL, 5, Supplement (Summer, 1969), 119-144.

6742 ________. "The Mythic Background of Faulkner's Horse Imagery," NCaFJ, 13 (1965), 135-146; repr., in *Folklore Studies in Honor of Arthur Palmer Hudson.* Chapel Hill: N. C. Folklore Soc., 1965, pp. 135-145.

6743 Fleishmann, Wolfgang Bernard. "Remarks," BA, 37 (Summer, 1963), 268-270.
Cf., James B. Meriwether. "Faulkner and the New Criticism," BA, 37 (Summer, 1963), 265-268.

6744 Fletcher, Mary Dell. "Jason Compson: Contemporary Villain," LaS, 15 (Fall, 1976), 253-261.

6745 ________. "William Faulkner: The Calvinistic Sensibility," DAI, 35 (La. St.: 1974), 5400A.

6746 Flint, R. W. "Faulkner as Elegist," HudR, 7 (Summer, 1954), 246-257.

6747 Flory, Joseph Weldon. *The New Rhetoric of Faulkner's Heroes in His Later Work.* Diss. Indiana U. of Pennsylvania. 1973.

6748 Flowers, Paul. "William Faulkner: Paradoxes or Contrasts," MissLN, 26 (September, 1962), 100-103.

6749 Folks, Jeffrey Jay. "Plot Materials and Narrative Form in Faulkner's Early Fiction," DAI, 38, #11 (Indiana: 1977), 6724A.

6750 Foote, Shelby. "Faulkner and Race," *The South and Faulkner's Yoknapatawpha*, Jackson, Miss.: Mississippi U. P., 1977, pp. 86-103.

6751 ________. "Faulkner and War," *The South and Faulkner's*

Yoknapatawpha. Evans Harrington, et al., eds. Jackson, Miss.: Mississippi U.P., 1977, pp. 152-167.

6752 _______. "Faulkner's Depiction of the Planter Aristocracy," The South and Faulkner's Yoknapatawpha, Jackson, Miss.: Evans Harrington, et al., eds. Jackson, Miss.: Mississippi U.P., 1977, pp. 40-61.

6753 Ford, Corey. The Time of Laughter. Boston: Little, Brown, 1967, passim.

6754 Ford, Daniel Gordon. "Comments on William Faulkner's Temporal Vision in Sanctuary, The Sound and the Fury, Light in August, Absalom, Absalom!" SoQ, 15 (April, 1977), 283-290.

6755 _______. "Uses of Time in Four Novels by William Faulkner," DAI, 35 (Auburn: 1974), 1654A.

6756 Ford, Margaret P., and Suzanne Kincaid. Who's Who in Faulkner. Baton Rouge: Louisiana U.P., 1963.

6757 Foster, Ruel E. "Dream As Symbolic Act in Faulkner," Perspective, 2 (Summer, 1949), 179-194.

6758 _______. Freudian Influences in the American Autobiographical Novel. Diss. Vanderbilt, 1941.

6759 _______. "Social Order and Disorder in Faulkner's Fiction," Approach 54 (Winter, 1965), 20-28.

6760 _______, and Mowrey, Sandra. "From Yoknapatawpha to Charlottesville," NatlObs (February 3, 1964), 22.

6761 Fouchet, Max-Pol. "Faulkner, ce monstre," Candide, No. 63 (July, 1962), 11-18.

6762 _______. "Littêrature amêricaine," Carrefour (24 octobre 1946), 7.

6763 Fowler, Doreen Ferland. "Faulkner's Changing Vision: Narrative Progress Toward Affirmation," DAI, 35 (Brown: 1974), 7302A.

6764 Frady, Marshall. "The Faulkner Place," FurmS, n.s., 13 (November, 1965), 1-6.

6765 Franc, M. "Babele olter le mura: Sartre e Marcel dopo il bivio Prokosch non ama Faulkner," FLe, 3 (January 15, 1950), 16.

6766 Francis, Thomas E. "News and Comments," FS, 1 (1952), 28, 41, 62.

6767 Frankel, Max. "The Worldwide Influence of William Faulkner: Reports from Six Capitals," NYTBR (November 15, 1959), 52-53.

6768 Franklin, Rosemary Futrelle. "Clairvoyance, Vision, and Imagination in the Fiction of William Faulkner," DA, 29 (Emory: 1968), 3135A.

6769 Franzen, Erich. "William Faulkners puritanischer Mythos," Merkur, 5 (1951), 629-641.

6770 Frederick, John. "New Techniques in the Novel," EJ, 24 (May, 1935), 355-363.

6771 Freedman, Morris. "Sound and Sense in Faulkner's Prose," CEA, 19 (September, 1957), 1, 4-5.

6772 French, Warren G. "The Background of Snopesism in Mississippi Politics," MASJ, 5 (Fall, 1964), 3-17.

6773 _______. The Social Novel at the End of an Era. Carbondale and Edwardsville: So. Ill. U. P., 1966, passim.

6774 _______, ed. The Twenties: Fiction, Poetry, Drama. DeLand, Florida: Everett/Edwards, 1975, passim.

6775 _______. "William Faulkner and the Art of the Detective Story," The Thirties: Fiction, Poetry, Drama. Warren French, ed. DeLand, Florida: Everett/Edwards, 1967, pp. 55-62.

6776 Frey, John R. "Post-War German Reactions to American Literature," JEGP, 54 (1955), 173-194.

6777 Friedling, Sheila. "Problems of Perception in the Modern Novel: The Representation of Consciousness in Works of Henry James, Gertrude Stein, and William Faulkner," DAI, 34 (Wisconsin: 1973), 3391A.

6778 Friedman, Alan. "The Myth of Openness," The Turn of the Novel. New York: Oxford U. P., 1966, pp. 183-184.

6779 Friedman, Melvin J. "Preface," RLM, 157/159 (1967), 7-31.
Faulkner's influence.

6780 _______. Stream of Consciousness: A Study of Literary Method. New Haven: Yale U. P., 1955, passim.

6781 _______. "William Styron (1925--)," The Politics of Twentieth Century Novelists. George A. Panichas, ed. New York: Hawthorn Bks., 1971, pp. 337-338.

6782 Friend, George L. "Levels of Maturity: The Theme of Striving in the Novels of William Faulkner," DA, 25 (Illinois: 1965), 6622-23.

6783 Frisé, Adolf. "Der junge amerikanische Roman," Die Tat, 27 (1936), 638, 639-640.

6784 Frohock, Wilbur Merrill. "Continuities in the 'New Novel,'" Style and Temper: Studies in French Fiction, 1925-1960. Cambridge: Harvard U.P., 1967, pp. 120-137.

6785 _______. "Faulkner and the 'Roman Nouveau': An Interim Report," BuR, 10 (March, 1962), 186-193.

6786 _______. "Faulkner in France: The Final Phase," Mosaic, 4 (Spring, 1971), 125-134.

6787 _______. "William Faulkner: The Private Versus the Public Vision," SWR, 34 (Summer, 1949), 281-294.

6788 _______. "William Faulkner: The Private Vision," The Novel of Violence in America. 2nd ed., rev. Dallas: So. Methodist U.P., 1957, pp. 144-165.

6789 Fuchs, Carolyn. "Words, Action, and the Modern Novel," Kerygma, 4, #1 (Winter, 1964), 3-11.
Comparison of Faulkner and Joseph Conrad.

6790 Fuller, Edmund. "The Bookshelf: Faulkner on Campus: Two Self Portraits," WallStJ (May 8, 1964), 14.

6791 _______. "Faulkner: The Man from Yoknapatawpha," WallStJ (March 18, 1964), 16.

6792 Fuller, Timothy. "The Story of Jack and Jill," SatRL, 15 (December 19, 1936), 10-11. Parody.

6793 Fumet, Stanislas. "La saveur poétique du roman," Confluences (1943), 312-321.

6794 Fusini, Nadia. "La caccia all'orso di Faulkner," SA, 14 (1968), 289-308.

6795 Gage, Duane. "William Faulkner's Indians," AIQ, 1 (1974), 27-33.

6796 Gale, Robert L. "Evil and the American Short Story," AION-SG, 1 (1958), 183-202.

6797 Galloway, David D. The Absurd Hero in American Fiction. Rev. ed. Austin: Texas U.P., 1966, pp. 10, 54.

6798 Gardiner, H. C. "Recalling Faulkner," America, 107 (July 21, 1962), 519.

6799 Gardner, Paul. "TV: Faulkner Country," NYTimes (April 24, 1965), 59.

6800 Garrett, George P., Jr. "Faulkner's Early Literary Criticism," TSLL, 1 (Spring, 1959), 3-10.

6801 _______. "The Influence of William Faulkner," GaR, 18 (Winter, 1964), 419-427.

6802 Garrique, Jean. "Six Writers of Crisis," Commentary, 27 (March, 1959), 270-272.

6803 Garson, Helen S. "The Fallen Woman in American Naturalistic Fiction: From Crane to Faulkner," DA, 28 (Maryland: 1968), 5052A.

6804 Garzilli, Enrico F. Circles Without Center: Paths to the Discovery and Creation of Self in Modern Literature. Cambridge: Harvard U.P., 1972, pp. 52-65, passim.

6805 _______. "Paths to the Discovery and the Creation of Self in Contemporary Literature," DAI, 31 (Brown: 1971), 6604A.
Faulkner, Joyce, and Beckett.

6806 Gass, W. H. "Mr. Blotner, Mr. Feaster, and Mr. Faulkner," in The World within the Word: Essays. New York: Alfred A. Knopf, 1978, pp. 45-62.

6807 Gassner, John. "Broadway in Review," ETJ, 11 (May, 1959), 117-126.

6808 Gaunt, Roger. "The Magic World Within the Mind: William Faulkner, James Joyce," Debonair, 1 (February, 1961), 57-64.

6809 Gegerias, Mary. "Michel Butor and William Faulkner: Some Structures and Techniques," DA, 30 (Columbia: 1968), 712A.

6810 Geismar, Maxwell. "A Cycle of Fiction," Sec. 77, Pt. 5, Literary History of the United States. Robert E. Spiller, et al., eds. New York: Macmillan, 1959, pp. 1304-08.

6811 _______. "Faulkner: den andra sidan," SamF, (Stockholm), 10 (1953), 32-33.

6812 _______. "A Rapt and Tumid Power," SatRL, 35 (July 12, 1952), 10-11.
Cf., Edith Hamilton. SatRL, 35 (July 12, 1952), 8-10, 9, 39-41.

6813 _______. "William Faulkner: Before and After the Nobel Prize," American Moderns: From Rebellion to Conformity.

New York: Hill & Wang, American Century Series, 1958, pp. 91-106.

6814 ________. "William Faulkner: The Negro and the Female," Writers in Crisis. Boston: Houghton Mifflin, 1942, pp. 141-183.

6815 Genova, Yvonne. "Elsa Triolet ou le nouveau rêalisme français," Fontaine (juin 1942), 214-218.
Comparisons with Faulkner.

Gêrard, Albert. See Guêrard, Albert Joseph.

6816 Gernes, Sonia Grace. "The Relationship of Storyteller to Community in the Tales of the Southwest Humorists, Mark Twain and William Faulkner," DAI, 36 (Washington: 1975), 3685.

6817 Gerould, Gordon Hall. The Patterns of English and American Fiction. Boston: Little, Brown, 1942, p. 460.

6818 Gerould, Katharine F. "A Yankee Looks at Dixie," AmMerc, 37 (February, 1936), 217-220.

6819 Geselbracht, Raymond Henry. "The Two New Worlds: The Arts and the Inspiration of Nature in Twentieth-Century America," DAI, 35 (Santa Barbara, California: 1973), 363A.

6820 Giannitrapani, Angela Minissi. "La New Orleans e la Louisiana del Faulkner," AION-SG, 2 (1959), 265-339.

6821 ________. "Il procedimento dello stupore in Faulkner," SA, 6 (1960), 275-305.

6822 ________. Wistaria: studi faulkneriani. Napoli: Istituto Universitario Orientale, Casa Editrice Cymba, 1963.
Said to be the first book-length study of Faulkner in Italian.

6823 ________. "Wistaria: Le immagini in Faulkner," SA, 5 (1959), 243-280.

6824 Gide, Andrê. "Interview imaginaire," Fontaine (27-28 aôut 1943), 7-11.

6825 ________. Imaginary Interviews. Malcolm Cowley, tr. New York: Knopf, 1944, passim.

6826 Gidley, G. "William Faulkner," N&Q, 14 (January, 1967), 25-26.

6827 Gidley, Mich. "Another Psychologist, a Physiologist and William Faulkner," ArielE, 2 (October, 1971), 78-86.

Discusses the possible influence on Faulkner of Havelock Ellis and Louis Berman.

6828 ________. "Elements of the Detective Story in William Faulkner's Fiction," JPC, 7 (Summer, 1973), 97-123.

6829 ________. "One Continuous Force: Notes on Faulkner's Extra-Literary Reading," MissQ, 23 (Summer, 1970), 299-314.

6830 ________. "Some Notes on Faulkner's Reading," JAmS, 4 (July, 1970), 91-102.

6831 Giles, Barbara. "The South of William Faulkner," Masses and Mainstream, 3 (February, 1950), 26-40.

6832 ________. "Whose South? A Reply to William Faulkner," Masses and Mainstream, 9 (May, 1956), 38-43.

6833 Gilman, Richard. "Faulkner's Yes and No," Cw, 76 (August 10, 1962), 449-450.

6834 Gindin, James. Harvest of a Quiet Eye: The Novel of Compassion. Bloomington: Indiana U.P., 1971, passim.

6835 Ginsberg, Elaine. "The Female Initiation Theme in American Fiction," SAF, 3 (Spring, 1975), 27-37.

6836 Giorgini, J. "Faulkner and Camus," DeltaR, 2 (July-August, 1965), 31, 74-79.

6837 Giudici, Giovanni. "Un incontro romano: Domande per Faulkner attorno ad una tavola," FLe, No. 38 (September 18, 1955), 1.

6838 Gladstein, Mimi Reisel. "The Indestructible Woman in the Works of Faulkner, Hemingway, and Steinbeck," DAI, 35 (New Mexico: 1974), 1655A.

6839 Glasgow, Ellen. "Heroes and Monsters," SatRL, 12 (May 4, 1935), 3-4.
Refers to the "fantastic nightmares" of Faulkner.

6840 ________. Letters of Ellen Glasgow. Blair Rouse, ed. New York: Harcourt, Brace, 1958, passim.

6841 Glick, Nathan. "Trends in the Modern American Novel," Amerika (Washington), No. 3 (March, 1959), 24-27.

6842 Glicksberg, Charles I. "The Art of Faulkner's Fiction," Meanjin, 12 (Autumn, 1953), 69-78.

6843 ________. The Tragic Vision in Twentieth Century Literature. Carbondale: So. Ill. U.P., 1963, pp. 3-4, 164.

6844 ________. "William Faulkner and the Negro Problem," *Phylon*, 10 (June, 1949), 153-160.

6845 ________. "The World of William Faulkner," ArQ, 5 (Spring, 1949), 46-57, 85-88.

6846 Gloster, Hugh M. "Southern Justice," Phylon, 10 (1949), 93-95.

6847 Godden, Richard. "So That's What Frightens Them Under the Tree?" JAmS, 11 (December, 1977), 371-377.
Rev.-art., of André Bleikasten's *The Splendid Failure* (1976).

6848 Gold, Joseph. "Dickens and Faulkner: The Uses of Influence," DR, 49 (Spring, 1969), 69-79.

6849 ________. "The Faulkner Game; or, Find the Author," SLJ, 1 (Spring, 1969), 91-97.

6850 ________. "The Humanism of William Faulkner," Humanist, 20 (March-April, 1960), 113-117.

6851 ________. "The Single Vision: A Study of the Philosophy and the Forms of Its Presentation in the Works of William Faulkner," DA, 20 (Wisconsin: 1959), 2289.

6852 ________. *William Faulkner: A Study in Humanism from Metaphor to Discourse*. Norman: Oklahoma U.P., 1966.

6853 ________. "William Faulkner's 'One Compact Thing,'" TCL, 8 (April, 1962), 3-9.

6854 Goldman, Arnold. *The American Novel and the Nineteen Twenties*. Malcolm Bradbury and David Palmer, eds. London: Edward Arnold, 1971, pp. 164-195; New York: Crane, 1971, pp. 165-195.

6855 ________. "Faulkner and the Revision of Yoknapatawpha History," *Ausgewählte Schriften zu deutschen Literaturgeschichte, germanischen Sprach- und Kulturgeschichte und zur deutschen Wort-, Mundart- und Volkskunde: Festschrift zum 75. Geburtstag von Hans-Friedrich Rosenfeld* (GAG 124, 125.) Göppingen: Kümmerle, 1974, pp. 165-195.

6856 Golub, L. S. "Syntactic and Lexical Problems in Reading Faulkner," EJ, 59 (April, 1970), 490-496.

6857 Goodenberger, Mary Ellen Marshall. "William Faulkner's Compleat Woman," DAI, 38, #8 (Lincoln, Nebraska: 1976), 4827A.

6858 Gordon, Caroline, and Allen Tate. *The House of Fiction*. New York: Scribners, 1950, pp. 531-534.

6859 _______. "Notes on Faulkner and Flaubert," HudR, 1 (Summer, 1948), 222-231.

6860 Goren, Leyla Melek. William Faulkner: An International Novelist. Diss. Harvard: 1963.

6861 Gorlier, Claudio. "Il pellegrinaggio del buon ribelle," SA, 10 (1964), 134-179.

6862 _______. "William Faulkner: La genesi e la redenzione," Approdo, 20 (October-December, 1962), 42-68.

6863 Gorman, Thomas R. "Faulkner's Ethical Point of View," CEA, 28 (June, 1966), 4-6.

6864 Gossett, Louise Young. "The Climate of Violence: Wolfe, Caldwell, Faulkner," Violence in Recent Southern Fiction. Durham, North Carolina: Duke U.P., 1965, pp. 29-47.

6865 Gott, Francis. "Only God Can Do It," Newsweek, 44 (September 13, 1954), 10.

6866 Gotten, H. B. "Oxford," Delta R, 5 (December, 1968), 14-16, 80-81.

6867 Grames, Bernice D. "The American Story," NS (1952), 140-143.

6868 Grant, Douglas. "The Last of William Faulkner," Purpose and Place: Essays on American Writers. London: Macmillan, 1965, pp. 183-188.

6869 Grantham, Dewey W., Jr. "Interpreters of the Modern South," SAQ, 63 (Autumn, 1964), 521-529.

6870 Graves, Allen Wallace. "Difficult Contemporary Short Stories: William Faulkner, Katherine Anne Porter, Dylan Thomas, Eudora Welty and Virginia Woolf," DA, 14 (Washington: 1954), 2067-68.

6871 Graves, John Temple. The Fighting South. New York: Putnam's, 1943, p. 207.

6872 Gray, Paul. "Yoknapatawpha Blues," Time, 108 (September 27, 1976), 92-93.
A survey of Southern writers including Faulkner.

6873 Gray, Richard. "The Individual Talent: William Faulkner and the Yoknapatawpha Novels," The Literature of Memory: Modern Writers of the American South. Baltimore and London: The Johns Hopkins U.P., 1977, pp. 197-256.
Rev. by Rayburn S. Moore. MissQ, 31, #4 (Fall, 1978), 656-660.

6874 Green, Martin Burgess. "Faulkner: The Triumph of Rhetoric," Re-Appraisals: Some Commonsense Readings in American Literature. London: Hugh Evelyn, 1963; New York: Norton, 1965, pp. 167-195.

6875 ______. "Style in American Literature," CamR, 89 (June 3, 1967), 385-387.

6876 Greenberg, Alvin. "Letter to the Editor," NCr, 1 (October, 1949), 120-121.

6877 ______. "Shaggy Dog in Mississippi," SFQ, 29 (1964), 284-287.

6878 Greene, Graham. "The Furies in Mississippi," LonMerc, 35 (March, 1957), 517-518.

6879 Greene, Robert Ira. "Innocence and Experience in Selected Major Fiction of William Faulkner," DAI, 40 (Indiana: 1978), 852A-53A.

6880 Greet, T. Y. "Toward the Light: The Thematic Unity of Faulkner's 'Cycle,'" CarQ, 3 (December, 1950), 38-44.

6881 Gregory, Charles T. "Darkness to Appall: Destructive Designs and Patterns in Some Characters of William Faulkner," DA, 30 (Columbia: 1969), 1565A-66A.

6882 Gregory, Horace. "Mutations of Belief in the Contemporary Novel," Spiritual Problems in Contemporary Literature. S. R. Hopper, ed. New York: Harper, 1957, pp. 43-44.

6883 Grenier, Roger. "La ténébreuse malédiction faulknérienne," FL, 17 (July 14, 1962).

6884 Grenzmann, Wilhelm. "Nobelpreisträger William Faulkner, sein Weg und seine Dichtung," Univ, 9 (Summer, 1959), 909-920.

6885 Gresham, Jewell H. "The Fatal Illusions: Self, Sex, Race, and Religion in William Faulkner's World," DAI, 31 (Columbia: 1970), 5402A.

6886 ______. "Narrative Techniques of William Faulkner's Form," NasR, 1, iii (1966), 103-119.

6887 Gresset, Michel. "Epithèse," Delta, 3 (November, 1976), 173-191.

6888 ______. "Faulkner, 1935," EA, 29 (July-Sept., 1976), 448-455.

6889 ______. "Faulkner essaysisté," NRF, 15 (1967), 309-313.

6890 _______. "Faulkner et l'océan," Sud, 14 (1975), 185-189.

6891 _______. "Faulkner par lui-même," MdF, 349, No. 1201 (November, 1963), 622-626.

6892 _______. "Faulkneriana," LanM, 59 (January-February, 1965), 107-113.

6893 _______. "Faulkneriana," MdF, 350 (April, 1964), 658-661.

6894 _______. Foreword. A French View of Modern America: Essays by Maurice Edgar Coindreau. George M. Reeves, ed. and tr. Columbia: South Carolina U.P., 1971, pp. ix-xiv.

6895 _______. "Le'parceque' chez Faulkner et le 'donc' chez Beckett," LetN, 19 (November, 1961), 124-138.

6896 _______. "Le regard et le désir chez Faulkner," Sud, 14 (1975), 12-61.

6897 _______. "Temps et destin chez Faulkner," Preuves, 155 (January, 1964), 44-49.

6898 _______. "Théorème," RANAM, 9 (1976), 73-94.

6899 _______, ed. "Valery Larbaud et les débuts de Faulkner en France," Preuves, No. 184 (juin 1966), 26-28.

6900 _______, ed. [Introduction.] William Faulkner. Paris: Armand Colin, 1970.

6901 Gribbin, Daniel V. "Men of Thought, Men of Action: A Pattern of Contrasts in Faulkner's Major Novels," DAI, 34 (North Carolina, Chapel Hill: 1974), 5969A.

6902 Griffin, Mary N. Coming to Manhood in America: A Study of Significant Initiation Novels, 1797-1970. Diss. Vanderbilt: 1971.

6903 Griffin, William J. "How to Misread Faulkner: A Powerful Plea for Ignorance," TSL, 1 (1956), 27-34.

6904 Griffith, Benjamin W. "Faulkner's Archaic Titles and the Second Shepherds' Play," NMW, 4 (1971), 62-63.

6905 Grillo, Giuseppe. "Faulkner autore 'proibito?'" Dialoghi, 10 (1962), 91-95.

6906 Grimwood, James Michael. "Pastoral and Parody: The Making of Faulkner's Anthology Novels," DAI, 37, #9 (Princeton: 1976), 5828A.

6907 Gross, Seymour, and J. E. Hardy, eds. Introduction. Images of the Negro in American Literature. Chicago: Chicago U. P., 1966, passim.

6908 _______, and Rosalie Murphy. "From Stephen Crane to William Faulkner: Some Remarks on the Religious Sense in American Literature," Cithara, 16 (May, 1977), 90-108.

6909 Gross, Theodore L. The Heroic Ideal in American Literature. London: Collier-Macmillan; New York: Free Press, 1971, passim.

6910 Grossman, Joel M. "The Source of Faulkner's 'Less Oft Is Peace,'" AL, 47 (November, 1975), 436-438.
The quotation is from Shelley (1822), "To Jane: The Recollection."

6911 Grove, James Leland. Visions and Revisions: A Study of the Obtuse Narration in American Fiction from Brockden Brown to Faulkner. Diss. Harvard: 1968.

6912 Guérard, Albert J., ed. Ecrit aux U. S. A. Anthologie des Prosateurs américains du XXe Siècle. Paris: Robert Laffont, 1947.

6913 _______. "Faulkner: Problems of Technique," The Triumph of the Novel. New York: Oxford U. P., 1976, pp. 204-234.

6914 _______. "Faulkner the Innovator," and "The Faulknerian Voice," The Maker and The Myth: Faulkner and Yoknapatawpha, 1977. Evans Harrington and Ann J. Abadie, eds. Jackson: U. P. of Miss.: 1977, pp. 71-88, 25-42.

6915 _______. "Forbidden Games (III): Faulkner's Misogyny," The Triumph of the Novel. pp. 109-135.

6916 _______. "French and American Pessimism," HarpersM, 191 (September, 1945), 267-272.
Comparison of Sartre's pessimism and Faulkner's.

6917 _______. "Justice in Yoknapatawpha County: Some Symbolic Motifs in Faulkner's Later Writing," FS, 2 (Winter, 1954), 49-57.

6918 _______. "Les Lettres: William Faulkner, ou le fardeau de l'Homme Noir," LRN, 24 (October, 1956), 331-338.

6919 _______. "Puritanisme, solitude et violence," Confluences (septembre 1945), 736-745.

6920 _______. "Le roman américain depuis 1939, "LMod (octobre 1945), 111-120.

6921 ________. "Les romanciers amêricains," TP (17 août 1945), 3.

6922 ________. "Voici l'etat actuel de la littêrature amêricaine," Le Monde Illustré (22 septembre 1945), 20.

6923 ________. "William Faulkner, Chroniquer de l'apocalypse," LRN, 13 (janvier 1951), 81-90.

6924 Guetti, James Lawrence, Jr. "The Failure of the Imagination: A Study of Melville, Conrad, and Faulkner," DA, 25 (Cornell: 1965), 4145-46.

6925 ________. The Limits of Metaphor: A Critical Study of Melville, Conrad, and Faulkner. Ithaca: Cornell U.P., 1967.

6926 Guicharnaud, Jacques, in collaboration with June Beckelman. Modern French Theatre from Giraudoux to Beckett. Paris: Presses Universitaires de France; New Haven: Yale U.P., 1961, passim.

6927 "Guides to Yoknapatawpha County," TLS (July 10, 1959), 408.

6928 Guidici, Giovanni. "Domande per Faulkner Attorno ad una Tavola," FLe, 38 (September 18, 1955), 1.

6929 Gurko, Leo. The Angry Decade. New York: Dodd, Mead, 1947; repr., Harper & Row, 1968, pp. 117-119, 128-136.

6930 ________. Heroes, Highbrows and the Popular Mind. Freeport, New York: Books for Libraries Press, repr., 1971, pp. 252-255, passim.

6931 Guth, Paul. "En remontant avec Faulkner les chemins de la vie et ceux de l'êcriture," FL, 10 (3 octobre 1955), 3.

6932 Guttman, Allen. "Collisions and Confrontations," ArQ, 16 (Spring, 1960), 46-52.
Faulkner's imagery and character contrasts.

6933 Guyard, Marius Françoise. "Faulkner le tragique," Études (Paris), 268 (fêvrier 1951), 172-183.

6934 Guyot, Charly. "Faulkner," Les romanciers amêricains d'aujourd'hui. Paris: Editions Labergerie, 1948, pp. 45-60.

6935 Gwynn, Frederick L. "Faulkner in the University," CE, 19 (October, 1957), 1-6.

6936 ________. "Faulkner's Prufrock," JEGP, 52 (January, 1953), 63-70.

6937 ________. "Faulkner's Raskolnikov," MFS, 4 (Summer, 1958), 169-172.
Cf., R. W. Flint. HudsonR, 7 (Summer, 1954), 249-50; Linton Massey. SB, 8 (1956), 196; Martha W. England, CE, 18 (August 2, 1954), 50; Vivian Mercier, Cw, 60 August 6, 1954), 443.

6938 ________. "William Faulkner," Cyclopedia of World Authors. Frank N. Magill, ed. New York: Harper, 1958, pp. 352-355.

6939 ________, and Joseph L. Blotner, eds. Faulkner in the University: Class Conferences at the University of Virginia, 1957-1958. Charlottesville: Virginia U. P., 1959.

6940 ________, and ________, eds. Gespräche mit Faulkner. Helmut Hilzheimer, tr. Stuttgart: Goverts, 1961.

6941 ________, and ________. "William Faulkner on Dialect," UVM, 2 (1958), 7-13, 32-37.

6942 Haas, Rudolf. "Faulkner und die Humanität," Univ, 18 (April, 1963), 347-362.

6943 Hafner, John H. "William Faulkner's Narrators," DAI, 30 (Wisconsin: 1970), 5445A.

6944 Hagopian, John V. "The Adyt and the Maze: Ten Years of Faulkner Studies in America," JA, 6 (1961), 134-151.

6945 ________. "Style and Meaning in Hemingway and Faulkner," JA, 4 (1959), 170-179.

6946 Hahn, Otto. "Le second Faulkner (à propos du Hameau et du Domaine)," TM, 195 (August, 1962), 347-357.

6947 Haight, Ann Lyon. Banned Books. 2nd ed., rev. New York: Bowker, p. 100; 3rd ed., 1970, p. 87.

6948 Haines, Helen E. What's in a Novel? New York: Columbia U. P., 1942, pp. 90-91.

6949 Hall, James. "Play, The Fractured Self, and American Angry Comedy: From Faulkner to Salinger," The Lunatic Giant in the Drawing Room: The British and American Novel Since 1930. Bloomington: Indiana U. P., 1968, pp. 56-77.

6950 Hall, Wade. The Smiling Phoenix: Southern Humor from 1865 to 1914. Gainesville, Florida: Florida U. P., 1965, passim.

6951 Hall, William. "Autopsy on Faulkner," CanL, 30 (Autumn, 1966), 59-60, 62-63.

6952 _______. "Presenting a United Front," NYTimes (October 20, 1957), IV, 10.

6953 Halley, Marianne. "News and Comments," FS, 2 (1953), 13-14, 27-28, 44, 64-65; 3 (1954), 16, 44.

6954 Halsband, Robert. "Faulkner and the Critics," SatRL, 38 (March 26, 1955), 19.

6955 Halsell, W. D. "A Bibliography of Theses and Dissertations Relating to Mississippi, 1970," JMissH, 33 (February, 1971), 59-68.

6956 Hamblin, Bobby Wayne. "William Faulkner's Theory of Action," DAI, 37 (Mississippi: 1976), 1546A-1547A.

6957 Hamilton, Edith. "Faulkner: Sorcerer or Slave?" SatRL, 35 (July 12, 1952), 419-429; repr., in Saturday Review Gallery. Jerome Beatty, ed. New York: Simon & Schuster, 1959, pp. 419-429.
Cf., Maxwell Geismar. SatRL, 35 (July 12, 1952), 10-11.

6958 _______. "Faulkner: Trollkarl eller slav?" Samtid och framtid (Stockholm), 10 (1953), 24-31.

6959 _______. "William Faulkner," The Ever-Present Past. New York: Norton, 1964, pp. 159-173.

6960 Hammond, Donald. "Faulkner's Levels of Awareness," FQ, 1, ii (1967), 73-81.

6961 Hanak, Miroslav J. "Nietzsche, Dostoevsky, and Faulkner: Rebellion against Society in the Light in the New Left," Actes du VI Congres de l'Association Internationale de Littérature Comparée/Proceedings of the 6th Congress of the International Comparative Literature Association. Michel Cadot, Milan V. Dimić, David Malone, and Miklós Szabolcsi, eds. Stuttgart: Bieber, 1975, pp. 739-743.

6962 Hanamoto, Kingo. Faulkner Kenkyu: Shudai no Tsuikyu. Vol. I. Tokyo: Manabu Shobo, 1971.

6963 Hancock, Maxine. "Fire: Symbolic Motif in Faulkner," EngQ, 3 (Fall, 1970), 19-23.

6964 Hand, Nancy W. The Anatomy of a Genre: The Modern Novelette in English. Diss. Kent State, 1971.

6965 Handy, William J. Modern Fiction: A Formalist Approach. Carbondale & Edwardsville: So. Ill. U.P., 1971, passim.

6966 Hanoteau, Guillaume. "Faulkner: Il s'est battu à Verdun et se souvient," Match, No. 474 (May 10, 1958), 14-17.

6967 Hansen, Harry. "Fashions in Fiction," Forum, 89 (March, 1933), 152-155.

6968 ________. "Faulkner Dodges Sun-Baked South," Chicago Sunday Tribune (August 8, 1954), Mag. Bks., 4.

6969 ________. "The Faulkner Enigma: Charmed, Baffled Critics," Chicago Sunday Tribune (August 15, 1954), Mag. Bks., 4.

6970 Harakawa, Kyoichi. "Bride of Quietness and Walking Shadow," Kamereon, No. 6 (June, 1963), 1-31.

6971 ________. Demon's Song: Essays on William Faulkner. Tokyo: Hyogensha, 1964.

6972 ________. "Faulkner Hihyo no Doko," EigoS, 119 (1973), 228-229.

6973 Harder, Kelsie B. "Charactonyms in Faulkner's Novels," BuR, 8 (May, 1959), 189-201.

6974 Harding, D. W. "Revenger's Tragedy," Spectator, No. 6918 (January 27, 1961), 110-111.

6975 Hardwick, Elizabeth. "Faulkner and the South Today," PR, 15 (October, 1948), 1130-1135; repr., in Two Decades of Criticism. Frederick Hoffman and Olga Vickery, eds. East Lansing: Michigan U.P., 1951, pp. 244-250.

6976 Hardy, John Edward. "William Faulkner: The Legend Behind the Legend," Man in the Modern Novel. Seattle: Washington U.P., 1964, pp. 137-155.

6977 Harkness, Bruce. "Faulkner and Scott," MissQ, 20 (Summer, 1967), 164.

6978 Harnack-Fish, Mildred. Entwicklung der amerikanischen Literatur der Gegenwart in einigen Vertretern des Romans und der Kurzgeschichte. Diss. Giessen: 1941.

6979 ________. "William Faulkner: Ein amerikanischer dichter aus grosser tradition," Literatur, 38 (October, 1935), 64-67.

6980 Harold, Brent. "The Value and Limitations of Faulkner's Fictional Method," AL, 47 (May, 1975), 212-229.

6981 Harrington, Catherine Steta. "Southern Fiction and the Quest for Identity," DA, 25 (Washington: 1963), 1210.

6982 Harrington, Evans, and Ann J. Abadie, eds. The Maker and the Myth: Faulkner and Yoknapatawpha, 1977. Jackson, Miss. U.P., 1978.

6983 ________, and ________, eds. The South and Faulkner's Yoknapatawpha. Jackson: Mississippi U. P., 1977.

6984 Hart, James D., ed. "William Faulkner," The Oxford Companion to American Literature. New York: Oxford U. P., 4th ed., rev. and enl., 1965, pp. 271-273.

6985 Hart, John A. "That Not Impossible He: Faulkner's Third-Person Narrator," (Carnegie Series in English No. 6), Pittsburgh: Carnegie Institute of Technology, 1961, pp. 29-41.

6986 Harter, Carol Clancey. "Recent Faulkner Scholarship: Five More Turns of the Screw," JML, 4 (September, 1974), 139-145.

6987 Hartt, Julian N. The Lost Image of Man. Baton Rouge: Louisiana State U. P., 1963, pp. 109-111.

6988 ________. "William Faulkner: An Appreciation," Christianity and Crisis, 22 (1962), [138].

6989 Hartwick, Harry. "The Cult of Cruelty," The Foreground of American Fiction. New York: American Book Co., 1934, pp. 160-166.

6990 Harwick, Robert Duane. "Humor in the Novels of William Faulkner," DA, 26 (Nebraska: 1965), 1646.

6991 Harzic, Jean. Faulkner. Paris: Borda, 1973.
Rev. by Ahmed Amriqua, MissQ, 31, #3 (1978), 494-496.

6992 Hassan, Ihab. Contemporary American Literature 1945-1972. New York: Frederick Ungar, 1973, passim.

6993 ________. The Dismemberment of Orpheus: Toward Postmodern Literature. New York: Oxford U. P., 1971, passim.

6994 ________. Radical Innocence: Studies in the Contemporary American Novel. Princeton: Princeton U. P., 1961, passim.

6995 Hastings, John. "Faulkner's Prose," SatRL, 37 (September 18, 1954), 23.

6996 Hatcher, Harlan Henthorne. "The Torches of Violence," EJ, 23 (February, 1934), 91-99.

6997 ________. "Ultimate Extensions," Creating the Modern American Novel. New York: Farrar & Rinehart, 1935; Russell & Russell, 1965, pp. 234-243.

6998 Hatcher, J. Wesley. "Appalachian America," Culture in the South. W. T. Couch, ed. Chapel Hill: North Carolina U. P., 1934, pp. 374-402.

6999 Hathaway, Baxter. "The Meanings of Faulkner's Structures," EngRec, 15 (December, 1964), 22-27.

7000 Hatzfeld, Helmut. *Trends and Styles in Twentieth Century French Literature*. Rev. and Enl. Washington, D.C.: Catholic Univ. of Amer. Press, 1966, *passim*.

7001 Hauck, Richard B. "The Prime Maniacal Risibility: William Faulkner," *A Cheerful Nihilism: Confidence and "The Absurd" in American Humorous Fiction*. Bloomington: Indiana U.P., 1971, pp. 167-200.

7002 Hawkins, E. O., Jr. "Faulkner's 'Duke John of Lorraine,'" AN&Q, 4 (1965), 22.

7003 _______. "A Handbook of Yoknapatawpha," DA, 21 (Arkansas: 1961), 3457-58.

7004 Hayakawa, Hiroshi. Faulkner Studies: *The Problem of Techniques and Styles*. Tokyo: Kenkyusha, 1961.

7005 _______. "Negation in William Faulkner," *Studies in English Grammar and Linguistics: A Miscellany in Honour of Takanobu Otsuka*. Kazuo Araki, et al., eds. Tokyo: Kenkyusha, 1958, pp. 103-113.

7006 Haydn, Hiram. "Personal Glimpses," Reader's Dig., 106 (January, 1975), 184.
An account of Faulkner at work in the offices of Random House.

7007 Hayes, Ann L., et al. *Studies in Faulkner*. Carnegie Series in English No. 6. Pittsburgh: Carnegie Institute of Technology, 1961.

7008 Hayes, Elizabeth Tracy. "Comedy in Faulkner's Fiction," DAI, 40 (Syracuse: 1978), 256A-57A.

7009 "He Will Prevail," Time, 80 (July 13, 1962), 85-86.

7010 Heilman, Robert B. "The Southern Temper," HopR, 6 (Fall, 1952), 5-15.

7011 _______. "The Southern Temper," *South: Modern Southern Literature in Its Cultural Setting*. Louis D. Rubin, Jr., and Robert D. Jacobs, eds. Garden City, New York: Doubleday, 1961, pp. 48-59.

7012 Heiney, Donald W. "William Faulkner," *Essentials of Contemporary Literature*. Great Neck, New York: Barron's Educational Series, 1955, pp. 133-143; repr., in *Recent American Literature*. Great Neck: Barron's, 1958, pp. 208-227.

7013 Heiseler, Bernt von. "Neue Amerikaner," Deutsche Zeitschrift, 49, i (1936), 468-469.

7014 Hell, Henri. "Critique du roman," Fontaine (mai 1942), 95-98.

7015 Hellman, Geoffrey Theodore. "Profiles," NY, 35 (May 16, 1959), 48-84.

7016 Hellman, Lillian. An Unfinished Woman--A Memoir. Boston: Little, Brown, 1969, pp. 177-179.

7017 Helsztyński, Stanislaw. "Okreg Yoknapatawpha w twórczości Williama Faulknera," KN, 6 (4th Qt., 1959), 305-320.
The regional element in Faulkner's work.

7018 Hemingway, Ernest. Death in the Afternoon. New York: Scribner's, 1932, p. 173.

7019 _______. Reply to Robert Coates. NY, 7 (November 5, 1932), 74-75.

7020 Henderson, Harry B., III. "Faulkner," Versions of the Past: The Historical Imagination in American Fiction. New York: Oxford U.P., 1974, pp. 253-269, passim.

7021 Henderson, Philip. "William Faulkner," The Novel Today: Studies in Contemporary Attitudes. London: Bodley Head, 1936, pp. 147-150.

7022 Hepburn, James G. Introduction. The Art of Arnold Bennett. Bloomington: Indiana U.P., 1963, p. 11.
Quotes Arnold Bennett as saying "... Faulkner is the coming man."

7023 Hernandez, Joan Loyd. "The Influence of William Faulkner in Four Latin American Novelists (Yáñez, Garcia, Márquez, Cepeda Samudio, Donoso)," DAI, 39 (La. State and A&M College: 1978), 6756A.

7024 Herron, Ima Honaker. "This Was Jefferson," The Small Town in American Drama. Dallas: So. Methodist U.P., 1969, pp. 377-389.

7025 _______. "William Faulkner," The Small Town in American Literature. Durham, North Carolina: Duke U.P., 1939, pp. 418-422.

7026 Hesse, C., and S. Hesse. "Faulkner Country," Travel, 134 (December, 1970), 68-70.

7027 Hickerson, Thomas F. The Falkner Feuds. Chapel Hill: Colonial Press, 1964.
Events in the lives of Faulkner's ancestors.

7028 Hicks, Granville. "Facets of Faulkner," SatRL, 51 (July 13, 1968), 23-24.
Comments that "The mass of Faulkner material grows steadily and, one might say, alarmingly...."

7029 ________. "Faulkner and His Town," SatRL, 48 (October 2, 1965), 37-38.

7030 ________. "Faulkner's South," GaR, 5 (Fall, 1951), 269-284.
Called a "Northern" interpretation.

7031 ________. "John Dos Passos," Bookman, 75 (April, 1932), 41.
"Faulkner isolates himself ... in a world of his own creation...."

7032 ________, ed. The Living Novel. New York: Macmillan, 1957, passim.

7033 ________. "The Past and the Future of William Faulkner," Bookman, 74 (September, 1931), 17-24.

7034 ________. "Pessimists: Krutch, Jeffers, Faulkner," The Great Tradition: An Interpretation of American Literature Since the Civil War. New York: Macmillan, 1935, pp. 262-268.

7035 ________. "Prizes Authors Seek," SatRL, 50 (May 20, 1967), 35-36.

7036 ________. "The Public and Private Faulkner," SatRL, 49 (July 30, 1966), 27-28.

7037 ________. "The Shape of a Career," SatRL, 41 (December 13, 1958), 16, 38.

7038 ________. "Trumpet Call," The Great Tradition. New York: Macmillan, 1933, pp. 257-292.

7039 ________. "The Writer in Critical Perspective," SatRL, 45 (July 28, 1962), 25.

7040 Higgins, Claire M. A Study of Metaphor and Simile in the American Literary Novel and the American Popular Novel, 1911-1940. Diss. N.Y. Univ., 1954.

7041 Hill, A. A. "Three Examples of Unexpectedly Accurate Indian Lore," TSLL, 6 (Spring, 1964), 80-83.
Includes note on Faulkner's word "Yoknapatawpha."

7042 Hinchcliffe, A. P. Symbolism in the American Novel, 1850-1950: An Examination of the Findings of Recent Literary Critics in Respect of the Novels of Hawthorne, Melville,

James, Hemingway, and Faulkner. Diss. Manchester, 1962-63.

7043 Hinchey, John J. *Implausible Motion: Generation and Regeneration in the Novels of William Faulkner.* Diss. Harvard: 1974.

7044 Hinteregger, Gerald. *Das Land und die Menschen in William Faulkners erzählenden Werken.* Diss. Graz, Germany, 1953.

7045 Hirano, Nobuyuki. "Reconsideration of Moral Order and Disorder in Faulkner's Works," HitJA&S (Tokyo), 8, i (September, 1967), 7-32.

7046 Hoadley, Frank Mitchell. "Folk Humor in the Novels of William Faulkner," TFSB, 23 (September, 1957), 76-82.

7047 ________. "The Theme of Atonement in the Novels of William Faulkner," NWR, 10 (Summer, 1970), 30-43.

7048 ________. "The World View of William Faulkner," DA, 16 (Oklahoma: 1956), 338.

7049 Hoar, Jere R. "William Faulkner of Oxford, Mississippi," WriterD, 42 (July, 1961), 15-16.

7050 ________. "William Faulkner of Oxford, Mississippi," Ed&Pub, 94 (January 7, 1961), 14.
Faulkner's expression of opinion on local issues.

7051 Hochberg, Mark Robert. "Narrative Forms in the Modern Southern Novel," DA, 31 (Cornell: 1970), 4773.

7052 Hofammann, Albert G., Jr. *Faulkner's Conflicting Galaxies: A Study in Literary Polarity.* Diss. Pennsylvania: 1951.

7053 Hoffman, Daniel G. *Form and Fable in American Literature.* New York: Oxford U.P., 1961, p. 359.

7054 Hoffman, Frederick J. *The Art of Southern Fiction: A Study of Some Modern Novelists.* London: Feffer & Simons; Carbondale and Edwardsville: So. Ill. U.P., 1967, 2nd pr., 1968, pp. 109-110, 166-167, *passim.*

7055 ________. *Freudianism and the Literary Mind.* Baton Rouge: Louisiana State U.P., 1957, pp. 129-130.

7056 ________. "Nostalgia and Christian Interpretation: Henry Adams and Faulkner," *The Imagination's New Beginning: Theology and Modern Literature.* Notre Dame: Notre Dame U.P., 1967, pp. 75-102.

7057 ________. "The Sense of Place," South: Modern Southern Literature in Its Cultural Setting. Louis D. Rubin, Jr., and Robert D. Jacobs, eds. Garden City, New York: Doubleday, 1961, pp. 60-75.

7058 ________. The Twenties. New York: Viking, 1955, passim.

7059 ________. "Violence and Rhetoric," The Modern Novel in America, 1900-1950. Chicago: Henry Regnery, 1951; rev. ed., 1963, pp. 154-164, passim.

7060 ________. "William Faulkner," American Winners of the Nobel Literary Prize. Warren G. French, ed. Norman, Okla.: Oklahoma U.P., 1968, pp. 138-157.

7061 ________. William Faulkner. New York: Twayne's United States Authors Series, 1961, 2nd ed. revised, 1966.

7062 ________. "William Faulkner: A Review of Recent Criticism," Renascence, 13 (1960), 3-9, 32.

7063 ________, and Olga W. Vickery, eds. William Faulkner: Two Decades of Criticism. East Lansing: Michigan State College, 1951, reprint, 1954.

7064 ________, and ________, eds. William Faulkner: Three Decades of Criticism. East Lansing: Michigan State U.P., 1960; Repr., New York: Harcourt, Brace, 1963.

7065 ________, and ________, eds. William Faulkner: venti anni di critica. Parma: Guanda, 1957.

7066 Hoffmann, Gerhard. "Die Rolle des Ich-Erzählers in Faulkners Kurzgeschichten," Archiv, 201 (February, 1965), 339-349.

7067 Hofmann, W. J. V. "Contemporary Portraits: William Faulkner," Literary America, 2 (March, 1935), 193-195.

7068 Hogan, Patrick G. "Critical Misconceptions of Southern Thought: Faulkner's Optimism," MissQ, 10 (January, 1957), 19-28.

7069 ________. "Faulkner: 'A Rejoinder,'" CEA, 28 (June, 1966), 3.
Cf., M. E. Bradford. CEA, 28 (June, 1966), 1-3.

7070 ________. "Faulkner Scholarship and the CEA," CEA, 26 (October, 1963), 1, 5, 7-8, 12.

7071 ________. "Faulkner's 'Female Line,'" SSF, 1 (1964), 63-65.

7072 _______. "Faulkner's New Orleans Idiom: A Style in Embryo," LaS, 5 (Fall, 1966), 171-181.

7073 Hollander, John. "The Voice of the Enemy," London Times (August 11, 1963), 23.
Review of Martin B. Green's Re-Appraisals. London: 1963.

7074 Holman, C. Hugh. "The Novel in the South," A Time of Harvest: American Literature, 1910-1960. Robert E. Spiller, ed. New York: Hill & Wang, American Century Series, 1962, pp. 83-94.

7075 _______, et al. "Rhetoric in Southern Writing," GaR, 12 (Spring, 1958), 74-86.

7076 _______. The Roots of Southern Writing: Essays on the Literature of the South. Athens: Georgia U.P., 1972, passim.

7077 _______. "'To Grieve on Universal Bones': The Past as Burden," The Immoderate Past: The Southern Writer and History. Athens, GA: Georgia U.P., 1977, pp. 72-79.

7078 _______. "William Faulkner: The Anguished Dream of Time," Three Modes of Modern Southern Fiction: Ellen Glasgow, William Faulkner, Thomas Wolfe. Athens: Georgia U.P., 1966, pp. 27-47.

7079 _______. "William Faulkner Wrote of the Heart in Conflict with Itself," MissLN, 26 (September, 1962), 99.

7080 Holmes, Edward Morris. "Faulkner's Twice-Told Tales: His Re-Use of His Material," DA, 23 (Brown: 1963), 2527.

7081 _______. Faulkner's Twice-Told Tales: His Re-Use of His Material. The Hague: Mouton, 1966.

7082 Honeywell, J. Arthur. An Enquiry into the Nature of Plot in the Twentieth-Century Novel. Diss. Chicago: 1964.

7083 Hopper, Vincent Foster. "Faulkner's Paradise Lost," VQR, 23 (Summer, 1947), 405-420.

7084 Hornback, Vernon Theodore, Jr. "William Faulkner and the Terror of History: Myth, History, and Moral Freedom in the Yoknapatawpha Cycle," DA, 25 (St. Louis: 1964), 476.

7085 Hornberger, Theodore. "Faulkner's Reputation in Brazil," FS, 2 (Spring, 1953), 9-10.

7086 Horsch, Janice. "Faulkner on Man's Struggle with Communication," KM (1964), 77-83.

7087 Hovde, Carl F. "Faulkner's Democratic Rhetoric," SAQ, 63 (Autumn, 1964), 530-541.

7088 Howard, Edwin. "The Faithful Smith," DeltaR, 2 (July-August, 1965), 34-35.
Faulkner's blacksmith.

7089 Howard, Leon. Literature and the American Tradition. Garden City: Doubleday, 1960, pp. 296-301, passim.

7090 Howe, Irving. "American Moderns," Paths of American Thought. Arthur M. Schlesinger, Jr., and Morton White, eds. Boston: Houghton Mifflin, 1963, pp. 320-322.

7091 _______. "Anarchy and Authority in American Literature," DenverQ, 2 (Autumn, 1967), 5-30.

7092 _______. "Faulkner and the Negroes: A Vision of Lost Fraternity," Commentary, 12 (October, 1951), 359-368.

7093 _______. "Faulkner and the Negroes," Images of the Negro in American Literature. Seymour Gross and J. E. Hardy, eds. Chicago: Chicago U. P., 1966, pp. 204-220.

7094 _______. "Faulkner and the Southern Tradition," William Faulkner. New York: Random House, 1951, pp. 22-29; repr., in Literature in America. Philip Rahv, ed. New York: Meridian Press, 1957, pp. 409-414.

7095 _______. "Faulkner: End of a Road," NR, 141 (December 7, 1959), 17-21.

7096 _______. "In Search of a Moral Style," NR, 145 (September 25, 1961), 26-27.

7097 _______. "Lonely White Man," NR, 151 (July 4, 1964), 19-21.

7098 _______. "The Quest for a Moral Style," A World More Attractive: A View of Modern Literature and Politics. New York: Horizon Press, 1963, pp. 59-76.

7099 _______. Sherwood Anderson. New York: Wm. Sloane Associates, 1951, passim.

7100 _______. "The Southern Myth and William Faulkner," AQ, 3 (Winter, 1951), 357-362.

7101 _______. "William Faulkner." Major American Authors. Perry Miller, ed. New York: Harcourt Brace, 1962, II, 825-841.

7102 _______. William Faulkner: A Critical Study. New York:

Random House, 1952; revised and expanded, New York: Vintage Bks., 1962; 3rd ed., Chicago U.P., 1975.

7103 _______. "William Faulkner: A Talent of Wild Abundance," Opinions and Perspectives. F. Brown, ed. Boston: Houghton Mifflin, 1964, pp. 194-198.

7104 _______. "William Faulkner and the Quest for Freedom," Tomorrow, 9 (December, 1949), 54-56.

7105 _______. "William Faulkner's Enduring Power," NYTBR, 19 (April 4, 1954), 1, 22.

7106 _______. "Yoknapatawpha County Was a World that Was Complete in Itself," NYTimes (July 22, 1962), 6-7, 24.

7107 Howe, Russell Warren. "Prejudice, Superstition and Economics," Phylon, 17 (3rd Qt., 1956), 215-226.

7108 Howell, Elmo. "Eudora Welty's Comedy of Manners," SAQ, 69 (Autumn, 1970), 469-479.
Asserts that Welty's work "is in a sense the feminine counterpart" of Faulkner's.

7109 _______. "Faulkner and Scott and the Legacy of the Lost Cause," GaR, 26 (1972), 314-325.

7110 _______. "Faulkner's Jumblies," ArQ, 16 (1960), 70-78.

7111 _______. "In Ole Mississippi: Faulkner's Reminiscence," KM, 30 (1965), 77-81.

7112 _______. "Mark Twain, William Faulkner and the First Families of Virginia," MTJ, 13 (Summer, 1966), 1-3, 19.

7113 _______. "A Name for Faulkner's City," Names, 16 (December, 1968), 415-421.

7114 _______. "A Note on Faulkner's Negro Characters," MissQ, 11 (Fall, 1958), 201-203.
"... It is to William Faulkner's credit that he has perhaps more than any other American writer treated the Negro as a human being and not merely as a member of a race...."

7115 _______. "President Jackson and William Faulkner's Choctaws," ChO, 45 (Fall, 1967), 252-258.

7116 _______. "William Faulkner and Pro Patria Mori," LaS, 5 (Summer, 1966), 89-96.

7117 _______. "William Faulkner and the Andrews Raid in Georgia, 1862," GHQ, 49 (June, 1965), 187-192.

7118 ________. "William Faulkner and the Chickasaw Funeral," AL, 36 (January, 1965), 523-525.

7119 ________. "William Faulkner and the Concept of Honor," NWR, 5 (Summer, 1962), 51-60.

7120 ________. "William Faulkner and the Mississippi Indians," GaR, 21 (December, 1967), 386-396.

7121 ________. "William Faulkner and the New Deal," MidwQ, 5 (Summer, 1964), 323-332.

7122 ________. "William Faulkner and the Plain People of Yoknapatawpha County," JMissH, 24 (April, 1962), 73-87.

7123 ________. "William Faulkner and Tennessee," THQ, 21 (September, 1962), 251-262.

7124 ________. "William Faulkner: The Substance of Faith," BYUS, 9 (Summer, 1969), 453-462.

7125 ________. "William Faulkner's 'Christmas Gift!'" KFR, 13 (1967), 37-40.

7126 ________. "William Faulkner's General Forest and the Uses of History," THQ, 29 (Fall, 1970), 287-294.

7127 ________. "William Faulkner's Mule: A Symbol of the Post-War South," KFR, 15 (October-December, 1969), 81-86.

7128 ________. "William Faulkner's New Orleans," LaH, 7 (Summer, 1966), 229-240.

7129 ________. "William Faulkner's Southern Baptists," ArQ, 23 (Autumn, 1967), 220-226.

7130 Howell, John Michael. "The Waste Land Tradition in the Modern Novel," DA, 24 (Tulane: 1964), 3337.
Influence of _The Waste Land_ on Faulkner and others.

7131 Hubank, Roger. "William Faulkner: A Perspective View," Delta, 10 (Autumn, 1956), 13-21.

7132 Hubbell, Jay B. _South and Southwest: Literary Essays and Reminiscences_. Durham: Duke U.P., 1965, _passim_.

7133 ________. _The South in American Literature_. Durham: Duke U.P., 1954, pp. 868-869, _passim_.

7134 ________. _Southern Life in Fiction_. Athens: Georgia U.P., 1960, _passim_.

7135 _______. "Who Are the Best American Writers? A Study of Some Critical Polls Sponsored by American Magazines," Anglo-American (Vienna-Stuttgart), No. 70 (1955), 80-81.

7136 _______. Who Are the Major American Writers? A Study of the Changing Literary Canon. Durham: Duke U.P., 1972, passim.

7137 Hudson, Bill. "Faulkner before Sanctuary," Carolina Magazine, 64 (April, 1935), 11-14.
Stresses Faulkner's indebtedness to Phil Stone.

7138 Hudson, Tommy. "William Faulkner: Mystic and Traditionalist," Perspective, 3 (Autumn, 1950), 227-235.

7139 Hughes, Richard, and P. Albert Duhamel. Rhetoric, Principles and Usage. Englewood Cliffs, New Jersey: Prentice-Hall, 1962, passim.

7140 _______. "Faulkner and Bennett," Encounter, 21 (September, 1963), 59-61.
Arnold Bennett's introduction of Faulkner to English readers.

7141 Hume, Robert D. "Gothic Versus Romantic: A Revaluation of the Gothic Novel," PMLA, 84 (March, 1969), 282-290.

7142 Humphrey, Robert. "Faulkner's Synthesis," Stream of Consciousness in the Modern Novel. Berkeley: California U.P., 1954, pp. 17-22, 36-37, 64-65, 72-73, 104-111.

7143 Hunt, J. A. "Thomas Mann and Faulkner: Portrait of a Magician," WSCL, 8 (Summer, 1967), 431-436.

7144 Hunt, John W., Jr. "The Theological Complexity of Faulkner's Fiction," Religious Perspectives of Faulkner's Fiction. J. R. Barth, ed. Notre Dame U.P., 1972, pp. 81-87.

7145 _______. William Faulkner: Art in Theological Tension. Syracuse, New York: Syracuse U.P., 1965. Repr., 1972.

7146 _______. William Faulkner's Rendering of Modern Experience: A Theological Analysis. Diss. Chicago: 1961.

7147 Hunt, Wallace. "The Stratagems of William Faulkner," Gambit, 1 (Spring, 1952), 8-12.

7148 Hunter, Edwin R. William Faulkner: Narrative Practice and Prose Style. Washington, D.C.: Windhover, 1973.

7149 Hunter, Marjorie. "Faulkner Sensed Impending Crisis," NYTimes (October 7, 1962), 61.

7150 Hutchens, John K. "Character Sketch," NYHTBR (December 3, 1950), 3.

7151 _______. "Gentleman from Mississippi," NYHTBR (October 10, 1948), 8.

7152 _______. "Mr. Faulkner and a Predecessor," NYHTBR (October 7, 1951), 3.

7153 _______. "With Honor," NYHTBR (December 24, 1950), 2.

7154 Hutcheon, Philip Loring. "Affirming the Void: Futilitarianism in the Fiction of Conrad and Faulkner," DA, 35 (Rice: 1974), 2271A.

7155 Hutcherson, D. R. "El mundo novelesco de William Faulkner," Arbor, 43 (January, 1959), 71-83.

7156 Hutchings, Winifred L. "Trends in Modern Fiction," LibJ, 60 (July, 1935), 556-561.

7157 Hutchinson, James D. "Time: The Fourth Dimension in Faulkner," SDR, 6 (Autumn, 1968), 91-103.

7158 Hutchinson, Stuart. "All Havens Astern: Selby's Exit to Brooklyn," LonM, 9 (April, 1969), 22-34.
Faulkner's influence.

7159 Hutton, Patrick H. "Companionship in Voltaire's Candide," EnlE, 4 (1973), 39-45.

7160 Huxley, Julian Sorell. "The Analysis of Fame: A Revelation of the Human Documents in Who'sWho," SatRL, 12 (May 11, 1935), 12.

7161 Hyde, Monique Raymond. "William Faulkner and Claude Simon: A Stylistic Study," DAI, 32 (Indiana: 1971) 5740A-41A.

7162 Hyman, Stanley Edgar. "Some Trends in the Novel," CE, 20 (October, 1958), 1-9.

7163 Ibuki, Takehiko. "On William Faulkner," World Literature, No. 8 (1948).

7164 Ilacqua, Alma Aquilino. "Faulkner and the Concept of Excellence," DAI, 36 (Syracuse: 1975), 314A.

7165 Illo, John. "Faulkner's Racial Views," NYTimes (August 13, 1967), IV, 11.

7166 Inge, M. Thomas. "Contemporary American Literature in Spain," TSL, 16 (1971), 155-167.

7167 _______, ed. "Donald Davidson on Faulkner: An Early Recognition," GaR, 20 (December, 1966), 454-462.
Cf., Donald Davidson. "A Meeting of Southern Writers," Bookman, 74 (January-February, 1932), 494-496.

7168 _______, ed. The Frontier Humorists: Critical Views. Hamden, Conn.: Archon Bks. (Shoe String Press), 1975, passim.

7169 _______. "The Virginia Face of Faulkner," Va. Cavalcade, 24 (Summer, 1974), 32-39.

7170 _______. "William Faulkner and George Washington Harris: In the Tradition of Southwestern Humor," TSL, 7 (1962), 47-59.

7171 Ingram, Forrest. Representative Short Story Cycles of the Twentieth Century: Studies in Literary Genre. (DPL, Ser. Major 19) The Hague: Mouton, 1971, passim.

7172 _______, and Barbara Steinberg. "On the Verge: An Interview with Ernest J. Gaines," NOrlR, 3 (1973), 339-344.
Faulkner's influence.

7173 Irizarry, Estelle. "Procedimientos estilisticos de J. C. Onetti," CHA, 292-94 (1974), 669-695.

7174 Irvine, Peter L. "Faulkner and Hardy," ArQ, 26 (Winter, 1970), 357-365.

7175 Irwin, John T. Doubling and Incest: Repetition and Re- A Speculative Reading of Faulkner. Baltimore: Johns Hopkins U.P., 1975. Rev-art., by James M. Cox, MLN, 91 (1976), 1120-31.

7176 Isaacs, Neil D. "Faulkner with a Vengeance," SAQ, 60 (Autumn, 1961), 427-433.
Faulkner's influence on Claude Simon.

7177 _______. "Götterdammerung in Yoknapatawpha," TSL, 8 (1963), 47-55.

7178 Ishi, Ichiro. "Introduction to the Study of Faulkner," Eibungaku Kenkyu, 15 (February, 1960), 75-175.

7179 Israel, Calvin. "The Last Gentleman," PR, 35 (Spring, 1968), 315-319.
A reminiscence.

7180 Ivǎnescu, Mircea. "Dostoievski si Faulkner," Secolul, 20, No. 4 (1969), 209-212.

7181 Izakov, B. Miatushchaiasia dusha. [A restless spirit.] Moskva: 1960, No. 2, pp. 97-98.

7182 Izzo, Carlo. "William Faulkner," Civiltà americana: saggi. Roma: Edizioni di Storia e Letteratura, 1967, I, 401-412.

7183 _______. "William Faulkner," La letteratura nordamericana. Rev. ed. Firenze: Sansoni-Accademia, 1967, pp. 569-573.

7184 Jackson, James Turner. "Delta Cycle: A Study of William Faulkner," Chimera, 5 (Autumn, 1946), 3-14.

7185 Jackson, Naomi. "Faulkner's Woman: 'Demon-Nun and Angel-Witch,'" BSUF, 8 (Winter, 1967), 12-20.

7186 Jacobs, Robert D. "Faulkner's Humor," The Comic Imagination in American Literature. Louis D. Rubin, Jr., ed. New Brunswick, New Jersey: Rutgers U. P., 1973, pp. 305-318.

7187 _______. "Faulkner's Tragedy of Isolation," HopR, 6 (Spring-Summer, 1953), 162-183; repr., in Southern Renascence. Louis D. Rubin and Robert D. Jacobs, eds. Baltimore: Johns Hopkins, 1953, pp. 170-191.

7188 _______. "How Do You Read Faulkner?" Provincial, 1 (April, 1957), 3-5.

7189 _______. "Southern Literature: The Historical Image," South: Modern Southern Literature in Its Cultural Setting. Louis D. Rubin, Jr., and Robert D. Jacobs, eds. Garden City: Doubleday, 1961, pp. 29-47.

7190 _______. "William Faulkner: The Passion and the Penance," South: Modern Southern Literature in Its Cultural Setting. Louis Rubin and Robert D. Jacobs, eds. Garden City: 1961, pp. 142-176.

7191 Jaffe, Evelyn. "Endure and Prevail: Faulkner's Social Outcasts," DAI, 38 (Boulder, Colorado: 1977), 2789.

7192 Jafford, Paul. "Le double aspect de l'oeuvre de Faulkner," Critique, 9 (June, 1953), 496-507.

7193 Jäger, Dietrich. "Die Darstellung des Kampfes bei Stephen Crane, Hemingway, Faulkner, und Britting," Amerikanische Erzählungen von Hawthorne bis Salinger: Interpretationen. Paul G. Buchloh, ed. (KBAA 6.) Neumünster, 1968, pp. 112-154.

7194 James, Stuart. "Faulkner's Shadowed Land," DQ, 6 (1971), 45-61.

7195 _______. "'I Lay My Hand on My Mouth': Religion in Yoknapatawpha County," IllQ, 40 (Fall, 1977), 38-53.

7196 Jameson, Fredric. "Three Methods in Sartre's Literary Criticism," _Modern French Criticism: From Proust and Valery to Structuralism._ John K. Simon, ed. Chicago U. P., 1972, pp. 195-198, 199.

7197 Janeway, Elizabeth. "Fiction's Place in a World Awry," NYTBR (August 13, 1961), 1.

7198 Janković, Mira. _Faulknerova alegorija moralne svijesti._ Zagreb: Staroslavenski Institut, 1963/1964.

7199 ______. "U kući Williama Faulknera," Forum (1967), 1-2, 277-289.

7200 Janson, Ake. "William Faulkner," BLM, 10 (December, 1950), 734-739.

7201 Janssens, G. A. M. _The American Literary Review: A Critical History, 1920-1950._ The Hague: Mouton, 1968, passim.

7202 Jarlot, Gérard. [William Faulkner] Fontaine (novembre 1946), 653-657.

7203 Jarrett-Kerr, Martin. _William Faulkner: A Critical Essay._ Contemporary Writers in Christian Perspective. Grand Rapids, Michigan: William B. Eerdmans, 1970.

7204 Jehlen, Myra. _Class and Character in Faulkner's South._ New York: Columbia U. P., 1975.

7205 Jelliffe, Robert A., ed. _Faulkner at Nagano._ Tokyo: Kenkyusha, Ltd., 1956.

7206 Jenkins, Clauston Levi. "Faulkner's Edition of Swift: A Textual Study of Volumes One and Three," DA, 27 (Virginia: 1966), 2499A.

7207 Jenkins, Lee Clinton. "Faulkner, the Mythic Mind, and the Blacks," L&P, 27, #2 (1977), 74-91.

7208 ______. "Images of the Negro in the Novels of William Faulkner," DAI, 34 (Columbia: 1973), 3403A.

7209 Jensen, Merrill, ed. "The South," _Regionalism in America._ Madison, Wisconsin: Wisconsin U. P., 1951, p. 149.

7210 Jepson, Hans Lyngby. "William Faulkner som novellist," Vindrosen, 4 (November, 1957), 465-482.

7211 Johannessen, Matthias. "'Rikisstjornir eru ekki osvipaðar versmiðjum.' Minnispunktar frá dvöl Faulkners á Islandi." ["Governments are not unlike factories." Reminiscence from

Faulkner's visit to Iceland.] Lesbôk Morgunblaðsins 46:42 (1971), 1-2.

7212 Johnson, Beulah V. "The Treatment of the Negro Woman as a Major Character in American Novels, 1900-1950," DA, 16 (New York: 1955), 528.

7213 Johnson, Ellwood C. "Some Versions of Individualism in American Literature and Thought," DA, 30 (Washington: 1969), 2486A-87A.

7214 Johnson, Gerald. "The Horrible South," VQR, 11 (April, 1935), 201-217.

7215 Johnson, James W. "The Adolescent Hero: A Trend in Modern Fiction," TCL, 5 (April, 1959), 3-11.

7216 Johnson, Pamela Hansford. *Books of the Month* (November, 1942), 9-10.

7217 Jones, Billy. Letter to the Editor. Memphis Commercial Appeal (April 24, 1955), V, 3.
Response to Faulkner on race issue.

7218 Jones, Howard Mumford. "Relief from Murder," Atl, 162 (July, 1938), 82.

7219 ________. "Social Notes on the South," VQR, 11 (July, 1935, 454.

7220 ________, and Walter Rideout, eds. *Letters of Sherwood Anderson.* Boston: Little, Brown, 1953, *passim.*

7221 Jones, Peter G. *The Developing Voice: An Appraisal of the Modern American War Novel.* Diss. New York U., 1970.

7222 ________. *War and the Novelist: Appraising the American War Novel.* Columbia: Missouri U.P., 1976, *passim.*

7223 Jonsson, Thorsten. "William Faulkner på tu man hand," Dagens nyheter (Stockholm), (April 17, 1946).

7224 Jordan, Peter Wilson. "Faulkner's Crime Fiction: His Use of the Detective Story and the Thriller," DAI, 34 (Connecticut: 1974), 2630A.

7225 Jordan, Robert M. "The Limits of Illusion: Faulkner, Fielding, and Chaucer," Criticism, 2 (Summer, 1960), 278-305.

7226 Josephs, Mary J. "The Hunting Metaphor in Hemingway and Faulkner," DAI, 34 (Michigan State: 1973), 1282A.

7227 Josephson, Matthew. "The Younger Generation: Its Young Novelists," VQR, 9 (April, 1933), 243-261.

7228 Jovine, F. Anthony. The Young Hero in American Fiction: A Motif for Teaching Literature. New York: Appleton-Century-Crofts, 1971, passim.

7229 Judson, Horace, A. T. Baker, and Martha McDowell. "The Curse and the Hope," Time, 84 (July 17, 1964), 17, 44-48.

7230 Juin, Hubert. "L'univers clos de William Faulkner," Esprit, 24 (November, 1956), 704-715.

7231 Julien, Andre. "Faulkner, l'homme du Sud," GLet (15 décembre 1950), 28-30.

7232 Junius, Junior. Pseudo Realist. New York: Outsider Press, 1931.

7233 Justo, Luis. "La Antropologia de Faulkner," Sur, 206 (December, 1951), 126-130.

7234 Justus, James H. "Beyond Gothicism: Wuthering Heights and an American Tradition," TSL, 5 (1960), 25-33.

7235 ________. "On the Restlessness of Southerners," SoR, 11 (Winter, 1975), 65-83.

7236 ________. "William Faulkner and the Southern Concept of Woman," MissQ, 15 (1962), 1-16.

7237 Kahn, Ludwig W. "William Faulkner: Das Romanwerk des Dichters als geistige Antwort auf unsere Zeit," Universitas, 16 (December, 1961), 1307-1318.

7238 Kalb, Bernard. "The Author," SatRL, 37 (July 31, 1954), 11.

7239 Kaluza, Irena. "William Faulkner's Subjective Style," KN, 11 (1st Qt., 1964), 13-30.

7240 Kantak, V. Y. "Faulkner's Technique," Studies in American Literature: Essays in Honour of William Mulder. Jagdist Chander and Narindar S. Pradhan, eds. Delhi: Oxford U.P., 1976, pp. 77-96.

7241 Kanters, Robert. "Son oeuvre est le nègro spirituel de l'homme blanc," FL, 17 (July 14, 1962), 8.

7242 ________. "William Faulkner," RdP, 69 (August, 1962), 152-154.

7243 Kaplan, Harold. The Passive Voice: An Approach to Modern Fiction. Athens, Ohio: Ohio U.P., 1966, passim.

7244 Karanikas, Alexander. Tillers of a Myth: Southern Agrarians as Social and Literary Critics. Madison: Wisconsin U. P., 1966, passim.

7245 Karasu, Bilge. "Faulkner cevirisi," Forum fikir meydandidir (Ankara), 6 (January, 1957), 23.

7246 Karsten, Otto. [William Faulkner] Kölnisck Zeitung cited in Die Literatur, 40 (July, 1938), 693.

7247 Kartiganer, Donald M. The Fragile Thread: The Meaning of Form in Faulkner's Novels. Mass. U. P., 1979.

7248 _______. "The Individual and the Community: Values in the Novels of William Faulkner," DA, 25 (Brown: 1965), 4701-02.

Cf., Donald M. Kartiganer. "Absalom, Absalom!: The Discovery of Values," AL, 37 (1965), 291-306.

7249 _______. "Process and Product: A Study in Modern Literary Form, [Part 2]," MR, 12 (1971), 789-816.

7250 Kashkin, Ivan. "Folkner--rasskazchik" [Faulkner--the story writer]. in Faulkner, W. Sem' rasskazov [Seven stories]. Moscow: 1958, pp. 162-178.

7251 Kauffman, Linda Sue. "The Madam and the Midwife: Reba Rivers and Sairey Gamp," MissQ, 30, #3 (Summer, 1977), 395-401.

7252 _______. "Psychic Displacement and Adaptation in the Novels of Dickens and Faulkner," DAI, 39, #6 (Santa Barbara, Calif.: 1978), 3573A.

7253 Kawin, Bruce F. Faulkner and Film. New York: Frederick Ungar, 1977.

7254 _______. "Faulkner Filmography," FilmQ, 30 (Summer, 1977), 12-21.

7255 _______. Telling It Again and Again: Repetition in Literature and Film. Ithaca: Cornell U. P., 1972.

7256 Kay, Wallace G. "Faulkner's Mississippi: The Myth and the Microcosm," SoQ, 6 (October, 1967), 13-24.

7257 Kazin, Alfred. "Faulkner: The Rhetoric and the Agony," VQR, 18 (Summer, 1942), 389-402.

7258 _______. "Faulkner: The Rhetoric and the Agony," [Rev. and enl., from VQR, 18 (1942), 389-402] in On Native Grounds. New York: Reynal & Hitchcock, 1942, pp. 453-484.

7259 _______. "Faulkner in His Fury," The Inmost Leaf: A Selection of Essays. New York: Harcourt, Brace, 1955, pp. 257-273. Also in Modern American Fiction. A. W. Litz, ed. New York: Oxford U.P., 1963, pp. 166-178.

7260 _______. "Faulkner's Vision of Human Integrity," HA, 135 (November, 1951), 8-9, 28-31.

7261 _______. "Faulkners vision av människans integritet," BLM (Sweden), 20 (May-June, 1951), 356-364.

7262 _______. "The Secret of the South: Faulkner to Percy," Bright Book of Life: American Novelists and Storytellers from Hemingway to Mailer. Boston: Little, Brown, 1973, pp. 21-67.

7263 _______. "William Faulkner: The Short Stories," Contemporaries. Boston: Little, Brown, 1962, pp. 130-158.

7264 _______. "Works of William Faulkner," VQR, 18 (Summer, 1942), 389-402.

7265 _______. "The Writer in Perspective," SatRL, 45 (July 28, 1962), 24.

7266 _______. "Young Man, Old Man," Reporter, 29 (December 19, 1963), 36-40.

7267 Kazula, Irene. "William Faulkner's Subjective Style," KN (Warsaw), (1964).

7268 Kehler, Joel R. "Faulkner, Melville, and a Tale of Two Carpenters," NMAL, 1 (1977), Item 22.

7269 Kellner, Bruce. Carl Van Vechten and the Irreverent Decades. Norman: Oklahoma: Okla. U. Pr., 1968, passim.

7270 Kellogg, Gene. The Vital Tradition: The Catholic Novel in a Period of Convergence. Chicago: Loyola U.P., 1970, pp. 135, 183.

7271 Kellogg, Jean Defrees. "William Faulkner and the Tyranny of Linear Consciousness," Dark Prophets of Hope: Dostoevsky, Sartre, Camus, Faulkner. Chicago: Loyola U.P., 1975, pp. 123-135.

7272 Kenner, Hugh. "The Last Novelist," A Homemade World. New York: Knopf [distr. by Random House], 1975, pp. 194-221.

7273 Kent, George. "The Black Woman in Faulkner's Works, with the Exclusion of Dilsey," Phylon, 35 (December, 1974), 430-441; Part II, Phylon, 36 (March, 1975), 55-67.

7274 Kent, Michael. "Realism and Reality," CathW, 163 (June, 1946), 224-229.

7275 Kerlin, Charles M., Jr. "Life in Motion: Genteel and Vernacular Attitudes in the Works of the Southwestern American Humorists, Mark Twain, and William Faulkner," DA, 29 (Colorado: 1968), 4492A.

7276 Kerr, Elizabeth M. "William Faulkner and the Southern Concept of Woman," MissQ, 15 (Winter, 1961-1962), 1-16.

7277 ________. "Yoknapatawpha and the Myth of the South," WissSL, No. 1 (1964), 85-93.

7278 ________. Yoknapatawpha: Faulkner's "Little Postage Stamp of Native Soil." New York: Fordham U.P., 1969.

7279 Kibler, James E., Jr. "William Faulkner and Provincetown Drama, 1920-1922," MissQ, 22 (1969), 226-236.

7280 Kikuchi, Takenobu. "Sartre's Critique on Faulkner," Sylvan, 8 (May, 1963), 61-68.

7281 Killingsworth, Kay. "L'hêritage mêridional dans l'oeuvre de William Faulkner et d'Albert Camus," Esprit, 9 (September, 1963), 209-234.

7282 King, Larry L. "Requiem for Faulkner's Home Town," Holiday (March, 1969), 60-61, 74-76.

7283 Kinney, Arthur. "Faulkner and Flaubert," JML, 6 (April, 1977), 222-247.

7284 ________. "Faulkner and the Possibilities for Heroism," SoR, 6 (October, 1970), 1110-1125.

7285 Kirk, Robert Warner. "An Index and Encyclopedia of the Characters in the Fictional Works of William Faulkner," DA, 20 (So. California: 1959), 2292-93.

7286 ________, and Marvin Klotz. Faulkner's People: A Complete Guide and Index to Characters in the Fiction of William Faulkner. Berkeley: California U.P., 1963.

7287 Klotz, Marvin. "The Triumph Over Time: Narrative Form in William Faulkner and William Styron," MissQ, 17 (Winter, 1964), 9-20.

7288 Knight, Arthur. "Land of the Pharaohs," SatRL, 38 (June 25, 1955), 24.

7289 Knight, Grant C. American Literature and Culture. New York: Ray Long and Richard R. Smith, 1932, passim.

7290 Kniskern, M. "Reply: 'In the Name of Allah, Figs,'' by Simeon Stylites [pseud.]," ChrC, 68 (January 10, 1951), 41.

7291 Knox, George. "William Faulkner: August Light," MissQ, 15 (1961-62), 138.
A poem about Faulkner.

7292 Kohler, Dayton. "William Faulkner and the Social Conscience," CE, 11 (December, 1949), 119-127; also in EJ, 38 (December, 1949), 545-553.

7293 Koljević, Svetozar. "Foknerov književni eksperimenat," Putevi (July 1, 1960), 538-550.

7294 Kolodny, Anette. The Lay of the Land: Metaphor as Experience and History in American Life and Letters. Chapel Hill: North Carolina U.P., 1975.
Rev., by Russel B. Nye, AL, 47 (1976), 651-652.

7295 ________. "'Stript, shorne and made deformed': Images on the Southern Landscape," SAQ, 75 (1976), 55-73.

7296 Kondravy, Connie Ranck. "Faulkner's Study of Youth," DAI, 36 (Lehigh: 1975), 6100A-01A.

7297 Korenman, Joan Smolin. "Faulkner and 'That Undying Mark,'" SAF, 4 (Spring, 1976), 81-91.

7298 ________. Faulkner's Grecian Urn. Diss. Harvard: 1970.

7299 ________. "Faulkner's Grecian Urn," SLJ, 7, i (1974), 3-23.

7300 Korn, Karl. "Moira und Schuld," DNR, 49, #2 (December, 1938), 603-609.

7301 ________. "Ubersetzungsernte," Die Tat, 29 (1937), 128, 129.

7302 Kornfeld, Milton H. "A Darker Freedom: The Villain in the Novels of Hawthorne, James, and Faulkner," DAI, 31 (Brandeis: 1970), 2883A.

7303 Kostiakov, V. A. Trilogija Uil'jama Folknera. Saratov, Russia: Saratovskogo Universiteta, 1969.

7304 Koury, Leon Z. "The Spark and the Flame," DeltaR, 2 (July-August, 1965), 46-47.

7305 Kowalczyk, Richard L. "From Addie Bundren to Gavin Stevens: The Direction of Reality," CEJ, 2 (Winter, 1966), 45-52.

7306 Krefft, James Harvey. "The Yoknapatawpha Indians: Fact and Fiction," DAI, 37 (Tulane: 1976), 1549A.

7307 Kreiswirth, Martin. "Faulkner as Translator: His Versions of Verlaine," MissQ, 30 (Summer, 1977), 429-432.

7308 Krishnamurthi, M. G. "The Distaff Faulknerians," LCrit, 8 (1967), 69-78.

7309 Kristensen, Sven Moller. "William Faulkner," Amerikansk litteratur, 1920-1947. Copenhagen: Athenaeum, 1948, pp. 64-75.

7310 ________. "William Faulkner," Lidt om amerikansk litteratur. Copenhagen: Carit Andersens Forlag [1950?], pp. 25-27.

7311 Kronenberger, Louis. "Gambler in Publishing: Horace Liveright," Atl, 215 (January, 1965), 94-104.
Anecdote.

7312 Kroner, Jack. "Une Discussion sur Faulkner chez les êtudiants communistes amêricains," NCr (juillet-août 1949), 87-96.

7313 Krutch, Joseph Wood. "In These Days Our Literature in All Its Might Came of Age," NYTBR (October 7, 1956), 6-9, 40.

7314 Kulin, Katalin. "Reasons and Characteristics of Faulkner's Influence on Modern Latin-American Fiction," ALit ASH, 13 (1971), 349-363.

7315 Kunitz, Stanley J., ed. "William Faulkner," Living Authors. New York: Wilson, 1931, pp. 121-122; superseded by Twentieth Century Authors. New York: Wilson, 1942, 2nd pr., 1944, pp. 438-439; First Supplement, 1955, pp. 316-317.

7316 Kunkel, F. L. "Christ Symbolism in Faulkner: Prevalence of the Human," Renascence, 17 (1965), 148-156.

7317 Kwiat, Joseph J., and Marc C. Turpie, eds. Studies in American Culture. Minneapolis: Minnesota U.P., 1960, passim.

7318 Kwiatek, Vivien Louise. "Moment of Truth: The Hunt in American Fiction," DAI, 35, #6 (Maryland: 1974), 3749A.

7319 Labatt, Blair P., Jr. "Faulkner the Storyteller," DAI, 34 (Virginia: 1974), 7761A.

7320 LaFrance, Marston, ed. Patterns of Commitment in American Literature. Toronto: Toronto U.P., 1967, passim.

7321 Lambert, J. W. "Faulkner's World," Sunday Times (London), (July 8, 1962), 25.

7322 Lampl, Nancy Williams. "The Decomposing Form: Studies in Faulkner," DAI, 37, #12 (Case Western Reserve: 1976), 7735A-36A.

7323 Landfield, Sidney. "William Faulkner at Home," Chicago Sun (June 23, 1946), Bk. Wk., 6.

7324 Landor, Mikhail. "Faulkner in the Soviet Union," SovL, 12 (1965), 178-185.

7325 ________. "Faulkner in the Soviet Union," Soviet Criticism of American Literature in the Sixties. Carl R. Proffer, ed., and tr. Ann Arbor: Ardis Pubs., 1972, pp. 173-180.

7326 ________. "Tvorčheskii metod Folknera v stanovlenii," [Faulkner's Creative Method in the Making.], VLit, 15, x (October, 1971), 110-135.

7327 ________. "William Faulkner: New Translations and Studies," SovL, 8 (1968), 180-185.

7328 Landrum, Larry N., Pat Browne, and Ray B. Browne, eds. Dimensions of Detective Fiction. Bowling Green, Ohio: Popular Pr., 1976.

7329 Lang, Eleanor M. "Hawthorne and Faulkner: The Continuity of a Dark American Tradition," DAI, 31 (Lehigh: 1970), 5410A.

7330 Lange, V., und H. Boeschenstein. Kulturkritik und Literaturbetrachtung in Amerika. Breslau: 1938.

7331 Langford, Gerald. "Insights into the Creative Process: The Faulkner Collection at the University of Texas," Proceedings of the Comparative Literature Symposium. Vol. IV. William Faulkner: Prevailing Verities and World Literature. Wolodymyr T. Zyla, and Wendell M. Aycock, eds. Lubbock: Interdept. Comm. on Comp. Lit. Texas Tech. U., 1973, pp. 115-133.

7332 Langford, Walter M. The Mexican Novel Comes of Age. Notre Dame: Notre Dame U.P., 1971; 2nd pr., 1972, pp. 134, 143.
Faulkner's influence on Carlos Fuentes.

7333 Langland, Richard E., and Wm. E. Taylor, eds. The Twenties: Poetry and Prose. DeLand, Florida: Everett/Edwards, 1966, pp. 95-98.

7334 Lannon, John M. "William Faulkner: A Study in Spatial Form," DAI, 33 (Massachusetts: 1973), 5184A.

7335 Larbaud, Valéry. "Un roman de William Faulkner--1897,"

Domaine anglais: Ce Vice Impuni, La Lecture. Paris: Gallimard, 1925; rev. and enlarged, 1936, repub., 1951, as Vol. III of his complete works, pp. 218-222.

7336 Larsen, Eric. "The Barrier of Language: The Irony of Language in Faulkner," MFS, 13 (Spring, 1967), 19-31.

7337 Las Vergnas, Raymond. "Faulkner: Un aristocrate sudiste," NL, 40 (12 juillet 1962), 3.

7338 _______. "Faulkner," NL (19 février 1946), 5.

7339 _______. "Lettres étrangères," HM (juillet 1946), 192-197.

7340 _______. "Regards sur les lettres américaines," TR, No. 105 (September, 1956), 91-92.

7341 Lauras, Antoine. "Paradoxical Faulkner," Etudes, 215 (October-December, 1962), 87-93.

7342 _______. "Vieille Europe, jeune Amérique," Etudes, 274 (July-August, 1952), 72-84.

7343 Lawson, Lewis Allen. "The Grotesque in Recent Southern Fiction," DA, 25 (Wisconsin: 1964), 2514.

7344 _______. "William Faulkner," The Politics of Twentieth-Century Novelists. George Andrew Panichas, ed. New York: Hawthorn Bks., 1971, pp. 278-295.

7345 Leary, Lewis. Introduction. Crowell's Handbook of Faulkner by Dorothy Tuck. Lewis Leary, advisory ed. New York: Thomas Y. Crowell, 1964, pp. vii-xx.

7346 _______. "William Faulkner and the Grace of Comedy," [Altered from Crowell's Handbook], Southern Excursions: Essays on Mark Twain and Others. Baton Rouge: Louisiana State U.P., 1971, pp. 209-229.

7347 _______. William Faulkner of Yoknapatawpha County. New York: Crowell, 1973.
Rev., by J. E. Kibler, MissQ, 28 (1975), 392-393.

7348 _______. "William Faulkner: The Grace of Comedy," Australian and New Zealand Am. Stud. Assn., 1 (1963), 18-29.

7349 Leaska, Mitchell A. "The Rhetoric of Multiple Points of View in Selected Contemporary Novels," DA, 29 (New York: 1969), 3145.

7350 Leaver, Florence. "Faulkner: The Word as Principle and Power," SAQ, 57 (Fall, 1958), 464-476; repr., in Three

Decades of Criticism. Frederick Hoffman and Olga Vickery, eds. East Lansing: Michigan St., 1960, pp. 199-209.

7351 Lebesque, M. [William Faulkner] Climats (1 dêcembre 1948), 12.

7352 Le Breton, Maurice. "Technique et psychologie chez William Faulkner," EA, 1 (septembre 1937), 418-438.

7353 ________. "Temps et per chez William Faulkner," JdP, 44 (January-June, 1951), 344-354.

7354 LeClair, Thomas. "Death and Black Humor," Critique, 17, #1 (1975), 5-40.

7355 Lehan, Richard Daniel. "Existentialism and the Modern American Novel," DA, 20 (Wisconsin: 1959), 1365.

7356 ________. "Existentialism in Recent American Fiction: The Demonic Quest," TSLL, 1 (Summer, 1959), 181-202.

7357 ________. F. Scott Fitzgerald and the Craft of Fiction. Carbondale and Edwardsville: So. Ill. U.P., 1966, pp. 45-48.

7358 ________. "French and American Literary Existentialism: Dos Passos, Hemingway, Faulkner," A Dangerous Crossing: French Literary Existentialism and the Modern American Novel. Carbondale and Edwardsville: So. Ill. U.P., 1973, pp. 35-79.

7359 Leibowitz, Rene. "L'art tragique de William Faulkner," CdSud, 17 (novembre 1940), 502-508.

7360 Leisy, Ernest E. "The Novel in America: Notes for a Survey," SWR, 22 (October, 1936), 88-89.

7361 Leiter, Louis. "Faulkner," CE, 24 (October, 1962), 66.

7362 Lemaire, Marcel. "Fiction in U.S.A.--From the South," RLV, 27, #3 (1961), 244-253.

7363 Lennox, Sara Jane K. "The Fiction of William Faulkner and Uwe Johnson: A Comparative Study," DAI, 34 (Madison, Wisconsin: 1974), 6647A.

7364 Lerman, Leo. "Faulkner's County: Yoknapatawpha," Mademoiselle (December, 1964), 55.

7365 Levin, Harry. "Some European Views of Contemporary American Literature," The American Writer and the European Tradition. Margaret Denny, ed. Minneapolis: Minnesota U.P., 1950, pp. 168-184.

7366 ________. Symbolism and Fiction. Charlottesville, Virginia: Virginia U. P., 1956, pp. 7-8.

7367 Levins, Lynn G. Faulkner's Heroic Design: The Yoknapatawpha Novels. Athens: Georgia U. P., 1976.
Rev., by D. L. Anderson. MissQ, 29 (1976), 466-470.

7368 ________. "William Faulkner: The Heroic Design of Yoknapatawpha," DAI, 34 (North Carolina, Chapel Hill: 1973), 2635A.

7369 Lewis, Clifford L. "William Faulkner: The Artist as Historian," MASJ, 10 (Fall, 1969), 36-48.

7370 Lewis, Flora. "The Worldwide Influence of William Faulkner: Report from Six Capitals [from Bonn, Germany]," NYTBR (November 15, 1959), 53.

7371 Lewis, R. W. B. The American Adam: Innocence, Tragedy, and Tradition in the Nineteenth Century. Chicago: Chicago U. P., 1955, passim.

7372 ________. "Hero in the New World," KR, 12 (Autumn, 1951), 641-660; repr., in Interpretations of American Literature. Charles Feidelson, ed. New York: Oxford U. P., 1959, pp. 332-348; Picaresque Saint: Representative Figures in Contemporary Fiction. Philadelphia: Lippincott, 1959, pp. 179-219.

7373 Lewis, Sinclair. A Sinclair Lewis Reader: The Man from Main Street: Selected Essays and Other Writings, 1904-1950. Harry E. Maule and Melville H. Cane, eds. New York: Random House, 1953, passim.
Contains Lewis's reference to Faulkner as the man "who has freed the South from hoop-skirts...."

7374 Lewis, Wyndham. "Criticism as Performance: Literary," The Profils in Literature Series. New York: Humanities Press, 1972, pp. 39-40.

7375 ________. "William Faulkner: The Moralist with a Corncob," Men Without Art. London: 1934; reissued, New York: Harcourt, Brace, 1934, 1964, pp. 42-64.

7376 ________. The Writer and the Absolute. London: Methuen, 1952, passim.

7377 Lewisohn, Ludwig. "The Crisis of the Novel," YR, 22 (March, 1933), 533-544.

7378 ________. Expression in America. New York: Harper, 1932, pp. 520-521; see also Creative America. New York: 1933, pp. xviii-xix.

7379 Libby, Anthony P. "Chronicles of Children: William Faulkner's Short Fiction," DA, 30 (Stanford: 1969), 1568A.

7380 Lilly, Paul R., Jr. "Silence and the Impeccable Language: A Study of William Faulkner's Philosophy of Language," DAI, 32 (Fordham: 1971), 973A.

7381 "The Limits of the Possible, Accepting the Reality of the Human Situation," TLS (November 6, 1959), xvi.

7382 Lincoln, Ruth Thompson. "Ontological Implications in Faulkner's Major Novels," DAI, 34 (Indiana: 1973), 1286A.

7383 Lind, Isle Dusoir. "Faulkner's Women," The Maker and The Myth: Faulkner and Yoknapatawpha, 1977. Evans Harrington and Ann J. Abadie, eds. Jackson, Miss.: Miss. U. P., 1978, pp. 89-104.

7384 ________. "The Teachable Faulkner," CE, 16 (February, 1955), 284-287, 302.
Cf., Robert E. Knoll. "The Unvanquished for a Start," CE, 19 (May, 1958), 338-343.

7385 Lind, L. Robert. "The Crisis in Literature," SR, 47 (January-March, 1939), 35-62.

7386 Lindell, Richard P. The Ritual of Survival: Landscape in Conrad and Faulkner. Diss. Yale: 1971.

7387 Link, Karl E. "William Faulkner: Form as Experience," SAQ, 53 (July, 1954), 384-403.

7388 Linn, Robert. "Robinson Jeffers and William Faulkner," AmSpec, 2 (November, 1933), 1; repr., in The American Spectator Yearbook. New York: Stokes, 1934, pp. 304-307.

7389 Linneman, William R. "Faulkner's Ten-Dollar Words," AS, 38 (May, 1963), 158-159.

7390 Linscott, Elizabeth. "Faulkner in Massachusetts," NEG, 10 (Winter, 1969), 37-42.

7391 Linscott, Robert N. "Faulkner without Fanfare," Esquire, 60 (July, 1963), 36-38.

7392 Littlejohn, David. "How Not to Write a Biography," NY, 170 (March 23, 1974), 25-27.
Essay-review of Joseph Blotner's Faulkner: A Biography.

7393/4 Litz, Walton. "William Faulkner's Moral Vision," SWR, 37 (Summer, 1952), 200-209.

7395 Lively, Robert A. *Fiction Fights the Civil War: An Unfinished Chapter in the Literary History of the American People.* Chapel Hill: North Carolina U. P., 1957, *passim.*

7396 Lloyd, James B. "The Oxford *Eagle*, 1902-1962: A Census of Locations," MissQ, 29 (1976), 423-431.

7397 Logan, John. "Nota sobre personaje balbuciente como hêroe," Sur, 322-23 (1970), 148-154.

7398 Loggins, Vernon. "Cleaving to the Dream," *I Hear America: Literature in the United States Since 1900.* New York: Crowell, 1937, pp. 109-112.

7399 Loghin, Georgeta. "William Faulkner şi problema populaţiei de culoare," ASUI, 13, #2 (1967), 245-248.

7400 Lohner, Edgar, ed. *Der Amerikanische Roman im 19. und 20. Jahrhundert.* Berlin: Erich Schmidt Verlag, 1974, *passim.*

7401 ________. *Thematik, Symbolik und Technik im Werk William Faulkner.* Diss. Bonn: 1950.

7402 Lombardo, Agostino. "Faulkner e Hawthorne," Il Mondo, 12 (February 2, 1960), 9-10; also in "La ricerca di Faulkner," *La ricerca del vero: saggi sulla tradizione letteraria americana.* Roma: Edizioni di Storia e Letteratura, 1961, pp. 317-346.

7403 ________. "I Negri e Gli Indiani," Il Mondo, 13 (May 2, 1961), 9.

7404 ________. "Il primo e l'ultimo Faulkner," *Realismo e simbolismo.* Rome: Edizioni di Storia e Letteratura, 1957, pp. 207-221.

7405 ________. *La Ricerca del vero: Saggi sulla tradizione letteraria americana.* Roma: Ed. di storia e letteratura, 1961, *passim.*

7406 ________. "I segreti di Faulkner," Il Mondo, 12 (July 12, 1960), 9-10; also in "La ricerca di Faulkner," *La ricerca del vero.* Roma: 1961.

7407 ________. "L'ultimo Faulkner," Lo Spettatore Italiano, 8 (January, 1955), 26-30.

7408 Longley, John. "Faulkner's Tragic Heroes," DA, 18 (New York: 1957), 1047.

7409 ________. *The Tragic Mask: A Study of Faulkner's Heroes.* Chapel Hill: North Carolina U. P., 1963.

7410 ________, and Robert Daniel. "Faulkner's Critics," Perspective, 3 (Winter, 1950), 202-208.

7411 López, Emilio Sosa. "El problema de mal en William Faulkner," Sur, (Buenos Aires), No. 247 (July-August, 1957), 55-63.

7412 Lopez, Guido (Ruth Feldman, tr.) "Letters and Comments: 'Faulkner and the Horses,'" YR, 64 (Spring, 1975), 468-476.
Faulkner's visit in Italy, September, 1955.

7413 Loreis, Hector-Jan. "De Wortels van de Nieuwe Roman [The Root of the New Novel]," NVT, 19, #4 (April, 1966), 379-408.

7414 Loughrey, Thomas Francis. "Values and Love in the Fiction of William Faulkner," DA, 23 (Notre Dame: 1963), 2915.

7415 Lovati, Georgia. "Faulkner, Soldati and America," LivA, 351 (September, 1936), 71-72.

7416 Loveman, Amy. "Southern Fiction," SatRL, 11 (December 8, 1934), 359.

7417 Lowrey, Perrin Holmes. The Critical Reception of William Faulkner's Work in the United States: 1926-1950. Diss. Chicago: 1957.

7418 Lowry, Malcolm. Selected Letters of Malcolm Lowry. Philadelphia and New York: Lippincott, 1965, p. 172, passim.

7419 Lowry, Thomas. "One Man's Faulkner," SatRL, 40 (May 4, 1957), 23.

7420 Luccock, Halford E. American Mirror: Social, Ethical and Religious Aspects of American Literature, 1930-1940. New York: Cooper Square Pubs., 1971, pp. 69-71, passim.

7421 ________. Contemporary American Literature and Religion. New York: Willett, Clark, 1932, passim.

7422 Lüdeke, Henry. "William Faulkner," Geschichte der amerikanischen Literatur. Bern: A. Francke AG Verlag, 1952, pp. 523-526.

7423 Ludington, Townsend, ed. The Fourteenth Chronicle: Letters and Diaries of John Dos Passos. Boston: Gambit, 1973, passim.

7424 Ludmer, Josefina. "Onetti: 'La novia (carta) robada (a Faulkner),'" Hispam, 9 (1975), 3-19.

7425 Lukács, George. Realism in Our Time: Literature and the Class Struggle. John and Necke Mander, trs. New York: Harper & Row, 1964, 1971, passim.

7426 Lundkvist, Artur. "Amerikansk prosa," BLM, 6 (March, 1937), 197-204.

7427 _______. "William Faulkner," Diktare och avslöjare i Amerikas moderna literatur. Stockholm: Kooperativa Förbundets Bokförlag, 1956, pp. 160-170.

7428 Lupan, Radu. "In Jefferson, acasă la Faulkner," Luc, 21 (April, 1973), 10.

7429 _______. "Sur l'esprit moderne dans l'art de traduire," The Nature of Translation: Essays on the Theory and Practice of Literary Translation. James S. Holmes, ed. The Hague, Paris: House of the Slovak Academy of Sciences, pub., 1970, p. 153.

7430 Lutwack, Leonard. Heroic Fiction: The Epic Tradition and American Novels of the Twentieth Century. London and Amsterdam: Feffer & Simons; Carbondale and Edwardsville: So. Ill. U.P., 1971, passim.

7431 Lyday, Charles Lance. "Faulkner's Commedia: An Interpretation of The Sound and the Fury, Sanctuary, As I Lay Dying, and Light in August," DAI, 39, #2 (Vanderbilt: 1977), 886A.

7432 Lydenberg, John. "American Novelists in Search for a Lost World," RLV, 27 (No. 4, 1961), 306-321.

7433 Lyons, Anne Ward. "Myth and Agony: The Southern Woman as Belle," DAI, 35, #11 (Bowling Green: 1974), 7314A.

7434 Lyons, Leonard. "The Lyon's Den," NYPost (May 3, 1962), 31.
Faulkner's meeting with Einstein.

7435 Lyra, Franciszek. William Faulkner. Warsaw: Wiedza Powszechna, 1969.

7436 Lytle, Andrew. "Regeneration for the Man," SR, 57 (Winter, 1949), 120-127; repr., in Two Decades of Criticism. Frederick Hoffman and Olga Vickery, eds. East Lansing: Michigan U.P., 1951, pp. 251-258.

7437 _______. "The Son of Man: He Will Prevail," SR, 63 (Winter, 1955), 114-137.

7438 McAleer, John J. "Biblical Symbols in American Literature: A Utilitarian Design," ES, 46, #4 (August, 1965), 310-322.

7439 McAlexander, Hubert, Jr. "General Earl Van Dorn and Faulkner's Use of History," JMissH, 39 (November, 1977), 357-361.

7440 ________. "History as Perception, History as Obsession: Faulkner's Development of a Theme," DAI, 34 (Madison, Wisconsin: 1974), 6596A-97A.

7441 ________. "William Faulkner--The Young Poet in Stark Young's The Torches Flare," AL, 43 (1972), 647-649.

7442 McCarthy, Mary. "One Touch of Nature," NY, 45, #49 (January 24, 1970), 39-57.
Faulkner saw Nature as "a force in human destiny."

7443 McClelland, Benjamin Wright. "Not Only to Survive but to Prevail: A Study of William Faulkner's Search for a Redeemer of Modern Man," DAI, 32 (Indiana: 1972), 6438-39A.

7444 McClennan, Joshua. "Why Read William Faulkner?" MAQR, 62 (Summer, 1956), 342-345.

7445 ________. "William Faulkner and Christian Complacency," PMASAL, 41 (1956), 315-322.

7446 McCole, Camille J. "The Nightmare Literature of William Faulkner," CathW, 141 (August, 1935), 576-583.

7447 ________. "William Faulkner: Cretins, Coffin-Worms and Cruelty," Lucifer at Large. London and New York: Longmans Green, 1937, pp. 203-228.

7448 McColgan, Kristin Pruitt. "The World's Slow Stain: The Theme of Initiation in Selected American Novels," DAI, 36 (Chapel Hill, North Carolina: 1974), 279A.

7449 McCormick, John. The Middle Distance: A Comparative History of American Imaginative Literature, 1919-1932. New York: Free Press, 1971, pp. 97-107.

7450 ________. "William Faulkner, the Past, and History," Fiction as Knowledge: The Modern Post-Romantic Novel. New Brunswick, N.J.: Rutgers U.P., 1975, pp. 88-108.

7451 McCorquodale, Marjorie K. "Alienation in Yoknapatawpha County," ForumH, 1, ii (January, 1957), 4-8.

7452 ________. William Faulkner and Existentialism. Diss. Texas (Austin): 1956.

7453 McCullers, Carson. "The Flowering Dream: Notes on Writing," Esquire, 52 (December, 1959), 162-164.

7454 ________. "The Russian Realists and Southern Literature," Decision, 2 (July, 1941), 15-19.

7455 McDonald, Walter R. "Coincidence in the Novel: A Necessary Technique," CE, 29 (February, 1968), 373-388.

7456 McElroy, Davis Dunbar. Existentialism and Modern Literature: An Essay in Existential Criticism. New York: Philosophical Library, 1963, pp. 24-25, 43-44.

7457 McElroy, John. "The Bequest of Hawthorne to James and Faulkner," ESQ, 19 (2nd Qt., 1973), 117-123.

7458 McGehee, Larry T. "The Southern Ethic of William Faulkner," Encounter (Indianapolis), 26 (Autumn, 1965), 461-469.

7459 McGrew, Julia. "Faulkner and the Icelanders," SS, 31 (February, 1959), 1-14.
Similarities between Faulkner's novels and 13th century Icelandic sagas.

7460 McHaney, Thomas L. "Faulkner Borrows from the Mississippi Guide," MissQ, 19 (1966), 116-120.

7461 ________. Review-art., Hans Bungert's William Faulkner und die humoristische Tradition des amerikanischen Südens. Heidelberg, Germany: Carl Winter, 1971, in MissQ, 26, # 3 (Summer, 1973), 451-454.

7462 McIlwaine, Shields. "Naturalistic Modes: The Gothic, the Ribald, and the Tragic: William Faulkner and Erskine Caldwell," The Southern Poor--White from Lubberland to Tobacco Road. Norman: Oklahoma U.P., 1939, pp. 217-240.

7463 McKean, Keith F. "Southern Patriarch: A Portrait," VQR, 36 (Summer, 1960), 376-389.

7464 Maclachlan, John Miller. "No Faulkner in Metropolis," Southern Renascence: The Literature of the Modern South. Louis D. Rubin and Robert D. Jacobs, eds. Baltimore: Johns Hopkins, 1953, pp. 101-111.

7465 ________. "William Faulkner and the Southern Folk," SFQ, 9 (September, 1945), 153-167.

7466 McLaughlin, Carrol Dee. "Religion in Yoknapatawpha County," DA, 23 (Denver: 1962), 2915-16.

7467 MacLean, Hugh. "Conservatism in Modern American Fiction," CE, 15 (March, 1954), 315-325.

7468 MacLeish, Archibald. "Faulkner and the Responsibility of the Artist," HA, 135 (November, 1951), 18, 43.

7469 MacLure, Millar. "Allegories of Innocence," DR, 40 (Summer, 1960), 145-156.

7470 _______. "William Faulkner: Soothsayer of the South," QQ, 63 (Autumn, 1956), 334-343.

7471 MacMillan, Duane Johnson. "The Non-Yoknapatawpha Novels of William Faulkner: An Examination of Soldiers' Pay, Mosquitoes, Pylon, The Wild Palms, and A Fable," DAI, 32 (Wisconsin: 1972), 6986A.

7472 MacMillan, Kenneth Douglas. "The Bystander in Faulkner's Fiction," DAI, 34 (British Columbia, Canada: 1972), 783A.

7473 McWilliams, David D. "The Influence of William Faulkner on Michel Butor," DAI, 31 (Oregon: 1969), 1282A-83A.

7474 _______. "William Faulkner and Michel Butor's Novel of Awareness," KRQ, 19 (1972), 387-402.

7475 Madden, David, ed. American Dreams, American Nightmares. Carbondale and Edwardsville: So. Ill. U.P., 1970, passim.

7476 _______, ed. Tough Guy Writers of the Thirties. Carbondale and Edwardsville: So. Ill. U.P., 1968, pp. 194-195.

7477 Maddocks, Gladys. "William Faulkner and the Evolution of V. K. Ratliff," CCTE, 33 (September, 1968), 24-28.

7478 Madge, Charles. "Time and Space in America," LonMerc, 32 (May, 1935), 83.

7479 Magill, Frank N., ed., and Dayton Kohler, assoc. ed. Cyclopedia of World Authors. New York: Harper, 1958, pp. 352-355.

7480 Magnan, Jean-Marie. "Inceste et mêlange des sangs dans l'oeuvre de William Faulkner," Sud, 14 (1975), 150-184.

7481 Magny, Claude Edmonde. "Faulkner o l'inversione teologica," Delta, 2 (January, 1950), 57-68.

7482 _______. "Faulkner or Theological Inversion," Faulkner: A Collection of Critical Essays. Robert Penn Warren, ed. Englewood Cliffs, New Jersey: 1966, pp. 66-78.

7483 _______. "Faulkner: ou l'inversion théologique," L'Age du Roman américain. Paris: Editions du Seuil, 1948, pp. 196-243; Eleanor Hochman, tr. New York: Ungar, 1972, pp. 178-223, 230-232.

7484 Mailer, Norman. "Modes and Mutations: Quick Comments

on the Modern Novel," Commentary, 41 (March, 1966), 39. "... Faulkner [wrote] about the dreams of the beast."

7485 Makuck, Peter Landers. "Faulkner Studies in France, 1953-1969," DA, 32 (Kent State: 1971), 3314A.

7486 Malcolm, Donald. "In Memoriam: G. Gissing Vines," NR, 136 (February 11, 1957), 19.
An account of Vines' reaction to Faulkner's stories.

7487 Malherbe, Henry. "L'avenir du roman," Confluences, numéro spécial, (1943), 394-397.

7488 _______. "Les français n'achètent plus les romans américains. Reflexions sur le déclin de la littérature commerciale," LF, (24 mars 1949), 1, 2.

7489 Malin, Irving, ed. Psychoanalysis and American Fiction. New York: Dutton, 1965, passim.

7490 _______. William Faulkner: An Interpretation. Stanford, California: Stanford U.P., 1957.

7491 _______. "William Faulkner: An Interpretation," DA, 21 (Stanford: 1960), 344.

7492 Mallard, William. The Reflection of Theology in Literature: A Case Study in Theology and Culture. San Antonio: Trinity U.P., 1977, passim.

7493 Mallonee, Helen H. "Land-Character Relationships in Selected Works of Faulkner's Yoknapatawpha Saga," DAI, 36 (So. Florida: 1975), 890A.

7494 Maloney, Michael F. "The Enigma of Time: Proust, Virginia Woolf, and Faulkner," Thought, 32 (Spring, 1957), 69-85.

7495 Malraux, André. "Faulkner's Tragedy of Isolation," NRF (November 1, 1933).

7496 Mamoli, Rosella. "Otto racconti inediti di William Faulkner," Annali della Facoltà di Lingue e Letterature Straniere di Ca' Foscari, iv (1965), pp. 65-75.

7497 Manchester, William. Disturber of the Peace: The Life of H. L. Mencken. New York: Harper, 1951, pp. 221-222.
States that Mencken could not understand Faulkner.

7498 Manheim, Leonard, and Eleanor, eds. Hidden Patterns: Studies in Psychoanalytic Literary Criticism. New York: Macmillan; London: Collier-Macmillan, 1966, pp. 243-258.

7499 Manley, Justine M. "The Function of Stock Humor and Grotesque Humor in Faulkner's Major Novels," DAI, 35, (Loyola [Chicago]: 1974), 1111A.

7500 Marceau, Felicien. "Etrange Amerique," TR, 54 (June, 1952), 152-156.

7501 Marichalar, Antonio. "William Faulkner," RdO, 42 (October, 1933), 78-86.

7502 Marshall, Emma Jo Grimes. "Scenes from Yoknapatawpha: A Study of People and Places in the Real and Imaginary Worlds of William Faulkner," DAI, 39, #4 (Alabama: 1978), 2276A.

7503 Marshall, Lenore. "The Power of Words," SatR, 45 (July 28, 1962), 16, 17.

7504 Marshall, Thomas. "Compasion, Sacrificio y Perseverancia": La Obra de William Faulkner. Mexico City: Facultad de Filosofía de la Univ. Nacional Autônoma de Mêxico, 1962.

7505 Martin, Harold. "Caravan to Faulkner Country ... And Beyond," Southern Living, 8 (May, 1973), 116-118, 120, 122-125.

7506 Martin, Jay. Nathanael West: The Art of His Life. New York: Farrar, Straus & Giroux, 1970, passim.

7507 Mascitelli, David W. "Faulkner's Characters of Sensibility," DA, 29 (Duke: 1969), 608A-09A.

7508 Massey, Tom Malcolm. "Faulkner's Females: The Thematic Function of Women in the Yoknapatawpha Cycle," DA, 30 (Nevada: 1970), 3468A.

7509 Materassi, Mario. "Faulkner e la presentazione del personaggio," SA, 7 (1961), 163-193.

7510 ________. "Faulkner Criticism in Italy, IQ, 57 (Summer, 1971), 47-85.

7511 ________. I romanzi di Faulkner. Biblioteca di studi Americani, 17. Rome: Edizioni di Storia e Letteratura, 1968.

7512 ________. "Le prime prove narrative di William Faulkner," Paragone, 17, No. 196 (June, 1966), 74-92.

7513 ________. "Ultima critica Faulkneriana," IlP, 23 (1967), 1495-1501.

7514 Matthews, John Thomas. "Creative Responses to Time in

the Novels of William Faulkner," DAI, 37, #10a (Johns Hopkins: 1977), 6486-87A.

7515 Mathieu-Higginbotham, Corina. "Faulkner y Onetti: Una visión de la realidad a través de Jefferson y Santa María," Hispano, 61 (1977), 51-60.

7516 Maugham, W. Somerset. "What Makes a Good Novel Great?" NYTBR (November, 1947), 1, 48-49.

7517 Maxwell, Desmond Ernest Stewart. "The Comprehensive Genius of William Faulkner," American Fiction: The Intellectual Background. London: Routledge & Kegan Paul, 1963, pp. 275-278.

7518 Mayes, Martha. "Faulkner's Juvenilia," New Campus Writing, No. 2, New York: 1957, pp. 135-144.

7519 Mayhew, Paul (pseud.) "Giving Racism the Sanctity of Law," NR, 134 (May 7, 1956), 13-16.

7520 Mayoux, Jean Jacques. "La création du réel chez William Faulkner," EA, 5 (February, 1952), 25-39; repr., in Three Decades of Criticism. Frederick Hoffman and Olga Vickery, eds. East Lansing: Michigan U.P., 1960, pp. 156-172.

7521 ______. "Faulkner et le sens tragique," Combat (6 mars 1952), 7.

7522 ______. "Le temps et la destinée chez William Faulkner," La Profondeur et le rythme (Cahiers du collège philosophique). Paris: Arthaud, 1948, pp. 303-331.

7523 ______. "The Writer in Perspective," SatR, 45 (July 28, 1962), 23-24.

7524 Mazars, Pierre. "Comment on boit le whisky à Yoknapatawpha," TR (Paris), No. 50 (février, 1952), 150-152.

7525 Mei, Francesco. "Ricordo di William Faulkner," FLe, 17 (July 15, 1962), 1.

7526 Meindl, Dieter. Bewusstsein als Schicksal: Zu Struktur und Entwicklung von Faulkners Generalionenromanen. Stuttgart: Metzler, 1974.
Rev. by André Bleikasten, MissQ, 28 (Summer, 1974), 395-398.

7527 Mellard, James Milton. "Humor in Faulkner's Novels: Its Development, Forms, and Functions," DA, 25 (Texas, [Austin]: 1964), 480-481.

7528 ______. "Racism, Formula, and Popular Fiction," JPC, 5 (Summer, 1971), 10-37.

7529 Memmott, Albert J. "The Theme of Revenge in the Fiction of William Faulkner," DAI, 34 (Minnesota: 1974), 4273A-74A.

7530 Mendel'son, M. "Ad na zemle i Uil'jam Folkner," Voprosy literatury, 7, No. 9 (September, 1963), 129-155.

7531 Mercier, Vivian. "Claude Simon: Order and Disorder," Shenandoah, 17 (Summer, 1966), 79-92.
The influence of Faulkner and others.

7532 Meriwether, James B., ed. "And Now What's to Do," MissQ, 26 (Summer, 1973), 399-402.
A two-page manuscript by Faulkner found in 1970 at Rowanoak.

7533 _______. "Early Notices of Faulkner by Phil Stone and Louis Cochran," MissQ, 17 (Summer, 1964), 136-164.

7534 _______. "Faulkner and the New Criticism," BA, 37 (Summer, 1963), 265-268.
Cf., Wolfgang B. Fleishmann. "Remarks," BA, 37 (Summer, 1963), 268-270.

7535 _______. "Faulkner and the South," The Dilemma of the Southern Writer: Institute of Southern Culture Lectures, Longwood College. Richard K. Meeker, ed. Farmville, Virginia: Longwood College, 1961, pp. 143-163. Also in Southern Writers: Appraisals in Our Time. R. C. Simonini, ed. Charlottesville: Virginia U.P., 1964, pp. 142-161.

7536 _______. "Faulkner and the World War II Monument in Oxford," A Faulkner Miscellany. James B. Meriwether, ed. Jackson, Miss.: Mississippi U.P., 1974, pp. 105-106.

7537 _______. "Faulkner's Essays on Anderson," Faulkner: Fifty Years after The Marble Faun. George H. Wolfe, ed. Tuscaloosa: University of Alabama Pr., 1976.

7538 _______, ed. Foreword. Special Faulkner Issue. MissQ, 26 (Summer, 1973), 243.
James B. Meriwether is editor of other Special Faulkner Issues, MissQ, Vols. 21, 22, 24, 25.

7539 _______. "Introduction: The Short Fiction of William Faulkner: A Bibliography," Proof, 1 (1971), 293-329.

7540 _______. "The Literary Career of William Faulkner," PULC, 21 (Spring, 1960), 111-164.

7541 _______. The Literary Career of William Faulkner. Princeton: Princeton U. Library, 1961; also Columbia: So. Carolina P., 1971.

7542 ________, ed. "Mac Grider's Son," MissQ, 28 (Summer, 1975), 347-351.
Meriwether's headnote provides information as to this Faulkner item in the Memphis Commercial Appeal.

7543 ________. The Merrill Checklist of William Faulkner. Columbus, Ohio: Chas. E. Merrill, 1970.

7544 ________. "The Novel Faulkner Never Wrote: His 'Golden Book' or 'Doomsday Book,'" AL, 42 (March, 1970), 93-96.

7545 ________. "A Proposal for a CEAA Edition of William Faulkner," Editing Twentieth Century Texts. Francess G. Halpenny, ed. Toronto: Toronto U.P., 1972, pp. 12-27.

7546 ________. "The Text of Faulkner's Books: An Introduction and Some Notes," MFS, 9 (Summer, 1963), 159-170.

7547 ________. "William Faulkner," PULC, 18 (Spring, 1957), 136-158.

7548 ________. "William Faulkner," Shenandoah, 10 (Winter, 1959), 18-24.

7549 ________. "William Faulkner," Fifteen Modern American Authors: A Survey of Research and Criticism. Jackson R. Bryer, ed. Durham: Duke U.P., 1969, pp. 175-210.

7550 ________. "William Faulkner," Sixteen Modern American Authors: A Survey of Research and Criticism. Jackson R. Bryer, ed. Durham: Duke U.P., 1974, pp. 223-275. (Revised ed. of Fifteen Modern American Authors.)

7551 ________. "William Faulkner," American Literary Scholarship: An Annual 1973. James Woodress, ed. Durham: Duke U.P., 1975, pp. 135-149.

7552 ________, and Michael Millgate, eds. Lion in the Garden: Interviews with William Faulkner, 1926-1962. New York: Random House, 1968.

7553 Merton, Thomas. "'Baptism in the Forest': Wisdom and Initiation in William Faulkner," CathW, 207 (June, 1968), 124-130; also in Mansions of the Spirit: Essays in Literature and Religion. George A. Panichas, ed. New York: Hawthorn Bks., 1967, pp. 17-44.

7554 Meyer, Norma Lee. "Syntactic Features of William Faulkner's Narrative Style," DAI, 32 (Nebraska, Lincoln: 1971), 6406A.

7555 Meyers, Harold B. "Faulkner," USA, 1 (August 3, 1962), 47-53.

7556 Michael, Thomas E. "Yoknapatawpha County Today," Mid-South Magazine: Memphis Commercial Appeal (Sunday, April 4, 1965), 6-7, 16-17.

7557 Michel, Laurence. "Faulkner: Saying No to Death," The Thing Contained: Theory of the Tragic. Bloomington: Indiana U. P., 1970, pp. 107-130.

7558 Mickelson, Joel C. "Faulkner's Military Figures of Speech," WisSL, 4 (1967), 46-55.

7559 Mikules, Leonard. "The Road of William Faulkner: A Reading of Southern Fiction," DA, 18 (Berkeley: 1957), 99.

7560 Milano, Paolo. "Faulkner in Crisis," Nation, 167 (October 30, 1948), 496-497.

7561 Miller, Arthur. "On Recognition," To the Young Writer. A. L. Bader, ed. Ann Arbor: Michigan U. P., 1965, pp. 166-180.

7562 Miller, Bernice Berger. "William Faulkner's Thomas Sutpen, Quentin Compson, Joe Christmas: A Study of the Hero-Archetype," DAI, 38 (Florida: 1977), 6728A.

7563 Miller, David M. "Faulkner's Women," MFS, 13 (Spring, 1967), 3-17.

7564 Miller, Douglas T. "Faulkner and the Civil War: Myth and Reality," AQ, 15 (Summer, 1963), 200-209.

7565 Miller, Henry. Henry Miller: Letters to Anaïs Nin. Gunther Stuhlmann, ed. New York: Putnam's, 1965, pp. 156, passim.

7566 Miller, James E., Jr. "William Faulkner: Descent into the Vortex," Quests Surd and Absurd: Essays in American Literature. Chicago: Chicago U. P., 1967, pp. 41-75.

7567 Miller, Nolan, ed. "Faulkner's Juvenilia," New Campus Writing. New York: Bantam Bks., 1957.

7568 Millett, Fred B. Contemporary American Authors. New York: Harcourt, Brace, 1940, 346-348, passim.

7569 Millgate, Michael. The Achievement of William Faulkner. New York: Random House, 1966.

7570 ________. American Social Fiction: James to Cozzens. New York: Barnes & Noble, 1965, p. 205.

7571 ________. "Faulkner," American Literary Scholarship: An Annual/1969. J. Albert Robbins, ed. Durham: Duke U. P., 1971, pp. 108-121.

7572 ______. "Faulkner," American Literary Scholarship: An Annual/1970. J. Albert Robbins, ed. Durham: Duke U.P., 1972, pp. 116-131.

7573 ______. "Faulkner," American Literary Scholarship: An Annual/1971. J. Albert Robbins, ed. Durham: Duke U.P., 1973, pp. 104-119.

7574 ______. "Faulkner," American Literary Scholarship: An Annual/1972. J. Albert Robbins, ed. Durham: Duke U.P., 1974, pp. 114-130.

7575 ______. "Faulkner," German Language and Literature: Seven Essays. Karl S. Weimar, ed. Englewood Cliffs, N.J.: Prentice-Hall, 1974, pp. 114-130.

7576 ______. "Faulkner and History," "Faulkner and the South: Some Reflections," The South and Faulkner's Yoknapatawpha: The Actual and the Apocryphal. Jackson: Miss. U.P., 1977, pp. 22-39; 195-210.

7577 ______. "Faulkner Criticism," Venture, 2 (June, 1961), 128-134.

7578 ______. "Faulkner in Toronto: A Further Note," UTQ, 37 (January, 1968), 197-202.

7579 ______. "Faulkner on the Literature of the First World War," MissQ, 26 (Summer, 1973), 387-393.

7580 ______. "Faulkner on the Literature of the First World War," A Faulkner Miscellany. James B. Meriwether, ed. Jackson, Miss.: Mississippi U.P., 1974, pp. 98-104.

7581 ______. Thomas Hardy: His Career As a Novelist. New York: Random House, 1971, pp. 345-351.

7582 ______. William Faulkner. New York: Grove Press, 1961. Revised, 1966; repr., Capricorn Bks., 1971.

7583 ______. "William Faulkner," BAASB, No. 5 (December, 1962), 43-46.

7584 ______. "William Faulkner: The Problem of Point of View," Patterns of Commitment in American Literature. Marston LaFrance, ed. Toronto: Toronto U.P., 1967, pp. 181-192; also in William Faulkner: Four Decades of Criticism. Linda W. Wagner, ed. Michigan State U.P., 1973, pp. 179-191.

7585 Milligan, Vincent. "Valery Larbaud, Anglicist," DA, 14 (Columbia: 1953), 1415.

"He [Larbaud] was one of the first European critics to recognize the importance of William Faulkner...."

7586 Milliner, Gladys W. "Faulkner's Young Protagonists: The Innocent and the Damned," DAI, 31 (Tulane: 1970), 2928A.

7587 Millis, Ralph Eugene. "Humanistic and Legal Values in Some Works of Faulkner," DAI, 38, #7 (Iowa: 1977), 4170A.

7588 Milner, Jay. "The Inaccessible Author," NYHTB (August 28, 1960), 3.

7589 Milton, John R. "Conversations with Distinguished Western American Novelists," SDR, 9 (Spring, 1971), 16-57.

7590 Milum, Richard A. "The Cavalier Spirit in Faulkner's Fiction," DAI, 33 (Indiana: 1973), 5737A.

7591 _______. "Faulkner and the Cavalier Tradition: The French Bequest," AL, 45 (January, 1974), 580-589.
Faulkner's use of French materials in his fiction.

7592 _______. "'The Horns of Dawn': Faulkner and Metaphor," AN&Q, 11 (1973), 134.

7593 Miner, Ward L. "Faulkner and Christ's Crucifixion," NM, 57 (1956), 260-269.

7594 _______. "The Southern White-Negro Problem through the Lens of Faulkner's Fiction," JHR, 14 (1966), 507-517.

7595 _______. The World of William Faulkner. Diss. Pennsylvania: 1951.

7596 _______. The World of William Faulkner. Durham: Duke U.P., 1952; reissued by Pageant Bks., 1959.

7597 Mirabelli, Eugene, Jr. The Apprenticeship of William Faulkner: The Early Short Stories and the First Three Novels. Diss. Harvard: 1964.

7598 "Mississippi Musings," America, 98 (March 29, 1958), 742.

7598a "Mr. Faulkner Exhausts the Future," Nation, 185 (October 26, 1957), 274-275.

7599 Mitani, Teiichiro. "The Language and Technique of William Faulkner," EngLit (Waseda Univ.), No. 22 (November, 1962), 57-65.

7600 Mizener, Arthur. The Far Side of Paradise. Boston: Houghton Mifflin, 1951, p. 313.
Quotes Fitzgerald as to Faulkner.

7601 _______. "The Thin Intelligent Face of American Fiction," KR, 17 (Autumn, 1955), 507-524; adaptation of The Sense of

Life in the Modern Novel. Boston: Houghton Mifflin, 1964, pp. 161-181.

7602 Möhl, Gertrud. Die Aufnahme Amerikanischer Literatur in der Deutschsprachigen Schweiz wahrend der Jahre 1945-1950. Zurich: Juris-Verlag, 1961.

7603 Mohrt, Michel. "Le 'domaine' de William Faulkner," Candide, No. 50 (April 12-19, 1962), 13.

7604 _______, ed. Jefferson, Mississippi, une anthologie éstablie et présentée par Michel Mohrt. Paris: Gallimard, 1956.

7605 _______. "Les lettres américaines: Les prisonniers du temps," TR, 59 (November, 1952), 160-165; also Preuves, 4 (April, 1954), 8-14.

7606 _______. "Le voice couché sur ce sol qu'il a tant aimé," FL, 17 (July 14, 1962).

7607 _______. "William Faulkner: ou, Démesure du souvenir," Preuves, 4 (April, 1954), 8-14.

7608 _______. "William Faulkner: ou, une religion du temps," Le nouveau roman américain. Paris: Gallimard, 1955, pp. 80-118; translation: "William Faulkner: o, Una religion del tiempo," La novela americana contemporánea. Madrid: Escelicer, 1956, pp. 99-145.

7609 Moloney, Michael Francis. "The Enigma of Time: Proust, Virginia Woolf, and Faulkner," Thought, 32 (Spring, 1957), 69-85.

7610 Momberger, Philip. "A Critical Study of Faulkner's Early Sketches and Collected Stories," DAI, 33 (Johns Hopkins: 1970), 2386A.

7611 _______. "Faulkner's 'Country' as Ideal Community," Individual and Community: Variations on a Theme in American Fiction. Kenneth H. Baldwin and David K. Kirby, eds. Durham, North Carolina: Duke U.P., 1975, pp. 112-136.

7612 Monat, Olympio. "Faulkner, a dimensão da tragédia," ESPSL, 1 (September, 1974), 1.

7613 Monroe, Elizabeth N. The Novel and Society: A Critical Study of the Modern Novel. Chapel Hill: North Carolina U.P., 1941, pp. 10, 44.

7614 Monteiro, George. "The Limits of Professionalism: A Sociological Approach to Faulkner, Fitzgerald and Hemingway," Criticism, 15 (Spring, 1973), 145-155.

7615 Montenegro, Ernesto. "Interpretación de William Faulkner," Revista de Educación, Año, 11, No. 58 (December, 1951), repr., in Panorama, 1 (1952), 71-75.

7616 Montgomery, Marion. "The Sense of Violation: Notes Toward a Definition of Southern Fiction," GaR, 19 (Fall, 1965), 278-287.

7617 Moore, Harry T. "The American Novel Today," LonMerc, 31 (March, 1935), 161-167.

7618 Moore, Nicolas, ed. Courtes Histoires américaines. Paris: Editions Corrêa, 1948.

7619 Moore, Robert. "The Faulkner Concordance and Some Implications for Textual and Linguistic Studies," U.S. Military Academy Library Occasional Papers, No. 2 (1974), 6-13.

7620 Moore, Robert Henry. "Perspectives on William Faulkner: The Author and His Work as Reflected in Surveys of American History, Works on Southern Life and History, and Works and Comments by Mississippians," DAI, 32 (Wisconsin: 1972), 5798A-99A.

7621 Moore, Stephen C. Review. GaR, 25 (Winter, 1971), 505-507. (Coindreau)

7622 Moreland, Agnes L. "A Study of Faulkner's Presentation of Some Problems that Relate to Negroes," DA, 21 (Columbia: 1960), 1192-3.

7623 Morell, Giliane. "Echec et Vol," RANAM, 9 (1976), 124-131.

7624 Morgan, Thomas B. "The Long Happy Life of Bennett Cerf," Esquire, 61 (March, 1964), 112-118.
Faulkner anecdotes.

7625 Moriarty, Jane V. The American Novel in France, 1919-1939. Diss. Wisconsin: 1954.

7626 Morita, Takashi. "Faulkner: 'Kuyashisa' Kokufuku no Kiseki," [Locus on Conquering Chagrin], America Shosetsu no Tenkai. Katsuji Takamura, and Iwao Iwamoto, eds. Tokyo: Shohakusha, 1977, pp. 244-255. [Development of American Novels.]

7627 Morra, Umberto. "William Faulkner," Letteratura, 3 (July, 1939), 173-174.

7628 Morris, Lloyd R. "Heritage of a Generation of Novelists," NYHTBR (September 25, 1949), 12-13, 74.

7629 ________. "Seven Pillars of Wisdom," Postscript to Yesterday--America: The Last Fifty Years. New York: Random House, 1947, pp. 134-171.

7630 Morris, Wright. "The Function of Rage: William Faulkner," The Territory Ahead. New York: Harcourt, Brace, 1958, pp. 171-184.

7631 ________. "The Violent Land: Some Observations on the Faulkner Country," Magazine of Art (New York), 45 (March, 1952), 99-103.

7632 Mortimer, Gail Linda. "Rhetoric of Loss: An Analysis of Faulkner's Perceptual Style," DAI, 37 (New York State, Buffalo: 1976), 971A-72A.

7633 Moseley, Edwin M. "Christ as Social Scapegoat," Pseudonyms of Christ in the Modern Novel. Pittsburgh: Pittsburgh U.P., 1962, pp. 135-151, passim.

7634 Moses, Edwin P. "Faulknerian Comedy," DAI, 36 (Binghamton, New York: 1975), 1507A.

7635 Moses, Henry C., III. "History as Voice and Metaphor: A Study of Tate, Warren, and Faulkner," DA, 29 (Cornell: 1969), 4014A.

7636 Moses, W. R. "The Limits of Yoknapatawpha County," GaR, 16 (Fall, 1962), 297-305.

7637 ________. "Where History Crosses Myth," Accent, 13 (Winter, 1953), 21-33.

7638 Mottram, Eric. "Mississippi Faulkner's Glorious Mosaic of Impotence and Madness," JAmS, 2 (April, 1968), 121-129.

7639 ________. William Faulkner. London: Profiles in Literature Series. Routledge & Kegan Paul, 1971.

7640 Motyleva, Tamara. "Dostoevskij i zarubežnye pisateli xx veka," VLit, 15, v (1971), 96-128.

7641 ________. "Dostojewski und die ausländischen Scriftsteller des 20, Jahrhunderts," KuL, 19 (1971), 938-955; translation of second part of article in VLit, 15, v (1971), 96-128.

7642 ________. "Reflections on an Article by Leon Edel," SovL, No. 5 (1965), 183-185.

7643 Muehl, Lois. "Faulkner's Humor in Three Novels and One 'Play,'" LibChron, 24 (Spring, 1968), 78-93.
Provides categories of Faulkner's humor.

7644 Mueller, Christopher. William Faulkner's Romane nach dem Zweiten Weltkrieg. Diss. Humboldt, Berlin.

7645 Muhlenfeld, Elisabeth. "Faulkner's Women," MissQ, 26 (Summer, 1973), 435-450.
Rev.-art., of Sally R. Page's Faulkner's Women. DeLand, Florida: 1972.

7646 Muir, Edwin. [William Faulkner], Listener, 21 (March 30, 1939), 701.

7647 Muller, Herbert Joseph. Modern Fiction: A Study of Values. New York: Funk & Wagnalls, 1937, pp. 405-407.

7648 Mulqueen, James E. "Foreshadowing of Melville and Faulkner," AN&Q, 6 (March, 1968), 102.

7649 Munson, Gorham. "Our Post-War Novel," Bookman, 74 (October, 1931), 141-144.
Agrees with Arnold Bennett's statement that Faulkner "writes like an angel," but adds that Faulkner was indebted to Sherwood Anderson, and others.

7650 ________. "Le Roman d'Après-Guerre aux Etats-Unis," Europe, No. 2 (1932), 617.

7651 Murphree, John Wilson, Jr. "A Study of William Faulkner's Informal Dialect Theory and His Use of Dialect Markers in Eight Novels," DAI, 36 (Ball State: 1975), 2177A.

7652 Murray, D. M. "Faulkner, the Silent Comedies, and the Animated Cartoon," SHR, 9 (Summer, 1975), 241-257.

7653 Murray, Edward. "The Stream-of-Consciousness Novel and Film, III--William Faulkner," The Cinematic Imagination: Writers and the Motion Pictures. New York: Ungar, 1972, pp. 154-167.

7654 Musil, Robert Kirkland. "The Visual Imagination of William Faulkner," DAI, 31 (Northwestern: 1970), 3558A.

7655 Nadeau, Maurice. Littérature présente. Paris: Corrêa, 1952, passim.

7656 ________. Le roman français depuis la guerre. Nouvelle édition-revue et augmentee. Paris: Gallimard, 1970, passim.

7657 Nadeau, Robert L. Motion and Stasis Time as Structuring Principle in the Art of William Faulkner. Diss. Florida: 1970.

7658 Nagy, László B. "William Faulkner eszmevilága," ["William Faulkner's World of Ideas,"] VF, 9 (1963), 237-241.

7659 Nagy, Peter. "William Faulkner," Kritika, 5, viii (1967), 10-18.

7660 Nash, Cristopher Weston. "A Modern Bestiary: Representative Animal Motifs in the Encounter between Nature and Culture in the English, American, French and Italian Novel, 1900-1950," DAI, 31 (New York: 1970), 6622A.

7661 Nathan, Monique. "Faulkner," Candide, No. 63 (July 11-18, 1962), 11.

7662 _______. Faulkner par lui-même. Paris: Seuil, 1963.

7663 _______. "Jeunesse de Faulkner," Preuves, No. 161 (July, 1964), 85-88.

7664 _______. "I personaggi femminili nei romanzi di Faulkner," La Stampa, 97 (September 28, 1963), 7.

7665 Nauman, Hilda. "How Faulkner Went His Way and I Went Mine," Esquire, 68 (December, 1967), 173-175.
A reminiscence.

7666 Newhall, Eric Luther. "Prisons and Prisoners in the Works of William Faulkner," DAI, 36 (California, Los Angeles: 1975), 5300A.

7667 Nichols, Lewis. "Faulkner," NYTBR (April 19, 1964), 8.

7668 Nicholson, Norman. "Morals and the Modern Novel," Theology, 40 (June, 1940), 412-420.

7669 _______. "William Faulkner," Man and Literature. London: S. C. M. Press, 1943, pp. 122-138.

7670 _______. "William Faulkner," The New Spirit. Ernest W. L. Martin, ed. London: Dobson, 1946, pp. 32-41.

7671 Nigliazzo, Marc A. Faulkner's Indians. DAI, 34 (New Mexico: 1973), 6650A-51A.
Rev. by Noel Polk, MissQ, 28, #3 (Summer, 1975), 387-392.

7672 Nilon, Charles H. "Faulkner and the Negro," UCSLL, No. 8 (September, 1962), 1-111.

7673 _______. Faulkner and the Negro. Boulder: Colorado U. P., 1962. (University of Colorado Series in Language and Literature No. 8); reprinted, New York: Citadel Press, 1965.

7674 _______. "The Treatment of Negro Characters by Representative American Novelists: Cooper, Melville, Tourgee, Glasgow, Faulkner," DA, 13 (Wisconsin: 1953), 385-387.

7675 Nishikawa, Masami, ed. Faulkner. Tokyo: Kenkyusha, 1967.

7676 ________. "The Worldwide Influence of William Faulkner: Reports from Six Capitals," NYTBR (November 15, 1959), 53. [Report from Tokyo.]

7677 Noble, David W. "After the Lost Generation: William Faulkner, Robert Penn Warren, James Gould Cozzens," The Eternal Adam and the New World Garden: The Central Myth in the American Novel Since 1830. New York: George Braziller, 1968, pp. 161-193.

7678 Noble, Donald R. "Southern Writers in General Studies in American Literature," MissQ, 28 (Fall, 1975), 521-530.

7679 Nochimson, Martha. "Against the Limitations of Rationalism: Undercurrents in the Works of William Faulkner," DAI, 37 (City Univ. of New York: 1976), 1551A.

7680 Nolte, William H. "Mencken, Faulkner, and Southern Moralism," SCR, 4 (December, 1971), 45-61.

7681 Nolting-Rauff, Lore. Sprachstil und Weltbild bei William Faulkner. Diss. Freiburg, 1958.

7682 Nonaka, Ryo. "Faulkner's 'Stream of Consciousness,'" SEL, 36 (October, 1959), 179-180.

7683 Nordell, Roderick. "Is Faulkner Now Standard?" CSMM (July 30, 1964), 5.

7684 Nores, Dominique. "Contre un Theatre d'Effraction," RT, 36 (1958), 46-52.

7685 Norris, Carolyn Brimley. "The Image of the Physician in Modern American Literature," DAI, 31 (Maryland: 1969), 765A.

7686 "Novelist on His Art," TLS, #2831 (June 1, 1956), 32.

7687 Nowell, Elizabeth, ed. The Letters of Thomas Wolfe. New York: Scribner's, 1956, p. 495.
Wolfe's letter to Stark Young about Faulkner.

7688 Noyes, C. E. "Welcome to Faulkner and Yoknapatawpha, 1977," in The Maker and The Myth: Faulkner and Yoknapatawpha, 1977. Evans Harrington and Ann J. Abadie, eds. Jackson, Miss.: Miss. U.P., 1978, pp. xi-xiv.

7689 Nummelin, Rolf. "William Faulkner:--Sydstatsman och romanförfattare," Finsk-Tidskrift, 163-164 (1958), 256-265.

7690 Nyren, Dorothy, ed. "Faulkner, William," A Library of Literary Criticism: Modern American Literature. Dorothy Nyren, comp. & ed. New York: Ungar, 1960, pp. 170-174.

7691 Oberhelman, Harley D. "Gabriel Garcia Marquez and the American South," Chasqui, 5, i (1975), 29-38.
Possible influence of Faulkner.

7692 O'Brien, Frances Blazer. "Faulkner and Wright, Alias S. S. Van Dine," MissQ, 14 (Spring, 1961), 101-107.

7693 O'Brien, Matthew C. "Faulkner, General Chalmers, and the Burning of Oxford," AN&Q, 12 (February, 1974), 87-88.
In a letter to the editor Faulkner mistakenly blamed General Chalmers.

7694 ________. "William Faulkner and the Civil War in Oxford, Mississippi," JMissH, 35 (May, 1973), 167-174.

7695 Ochi, Michio. "Kuhaku wo toshite minaoshita Faulkner," EigoS, 115 (1969), 558-560.

7696 O'Connor, Frank [pseud. for Michael O'Donovan]. The Mirror in the Roadway: A Study of the Modern Novel. New York: Knopf, 1964, pp. 191, 267, 294.

7697 O'Connor, William Van. "Faulkner," GaR, 12 (Spring, 1958), 83-86.

7698 ________. "Faulkner, Hemingway, and the 1920's," The Twenties, Poetry and Prose: Twenty Critical Essays. Richard E. Langford and William E. Taylor, eds. DeLand, Florida: Everett/Edwards, 1966, pp. 95-98.

7699 ________. "Faulkner's Legend of the Old South," WHR, 7 (Autumn, 1953), 293-301.

7700 ________. "Faulkner's One-Sided 'Dialogue' with Hemingway," CE, 24 (December, 1962), 208-215.

7701 ________. "The Grotesque in Modern American Fiction," CE, 20 (April, 1959), 342-346.

7702 ________. "Hawthorne and Faulkner: Some Common Ground," VQR, 33 (Winter, 1957), 105-123. Also in The American Literary Scene. Manning Hawthorne, ed. Bombay: Popular Bk. Depot, 1962, pp. 35-53; The Grotesque: An American Genre, and Other Essays. Carbondale: So. Ill. U.P., 1962, pp. 59-77.

7703 ________. "The Novel and the 'Truth' about America," ES, 35 (October, 1954), 204-211.

7704 _______. "The Novel as a Social Document," AmQt, 4 (Summer, 1952), 169-175.

7705 _______. "The Old Master, the Sole Proprietor," VQR, 36 (Winter, 1960), 147-151.

7706 _______. "Protestantism in Yoknapatawpha County," HopR, 5 (Spring, 1952), 26-42; repr., in Southern Renascence. L. D. Rubin and Robert Jacobs, eds. Baltimore: Johns Hopkins, 1966, pp. 153-169; repr., with modification, "A Part of the Southern Mores: Protestantism," The Tangled Fire of William Faulkner. Minneapolis: Minnesota U.P., 1954, pp. 72-87.

7707 _______. "Rhetoric in Southern Writing: Faulkner," GaR, 12 (Spring, 1958), 83-86.

7708 _______. "The State of Faulkner Criticism," SR, 60 (Winter, 1952), 180-186; repr., with modifications as "Period of Apprenticeship," The Tangled Fire of William Faulkner. 1954, pp. 16-36.

7709 _______. The Tangled Fire of William Faulkner. Minneapolis: Minnesota U.P., 1954. Repr., Gordian Press, 1968.

7710 _______. "William Faulkner," Encyclopedia of World Literature in the 20th Century. W. B. Fleischmann, ed. New York: Ungar, 1967, I, 373-376.

7711 _______. "William Faulkner," Quatre visages du roman Americaine. Strasbourg and Paris: Nouveaux Horizons, 1970, pp. 121-171.

7712 _______. William Faulkner. (Univ. of Minnesota Pamphlets on American Writers, No. 3.) Minneapolis: Minnesota U.P., 1959, 1961.

7713 _______, ed. "William Faulkner," Seven Modern American Novelists. Minneapolis: Minnesota U.P., 1964, pp. 118-152.

7714 _______. "William Faulkner," Tres escritores Norteamericanos. Madrid: Gredos, 1961, pp. 51-93.

7715 _______. "William Faulkner's Apprenticeship," SWR, 38 (Winter, 1953), 1-14.

7716 O'Dea, Richard J. "Faulkner's Vestigial Christianity," Renascence, 21 (Autumn, 1968), 44-54.

7717 O'Donnell, George Marion. "Correspondence," SR, 51 (Summer, 1943), 446-447.
Cf., O'Donnell's essay "Faulkner's Mythology."

7718 ________. "Faulkner's Mythology," KR, 1 (Summer, 1939), 285-299. Repr., in Two Decades of Criticism. Frederick Hoffman and Olga Vickery, eds. East Lansing: 1951, pp. 49-62; Three Decades of Criticism. East Lansing: 1960, pp. 82-93; William Faulkner: Four Decades of Criticism. Linda W. Wagner, ed. Michigan St. U.P., 1973, pp. 83-93.

7719 ________. "The Writer in Critical Perspective," SatRL, 45 (July 28, 1962), 22.

7720 Odum, Howard W. "On Southern Literature and Southern Culture," HopR, 7 (Winter, 1953), 60-76. Also in Folk Religion and Society: Selected Papers of Howard W. Odum. Katherine Jocher, ed. Chapel Hill: North Carolina U.P., 1964, pp. 202-218; in Southern Renascence. L. D. Rubin and Robt. Jacobs, eds. Baltimore: 1953, pp. 84-100.

7721 O'Faolain, Sean. "Fiction," Spectator, (April 19, 1935), 668.

7722 ________. "Pigeon-Holing the Modern Novel," LonMerc, 33 (December, 1935), 159-164.

7723 ________. "The Proletarian Novel," LonMerc, 35 (April, 1937), 583-589.

7724 ________. "William Faulkner: More Genius than Talent," The Vanishing Hero: Studies in Novelists of the Twenties. Boston: Little, Brown, 1957, pp. 73-111; London: Eyre & Spottiswoode, 1956, pp. 99-134.

7725 Ohashi, Kenzaburo. Faulkner Kenkyu 1: Shiteki Genso kara Shosetsuteki Genso e. [Faulkner: From Poetic Vision to Fictional Vision.] Tokyo: Nan'undo, 1977.

7726 ________, ed. Gendai Sakka Ron--William Faulkner. [Study of a Modern Writer--William Faulkner.] Tokyo: Hayakawa Shobo, 1973.

7727 Okaniwa, Noboru. Faulkner: Tsurusareta Ningen no Yume. [Faulkner: Dream of Hanged Man.] Tokyo: Chikuma Shobo, 1976.

7728 Oldenburg, Egbert W. "William Faulkner's Early Experiments with Narrative Techniques," DA, 27 (Michigan: 1967), 2158A.

7729 O'Leary, Jerry. "Faulkner Mississippi Thing of the Past," Washington Sunday Star (October 21, 1962), B-3.

7730 Oliver, Maria Rosa. "La novela norteamericana moderna," Sur (Buenos Aires), 9 (August, 1939), 33-47.

7731 Olson, Ted. "Faulkner and the Colossus of Maroussi," SAQ, 71 (Spring, 1972), 205-212.
A reminiscence.

7732 Onimus, Jean. "Camus adapte à la scène Faulkner et Dostoievski," RSH (facsimile 104), (October-December, 1961), 607-621.

7733 Onis, Harriet de. "William Faulkner," Torre, 3 (October-December, 1955), 11-26.

7734 ______. "William Faulkner y su Mondo," Sur, 202 (August, 1951), 24-33.

7735 Onoue, Masaji. "Coined Words in Faulkner," EigoS, 98 (1952), 105-106.

7736 Oppewall, Peter. "The Critical Reception of American Fiction in The Netherlands, 1900-1953," DA, 21 (Michigan: 1961), 3790.
"... [T]heir [the Dutch] 'discovery' of him [Faulkner] paralleled his reception in France...."

7737 Orlova, Raisa, and Lev Kopelev. "Myths and Truths about America's South," ForLit, 3 (March 1958), 206-222.

7738 Orvis, Mary B. "William Faulkner," The Art of Writing Fiction. New York: Prentice-Hall, 1948, passim.

7739 Ott, Friedrich Peter. The Literature of the Air: Themes and Imagery in the Work of Faulkner, Saint-Exupery, and Gaiser. Diss. Harvard: 1968.

7740 Overly, Dorothy N. The Problem of Character in the Development of Theme in the Novels and Short Stories of William Faulkner. Diss. Chicago: 1950.

7741 Page, Sally R. "Faulkner's Sense of the Sacred," Faulkner: Fifty Years After The Marble Faun. George H. Wolfe, ed. University: University of Alabama Press, 1976, pp. 101-121.

7742 ______. Faulkner's Women: Characterization and Meaning. DeLand, Florida: Everett/Edwards, 1972.

7743 ______. "Woman in the Works of William Faulkner," DAI, 31 (Duke: 1969), 2395A.

7744 Palievsky, Pyotr. "Chelovek pobedit," ["Man Is Victorious"], Literaturnaia gazeta (July 10, 1962).

7745 ______. "Die Entdeckung William Faulkners," KuL, 13 (1965), 968-982.

7746 ________. "Faulkner's Road to Realism," Soviet Criticism of American Literature in the Sixties. Carl R. Proffer, ed. and tr. Ann Arbor: Ardis Pub., 1972, pp. 150-168.

7747 ________. "Hemingway and Faulkner: A Russian View," Soviet Life (June, 1966), 58-59.

7748 ________. "Otkrytija Uil-jama Folknera," ["The Discoveries of William Faulkner,"], Znamya, 3 (1965), 222-232.

7749 ________. Uil'yam Folkner. Moscow: Vysšhaya shkola, 1970.

7750 Pallyevsky, P. "Faulkner's America," SovL, 8 (1977), 177-180.

7751 Palumbo, Donald Emanuel. "Faith, Identity, and Perception: Three Existential Crises in Modern Fiction and Their Artistic Reconciliation: A Comparison of the Fiction of Dostoevsky, Joyce, Kafka, and Faulkner from the Perspective of the Works of Sartre and Camus," (Volumes I-III), DAI, 37 (Michigan: 1976), 3616A.

7752 Panichas, George A., ed. The Politics of Twentieth Century Novelists. New York: Hawthorn Books, 1971, pp. 278-295, 337-338, passim.

7753 Parkes, H. B. "The American Cultural Scene (IV): The Novel," Scrutiny, 9 (June, 1940), 2-8.

7754 Parks, Edd Winfield. "Faulkner and Hemingway: Their Thought," SAB, 22 (March, 1957), 1-2.

7755 ________. "Hemingway and Faulkner: The Pattern of Their Thought," Dagens Nyheter (Copenhagen), (February 12, 1956), 4-5.

7756 Parrot, Louis. "Les livres et l'homme: De Faulkner à Henry Miller," LF (9 août 1946), 5.

7757 Pate, Frances W. "Names of Characters in Faulkner's Mississippi," DAI, 30 (Emory: 1969), 2036A-37A.

7758 Pate, Willard. "Pilgrimage to Yoknapatawpha," FurmanM (Winter, 1969), 6-13.

7759 Paterson, John. "Hardy, Faulkner, and the Prosaics of Tragedy," CRAS, 5 (Spring, 1961), 156-175.

7760 Patil, Vimala. "William Faulkner: America's Literary Giant," United Asia, 14 (September, 1962), 523-525.

7761 Paulding, G. "Many Souths," Reporter, 17 (September 19, 1957), 47-48.

7762 Pavese, Cesare. Lettere 1924-1944. Lorenzo Mondo, ed. 3rd ed. Torino: Einaudi, 1966, p. 326.

7763 Pavilioniené, Marija-Aušriné. "Apie amerikiečių romantiku įtaką V. Folknerio kūrybai," Literatūra, 15, iii (1973), 95-108.

7764 _______. "Laikas ir V. Folknerio žmogus," Pergale, 3 (1973), 132-137. ["Time and Man in Faulkner's Works."]

7765 _______. "Malen'kij celovek v tvorčestve V. Folknera," Literatura, 16, iii (1974), 75-88.

7766 Peabody, Henry W. "Faulkner's Initiation Stories: An Approach to the Major Works," DAI, 33 (Denver: 1973), 3663A.

7767 Pearce, Richard. "Faulkner's One Ring Circus," WSCL, 7 (Autumn, 1966), 270-283.

7768 _______. "Reeling Through Faulkner: Pictures of Motion, Pictures in Motion," MFS, 24, #4 (Winter, 1978-79), 483-495.

7769 Pearce, Roy Harvey. Historicism Once More: Problems and Occasions for the American Scholar. Princeton, New Jersey: Princeton U.P., 1969, pp. 133-136.

7770 Pearson, Norman H. "The American Writer and the Feeling for Community," ES, 43 (October, 1962), 403-412.

7771 Peavy, Charles D. Go Slow Now: Faulkner and the Race Question. Eugene: Oregon Univ. Bks., 1971.

7772 Peden, William. The American Short Story. Boston: Houghton Mifflin; Cambridge: Riverside, 1964, passim.

7773 Pegler, Westbrook. "Faulkner Slanders the South," Times-Dispatch (Richmond) (October 5, 1955), 16.

7774 Pego, Aurelio. "Lo que se desconocia de William Faulkner," Horizontes, 6 (February 15-April 15, 1963), 6-7.

7775 Pells, Richard H. Radical Visions and American Dreams: Culture and Social Thought in the Depression Years. New York: Harper & Row, 1973, pp. 172-173, 240-246, passim.

7776 Penick, Edwin A., Jr. "The Testimony of William Faulkner," ChS, 38 (June, 1955), 121-133.

7777 _______. A Theological Critique of the Interpretation of Man in the Fiction and Drama of William Faulkner, Ernest Hemingway, Jean-Paul Sartre, and Albert Camus. Diss. Yale: 1954.

7778 Peper, Jürgen. Bewusstseinslage des Erzählens und erzählte Wirklichkeit: Bermuhüngen um ein geisteswissenschaftliches und literarhistorisches Verständnis für wirklichkeitsbildendes Erzählen bei William Faulkner. Diss. Freie Universität, Berlin: 1962.

7779 ______. Bewusstseinslagen des Erzählens und erzählte Wirklichkeiten. Leiden: E. J. Brill, 1966. (Studien zur amerikanischen Literatur und Geschichte, 3.)

7780 Percy, Walker. "Mississippi: The Fallen Paradise," HM, 230 (April, 1965), 166-172.

7781 Perluck, Herbert A. "The Heart's Driving Complexity," Accent, 20 (1960), 23-46.

7782 Perry, Bradley. "Faulkner Critics," FS, 2 (1953), 11-13, 30-32, 60-64.

7783 Perry, J. Douglas, Jr. "Gothic as Vortex: The Form of Horror in Capote, Faulkner, and Styron," MFS, 19 (Summer, 1973), 153-167.

7784 Perry, Thomas Edmund. "Knowing in the Novels of William Faulkner," DAI, 35 (Rochester: 1974), 2289A.

7785 Peskin, S. G. "William Faulkner: A 'Failed' Poet," Unisa ES (May, 1969), 39-45.

7786 Peters, Erskine Alvin. "The Yoknapatawpha World and Black Being," DAI, 37 (Princeton: 1976), 5831A.

7787 Petersen, Carl. Foreword and Introduction. Each in Its Ordered Place: A Collector's Notebook. Ann Arbor, Michigan: Ardis, 1975.

7788 Peterson, Richard Frank. "Time As Character in the Fiction of James Joyce and William Faulkner," DA, 31 (Kent State: 1969), 1285A-86A.

7789 Petesch, Donald A. "Faulkner on Negroes: The Conflict Between the Public Man and the Private Art," SHR, 10 (Winter, 1976), 55-64.

7790 ______. "Some Notes on the Family in Faulkner's Fiction," NMW, 10 (Spring, 1977), 11-18.

7791 Peyre, Henri. "American Literature Through French Eyes," VQR, 23 (Summer, 1947), 421-438.

7792 ______. "La culture et la littérature aux Etats-Unis," MonF (septembre 1948), 485-490.

7793 _______. *The Failures of Criticism.* Emended edition of *Writers and Their Critics,* [1944]. Ithaca, New York: Cornell U. P., 1967, *passim.*

7794 _______. *French Novelists of Today.* New York: Oxford U. P., 1967, *passim.*

7795 _______. "The Impact of the American Novel," *The Contemporary French Novel.* New York: Oxford U. P., 1955, pp. 263-278.

7796 _______. "Literature," BA, 21 (Spring, 1947), 175.
Review-art., Maurice Coindreau's *Aperçus de littêrature amêricaine.* Paris: Gallimard, 1946.

7797 Pfaff, William. "Future That Is Already Here," Cw, 54 (September 28, 1951), 601.

7798 Pfeiffer, Andrew H. "Eye of the Storm: The Observers' Image of the Man Who Was Faulkner," SoR, n. s. 8 (October, 1972), 763-773.

7799 Phillips, John, and Anne Hollander. "The Art of the Theatre I," ParisR, 9 (Winter-Spring, 1965), 65-94.
Interview of Lillian Hellman in which she discussed William Faulkner and other writers.

7800 Phillips, William L. "Sherwood Anderson's Two Prize Pupils," UCM, 47 (January, 1955), 9-12.
The Anderson-Faulkner-Hemingway relationship.

7801 Picchi, Mario. "William Faulkner: discorsi inediti sull arte e testimonianze di grandi critici sulla sua figura," FLe, 17 (October 17, 1962), 3.

7802 _______. "William Faulkner si confessa," FLe, 3 (January 20, 1957), 3.

7803 Pick, Robert. "Old World Views on New World Writing," SatRL, 32 (August 20, 1949), 7-9, 35-38.
More recognition of Faulkner abroad than at home.

7804 Picon, Gaëtan. *Contemporary French Literature: 1945 and After.* New York: Ungar, 1974, pp. 101-102, 167.

7805 _______. "Faulkner: L'agoisse et le dêsordre," NL, 40 (July 12, 1962), 3.

7806 Pieper, Janet Leah Steffen. "Black Characters in Faulkner's Fiction," DAI, 37 (Nebraska: 1976), 2877A.

7807 Pierce, Constance M. "Earth, Air, Fire, and Water: The Elements in Faulkner's Fiction," DAI, 33 (Penn. State: 1973), 6927A.

7808 Pilkington, John. "History and Literature in Mississippi since 1900," JMissH, 20 (October, 1958), 234-243.

7809 _______. "Nature's Legacy to William Faulkner," The South and Faulkner's Yoknapatawpha: The Actual and the Apocryphal. Harrington, Evans, and Ann J. Abadie, eds. Jackson: U.P. of Miss., 1977, pp. 104-127.

7810 _______. "William Faulkner and the University," UMissAR, 15 (October, 1962), 2-5.

7811 Pinckney, Josephine. "Southern Writers' Congress," SatRL, 8 (November 7, 1931), 266.

7812 Pindell, Richard P. "The Ritual of Survival: Landscape in Conrad and Faulkner," DAI, 32 (Yale: 1971), 3324A.

7813 Pineda, Rafael. "Yoknapatawpha, el condado de William Faulkner," Farol (Caracas), 22 (May-June, 1961), 9-12.

7814 Pires, Alves. "Faulkner: Um humanismo da existência trágica," Brotéria, 81 (1965), 393-401.

7815 Pisani, Assunta Sarnacchiaro. "The Raging Impotence: Humor in the Novels of Dostoevsky, Faulkner and Beckett," DAI, 38 (Brown: 1976), 248A-249A.

7816 Pitavy, François L. "Faulkner Poete," EA, 29 (1976), 456-467.

7817 _______. "Le Reporter: Tentation et Dérision de l'Ecriture," RANAM, 9 (1970), 95-108.

7818 Pivano, Ferñanda. Introduzione. Tutte le opere di William Faulkner. Milano: A. Mondadori, 1961.

7819 Pladott, Dinah. Absurd and Romantic Elements in the Writing of William Faulkner. Tel-Aviv: 1973. Diss.

7820 Player, Ralph Preston, Jr. "The Negro Character in the Fiction of William Faulkner," DA, 27 (Michigan: 1966), 483A-4A.

7821 Podhoretz, Norman. "Faulkner in the 50's," Doings and Undoings in the Fifties and After in the American Writing. New York: Farrar, Straus & Giroux, 1953; 2nd pr., 1964, pp. 13-29.

7822 _______. "William Faulkner and the Problem of War," Commentary, 18 (September, 1954), 227-232.

7823 Poirier, Richard. A World Elsewhere: The Place of Style in American Literature. New York: Oxford U.P., 1966,

pp. 78-84, passim.
Cf., Martin Green. "Style in American Literature," CamR, 89 (1967), 385-389.

7824 Polek, Fran James. "From Renegade to Solid Citizen: The Extraordinary Individual and the Community," SDR, 15, i (1977), 61-72.

7825 _______. "Tick-Tocks, Whirs, and Broken Gears: Time and Identity in Faulkner," Renascence, 29 (Summer, 1977), 193-200.

7826 _______. "Time and Identity in the Novels of William Faulkner," DA, 29 (So. California: 1969), 3151A.

7827 Polk, Noel. "The Critics and Faulkner's 'Little Postage Stamp of Native Soil,'" MissQ, 23 (Summer, 1970), 323-335.

7828 _______. "Some Recent Books on Faulkner," SNNTS, 9 (1976), 201-210.

7829 Pollock, Agnes Schelling. "The Current of Time in the Novels of William Faulkner," DA, 25 (U. C. L. A.: 1965), 7276-77.

7830 Pomeroy, Charles William. "Soviet Russian Criticism 1960-69 of Seven Twentieth Century American Novelists," DA, 32 (So. California: 1971), 449A.

7831 Poore, Charles J. "Books of the Times," NYTimes (November 11, 1950), 13.
Satiric verses about writers including Faulkner.

7832 Porter, Carolyn J. "Form and Process in American Literature," DAI, 34 (Rice: 1972), 1291A.

7833 Portuondo, Josê Antonio. "Brush of Faulkner," Americas, 7 (June, 1953), 40-41.

7834 _______. "Portraits of Crises," Americas, 3 (February, 1951), 20-23; (August 20, 1949), 7-9, 35-38.

7835 _______. "Retrato de Faulkner," Americas, 3 (March, 1951), 20-23, 45.

7836 _______. "William Faulkner y la conciencia sureña," El Heroismo intellectual. Mexico City: Tezontle, 1955, pp. 73-81.

7837 Potter, David M. "On Understanding the South: A Review Article," JSH, 30 (November, 1964), 451-462.

7838 Pouillon, Jean. "Temps et destinée chez Faulkner, Temps et roman. Paris: Gallimard, 1946, pp. 238-260. Repr., in Faulkner: A Collection of Critical Essays. Robert Penn Warren, ed. Englewood Cliffs, New Jersey: Prentice-Hall, 1966, pp. 79-87.

7839 _______. "William Faulkner, un témoin," TM, 2 (October 11, 1946), 172-178.

7840 Pound, Reginald. Arnold Bennett: A Biography. New York: Harcourt, Brace & Co., 1953, p. 204.

"... Bennett rendered ... service to American letters by being the first British critic to 'discover' William Faulkner...."

7841 Powell, William J. "The Personality of William Faulkner," Virginia Spectator, 117 (April, 1957), 10-11, 28.

7842 Powers, Lyall H. "Hawthorne and Faulkner and the Pearl of Great Price," PMASAL, 52 (1967), 391-401.

7843 Pozner, Vladimir. "Lettre à William Faulkner et à quelques autres," LF, (31 août 1951), 1, 6.

7844 Prasad, V. R. N. "William Faulkner and the Southern Syndrome," Indian Studies in American Fiction. M. K. Naik, S. K. Desai, and S. Mokashi-Punekar, eds. Dharwar: Karnatak Univ.: Delhi: Macmillan, India, 1974, pp. 185-202.

7845 Pratt, Branwen Bailey. "The Novel as Art: Criticism as Illumination," HSL, 9, #2 and 3 (1977), 223-231.

Essay-rev. of Albert J. Guerard's The Triumph of the Novel: Dickens, Dostoevsky, Faulkner (1976).

7846 Preece, Harold. "Some Aspects of Southern Culture," SWR, 21 (Winter, 1930), 217-222.

7847 Prescott, Herman. "Hemingway versus Faulkner: An Intriguing Feud," Lost Generation Journal, 3, #3 (1975), 18-19.

7848 Prescott, Joseph. "William Faulkner," FS, 2 (Summer, 1953), 28.

7849 Prescott, Orville. "The Eminently Obscure: Mann, Faulkner," In My Opinion: An Inquiry into the Contemporary Novel. New York, and Indianapolis: Bobbs-Merrill, 1952, pp. 75-91.

7850 Price, Lawrence Marsden. The Reception of United States Literature in Germany. (North Carolina University Studies in Comparative Literature, No. 39.) Chapel Hill: North Carolina U.P., 1966, pp. 217-218, passim.

7851 Price, Reynolds. "Clearer Road Signs in His County," BookW, (January 12, 1964), 5.

7852 Price-Stephens, Gordon. "The British Reception of William Faulkner, 1929-1962," MissQ, 18 (Summer, 1965), 119-200.

7853 Priestley, John Boynton. "William Faulkner," Literature and Western Man. London: Heinemann, pp. 436-438; New York: Harper, 1960, pp. 436-437.

7854 Prince, John. "André Dhotel, Steinbeck et Faulkner: Quelques similitudes," Caliban, 6 (January, 1969), 85-90.

7855 Prins, A. P. "Faulkner en het Negervraagstuk," Critisch Bulletin (1950), 126-127.

7856 Pritchett, V. S. "Books in General," NSt, 41 (June 2, 1951), 624-626.

7857 ________. "The Hill-billies," NS&N, 41, #1056 (June 2, 1951), 624-626; repr., with revisions in Books in General," New York: Harcourt, Brace, 1953, pp. 242-247.

7858 ________. "That Time and That Wilderness," NSt, 64 (September 28, 1962), 405-406.

7859 ________. "Time Frozen," PR, 21 (September-October, 1954), 557-561.

7860 "Professional Notes and Comment," PMLA, 89 (September, 1974), 882-883.

In number of dissertations (September 1968 to December 1973) about individual authors, Faulkner held second place to Shakespeare.

7861/3 Proffer, Carl R., ed. and tr. Preface and Introduction. Soviet Criticism of American Literature in the Sixties. Ann Arbor: Ardis Pubs., 1972, pp. xiii-xxxi.

7864 Pusey, William Webb. "William Faulkner's Works in Germany to 1940: Translations and Criticism," GR, 30 (October, 1955), 211-226.

7865 Putney, Michael. "Yoknapatawpha's Mr. Bill," NatlObserv (February 16, 1974), 22.

7866 Putzel, Max. "Faulkner's Short Story Sending Schedule," PBSA, 71 (1977), 98-105.

7867 Quasimodo, Salvatore. "L'epica del Faulkner maggiore," Il poeta e il Politico, e altri saggi. Milano: Schwartz, 1960, pp. 149-152.

7868 "Qui est Faulkner?--Un success qui ne doit rien à la complaisance," Réforme (16 février 1952), 7.

7869 Quinn, Arthur Hobson, ed. *The Literature of the American People*. New York: Appleton-Century, 1951, pp. 884-885, *passim*.

7870 Quiñonero, Juan Pedro. "Faulkner, aquel viejo lobo," La Estafeta Literaria, No. 385 (December 16, 1967), 13.

7871 R., W. M. "Footnotes," Kansas City Star (April 6, 1940), 14.

7872 "Rabi." "Faulkner au Natural," Gazette des Lettres (September 14, 1946), 15.

7873 _______. "Faulkner et la génération de l'exil," Esprit, 175 (January, 1951), 47-65; repr., *Three Decades of Criticism*. Frederick Hoffman and Olga Vickery, eds. East Lansing: 1956, pp. 118-138.

7874 Rabinovitz, Rubin. *The Reaction against Experiment in the English Novel, 1950-1960*. New York and London: Columbia U.P., 1967, pp. 50-51, *passim*.

7875 Radomski, James Louis. "Faulkner's Style: A Syntactic Analysis," DAI, 35 (Kent State: 1974), 6154A.

7876 Rahv, Philip. "The Cult of Experience in American Writing," PR, 7 (November-December, 1940), 412-424.

7877 _______. *Literature in America*. New York: Meridian Books, 1965, *passim*.

7878 Raimbault, René-Noel. "Faulkner au naturel," GLet (14 septembre 1946), 15.

7879 _______, tr. *Histoires diverses*. Paris: Gallimard, 1967.

7880 _______. *William Faulkner*. Paris: Editions Seuil, 1963.

7881 Raimondi, E. "Note sulla narrativa americana contemporanea," Convivium, 1 (1947), 65-77.

7882 Raines, Charles A. "Faulkner and Human Freedom: A Neglected Theme in the Yoknapatawpha Sagas," Forum, 3 (Fall, 1959), 50-53.

7883 Rakić, Bogdan. "Rodenje Yoknapatawphe: Niličja Faulknerove prošlosti," Izraz, 42, v (1977), 589-97.

7884 Ranald, Ralph A. "William Faulkner's South: Three Degrees of Myth," Landfall, 18 (December, 1964), 329-338.

7885 Randolph, Linda Scott. "A Question of Responsibility: The Villain in the Yoknapatawpha Fiction of William Faulkner," DAI, 36 (Mississippi: 1975), 7425A-26A.

7886 Ransom, John Crowe. "The Content of the Novel: Notes Toward a Critique of Fiction," AmR, 7 (Summer, 1936), 301-318.

7887 _______. "Modern with a Southern Accent," VQR, 11 (April, 1935), 184-200.
Faulkner "the most exciting figure in our contemporary literature."

7888 _______. "William Faulkner: An Impression," HA, 135 (November, 1951), 17.

7889 Rao, N. Krishna. "The Christ Image in Two Novels of Wilian Faulkner," Andhra Univ. Mag. (Waltair, India), 20 (1959-1960), 55-59.

7890 Rascoe, Burton. "Faulkner's New York Critics," AmMerc, 50 (June, 1940), 243-247.

7891 Ratner, Marc L. "Rebellion of Wrath and Laughter: Styron's Set This House on Fire," SoR, 7 (October, 1971), 1007-1020.
Briefly compares Styron and Faulkner.

7892 Ray, David. "What Mr. Faulkner Meant Writing 'Wump-Wump-Wump,'" Kans. City Star (October 17, 1976), 10D.
Art.-Rev. of Calvin S. Brown's A Glossary of Faulkner's South. Yale U.P., 1976.

7893 Reaver, J. Russell. "This Vessel of Clay," FSUS, 14 (1954), 131-140.

7894 Reed, Joseph W., Jr. Faulkner's Narrative. New Haven and London: Yale U.P., 1973.

7895 Reed, Richard A. "A Chronology of William Faulkner's Yoknapatawpha County," DAI, 32 (Emory: 1971), 2101A.

7896 _______. "The Role of Chronology in Faulkner's Yoknapatawpha Fiction," SLJ, 7 (Fall, 1974), 24-48.

7897 Reeves, George M. Introduction. The Time of William Faulkner: A French View of Modern American Fiction. George M. Reeves, ed. and tr. Columbia: South Carolina U.P., 1971, pp. xv-xxi.

7898 "'Resist the Mass'--William Faulkner at the University of Virginia" Time, 69 (June 3, 1957), 39-40.

7899 Reval, François. "Faulkner, deuxième manière," TM, 10 (November, 1954), 750-754.

7900 Revol, E. L. "Faulkner," Panorama de la literatura norteamericana actual. Córdoba, Spain: Editorial Assandri, 1945, pp. 63-66.

7901 Reynolds, Gordon Duncan. "Psychological Rebirth in Selected Works by Nathaniel Hawthorne, Stephen Crane, Henry James, William Faulkner, and Ralph Ellison," DAI, 34 (California, Irvine: 1974), 7719A.

7902 Rhode, Robert Huff. "William Faulkner and the Gods of Yoknapatawpha: An Essay in Comparative Mythopoesis," DAI, 36 (Syracuse: 1975), 6761A-62A.

7903 Ribeiro, Leo Gibson. "Brazil: Between Dogpatch and Yoknapatawpha," KR, 23 (Summer, 1961), 394-407.

7904 Ricard, Jean-François. "Faulkner en France," Confluences, nouvelle serie, 1 (January-February, 1945), 82-85.

7905 Rice, Charles D. "Faulkner Failed in English," This Week Mag. (January 31, 1960), 14.

7906 Richards, Lewis Alva. "The Literary Style of Jean-Paul Sartre and William Faulkner: An Analysis, Comparison, and Contrast," DA, 24 (So. California: 1963), 3755-56.

7907 Richardson, H. Edward. "Anderson and Faulkner," AL, 36 (November, 1964), 298-314.

7908 _______. "Faulkner, Anderson, and Their Tall Tale," AL, 34 (May, 1962), 287-291.

Cf., Walter B. Rideout and James B. Meriwether. "On the Collaboration of Faulkner and Anderson," AL, 35 (March, 1963), 85-87.

7909 _______. "Oxford, Mississippi," Books and Bookmen, 10 (February, 1965), 39-40, 48.

7910 _______. "The Ways that Faulkner Walked: A Pilgrimage," ArQ, 21 (Summer, 1965), 133-145.

7911 _______. "William Faulkner: From Past to Self-Discovery; A Study of His Life and Work through Sartoris (1929)," DA, 24 (So. California: 1963), 3756.

7912 _______. William Faulkner: The Journey to Self-Discovery. Columbia: Missouri U.P., 1969.

7913 Richardson, Kenneth E. Force and Faith in the Novels of William Faulkner. The Hague: Mouton, 1967.

7914 _______. "Quest for Faith: A Study of Destructive and Creative Force in the Novels of William Faulkner," DA, 23 (Claremont: 1963), 3384.

7915 Riche, James. "Pragmatism: A National Mode of Thought," L&I, 9 (1971), 37-44.

7916 Richter, Barbara. "Per Arcdua ad Astra: Perversity in the Morality Puzzle of William Faulkner," RUCR, 39 (1974), 139-147.

7917 Rideout, Walter B., and James B. Meriwether. "On the Collaboration of Faulkner and Anderson," AL, 35 (March, 1963), 85-87.
Cf., Edward Richardson. "Faulkner, Anderson, and Their Tall Tale," AL, 34 (May, 1962), 287-291.

7918 Riedel, Frederick Carl. "Faulkner As Stylist," SAQ, 56 (Autumn, 1957), 462-478.

7919 Riese, Utz. "Das Dilemma eines dritten Weges: William Faulkners widerspruchlicher Humanismus," ["The Dilemma of the Third Way: William Faulkner's Contradictory Humanism"], ZAA, 16, (1968), I, 138-155; II, 257-273.

7920 Rigsby, Carol Anne Roscoe. "The Vanishing Community: Studies in Some Late Novels by William Faulkner," DAI, 36 (Toronto: 1973), 1509A-10A.

7921 Rinaldi, Nicholas Michael. "Game-Consciousness and Game-Metaphor in the Work of William Faulkner," DA, 24 (Fordham: 1964), 4196-97.

7922 ________. "Game Imagery and Game-Consciousness in Faulkner's Fiction," TCL, 10 (October, 1964), 108-118.

7923 Ringold, Francine. "The Metaphysics of Yoknapatawpha County: 'Airy Space and Scope for Your Delirium,'" HSL, 8 (1976), 223-240.

7924 Riskin, Myra J. "Faulkner's South: Myth and History in the Novel," DA, 30 (California, Berkeley: 1968), 1148A-49A.

7925 Robb, Mary Cooper. William Faulkner: An Estimate of His Contribution to the Modern Novel. (Critical Essays in English and American Literature, No. 1). Pittsburgh: Pittsburgh U.P., 1957.

7926 Robbins, Deborah Lynn. "Characters in Crisis: Communication and the Idea of Self in Faulkner," DAI, 37 (Northwestern: 1976), 7132A.

7927 Roberts, E. F. "Faulkner," Cw, 60 (August 27, 1954), 514.

7928 Roberts, James L. "Experimental Exercises: Faulkner's Early Writings," Discourse, 6 (Summer, 1963), 183-197.

7929 ________. "The Individual and the Community," Studies in American Literature. W. F. McNeir, ed. Baton Rouge: Louisiana State U. P., 1960, pp. 132-153.

7930 ________. "The Individual and the Family," ArQ, 16 (1960), 26-38.

7931 ________. "William Faulkner: A Thematic Study," DA, 17 (Iowa: 1957), 3023.

7932 Roberts, Kenneth. I Wanted to Write. Garden City: Doubleday, 1949, passim.

7933 Robinson, Clayton. "Faulkner and Welty and the Mississippi Baptists," Interpretations, 5 (1973), 51-54.

7934 ________. "Memphis in Fiction: Rural Values in an Urban Setting," Myths and Realities: Conflicting Values in America. Berkley Kalin, and Clayton Robinson, eds. Memphis, Tennessee: John Willard Brister Lib., Memphis State U., 1972, pp. 29-38.

7935 Robinson, Evalyne Carter. "The Role of the Negro in William Faulkner's Public and Private Worlds," DAI, 32 (Ohio State: 1971), 2704A.

7936 Robinson, Frederick M. "The Comedy of Language: Studies in Modern Comic Literature," Diss. Washington: 1972.

7937 Robson, W. W. "William Faulkner," Spectator (London), 200 (February 14, 1958), 206.

7938 Rodewald-Grebin, Von V. "Eine Königin: Novelle Ubers," NRs, 44 (Pt. 2 (October, 1933), 527-541.

7939 Rodnon, Stewart. "Sports, Sporting Codes, and Sportsmanship in the Work of Ring Lardner, James T. Farrell, Ernest Hemingway and William Faulkner," DA, 23 (N. Y. U.: 1962), 634-635.

7940 Rogers, Katharine M. The Troublesome Helpmate: A History of Misogyny in Literature. Seattle: Washington U. P., 1966, pp. 252-257.

7941 Rohrberger, Mary. Hawthorne and the Modern Short Story: A Study in Genre. (Studies in General and Comparative Literature, Vol. 2) The Hague and Paris: Mouton, 1966, passim.

7942 Rolle, Andrew F. "William Faulkner: An Inter-disciplinary Examination," MissQ, 11 (Fall, 1958), 157-159.

7943 Rollyson, Carl Edmund, Jr. "The Uses of the Past in the

Novels of William Faulkner," DAI, 37 (Toronto, Canada: 1975), 6488A.

7944 Rolo, Charles J. "The World of Faulkner," Atl, 190 (August, 1952), 85-86.

7945 Romanova, Elena. "Antivoennye motivy v tvorchestve Uil'iama Folknera," ["Anti-war Themes in the Work of William Faulkner,"] Inostrannaia Literatura, #6 (1955), 170-176; and SovLit, 12 (1965), 178.

7946 Romig, Evelyn Matthews. "Women as Victims in the Novels of Charles Dickens and William Faulkner," DAI, 39 (Rice: 1978), 1600A.

7947 Rosati, Salvatore. "Faulkner, William," Dizionario Letterario Bompiani degli autori di tutti i tempi e di tutte le letterature. Milano: Bompiani, 1956, I, 750-751.

7948 _______. "Letteratura americana: William Faulkner, Nuova antologia, 395 (Florence), (January 16, 1938), 225-230.

7949 _______. "Valori e tendenze nella prosa americana d'oggi," Le Tre Venezie, 21 (October-November-December, 1947), 329-337.

7950 _______. "William Faulkner," L'ombra dei padri: studi di letteratura americana. Roma: Edizioni di Storia e Letteratura, 1958, pp. 99-109.

7951 Rose, Alan Henry. "The Evolution of the Image of the Negro as Demon in Southern Literature," DAI, 31 (Indiana: 1970), 4732.

7952 _______. "The Limits of Humanity in the Fiction of William Faulkner," Demonic Vision: Racial Fantasy and Southern Fiction. Hamden, Conn.: Archon Books, 1976, pp. 101-118.

7953 Rosenberg, von K. "Heute nacht: Erzählung, Übers," Neue Rundsch, 44, Pt. 1 (May, 1933), 652-669.

7954 Rosenfeld, Isaac. "Faulkner and His Contemporaries," PR, 18 (January-February, 1951), 106-109.

7955 _______. "Faulkner's Two Styles," An Age of Enormity. Theodore Solotaroff, ed. New York: World, 1962, pp. 268-272.

7956 Rosenman, John B. "A Matter of Choice: The Locked Door Theme in Faulkner," SAB, 41, ii (1976), 8-12.

7957 Rosenzweig, Paul Jonathan. "The Wilderness in American

Fiction: A Psychoanalytic Study of a Central American Myth," DAI, 33, #9 Michigan: 1972), 5140A.
Discussion of "The Bear," "Delta Autumn," and "The Old People."

7958 Ross, Danforth R. "William Faulkner," The American Short Story. (University of Minnesota Pamphlets on American Writers, No. 14.). Minneapolis: Minnesota U.P., 1961, pp. 36-37.

7959 Ross, Maude Cardwell. "Moral Values of the American Woman As Presented in Three Major American Authors (Hawthorne, James, Faulkner)," DA, 25 (Texas: 1965), 5262-63.

7960 Ross, Stephen M. "The 'Loud World' of Quentin Compson," SNNTS, 7 (Summer, 1975), 245-257.

7961 ________. "A World of Voices: 'Talking' in the Novels of William Faulkner," DAI, 32 (Stanford: 1972), 7002A.

7962 Ross, Werner. "Der amerikanische Roman der Gegenwart," Hockland, 46, #1 (1953), 153-163.

7963 Ross, Woodburn O. Short Stories in Context. New York: American Bk. Co., 1953, pp. 337-341.

7964 Roth, Richard Allen. "From Gap to Gain: Outrage and Renewal in Faulkner and Mailer," DAI, 37 (Washington: 1976), 1554A-1555A.

7965 Roth, Russell. "The Brennan Papers: Faulkner in Manuscript," Perspective, 2 (Summer, 1949), 219-224.

7966 ________. "The Centaur and the Pear Tree," WestR, 16 (Spring, 1952), 199-205.
Cf., Harry Campbell. "Mr. Roth's Centaur and Faulkner's Symbolism," WR, 16 (1952), 320-321.

7967 ________. "Ideas and Queries," FS, 1 (Summer, 1952), 23-26.

7968 ________. "The Inception of a Saga: Frederick Manfred's 'Buckskin Man,'" SDR, 7, #4 (Winter, 1969-70), 87-99.
Faulkner's influence.

7969 ________. "William Faulkner: The Pattern of Pilgrimage," Perspective, 2 (Summer, 1949), 246-254.

7970 Rouberol, Jean. "Faulkner et l'histoire," RANAM, 9 (1976), 7-17.

7971 ________. "Les Indiens dans l'oeuvre de Faulkner," EA, 26 (March, 1973), 54-58.

7972 Rougé, Robert. L'Inquiétude Religieuse dans le Roman Américain Moderne. (Publications de l'universite- de Haute-Bretagne 4.) Paris: Librairie C. Klincksieck, 1973[?]

7973 Rourke, Constance. American Humor. New York: Harcourt, Brace, 1931, passim.

7974 Rouse, Blair. Ellen Glasgow. New York: Twayne, 1962, passim.
Comparison of Glasgow and Faulkner.

7975 _______, ed. Letters of Ellen Glasgow. New York: Harcourt, Brace, 1958, passim.

7976 _______. "Time and Place in Southern Fiction," Southern Renascence: The Literature of the Modern South. Louis D. Rubin and Robt. Jacobs, eds. Baltimore: Johns Hopkins, 1953; 2nd pr., 1954, pp. 126-150.

7977 Rousseaux, André. "Faulkner," Littérature du vingtième siècle. Paris: Albin Michel, 1949, pp. 238-246.

7978 _______. "Le monde infernal de Faulkner, FL, 15 (January 16, 1960), 2.

7979 _______. "Parabole de Faulkner," FL, 13 (June 14, 1958), 2.

7980 Rovit, Earl. "Faulkner, Hemingway, and the American Family," MissQ, 29, #4 (Fall, 1976), 483-497.

7981 Rubel, Warren Gunter. "The Structural Function of the Christ Figure in the Fiction of William Faulkner," DA, 25 (Arkansas: 1965), 5941-42.

7982 Rubin, Louis D., Jr. "Chronicles of Yoknapatawpha: The Dynasties of William Faulkner," The Faraway Country: Writers of the Modern South. Seattle: Washington U.P., 1963, pp. 43-71.

7983 _______. "The Difficulties of Being a Southern Writer Today: Or, Getting Out from Under William Faulkner," The Curious Death of the Novel: Essays in American Literature. Baton Rouge: Louisiana U.P., 1967, pp. 282-293.

7984 _______. "Don Quixote and Selected Progeny: Or, the Journey-man As Outsider," SoR, 10 (Winter, 1974), 31-58.

7985 _______, ed. Introduction: "The Great American Joke," The Comic Imagination in American Literature. New Brunswick: Rutgers U.P., 1973, pp. 14-15.

7986 _______. "Thomas Wolfe in Time and Place," Southern

Renascence. L. D. Rubin and Robt. Jacobs, eds. Baltimore: 1966, pp. 291-294, 297-300.

7987 _______. William Elliott Shoots a Bear: Essays on the Southern Literary Imagination. Baton Rouge: Louisiana St. U. P., 1975, passim.

7988 _______. "William Faulkner: The Discovery of a Man's Vocation," Faulkner: Fifty Years after The Marble Faun. George H. Wolfe, ed. University, Alabama: Alabama U. P., 1976, pp. 43-68.

7989 _______. The Writer in the South: Studies in a Literary Community. (Mercer Univ. Lamar Memorial Lectures, No. 15.) Athens: Ga. U. P., 1972, passim.

7990 _______, and C. Hugh Holman. Southern Literary Study: Problems and Possibilities. Durham: North Carolina U. P., 1975, passim.

7991 _______, and Robert D. Jacobs, eds. Introduction. South: Modern Southern Literature in Its Cultural Setting. Garden City, New York: Doubleday, 1961, pp. 11-25.

7992 _______, and _______, eds. Preface. Southern Renascence: The Literature of the Modern South. Baltimore: Johns Hopkins, 1953.

7993 _______, et al. "Modern Novelists and Contemporary American Society: A Symposium," Shenandoah, 10 (Winter, 1959), 3-31.

7994 Runyan, Harry. A Faulkner Glossary. New York: Citadel: 1964.

7995 _______. "Faulkner's Non-Fiction Prose," FS, 3 (Winter, 1954), 67-69.

7996 Ruoff, G. W. "Faulkner: The Way out of the Waste Land," The Twenties: Fiction, Poetry, Drama. Warren G. French, ed. DeLand, Florida: Everett/Edwards, 1975, pp. 235-248.

7997 Rupe, James E. "They Endure and Prevail," MSCS, 1, #1 (May, 1966) 87-102. [Mankato Studies in English, No. 1.]

7998 Rupp, Richard H. "Subversions of the Pastoral: The Hero in Our Time--A Review Essay," SHR, 10 (Winter, 1976), 74-80.

7999 Ruppersburg, Hugh Michael. "Narrative Mode in the Novels of William Faulkner," DAI, 39 (South Carolina: 1978), 1576A.

8000 Russell, Bertrand, et al. The Impact of America on European Culture. Boston: Beacon, 1951, pp. 88-89, 90.

8001 Rutledge, Wilmuth S. "How Colonel Faulkner Built His Railroad," MissQ, 20 (Summer, 1967), 166-170.

8002 Saal, Hubert D. "Faulkner: Chronicler and Prophet," YLM, 115 (December, 1947), 8-15.

8003 _______. "The Style of William Faulkner," YLM (December, 1946), 19-22.

8004 Saavedra, Vargas. "La afinidad de Onetti a Faulkner," Cuadernos Hispanoamericanos, 292-294 ([1974]), 257-265.

8005 Sachs, Viola, ed. Le Blanc et le Noir chez Melville et Faulkner. Paris: Mouton, 1974.

8006 _______. "Contemporary American Fiction and Some Nineteenth Century Patterns," KN, 13, #1 (First Qt., 1966), 3-29.

8007 _______. The Myth of America: Essays in the Structure of Literary Imagination. The Hague and Paris: Mouton, 1973, passim.

8008 Saito, Kazue. "Ethics in Faulkner's Works," Ushione, 10 (1957), 1-12.

8009 Sale, Richard B. "An Interview in New Haven with Robert Penn Warren," SNNTS, 2 (Fall, 1970), 325-354.

8010 Samuels, Charles T. "He Made the Books and He Died," Nation, 203 (September 12, 1966), 220-222.

8011 Samway, Patrick. [Untitled essay-review of books on Faulkner], Cw, 104 (August 5, 1977), 507-509.

8012 _______. "War: A Fulknerian Commentary," ColQ, 18 (Spring, 1970), 370-378.

8013 Sandeen, Ernest. "William Faulkner: A Glance in Retrospect," Books on Trial, 14 (March, 1956), 281-282, 325-327.

8014 _______. "William Faulkner: Tragedian of Yoknapatawpha," Fifty Years of the American Novel, 1900-1950. Harold Charles Gardiner, ed. New York and London: Scribner's, 1951, pp. 165-182.

8015 Sanderson, Jane. "A Kind of Greatness," DeltaR, 2 (July-August, 1965), 15-17.

8016 Sans, Julien. "Compte rendu d'Aperçus de littérature américaine," Climats, (25 juillet, 1946), 8.

8017 _______. "D'un nouveau poncif," Climats (3 décembre 1947), 4.

8018 Saporta, Marc. "Après Faulkner," IeD, No. 166 (September 1, 1962), 24-28.

8019 Saroyan, William. "Myself Upon the Earth," The Daring Young Man on the Flying Trapeze and Other Stories. London: Faber & Faber, 1935, pp. 283-302. Also in William Saroyan: The Saroyan Special; Selected Short Stories. Freeport, New York: Bks for Libraries, repr., 1970, p. 5. Note also parody in Inhale and Exhale. New York: 1935, p. 212.

"... [I]f I felt inclined, I could write like John Dos Passos or William Faulkner...."

8020 Sartre, Jean-Paul. "A propos de Dos Passos," NRF, 26 (August, 1938), 292-301; repr., in Situations, pp. 14-25.

8021 _______. "American Novelists in French Eyes," Atl, 178 (August, 1946), 114-118.

8022 _______. What Is Literature? Bernard Frechtman, tr. New York: Philosophical Libr., 1949, p. 228.

8023 _______. "The Writer in Perspective," SatRL, 45 (July 28, 1962), 24.

8024 Satin, Joseph Henry. "Resist the Mass," Ideas in Context. Boston: Houghton Mifflin, 1958, pp. 96-98.

8025 Savarese, Sister Paul C. "Cinematic Techniques in the Novels of William Faulkner," DAI, 33 (St. Louis U.: 1972), 1179A.

8026 Savelli, Giovanni. "Paràbola di Faulkner," LetM (Milan), 4 (May-June, 1953), 337-342.

8027 Scaffella, Frank. "Models of the Soul: Authorship as Moral Action in Four American Novels," Journal of American Academy of Religion, 44 (September, 1976), 459-475.

8028 Scanlan, Margaret C. T. "William Faulkner and The Search for Lost Time: Three Aspects of Literary Deformation," DAI, 33 (Iowa: 1972), 1741A-42A.

8029 Schérer, Olga. "La contestation du jugement sur pièces chez Dostoïevski et Faulkner," Delta, 3 (November, 1976), 47-61.

8030 _______. "Faulkner et le fratricide pour une théorie des titres dans la littérature," EA, 30 (1976), 329-336.

8031 Scherman, David Edward. "William Faulkner," Literary America. New York: Dodd, Mead, 1952, pp. 148-151.

8032 Schermbrucker, William Gerald. "Strange Textures of Vision: A Study of the Significance of Mannered Fictional Techniques in Six Selected Novels of D. H. Lawrence, William Faulkner, and Patrick White together with a Theoretical Introduction on "The Novel of Vision," DAI, 35 (British Columbia: 1974), 473A.

8033 Schevill, James. "The Meeting of Nathaniel Hawthorne and William Faulkner," The American Fantasies. Agana, Guam: Bern Porter Bks., 1952, pp. 10-11.

8034 ________. Sherwood Anderson: His Life and Work: Denver: Denver U.P., 1951, passim.

8035 Schirmer, Walter Franz. Geschichte der englischen literatur von den Anfängen bis zur Gegenwart. Halle/Saale: Max Niemeyer Verlag, 1937, passim.

8036 Schlesinger, Arthur M., and Morton White, eds. Paths of American Thought. Boston: Houghton Mifflin, 1963, passim.

8037 Schlumpf, Otto Norman. "William Faulkner: Myth-Maker and Morals-Monger; Esthetics and Ethics in Yoknapatawpha County," DAI, 35 (Santa Barbara, California: 1974), 7327A.

8038 Schmidt, Albert-Marie. ["William Faulkner"], Rêforme (16 fêvrier 1952), 7.

8039 Schmitter, Dean Morgan, ed. William Faulkner: A Collection of Criticism. New York: McGraw-Hill Bk. Co., 1973.

8040 Schmitz, Neil. "The Difficult Art of American Political Fiction: Henry Adams' 'Democracy' as Tragical Satire," WHR, 25 (Spring, 1971), 147-162.

8041 Scholes, Robert E. The Fabulators. New York: Oxford U.P., 1967, passim.

8042 ________, ed. Introduction. Some Modern Writers: Essays and Fiction by Conrad, Dinesen, Lawrence, Orwell, Faulkner, and Ellison. New York: Oxford U.P., 1971, pp. xi-xiii.

8043 ________. "The Modern American Novel and the Mason-Dixon Line," GaR, 14 (Summer, 1960), 193-204.

8044 ________. "Understanding Faulkner," YR, 53 (Spring, 1964), 431-435.

8045 ________, and Robert Kellogg. The Nature of Narrative. New York: Oxford U.P., 1966, pp. 199-200, passim.

8046 Schorer, Mark. The Story: A Critical Anthology. New York: Prentice-Hall, 1950, pp. 418-419.

8047 Schultz, William J. "Motion in Yoknapatawpha County: Theme and Point of View in the Novels of William Faulkner," DA, 29 (Kansas State: 1969), 3154A.

8048 Schwartz, Delmore. "The Fiction of William Faulkner," SoR, 7 (Summer, 1941), 145-160.

8049 ________. "The Fiction of William Faulkner," Selected Essays of Delmore Schwartz. Donald A. Dike and David H. Zucker, eds. Chicago: Chicago U.P., 1970, pp. 274-289.

8050 Scott, Arthur L. "The Faulknerian Sentence," PrS, 27 (Spring, 1953), 91-98.

8051 Scott, Nathan A., Jr. "Judgment Marked by a Cellar: The American Negro Writer and the Dialectic of Despair," DenverQ, 2 (Summer, 1967), 5-35.

8052 ________. Modern Literature and the Religious Frontier. New York: Harper, 1959, passim.

8053 ________. Three American Moralists: Mailer, Bellow, Trilling. Notre Dame, London: Notre Dame U.P., 1973, passim.

8054 ________. "Vision of William Faulkner," ChrC, 74 (September 18, 1957), 1104-1106.

8055 ________. "Warren: The Man to Watch," ChrC, 73 (February 29, 1956), 272-273.

8056 Scura, Dorothy. "Glasgow and the Southern Renaissance: The Conference at Charlottesville," MissQ, 27 (Fall, 1974), 415-434.

Description of the meeting in Charlottesville, Virginia, October 23-24, 1931, which Faulkner attended.

8057 Sedenberg, Nancy Belcher. "William Faulkner's World War I and Flying Short Fiction: An Imaginative Appropriation of History," DAI, 38, # 9 (South Carolina: 1977), 5484A.

8058 Seiden, Melvin. "Faulkner's Ambiguous Negro," MassR, 4 (Summer, 1963), 675-690.

8059 Seidensticker, Edward. "Through Foreign Eyes: Redskins in Japan," KR, 22 (Summer, 1960), 374-391.

Reception of American literature in Japan. Faulkner's work suffers in translation.

8060 Seltzer, Alvin Jay. "Chaos in the Novel--The Novel in Chaos," DAI, 32, # 2 (Penn. State: 1970), 984A.

8061 ________. Chaos in the Novel--The Novel in Chaos. New York: Schocken Books, 1974.

8062 Sengelli, Nazan Feride. "Literary Continuity Traced through the Progression in the Use of Time in Wordsworth, Faulkner, Virginia Woolf, T. S. Eliot and Yeats," DAI, 38 (George Peabody: 1977), 2766A.

8063 Sequeira, Isaac J. F. "The Theme of Initiation in Modern American Fiction," DAI, 31 (Utah: 1970), 2354A-55A.

8064 Serafin, Sister Joan M. "Faulkner's Uses of the Classics," DA, 29 (Notre Dame: 1969), 3155A-56A.

8065 Sewall, Richard B. The Vision of Tragedy. New Haven: Yale U.P., 1960, pp. 133-147, passim.

8066 Seward, William W., Jr. "William Faulkner: Folk Legends of Frenchman's Bend," Contrasts in Modern Writers. New York: Frederick Fell, 1963, pp. 59-61.

8067 Sewell, Elizabeth. "Portraiture and Pedagogics," Tablet (November 21, 1959).

8068 Seyppel, Joachim. "Faulkner's Dichtung," NZ, 4 (1952), 369-372.

8069 ________, tr. William Faulkner. New York: Ungar, 1962; Berlin: Colloquium Verlag, 1962.

8070 Shanaghan, Malachy M. "A Critical Analysis of the Fictional Techniques of William Faulkner," DA, 20 (Notre Dame: 1960), 4663.

8071 Sharma, P. P. "William Faulkner's South and the Other South," IJAS, 7 (January, 1977), 79-93.

8072 Shaw, Joe C. "Sociological Aspects of Faulkner's Writing," MissQ, 14 (Summer, 1961), 148-152.

8073 Shelton, Frank Wilsey. "The Family in the Novels of Wharton, Faulkner, Cather, Lewis and Dreiser," DAI, 32 (North Carolina, Chapel Hill: 1971), 5244A.

8074 Sherwood, John C. "The Traditional Element in Faulkner," FS, 3 (Summer-Autumn, 1954), 17-23.

8075 ________. "Thirty-three," FS, 2 (Summer, 1953), 29.

8076 Sherwood, Robert Emmett. "Of Durability," SatRL, 34 (March 17, 1951), 22-23.

8077 Showett, H. K. "Faulkner and Scott: Addendum," MissQ, 22 (Spring, 1969), 152-153.

8078 Shulman, Irving. "A Study of the Juvenile Delinquent as

Depicted in the Twentieth-Century American Novel to 1950," DAI, 33 (Los Angeles: 1972), 329A-30A.

8079 Sidney, George R. "An Addition to the Faulkner Canon: The Hollywood Writings," TCL, 6 (January, 1961), 172-174.

8080 ________. "Faulkner in Hollywood: A Study of His Career as a Scenarist," DA, 20 (New Mexico: 1960), 2810.

8081 ________. "William Faulkner and Hollywood," ColQ, 9 (Spring, 1961), 367-377.

8082 Sieben, John Kenneth. "The Presentation of the Negro Character in the Best-Selling Novels of the Postwar Period 1946 through 1965 in the United States," DAI, 32 (New York: 1971), 2709A.

8083 Siegel, Roslyn. "Faulkner's Black Characters: A Comparative Study," DAI, 35 (New York City University: 1974), 3009A.

8084 Sigaux, Gilbert. "Sur Faulkner," Nef, 6 (February, 1949), 117-120.

8085 Silver, James W. "Faulkner's South," SHR, 10 (Fall, 1976), 301-312.

8086 ________. Preface. *Mississippi: The Closed Society*. New York: Harcourt, Brace & World, 1964, pp. xi-xiv.

8087 Simkins, Francis Butler. *A History of the South*. New York: Knopf, 1947, pp. 347-348.

8088 ________. "Literature since the Civil War," *The South Old and New*. New York: Knopf, 1949, pp. 347-348.

8089 ________. "The South," *Regionalism in America*. Merrill Jensen, ed. Madison: Wisconsin U.P., 1951, p. 149.

8090 Simmons, Edgar. "Faulkner," YR, 57 (Summer, 1968), 586-587.
A poem about Faulkner.

8091 Simon, Jean. "Romanciers américains et critiques français," RSH (janvier-mars, 1948), 60-64.

8092 ________. "William Faulkner," *Le roman américain au XXe siècle*. Paris: Boivin & Cie., 1950, pp. 119-131.

8093 Simon, John K. "Faulkner and Sartre: Metamorphosis and the Obscene," CL, 15 (Summer, 1963), 216-225.

8094 ________. "The Glance of the Idiot: A Thematic Study of

Faulkner and Modern French Fiction," DA, 25 (Yale: 1964), 1220.

8095 Simonini, R. C., Jr., ed. Southern Writers: Appraisals in Our Time. Charlottesville: Virginia U.P., 1964, passim.

8096 Simpson, Hassell A. "The Short Stories of William Faulkner," DA, 23 (Florida State: 1962), 1709.

8097 ________. "Yoknapatawpha: Faulkner's 'Little Postage Stamp of Native Soil,'" NMW, 3 (Spring, 1970), 43-47.

8098 Simpson, Lewis P. "Faulkner and the Legend of the Artist," Faulkner: Fifty Years After The Marble Faun. George H. Wolfe, ed. University, Alabama: Alabama U.P., 1976, pp. 69-100.

8099 ________. "Faulkner and the Southern Symbolism of Pastoral," MissQ, 28 (Fall, 1975), 401-415.

8100 ________. "O'Donnell's Wall," SoR, 6 (October, 1970), xix-xxvii.

8101 ________. "Sex & History: Origins of Faulkner's Apocrypha," and "Yoknapatawpha & Faulkner's Fable of Civilization," in The Maker and The Myth: Faulkner and Yoknapatawpha, 1977. Evans Harrington and Ann J. Abadie, eds. Jackson, Miss.: U.P. of Miss., 1978, pp. 43-70, 122-145.

8102 ________. "The Southern Recovery of Memory and History," SR, 82 (Winter, 1974), 1-32.

8103 ________. "William Faulkner and the Fall of New World Man," The Man of Letters in New England and the South. Baton Rouge: Louisiana State U.P., 1973, pp. 167-191.

8104 Sims, Barbara B. "Jaybirds as Portents of Hell in Percy and Faulkner," NMW, 9 (1976), 24-27.

8105 Skaggs, Merrill Maguire. "The Tradition in the Twentieth Century," The Folk of Southern Fiction. Athens: Georgia U.P., 1972, pp. 221-234, passim.

8106 Skard, Sigmund. American Studies in Europe: Their History and Present Organization. 2 vols. Philadelphia: Pennsylvania U.P., 1958, pp. 156, 184, 372, 528, 610.

8107 Skelton, B. J. "Double-Take on Mississippi," SatRL, 34, Pt. 1 (May 19, 1951), 20-21, 33-35.

8108 Skenazy, Paul N. "Inarticulate Characters in Modern American Fiction: A Study of Fitzgerald, Hemingway, and Faulkner," DAI, 34 (Stanford: 1974), 7783A.

8109 Skou-Hansen, Tage. "To slags kaerlighed," Dansk Udsyn, 45 (1965), 241-258.

8110 _______. "William Faulkner," Fremmedc Digtere 1 Det 20 Århundrede. Sven M. Kristensen, ed. Copenhagen: G. E. C. Gad., 1968, II, 279-295.

8111 Skulima, Loni. "Der Nobelpreisträger fur Literature: Versuch einer Darstellung. Der Dichter William Faulkner," DLD, (November 20, 1950), 4.

8112 Slabey, Robert M. "William Faulkner: The 'Waste Land' Phase (1926-1936)," DA, 22 (Notre Dame: 1961), 1632.

8113 Slater, John R. Recent Literature and Religion. New York: Harper, 1938, p. 40.

8114 Slatoff, Walter Jacob. "The Edge of Order: The Pattern of Faulkner's Rhetoric," TCL, 3 (October, 1957), 107-127; repr., in William Faulkner: Four Decades of Criticism. Linda W. Wagner, ed. Michigan State U. P., 1973, pp. 155-179.

8115 _______. "Emphases and Modes of Organization in the Fiction of William Faulkner: A Study in Patterns of Rhetoric and Perception," DA, 16 (Michigan: 1956), 2461-62.

8116 _______. Quest for Failure: A Study of William Faulkner. Ithaca: Cornell U. P., 1960; 2nd pr., 1961.

8117 _______. "The Writer in Perspective," SatRL, 45 (July 28, 1962), 24.

8118 Sleeth, Irene L. "William Faulkner: A Bibliography of Criticism," TCL, 8 (April, 1962), 18-43.

8119 Smart, George K. Religious Elements in Faulkner's Early Novels: A Selective Concordance. (UMPEAL, No. 8.) Coral Gables, Florida: Miami U. P., 1965.

8120 Smith, Bradley. "The Faulkner Country," '48, the Magazine of the Year, 2 (May, 1948), 85-89.

8121 [Smith, Harrison]. "The Duty of the Writer," SatRL, 34 (February 3, 1951), 5.

8122 _______. "Time for a Change," SatRL, 32 (September 17, 1949), 24.

8123 _______. "William Faulkner Versus the Literary Conference," SatRL, 39 (July 7, 1956), 16.

8124 Smith, Helena Maude. "Negro Characterization in the American Novel: A Historical Survey of Work by White Authors," DA, 20 (Pennsylvania State: 1959), 3284.

8125 Smith, Henry Nash. "Notes on Recent Novels," SoR, 2 (1936-37), 583-585.

8126 _______. "William Faulkner and Reality," FS, 2 (Summer, 1953), 17-19.

8127 _______. "Writing Right Smart Fun, Says Faulkner," Dallas Morning News (February 14, 1932), IV, 2.

8128 Smith, James Frederick, Jr. "From Symbol to Character: The Negro in American Fiction of the Twenties," DAI, 33 (Penn. State: 1972), 3672A-73A.

8129 Smith, Kearney I. "Some Romantic Elements in the Works of William Faulkner," DAI, 34 (Georgia: 1974), 4286A.

8130 Smith, Lewis A. "William Faulkner and the Racist Virus," *Annual Reports of Studies. Doshisha Women's College of Liberal Arts.* Vol. 21. Kyoto: Doshisha Women's College, 1970, pp. 388-398.

8131 Smith, Maxwell A. "A Visit to Giono," BA, 33 (Winter, 1959), 23-26.
Jean Giono admired Faulkner as "the greatest of American contemporaries."

8132 Smith, Stella P. "The Evolution of Patterns of Characterization from Faulkner's *Soldiers' Pay* (1926) Through *Absalom, Absalom!* (1936)," DAI, 37 (Texas Tech: 1976), 2881A.

8133 Smith, Thelma M., and Ward L. Miner. "Faulkner," *Transatlantic Migration: The Contemporary American Novel in France.* Durham, North Carolina: Duke U.P., 1955, pp. 122-145.

8134 Smithey, Robert A. "Faulkner and the Status Quo," CLAJ, 11 (December, 1967), 109-116.

8135 Smyth, Joseph Hilton. *To Nowhere and Return: The Autobiography of a Puritan.* New York: Garrick & Evans, 1940, pp. 148-149.

8136 Snell, George. "The Fury of William Faulkner," WestR, 11 (Autumn, 1946), 29-40; repr., in *Shapers of American Fiction.* New York: Dutton & Co., 1947, pp. 87-104.

8137 Snyder, Stephen. "From Words to Images: Five Novelists in Hollywood," CRevAS, 8 (1977), 206-213.

8138 Söderberg, Sten. "Nazismen och den moderna realismen," SamF, (Stockholm), 2 (June-August, 1945), 376-379.

8139 Solomon, Robert H. "Classical Myth in the Novels of William Faulkner," DAI, 36 (Pennsylvania State: 1975), 7428A-29A.

8140 Sosa Lôpez, Emilio. "El problema del mal en William Faulkner," Sur, No. 247 (July-August, 1957), 55-63.

8141 Soulac, Anne-Marie. "William Faulkner," Romanciers amêricains contemporains. (Cahiers des langues modernes, 1.) Paris: Librairie Didier, 1946, pp. 239-249.

8142 "The South: The Authentic Voice," Time, 67 (March 26, 1956), 26-29.

8143 Sowder, William J. "The Concept of Endurance in the Characters of William Faulkner," HPCS, 1 (Spring, 1961), 15-30.

8144 ________. "Faulkner and Existentialism: A Note on the Generalissimo," WSCL, 4 (Spring-Summer, 1963), 163-171. Cf., Walter F. Taylor, ASch, 26 (1957), 471-477.

8145 Spears, James E. "William Faulkner, Folklorist: A Note," TFSB, 38 (December, 1972), 95-96.

8146 Spears, Monroe K. "Les romanciers amêricains devant le public et la critique des Etats-Unis," CLM (dêcembre 1946), 287-313.

8147 Spencer, Benjamin T. "An American Literature Again," SR, 57 (Spring, 1949), 56-72.

8148 ________. "Wherefore This Southern Fiction?" SR, 47 (October-December, 1939), 500-513.

8149 Spender, Stephen. The Destructive Element. Boston: Houghton Mifflin, 1936, pp. 42, 104, 205.

8150 Spiller, Robert, et al. Literary History of the United States. New York: Macmillan, 1948, pp. 1304-1306.

8151 ________. The Third Dimension. New York: Macmillan, 1965, passim.

8152 ________. "The Uses of Memory: Eliot, Faulkner," Cycle of American Literature. New York: Macmillan, 1955, pp. 275-303.

8153 Spinucci, Pietro. "La 'citta' nella narrativa di William Faulkner," Humanitas, 17 (April, 1962), 346-356.

8154 Spivey, Herman E. "Faulkner and the Adamic Myth: Faulkner's Moral Vision," MFS, 19 (Winter, 1973-74), 497-505.

8155 Spratling, William. "Chronicle of a Friendship: William Faulkner in New Orleans," TQ, 9 (Spring, 1966), 34-40.

8156 ________. File on Spratling. Boston: Little, Brown, 1967, pp. 21-34.

8157 ________. Sherwood Anderson and Other Famous Creoles. Austin: Texas U. P., 1966, p. 11, passim.

8158 Springer, Anne Marie. "The American Novel in Germany: A Study of the Critical Reception of Eight American Novelists between the Two World Wars," DA, 20 (Pennsylvania: 1959), 308.

8159 ________. The American Novel in Germany. Hamburg: Cram, de Gruyter & Co., 1960, passim.

8160 Stafford, William T. "Hemingway/Faulkner: Marlin and Catfish?" SoR, 6 (October, 1970), 1191-1200.

8161 Stallman, Robert W. "William Faulkner," Critiques and Essays on Modern Fiction, 1920-1951. John W. Aldridge, ed. New York: Ronald P., 1952, pp. 582-586.

8162 Stanford, Raney. "Of Mules and Men: Faulkner and Silone," Discourse, 6 (Winter, 1962-63), 73-78.

8163 Starke, Aubrey. "An American Comedy," Colophon, 5 (December, 1934), 19.

8164 Starke, Catherine J. Black Portraiture in American Fiction. New York: Basic Bks., 1971, passim.

8165 Stateman, Robert. "William Faulkner," Critiques and Essays on Modern Fiction. John W. Aldridge, ed. New York: Ronald P., 1952, pp. 582-586.

8166 Stavrou, C. N. "Ambiguity in Faulkner's Affirmation," Personalist, 40 (Spring, 1959), 169-177.

8167 Stecenko, E. A. "Xudožestvennoe vremja v romanax U. Folknera," FN, 19, iv (1977), 36-46.
Artistic time in Faulkner's novels.

8168 Steene, Birgitta. "William Faulkner and the Myth of the American South," ModSpr, 54, #3 (1960), 271-279.

8169 Stegner, Wallace, ed. Preface. The American Novel: From James Fenimore Cooper to William Faulkner. New York: Basic Books, 1965, pp. 219-228.

8170 ________. The Writer in America. Tokyo: Hokuseido Press, 1952, passim.

8171 Stein, Jean. "The Art of Fiction: William Faulkner," ParisR, 12 (Spring, 1956), 28-52; repr., in Writers at Work.

Malcolm Cowley, ed. New York: Viking, 1958, pp. 119-141.

8172 _______. "El arte de novelar: Diálogo con William Faulkner," Sur, No. 245 (Spring, 1957), 39-56.

8173 Stein, Randolph E. "The World Outside Yoknapatawpha: A Study of Five Novels by William Faulkner," DA, 26 (Ohio: 1965), 2225.

8174 Steinbeck, Elaine, and Robert Wallsten, eds. <u>Steinbeck: A Life in Letters</u>. New York: Viking, 1975.
Letters comment on Faulkner, and a letter from Faulkner is quoted.

8175 Steinberg, Aaron. "Faulkner and the Negro," DA, 27 (N. Y. U.: 1966), 1385A.

8176 Steinmetz-Schünemann, H. <u>Die Bedeutung der Zeit in den Romanen von Marguerite Duras: Unter besonderer Berücksichtigung des Einflusses von Faulkner und Hemingway</u>. Amsterdam: Rodopi, 1976.

8177 Stern, Richard G. "Faulkner at Home," BA, 39 (Autumn, 1965), 409-411.
Faulkner from the Italian point of view.

8178 Stevick, Philip, ed. <u>The Theory of the Novel</u>. New York: Free Press, 1967; London: Collier-Macmillan, 1967, <u>passim</u>.

8179 Stewart, David H. "Faulkner, Sholokhov, and Regional Dissent in Modern Literature. <u>Proceedings of the Comparative Literature Symposium</u>. Vol. IV. <u>William Faulkner: Prevailing Verities and World Literature</u>. Wolodymyr T. Zyla and Wendell M. Aycock, eds. Lubbock: Interdept. Comm. on Comp. Lit. Texas Tech U., 1973, pp. 135-150.

8180 _______. "William Faulkner and Mikhail Sholokhov: A Comparative Study of Two Representatives of the Regional Conscience, Their Affinities and Meanings," DA, 19 (Michigan: 1959), 3309-10.

8181 Stewart, Jean. "The Novels of William Faulkner," CamR, 54, #1330 (March 10, 1933), 310-312.

8182 Stewart, Randall. <u>American Literature and Christian Doctrine</u>. Baton Rouge: Louisiana State U. P., 1958, pp. 136-142.

8183 _______. "Hawthorne and Faulkner," CE, 17 (February, 1956), 258-262.

8184 _______. "1956: Hawthorne and Faulkner," CE, 22 (No-

vember, 1960), 128-132.
"... We see these two writers, ... as working in the orthodox Christian tradition, a tradition which posits original sin...."

8185 _______. "The Old Cost of Human Redemption," Regionalism and Beyond: Essays of Randall Stewart. George Core, ed. Nashville: Vanderbilt U.P., 1968, pp. 204-211.

8186 _______. "The Outlook for Southern Writing: Diagnosis and Prognosis," VQR, 31 (Spring, 1955), 252-263.

8187 _______. "Poetically the Most Accurate Man Alive," ModA, 6 (Winter, 1961-62), 81-90.

8188 _______. "The Vision of Evil in Hawthorne and Faulkner," The Tragic Vision and the Christian Faith. Nathan A. Scott, Jr., ed. New York: Association Press, 1957, pp. 238-263.

8189 Stineback, David Ceburn. "Social Change and Nostalgia in Ten American Novels," DAI, 31 (Yale: 1969), 1242A-43A.

8190 Stone, Edward. Voices of Despair: Four Motifs in American Literature. Athens: Ohio U.P., 1966, passim.

8191 _______. "William Faulkner," A Certain Morbidness: A View of American Literature. Carbondale and Edwardsville: Southern Ill. U.P., 1969; London: Feffer & Simons, 1969, pp. 85-120.

8192 Stone, Emily W. "Faulkner Gets Started," TQ, 8 (Winter, 1965), 142-148.

8193 _______. "How a Writer Finds His Material," Harpers, 231 (November, 1965), 157-161.

8194 Stone, Phil. "Faulkner Classified," Memphis Commercial Appeal (November 19, 1950), V, 3.

8195 _______. "Faulkner Publication," SatRL, 42 (June 27, 1959), 23.

8196 _______. "William Faulkner and His Neighbors," SatRL, 25 (September 19, 1942), 12.

8197 _______. "William Faulkner, the Man and His Work," Oxford Mag., Copies 1, 2, 3 (1934); repr., by James B. Meriwether, "Early Notices of Faulkner by Phil Stone and Louis B. Cochran," MissQ, 17 (Summer, 1964), 136-164.

8198 Stoneback, Harry Robert. "The Hillfolk Tradition and Images of the Hillfolk in American Fiction Since 1926," DAI, 31 (Vanderbilt: 1970), 2942A.

8199 Stonum, Gary Lee. "William Faulkner: The Dynamics of Form," DAI, 34 (Johns Hopkins: 1973), 3433A.

8200 Strandberg, Victor. "Between Truth and Fact: Faulkner's Symbols of Identity," MFS, 21 (Autumn, 1975), 445-457.

8201 ________. "Faulkner's Poor Parson and the Technique of Invasion," SR, 73 (Spring, 1965), 181-190.

8202 Strauch, Carl F. "The Crisis in Modern Literature," CE, 5 (May 5, 1944), 423-428.

8203 Straumann, Heinrich. "The Early Reputation of Faulkner's Work in Europe: A Tentative Appraisal," _English Studies Today_. Ilva Cellini and Giorgio Melchiori, eds. 4th Series. Roma: Edizioni di Storia e Letteratura, 1966, pp. 443-459.

8204 ________. "The Psychological Approach to Fiction: William Faulkner," _American Literature in the Twentieth Century_. 3rd ed., rev. New York and Evanston: Harper & Row, 1965, pp. 86-93, _passim_.

8205 ________. "William Faulkner," _American Literature in the Twentieth Century_. London: Hutchinson House, 1951, pp. 86-89.

8206 ________. _William Faulkner_. Frankfurt: Athenäum, 1968.

8207 Strickland, Carol Ann C. "The Search for the Father in Selected American Novels," DAI, 35 (Michigan: 1973), 418A-19A.

8208 Strong, L. A. G. "Mr. Faulkner Again," Spectator, 146 (April 25, 1931), 674.

8209 Strozier, Robert. "Some Versions of Faulkner's Pastoral," ForumH, 5 (Summer, 1967), 35-40.

8210 Stubblefield, Charles F. "A Freight of Faith and Hope: A Study of the Quest in the American Novel," DA, 28 (Denver: 1968), 4146.

8211 Stuckey, W. J. _The Pulitzer Prize Novels: A Critical Backward Look_. Norman: Oklahoma U.P., 1966, pp. 151-152, _passim_.

8212 Stylites, Simeon (pseud.). "In the Name of Allah, Figs!" ChrC, 68 (January 10, 1951), 41.
Cf., Maynard Kniskern. "In Defense of Faulkner," ChrC, 68 (January 24, 1951), 114.

8213 Styron, William. "The Art of Fiction," ParisR, 5 (Spring, 1954), 42-57.

8214 ________. "William Faulkner's Beisetzung," Englische Jahrbuch (1963), 124-130.

8215 Subramanyam, N. S. "William Faulkner's Prose Style," Calcutta Review, 1 (April-June, 1976), 41-53.

8216 Sugg, Redding S., Jr. "John Faulkner's Vanishing South," AH, 22 (April, 1971), 65-75.
References to William Faulkner.

8217 ________. "John Faulkner's Yoknapatawpha," SAQ, 68 (Summer, 1969), 343-362.

8218 Sullivan, Barbara White. "A Gallery of Grotesques: The Alienation Theme in the Works of Hawthorne, Twain, Anderson, Faulkner, and Wolfe," DA, 30 (Georgia: 1969), 698A-99A.

8219 Sullivan, Frank. "A Distinguished Commuter," SatRL, 34 (June 9, 1951), 4.

8220 Sullivan, Walter. "Allen Tate, Flem Snopes, and the Last Years of William Faulkner," Death by Melancholy: Essays on Modern Southern Fiction. Baton Rouge: Louisiana State U.P., 1972, pp. 3-21, passim.

8221 ________. "The Decline of Myth in Souther Fiction," SoR, 12, #1 (Winter, 1976), 16-31.

8222 ________. A Requiem for the Renascence: The State of Fiction in the Modern South. Athens: Univ. of Georgia Press, 1976.

8223 ________. "Southern Novelists and the Civil War," Southern Renascence. L. D. Rubin and Robt. Jacobs, eds. Baltimore: Johns Hopkins U.P., 1953, 1966, pp. 112-125.

8224 ________. "Southern Writers in the Modern World: Death by Melancholy," SoR, 6 (October, 1970), 907-919.

8225 Sullivan, William Patrick. "William Faulkner and the Community," DA, 22 (Columbia: 1961), 4355.

8226 Summers, Marcia P. "The Use of Subordinate Characters as Dramatized Narrators in Twentieth-Century Novels," DAI, 30 (Illinois: 1970), 3024A-25A.

8227 Sutherland, Donald. "Time on Our Hands," YFS, No. 10 (1953), 5-13.

8228 Sutton, George William. "Primitivism in the Fiction of William Faulkner," DA, 28 (Mississippi: 1967), 695A-96A.

8229 Suyama, Shizuo. "William Faulkner," Eibei Bungaku (Meiji University) 4 (August, 1959), 68-98.
The doomed characters in Faulkner's novels.

8230 Swallow, Alan. "A General Introduction to Faulkner Studies," FS, 1 (Spring, 1952), 1-3.

8231 Swanson, William J. "William Faulkner and William Styron: Notes on Religion," CimR, No. 7 (March, 1969), 45-52.

8232 Swiggart, Peter. The Art of Faulkner's Novels. Austin: Texas U. P., 1962.

8233 _______. Time and Structure in the Novels of William Faulkner. Diss. Yale: 1954.

8234 _______. "Time in Faulkner's Novels," MFS, 1 (May, 1955), 25-29.

8235 _______. "Two Faulkner Critics," SR, 62 (Autumn, 1954), 696-705.
Irving Howe. William Faulkner: A Critical Study, and William Van O'Connor. The Tangled Fire of William Faulkner.

8236 Swink, Helen M. "The Oral Tradition in Yoknapatawpha County," DA, 30 (Virginia: 1970), 3920A.

8237 _______. "William Faulkner: The Novelist as Oral Narrator," GaR, 26 (Summer, 1972), 183-209.

8238 Szpotanski, Zenon. "Slowacki a Faulkner," Znak, 20, iv (1968), 495-501.

8239 Takahashi, Masao. The World of William Faulkner. Tokyo: Kenkyusha, 1958.

8240 Takigawa, Motoo. "From Anderson to Hemingway and Faulkner," English and American Literature (Kwansel Gakuin University), 7 (October, 1962), 68-75.

8241 _______. "The Relationship between God and Human Beings in American Literature," SELit, 53 (1976), 59-73.

8242 Tallack, Douglas G. "William Faulkner and the Tradition of Tough-Guy Fiction," Dimensions of Detective Fiction. Larry N. Landrum, Pat Browne, and Ray B. Browne, eds. Bowling Green, OH: Popula Pr., 1976, pp. 247-264.

8243 Tanner, Jimmie Eugene. "The Twentieth Century Impressionistic Novel: Conrad and Faulkner," DA, 25 (Oklahoma: 1964), 1927.

8244 Tanner, Tony. "Butterflies and Beetles: Conrad's Two Truths," ChiR, 16, i (1963), 123-140.

8245 Tarrant, Desmond. "The Rise of the American Novel," Humanist, 76 (August, 1961), 235-236.

8246 Tate, Allen. Collected Essays. Denver: Swallow, 1959, passim.

8247 _______. Memoirs and Opinions, 1926-1974. Chicago: Swallow Press, 1975, pp. 82-86.

8248 _______. "The New Provincialism," VQR, 21 (Spring, 1945), 262-272.

8249 _______. "The Novel in the American South," NSt, 57 (June 13, 1959), 831-832.

8250 _______. On the Limits of Poetry: Selected Essays, 1928-1948. New York: Swallow and Wm. Morrow, 1948, p. 303.

8251 _______. "A Southern Mode of the Imagination," Essays of Four Decades. Chicago: Swallow Press, 1968, pp. 577-592.

8252 _______. "William Faulkner," NSt, 64 (September 28, 1962), 408.

8253 _______. "William Faulkner: 1897-1962," SR, 71 (January-March, 1963), 160-164.

8254 Taylor, Nancy Dew. "The River of Faulkner and Mark Twain," MissQ, 16 (Fall, 1963), 191-199.

8255 Taylor, Walter. "Faulkner: Nineteenth-Century Notions of Racial Mixture and the Twentieth-Century Imagination," SCR, 10 (November, 1977), 57-66.

8256 Taylor, Walter Fuller. "Faulkner: Social Commitment and Artistic Temperament," SoR, 6 (Autumn, 1970), 1075-1092.

8257 _______. "The Roles of the Negro in William Faulkner's Fiction," DA, 25 (Emory: 1965), 2990.

8258 _______. "William Faulkner: A Wider Range," The Story of American Letters. Chicago: Henry Regnery, 1956, pp. 471-481.

8259 "This Is William Faulkner's Homeland, People," Newsweek, 49 (May 6, 1957), 116-117.

8260 Thomas, Frank H., III. "The Search for Identity of Faulkner's Black Characters," DAI, 33 (Pittsburgh: 1972), 6935A.

8261 Thomas, Henri. "Notre grand-père Faulkner," NRF, 9 (January, 1961), 30-40.

8262 Thompson, Alan R. "The Cult of Cruelty," Bookman, 74 (January-February, 1932), 477-487.

8263 Thompson, Evelyn J. "William Faulkner's Yoknapatawpha: The Land of Broken Dreams," DAI, 33 (Texas Tech.: 1972), 4435A-36A.

8264 Thompson, James, et al. "A Very Stern Discipline," Harpers, 234 (March, 1967), 76-95.

8265 Thompson, Lawrance. "A Defense of Difficulties in William Faulkner's Art," Carrell, 4 (December, 1963), 7-19.

8266 ________. "Redeemed and Unredeemed," NYTBR (December 8, 1963), 4.

8267 ________. William Faulkner: An Introduction and Interpretation. New York: Barnes & Noble, 1963; 2nd ed. Holt, Rinehart & Winston, 1967.

8268 Thornton, Patricia Elizabeth. "The Prison of Gender: Sexual Roles in Major American Novels of the 1920's," DAI, 37 (New Brunswick, Canada: 1976), 7133A-34A.

8269 Thorp, Willard. "Mr. Faulkner in the Classroom," NYHTBR (January 31, 1960), 1, 11.

8270 ________. "Southern Renaissance: William Faulkner," American Writing in the Twentieth Century. Cambridge: Harvard U.P., 1960, pp. 263-274.

8271 ________. "What Have American Novelists Achieved?" NYHTBR (April 3, 1960), 5.

8272 Tindall, George Brown. "Tradition and Transition: The Southern Renaissance," The Emergency of the New South: 1913-1945. Wendell Holmes Stephenson, and E. Merton Coulter. Louisiana St. U.P., 1967, pp. 653-657, 669-670, passim.

8273 Tinkle, Lon. "William Faulkner and the Dallas News," Dallas Morning News (July 14, 1957), VII, 5.

8274 Tischler, Nancy M. Black Masks: Negro Characters in Modern Southern Fiction. University Park: Penn. St. U.P., 1969, passim.

8275 Tischler, Nancy P. "William Faulkner and the Southern Negro," SUS, 7 (June, 1965), 261-265.

8276 Tolliver, Kenneth R. "Truth and the Poet," DeltaR, 2 (July-August, 1965), 48, 67-69.

8277 Tololyan, Khachig. "The Cosmographic Strain in Narrative: From Homer to Faulkner, Joyce and Butor," DAI, 37 (Brown: 1975), 303A.

8278 Tomlinson, T. B. "Faulkner and American Sophistication," MCR, No. 7 (1964), 92-103.

8279 Toynbee, Philip. "Faulkner: Poet of the South," Observer (London), (July 8, 1962), 24.

8280 _______. "William Faulkner, Alas!" Observer (February 1, 1959).

8281 Tran, Phiet Qui. "The French and Faulkner: The Reception of William Faulkner's Writing in France and Its Influence on Modern French Literature," DAI, 38, #7 (Austin, Texas: 1977), 4162A.

8282 Trêdant, Paul. "Faulkner à Paris," NL (14 dêcembre 1950), 1.

8283 Trilling, Lionel. "Contemporary American Literature in Its Relation to Ideas," AmQ, 1 (Fall, 1949), 195-208; repr., in The American Writer and the European Tradition. Margaret Denney, ed. Minneapolis: Minnesota U. P., 1950, pp. 132-153; revised for The Liberal Imagination. Garden City: Doubleday, 1950, pp. 281-303.

8284 _______. "Manners, Morals, and the Novel," KR, 10 (Winter, 1948), 11-27; repr. Forms of Modern Fiction. William Van O'Connor, ed. Minneapolis: Minnesota U. P., 1948.

8285 Trimmer, Joseph Francis. "A portrait of the Artist in Motion: A Study of the Artist-Surrogates in the Novels of William Faulkner," DA, 29 (Purdue: 1968), 3623A.

8286 _______. Review: Elizabeth Kerr's Yoknapatawpha: Faulkner's 'Little Postage Stamp of Native Soil,' MFS, 17 (Summer, 1971, 284.

8287 Tritschler, Donald H. "The Unity of Faulkner's Shaping Vision," MFS, 5 (Winter, 1959-60), 337-343.

8288 _______. "Whorls of Form in Faulkner's Fiction," DA, 17 (Northwestern: 1957), 3025.

8289 Trobaugh, Robert J. "The Nature of Man in the Writings of Reinhold Niebuhr and William Faulkner," DA, 27 (Vanderbilt: 1966), 1441A-42A.

8290 Trowbridge, William Leigh. "Myth and Dream in the Novels of William Faulkner," DAI, 36 (Vanderbilt: 1975), 4498A-99A.

8291 Tuck, Dorothy. Crowell's Handbook of Faulkner. New York: Crowell, 1964. Repr., 1969.

8292 Tumulty, Michael J., C.M. "Youth and Innocence in the Novels of William Faulkner," DAI, 34 (St. John's: 1974), 4292A.

8293 Turner, Arlin. "The Southern Novel," SWR, 25 (January, 1940), 205-212.

8294 _______. "William Faulkner and the Literary Flowering in the American South," DUJ, 29 (March, 1968), 109-118.

8295 _______. "William Faulkner, Southern Novelist," MissQ, 14 (Summer, 1961), 117-130.

8296 Turner, Darwin T. "Faulkner and Slavery," The South and Faulkner's Yoknapatawpha. Harrington, Evans, and Ann J Abadie, eds. Jackson: Miss. U.P., 1977, pp. 62-85.

8297 Tuttleton, James W. "The American Novelist: His Time and Place," YR, 62 (December, 1972), 305-307.

8298 Twigg, Carol Ann. "The Social Role of Faulkner's Women: A Materialist Interpretation," DAI, 39, #3 (Buffalo, New York: 1978), 1578A.

8299 Ulanov, Barry. "The Novel," and "The Short Story," The Two Worlds of American Art: The Private and the Popular. New York: Macmillan, 1965, pp. 196-198, 272-275.

8300 Ulich, Michaela. Perspektive und Erzählstruktur in William Faulkners Romanen. Beihefte zum Jahrbuch für amerika-studien. Heidelberg: Carl Winter, 1972.

8301 Ulmann, André. "Sur la littérature américaine: Faulkner," Etoiles (15 octobre 1946), 5.

8302 Untermeyer, Louis. "William Faulkner," Makers of the Modern World. New York: Simon & Schuster, 1955, pp. 702-711.

8303 Urie, Margaret Ann. "The Problem of Evil: The Myth of Man's Fall and Redemption in the Works of William Faulkner," DAI, 39 (Nevada, Reno: 1978), 4943A.

8304 Utterback, Sylvia W. "Kierkegaard and Faulkner," MissQ, 26, #3 (Summer, 1973), 421-435.

8305 Vallette, Jacques. "Un Apologue à la gloire de l'homme," MdF, 325 (October, 1955), 330-334.

8306 Vance, Eleanor Graham. "Modern Men of Letters: William Faulkner," SatRL, 32, Pt. 1 (January 22, 1949), 30.
Satiric verse.

8307 Van Cromphout, Gustaav V. "Faulkner: Myth and Motion," ES, 53 (December, 1972), 572-574.
Essay-review of Richard P. Adams. Faulkner: Myth and Motion.

8308 Van Der Krolf, J. M. "Zen and the American Experience," VBQ, 25 (Autumn, 1959), 122-132.

8309 Vandiver, Frank L., ed. The Idea of the South. Chicago: Chicago U.P., 1964, passim.

8310 Van Doren, Carl. The American Novel. New York: Macmillan, 1955, pp. 325, 354-356, 359.

8311 ________, and Mark Van Doren. American and British Literature Since 1890, 2nd ed. New York: Appleton-Century, 1939, pp. 102-103, 365.

8312 Van Doren, Mark. "The Art of American Fiction," Nation, 138 (April 25, 1934), 471-474.

8313 Van Nostrand, Albert D. "The Poetic Dialogues of William Faulkner," Everyman His Own Poet: Romantic Gospels in American Literature. New York: McGraw-Hill, 1968, pp. 175-196.

8314 Vare, Robert. "Oxford, Miss., Which William Faulkner Transcended, Is As He Left It," NYTimes (January 14, 1973), Sec. 20, 3, 11.

8315 Vargas Saavedra, Luis. "La afinidad de onetti a Faulkner," CHA, 292-94 (1974), 257-265.

8316 Vaucher-Zananiri, Nelly. "William Faulkner, romancier saturnin," Voix d'Amérique: Etudes sur la Litterature americaine d'aujourd'hui. Le Caire: R. Schindler, 1945, pp. 29-31.

8317 Vernon, Grenville. "Fallen Angel?" Cw, 15 (January 20, 1932), 332-333.

8318 Vest, David C. "Perpetual Salvage: The Historical Consciousness in Modern Southern Literature," DAI, 34 (Vanderbilt: 1974), 5209A-10A.

8319 Vickery, John B., ed. Introduction. Myth and Literature:

Contemporary Theory and Practice. Lincoln: Nebraska U. P., 1966, *passim*.

8320 ________. "William Faulkner and Sir Philip Sidney," MLN, 70 (May, 1955), 349-350.

8321 Vickery, Olga W. "Faulkner," *American Literary Scholarship: An Annual/1968*. J. Albert Robbins, ed. Durham, North Carolina: Duke U. P., 1970, pp. 100-106.

8322 ________. "Faulkner and the Contours of Time," GaR, 12 (Summer, 1958), 192-201.

8323 ________. "Language As Theme and Technique," *Modern American Fiction: Essays in Criticism*. A. Walton Litz, ed. New York: Oxford U. P., 1963, pp. 179-193.

8324 ________. *The Novels of William Faulkner: A Critical Interpretation*. Rev. ed. Baton Rouge: Louisiana State U. P., 1964.

8325 ________. *The Novels of William Faulkner: Patterns of Perspective*. Diss. Wisconsin: 1955.

8326 ________. The Novels of William Faulkner: Patterns of Perspective," SDD-UW, 15 (1955), 624-626.

8327 ________. "William Faulkner," ConL, 9 (Spring, 1968), 254-260.

8328 ________. "William Faulkner and the Figure in the Carpet," SAQ, 63 (Summer, 1964), 318-335; repr., SAQ, 76 (Autumn, 1977), 479-496.

8329 Viertel, Tom. "Mr. Faulkner's Position on Equality," Coastlines, 5 (Summer, 1956), 33-43.

8330 Visentin, Giovanni. "Considerazioni su un ladro di cavilli," FLe, 23 (June 10, 1951), 1.

8331 "The Visitor to the University of Virginia," Time, 69, #8 (February 25, 1957), 72, 75.

8332 Vittorini, Elio. "Da Conrad a Faulkner," Omnibus, 4 (October, 1938); a shorter version in *Diario in pubblico*. Milano: Bompiani, 1957, p. 97.

8333 ________. "Faulkner come Picasso?" La Stampa (Dicembre 8, 1950); repr., in *William Faulkner: Venti Anni Di Critica*. Frederick J. Hoffman and Olga Vickery, eds. Parma: Guanda, 1957, pp. 162-164.

8334 ________. "William Faulkner: *Oggi si vola*," Letteratura, 1 (July, 1937), 174-175.

8335 Vizioli, Paolo. "Guimarães Rosa e William Faulkner, ESPSL, 11 (April, 1970), 1.

8336 Vogel, Stanley M., and Ella M. Murphy. "William Faulkner," An Outline of American Literature. Boston: Student Outlines, 1961, II, 268-281.

8337 Volpe, Edmond L. A Reader's Guide to William Faulkner. New York: Farrar, Straus and Giroux, 1964; Noonday Press, 1971.

8338 Von Einsiedel, Wolfgang. "Revolte des Menschensohnes: zu William Faulkners 'Eine Legende,'" Merkur, 10 (March, 1955), 282-290.

8339 _______. "William Faulkner," Europäische, 11 (1935), 707-708.

8340 Von Heiseler, Bernt. "Neue Amerikaner," Deutsche Zeitschrift, 49 (1936), 468-469.

8341 Vorpahl, Ben Merchant. "Such Stuff As Dreams Are Made On: History, Myth and the Comic Vision of Mark Twain and William Faulkner," DA, 28 (Wisconsin: 1966), 698A.

8342 Voss, Arthur. "Virtuoso Storyteller: William Faulkner," The American Short Story. Norman, Oklahoma U.P., 1973, pp. 242-261, passim.

8343 Wagenknecht, Edward Charles. "William Faulkner," Cavalcade of the American Novel. New York: Henry Holt, 1952, repr., 1962, pp. 417-425.

8344 Wager, Willia. American Literature: A World View. New York: New York U.P., 1968, pp. 235-238.

8345 Waggoner, Hyatt H. "Faulkner's Critics," Novel, 3 (Fall, 1969), 94-96.

8346 _______. "Hemingway and Faulkner: The End of Something," SoR, 4 (Spring, 1968), 458-466.

8347 _______. "Romanticism and Stoicism in the American Novel: From Melville to Hemingway, and After," Diogenes, No. 23 (Fall, 1958), [105].

8348 _______. "William Faulkner: The Definition of Man," BBr, 18 (March, 1958), 116-124.

8349 _______. William Faulkner: From Jefferson to the World. Lexington: Kentucky U.P., 1959.

8350 _______. "William Faulkner's Passion Week of the Heart,"

The Tragic Vision and the Christian Faith. Nathan A. Scott, ed. New York: Association Pr., 1957, pp. 306-323; revised, 1959, pp. 238-266.

8351 Wagner, Geoffrey. "American Fiction in England," Adelphi, 28, #4 (3rd Qt., 1952), 663-672.

8352 Wagner, Linda Welshimer. "Codes and Codicils: Faulkner's Last Novels," *Itinerary, 3: Criticism.* Frank Baldanza, ed. Bowling Green, Ohio: Bowling Green U.P., 1977, pp. 1-9.

8353 ________. "Faulkner and Women" and "Faulkner and Southern Women," *The South and Faulkner's Yoknapatawpha.* Evans Harrington, ed. Jackson, Miss.: Miss. U.P., 1977, pp. 147-151, 128-146.

8354 ________. "Faulkner's Fiction: Studies in Organic Form," JNT, 1 (January, 1971), 1-14.

8355 ________. *Hemingway and Faulkner: Inventors/Masters.* Metuchen, New Jersey: Scarecrow Press, 1975.
Technique and theme in the two writers compared.

8356 ________, ed. Introduction. *William Faulkner: Four Decades of Criticism.* East Lansing: Michigan St. U.P., 1973.

8357 ________. "The Poetry in American Fiction," *Prospects: Annual of American Cultural Studies,* 2. New York: Burt Franklin & Co., Inc., 1975, pp. 513-526.

8358 ________. "Tension and Technique: The Years of Greatness," SAF, 5 (Spring, 1977), 65-77.

8359 Walcutt, Charles C. *American Literary Naturalism: A Divided Stream.* Minneapolis: Minnesota U.P., 1956, pp. 64-65, 300-301.

8360 ________. *Man's Changing Mask: Modes and Methods of Characterization in Fiction.* Minneapolis: Minnesota U.P., 1966, *passim.*

8361 Wald, Jerry. "Faulkner and Hollywood," Films in Review, 10 (March, 1959), 129-133.

8362 ________. "From Faulkner to Film," SatRL, 42 (March 7, 1959), 16, 42.

8363 Waldman, Milton. "Tendencies of the Modern Novel, America," FnR, 140 (December, 1933), 717-725; repr., *Tendencies of the Modern Novel.* Freeport, New York: Bks. for Libraries P., 1967. 50, 56-59.

8364 Walhout, Clarence. "The Earth Is the Lord's: Religion in Faulkner," CSR, 4 (1975), 26-35.

8365 Walker, Emma Clement. "A Study of the Fiction of Hemingway and Faulkner in a College Sophomore English Class," DAI, 30 (Ohio State: 1969), 4212A-13A.

8366 Wall, Carey G. "Faulkner's Rhetoric," DA, 25 (Stanford: 1965), 5947.

8367 Walravens, Jan. "Faulkner, na overlijden," VlG, 46 (1962), 677-678.

8368 Walser, Richard, ed. Preface. The Enigma of Thomas Wolfe. Cambridge: Harvard U.P., 1953, p. vii.
Quotes letter from Faulkner as to Faulkner's estimate of Thomas Wolfe.

8369 _______. Thomas Wolfe: An Introduction and Interpretation. New York: Barnes & Noble, 1961, passim.

8370 Ward, Alfred Charles. "William Faulkner," American Literature, 1880-1930. London, New York: Methuen & Co., 1932, pp. 153-156.

8371 Warren, Robert Penn. "Cowley's Faulkner," NR, 115 (August 12, 1946), 176-180; repr., in Three Decades of Criticism. Hoffman and Vickery, eds. 1960, pp. 109-124; Literature in America. P. Rahv, ed., pp. 415-430.

8372 _______. "Faulkner: The South and the Negro," SoR, 1, n.s. (July, 1965), 501-529.

8373 _______. "Introduction: Faulkner, Past and Present," Faulkner: A Collection of Critical Essays. Englewood Cliffs, New Jersey: Prentice-Hall, 1966, pp. 1-22.

8374 _______. "Introduction à William Faulkner," RLM, Part II, Nos. 40-42 (1958-59), 205-230.

8375 _______. "The Portable Faulkner," The Critic as Artist: Essays on Books, 1920-1970. Gilbert A. Harrison, ed. New York: Liveright, 1972, pp. 358-377.

8376 _______. "T. S. Stribling: A Paragraph in the History of Critical Realism," AmR, 2 (November, 1933; March, 1934), 483-486.

8377 _______. "Thèmes de William Faulkner," Revue Internationale (février 1947), 140-148.

8378 _______. "William Faulkner," Literature in America. Philip Rahv, ed. New York: Meridian, 1957, pp. 415-430.

8378a ________. "William Faulkner: A Life on Paper," TV Guide, 27, # 50 (December 15, 1979), 12-14, A43.

8379 ________. "William Faulkner (1946-1950)," Selected Essays of Robert Penn Warren. L. W. Wagner, ed. New York: Random House, 1958, pp. 59-79.

8380 ________. "William Faulkner," Forms of Modern Fiction. Wm. Van O'Connor, ed. Minneapolis: Minnesota U. P., 1948, pp. 125-143.

8381 ________. "Within the Traditional World There Had Been a Notion of Truth," Idea of the American Novel. Louis D. Rubin, Jr., and J. R. Moore, eds. New York: Crowell, 1961, pp. 359-363.

8382 ________. "William Faulkner," Modern American Fiction: Essays in Criticism. A. Walton Litz, ed. New York: Oxford U. P., 1963, pp. 150-165.

8383 ________. "The Writer in Perspective," SatRL, 45 (July 28, 1962), 22-23.

8384 Wasiolek, Edward. "The Past Reconstituted," Novel, 10 (Winter, 1977), 182-184.

8385 Wasser, Henry. "Faulkner as Artist," Commentary, 18 (December, 1954), 569-570.

8386 ________. "Reply," Commentary, 18 (September, 1954), 569-570.

Cf., N. Podhoretz. "William Faulkner and the Problem of War," Commentary, 18 (September, 1954), 227-232.

8387 Waters, Maureen Anne. "The Role of Women in Faulkner's Yoknapatawpha," DAI, 36 (Columbia: 1975), 332A.

8388 Watkins, Evan. The Critical Act: Criticism and Community. New Haven: Yale U. P., 1978, pp. 188-212.

8389 Watkins, Floyd C. "Delta Hunt," SWR, 45 (Summer, 1960), 266-272.

Description of setting and models for characters in Faulkner's hunting stories.

8390 ________. "Faulkner and His Critics," TSLL, 10 (Summer, 1968), 317-329.

8391 ________. The Flesh and the Word: Eliot, Hemingway, Faulkner. Nashville: Vanderbilt U. P., 1971.

8392 ________. "The Gentle Reader and Mr. Faulkner's Morals," GaR, 13 (Spring, 1959), 68-75.

8393 ________. "Habet: Faulkner and the Ownership of Property," Faulkner: Fifty Years After The Marble Faun. George H. Wolfe, ed. Tuscaloosa: Alabama U.P., 1976, pp. 123-137.

8394 ________. "Through a Glass Darkly: Recent Faulkner Studies," SR, 85 (Summer, 1977), 484-493.

8395 ________. "William Faulkner in His Own Country," EUQ, 15 (December, 1959), 228-239.

8396 ________. "William Faulkner, the Individual, and the World," GaR, 14 (Fall, 1960), 238-247.

8397 Watson, James G. "Faulkner: Short Story Structures and Reflexive Forms," Mosaic, 11 (Summer, 1978), 127.

8398 ________. "'If Was Existed': Faulkner's Prophets and the Patterns of History," MFS, 21 (Winter, 1975-76), 499-507.

8399 Way, Brian. "William Faulkner," CritQ, 3 (Spring, 1961), 42-53.

8400 Weatherby, Hal L. "Jude the Victorian," SHR, 1 (Summer, 1967), 158-169.
Comparison of Jude and Quentin Compson.

8401 Webb, Gerald F. "Jeffersonian Agrarianism in Faulkner's Yoknapatawpha: The Evolution of Social and Economic Standard," DAI, 33 (Florida State: 1973), 5754A.

8402 Webb, James W. "A Review: Elizabeth Kerr's Yoknapatawpha: Faulkner's 'Little Postage Stamp of Native Soil,'" SAQ, 66 (Spring, 1970), 300-301.

8403 ________. "Rowan Oak, Faulkner's Golden Bough," UMSE, 6 (1965), 39-47.

8404 ________, and A. Wigfall Green, eds. Preface. William Faulkner of Oxford. Baton Rouge: Louisiana St. U.P., 1965.

8405 Weber, Robert. "Aspekte der Faulkner-Kritik in Frankreich," JA, 6 (1961), 152-167.

8406 Weeks, Willis Earl. "Faulkner's Young Males: From Futility to Responsibility," DAI, 34 (Arizona St: 1973), 2663A.

8407 Wegelin, Christof. "'Endure' and 'Prevail': Faulkner's Modification of Conrad," N&Q, 21 (October, 1974), 375-376.

8408 Weidlé, Wladimir. "Notes," Cahiers de la Pléiade (printemps 1949), 52-53.

8409 Weigel, John A. "Teaching the Modern Novel: From *Finnegans Wake* to *A Fable*," CE, 21 (December, 1959), 172-173.

8410 Weingart, Seymour Leonard. "The Form and Meaning of the Impressionist Novel," DA, 26 (California, Davis: 1965), 1656.

8411 Weinstein, Arnold Louis. *The Reconstructive Mode in Fiction: A Study of Faulkner and the French New Novel*. Diss. Harvard: 1968.

8412 _______. *Vision and Response in Modern Fiction*. Ithaca: Cornell U. P., 1974, *passim*.

8413 Weinstein, Philip M. "Caddy *Disparue*: Exploring an Episode Common to Proust and Faulkner," CLS, 14 (1977), 38-52.

8414 Weisgerber, Jean. *Faulkner and Dostoevsky: Influence and Confluence*. Dean McWilliams, tr. Athens: Ohio U. P., 1974.

8415 _______. "Faulkner et Dostoievski," RLC, 39 (July-September, 1965), 406-421.

8416 _______. *Faulkner et Dostoievski: Confluences et influences*. Travaux de la Faculté de Philosophie et Lettres Tome 39. Bruxelles: Presses Universitaires de Bruxelles, 1968.

8417 _______. "Faulkner's Monomaniacs: Their Indebtedness to Raskolnikov," CLS, 5 (June, 1968), 181-193.

8418 _______. "Metamorphoses du réalisme: Dostoevskij et Faulkner," RusL, 4 (1973), 37-50.

8419 Weiss, Daniel. "William Faulkner and the Runaway Slave," NWR, 6 (Summer, 1963), 71-79.

8420 Welker, Robert L. "*Liebestod* with a Southern Accent," *Reality and Myth: Essays in Memory of Richard Croom Beatty*. William E. Walker and Robert L. Welker, eds. Nashville: Vanderbilt U. P., 1964, pp. 179-211.

8421 Wellek, Rene, and Austin Warren. "Literature and Psychology," *Theory of Literature*. New York: Harcourt, Brace, 1949, 1956, pp. 69-81.

8422 Wells, Dean Faulkner, and Lawrence Wells. "The Trains Belonged to Everybody: Faulkner As a Ghost Writer," SoR, 12 (Autumn, 1976), 864-871.

Account of an anecdote ghost story written by Faulkner in 1928 for a student.

8423 Welty, Eudora. "Departure of Amplification," NY, 24 (January 1, 1949), 50-51.
Cf., Edmund Wilson. "William Faulkner's Reply to the Civil-Rights Program," NY, 24 (October 23, 1948), 120.

8424 ________. "In Yoknapatawpha," HudR, 1 (Winter, 1948), 596-598.

8425 ________. "Must the Novelist Crusade?" Atl, 216 (October, 1965), 104-108; Writer's Dig., 50 (February, 1970), 32-35.

8426 ________. On Short Stories. New York: Harcourt, Brace, 1949, pp. 39-47.

8427 ________. "Place in Fiction," SAQ, 55 (January, 1956), 57-72.

8428 Wenstrand, Thomas E. "An Analysis of Style: The Application of Sector Analysis to Examples of American Prose Fiction," DA, 28 (Columbia: 1967), 1799.

8429 West, Anthony. "Remembering William Faulkner," Gourmet, 29 (January, 1969), 22-23, 74-75.

8430 ________, et al. "William Faulkner: A Critical Consensus," Study of Current English (Tokyo), 10 (September, 1955), 28-29.

8431 West, Paul. "A Mystique of Documentary," The Modern Novel. London: Hutchinson, 2nd. ed., 1965, II, 253-258, passim.

8432 West, Ray B., Jr. "Hemingway and Faulkner: Two Masters of the Modern Short Story," The Short Story in America, 1900-1950. Chicago: Regnery, 1952, pp. 85-106.

8433 ________. "Hemingway and Faulkner: Two Masters of the Modern Short Story," The Short Stories of Ernest Hemingway: Critical Essays. Jackson J. Benson, ed. Duke U.P., 1975, pp. 2-14.

8434 ________. "William Faulkner: Artist and Moralist," WestR, 16 (Winter, 1952), 162-167.

8435 ________, and Robert Wooster Stallman. "Theme Through Atmosphere," Art of Modern Fiction. New York: Rinehart & Co., 1949, pp. 263-276.

8436 Westbrook, Andrew J. "The Commitment of Self in the Works of William Faulkner," DAI, 31 (Austin, Texas: 1970), 3568A-69A.

8437 Westbrook, John T. "Twilight of Southern Regionalism," SWR, 42 (Summer, 1957), 231-234.

8438 Westbrook, Max, ed. Introduction. The Modern American Novel: Essays in Criticism. (Studies in Language and Literature, No. 6) New York: Random House, 1966, passim.

8439 Weston, Robert V. "Faulkner and [Andrew] Lytle: Two Modes of Southern Fiction," SoR, 15, #1 (January, 1979), 34-51.

8440 Weybright, Myron Duane. "A Study of Tensiveness in Selected Novels of William Faulkner " DAI, 32 (Northwestern: 1971), 5389A.

8441 Wharton, Don, Coll. "William Faulkner: The Man Behind the Genius," ReadD, 108 (June, 1976), 51-58.

8442 Wheeler, Otis B. "Faulkner's Wilderness," AL, 31 (May, 1959), 127-136.

8443 _______. "Some Uses of Folk Humor by Faulkner," MissQ, 17 (Spring, 1964), 107-122.

8444 Whicher, George F. "Analysts of Decay," The Literature of the American People: An Historical and Critical Survey. Arthur Hobson Quinn, ed. New York: Appleton-Century-Crofts, 1951, pp. 884-885.

8445 Whipple, T. K. "Literature in the Doldrums," NR, 90 (April 21, 1937), 311-314.

8446 Whitaker, Charles Francis. "Psychological Approaches to the Narrative Personality in the Novels of William Faulkner," DAI, 35 (Purdue: 1974), 7276A-77A.

8447 White, John. "The Hamilton Way," GaR, 24 (Summer, 1970), 132-157.

8448 White, Ray Lewis, ed. The Achievement of Sherwood Anderson. Chapel Hill: North Carolina U. P., 1966, passim.

8449 White, Robert. "Robert Penn Warren and the Myth of the Garden," FS, 3 (Winter, 1954), 59-67.

8450 White, Robert Lee. "Five Expotitions [sic] into Americana," SoR, 5 (Winter, 1969), 288-289.

8451 White, William. "Faulkner, q. v. (qq. v.) and the OCAL," AmBC, 16 (March, 1966), 7.

In the Oxford Companion to American Literature, notes that Faulkner received 238 lines in 1941, 1359 lines in 1966, which indicated current interest in American literary figures.

8452 _______. "One Man's Meat: Societies and Journals Devoted to a Single Author," AmBC, 8 (November, 1957), 22-24.

8453 ________. "Unpublished Faulkner: Reply to Nathanael West Questionnaire," AmBC, 17 (September, 1966), 27.

8454 Whittemore, Reed. "Notes on Mr. Faulkner," Furioso, 2 (Summer, 1947), 18-25.

8455 Whittington, Joseph R. "The Regional Novel of the South: The Dilemma of Innocence," DA, 24 (Oklahoma: 1964), 4202-03.

8456 Wiggins, Robert A. "Ambrose Bierce: A Romantic in an Age of Realism," ALR, 4 (Winter, 1971), 1-10.

8457 ________. "Faulkner," American Literary Scholarship: An Annual/1965. James Woodress, ed. Duke U.P., 1967, pp. 82-89.

8458 ________. "Faulkner," American Literary Scholarship: An Annual/1966. Durham: Duke U.P., 1968, pp. 79-84.

8459 ________. "Faulkner," American Literary Scholarship: An Annual/1967. James Woodress, ed. Durham: Duke U.P., 1969, pp. 86-95.

8460 Wilder, Amos N. "Faulkner and Vestigial Moralities," Theology and Modern Literature. Cambridge: Harvard U.P., 1958, pp. 112-131.

8461 Wiley, Electa C. "A Study of the Noble Savage Myth in Characterization of the Negro in Selected American Literary Works," DA, 25 (Arkansas: 1964), 5914.

8462 "William Faulkner and the Problem of War," Commentary, 18 (September, 1954), 227-232; (December, 1954), 569-570.

8463 "William Faulkner: Man and Writer," SatRL, 45 (July 28, 1962), 11ff.

8464 Williams, David L. Faulkner's Women: The Myth and the Muse. Montreal, Quebec, Canada: McGill-Queen's U.P., 1977.
Rev., by Michael A. Haynes, MFS, 24 (Winter, 1978-79), 637-641.

8465 ________. "William Faulkner and the Mythology of Woman," DAI, 34 (Massachusetts: 1974), 6610A.

8466 Williams, Mina Gwen. "The Sense of Place in Southern Fiction," DAI, 34 (LaState: 1973), 3440A-41A.

8467 Williams, Philip Eugene. "The Biblical View of History: Hawthorne, Mark Twain, Faulkner, and Eliot," DA, 25 (Pennsylvania: 1965), 4159-60.

8468 Willingham, John R. "Faulkner and His Critics," Nation, 179, No. 24 (December 11, 1954), 512.

8469 Wilson, Colin. "Existential Criticism," ChiR, 18 (Summer, 1959), 152-181.

8470 ________. "William Faulkner (The Implications of Realism)," The Strength to Dream: Literature and the Imagination. Boston: Houghton, Mifflin, 1962, pp. 36-40.

8471 Wilson, Edmund. "The James Branch Cabell Case Reopened," NY, 32 (April 21, 1956), 140-168.

8472 ________. Letters on Literature and Politics 1912-1972. Elena Wilson, ed. New York: Farrar, Straus, & Giroux, 1977, pp. 262-263, passim.

8473 ________. "William Faulkner's Reply to the Civil Rights Program," NY, 24 (October 23, 1948), 106, 109-112; repr., Classics and Commercials. New York: Farrar, 1950, pp. 460-470.

Cf., Eudora Welty. "Department of Amplifications," NY, 24 (January 1, 1949), 50-51.

8474 Wilson, Gillian Jennifer. "The Uncreating Word: Creators of Fiction in William Faulkner's Major Novels," DAI, 38 (Santa Barbara, Calif.: 1977), 6719A.

8475 Wilson, Herman Oland. A Study of Humor in the Fiction of William Faulkner. Diss. South California, Los Angeles: USCAD 1956 (1957), pp. 38-41.

8476 Wilson, James Southall. "The Novel in the South," SatRL, 26 (January 23, 1943), 11-12.

8477 Wilson, Jennifer G. "Faulkner's 'Riposte in Tertio,'" AN&Q, 16 (February, 1978), 88.

8478 Wilson, John W. "Delta Revival," EJ, 38 (March, 1949), 117-124.

8479 Winn, James A. "Faulkner's Revisions: Stylist at Work," AL, 41 (May, 1969), 231-250.

8480 Witham, W. Tasker. The Adolescent in the American Novel, 1920-1960. New York: Ungar, 1964, passim.

8481 ________. Living American Literature. New York: Stephen Daye, 1947, pp. 322-324.

8482 Wittenberg, Judith Bryant. Faulkner: The Transfiguration of Biography. Diss. Brown: 1977.

8483 ________. "Second Generation," Novel, 11 (Winter, 1978), 186-188.

8484 Wodehouse, P. G., A. Woollcott, and T. Fuller. "Story of Jack and Jill as It Might be Told by William Faulkner," SatRL, 15 (December 19, 1936), 10.

8485 Wolfe, Don Marion. "Faulkner and Hemingway: The Image of Man's Desolation," The Image of Man in America. Dallas: So. Methodist U.P., 1957, pp. 344-361; 2nd ed., New York: Crowell, 1970, pp. 344-361.

8486 Wolfe, George H., ed. Faulkner: Fifty Years After The Marble Faun. University, Alabama: University of Alabama Pr., 1977.

8487 Wolpers, Theodor. "Formen mythisierenden Erzählens in der modernen Prosa: Joseph Conrad im Vergleich mit Joyce, Lawrence und Faulkner," Lebend Antike: Symposion für Rüdolf Suhnel. Horst Meller, and Hans-Joachim Zimmermann, eds. Berlin: E. Schmidt, 1967, pp. 397-422.

8488 Woodruff, Neal Jr., ed. Studies in Faulkner. (CaSE, No. 6.) Pittsburgh: Carnegie Institute of Technology, 1961.

8489 Woodward, C. Vann. "Why the Southern Renaissance?" VQR, 51 (Winter, 1975), 223-239.

8490 Woodworth, Stanley D. "La Critique Faulknérienne en France: Essai de synthèse," RLM, Nos. 27-29 (2e Trim., 1957), 178-190.

8491 ________. "Problèmes de traduction des romans américains contemporains," RLM, 5 (hiver 1958-59), 345-364.

8492 ________. "Sélection bibliographique d'ouvrages ou d'articles sur 'William Faulkner en France, (1931-1952),'" RLM, Part I, Nos. 27-29 (1957), 191-196.

8493 ________. William Faulkner en France, (1931-1952). Paris: M. J. Minard, 1959.

8494 Wormley, Margaret J. The Negro in Southern Fiction, 1920-1940. Diss. Boston: 1948.

8495 Wouters, Alfredie F. M. America in Literature, 1920-1940. Diss. Cornell: 1950.

8496 Wright, Austin McGiffert. The American Short Story in the Twenties. Chicago: Chicago U.P., 1961, passim.

8497 ________. "Studies in Faulkner," CaSE, 6 (1961), 3-91.

8498 Wright, Louis B. "Myth-Makers and the South's Dilamma," SR, 53 (Autumn, 1945), 544-558.

8499 Wright, Ona Roberts. "Though Much Has Changed, Much Endures: Concepts of the Epic Hero in Selected Modern American Novels," DAI, 35 (Texas Woman's: 1974), 6738A-39A.

8500 Wykes, Alan. "The Perspective View and the Lost Generation," A Concise Survey of American Literature. London: Arthur Baker, 1955, pp. 165-174.

8501 Wyld, Lionel D. "Faulkner and Yoknapatawpha: Out of the 'Waste Land,'" AmLR, (Japan), 30, (December, 1959), 4-12.

8502 Wylie, Philip. "Five Decades of 'Writing Trends,'" NYTBR (October 6, 1946), 8, 58.

8503 Wynn, Lelia C. "A Bookman's Faulkner," DeltaR, 2 (July-August, 1965), 33-35, 57.

8504 Wynne, Carolyn. "Aspects of Space: John Marin and William Faulkner," AQ, 16 (Spring, 1964), 59-71.

8505 Wyrick, Green D., ed. "Faulkner: Three Studies," ESRS, 11 (September, 1962), 5-61; (December, 1962), 5-45.

8506 Yamada, Agnes A. "The Endless Jar: 'Contraries' in William Faulkner," DAI, 32 (Oregon: 1971), 5249A.

8507 Yates, Norris W. The American Humorist: Conscience of the Twentieth Century. Ames, Iowa: Iowa St. U.P., 1964, passim.

8508 Yep, Laurence Michael. "Self-Communion: The Early Novels of William Faulkner," DAI, 36 (Buffalo, New York: 1975), 1513A.

8509 Yglesias, Jose. "Neurotic Visions," Masses and Mainstreams, 2 (December, 1949), 76.

8510 Yndurain, Francisco. La obra de William Faulkner. Madrid: Ateneo (La Editora Nacional), 1953.

Cf., Emmanuel Carballo. "William Faulkner," Novedades, Supplement Mexico en la Cultura, No. 349 (November 27, 1955).

8511 "Yoknapatawpha Blues," Time, 108, #13 (September 27, 1976), 92-94.

"Writers who now elect to deal in moldering mansions and history-whipped alcoholics risk unfavorable comparisons with Faulkner...."

8512 "Yoknapatawpha Possum: William Faulkner's Visit," Newsweek, 59 (April 30, 1962), 58.

8513 Yonce, Margaret. "'Shot Down Last Spring': The Wounded Aviators of Faulkner's Wasteland," MissQ, 31 (Summer, 1978), 359-368.

8514 Yorks, Samuel A. "Faulkner's Women: The Peril of Mankind," ArQ, 17 (Summer, 1961), 119-129.

8515 Yoshida, Michiko. "The Voices and Legends in Yoknapatawpha County," SELit (Eng. No.) 174-176 [Abstracts of Art in Japan No.], 1971.

8516 Young, Stark. "New Year's Craw," NR, 93 (January 12, 1938), 283-284.

An account of Young's acquaintance with William Faulkner.

8517 ________. The Pavilion. New York: Scribner's, 1951, pp. 59-60.

8518 Young, Thomas Daniel. "Book Reviews," JMissH, 22 (July, 1960), 208-211.

8519 Zappulla, Giuseppe. "Lettera da New York: Pareri contrastanti su William Faulkner," FLe, 17 (July 22, 1962), 2.

8520 ________. "Lo Spirito Feudale nel Costume e nella Letteratura Americana," FLe, 16 (January 8, 1961), 4.

8521 Zavaleta, Carlos Eduardo. "The Hemingway Novel" EsAm, 16 (July-August, 1958), 47-52.

8522 ________. William Faulkner: novelista trágico. Lima: Universidad Nacional Mayor de San Marcos, 1959.

8523 Zellefrow, Ken. "Faulkner's Flying Tales: A View of the Past," Descant, 16 (Summer, 1972), 42-48.

8524 Zender, Karl F. "Jason Compson and Death by Water," MissQ, 31 (Summer, 1978), 421-422.

8525 Ziegfeld, Richard Evan. "A Methodology for the Study of Philosophy in Literature: Philosophy and Symbol in Selected Works of William Faulkner and Thomas Mann," DAI, 37, #8 (Austin, Texas: 1976), 5105A.

8526 Zindel, Edith. William Faulkner in den deutschsprachigen Ländern Europas: Untersuchungen zur Aufnahme seiner Werke nach 1945. Hamburg: Lüdke, 1972.

8527 Zink, Karl E. "Faulkner's Garden: Woman and the Immemorial Earth," MFS, 2 (Autumn, 1956), 139-149.

8528 ________. "La femme et la terre immêmoriale," RLM, Part I, Nos. 27-29 (June, 1957), 131-153.

8529 ________. "Flux and the Frozen Moment: The Imagery of Stasis in Faulkner's Prose," PMLA, 71 (June, 1956), 285-301.

8530 ________. "William Faulkner: Form as Experience," SAQ, 53 (July, 1954), 384-403.

8531 ________. William Faulkner: Studies in Form and Idea. Diss. Washington, Seattle: 1952.

8532 Ziolkowski, Theodore. Fictional Transfigurations of Jesus. Princeton: Princeton U.P., 1972, passim.

8533 Zrimc, Marie-Antoinette U. Creation of Atmosphere in the Novels of Hawthorne, Faulkner, and Julien Green. Diss. Harvard: 1969.

8534 Zyla, Wolodymyr T., and Wendell M. Aycock, eds. William Faulkner: Prevailing Verities and World Literature. Proceedings of the Comparative Literature Symposium. Vol. IV. Lubbock: Texas Tech. U., 1973.

Faulkner's foreign reception and reputation.

IV. BIBLIOGRAPHY

8535 Adams, Richard P. "Faulkner," American Literary Scholarship: An Annual/1963. James Woodress, ed. Durham: Duke U. P., 1965, pp. 72-80.

8536 _______. "Faulkner," American Literary Scholarship: An Annual, 1964. James Woodress, ed. Durham: Duke U. P., 1966, pp. 73-81.

8537 _______. "Recent Scholarship on Faulkner and Hemingway," The Teacher and American Literature. Lewis G. Leary, ed. Champaign, Ill.: National Council of Teachers of English, 1965, pp. 149-156.

8538 Adelman, Irving, and Rita Dworkin. The Contemporary Novel: A Checklist of Critical Literature on the British and American Novel Since 1945. Metuchen, New Jersey: The Scarecrow Press, 1972, pp. 134-196.

8539 Allen, Walter, et al. "The Worldwide Influence of William Faulkner: Reports from Six Capitals," NYTBR (November 15, 1959), pp. 52-53.

8540 Anon. "New and Notable: The William Faulkner Collection," PULC, 18 (Spring, 1957), 166-167.

8541 Anon. "Polish Popularity," New Orleans Times-Picayune (July 24, 1960), III, 16.

8542 Anon. The Saturday Review of Literature Index: 1924-1944. New York: R. R. Bowker, 1971.

8543 Archer, H. Richard. "Collecting Faulkner Today," FS, 1 (Fall, 1952), 42-43.

8544 _______. "The Ups and Downs of a Faulkner Collector," Antiquarian Bookman (January 5, 1952), 13-14.

8545 _______. "The Writings of William Faulkner: A Challenge to the Bibliographer," PBSA, 50 (3rd Qt., 1956), 229-242.

8546 Avni, Abraham. "The Influence of the Bible on American Literature: A Review of Research from 1955 to 1965," BB, 27 (October-December, 1970), 101-106.

8547 Baker, James R., John R. Marvin, and Tom E. Francis, eds. *Faulkner Studies.* Denver-Minneapolis: 1952-1954, Eleven Issues. I, (1, 2-3, 4), 1952; II, (1, 2, 3, and 4), 1953-54; III, 1, 2-3, and 4, 1954.

8548 ________. "Mr. H. Richard Archer," FS, 1 (Summer, 1952), 27-28.

8549 Bassett, John E., comp. *William Faulkner: An Annotated Checklist of Criticism.* New York: David Lewis, 1972.

8550 ________. *William Faulkner: The Critical Heritage.* London; Boston: Routledge & Kegan Paul, 1974.

8551 ________. "William Faulkner's *The Sound and the Fury*: An Annotated Checklist of Criticism," RALS, 1 (Autumn, 1971), 217-246.

8552 Beebe, Maurice. "Criticism of Faulkner: A Selected Checklist with an Index to Studies of Separate Works," MFS, 2 (Autumn, 1956), 150-164.

8553 ________. "Criticism of William Faulkner: A Second Checklist," MFS, 13 (Spring, 1967), 115-161.

8554 "Bibliography of Mississippi Writers," NMW, 1, #3 (Winter, 1969), 117-124.

8555 Blanck, Jacob, ed. *Merle Johnson's American First Editions.* 4th rev., and enlarged. Waltham, Massachusetts: Mark Press, 1965, pp. 170-172.

8556 Blotner, Joseph, comp. *William Faulkner's Library: A Catalogue.* Charlottesville, Virginia: Virginia U.P., 1964.

8557 "Books by William Faulkner," SatRL, 45 (July 28, 1962), 26.

8558 Broughton, Panthea Reid. "Faulkner," *American Literary Scholarship: An Annual/1976.* J. Albert Robbins, ed. Durham, North Carolina: Duke U.P., 1978, pp. 119-140.

8559 Brown, Calvin S. *A Glossary of Faulkner's South.* New Haven: Yale U.P., 1976.
Cf., art.-rev., by David Ray, Kansas City Star (Oct. 17, 1976), 10D; by Leland H. Cox, Jr., MissQ, 30 (1977), 483-489.

8560 Bryer, Jackson R., ed. "William Faulkner," *Fifteen Modern American Authors: A Survey of Research and Criticism.* Durham: Duke U.P., 1969, pp. 175-210.

8561 ________, ed. "William Faulkner. *Sixteen Modern American Authors.* Durham: Duke U.P., 1974, pp. 223-275.

8562 Bush, Alfred L. "Literary Landmarks of Princeton," PULC, 29, #1 (Autumn, 1967), 1-90.
Faulkner one of the 132 authors represented in a catalogue of an exhibition of imaginative writing done in Princeton.

8563 Cantrell, Clyde Hull, and Walton R. Patrick, eds. Southern Literary Culture: A Bibliography of Masters' and Doctors' Theses. University: University of Alabama Pr., 1955, p. 107.

8564 Capps, Jack L. "Auxiliary Faulkner: Six New Volumes, 1976-1977," SLJ, 10, #1 (Fall, 1977), 106-114.

8565 Chapman, Arnold. "William Faulkner: The Demonic Novel," The Spanish-American Reception of United States Fiction, 1920-1940. Berkeley: California U.P., 1966, pp. 127-150, 216-220.
Comprehensive list of Spanish-American items on Faulkner.

8566 Cofield, Jack. William Faulkner: The Cofield Collection. Lawrence Wells, ed. Introduction by Carvel Collins. Oxford, Miss.: Yoknapatawpha Pr., 1978.

8567 Coindreau, Maurice E. "France and the Contemporary American Novel," UKCR, 3 (Summer, 1937), 273-279.

8568 _______. "On Translating Faulkner," PULC, 18 (Spring, 1957), 108-113.

8569 _______. The Time of William Faulkner: A French View of Modern American Fiction. George M. Reeves, ed., and tr. Columbia: South Carolina U.P., 1971.

8570 _______. "William Faulkner: Translated from the English," University, 4 (Spring, 1960), 25-26.

8571 _______. "William Faulkner in France," YFS, 10 (Fall, 1952), 85-91.

8572 Collins, Carvel. "A Fourth Book Review by Faulkner," MissQ, 28, #3 (Summer, 1975), 339-342.

8573 Crane, Joan St. C. "Rare or Seldom-Seen Dust Jackets of American First Editions: III," Serif, 7, #4 (December, 1970), 64-66.
In Linton R. Massey's Faulkner collection, Virginia University.

8574 _______, and Anne E. H. Freudenberg, comps. Man Collecting: Manuscripts and Printed Works of William Faulkner in the University of Virginia Library - Honoring Linton Reynolds Massey (1900-1974). Foreword by Joseph Blotner. Charlottesville, Virginia: Virginia U.P., 1974.

8575 Daniel, Robert W. *A Catalogue of the Writings of William Faulkner*. New Haven: Yale U. P., 1942.

8576 _______, and John L. Longley, Jr. "Faulkner's Critics: A Selective Bibliography," Perspective, 3 (Winter, 1950), 202-208.

8577 Emerson, O. B. "Faulkner and His Bibliographers," BB, 30 (April-June, 1973), 90-92.

8578 _______. "Prophet Next Door," *Reality and Myth*. W. E. Walker and R. L. Welker, Nashville: Vanderbilt U. P., 1964, pp. 237-274.

8579 _______. "William Faulkner's Literary Reputation in America," DA, 23 (Vanderbilt: 1962), 631.

8580 _______, and Marion C. Michael, comps. "William Faulkner," *Southern Literary Culture: A Bibliography of Masters' and Doctors' Theses and Dissertations*. Rev. & enl. University: Alabama U. P., 1979.

8581 Everett, W. K. *Faulkner's Art and Characters*. Woodbury, New York: Barron's Educational Series, 1969.

8582 "The Faulkner Concordance Project," FCN 1 (1972), 1-5.

8583 Faulkner Scholarship Survey Committee. "Faulkner 1977: A Survey of Research and Criticism," MissQ, 31 (Summer, 1978), 429-447.

8584 Fitzgerald, James R. "William Faulkner's Literary Reputation in Britain, with a Checklist of Criticism, 1929-1972," DAI, 34 (Georgia: 1974), 5965A-66A.

"This dissertation is primarily a bibliography of approximately one thousand entries charting William Faulkner's literary reception in Britain from 1929 when he received his first press notice there to 1972, ten years after his death...."

8585 Frey, John R. "America and Her Literature Reviewed by Post-War Germany," AGR, 20 (1954), 4-6, 31.

Lists available books on American literature.

8586 _______. "Post-War Germany: Enter American Literature," AGR, 21 (1954), 9-12.

8587 _______. "Post-War German Reactions to American Literature," JEGP, 54 (April, 1955), 173-195.

8588 Frohock, W. M. "Faulkner and the Roman Nouveau: An Interim Report," BuR, 10 (March, 1962), 186-193.

8589 ________. "Faulkner in France: The Final Phase," Mosaic, 4 (Spring, 1971), 125-134.

8590 Fukuda, R. "Bibliography of William Faulkner in Japan," Hikaku bungaki, 3 (1960), 122-131.

8591 Gerstenberger, Donna, and George Hendrick. The American Novel, 1889-1959. Denver: Swallow, 1961, I, 71-89.

8592 ________, and ________. The American Novel, 1960-1968. Chicago: Swallow: 1970, II, 84-116.

8593 Gresset, Michel. "Faulkneriana," LMod, 59 (January-February, 1965), 107-113.

8594 Hagopian, John V. "The Adyt and the Maze: Ten Years of Faulkner Studies in America," JA, 6 (1961), 134-151.

8595 Halsell, W. D. "A Bibliography of Theses and Dissertations Relating to Mississippi, 1970," JMissH, 33 (February, 1971), 59-68.

8596 Harter, Carol Clancey. "Recent Faulkner Scholarship: Five More Turns of the Screw," JML, 4 (September, 1974), 139-145.

8597 Havlice, Patricia Pate. "Faulkner, William," Index to American Author Bibliographies. Metuchen, New Jersey: Scarecrow Press, 1971, pp. 56-57.

8598 Hayhoe, George F. "Faulkner in Hollywood: A Checklist of His Film Scripts at the University of Virginia," MissQ, 31, #3 (Summer, 1978), 407-419.

8599 Hicks, Granville. "Our Novelists' Shifting Reputations," CE, 12 (January, 1951), 187-193.

8600 Hoffman, Frederick J. "William Faulkner: A Review of Recent Criticism," Renascence, 13 (Fall, 1960), 3-9, 32.

8601 ________, and Olga W. Vickery, eds. William Faulkner: Two Decades of Criticism. East Lansing: Michigan State U.P., 1951.

8602 ________, and ________, eds. William Faulkner: Three Decades of Criticism. East Lansing: Michigan St. U.P., 1960.

8603 Hornberger, Theodore. "Faulkner's Reputation in Brazil," FS, 2 (Spring, 1953), 9-10.

8604 Inge, M. Thomas. "Contemporary American Literature in Spain," TSL, 16 (1971), 155-167.

8605 ________. "William Faulkner's *Light in August*: An Annotated Checklist of Criticism," *RALS*, 1 (Spring, 1971), 30-57.

8606 ________, ed. "Donald Davidson on Faulkner: An Early Recognition," GaR, 20 (Winter, 1966), 454-462.

8607 Johnson, Merle, comp. "American First Editions," PubW, 120 (August 15, 1931), 615.

8608 ________. "A Checklist of William Faulkner," *American First Editions*. New York: R. R. Bowker, 1932, pp. 119-120.

8609 Kawin, Bruce F. *Faulkner and Film*. New York: Frederick Ungar Pub. Co., 1977.

8610 Landor, Mikhail. "Faulkner in the Soviet Union," *Soviet Criticism of American Literature in the Sixties*. Carl R. Proffer, ed. and tr. Ann Arbor: Ardis Pubs., 1972, pp. 173-180.

8611 ________. "Faulkner in the Soviet Union," SovL, #12 (1965), 178-185.

8612 ________. "William Faulkner: New Translations and Studies," SovR, 8 (1968), 180-185.

8613 Leary, Lewis. *Articles on American Literature, 1900-1950*. Durham: Duke U. P., 1954, pp. 97-100.

8614 ________, Carolyn Bartholet, and Catharine Roth. *Articles on American Literature, 1950-1967*. Durham: Duke U. P., 1970, pp. 165-194.

8615 Lenormand, H. "American Literature in France," SatRL, 11 (October 27, 1934), 244-245.

8616 Levin, Harry. "Some European Views of Contemporary American Literature," The American Writer and the European Tradition. Margaret Denny and William H. Gilman, eds. Minneapolis: Minnesota U. P., 1950, pp. 168-184.

8617 Libman, Valentina A. "Folkner, Vil'iam," *Russian Studies of American Literature: A Bibliography*. Robert V. Allen, tr. Clarence Gohdes, ed. Chapel Hill: North Carolina U. P., 1969, pp. 38, 81-82.

8618 Lloyd, James Barlow. "An Annotated Bibliography of William Faulkner, 1967-1970," UMSE, 12 (1971), 1-57.

8619 ________. *The Oxford "Eagle," 1900-1962: An Annotated Checklist of Material on William Faulkner and the History of Lafayette County*. Mississippi State University: Published by the Mississippi Quarterly, 1977. Rev. by Noel Polk, MissQ, 31 (Summer, 1978), 486-487.

8620 _______. "The Oxford Eagle, 1902-1962: A Census of Locations," MissQ, 29 (Summer, 1976), 423-431.
A shortened version of a checklist of all Faulkner material in the Eagle.

8621 Longley, John L., Jr., and Robert Daniel. "Faulkner's Critics: A Selective Bibliography," Perspective, 3 (Autumn, 1950), 202-208.

8622 Luke, Myron H., ed. [William Faulkner], "Articles in American Studies," AmQ, 19 (Spring, 1967), 338-399; 20 (Summer, 1968), 397-466; 21 (Summer, 1969), 410-491; 25 (August, 1973), 261-314.

8623 McDonald, W. U., Jr. "Bassett's Checklist of Faulkner Criticism: Some 'Local' Addenda," BB, 32 (1975), 76.

8624 McHaney, Thomas L. "Faulkner 1977: A Survey of Research and Criticism," MissQ, 31 (Summer, 1978), 429-447.

8625 _______. William Faulkner: A Reference Guide. Boston: G. K. Hall, 1976. A most significant bibliography.
A most significant bibliography.

8626 McIntosh, William A., and Walton D. Stallings. "A Selective Listing of the William Faulkner Collection at the United States Military Academy," Die deutsche Literatur in der Weimarer Republik. Wolfgang Rothe, ed. Stuttgart: Reclam, 1974, pp. 20-28. Also in U.S. Military Academy Library Occasional Papers, No. 2 (1974), 20-28.

8627 McNamee, Lawrence F., ed. Dissertations in English and American Literature: Theses Accepted by American, British and German Universities, 1865-1964. New York; London: R. R. Bowker Co., 1968, pp. 779-781; Supplement One, 1964-1968, 1969, pp. 325-327; Supplement Two, 1969-1973, 1974, pp. 484-490.

8628 Makuck, Peter. "Faulkner Studies in France, 1953-1969," DA, 32 (Kent State: 1971), 3314A.

8629 Massey, Linton R., comp. William Faulkner: "Man Working," 1919-1962: A Catalogue of the William Faulkner Collections at the University of Virginia. Charlottesville: Bibliographic Society of the University of Virginia, 1968.
Cf., Joan St. C. Crane and Anne E. H. Freudenberg, comps. Man Collecting: Manuscripts and Printed Works of William Faulkner.... Honoring Linton Reynolds Massey (1900-1974). Charlottesville, Va.: Virginia U.P., 1974.

8630 Materassi, Mario. "Faulkner Criticism in Italy," ItalianQt, 57 (Summer, 1971), 47-85.

8631 Meriwether, James B. "The Books of William Faulkner: A Guide for Students and Scholars," MissQ, 30 (Summer, 1977), 417-428.
Brings up to date "The Texts of Faulkner's Books," MFS, 9 (1963), 159-170, No. 5779 herein.

8632 ________. "Early Notices of Faulkner by Phil Stone and Louis Cochran," MissQ, 17 (Summer, 1964), 136-164.

8633 ________. "Faulkner (1897-1962)," A Bibliographical Guide to the Study of Southern Literature. Louis D. Rubin, Jr., ed. Baton Rouge: Louisiana State U.P., 1969, pp. 192-196.

8634 ________. "Faulkner," American Literary Scholarship: An Annual/1973. James Woodress, ed. Durham: Duke U.P., 1973, pp. 135-149.

8635 ________. "Faulkner and the New Criticism," BA, 37 (Summer, 1963), 265-268.

8636 ________, ed. A Faulkner Miscellany. Jackson: Mississippi U.P., 1974.

8637 ________. The Literary Career of William Faulkner: A Bibliographical Study. Columbia: Southern Carolina U.P., 1961, reissue, 1971.

8638 ________. "The Literary Career of William Faulkner: Catalogue of an Exhibition," PULC, 21 (Spring, 1960), 111-164.

8639 ________. The Merrill Checklist of William Faulkner. Columbus: Charles E. Merrill, 1970.

8640 ________. "The Short Fiction of William Faulkner: A Bibliography," Proof, 1 (1971), 293-329.

8641 ________. "The Text of Faulkner's Books: An Introduction and Some Notes," MFS, 9 (Summer, 1963), 159-170.

8642 ________. "William Faulkner: A Check List," PULC, 18 (Spring, 1957), 136-158.

8643 ________. William Faulkner: A Checklist. Princeton: Princeton U. Library, 1957.

8644 ________. "William Faulkner," Fifteen Modern American Authors. Jackson R. Bryer, ed. Durham: Duke U.P., 1969, pp. 175-210.

8645 ________. "William Faulkner," Sixteen Modern American

Authors. Jackson R. Bryer, ed. Durham: Duke U.P., 1973, pp. 223-275.

8646 ________, and Michael Millgate, eds. Lion in the Garden: Interviews with William Faulkner (1926-1962). New York: Random House, 1968.

8647 Michael, Marion C. "Southern Literature in Academe," MissQ, 32 (Winter, 1978-79), 3-11.

8648 Millett, Fred B. Contemporary American Authors: A Critical Survey and 219 Bio-Bibliographies. New York: Harcourt, Brace & World, 1940, pp. 346-348.

8649 Millgate, Michael. "Faulkner," American Literary Scholarship: An Annual/1969. J. Albert Robbins, ed. Durham: Duke U.P., 1971, pp. 108-121.

8650 ________. "Faulkner," American Literary Scholarship: An Annual/1970. J. Albert Robbins, ed. Durham: Duke U.P., 1972, pp. 116-131.

8651 ________. "Faulkner," American Literary Scholarship: An Annual/1971. J. Albert Robbins, ed. Durham: Duke U.P., 1973, pp. 104-119.

8652 ________. "Faulkner," American Literary Scholarship: An Annual/1972. J. Albert Robbins, ed. Durham: Duke U.P., 1974, pp. 114-130.

8653 ________. "Faulkner Criticism: An Annotated Bibliography," Venture, 2 (June, 1961), 128-134.

8654 Moore, Robert H. "The Faulkner Concordance and Some Implications for Textual and Linguistic Studies," Die deutsche Literatur in der Weimarer Republik. Wolfgang Rothe, ed. Stuttgart: Reclam, 1974.

8655 Mugridge, Donald H., and Blanche P. McCrum. A Guide to the Study of the United States of America: Representative Books Reflecting American Life and Thought. Washington, D.C.: Library of Congress, 1960, pp. 1379-96, 1397-1402, passim.

8656 Nevius, Blake. "William Faulkner," The American Novel: Sinclair Lewis to the Present. New York: Meredith, 1970, pp. 37-48.

8657 Nilon, Charles H. Bibliography of Bibliographies in American Literature. New York: Bowker, 1970, pp. 194-196.

8658 O'Connor, William Van. William Faulkner. Minneapolis: Minnesota U.P., 1959, pp. 41-43.

8659 ________. "William Faulkner," Tres escritores norteamericanos. Madrid: Editorial Gredos, 1961, pp. 148-152.

8660 Page, Sally R. "Bibliography," Faulkner's Women. DeLand, Florida: Everett/Edwards, 1972, pp. 189-225.

8661 Perry, Bradley T. "Faulkner Critics: A Bibliography Breakdown," FS, 2 (Spring-Summer-Winter, 1953), 11-13, 30-32, 60-64.

8662 ________. "A Selected Bibliography of Critical Works on William Faulkner," UKCR, 18 (Winter, 1952), 159-164.

8663 Petersen, Carl. Each in Its Ordered Place: A Collector's Notebook. Ann Arbor, Michigan: Ardis, 1975

Description of a very large private collection of Faulkneriana.

8664 Peyre, Henri. "American Literature Through French Eyes," VQR, 23 (Summer, 1947), 421-438.

8665 Pick, Robert. "Old-World Views on New-World Writing," SatRL, 32 (August 20, 1949), 7-8, 35-38.

8666 Plummer, William. "Three Versions of Faulkner," HudR, 31 (Autumn, 1978), 466-482.

8667 Polk, Noel. "Some Recent Books on Faulkner," SNNTS, 9 (Summer, 1977), 201-210.

8668 Price, Lawrence M. The Reception of U.S. Literature in Germany. Chapel Hill: North Carolina U.P., 1966, pp. 152-157, 217-218.

8669 Price-Stephens, Gordon. "The British Reception of William Faulkner, 1929-1962," MissQ, 18 (Summer, 1965), 119-200.

8670 Pusey, William Webb, III. "William Faulkner's Works in Germany to 1940: Translations and Criticism," GermR, 30 (October, 1955), 211-226.

8671 Rehrauer, George. Cinema Booklist. Metuchen, New Jersey: Scarecrow Press, 1972.

8672 Richardson, H. Edward. "Bibliography," William Faulkner: The Journey to Self-Discovery. Columbia: Missouri U.P., 1969, pp. 230-245.

8673 Rollins, Peter C. "Film and American Studies: Questions, Activities, Guides," AmQ, 26 (August, 1974), 245-265.

8674 Rubin, Louis D., Jr., ed. A Bibliographical Guide to the Study of Southern Literature. Baton Rouge: Louisiana State U.P., 1969, pp. 192-196.

8675 Runyan, Harry. "Faulkner's Non-Fiction Prose: An Annotated Checklist," FS, 3 (Winter, 1954), 67-69.

8676 Sartre, Jean-Paul. "American Novelists in French Eyes," Atl, 158 (August, 1946), 114-118.

8677 Schmitter, Dean Morgan, comp. "Bibliography," *William Faulkner: A Collection of Criticism*. New York: McGraw-Hill, 1973, pp. 147-153.

8678 Schwartz, H. Warren, and Romaine Paul. *Checklists of Twentieth Century Authors*. First Series. Milwaukee: Casanova Booksellers, 1931, pp. 7-9.

8679 "A Selected Listing of Recent Works of Special Interest to the Faulkner Concordance Project," FCN, 2 (1973), 6-7.

8680 Sidney, George. "An Addition to the Faulkner Canon: The Hollywood Writings," TCL, 6 (January, 1961), 172-174.

8681 Skou-Hansen, Tage. "William Faulkner," *Fremmede digtere i det 20 århundrede*. Sven M. Kristensen, ed. Copenhagen: 1968, Vol. II.
Lists translation of Faulkner's works into Danish.

8682 Sleeth, Irene Lynn. *William Faulkner: A Bibliography of Criticism*. Denver, Colorado: Alan Swallow, 1962.

8683 ________. "William Faulkner: A Bibliography of Recent Criticism," TCL, 8 (April, 1962), 18-43.

8684 Smith, Thelma M., and Ward L. Miner. "Faulkner Checklist and Bibliography," *Transatlantic Migration: The Contemporary American Novel in France*. Durham: Duke U. P., 1955, pp. 227-235.

8685 Spiller, Robert Ernest, et al. "William Faulkner," *Literary History of the United States*. 2 Vols. New York: Macmillan, 1962, pp. 502-503; Supplement, pp. 119-121.

8686 Springer, Anne. "Bibliography," *The American Novel in Germany*. Hamburg: Cram, de Gruyter, 1960, pp. 85-87.

8687 Stallman, Robert W. "William Faulkner," *Critiques and Essays on Modern Fiction, 1920-1951*. John W. Aldridge, ed. New York: Ronald Press, 1952, pp. 582-586.

8688 Starke, Aubrey. "An American Comedy: An Introduction to a Bibliography of William Faulkner," Colophon, 5, Part 19 (1934).

8689 Terrey, John N. "Faulkner and Hemingway: Implications for School Programs," *The Teacher and American Literature*.

L. G. Leary, ed. Champaign, Ill.: National Council of Teachers of English, 1965, pp. 157-162.

8690 Thompson, Lawrance Roger. "Selected Bibliography," William Faulkner: An Introduction and Interpretation. New York: Barnes & Noble, 1963; Holt, Rinehart & Winston, 1967, pp. 177-179.

8691 Thurston, Jarvis, O. B. Emerson, et al. Short Fiction Criticism: A Checklist of Interpretations Since 1925 of Stories and Novelettes, 1800-1958. Denver: Swallow, 1960, pp. 49-56.

8692 Vickery, Olga W. "Bibliography," William Faulkner: Two Decades of Criticism. Frederick Hoffman and Olga Vickery, eds. East Lansing: Michigan State U.P., 1951, pp. 269-280.

8693 _______. "Bibliography," William Faulkner: Three Decades of Criticism. East Lansing: Michigan State U.P., 1960, pp. 393-428.

8694 _______. "Faulkner," American Literary Scholarship: An Annual/1968. J. Albert Robbins, ed. Durham: Duke U.P., 1970, pp. 100-106.

8695 Wages, Jack D., and William L. Andrews. ["William Faulkner"] "Southern Literary Culture: 1969-1975," MissQ, 32 (Winter, 1978-79), 13-20; 49-70.

8696 Waggoner, Hyatt H. "Hemingway and Faulkner: 'The End of Something,'" SoR, 4 (April, 1968), 458-466.

8697 Walker, Warren S., comp. "William Faulkner," Twentieth-Century Short Story Explication, Supplement II to 2nd Edition, 1970-1972. Hamden, Connecticut: Shoe String Press, 1973, pp. 36-41.

8698 Warren, Robert Penn. Faulkner: A Collection of Critical Essays. Englewood Cliffs: Prentice Hall, 1966, pp. 310-311.

8699 Watkins, Floyd C. "Faulkner and His Critics," TSLL, 10 (Summer, 1968), 317-329.

8700 White, Helen, and Redding S. Sugg, Jr. "John Faulkner: An Annotated Check List of His Published Works and of His Papers," SB, 23 (1970), 217-229.

8701 Wiggins, Robert A. "Faulkner," American Literary Scholarship: An Annual/1965. James Woodress, ed. Durham: Duke U.P., 1967, pp. 82-89.

8702 _______. "Faulkner," American Literary Scholarship: An Annual/1966. James Woodress, ed. Durham: Duke U. P., 1968, pp. 79-84.

8703 _______. "Faulkner," American Literary Scholarship: An Annual/1967. James Woodress, ed. Durham: Duke U. P., 1969, pp. 86-95.

8704 Woodress, James. American Fiction, 1900-1950: A Guide to Information Sources. Detroit: Gale Research, 1974, pp. 91-97.

8705 _______. Dissertations in American Literature, 1891-1966. Newly Revised and enlarged with assistance of Marian Koritz. Durham: Duke U. P., 1968, pp. 844-930, passim.

8706 Woodworth, Stanley D. "La critique Faulknérienne en France: Essai de synthèse," RLM, 4 (2e Trim., 1957), 354-366.

8707 _______. "Problèmes de traduction des romans amêricains contemporains," RLM, Nos. 40-42 (1958-59), pp. 345-364.

8708 _______. Selection bibliographique d'ouvrages ou d'articles sur 'William Faulkner en France' (1931-1952)," RLM, Nos. 40-42 (2e Trim., 1957), 191-196.

8709 _______. William Faulkner en France (1931-1952). Paris: Lettres Modernes, 1959.

8710 "Worldwide Influence of William Faulkner: Reports from Six Capitals, NYTBR, 64 (November 15, 1959), 52-53.

8711 Zender, Karl F. "Faulkner," American Literary Scholarship: An Annual/1974. James Woodress, ed. Durham, North Carolina: Duke U. P., 1976, pp. 123-138.

8712 _______. "Faulkner," American Literary Scholarship: An Annual/1975. James Woodress, ed. Durham, North Carolina: Duke U. P., 1977, pp. 143-165.

TOPICAL INDEX

INDEX OF CRITICS